Civil Litigation

Civil Litigation

Craig Osborne BA, MA (Econ), Solicitor

formerly Senior Lecturer at Manchester Metropolitan University and Visiting Lecturer
at the University of Hong Kong and the Institute of Commerce, Singapore

OXFORD
UNIVERSITY PRESS

OXFORD

UNIVERSITY PRESS

Great Clarendon Street, Oxford OX2 6DP

Oxford University Press is a department of the University of Oxford.
It furthers the University's objective of excellence in research, scholarship,
and education by publishing worldwide in

Oxford New York

Auckland Cape Town Dar es Salaam Hong Kong Karachi
Kuala Lumpur Madrid Melbourne Mexico City Nairobi
New Delhi Shanghai Taipei Toronto

With offices in

Argentina Austria Brazil Chile Czech Republic France Greece
Guatemala Hungary Italy Japan Poland Portugal Singapore
South Korea Switzerland Thailand Turkey Ukraine Vietnam

Oxford is a registered trade mark of Oxford University Press
in the UK and in certain other countries

Published in the United States
by Oxford University Press Inc., New York

First published 1993
Second edition 1994
Third edition 1995
Fourth edition 1996
Fifth edition 1997
Sixth edition 1998
Seventh edition 1999
Eighth edition 2000
Ninth edition 2001
Tenth edition 2002
Eleventh edition 2003
Twelfth edition 2004
Thirteenth edition 2005
Fourteenth edition 2006

British Library Cataloguing in Publication Data
Data available

Library of Congress Cataloging in Publication Data
Data available

Typeset by Newgen
Printed in Great Britain
on acid-free paper by
Antony Rowe Ltd, Chippenham, Wiltshire

ISBN 0–19–928962–X   978–0–19–928962–2

10 9 8 7 6 5 4 3 2 1

OUTLINE CONTENTS

DETAILED CONTENTS

Chapters 7 to 13   93

Chapters 25 and 26: Bringing a case to an early conclusion   345

Chapters 27 to 32: Procedural complications   385

PREFACE

This text is intended to be a 'legal resource book' for the Legal Practice Course in Civil Litigation. It covers all aspects of the written standards produced by the Law Society for that course, but it is the writer's hope that it also goes well beyond them. It is intended to be a legal resource book in the fullest sense, being a full and self-contained treatment of all relevant aspects of mainstream civil litigation. It includes not only a description of procedure but also a discussion of practical and tactical matters which commonly arise, together with a treatment of the more academic aspects, such as the law of remedies and limitation and civil evidence.

That is not of course to claim that students will not often benefit from referring direct to the original sources referred to in the text.

Although the text deals with mainstream aspects of litigation generally, I have in particular dealt with some aspects of personal injury actions in some depth in the hope that this guide will also be of use to students in the many institutions which offer personal injury litigation as a separate elective. I also hope that this guide will prove of some use to students during their training contracts.

I have been grateful to a number of people who have written, sometimes at considerable length, with suggestions. Unfortunately, some of the suggestions are diametrically opposed to each other, in particular, on the vexed question of how much depth and detail is appropriate for a text for LPC students. No doubt the differences reflect differences in individual courses or the type of students at the institutions concerned. My own experience in teaching the LPC course for several years at Manchester, as well as being external examiner of three other courses, does indeed show that there is a very wide variation amongst institutions in how they approach the LPC. One of my correspondents in particular suggested wholesale truncating of the text on the basis that LPC students did not need to know a great deal of the information contained here; another, however, actually suggested increasing the depth and detail, even in more purely academic areas, such as limitation of actions.

Notwithstanding that the text is now very long, I have generally preferred to leave in material which may be useful for further reference for use on electives or even during training contracts, which is one advantage of the book which a number of reviewers have mentioned. I have thus favoured an inclusive approach rather than a too restricted one. Statistics apparently show that as many as 44 per cent of all solicitors do some civil litigation. Obviously some students will go from this course to training contracts where they do heavyweight civil litigation from the start and for much of the two years; and others will do no civil litigation at all. For that reason the text has been organised in such a way as to concentrate on mainstream litigation in the central chapters. It is these of course on which most institutions will concentrate for the relatively short span of an LPC course.

The first six chapters deal with what is in effect substantive law, namely remedies, limitation of actions, and the law of civil evidence. Some institutions will want to teach, or persuade the students to teach themselves, from these chapters at the very outset of the course since a knowledge of the matters contained in them does underlie the whole of the civil litigation process. Others may choose to dip into them at later stages and progress immediately to the rest of the book from Chapter 7 onwards which deals with the litigation process. When describing the course of a claim under the Civil Procedure Rules the usual problems of organisation of a civil litigation textbook have been encountered, in particular to know when to continue with the description of the course of a mainstream claim so as to keep a coherent narrative, and when it may be appropriate to describe procedural sidetracks which may arise at the various stages. It is hoped that the organisation of this book is user-friendly.

A description of the mainstream civil litigation process ends at Chapter 26. Chapters 27 to 32 deal with specialised aspects of litigation which may not be material on many LPC courses, although even here it is suggested that one cannot really teach litigation without at least adverting in passing to the particular difficulties, for example, in acting for limited companies or children.

The Civil Procedure Rules 1998 have been in force since 26 April 1999. They provide a wholly new code for procedure, and in case after case the Court of Appeal has stressed that reference to pre-CPR authorities may be of little use even where the wording of the Civil Procedure Rule is the same as that of the rules which preceded it. The present text therefore now makes little mention, even in passing, of the pre-CPR situation. Although the CPR have now been in force at the time of writing for seven years, it is quite apparent that one of their objectives, namely, to unify practice between courts, has not been universally achieved. Indeed, some of those who have written to me have described remarkably different local approaches to

some aspects of procedure under the CPR and even to the way in which local solicitors have adapted to them, particularly in the matter of the degree of cooperation which they are prepared to demonstrate, something which has clearly not come easily to those with decades of experience of the purely adversarial approach to litigation.

Lastly, there is a chapter in this book on the effect of the Human Rights Act 1998. This is now a vitally important aspect of English law, and although its immediate impact is more strongly felt in areas such as criminal litigation, immigration, and public law cases generally, the impact on civil litigation is not negligible. In those cases decided up to the time of writing (summer 2006) it is fair to say that the courts have considered that English civil procedure in the main is perfectly compatible with the European Convention. There are, however, a number of observations about the way in which the Act may impact upon civil litigation, both in terms of causes of action and procedure.

In conclusion I am very grateful to Oxford University Press for their patience in awaiting delivery of this text which was substantially delayed by a desire to be as up to date as possible.

It is hoped that the text is up to date as at July 2006.

Craig Osborne
May 2006

TABLE OF CASES

TABLE OF STATUTES

TABLE OF STATUTORY INSTRUMENTS

Chapters 1 to 6

Chapters 1 to 6 are intended to stand separately from the rest of the text. They are intended to be a 'resource' in that they set out in a very brief form some aspects of what is in effect substantive law that are always important in civil litigation.

Chapter 1 deals with remedies and the principles on which they can be sought in a claim. Chapter 2 deals with the vitally important topic of limitation, a source of problems for the practising profession all too often.

Four brief chapters follow on the substantive law of evidence. It is obvious that there is little point in having an excellent case if one does not have the evidence to prove it, or if the evidence available is not admissible.

These chapters on substantive law end with Chapter 6, which deals in a practical way with the preparation of evidence for proceedings.

These chapters are very important and may perhaps best be studied at the start of a course. Alternatively they can be dipped into later. It is vital to appreciate, however, that the principles in them underlie the later chapters on the practicalities of evidence in the course of proceedings, in particular those chapters concerning disclosure of documents, preparation of witness statements, and expert evidence. Without an appreciation of the underlying rules of evidence, it may be difficult to see the point of some of the procedures and practical aspects later described.

Remedies

This chapter will consider some aspects of the remedies available in tort and contract, in particular, the principles for the award of damages and interest on damages, and injunctions and interim injunctions.

Although this is mainly a description of substantive law, there will be some passing references to procedural matters. It will be important, therefore, to know that procedure in the English and Welsh civil courts is now governed by the Civil Procedure Rules 1998 (CPR). The nature and function of these Rules is more particularly described at **Chapter 10**. The Rules appear in a number of Parts, and references to them describe the Part concerned by rule number (e.g., Part 25.2). Many Parts are supplemented by Practice Directions, the abbreviation for which is PD.

1.1 Damages in tort

1.1.1 Assessment

Damages in tort are compensatory in nature and are designed to put the claimant into the position in which he would have been but for the tort being committed. Thus an injured claimant will receive a sum deemed to be sufficient to compensate him for the type of injury he has received in terms of loss of quality of life and pain and suffering, but he will also receive a sum for financial loss flowing from that injury. For example, if the injury has totally disabled him from working again, the claimant will receive a sum deemed to be sufficient to compensate him for loss of income throughout his working life. Obviously, a very substantial element of informed guesswork will have to go into the assessment of damages in such cases.

In torts not involving personal injury, such as false imprisonment, malicious prosecution, defamation or nuisance, there may be little in the way of financial loss and a figure is fixed by the court deemed to be a fair sum for compensation for the injury to feelings, inconvenience or as the case may be. In the case of damaged property, there are two alternative modes of assessing damages, one being the cost of rectification of the problem, e.g., awarding a claimant whose vehicle has been damaged the amount needed to repair it; the other being the *diminution in value* basis, i.e., awarding the claimant a sum deemed to be the difference between the value of a chattel as damaged and its previous value. The case law is far from consistent as to which of the two bases for compensation will be awarded, though in many circumstances there will be no difference between the two.

It is appropriate to mention three further matters in connection with damages.

1.1.2 Contributory negligence

By virtue of s. 1 of the Law Reform (Contributory Negligence) Act 1945:

Where any person suffers damage as the result partly of his own fault and partly of the fault of any other person or persons . . . damages recoverable in respect thereof shall be reduced to such extent as the court thinks just and equitable having regard to the claimant's share in the responsibility for the damage.

The word 'fault' is defined in s. 4 as:

negligence, breach of statutory duty or other act or omission which gives rise to a liability in tort or would, apart from this Act, give rise to the defence of contributory negligence.

Contributory negligence therefore operates by way of reduction of damages. It must be remembered that contributory negligence may relate not only to fault in the *causation* of an accident, but may operate to reduce damages where the contributory fault merely aggravates the *amount of damage* suffered (e.g., failure to wear a seat belt). It is for a person raising an allegation of contributory negligence to prove it, and once established the reduction of damages will be by a round percentage or fraction, usually expressed as 25 per cent, one-third, 50 per cent, etc. It must be remembered that if there is a collision involving two vehicles and driver A is assessed as being contributorily negligent by 25 per cent in respect of causation of the accident, driver B will be negligent by 75 per cent. Thus each will recover some damages, and if driver B should prove to be much more seriously injured than driver A, then driver B may recover a larger sum in damages notwithstanding that the accident was primarily his fault.

1.1.3 Mitigation

The claimant has a duty to mitigate damages. All that this requires in fact is that he must take all *reasonable* steps to do so. Thus, for example, a claimant who is injured so badly that he cannot return to his previous job is expected to take any job that he can reasonably take in order to mitigate his continuing loss of earnings. If expenses are incurred in order to be able to mitigate (such as the cost of retraining for some other career), then these may be recovered as damages.

In questions of mitigation the tests are not entirely clear. In principle there is a subjective test, i.e., was it reasonable for *this* claimant to have behaved as he did. This applies in the case of damage to property as well as to personal injury damages. Though the case law is unclear, it is probably for the defendant to prove that the claimant did *not* act reasonably to mitigate rather than for the claimant to prove that he did act reasonably.

EXAMPLE

C's vehicle is damaged by D and while it is being repaired he hires a comparable vehicle. Unfortunately, due to a strike in the manufacturer's factory, parts prove difficult to obtain for many weeks. D's insurers contend that C should have mitigated his loss by selling the vehicle in its unrepaired state and buying a replacement, rather than hiring at great expense over the period. Will the courts hold that C should have acted thus to mitigate his damages?

The answer from the case law is that the defendant's insurers' contention will be unsuccessful. C is only expected to act reasonably in the circumstances and, the defendant's negligence having caused him to face the dilemma, the defendant's insurers cannot claim that C should have had the benefit of extraordinary foresight about the strike. The fact that some other course might look better with hindsight is irrelevant. Much the same arises in situations where the claimant, until he receives the compensation, cannot mitigate by having a damaged chattel repaired and so must hire. The famous case of *Liesbosch Dredger* v *SS Edison* [1933] AC 449, holding to the contrary, is now rarely followed (see *Martindale* v *Duncan* [1973] 1 WLR 573; *Perry* v *Sidney Phillips & Son* [1982] 1 WLR 1297; *Mattocks* v *Mann* [1993] RTR 13).

1.1.4 Exemplary damages

Exemplary damages are designed not to compensate the claimant but to punish the defendant, albeit that the claimant receives them. They can be awarded in three situations laid down in *Rookes* v *Barnard* [1964] AC 1129, namely:

(a) Where there has been oppressive or unconstitutional action by the servants of the government, which is taken to include civil servants, politicians, officers of a local authority and the police.

(b) Where the defendant's conduct has been calculated to make a profit which may well exceed the compensation payable to the claimant. This includes situations such as where a libel is calculated to obtain such publicity and extra sales that it will exceed any damages normally payable, or where a landlord harasses a tenant so that he leaves, thus freeing a property for sale on the open market.

(c) In cases where exemplary damages are expressly authorised by statute. Such statutes are not uncommon in the United States but there are few examples in the UK. One is the Protection from Eviction Act 1977.

1.2 Damages in personal injury cases

As indicated earlier, there are two elements of such damages. The first element is an attempt to compensate the claimant for his injuries by awarding him a sum of money. This is usually expressed as a conventional award, an approximately similar figure being given in respect of similar injuries to the same part of the body, notwithstanding individual characteristics of any given claimant (see **1.2.2.2**). Secondly, there is recompense for provable financial loss. In a simple case this can be computed as an exact figure (e.g., a claimant who suffers minor injuries necessitating a month off work without pay for which he can be recompensed by the precise net amount of his loss). In more complex cases, however, especially where a claimant will never return to work, compensation is based on predictions of future loss which, notwithstanding a great deal of factual information and semi-scientific projections (e.g., actuarial tables demonstrating average longevity), often end up being relatively arbitrary assessments. It is important for this purpose to divide damages in a personal injuries case into two parts, namely *general damages* and *special damages*.

General damages are the compensatory amounts which have to be assessed by the court of trial; *special* damages are the specific amounts which represent provable actual financial loss to the claimant. In the claimant's particulars of claim (see **Chapter 11**), he need only claim general damages by adding the words 'and the claimant claims damages' at the end of the document. While it is usual in the particulars of claim to give particulars of the injuries suffered and to indicate any special factors which apply, for example, the loss of career prospects, it is not necessary to put an exhaustive list of the aspects of the claimant's life which have been affected by the injury he has suffered, nor to suggest figures which are appropriate for each. Having said that it is not necessary to do so, it is in fact not uncommon to put this extra information in a modern statement of case, e.g., for a claimant whose leg has been broken to indicate in the document itself that his life has been affected in so far as his mobility is concerned so that his favourite sporting hobbies are now impossible. Nonetheless, he does not attribute a specific sum to these, the assessment of damages for such amounts being carried out by the judge at trial after hearing oral evidence.

Special damages do have to be set out in the particulars of claim, however, or in a separate document annexed to it. Moreover, as precise as possible a computation has to be given of the exact amounts which he is claiming. If accurate figures are given it may be that the claimant and defendant, however strenuously the action may be contested on liability, may be able to agree the basis of the computation to be used by the judge in the event of his finding liability established.

The above is a general indication of the difference between general and special damages. In personal injury litigation, however, it is for the claimant to supply, when serving his first particulars of claim a computation of special damages and of some elements of general damages, in particular, future loss of earnings.

1.2.1 Special damages

Special damages include actual loss incurred between the accident and the trial. Items of expense which are to be incurred *after* trial, even if the amount is known with precision, such as the amount it will take to adapt a badly injured claimant's house for wheelchair access and install a lift, are not, as such, special damages because they arise in the future. Special damages in the main include things such as:

(a) provable loss of earnings until trial;

(b) damage to clothing, repairs to vehicles, hire of alternative transport;

(c) extra travel costs occasioned by the accident, e.g., by the claimant having frequently to visit hospitals as an outpatient, or by relatives having to visit him in hospital;

(d) private medical or nursing treatment.

1.2.1.1 Loss of earnings

Loss of earnings in the period between the accident and the trial forms part of the special damages. It is not, of course, possible to specify the loss fully in the particulars of claim, because these are likely to be served quite soon after the accident and thus many months, if not years, before the trial. However, it is necessary to compute the loss of earnings up to the date of service of the particulars of claim, and these figures must then be updated and worked out again just before trial. Loss of earnings *after* the trial is part of the claim for general damages, and we shall come to this in due course.

The claimant may claim only what he has actually lost, that is, his *net* loss. Accordingly, his tax and national insurance contributions must be deducted from his gross earnings. The usual method of computing loss of earnings is to obtain details from the claimant's employer of his actual gross and net earnings over a recent typical period, e.g., the 6 months up to the date of the accident (choosing such a long period to allow seasonal fluctuations or overtime variations to even themselves out to a true average). The figure for one week's average net loss of earnings is then used as a basis for computing his continuing loss of earnings. It is important to find out when writing to the employer whether there have been any increases in pay since the accident for which the claimant would have been eligible, or indeed whether any promotion opportunities have arisen for which the claimant would have been a likely candidate. So, to take a simple example, suppose the claimant is injured on 1 January 2006 and you wish to compute his loss of earnings on 20 May 2006, a period of 20 weeks. His employers provide information which tells you that his pre-accident weekly average net pay was £200 but on 12 March 2006 (i.e., after he had been absent for 10 weeks) employees in his category received a pay rise giving a further £20 net per week. It is therefore very simple to work out the 20 weeks' loss of earnings, namely:

10 weeks @ £200 = £2,000
10 weeks @ £220 = £2,200
                          £4,200

Clearly this is a simple example, and to work out the loss of earnings can be complex where you are dealing with a long period. It is this item in particular which needs to be updated if the claimant has not returned to work before trial.

1.2.1.2 The claimant's contract of employment

It is necessary to consider carefully the claimant's contract of employment. It may be that his employer pays him for certain periods while he is off sick, and the defendant benefits from this since it is only actual loss for which he is liable to compensate the claimant. Suppose that in the previous example the employer had a private scheme negotiated with the claimant's trade union whereby he paid all employees who were off work regardless of whether the cause was accident or sickness for a period of, say, 20 weeks and the claimant returned to work after 20 weeks. The claimant would have no claim for loss of earnings in that time. In this situation only the claimant's employer loses because he has paid for 20 weeks' work which he has not received. He has of course no direct cause of action against the defendant.

Some employers have a provision in the contract of employment which is no less generous to their employees but does provide a sensible means of ensuring that they are reimbursed by the defendant. The contract provides that the employer will make the employee an interest-free loan equivalent to the amount of his net earnings while he is off work for a certain specified period. If the cause of absence is merely sickness, or some accident in respect of which the claimant is not able to recover any damages from some other person (e.g., an accident caused by the employee's own negligence), then he will usually not be asked to repay this loan. If, however, the employee is able to recover damages from some third party, he is expected to include loss of earnings in the claim and is then obliged to reimburse his employer.

1.2.1.3 Tax rebates

Because it is only loss of *net* earnings for which one can sue, credit must be given for any tax rebates received. This is because tax allowances are worked out over a whole year and the allowance is given in the form of a weekly amount set against weekly salary. A person is entitled to the whole tax allowance, however, even if he does not work for the whole year. Suppose that an individual has tax allowances equivalent to, say, £90 per week when spread over the whole year. He works for three months or so into the tax year and is injured in July. He does not work thereafter. Taking into account the £90 per week which has hitherto been credited to him as his allowance, he is credited now with the balance of the whole of his tax allowance for the year. When offset against his salary received for only three months, he will then clearly be entitled to a substantial tax rebate. This must be brought into account and deducted from his claim for loss of earnings.

1.2.1.4 Benefits received

The way in which compensation is affected by taking into account benefits received was radically changed in 1990. The need for special provisions about this is obvious. For example, where a claimant is injured and thus not able to work and earn his usual salary, he will generally receive benefits of various kinds. If at the end of the case the claimant recovers in full for his loss of earnings, but without having the benefits which he has received taken into account, then there will be two losers—the defendant, who will have had to compensate the claimant for a loss which he has not in fact sustained (since he will have received the benefits which ought partially to offset his loss of earnings), and the State, which will have paid out benefits to the claimant which will be irrecoverable. The statutory provisions attempt to rectify this apparent injustice.

The provisions are now contained in the Social Security (Recovery of Benefits) Act 1997 (as amended). This has been correctly described as an extremely contorted piece of legislation.

The current position is that in any case where a defendant (*the compensator*) is to pay damages for personal injury to a claimant, whether in consequence of a judgment at the end of a trial, or by settlement or compromise during or before a case, benefits received by the claimant will be taken into account. The procedure is as follows:

(a) When the solicitor for a claimant writes to the defendant notifying him of the claim which is to be made, the solicitor should inform the defendant of the claimant's date of birth, national insurance number, address and the name and address of the claimant's employer. Thereupon the defendant will notify a body called the Compensation Recovery Unit (CRU) who are part of the Department of Social Security by forwarding to them a certain form. This form will be acknowledged and thereupon the CRU will maintain records of all relevant benefits claimed and paid in respect of the injury in question.

(b) When the compensator is ready to make an offer of payment to the claimant, he should apply to the CRU for what is called a Certificate of Total Benefit. This certificate will then be issued by the CRU and will show the amount of total benefits paid to the claimant in respect of that injury since it occurred. Moreover, details will be given of future payments over eight weeks after the date of the certificate, thus enabling the compensator to know with precision what amount of benefits will have been paid on any given date for the following few weeks.

(c) Thereafter, when the payment is made to the claimant whether by way of court order or agreed compromise, the appropriate amount of benefit must be deducted from it by the compensator and this amount must then be remitted to the CRU. Thus the government is reimbursed for the benefits paid out and the claimant has no element of double compensation.

When negotiating settlement of claims or advising a claimant about likely future compensation, it is accordingly vital that a claimant's solicitor remembers to take into account the repayment of benefit element so that a claimant is not left with the mistaken belief that these payments will not be brought into account by way of deduction from his total compensation.

It is vital not to lose sight of this. A claimant who is the main breadwinner of his family and is receiving possibly several different kinds of benefit over a period may well be getting £200 per week or even more. Thus benefits may be running at more than £10,000 per year and this will have a dramatic effect on the net eventual amount of compensation.

Until October 1997 recoupment of benefits by the State was offset not only against loss of earnings, but also against any other heads of damages so that, for example, a poorly paid employee who was the main breadwinner and who was injured in an accident may have received substantially more in benefits than his loss of earnings claim would have been. The amount of benefits he had received would have been recouped by the State, not only from his loss of earnings claim, but from his general damages claim for pain and suffering and loss of amenity. This might indeed have exhausted the whole of his damages so that, although having a bad injury, he actually received nothing in compensation from the defendant. The injustice of that led to a great deal of complaint and this in turn led to the 1997 Act referred to above. In general this provides that recoupment does not attach to all damages, but only to compensation for loss of earnings, compensation for care costs and compensation for loss of mobility. General damages for pain, suffering and loss of amenity are therefore 'ring-fenced' against deduction of benefits. Moreover, types of benefits are recouped only against certain heads of pecuniary loss on a 'like for like' basis.

The defendant's insurers are responsible for repaying *all* relevant benefits received by the claimant since the accident, even those which cannot be recouped from the claimant's damages, and, moreover, there is no provision for contributory negligence so that even if, for example, a claimant has a deduction of 75 per cent for contributory negligence, the defendant is still obliged to reimburse the State for the whole of the benefits.

EXAMPLE

The claimant is injured in an accident and off work for some months. His general damages for pain, suffering and loss of amenity are £10,000; his special damages for loss of earnings are £6,000 and he receives benefits totalling £8,000. The court holds him 50 per cent to blame for the accident.

The result is that as the benefits exceed the loss of earnings the claimant will recover nothing for his loss of earnings claim; the defendant will be liable to reimburse the State for the whole of the claimant's benefits during the period (£8,000); the claimant will recover 50 per cent of his general damages from the defendant (£5,000). The defence insurers will thus be liable on the claim to pay out a total of £13,000 even though their insured was found only 50 per cent to blame for damages of £16,000.

There is no deduction from damages for future losses and the cut-off point is the date of the compensation payment itself or five years following the accident injury or first claim for a listed benefit in the case of industrial diseases.

There is a schedule to the Act which indicates what kinds of benefit may be deducted from what heads of claim and for ease of reference this appears below.

Schedule 2 — Calculation of compensation payment

(1) Head of Compensation	(2) Benefit
1. Compensation for earnings lost during the relevant period	Disability working allowance
	Disablement pension payable under s. 103 of the Social Security Contributions and Benefits Act 1992

cont'd

(1) Head of Compensation	(2) Benefit
	Incapacity benefit
	Income support
	Invalidity pension and allowance
	Jobseeker's allowance
	Severe disablement allowance
	Sickness benefit
	Statutory sick pay
	Unemployability supplement
	Unemployment benefit
2. Compensation for cost of care incurred during the relevant period	Attendance allowance Care component of disability living allowance Disablement pension increase payable under s. 104 or 105 of the 1992 Act
3. Compensation for loss of mobility during the relevant period	Mobility allowance Mobility component of disability living allowance

1.2.1.5 Other amounts received due to the accident

Some money received as a result of an accident is *not* deductible from damages, i.e., the defendant does not obtain the benefit of these payments:

(a) Any sums paid under private accident insurance. Even if these come about *factually* because of an accident, the *legal* cause is the claimant's own prudence in arranging to have personal accident insurance. It is therefore wrong for the defendant to get the benefit of this by having it offset against his liability.

(b) The results of public benevolence, e.g., public collection. Likewise, it would be wrong for the defendant to gain the benefit of this by having his liability to pay damages reduced.

(c) The result of private benevolence, e.g., gifts from friends or relatives.

(d) Redundancy payment. If, for example, a person is away from work because of disablement and during that time he is made redundant, then, unless the cause of the redundancy relates to his incapacity resulting from the accident (which is unlikely), no credit should accrue to the defendant.

(e) Pensions. If the claimant receives a pension as a result of his or her injuries, no deduction is made whether the pension was contributory or non-contributory (see *Smoker* v *London Fire and Civil Defence Authority* [1991] 2 AC 502). Nor are State retirement pensions deductible (*Hewson* v *Downs* [1981] QB 73).

(f) Other earnings. Credit must be given for earnings obtained while off work due to incapacity if they would not otherwise have been earned.

EXAMPLE

The claimant is a games teacher who is injured and unable to work. His claim includes loss of earnings. Suppose, however, that his second subject is French and he is able to give some daytime tuition at home to private students. The amount of income earned from this must be off-set against his claim for loss of earnings since he would not have earned it had he been at work. If, however, it had always been his practice to offer private tuition in his own time (i.e., in the evening) to obtain extra income, then since he would have earned the sums in any event he would not be obliged to give credit for them.

1.2.1.6 Maintenance at public expense

Section 5 of the Administration of Justice Act 1982 provides that any saving to an injured person which is attributable to his maintenance wholly or partly at public expense (i.e., in a National Health Service hospital) must be calculated and set off against any income lost as a result of the injuries. This is to be set off in fact against both loss of earnings incurred up to trial and loss thereafter, which forms part of general damages as we shall shortly see. In other words, where a claimant is fed and saves rent, rates, lighting and heating, etc., by being in hospital rather than at home, the amount saved should be calculated and brought into account.

The circumstances in which this will be applied vary very greatly from case to case. Suppose, for example, that the claimant is a single man living in a bedsitter. Whilst he will still have to pay rent he is entirely relieved of the cost of lighting, heating and food, etc. while in hospital. The amount saved may be reasonably substantial and of the order of, say, £100 per week. If, however, the claimant is a family man living in a three-bedroomed house with his wife and children, then the amount saved in terms of rent and council tax will be nil since the house will still be needed as a family home, and the amount saved with regard to heating, lighting and food will also be negligible.

This provision was designed to give the defendant some compensation where a claimant is in hospital for a lengthy period. In the case of the single man, if his stay in hospital lasted a few weeks, it is most unlikely that the defendants would bother to argue for or compute the amount saved. If the period of hospitalisation is longer, however, then it may be that in individual cases it will be worth negotiating figures, which will usually be done in modest round figures. There is no need to refer to this item in the particulars of claim. The defendant should be left to claim and argue for this if he wishes to.

1.2.1.7 Other losses

(a) *Repairs to vehicle*

Naturally the cost of repairs to a motor vehicle damaged in an accident and the cost of a hired car of a similar type can be claimed for the period when the vehicle is off the road awaiting repair. There is no restriction on the right to hire an alternative vehicle to cases where the car is needed for business use. If a claimant chooses not to hire a car for the intervening period he will be entitled to general damages for inconvenience caused by the necessity to walk, use public transport and the extra time which these things will take over the convenience of motoring. For the law relating to any claim by the defendant that the period of hire is excessive, see **1.1.3** above.

(b) *Damage to clothes and property damaged in the accident*

As there is no ready market for secondhand or damaged clothes, wrist watches, stereos, etc., it is usual to negotiate about these items. The value of such things is usually too small for there to be much case law, though points of principle of some difficulty may arise. For example, if the claimant's suit, which cost a substantial sum of money but is a year old, is damaged, then clearly, since repair of a suit is unlikely to be a viable option, an appropriate figure for recompense will be sought. This is unlikely to be the cost of a new suit, but will be more than the cost of a suit from a charity shop.

(c) *Other expenses*

Other more unusual expenses might involve, for example, adapting a car for disabled driving, or even adapting a house for wheelchairs by installing a lift. When arguing for these more esoteric things one should look carefully at the picture in the round. Putting ramps in a house and installing a lift not only costs a great deal, but will also actually diminish the value of the property since a future owner, unless also disabled, is unlikely to consider that these are attractive extra features. If the claimant has to move from a house to a bungalow, then expenses in the nature of estate agent's commission, solicitors' fees and removal expenses should be claimed.

(d) *Medical expenses*

By s. 2(4) of the Law Reform (Personal Injuries) Act 1948, a claimant is entitled to claim the cost of private medical treatment (even if National Health Service treatment is readily available). The claimant thus has the right to his choice of specialist in hospital, and even if the claimant is not someone who would ever otherwise have had private medical treatment, he will be entitled to reclaim the cost of it. 'Medical treatment' includes not merely surgery but aftercare, including nursing and convalescence. If a spouse rather than a relative has given up work to nurse the injured claimant at home, then either a sum equivalent to the commercial cost of nursing care may be claimed, or alternatively the spouse's or relative's loss of earnings (in an extreme case including full loss of earnings for an interrupted or a forfeited career) may be claimed and will be treated as the damages of the claimant.

(e) *Expenses incurred by other persons*

By convention, even though expenses are actually incurred by other people rather than the claimant personally, if travelling expenses are incurred for the purpose of visiting the claimant these are allowable in the claim against the defendant as if they were the claimant's own loss. Obviously there will be a test of basic reasonableness, so that for a very close relative to fly back from the other side of the world to visit an injured claimant the fares may be allowable, whereas the same would not be true of a distant relative who had never previously seen the claimant but suddenly was overwhelmed by the desire to be with him in his hour of need.

1.2.2 General damages

1.2.2.1 Pain and suffering

An amount is awarded to compensate the claimant for the pain and suffering which has been suffered, not only in the past, i.e., the agony of the accident itself and its immediate aftermath, but also that consequent upon any medical or surgical treatment. Compensation will take into account mental suffering and matters personal to the claimant which may increase that suffering. In addition, if the claimant's life expectancy has been reduced, the award for pain and suffering should take into account the claimant's knowledge of this. The award may also take into account other factors such as embarrassment (e.g., consequent upon facial scarring). The claimant's age and life expectancy may also be relevant if there is to be a substantial continuing period of pain and suffering. All necessary evidence on this must be produced (and should be put in detail in the claimant's witness statement for exchange with the defendant). Full medical evidence must be provided for the trial judge.

1.2.2.2 Loss of amenity

Loss of amenity damages are meant to compensate the claimant for the loss of quality or reduced enjoyment of life. Thus, for example, a claimant who has lost a leg, whatever his age, will clearly have the quality of his life considerably impaired in relation to his ordinary, everyday activities. Almost everything will be more uncomfortable and inconvenient, and many normal things that an individual might want to do will be impossible for him.

In general, relatively conventional awards are given so that a basic figure is fixed by reference to the nature of the injury, and this figure, the so-called 'tariff' for that type of injury, will not differ between individuals. There is some logic in this because, for example, although age is a subjective factor it may cut both ways. Thus an elderly man who is suddenly severely disabled by the loss of a leg may well be thought to have lost more in terms of quality of life for the few years remaining to him than a child; whereas the child, even though he may adjust better to disability, has to cope with disability over a longer period and may thus never be able to enjoy sporting and other activities of which the elderly man has had the advantage over most of his life.

Nonetheless, it is increasingly common now to stress individual and subjective factors in making a claim for loss of amenity. Thus if the claimant's hobby is, say, playing the violin, loss of a single finger may be a crucial impairment, whereas it may be of marginal consequence to the quality of life of others. Similarly, a leg injury will matter much more to someone whose hobbies were sporting than to someone who has a relatively sedentary life. It is important to call as much evidence as possible on these subjective matters to demonstrate to the judge that there is no element of exaggeration. Thus if it is claimed that the claimant's whole leisure time was given over to amateur sport, this should be demonstrated by calling evidence from other members of sports teams or clubs to which the claimant belonged.

The two sums for pain and suffering and loss of amenity are assessed together by the trial judge. The three most important sources are, first, a publication by the Judicial Studies Board, *Guidelines for the Assessment of General Damages in Personal Injury Cases* published by Blackstone Press and now in its 7th edition. This was published to assist judges to achieve consistency in awards for similar types of injuries. The book is brief but invaluable, although its brevity inevitably leaves room for argument since fairly broad brackets are given for each of the many possible types of injury. It is essential as a starting point, however, and is used by all judges. A very much weightier book is Kemp and Kemp, *Quantum of Damages*, a substantial loose-leaf work which contains a great deal of case law showing awards for various parts of the body. *Current Law* is also useful because it has a monthly section on quantum of damages, which keeps the reader up to date although the reports of cases are brief. It must be stressed that even using these three texts together, there is still plenty of room for distinguishing cases and for argument to contend that a given set of facts indicates that a case should be at one end of the bracket rather than the other.

Quite apart from any other aspects which may cause uncertainty in quantifying a claim (such as doubts about loss of earnings and the like), as will be observed there is a huge scope for negotiation and argument on the heads of pain, suffering and loss of amenity. Moreover, in accidents of any seriousness there may be two, three or more different parts of the body injured and different brackets of award needing to be considered for each.

1.2.2.3 Loss of future earnings

This is the most difficult head of damages of all, and in a case of serious injury to a young claimant is likely to be by far the largest element of damages. From the basic assessment of loss of present net earnings previously explained (**1.2.1.1**), you may have to launch off into many speculative areas.

The court works on the basis of two figures known as *multiplier* and *multiplicand*. *Multiplicand* is the net annual loss that the claimant has suffered. If the claimant is likely to be able to return to work in the same job in a year or two, then no great problem is involved, but what if he will not work for five years, or will never work again? Here there is great difficulty in picking the appropriate multiplicand. Suppose that the claimant is relatively young. Is it fair to take as his net loss of earnings the sum he is presently earning, when he might have had a glowing career before him with eventual promotion to the highest level? How can a figure be arrived at based on what a claimant of 23 earns and what the claimant might have earned at 60? Even in the case of apparently highly structured and stratified professions with annual increments such as local government or the civil service, assessing this figure can be an enormously difficult task (in fact the matrix of increments and promotion in the civil service is extremely complex). If faced with more volatile professions such as entertainment or sport, the difficulties seem virtually insuperable.

EXAMPLE

Suppose that the claimant is a 17-year-old professional footballer who has suffered a foot injury and will never play again. The evidence is that the claimant, who was a youth international and is currently in the first team of a lower division football club, was attracting great interest from several Premier League clubs, though none had actually made an offer for him. Are his damages to be assessed on the basis that he would have eventually become a Premier League professional with a top club, or even an England international? Moreover, what of the fact that the promise shown by very young footballers is often not maintained and that it is a short and injury-prone career likely to last less than 20 years? How is one to take into account the possibilities now open to the claimant in other fields? What is one to make of the fact that he would probably not have been a professional footballer much after his mid 30s and therefore could have had a further 30-year career in some unknown field?

An interesting factual example appeared as a news item in *The Times*, 7 May 1999, where a sum of more than a million pounds was awarded to a very promising footballer whose career had been affected by a relatively small, but permanent injury which deprived him of the ability to become a top-flight player, while still leaving him able to earn a living as a professional footballer in the lower divisions.

The same problems may apply to the learned professions. How does one compensate a barrister of 24 who has been in an accident and suffered brain damage so he will never work again? To take his last annual earnings which may be very modest would clearly be unfair, but is he to be compensated on the basis that he would inevitably have become a Queen's Counsel earning at the highest level?

In deciding these questions all that can be done is to present all available evidence about the claimant's future career. Full statements need to be taken from present employers or any other persons who might have been interested in the claimant. Whatever evidence is available will still provide a less than full picture for the trial judge, especially in the case of young claimants where income could vary greatly. In the case, for example, of an injured schoolboy, in assessing future loss of earnings the courts will have to have regard to school reports and other available evidence, however vague.

In fixing on this multiplicand judges will use their experience and common sense. Employment consultants, who specialise in providing evidence of earnings and job availability related to locality and profession, may be extremely useful.

After fixing the *multiplicand* the judge then needs to select the *multiplier*. This represents the number of years for which the claimant is to be awarded his net annual loss of earnings (the *multiplicand*). Let us take an example. Suppose the claimant is 25 and is earning £10,000 net per year. In principle, if he is never to work again he has lost 40 working years until 65 (possibly longer if he was self-employed). On the face of it the computation is simple and he should receive an award of £400,000. That is fallacious, however. If the claimant did indeed receive £400,000 now, if invested sensibly that would yield an annual income of several times the £10,000 which has been lost. Accordingly a multiplier is fixed to take into account accelerated receipt and other contingencies such as early death, and the risk of unemployment or injury from other sources. It must be remembered, moreover, that in the above example the fact that the claimant's present income was £10,000 net would not in itself necessarily provide the appropriate multiplicand either, and one would be attempting to persuade the court to fix a higher multiplicand if the claimant had good promotion prospects or might switch to a better-paid career.

Hitherto the maximum multiplier even for a very young claimant tended to be about 18. This was on the basis that such a gross lump sum, properly invested and allowing for certain assumptions about the rates of interest obtainable and the fall in the value of money, would produce an amount equivalent to the claimant's loss over his working lifetime. The figures previously used have been criticised for some years as relatively unscientific and a Law Commission Report in 1994 proposed approaches based on more scientific actuarial evidence. For some years the Government Actuaries Department have published a set of tables known as the *Ogden Tables* which have given more precise data about longevity, interest rates, work patterns and the like. Despite the availability of these tables, courts were still reluctant to use them, but s. 10 of the Civil Evidence Act 1995 provides that a court may have regard to the Ogden Tables in assessing multipliers. The effect of this will be that the previous maximum multiplier of 18 may be significantly uplifted, possibly to about 24 or 25 in appropriate cases.

The matter of multipliers is therefore governed by the investment return on lump sums. Section 1 of the Damages Act 1996 empowers the Lord Chancellor to prescribe expected rates of return on damages and thus to affect the multiplier. Following a consultation process, the Lord Chancellor made an order, namely the Damages (Personal Injury) Order 2001 (SI 2000/2301), on 25 June 2001, prescribing the rate of return at 2.5 per cent per annum. This is intended to be the safe net return on lump sums invested and, for the time being anyway, will lead to the outcome that multipliers will be significantly higher than they have been in the past.

1.2.2.4   Other factors affecting claims for loss of future earnings

(a) *Claimant's life expectancy*

If the claimant would have been unlikely to live until the usual retirement age, that is a factor affecting future loss of earnings. However, where the life expectancy has been reduced as a result of the injury, no reduction is made because to make such a reduction would be to allow the defendant to benefit from his tort.

(b) *Female claimants*

Sometimes a lower multiplier may be applied to annual loss because of the possibility of an interrupted career in order to have children and raise a family. Nonetheless, this is an individual matter and if a claimant is able to satisfy the court that she will never marry, e.g., if her religion requires chastity or she is a lesbian, then the court may not make any such deduction. In the normal case of an unmarried or young married woman there will be some reduction in the multiplier, although an individual is perfectly entitled to state that she would *not* sacrifice her career even if she has a family.

(c) *Ill health*

If the claimant had ill health before his injury and the defendants are able to show that he had lengthy periods off work or was unemployed, then this will naturally be taken into account to the extent that it is reasonable to do so.

(d) *The claimant's employment*

Individual factors relating to the claimant's career can make a difference. Some jobs (e.g., in professional sport) have low retirement ages and the multiplier will be accordingly reduced. On the other hand, a self-employed claimant who may well have continued beyond retirement age may obtain a higher multiplier. It is always vital to bring firm evidence on these matters.

(e) *Inflation*

No adjustment is made for inflation. This is because high inflation is usually followed by higher interest rates, and therefore the lump sum, when sensibly invested, ought to bring in a higher return to compensate for inflation.

(f) *Maintenance at public expense*

It must not be forgotten that from loss of future earnings credit must be given for maintenance at the public expense under s. 5 of the Administration of Justice Act 1982 (see **1.2.1.6**).

1.2.2.5 Risk on the labour market, or loss of earning capacity

(a) *The nature of the award*

This head of damages has long been recognised but was re-emphasised in the leading modern case of *Smith* v *Manchester Corporation* (1974) 17 KIR 1. The facts of that case provide a good example of the principle.

Mrs Smith was a cleaner employed by the defendants. Due to their negligence she suffered injury to her shoulder. This made her a considerably less efficient cleaner, but the defendants did undertake to keep her on and thus she had no apparent future loss of earnings. She did, however, receive a separate sum of money as compensation. This was because, should she ever lose or give up her job she would be at risk on the labour market because she would be competing with fully fit cleaners. She had thus lost her freedom of mobility of labour.

This award, often now called a *Smith* award, is appropriate in the following situations:

(i)   where the claimant has returned to his or her pre-accident employment with no net future loss but will some time in the future be at risk of early retirement or a less well paid job. See *Moeliker* v *Reyrolle & Co. Ltd* [1976] ICR 252;

(ii) where the claimant is back in pre-accident employment and will not lose it, but nonetheless the injury may have damaged prospects of promotion, ability to advance career, or the chance of moving to better employment;

(iii) where the claimant is handicapped on the labour market by the injury, e.g., where the claimant may have been unemployed at the time of accident and will now find work harder to obtain;

(iv) where the claimant is too young to have yet entered the labour market.

(b) *Quantification of the award*

There is a table in Kemp and Kemp, para. 5-009, which is of some assistance. Judges nonetheless tend to pick a 'conventional' award which is often within the range of one to one and a half year's gross salary. Nonetheless, a higher sum can be appropriate where clear evidence is provided, e.g., *Foster* v *Tyne and Wear County Council* [1986] 1 All ER 567, where a lump sum of five times annual net pay was approved.

(c) *Practical problems*

It is not uncommon for judges to fail to draw a clear distinction between damages for loss of earnings and damages for loss of earning capacity, but in general, for the years involved, the two heads are normally alternative to each other. Nonetheless, there may be cases where an award under both heads is appropriate, e.g., where a claimant has not yet gone back to work but is expected to do so in the future, at which stage he may be handicapped on the labour market.

The possibility of claiming damages for loss of earning capacity may not be immediately apparent. Suppose, for example, that the claimant, amongst other injuries, has suffered a head injury giving him an unpleasant and aggressive personality change. This may be covered by the damages for pain and suffering and loss of amenity, and for loss of future earnings; but it also may attract an award on the basis that if the claimant is to be a difficult and unpleasant colleague, there may be reasonable probability of prolonged unemployment and changes of job.

1.2.2.6   Loss of pension rights

Pension rights for an employee who will not return to work are an extremely difficult matter to compute and it is essential to employ a forensic accountant to assist. If a claimant has lost employment because of injury, or even if employment has been substantially interrupted, the claimant's own and his or her employer's contributions towards a retirement pension will be lost and the pension will be substantially reduced. This reduction must be taken into account by payment of a lump sum as part of the overall damages. In calculating this lump sum, which may well be received some decades before a pension would have been, account will be taken of the comparable pension that can be purchased with the lump sum now being made available.

1.2.2.7   Future expenses

If the claimant is likely to need to disburse specified future amounts, e.g., for future medical treatment, further adaptations of a car for disabled driving, moving house, a new wheelchair every five years, then these are quantified on an appropriate cost basis at present-day values. In such cases the fact that the claimant receives the money now (e.g., for six purchases of wheelchairs over a lifetime at present cost) is discounted by the fact that the wheelchairs will have risen in price.

Recurring items such as future nursing care, the cost of a care regime generally, the cost of a housekeeper and, where appropriate, gardener, and the value of voluntary services are quantified on a multiplier/multiplicand basis giving the value at the date of trial. The multiplier is unlikely to be the same as that applied to the annual loss of earnings because in principle the period will last until the claimant's death rather than just to the date of his retirement and therefore reference to actuarial tables for longevity may be needed.

1.3 Interest on damages in tort

Once damages have been awarded by a court at trial, the sum so awarded automatically carries interest under the Judgments Act 1838 at a prescribed rate (currently 8 per cent) until they are paid. Quite separately, however, by virtue of s. 35A of the Supreme Court Act 1981 or s. 69 of the County Courts Act 1984, either court has a discretion in every case to award interest on damages from the date when the cause of action arose to the date when judgment is given or earlier payment. The rate of interest chosen is within the court's discretion. In cases involving commercial loss, for example, in passing off or similar economic torts, the rate chosen may be a high one representing the cost to the claimant of interest on the financial loss caused to his business, especially if he has had to borrow money from a bank at a high rate in the light of the business difficulties caused to him by the defendant's action. In torts involving only injury to feelings, such as libel and malicious prosecution, there is usually no award of interest at all. In cases such as nuisance which may, for example, have involved physical injury to property as well as distress and inconvenience, the court may adopt different rates of interest on different aspects of the damages. We shall now turn to personal injury cases where there is a set of very specific rules provided by case law.

1.3.1 Personal injury cases

The Supreme Court Act 1981, s. 35A, and the County Courts Act 1984, s. 69, provide that in an action for damages for personal injuries or death where judgment is given for a sum which exceeds £200, the court *shall* award interest unless it is satisfied that there are special reasons to the contrary. Thus there is a presumption in favour of the award of interest on damages for personal injuries; indeed, from modern case law it is difficult to envisage circumstances in which interest would *not* be awarded, unless perhaps there had been wilful delay in the conduct of the case by the claimant. The prevailing rates are now specified in case law on the authority of *Wright* v *British Railways Board* [1983] 2 AC 773, and this case provides the following straightforward, if not entirely logical, rules.

(a) Interest is awarded on damages for pain and suffering and loss of amenities from the date of *service of the claim* to the date of trial. The current rate is 2 per cent per annum, although there is an argument, based on *Wells* v *Wells* [1999] 1 AC 345, that 3 per cent might be appropriate in future. Such arguments in the first instance case law have so far not met with any success. This rate is low because damages are valued as at the date of trial and thus, as awards of damages constantly creep up, a claimant would obtain slightly more in, say, 2006 than he would have obtained in 2004 for the same injury.

(b) Damages for future loss carry no interest because the claimant has not yet lost or expended the money.

(c) Special damages carry interest which will be awarded at half the prevailing court Special Account rate from the *date of accident* to the date of trial. This Account rate is fixed from time to time by statutory instrument. It is the rate of interest on funds in court and at the time of writing is 6 per cent per annum. The reason for awarding interest at *half* the appropriate rate is that the majority of such claims will be for loss of earnings. Accordingly, the loss will have been incurred gradually over the whole period from accident to trial, but clearly it would be unfair on the defendant to award interest at a high rate on the whole amount. Thus by awarding it at half the rate rough and ready justice is done and a great deal of difficult calculation avoided, because the rate will in effect be equivalent to the award of interest at the full rate on the figure due at the halfway point between accident and judgment.

The justification for that is thus easy to see. What is less easy to see, and indeed is quite arbitrary, is the reason why interest is usually only payable at half the Special Account rate on all other items which have been paid out in full, perhaps quite early in the period in respect of which the claimant has been out of pocket for a very considerable time (e.g., private medical treatment a few weeks after the accident). The court therefore does have a discretion to depart from the guidelines and, in exceptional cases, interest at the full rate, or indeed at some other commercial rate, may be allowed on the item in question from the date it was incurred. See *Dexter* v *Courtaulds Ltd* [1984] 1 WLR 372 and *Prokop* v *Department of Health and Social Security* [1985] CLY 1037. Where the items in question are reasonably substantial it is well worthwhile, therefore, producing a specific argument aimed at increasing the rate of interest. Surprisingly, defendants' insurers in negotiations quite often concede the interest element at higher rates on such items as car hire, repair or private medical treatment in recognition of the arbitrary nature of the prima facie rule.

1.4   Alternatives in personal injury cases to once and for all settlement

Until 2005 in litigation of all kinds in England the award of damages to a claimant was basically a 'once and for all' award. Thus if an injured claimant received judgment on the basis that his condition had a certain prognosis and then found to his dismay that his condition rapidly deteriorated, he could not appeal against the original judgment or go back to the original court to seek further award. There was no provision, until 2005, for the court to award damages in the form of periodical payments, which could be adjusted in view of changes to the claimant's condition over the foreseeable future. This sometimes favoured claimants of course. Sometimes the prognosis on which the claim had been settled would be much too pessimistic and the claimant would recover much earlier than the date suggested in the prognosis. Sometimes indeed a prognosis might suggest that a claimant would never recover or get back to work, but in fact a claimant might have a remarkable recovery. Defendants in that situation were unable to appeal. This position has changed in view of remarkable developments which came into force in April 2005.

When settling a case on behalf of a claimant, or arguing for an award at trial, it is important, to have as clear a view as possible of his medical prognosis and future career prospects. It would thus generally be considered negligent to attempt to settle a case before it was clear that the claimant's medical condition had stabilised to the point where a reasonably firm prognosis was available. However, where there is a great measure of uncertainty despite the lapse of time since the accident, there are now four options open to the claimant's solicitor. These are respectively:

(a) structured settlements;

(b) split trials;

(c) provisional damages;

(d) periodical payments of damages.

1.4.1   Structured settlements

Structured settlements are a relatively recent invention. They provide for periodical payments of compensation. It must be stressed that the court itself has at present no power whatsoever to *order* a structured settlement, and if the case goes to trial, the judge must in essence make a 'once and for all' award. In some recent complex cases, however, where the claimant's and the defendant's legal advisers have been able to reach agreement, settlements have been arrived at in structured form, particularly in cases where claimants will need a great deal of expensive medical and nursing care over the years to come. Although the court of its own motion has no power to give judgment in this form, the court does have power to make a consent judgment incorporating an agreement between the parties for damages to be paid in this way, which is known as a '*Tomlin*' order. Indeed, if the claimant is a mental patient or a child, the court's approval to the agreement will be positively required.

The drafting of these settlements requires very specialist tax, pensions and insurance advice. In essence, the defendants usually pay to the claimant a substantial lump sum but also purchase an annuity, index linked for protection against inflation. The settlement must be submitted for the agreement of the Inland Revenue so that they will accept the scheme as periodical payments of capital rather than income, and thus income tax is avoided.

The drafting of structured settlement agreements was very greatly assisted by provisions in the Finance Act 1996 which have considerably simplified the law and provide positively that appropriate schemes are to be treated as periodical instalments of capital. Help has also been given by the Damages Act 1996, which provides that if the parties consent, the court may order damages to be paid as periodical payments, and contains other detailed provisions concerning structured settlements.

Because of the complexities of setting them up and the cost involved, notwithstanding that the latter is usually borne by the defendants as part of the agreement, it is probably not worthwhile for there to be a structured settlement unless a sum of at least £250,000 is involved, although the writer is aware of one such case where the amount involved was only £80,000. There are said to have been fewer than 400 structured settlements since 1980.

1.4.2   Split trials

By virtue of the Civil Procedure Rules 1998 (CPR), r. 3.1(2)(i), the court has very wide powers to order split trials, that is, separate trials of the issues of liability and quantum. The court is likely to give its mind to the possibility of split trials particularly in personal injury cases, but may do so in any kind of case and is likely to do so at an early stage. As will be discussed in **Chapters 10 and 13**, it may then be possible for the court to direct that one issue be tried on one particular track and the other on another.

If this order is made, cases can proceed swiftly to a trial of liability while the memories of the witnesses of fact are fresh, and without the added expense of calling expert evidence to court on matters relevant only to quantum, particularly medical matters. Where a claimant wins on liability he can then obtain a substantial *interim payment* on account of eventual damages. If, on the other hand, the claimant loses on liability, a great deal of legal costs in obtaining medical and other evidence relevant only to quantum of damages and the lengthy part of the trial that would have been devoted to assessment of such damages will be totally avoided.

The opportunity to apply for split trials is a very useful procedural provision. In a case where a defendant purports to be defending strongly merely to avoid an application for an interim payment matters can often usefully be brought to a head by an application immediately after issue of proceedings for split trials, which may sometimes have the effect of concentrating the defendant's mind wonderfully on the desirability of admitting liability and making a sensible interim payment.

1.4.3 Provisional damages

There are many kinds of cases where the claimant's prognosis is reasonably certain in every respect but one. The one which is uncertain may well cause a great deal of worry to a claimant and his legal advisers, however.

Let us take two common examples. After a bone or joint injury most claimants make full recoveries. A small proportion of claimants may, however, often in the distant future, contract osteoarthritis in the joint affected. This is a painful, and indeed crippling, condition but it is often impossible to predict with any certainty whether a given claimant will sustain this deterioration. Similarly, in accidents which have involved a bad concussion, statistically a small minority of claimants develop epilepsy. The precise medical causes of this are unknown.

In either case, what may have appeared a relatively modest accident involving only a moderate level of damages will be seen in retrospect as having disastrous social and professional consequences. For example, a lorry driver who has apparently recovered completely from minor injuries involving concussion and has returned to work as a driver, but who, five years later, develops epilepsy, will be forced to give up his driving licence and will have a substantial loss of future earnings. If settlement had been accepted on a 'once and for all' basis earlier, nothing more could be done for such a claimant. The solution to the problem, however, is to apply for *provisional damages*.

Provisional damages were introduced by s. 32A of the Supreme Court Act 1981, which provides:

This section applies to an action for damages for personal injuries in which there is proved or admitted to be a chance that at some definite or indefinite time in the future the injured person will . . . develop some serious disease or suffer some serious deterioration in his physical or mental condition.

The relevant procedural rules are in CPR, r. 16.4(1)(d), and PD 16. The principles are contained in the case of *Wilson* v *Ministry of Defence* [1991] 1 All ER 638. This case holds:

(a) that the risk of serious disease or deterioration must be measurable rather than speculative;

(b) the 'serious deterioration' must be something which is quite distinct and severable and beyond the ordinary deterioration that may be a normal part of the claimant's condition.

Where the claimant can come within these provisions:

(a) The claimant must set out his claim for provisional damages in his particulars of claim, though no great detail need be given.

(b) At trial he will obtain judgment as to liability and, if successful, go on to be given an award of damages which will be made on the assumption that his medical condition in relation to the determined matters will *not* deteriorate in the way feared.

(c) The court must specify the type of disease or deterioration which it has been assumed will *not* occur for the purposes of the foregoing award of damages; the court may then prescribe that if the disease or deterioration *does* later occur a further application to the court for damages may be made and further damages will then be assessed.

This is a tactical option available to the claimant only and the defendant may not argue that a provisional award should be made if the claimant does not seek one.

It is always open, as an alternative, for a claimant to accept a so-called 'risk' award, i.e., a modest further award at trial to account for the risk of epilepsy etc. Should the claimant be in the lucky majority who do not then sustain epilepsy, the claimant will have received a little windfall. Should he be in the small minority who do contract epilepsy, he will prove to have been drastically undercompensated.

1.4.4   Periodical payments of damages

A complicated package of statutory provisions bring a new regime into force with effect from April 2005. The provisions have been available since the Damages Act 1996 and are brought in by sections 100 and 101 of the Courts Act 2003. There are new provisions in Part 41 of the CPR to provide the rule structure.

The new provisions are extremely complicated. There are differences of opinion as to how they will work from the judiciary, and from the representatives of claimants and insurance companies solicitors. A detailed discussion of the provisions is beyond the scope of this text, but the following is a bare outline:

(i) Unlike with structured settlements, the court can impose periodical payments of damages in personal injury cases whether the parties want it or not.

(ii) The court can provide that all or part of the claimant's damages can be by way of periodical payments and subject to a provision for future variation. This is to accommodate the position of a claimant who may suffer serious deterioration or enjoy some significant improvement, enabling either side to apply later for changes in the periodical payments.

(iii) It is envisaged generally speaking that this will only be appropriate for fairly high value claims, particularly for those where there is a significant item of special damages, in particular continuing loss of earnings over a substantial period; or the cost of care, the expense of which can vary dramatically dependent on the degree of recovery or partial recovery by a claimant.

(iv) There is provision for the funding of periodical payments by insurance in order to protect a claimant against any risk that the defendant or its immediate insurers become insolvent, if for example the periodical payments last for a long period.

(v) The claimant should include within his particulars of claim his view as to whether or not periodical payments or lump sums are more appropriate and must give 'relevant particulars of the circumstances relied on'. The court must give early consideration to whether it considers periodical payments are likely to be practicable (presumably at some case management stage). The court is likely to be primarily guided by the form of award which best meets the claimant's apparent needs.

(vi) If the court decides to make an order, it must specify the amount and frequency of payments and break down the amounts between income losses and other expenses. The period over which payments are to be made must be mentioned and there must be some mechanism to link the payments to the retail price index.

The Act is immediately in force in April 2005 in relation to cases coming before the trial court, but it will be a bold trial court who will impose a periodical payments order in litigation, which began before April 2005. Certainly in cases *issued* after April 2005 the court will be much more ready to deal both with periodical payments and with the crucial provision permitting the court to vary them.

It should be noted that because of the flexibility that the trial court will now have in deciding on the outcome of the case, there are substantial amendments to Part 36 so as to enable a defendant to express the nature of the offer to be made more exactly. See **25.4.7**.

1.5 Remedies for breach of contract

The right to monetary compensation will arise in a contract case where there has been a failure to perform, without proper excuse, one or more of the obligations contained in the contract. The innocent party may also have the right to rescind (i.e., terminate) the contract, or alternatively to affirm it, go on to perform his part, and claim damages.

1.5.1 Debt actions

The simplest case of breach of contract is undoubtedly debt, where typically goods have been sold for a prescribed sum, there is no dispute whether or not the contract has been performed by the seller, but the purchaser does not pay the price. In such a case the action is a simple one for recovery of a specified sum from the defendant, and usually for interest on that sum computed from the date when payment was due. The majority of all litigation comprises simple debt cases.

1.5.2 Other cases: damages

The principle of damages in contract is *restitution*, that is, to put the aggrieved party in the situation in which he would have been but for breach of contract. This may involve repayment of the whole of the price or payment for diminution in value, e.g., where a disgruntled consumer has had to spend a sum of money to put right a purchased item, and perhaps to hire a replacement item during the period of repair. Such items are precisely quantifiable. It may well be, however, that a claim for breach of contract may involve *general* damages which have to be assessed by the court, e.g., for distress, inconvenience or even personal injuries. For example, if a newly purchased television set suddenly explodes causing a fire, which in its turn damages the claimant's house and injures one of his children, not only can the cost of repairing the house be recovered as special damages, but the personal injury claim and a further sum for distress and inconvenience can be recovered.

The above is a fairly straightforward situation but it is obvious that the computation of damages can become nearly as complex as in the case of personal injuries. Thus damages may include:

(a) loss of the bargain or expectation, e.g., where, had the contract been completed, the result would have had a certain benefit to the claimant;

(b) wasted expenditure such as out-of-pocket expenses;

(c) loss of profit, e.g., where the business use of goods or services contracted for is impaired as a result of the breach of contract such as where the contract was for hire.

EXAMPLE

C contracts with D for the hire of some earth-moving equipment so that he can carry out some improvements to his garden centre before the profitable summer season opens. D fails to supply the equipment and it takes C an extra month to hire it elsewhere. In principle C can claim for the cost of hire over and above what the cost would have been from D, and for loss of profits should he be unable to open his garden centre until a month later than would otherwise have been the case.

1.5.3 Specific performance

It may be that financial compensation is not enough for the claimant and some other remedy of an equitable nature is required. Specific performance is a discretionary remedy requiring a party to honour his contract to perform obligations. The effect of this order is therefore to put the parties literally in the position in which they would have been had the contract been performed, though if there has been some delay past the proper contractual date, damages may be awarded in addition to specific performance. Specific performance will usually be awarded only in the situation where damages would not be an adequate remedy. Thus in purely business or monetary contexts, since damages are usually adequate, specific performance will not be ordered.

The claimant has to demonstrate the individual qualities of the thing contracted for and the financial ineffectiveness of damages. Consequently, a contract for, say, the purchase of a common type of motor car is unlikely to be enforced by specific performance, whereas a contract for the purchase of a given house may be enforced by specific performance notwithstanding that it may be one of several on a housing estate all virtually indistinguishable. The individual nature of the decoration, garden layout, etc. will be sufficient to make the contract enforceable by specific performance.

1.5.4 Other considerations

Damages may well be an adequate recompense, and the fact that it will be difficult to assess them does not necessarily mean that they are an inadequate remedy. The defendant's inability to pay rather than to perform the contract with the specific chattel may, however, be relevant. Regard should be had, on the question of adequacy of specific performance, to some of the material on injunctions which appears hereafter. In particular, specific performance is unlikely to be ordered of any contract requiring the performance of services where the court would have difficulty in supervising the adequacy of their performance. In addition, since the remedy is an equitable one, the court will usually have regard to general equitable principles.

Regard should finally be had to the other remedies available for breach of contract, in particular rescission, rectification and the special case of remedies for misrepresentation, which are beyond the scope of the present text but which are discussed in some detail in any contract textbook.

1.6 Interest on damages in contract

In cases where a claim is made in respect of a debt or breach of contract, the question of interest arises in two situations:

1.6.1 Where interest is payable as of right under the contract

The contract may provide that unless the amount due is paid in full on a certain date, interest on the whole amount begins to run at a rate fixed by the contract. In this case interest arises as of right as part of the contract and damages for breach of contract will include interest at the contractually agreed rate. In such a case interest may run at a higher rate than a court would ever award (subject to the term not being set aside under the Unfair Contract Terms Act 1977), and may even run past the date of judgment until the date of payment in full following enforcement. Such cases therefore provide no difficulty.

1.6.2 Interest payable under the court's discretion

It will be recalled that under s. 35A of the Supreme Court Act 1981 and s. 69 of the County Courts Act 1984, the court has a discretion to award interest, from the time when the cause of action arose, on the amount of the debt or damages for which judgment is given. In the case of personal injuries there is a presumption in favour of the award of interest, but in the case of contract actions there is merely a provision that the court *may* award interest. However, established principles now usually require the court to award interest since justice demands it. The court will have decided in its judgment that the claimant ought to be put in the same position as he would have been in but for the breach of contract, and thus, since he will have been kept out of monies which should have been his since the cause of action arose, he ought to receive compensation in the form of an award of interest. The rate which the court will choose is not specified as such, though s. 35A(5) of the 1981 Act provides:

. . . rules of court may provide for a rate of interest by reference to the rate specified in section 17 of the Judgments Act 1838 as that section has effect from time to time or by reference to a rate for which any other enactment provides.

Section 17 of the 1838 Act provides for interest on *judgment debts*. This is of course a different matter from interest on the *claim* itself until judgment. In the High Court, where judgment is given, interest continues to run until the sum is paid at a specified rate (currently 8 per cent per annum), and this is known as the *judgment debt* rate. The section merely adopts this rate as a convenient one, and the court will take that to be the appropriate rate unless there are special circumstances. The court will not adopt that rate in personal injury cases because of the case law principles previously mentioned (see **1.3.1**).

The judgment debt rate will be adopted unless either party can successfully argue to the contrary. It might, for example, be that the sum involved is a very large one which, if placed on the money market might have procured for the person who has been wrongfully deprived of it over the period a much higher return than 8 per cent per annum. Alternatively, a person may prove that because he has been kept out of his money he has had to have recourse to bank borrowing himself at a higher rate than 8 per cent, and that he should receive restitution for this precise amount which he has had to expend. Similarly, it is open to a defendant to argue that 8 per cent is too high a rate given the prevailing financial climate. In the case of substantial sums it may be worth either party arguing the matter fully before the court rather than adopting the norm. The matter is within the court's discretion and the court will have regard in every case to the evidence adduced to it of the financial realities of the situation when fixing the rate.

In the county court the same rate is usually adopted by analogy with High Court practice.

1.6.3   Interest on late payment of commercial debts

The general provisions in the Supreme Court Act 1981 and County Courts Act 1984 entitling one to claim interest in any kind of case are described above. There is, however, another vitally important provision which provides for interest at a more generous rate on those cases to which it applies. This is interest under the Late Payment of Commercial Debts (Interest) Act 1998.

This Act provides businesses (but not individuals, unless suing on business debts) with a statutory right to claim interest on commercial debts which are overdue. In the main, it took effect on 1 November 1998. It provides for what is called 'late payment interest', which is an alternative to statutory interest under the County Courts Act or Supreme Court Act. It can only be claimed from the date the debt became overdue until the date of judgment, although after judgment a commercial debt will continue to accrue interest at the statutory rate (currently 8 per cent) described above.

The Act now provides that all businesses and the public sector can use this Act against all other businesses and the public sector.

The debt must be a *commercial debt*, that is, one arising from an agreement between two businesses for the supply of goods and services. It should be noted that 'late payment interest' can only be claimed if a contract does not provide for contractual interest and it can then be claimed from the first day after any agreed credit period has ended or, if there is no credit period, 30 calendar days after delivery of goods, performance of the service, etc.

The particulars of claim (see **Chapter 11**) for a commercial debt should state that late payment interest is claimed.

1.6.3.1   The rate of interest

The different feature is the rate of interest that applies, which is meant to be of a semi-punitive nature. This provides for interest at the official dealing rate of the Bank of England ('the base rate') plus 8 per cent. At the time of writing the base rate is 4.5 per cent and therefore this would give the very healthy return of 12.5 per cent per annum on unpaid debts.

1.6.3.2 Interest after judgment

After judgment, if a judgment debt includes a claim for late payment interest or includes a claim for contractual interest and the business would otherwise have been able to claim 'late payment interest', further interest at the statutory rate of 8 per cent can be claimed from the date of judgment to the date and issue of enforcement. It should be noted that this applies even to county court judgment debts of under £5,000, which normally do not incur interest.

This is a very useful provision to be used by businesses which have to sue for debts. A typical situation is where a small business spends a great deal of its time working for a larger one and the larger one quite cavalierly fails to pay for many months after any agreed credit period. Of course in such a situation the small business may be very reluctant to sue for fear of alienating one of its main customers, but if it does take action, then interest at the higher rate is available. Careful notes should be taken of the dates for extension of the Act to all kinds of business debts.

1.6.4 Claiming interest

The CPR r. 16.4(2) provides that a party who wishes to claim interest must set out his claim. If no claim for interest is set out, then unless permission to amend is given at the trial no interest can be awarded. (The way in which interest should be set out is more particularly described in the material on statements of case.) In a personal injury case it is sufficient to claim interest generally, since interest is not capable of exact calculation in view of the fact that general damages are being claimed. In a debt case the claim should be set out precisely where the right to interest arises under contract, giving details of the amount accrued due at the contractual rate up to the date of issue of proceedings, together with a daily rate thereafter. Similarly, if there is no contractual provision for interest but the claimant is willing to accept the judgment rate of 8 per cent, it is both convenient and tactically wise for interest to be claimed at that rate in the statement of case, for the computations to be made in the same way. This will enable the claimant to obtain interest should the case terminate before trial in one of the ways described below (see **Chapter 26**).

1.7 Injunctions in tort and contract cases

The procedure for obtaining an injunction will be discussed in **Chapter 22**. At this point it is necessary to discuss the nature of injunctions.

An injunction is an order of the court requiring some person to do, or refrain from doing, some act. Breach of an injunction is a contempt of court, the penalty for which may be committal to prison or sequestration of assets. Injunctions are either:

(a) *prohibitory*, i.e., orders prohibiting or restraining a party from taking such steps as are named in the order (e.g., restraining further defamation, breach of copyright, continuation of a nuisance, etc.); or

(b) *mandatory*, i.e., orders compelling a party to take specified steps (e.g., to pull down a wall which has been wrongly erected across a right of way).

An injunction is a discretionary remedy and the usual equitable bars to its grant apply. However, the hurdles may not be as difficult to surmount as in the case of some other equitable remedy (e.g., an order of specific performance). It will often be appropriate, however, for the claimant to establish that damages alone would not be an adequate remedy.

1.7.1 Types of injunction

1.7.1.1 Final or 'perpetual' injunctions

This is a remedy granted at trial after the substantive rights of the parties have been determined. The effect of such an injunction lasts until some specified date or, if no date is given, in perpetuity.

1.7.1.2 Interim injunction

This is an order made at some stage of a claim before trial the object of which is to prevent some abuse pending full trial. Applications for interim injunctions may be made either:

(a) *without notice* (i.e., without informing the other party in a case of great urgency, or where some element of secrecy in the application is required); or

(b) *on notice* (i.e., having given the other party formal indication of the application).

An interim injunction which is granted at a hearing without notice will usually need to be supported by very strong evidence. The court will usually only order that it continue in force until an early hearing can be fixed at which the other party can be represented. The form of the order may therefore say that the injunction is granted e.g., 'until 4 p.m. on 1 December 2004 or until further order'.

1.7.1.3 *Quia timet* injunction

This is an order sought to prevent the commission of some legal wrong which has not yet occurred but is threatened (e.g., by one landowner to prevent a neighbour running a pop festival on his land for a weekend, which the first landowner contends will amount to an actionable nuisance). In such a case the claimant will have to prove a high probability of the breach occurring and the likelihood of substantial damage.

1.7.2 Possible alternatives to an injunction

The court will often consider alternatives. In particular:

1.7.2.1 Declaration

It may be that since the court will assume that its declarations will be honoured, it will find that to grant a declaration will be sufficient without the necessity for an injunction. Claimants will not usually find declarations to be such a satisfactory remedy because non-observance of a declaration does not amount to a contempt, but in some cases it may be sufficient for the parties to have an authoritative pronouncement as to whether the defendant's conduct did or does amount to a tort or breach of contract.

1.7.2.2 Specific performance

This is likely to be most appropriate in breach of contract for the sale of some unique item. As has been observed earlier, for example, non-performance of a contract to sell a house is usually enforced by specific performance, although in fact an injunction in the same terms could quite easily be given.

1.7.2.3 Undertaking

Where the defendant is willing to give an *undertaking* to the court, this is as satisfactory as an injunction, and indeed procedurally is preferable because there is then no need to incorporate it into a court order and it will remain enforceable by committal in the event of breach. It must be clearly understood that what is meant here by 'undertaking' is one given in the face of the court, and undertakings *between the parties* or their solicitors, unless incorporated in an appropriate order, would not suffice to ground an application for committal if dishonoured.

1.7.2.4 Other remedies

There are specific remedies in CPR, r. 25.1, for the detention, preservation, sampling and delivery up of goods, and it may be that in a given context these remedies are adequate to achieve the claimant's requirements.

1.7.3 The principles for the grant of an injunction

1.7.3.1 An injunction must support a legal right

An injunction can only be granted in support of a legal right which is capable of being established in the general law, thus:

(a) a claimant's failure to establish that he has a legal right will lead to his application being unsuccessful, e.g., *Gouriet* v *Union of Post Office Workers* [1978] AC 435;

(b) a person entitled to an injunction must be the person whose legal right has been or will be infringed (i.e., he must have *locus standi*);

(c) a local authority, however, can seek an injunction in its own name to enforce a public right for the benefit of the inhabitants of its area, by virtue of s. 222 of the Local Government Act 1972;

(d) the legal right infringed may be one in tort, contract, breach of trust or any other head of substantive English law. It can also include a right which can only be established by reference to the Treaty of Rome, e.g., art. 82, which governs the duty not to abuse a dominant market position. Thus a person who contends that he will suffer by such abuse may obtain an injunction (*Garden Cottage Foods Ltd* v *Milk Marketing Board* [1984] AC 130).

1.7.3.2 Application of equitable principles

Since an injunction is an equitable remedy it is discretionary and thus the usual equitable principles apply, in particular:

(a) He who comes to equity must come with clean hands. See *Armstrong* v *Sheppard and Short Ltd* [1959] 2 QB 384; *Argyll* v *Argyll* [1967] Ch 302.

(b) Acquiescence may deprive the claimant of an injunctive remedy if:

   (i)   he was aware he had a legal right; and

   (ii) was aware of the defendant's conduct; and

   (iii) it would be unjust and unconscionable after the claimant's delay for him now to be allowed to enforce his rights, e.g., where he had led the defendant to believe that there would be no objection to the defendant's conduct. See *Re Pauling's Settlement Trusts* [1964] Ch 303.

1.7.3.3   The power to award damages in lieu of an injunction

By s. 50 of the Supreme Court Act 1981, the court has a discretion to award damages in lieu of an injunction even though the claimant may have established a basic right to a remedy. Damages may be awarded instead of an injunction where:

(a) the injury to the claimant's right is small; and

(b) the injury is capable of being quantified in monetary terms; and

(c) the injury is one which can adequately be compensated by a small money payment; and

(d) the case is one in which it would be oppressive to the defendant to grant an injunction (see *Shelfer* v *City of London Electric Lighting Co.* [1895] 1 Ch 287 confirmed in *Jaggard* v *Sawyer* [1995] 1 WLR 269).

It should further be noted that:

(a) Damages in lieu of an injunction are not limited to losses accrued up to the date of issue of proceedings. Damages can be awarded in respect of an injury which will continue, and the amount can be quantified once and for all by the court of trial according to *Miller* v *Jackson* [1977] QB 966 (although that case has subsequently been doubted in *Kennaway* v *Thompson* [1981] QB 88 by a different Court of Appeal which indicated that the approach appeared irreconcilable with *Shelfer's* case).

(b) It is usually inappropriate to award damages in lieu of an injunction in the following cases:

   (i)   where the defendant is in breach of an express restrictive covenant (*Doherty* v *Allman* (1878) 3 App Cas 709); or

   (ii) the injury cannot fairly be compensated by money, or the defendant has acted in an oppressive or high-handed manner; or

   (iii) the defendant is wrongfully interfering with the claimant's property and clearly intends to continue to do so (though see *Miller* v *Jackson* above).

1.7.3.4   Scope of an injunction

An injunction is a flexible remedy. It is not necessarily a case of all or nothing. The court may merely restrict the defendant's activities in some way rather than prohibiting them entirely (see, e.g., *Kennaway* v *Thompson* (above) where powerboat racing on a lake adjacent to a claimant's house was restricted to certain weekends rather than banned entirely). The court has powers to grant an injunction but to suspend its operation to give the defendant time to rectify matters or change his industrial practices, e.g., *Halsey* v *Esso Petroleum Co. Ltd* [1961] 1 WLR 683.

1.7.3.5   Actionable nuisances

In regard to actionable nuisances, no matter how much the apparent public interest may be in favour of the activity continuing, the public interest should not always prevail over the private interest in the grant of an injunction. See *Kennaway* v *Thompson* above, expressly disapproving Lord Denning's views to the contrary in *Miller* v *Jackson*. Also see *Pride of Derby & Derbyshire Angling Association Ltd* v *British Celanese Ltd* [1953] Ch 149.

1.7.3.6   Mandatory and *quia timet* injunctions

There are some additional principles especially applicable to mandatory and *quia timet* injunctions. These are:

(a) A mandatory injunction will not be granted if it is difficult or impossible to supervise its carrying out (*Ryan* v *Mutual Tontine Westminster Chambers Association* [1893] 1 Ch 116).

(b) No injunction will usually be granted if the effect is to order specific performance of a contract of employment or for personal services. There are significant exceptions to this principle in employment case law, in particular those involving 'public office holders' or where there are certain procedures specified by statute which must be put in force before a person can be dismissed from office.

(c) In relation to *quia timet* injunctions, according to the leading case of *Redland Bricks Ltd* v *Morris* [1970] AC 652, there are four principles:

  (i)   There must be a very strong possibility that grave damage will be caused in the future.

  (ii)   Damages will be an insufficient remedy.

  (iii) The court must consider the cost to the defendant of preventing the apprehended wrong.

  (iv)   The injunction must be in terms which clearly indicate to the defendant what it is that he must do or refrain from doing.

1.7.4   Interim injunctions

An interim injunction is one given prior to trial and is intended to last until the trial itself or some earlier event. Such an injunction is intended as an urgent measure to cure some abuse or prevent some act pending full trial. A claimant may apply for an interim injunction at any stage, but in the vast majority of cases application for an interim injunction is made very early in a case, typically contemporaneously with the issue of the claim.

Although an interim injunction is intended to be a temporary remedy, in the majority of cases the grant or refusal of the injunction decides the outcome of the case and the matter never proceeds to trial, both parties accepting the outcome of the interim injunction application as conclusive and thereafter negotiating settlement of other outstanding matters. This is because in most cases where an interim injunction is sought, it will be considered vital for the preservation of the rights of one or other of the parties; and if the intended act is not restrained, the position of both parties will have changed materially by the time the claim comes to trial. This is pre-eminently the case in claims such as for passing off, or in support of a restraint of trade covenant.

1.7.4.1   The modern law

Few areas of procedural law have been the subject of as much practitioner and academic criticism as the law on interim injunctions, which were formerly called *interlocutory* injunctions. Because the need for interim injunctions may arise in a very wide range of kinds of proceedings, the rules relating to the grant or refusal of such injunctions may vary depending on the field of substantive law with which they are concerned. Most leading cases have to do with issues of infringement of intellectual property rights, defamation or employment law. For a first instance decision, which thoroughly reviews the law in an accessible form see *Series 5 Software Ltd* v *Clarke* [1996] FSR 273. This case usefully reviews the leading case, which is the House of Lords' decision in *American*

Cyanamid Ltd v *Ethicon Ltd* [1975] AC 396. One of the difficulties with this leading case is that there is only one speech, that of Lord Diplock, with which the other law lords concurred without contributing. An enormous amount of subsequent case law has been devoted to the question of whether the principles in the *American Cyanamid* case are of universal application or subject to exceptions and, if so, when and how. The test formulated in that case for the grant of an interim injunction in most instances (see **1.7.4.2** for exceptions) is as follows:

(a) Is there a *serious question* to be tried? In other words, the claim should not be frivolous or vexatious (this is *not* the same as a requirement to establish a prima facie case).

(b) Would *damages be an adequate compensation* to the claimant for his interim loss pending trial and, if so, is the defendant in a position to pay them? If the answer is 'yes', an injunction should not be granted.

(c) If the answer to the above is 'no', the court must then investigate whether, if the interim injunction were granted, the claimant is able to give an *undertaking* adequately to compensate the defendant for any loss if, at the eventual trial, the court finds the claimant was not entitled to the injunction (see further **1.7.4.3**). If the claimant is able to give such an undertaking effectively, there is a strong case for the interim injunction, for no eventual injustice is likely to be caused.

(d) If there is doubt as to the adequacy of the respective positions with regard to damages, then the case depends on the *balance of convenience* generally. The test is whether it would cause greater hardship to grant or to refuse the injunction. If even this consideration is evenly balanced, then other factors may be taken into account, e.g.:

    (i) the desirability of maintaining the status quo in general (*Attorney-General* v *Guardian Newspapers Ltd* [1987] 1 WLR 1248);

    (ii) the strength of one party's case being apparently disproportionate to that of the other. One must always bear in mind, however, the difficulty of embarking upon an investigation resembling a trial of the action based on conflicting affidavits when evaluating the strength of the parties' cases;

    (iii) the effect on the general public (*Smith* v *Inner London Education Authority* [1978] 1 WLR 411).

1.7.4.2   Exceptions to the *American Cyanamid* principle

The principle is said not to apply in the following kinds of case. In these cases something similar to the old law is applied. In the previous law there was what amounted to a short trial conducted on written evidence, where the key test was whether the claimant could establish a prima facie case; whether he would be entitled to a final injunction at trial; and who was favoured by the balance of convenience. These tests will still usually be applied in the following types of case:

(a) Where no action for a final injunction is likely to reach trial because the timing and circumstances mean that the grant of the interim injunction will be conclusive of the issue. Important examples of this are:

    (i) enforcement of covenants in restraint of trade (*Office Overload* v *Gunn* [1977] FSR 39; *Fellowes* v *Fisher* [1976] QB 122), at least where the covenant in restraint of trade is clearly valid: if there is a serious dispute about the validity of the covenant, the *American Cyanamid* approach may be preferred;

(ii)   passing off or similar commercial cases in appropriate circumstances;

(iii) defamation cases (*Herbage* v *Pressdram Ltd* [1984] 1 WLR 1160).

(b) Breach of confidence cases (*Woodward* v *Hutchins* [1977] 1 WLR 760, although on its facts this case might now be decided differently; see *Attorney-General* v *Guardian Newspapers Ltd* [1987] 1 WLR 1248).

(c) Where a statute prescribes an additional test to be followed, e.g., Trade Union and Labour Relations (Consolidation) Act 1992, s. 221(2): '*. . . the court shall, in exercising its discretion whether or not to grant [an interim injunction against a person claiming to act in contemplation or furtherance of a trade dispute], have regard to the likelihood of that party's succeeding at the trial of the action in establishing any matter which would afford a defence to the action under [s. 219 or s. 220]*'. According to the leading case on this (*NWL Ltd* v *Woods* [1979] 1 WLR 1294) the court must in this situation consider:

(i)   whether there is a serious question to be tried;

(ii)   the balance of convenience; and

(iii) the likelihood of establishing the statutory defence.

(d) Where neither side is interested in monetary compensation and the decision on an application for an interim injunction will be equivalent to final judgment (e.g., an application to prevent the transmission of a broadcast or publication of an article, the whole impact and value of which depend on the timing of the transmission or publication) a different approach is necessary. The court should assess the relative strength of the parties' cases in such an instance (*Cambridge Nutrition Ltd* v *British Broadcasting Corporation* [1990] 3 All ER 523).

1.7.4.3   The claimant's undertaking

In every case where an interim injunction is sought the applicant will be required to give an undertaking to pay the defendant damages for any loss sustained by the defendant as a consequence of the interim injunction if in the event the claimant fails to obtain a final injunction at trial. The following should be noted:

(a) The claimant must almost always demonstrate that he has the means to perform that undertaking in damages.

(b) However, in certain circumstances a publicly funded claimant will not be denied an interim injunction even if his undertaking will be of limited value (*Allen* v *Jambo Holdings Ltd* [1980] 1 WLR 1252).

(c) In *Blue Town Investments Ltd* v *Higgs & Hill plc* [1990] 1 WLR 696, the claimants' claim to a permanent injunction was struck out at an interim stage because of their refusal to apply for an interim injunction. They had refused to apply for the interim injunction because of the danger of giving the undertaking in damages. This refusal to apply was considered almost an abuse of process. However, doubt was cast on this result in the later case of *Oxy-Electric Ltd* v *Zainuddin* [1991] 1 WLR 115, where in somewhat similar circumstances the Court of Appeal doubted whether the court had had the jurisdiction to act as it did in the *Blue Town* case since the effect would be to restrict the availability of interim injunctions to the wealthy.

(d) In an action by a local authority for an injunction to restrain breaches of a statute, the court has a discretion to grant an interim injunction without requiring an undertaking in damages since in such an action the local authority is exercising the function of law enforcement (*Kirklees Metropolitan Borough Council* v *Wickes Building Supplies Ltd* [1993] AC 227).

(e) Where a local authority or the Crown applies for an interim injunction, it will ordinarily be required to give such an undertaking in damages unless the action is one to enforce the law (*F Hoffmann-La-Roche AG* v *Secretary of State for Trade and Industry* [1975] AC 295).

(f) Sometimes a defendant is willing to undertake to do, or refrain from doing something instead of there being an injunction. In such a case the claimant will usually have to give an undertaking of his own as to damages just as in an injunction case.

(g) If at the end of the trial an injunction is refused so that the claimant must perform his undertaking, then an *enquiry as to damages* will be held. This will usually be referred to a master or district judge, although the trial judge himself may undertake the investigation. If the investigation as to the amount of damage sustained appears very complex, the matter may be referred to a specially appointed judge with expertise in the area concerned. The defendant must rely on the outcome of this enquiry into damages and will not be permitted to issue a separate claim in respect of any loss which he had sustained.

The procedure for applying for interim injunctions is described in **Chapter 22**.

1.8   Injunctions and human rights

Readers are referred specifically to **Chapter 37** on human rights. There are specific problems in injunction cases caused by the fact that interim injunctions may be granted as a matter of urgency without very thorough investigation of the merits. Section 12 of the Human Rights Act 1998, in requiring the court to balance the right to freedom of expression under Article 10 of the European Convention on Human Rights with any other competing interests, such as the right to respect for privacy under Article 8, provides that the court must have particular regard to the importance of the Convention right of freedom of expression; and s. 12(2) provides that interim injunctions prohibiting publication may not be made on a without notice basis unless there are compelling reasons. The effect of s. 12 as a whole is to provide considerable assistance for those, such as newspapers, against whom interim injunctions without notice are often sought to prevent publication of allegedly defamatory articles.

Limitation of actions

2.1 Limitation periods

The rules on limitation of actions are laid down in the Limitation Act 1980, as amended, in particular, by the Latent Damage Act 1986. The rules provide a series of different periods in respect of different causes of action. They must also be read in conjunction with a number of specific statutes which lay down shorter periods, in particular, those for claims arising out of international trade or travel. There are also specific procedural rules applicable to individual types of action which lay down different periods—often very short periods—as, for example, under CPR, r. 54.5, by virtue of which an application for judicial review must be made within three months of the event complained of, and applications in respect of unfair dismissal for which an application must be lodged at the Central Office of Employment Tribunals within three months of the event claimed to constitute unfair dismissal.

Limitation is a procedural defence. The court will not take a limitation point of its own volition and the defence must be specifically alleged by a party wishing to rely on it (CPR, PD 16, para. 1). If successfully claimed, it is a complete defence.

The basic time limits are as follows:

(a) For all actions in contract—six years.

(b) For actions for recovery of land or for the recovery of money secured by a mortgage—12 years.

(c) Actions by beneficiaries to recover trust property or in respect of breach of trust—six years.

(d) Actions in tort not involving personal injuries—six years.

(e) Actions involving personal injuries—three years.

(f) Actions under the Defective Premises Act 1972—six years from completion of the house (Defective Premises Act 1972, s. 1(5)).

2.2 Miscellaneous exceptions to the rule

2.2.1 Under the Human Rights Act 1998

By s. 7(5) of the Human Rights Act 1998 a person who claims that a public authority has acted in a way which is made unlawful by the Act and who wishes to bring proceedings must do so before the end of:

(a) the period of one year beginning with the date on which the Act complained of took place; or

(b) such longer period as the court or tribunal considers equitable having regard to all the circumstances.

This is subject to any rule imposing a stricter time limit in relation to the procedure in question so, for example, if a claim were to be added to an application for judicial review the time limit would be that for judicial review (three months).

2.2.2 Defamation

Actions in respect of defamation must be brought within one year (Limitation Act 1980, s. 4, as amended by the Defamation Act 1996).

2.2.3 Consumer Protection Act 1987

Actions under the Consumer Protection Act 1987 must normally be brought within three years of suffering the relevant damage, or within three years of acquiring the necessary knowledge of the facts to sue if later. However, there is an absolute cut-off date of 10 years from the date the product was first put into circulation (Consumer Protection Act 1987, s. 5(5) and sch. 1). This relates only to claims in respect of the strict liability under the Act. If the actions in question also amount to negligence, the more generous limitation period of three years from *date of knowledge* applies, even if that should be outside the 10-year period.

2.2.4 Latent Damage Act 1986

The Latent Damage Act 1986 inserted a new s. 14A in the Limitation Act 1980. This applies to negligence actions other than for personal injuries. It has a particular application in claims relating to defective buildings but may also cover other kinds of claims, e.g., against solicitors for negligent drafting of documents. The practical scope of these provisions, which were viewed as of great importance at the time, has been reduced by the overruling of the former leading authority, *Anns* v *Merton London Borough Council* [1978] AC 728, by the case of *Murphy* v *Brentwood District Council* [1991] 1 AC 398.

Section 14A provides for two alternative periods:

(a) six years from accrual of cause of action; and

(b) three years from the 'starting date'.

Both these periods are subject to a final cut-off period of 15 years.

(a) *Accrual*

Damage accrues when it is initially suffered. So in the case of an action against a solicitor for negligently drafting a will, the claimant's cause of action accrues when the will takes effect.

(b) *Starting date*

The period of three years runs from the earliest date on which the claimant was aware of the following:

(i)   that the relevant damage was sufficiently serious to justify commencing proceedings;

(ii) that the damage was attributable to the negligence of the defendant; and

(iii) the defendant's identity.

The Limitation Act 1980, s. 14B, provides a 15-year final cut-off date for negligence actions, after which such actions shall not be brought even if the cause of action has not yet accrued or the starting date has not yet arrived. The 15-year period runs from the actual act or omission constituting the negligence resulting in the claimant's damage (e.g., in the case of solicitors drafting a will negligently, from the date on which the will was drafted or executed).

2.3 Personal injuries and fatal accidents

The law on limitation periods for damages for personal injuries and fatal accidents is now contained in ss. 11–14 of the Limitation Act 1980 as supplemented by s. 33 of that Act, which gives the court a discretion to disregard the prima facie time limits.

The three-year period of limitation for personal injuries applies to:

any action for damages for negligence, nuisance or breach of duty (whether the duty exists by virtue of a contract or of provision made by or under a statute or independently of any contract or any such provision).

It follows, therefore, that the reduced limitation period of three years applies in respect of the personal injuries caused by breach of contract just as much as to those caused in a road or factory accident. In *Stubbings* v *Webb* [1993] AC 498, it was held that where an action for personal injuries was based on *trespass* rather than negligence, the longer period of six years applied. This overruled the old authority of *Letang* v *Cooper* [1965] 1 QB 232.

The term 'personal injuries' is defined to include any disease and any impairment of a person's physical or mental condition (Limitation Act 1980, s. 38(1)). Whether distress and injury to feelings, where they do not amount to impairment of a mental condition in a defined medical sense, come within the Act is undecided.

In personal injury cases, time initially begins to run on the date of the cause of action in negligence. This is an easy enough matter in the case of a physical accident, but in the case of industrial diseases or industrial deafness, which may have occurred over decades early in a claimant's working life, considerable injustice would be caused by a strict three-year cut-off date. Accordingly, the limitation period of three years runs either from the date of the *cause of action* arising or from the date of the claimant's *knowledge* of the cause of action if later. If the claimant dies before that period expires, the period survives for the benefit of the estate and becomes three years from the date of death, or the date of knowledge of the personal representative (s. 11(5)).

2.3.1 What is knowledge?

The definition of 'knowledge' is provided in s. 14 of the Act, and the relevant date is the date on which the claimant had knowledge of the following:

(a) That the injury in question was *significant*, that is to say, sufficiently serious to justify instituting proceedings for damages against a defendant who did not dispute liability and was able to satisfy a judgment. It is suggested that the level of intelligence of the claimant in considering these matters may be taken into account (*McCafferty* v *Metropolitan Police District Receiver* [1977] 1 WLR 1073) but a personal reason such as unwillingness to sue one's employer may not be taken into account (*Miller* v *London Electrical Manufacturing Co. Ltd* [1976] 2 Lloyd's Rep 284). That the claimant's level of intelligence in understanding the facts available to him would be taken into account was further confirmed in *Nash* v *Eli Lilly and Co.* [1993] 1 WLR 782, although whether a subjective test at all was appropriate was further doubted in *Forbes* v *Wandsworth Area Health Authority* [1997] QB 402.

(b) That the injury was *attributable* in whole or in part to the alleged wrongful act or omission. This means that the claimant must in essence know what was the cause of his injury. However, the fact that the claimant did not know that he had a cause of action as a matter of law is not relevant (*Brooks* v *J & P Coates (UK) Ltd* [1984] 1 All ER 702). A subjective test for this part of the section was positively approved in *Spargo* v *North Essex District Health Authority* (1997) *The Times*, 21 March 1997, where it was shown that the claimant had been clear in her own mind when she first consulted solicitors that there was a causal connection between her suffering and the mistaken medical diagnosis, concerning which she brought her claim.

(c) The identity of the defendant.

(d) If it is alleged that the act or omission was that of a person other than the defendant, the identity of that person and the additional facts supporting the bringing of an action against the defendant (i.e., if the claimant wishes to hold the defendant vicariously liable, time does not run until he identifies the relevant employee and ascertains that he was acting in the course of his employment).

Section 14(1) expressly states that knowledge that any acts or omissions did or did not as a matter of law involve negligence, nuisance or breach of duty is irrelevant. In other words, a claimant is deemed to know the legal significance of facts.

2.3.2 Constructive knowledge

The claimant's actual state of knowledge is not necessarily what matters. There is a deeming provision in s. 14(3) which states that for the purpose of the section a person's knowledge includes knowledge which he might reasonably have been expected to acquire:

(a) from facts observable or ascertainable by him; or

(b) from facts ascertainable by him with the help of medical or other appropriate expert advice which it is reasonable for him to seek.

Nonetheless, so long as he acts appropriately he is not prejudiced if the expert whom he consults fails to find ascertainable facts. It is important to note that this deeming provision relates only to *facts*. If a claimant obtains incorrect *legal advice*, time will continue to run against him.

2.4   The discretion to extend the limitation period

2.4.1   Matters the court will take into account

In the case of damages for personal injury and death only, the court may still allow an action to proceed notwithstanding that the limitation period has expired (Limitation Act 1980, s. 33). The court has a discretion to extend the time limit if it considers it equitable to do so having regard to the degree to which the ordinary limitation periods would prejudice the claimant and to which any exercise of the power to extend the period would prejudice the defendant. The court must have regard to all the circumstances, including:

(a) the length of and the reasons for the delay on the part of the claimant;

(b) the effect of the delay on the cogency of the evidence in the case;

(c) the conduct of the defendant after the cause of action arose, including his response to any request by the claimant for information;

(d) the duration of any disability of the claimant arising after the cause of action;

(e) the extent to which the claimant acted promptly and reasonably once he knew of the facts which afforded him a cause of action;

(f) the steps taken by the claimant to obtain medical, legal or other expert advice and the nature of any such advice received.

This provision gives the court a very wide mandate indeed to enquire into all the surrounding circumstances concerning the apparent delay. Although all the factors must be weighed, a key question will be 'the effect of the delay on the cogency of the evidence in the case'. Thus if the case depends on eyewitness recollection, it may be more difficult for the claimant to have the period extended than if there is a wealth of evidence in documentary form, e.g., in the case of a factory accident where there may be prompt reports and statements made at the time, or a conviction of the defendants for breach of regulations made under the Health and Safety at Work etc. Act 1974.

It should also be noted that the claimant will have to waive his privilege and reveal the nature of the legal advice he asked for and received. The court will thereupon have regard to the question of whether the claimant acted reasonably promptly after he had the relevant advice. The fact that the claimant may have an excellent case against his solicitors in respect of negligent advice or delay is not necessarily relevant. It must be borne in mind that an action against one's solicitors may be less advantageous than an action against the defendant because, after all, those solicitors may have knowledge of the weaknesses of the claimant's original case.

2.4.2   The procedure

Where a claimant wishes to apply to the court to extend the limitation period, there are two main possibilities in terms of procedure. One is for the claimant to apply to the court after the defendant has filed his defence, taking the Limitation Act point for a preliminary hearing on the issue of limitation. The court itself has power of its own initiative under CPR, r. 3.1(2)(i), to 'direct a separate trial of any issue'. An application may therefore be listed and both parties directed to file evidence in the form of witness statements on the issues arising out of the delay. If the limitation point is dealt with at an early stage and is decided in the defendant's favour then, subject to appeals, the case will be over and a good deal of cost saved. Alternatively, and perhaps more commonly, the matter is left to be taken as a preliminary issue at the trial itself. This may be better where it is necessary to investigate a good deal of the factual background including 'the cogency of the evidence' (one of the factors under the Limitation Act 1980, s. 33) and this may be best left until trial. Otherwise there is a risk of duplication with a great deal of the court's time being taken up with repetition of issues. In addition, all the factors in the case may not become apparent until after all the relevant directions, in particular for disclosure of documents, have been carried out.

2.5   Disability

Under the Limitation Act 1980, s. 28, time does not begin to run against a person *under a disability* until the expiry of the disability. In this context 'disability' means legal disability, and therefore that the potential claimant is either:

(a) a child, i.e., a person under the age of 18; or

(b) a mental patient, i.e., a person who by reason of mental disorder within the meaning of the Mental Health Act 1983 is incapable of managing and admin istering his property and affairs.

Where a claimant suffers from a legal disability, the usual limitation period applicable to the kind of claim will begin to run only at the cessation of that disability. Thus if a mental patient recovers so as to become capable of administering his affairs, time will start to run from that point; in the case of a child time will start to run from his 18th birthday, though in a personal injury case it may be the date of knowledge that is relevant rather than the date of the accident. It may be that a claimant, injured when young, does not obtain the relevant knowledge of the circumstances of the accident, the identity of the potential defendant, etc., until well after his 18th birthday, in which case time will begin to run from then.

2.6   The relevant date for the limitation period

The action that must be taken within the limitation period is the *issue* of the claim, not its service. Similarly, in Part 20 claims against a new party, what matters is the date on which the Part 20 claim is issued at court (Limitation Act 1980, s. 35(1)(a)). (See **Chapter 27**.)

Civil evidence (1)

3

The law of evidence is notoriously a difficult and technical subject. It has reached its present confused state by piecemeal statutory reforms and tinkerings grafted on to a base of common law principles. In a few respects the law of civil evidence is almost the same as that of criminal evidence but the overwhelming majority of the rules are now radically different. One of the main purposes of the law of evidence is to prevent the trier of fact hearing evidence which he or she would be incompetent to assess properly. This is still a dominant feature of the rules of criminal evidence in the light of the supposed naivety of the average jury. That principle, however, may have little relevance in the ordinary civil case where the trial is conducted by a judge well able, in principle, to sift the evidence and discard what is unreliable, even if superficially attractive. For that, amongst other reasons, there has been considerable slackening in the former strictness of the rules of evidence in relation to civil proceedings. This has led to the more widespread acceptance of, for example, hearsay evidence (that trend reaching its zenith in the Civil Evidence Act 1995) and evidence of opinion in civil cases. In addition, although no legal authority states this, every practitioner in the civil courts will confirm that advocates are less ready to take purely technical points of admissibility and that a great deal of evidence which might well technically fall foul of one or other rule of admissibility is often admitted without challenge or comment.

In **Chapters 3 to 6** we shall be considering the rules of civil evidence in a straightforward and practical way including giving consideration to the stages in a civil case at which matters of evidence may arise and how the evidence in a civil case should be handled.

3.1 Introduction

The essence of the law of evidence is that it regulates what material may or may not be put before the person who is trying the facts, i.e., in an ordinary civil case the district judge, circuit judge or High Court judge. It also regulates the manner in which those facts may be proved.

To succeed in a case, the party who wishes to establish his case (usually, but not invariably, the claimant) must prove 'the facts in issue'. In most cases the 'facts in issue' can be determined by looking at the substantive law and at the statements of case, the whole point of which is to set out the factual case on which each party relies. So in a straightforward negligence case the claimant must prove that the defendant owed him a duty, breached that duty, and caused him foreseeable damage flowing from it; or that the defendant had a contractual relationship with him which the defendant breached and as a result of which the claimant suffered loss.

3.2   Types of evidence

3.2.1   In general

The kinds of evidence which may be adduced are usually divided into four categories:

(a) *Testimony*

This is an assertion by a witness in court, which in civil cases must in principle be on oath, of what he has himself perceived by one or more of his five senses.

(b) *Hearsay*

Hearsay is 'a statement other than one made by a person while giving oral evidence in proceedings and tendered as evidence of the truth of the fact stated'. Matters have been greatly simplified and clarified by the coming into force of the Civil Evidence Act 1995, which has the simple effect of making all hearsay admissible in civil proceedings (though see **4.3** for criteria to be applied by the court and practical considerations).

(c) *Documents*

Documents may be produced for inspection by the court. These may be either hearsay documents (for example, a witness statement), or a piece of real evidence (see (d) below). Thus, for example, the very contract, or will or lease may be proved in court to show the court what its terms were where that is relevant to the litigation. Similarly, public documents such as marriage certificates or certificates of conviction may be used in this way.

(d) *Real evidence*

This includes producing actual objects to the court, such as the very piece of machinery which caused an injury, or the shoes that the claimant was wearing when he slipped on a factory floor. It may also include going out of court to a 'view' of a material place, as in the famous case of *Tito v Waddell (No. 2)* [1977] Ch 106 where, in a dispute to do with mining rights on Ocean Island in the South Pacific, the judge, accompanied by lawyers from both sides, adjourned for several days to visit the island in question. This is not to say that going on a view takes place only in bizarre circumstances. In fact a view is very common even in the most mundane cases where something in question cannot be brought to court, such as disputes about the positioning of hedges, road layout at the occurrence of an accident, whether a certain piece of carpet is a proper match for another piece and the like. Most district judges have ample experience of going on a view, even in small claims cases (see **Chapter 17**).

3.2.2   Direct or circumstantial evidence

There are alternative ways of classifying evidence. The most useful way is perhaps to consider whether each piece of evidence is either *direct* or *circumstantial.*

3.2.2.1   Direct evidence

Direct evidence is evidence in the form usually of the testimony of the witness who has perceived a relevant fact (e.g., an eyewitness who saw exactly how an accident occurred).

Similarly, if the terms of a lease are disputed, the production of the actual executed and stamped lease is direct evidence.

3.2.2.2 Circumstantial evidence

This is evidence which does not directly establish a fact but is still admissible in order to enable the court to decide whether or not it did exist. Circumstantial evidence usually assists by enabling the trier of fact to make some deduction from generalisations, often about ordinary matters of human behaviour. So, for example, if the dispute concerns whether an individual, B, visiting his dangerously ill elderly relative T in hospital, used undue influence to get the latter to change his will to B's advantage, evidence that B's business was in grave financial difficulties at the time might be a relevant piece of circumstantial evidence. The reason is obvious, that persons in financial difficulties may be forced to go to unusual lengths to attempt to extricate themselves, and that the coincidence of the two events is of significance. On the other hand, this is just a generalisation about human behaviour and the conclusion that B *did* employ undue influence is far from inevitable.

Naturally a prolonged examination of circumstantial evidence can lead to sidetracks, and it is part of the function of the judge to control the relevance of testimony in the trial before him.

3.2.3 The facts in issue

The facts in issue are what the claimant needs to prove to succeed. These are not just the facts relevant to liability. Even though the claimant may establish liability easily, for example, that the defendant breached his contract, or caused a road accident in which the claimant was injured, the claimant always needs to go on to prove the damage which he claims to have suffered and that this flowed from the breach of contract or tort. For example, notwithstanding that a claimant can adduce sufficient evidence to prove that the defendant collided with his car, it might be the defendant's contention that, although he is liable for vehicle damage, the impact was so minimal that the personal injuries claimed by the claimant do not flow from it and are either the result of some pre-existing condition, or that the claimant is malingering. In such a case the claimant will have to call expert evidence about medical matters and also prove under the strict rules of admissibility each and every pecuniary item for which he is claiming such as loss of earnings, past and future, the cost of private medical treatment or nursing care, the cost of his mother travelling to visit him in hospital from the other end of the country and so on, as the case may be. As much time (or more) may be given over in some civil trials to questions of quantum as to questions of liability, and it is easy to overlook the fact that the rules of evidence are the same for matters of quantum.

3.3 The burden of proof

As indicated in **3.2.3**, in principle a party has the obligation of proving the facts which he needs to establish for success in his case. It is necessary to subdivide the term 'burden of proof' into two elements, the legal burden and the evidential burden.

3.3.1 The legal burden

The legal burden of proof is borne by the person who asserts a fact. This is normally the claimant. Much may depend upon the statement of case, however. A defendant who merely does not admit the claimant's case is not positively asserting anything of his own and therefore does not have the burden of proving alternative versions of how an accident came about. On the other hand, if the defendant goes so far as to assert contributory negligence, he is making a positive allegation against the claimant and it is then for him to prove that contributory negligence.

In some cases the incidence of a legal burden may be fixed by statute, e.g., if a debtor alleges that a credit bargain is extortionate, the burden of proof is switched to the creditor to prove the contrary (Consumer Credit Act 1974, s. 171(7)). The terms of a contract may also fix where the burden is to fall in litigation under the contract. This is quite common, for example, in insurance contracts and international trade contracts.

Outside the run of routine litigation it is often difficult to know on which party a burden falls. Sometimes the courts have placed the legal burden on one party because the other party would have had to prove a negative state of affairs and it is difficult to prove a negative. A good example is the following case which, although it is the case that went the furthest in the judicial system, could hardly be called a leading case in the sense that it enunciates any clear principle.

Joseph Constantine Steamship Line Ltd v *Imperial Smelting Corporation Ltd* [1942] AC 154

The appellants were shipowners who had chartered a cargo ship to the respondents. Immediately before the charter was about to start there was a great explosion on board the ship, such that the charter could not proceed and the contract was frustrated. There was no evidence at all about the cause of the explosion. A question arose as to whether it was for the charterers, in their claim for damages against the shipowners for failure to provide a ship, to prove that the explosion had occurred because of the shipowners' negligence, or whether it was for the shipowners to prove absence of negligence on their part. As there was no evidence at all about the cause of the explosion, whichever party bore the burden of proof was bound to lose. The House of Lords held that it was not for the shipowners to prove that the explosion was *not* due to their negligence or default because of the difficulty of proving a negative state of affairs. Thus the defence of frustration succeeded.

3.3.2 The evidential burden

The evidential burden is the obligation to bring sufficient evidence on the facts in issue to justify, as a possibility, a favourable finding on that issue by the ultimate trier of fact. Whether this burden has been discharged is decided during the course of the trial by the judge. The evidential burden, for this reason, is sometimes known as 'the burden of passing the judge'.

This term is much more relevant in a criminal context where there is a judge deciding on matters of law and evidence and a jury deciding on matters of fact. It leads to the position in criminal trials that a judge may decide that the evidential burden has not been discharged by the prosecution, and he may then stop the case in favour of the defence rather than leaving it to the jury. In civil cases, which are tried without a jury, the position still arises in principle at the end of the claimant's case. If by that stage the claimant's case is so weakened that there is no case for the defendant to meet, the judge may be asked to rule on a submission that there is no case for the defendant to be called upon to answer. If he so rules then the case is over.

3.4 The standard of proof

3.4.1 Proof on a preponderance of probabilities

In civil cases the standard of proof is proof 'on a preponderance of probabilities', which in ordinary English simply means that the claimant must prove that it is *more likely than not* that his version of the facts is right.

In simple terms it might be thought that this means a claimant need only prove matters to 51 per cent probability. In fact a wealth of case law has introduced a great deal of confusion into this area. The courts have often considered whether the conduct alleged against the defendant was in some way so reprehensible that it would be right to throw upon the claimant a burden of proof to a higher standard, perhaps even to the equivalent of the criminal standard, i.e., proof beyond reasonable doubt. Examples are an allegation that the defendant's director made a fraudulent misrepresentation (*Hornal* v *Neuberger Products Ltd* [1957] 1 QB 247); and a serious allegation of medical negligence (*Whitehouse* v *Jordan* [1980] 1 All ER 650 (CA), [1981] 1 WLR 246 (HL)), where Denning MR and Lawton LJ in the Court of Appeal considered that allegations of medical negligence were of such a serious nature in view of the doctor's future career and public confidence in the medical profession that they should be proved to a higher standard, but these observations were expressly disapproved when the case reached the House of Lords). The best view is probably that of the High Court of Australia in *Rejfek* v *McElroy* (1965) 112 CLR 517 at pp. 521–2, which was approved by Edmund Davies LJ in *Bastable* v *Bastable* [1968] 1 WLR 1684:

The difference between the criminal standard of proof and the civil standard of proof is no mere matter of words: it is a matter of critical substance. No matter how grave the fact which is to be found in a civil case, the mind has only to be reasonably satisfied and has not with respect to any matter in issue in such a proceeding to attain that degree of certainty which is indispensable to the support of a conviction upon a criminal charge.

The matter ought finally to have been decided by a case where the allegation was one of murder in a civil context:

Re Dellow's Will Trusts [1964] 1 WLR 451

D, the testator, left his whole estate to his wife with gifts over should she not survive. D suffered cerebral thrombosis and was disabled. He was cared for by his wife who eventually became acutely depressed. Both were found in a gas-filled room having taken sleeping tablets. The issue was whether Mrs Dellow killed herself and the testator, or whether it had been a genuine suicide pact. If she had killed the testator, his estate would pass to the subject of his gifts over, whereas if she had not killed him and it had been a genuine suicide pact, his estate would have passed to her and through her to her own beneficiaries. It was held that even though the crime alleged in the civil proceedings was murder, the standard of proof did not need to reach the very high standard required by the criminal law. On the evidence the only reasonable conclusion was that Mrs Dellow did kill her husband, and the court so found.

Despite this clear outcome a number of cases since have confused the position. For example, *Bahai* v *Rashidian* [1985] 1 WLR 1337, where it was suggested that an allegation of serious misconduct against a solicitor in a civil case involved a higher standard of proof; the celebrated defamation action between Neil Hamilton and Mohamed Al Fayed, where the judge directed the jury that it had to be satisfied 'on highly convincing evidence' that Hamilton was corrupt (and the jury so found); and *Miles* v *Cain* (1989) *The Times*, 15 December 1989 where a civil action for sexual assault was brought against a defendant whom the police had refused to prosecute. At the trial by judge alone, although the judge purported to direct himself on corroboration as if it were a criminal case, he found in favour of the claimant. The Court of Appeal found that the judge's sympathy for the claimant had coloured his view and that a higher degree of probability was required to prove that a defendant in a civil action had committed serious criminal assaults.

The best view of these cases is that there is only one standard, namely proof on a balance of probabilities. It is therefore wrong to say that the more serious the allegation the higher the degree of probability that is required. It is better to say that the more serious the allegation the more cogent is the evidence required to overcome the inherent improbability of what is alleged and thus to prove it.

3.4.2   What if the court is undecided?

The court re-visited this issue in *Cooper* v *Floor Cleaning Machines Ltd and Another* (2003) *The Times*, 24 October 2003. This case involved a collision between two vehicles where there were no independent witnesses and both parties were injured. The judge having heard evidence from both motorists found that neither were to be disbelieved and said that the only fair decision he could reach was the conclusion that on the balance of probabilities neither had discharged the onus of proving negligence against the other. The Court of Appeal observed that the collision could not have happened without one of the parties being negligent and that the judge had failed to analyse the evidence properly. It repeated that except in the most exceptional case it was incumbent on a judge hearing an action for negligence to analyse the evidence and decide which party was more likely to be correct. The Court of Appeal imposed its own view of the facts and found in favour of the defendant 'as a matter of broad probability'.

3.5   Methods of proof

The facts in issue must normally be proved by admissible evidence. This usually takes the form of a witness testifying on oath as to matters which he has himself perceived. It may also, as we mentioned in **3.2.1**, involve actual documents being put before the court because their very contents are in issue, e.g., the terms of a lease or will, or a document being produced as admissible hearsay evidence in instances where this is permissible, or an object being brought to court for the judge to see.

There are four examples of situations, however, where a court may treat matters as established without evidence being brought to court at all. These instances are:

(a) facts of which *judicial notice* is taken;

(b) facts which are *formally admitted* by a party;

(c) facts which are the subject of a *presumption*;

(d) facts which may be *inferred*.

3.5.1 Judicial notice

Facts which will be judicially noticed are those which are incapable of dispute, either because they are so notorious or because they are readily ascertainable by reference to a proper source. When a court takes judicial notice it declares that it will find that a fact exists even though no evidence has been called to establish it. For example:

(a) that a fortnight is too short a period for human gestation (*R* v *Luffe* (1807) 8 East 193);

(b) that a defamatory postcard is likely to be read by anyone (*Huth* v *Huth* [1915] 3 KB 32);

(c) that criminals have unhappy lives (*Burn* v *Edman* [1970] 2 QB 541).

A judge may also act upon facts which he has ascertained from sources to which it is proper for him to refer. For example:

(a) where a certificate is received from the Secretary of State on a matter of foreign policy, e.g., the recognition of a foreign sovereign, or whether a state of war exists (*Duff Development Co. Ltd* v *Government of Kelantan* [1924] AC 797);

(b) matters of historical fact, e.g., *Read* v *Bishop of Lincoln* [1892] AC 644, a case to do with the historical basis of a church practice;

(c) custom and professional practice, e.g., the practice of conveyancers, shipping customs and commercial customs.

3.5.2 Formal admissions

Facts may be formally admitted in civil cases by a party before trial. The opposite party is then relieved of the obligation of proving the matters admitted and they are taken to be established without formal evidence. Such admissions may be made by any document, e.g., letters between the parties, but more normally are admitted either:

(a) in the statement of case; or

(b) in response to a 'notice to admit facts'.

There is a necessary link between this topic of 'pure' evidence and practical civil procedure. For that reason reference back to this section is suggested after reference to **Chapters 11, 12** and **19**.

3.5.2.1 In the statement of case

EXAMPLE

The claimant pleads the existence of an oral contract and says that a certain term is imported into the contract, because of previous dealings between the parties. In his defence the defendant admits the existence of previous contracts containing the disputed term but goes on to say that the term was expressly varied here by subsequent agreement. The effect of this is thus to relieve the claimant of the obligation of proving the preliminary facts to do with the existence of other contracts and the term that was imported into them. The dispute now centres entirely on the question of whether and how the term was expressly varied in the present case.

3.5.2.2 In response to a 'notice to admit facts'

Under CPR, r. 32.18, a party who wishes his opponent to admit some fact without the need to call a witness at trial to prove it, may serve on his opponent a 'notice to admit facts' which specifies the fact required to be admitted. A party may use this procedure if for any reason he wishes to avoid calling a witness, for example, in order to save time and costs. Examples are where the fact appears to be uncontroversial and the witness will be expensive to call because he will demand a substantial expert witness fee, or perhaps will have to be brought from abroad. In addition, it may be useful to use this method to get the opposing party to admit facts which it would be very time-consuming to prove.

Such notices may in principle be served at any time up to 21 days before trial. A party who receives such a notice may then either:

(a) Admit the fact. This means that the other party is relieved from calling evidence about the fact at trial and it is taken as established. Thus the first party has succeeded in his object.

(b) Not admit the fact. In this case the first party must call the necessary evidence properly to prove the facts at trial. However, if the first party *succeeds* in proving the facts at trial, then, whoever wins the case at trial on the main issue, the court is likely to order that the costs of proving the facts shall be paid by the party who refused to admit them (CPR, r. 44.3).

Thus the sanction for a party failing to admit the fact that he should have admitted is a penalty in costs. Of course, if the party who serves the notice to admit *fails* to prove the facts at trial, the notice is of no effect whatever on costs.

EXAMPLE

The claimant is injured in a road accident caused by a collision at a crossroads. The claimant is self-employed, and in the period while he is injured he loses some particularly profitable work which he would otherwise have had. It will, however, take a lot of time and expense at trial to prove the existence of these contracts and the precise net amounts which they would have brought him, and the evidence on this aspect, including evidence of an accountant, might take some hours. Accordingly, the claimant serves a notice to admit the amounts which he would have lost during his period of incapacity. The defendant does not accept the notice to admit facts and the claimant is obliged to call all the relevant evidence at trial a process which takes several hours. The judge finds that the claimant has established the exact amount of his loss but finds for the defendant on *liability*, i.e., that the accident was caused by the claimant himself. Although the claimant will therefore inevitably be ordered to pay the defendant's costs of everything else in the trial, the judge may order that the defendant pays the claimant's costs of calling the evidence on these items of quantum if the defendant should reasonably have admitted them.

On the same facts, if the judge had *not* accepted all the evidence but had found, for example, that the claimant's actual loss in the period was rather less than he had claimed, the costs of the evidence would have formed part of the general costs, awarded to the defendant.

The possibility of using a notice to admit facts always worth considering. The CPR stress the importance of the parties doing their best to make the trial as brief and efficient as possible by agreeing all matters about which reasonable agreement is possible. A notice to admit facts should not, of course, be abused. There is little point in serving a notice on the defendant requiring him to admit some fact so central that the whole of liability and quantum flows from it. If the defendant is continuing to defend then no response will be received. Nor should one behave unreasonably in general with regard to such notices. In the above example it would have been wrong for the claimant to have served his notice to admit facts before he had himself given full disclosure of the documentary evidence relevant to the claims which he was advancing so that the defendant could have a reasonable chance to consider it.

3.5.3 Presumptions

Certain matters may be presumed by the court to exist without formal proof. This means that a person challenging the existence of a certain state of affairs has the burden of disproving it rather than vice versa, no matter which of them is claimant and which defendant. An example is the well-known presumption of legitimacy, which is that a child born during the existence of a marriage is presumed to be legitimate so that a party wishing to dispute that fact has the burden of proving it. Another example is the presumption of regularity in official matters, expressed in the Latin maxim *omnia praesumuntur rite esse acta*. This means that there is a presumption, unless the contrary is proved, that public officials have been properly appointed and public acts properly carried out.

Neither of the presumptions mentioned above is irrebuttable. They are merely what a court will take to be the case if there is no evidence sufficient to overturn the presumption. Thus if, for example, the whole point of a case is that it is alleged that a certain public official was not properly appointed so that some act done by him is a nullity, provided the person making this allegation can prove it on a balance of probabilities, the presumption will be displaced. In the case of the presumption of legitimacy, this is expressed in s. 26 of the Family Law Reform Act 1969, which provides that:

Any presumption of law as to the legitimacy . . . of any person may in any civil proceedings be rebutted by evidence which shows that it is more probable than not that that person is illegitimate.

There is only one presumption of much importance in civil cases. Namely *res ipsa loquitur*.

3.5.3.1 *Res ipsa loquitur*

Res ipsa loquitur is a presumption of negligence which arises where the whole activity is under the management of the defendant and the accident is such as in the ordinary course of things does not happen if those who have the management of the activity use proper care. Thus, in the absence of explanation by the defendants, there is a presumption that the accident arose from negligence, and the effect of this is to shift the burden of proof onto the defendants once the primary facts are established. See *Scott* v *London and St Katherine Docks Co.* (1865) 3 Hurl & C 596, 159 ER 665 where, while S was passing through the defendant's dock, a bag of sugar fell on him from a crane and injured him. In the normal course of things the claimant would have had the burden of proof on all issues of fact, and thus would have had to put his finger on precisely which employee loading the hoist from which the sugar fell had been negligent and in what way. The operation of the presumption, however, once the primary fact was proved, shifted the burden to the defendant to show positively that there was an absence of negligence.

The results of the many decided cases on this presumption leave it unclear precisely what elements of the burden of proof are discharged by its operation. The clearest statement is said to be *Barkway* v *South Wales Transport Co. Ltd* [1948] 2 All ER 460, in the judgment of Asquith LJ at p. 471. On this view where the maxim applies it is for the defendant to do more than show an equally possible non-negligent explanation—he must show positively that the cause did *not* connote negligence. This case was considered in *Henderson* v *Henry E. Jenkins & Sons* [1970] AC 282, which, although a House of Lords case, puts the matter in a somewhat less clear way.

This presumption of law, if it is one, is now of considerably less importance in practical litigation. Recent cases have tended to play down its importance. It was said in one case, for example, that it is 'merely a way of helping to evaluate evidence . . . not bound by technical rules' and in another case that it would never have been considered to be a rule of law at all if it had not been expressed in Latin.

3.5.4 Inferences of fact

These are merely examples of the court being prepared to draw common-sense conclusions from primary facts without subjecting the matter to the need for formal proof. They should thus be contrasted with the question of presumptions, or the strict rules of evidence as indicated above.

An example of an inference of fact is when a judge, in arriving at his decision on negligence, draws conclusions as to what the 'reasonable man' ought to have done in the situation which confronted the defendant. This very non-specific way of establishing matters is inadequately analysed in most evidence textbooks, and it passes without mention in many judgments where judges draw these kind of conclusions. So, for example, in *R* v *Thompson* [1918] AC 221, a case to do with an allegation of homosexual conduct involving young boys, the court treated it as a matter of common sense that where indecent photographs of young boys were found in the home of the accused he was likely to be a homosexual with such leanings.

When analysing the relevant facts in a civil case it is always vital to bear in mind how many of the primary facts need to be established before the court can be called upon to make reasonable inferences.

3.6 Competence and compellability

A witness is *competent* if he can lawfully be called to give evidence; *compellable* if he can be made to give evidence even if he is unwilling to do so.

3.6.1 The general rule

The general rule is that all persons in civil cases are competent to give evidence and all competent persons are also compellable. One can compel a witness to attend court and to answer questions by a witness summons. Failure to attend court is a contempt and will result in arrest. Similarly, if having come to court the witness refuses to answer questions, this will again be a contempt leading to criminal penalties. A witness may claim *privilege* not to answer certain questions in certain situations, which will be further discussed in 5.2. Subject to that, however, a witness, once called, must cooperate fully in the proceedings.

The rule concerning competence and compellability extends to the opposing party and his/her spouse. Thus if one finds that one's opponent is not proposing to testify, it is perfectly in order to serve a witness summons on him to compel him to testify.

3.6.2   Evidence on oath

In civil cases oral evidence must in general be given on oath. (This is not entirely logical, for in the situations where hearsay evidence is admitted, e.g., under the Civil Evidence Act 1995, evidence in the form of written statements may be put in, and this evidence does not have to be in the form of an affidavit (a sworn statement) but can simply be a witness statement.) The only substantial exception to the rule that all evidence must be sworn is that of children (see **3.6.3** below).

3.6.3   Children

In civil cases, by virtue of s. 96 of the Children Act 1989, children may now give *unsworn* evidence if they are possessed of sufficient intelligence to justify the reception of the evidence and understand the duty of speaking the truth. There will therefore be an initial test by the judge to see how intelligent the child is, and no matter how basically intelligent it is, what its state of awareness is in relation to the proceedings generally and the particular need to speak the truth.

A judge will test a child for its competence by asking it questions, naturally in a friendly and sympathetic manner, in open court. It is impossible to say, from the case law, that there is any hard and fast age at which a child is too young to testify. All the relevant cases deal with criminal evidence, and although previously it had been held undesirable to call a child as young as five years old, later cases have held that at present the public generally have confidence in the evidence of children and that, provided proper precautions are taken by adequately testing the intelligence and awareness of the child, the evidence of a child may be just as reliable as that of an adult. See in particular *R* v *Wright* (1987) 90 Cr App R 91 and *R* v *Z* [1990] 2 QB 355.

3.7   Testimony

The general rule is, as mentioned at **3.6.2**, that all evidence must be given on oath or by a witness who has made an affirmation. The law is governed by the Oaths Act 1978. The oath will be administered to Christians or Jews unless the witness objects. A solemn affirmation may be administered instead if the witness is not a believer or taking an oath is contrary to his religion, or if it is impracticable to administer the oath in a manner appropriate to a witness's religion. What matters in these cases is whether the witness agrees that the form of oath or affirmation is binding on his conscience.

Evidence at trial proceeds in three stages—examination-in-chief, cross-examination and re-examination—which we shall now consider in turn.

3.7.1   Examination-in-chief

The purpose of examination-in-chief is for the advocate calling the witness to obtain evidence to support his client's case. Inevitably, therefore, an advocate will only call witnesses who he anticipates will provide helpful evidence. Under a procedure described at **19.3** below, in all civil claims the statements of the parties and their witnesses are exchanged in advance. Under the CPR in general the judge should take steps to shorten the trial by dispensing with examination-in-chief altogether, and thus requiring each witness merely to swear as to the truth of his previously exchanged written statement and then be tendered for cross-examination.

To the writer's knowledge some judges dislike this procedure, believing that to see a witness telling his own story in his own words in the course of examination-in-chief is very helpful in getting the full facts and in testing the witness's credibility. To the extent, therefore, that judges of this persuasion permit it, there will continue to be evidence-in-chief in civil trials.

In examination-in-chief the general rule is that *leading questions* may not be used. A leading question is one which:

(a) assumes the existence of disputed facts as to which the witness is to testify; or

(b) suggests the required answer.

Leading questions are improper because constant reiteration of facts which are really in dispute may influence the trier of fact to regard them as established, or because they coach the witness. Thus questions which generally require only the answer 'Yes' or 'No' are often improperly leading. Leading questions may be permitted in respect of formal or introductory matter, or by agreement.

It is necessary to consider three separate topics in relation to one's own witnesses' examination-in-chief, namely:

(a) refreshing the memory;

(b) previous consistent statements by the witness;

(c) unfavourable and hostile witnesses.

3.7.1.1   Refreshing the memory

The witness may refresh his or her memory *out of court* whether outside the courtroom immediately before the trial, or at home previously—from any document. Thus it is perfectly proper to post a witness his witness statement, perhaps made some years previously, shortly before a civil trial. According to the criminal case of *Owen* v *Edwards* (1983) 77 Cr App R 191, in such a case there is a duty to inform one's opponent that the memory refreshing has occurred and the opponent has the right to see the statement in question. This is of less importance now that the exchange of witness statements in advance is the norm in civil claims. A witness may also refresh his memory from a document outside the courtroom, and be permitted to withdraw to do so, even after he has begun to give evidence, in a proper case. See *R* v *Da Silva* [1990] 1 WLR 31.

In court a witness may refresh his or her memory in the witness-box by reference to a document that that witness has made or verified, provided the following conditions are satisfied:

(a) The document must have been made at substantially the same time as the occurrence of the events about which the witness is testifying. This is a question of fact on which case law is inconsistent. Certainly a delay of a few hours will be in order, but longer delays will be fatal.

(b) The document must have been made by the witness himself, or supervised or verified by him immediately afterwards. See, for example, *Burrough* v *Martin*

(1809) 2 Camp 112, 170 ER 1098, where a captain who had inspected his ship's log throughout the voyage was allowed to refresh his memory from it although the entries had been made by the mate.

(c) The document must be produced in court for inspection by the opposing advocate, and the judge may also see it. If opposing counsel cross-examines on the parts which have been used to refresh the memory, that does not make the document 'evidence' in itself so that it does not become a separate piece of testimony as to the facts; however, if the opposing counsel cross-examines on other parts of the document he makes it evidence and the document may then be put before the judge, who may take note of the whole of its contents notwithstanding that the document may contain hearsay, since that will now generally be admissible by virtue of the Civil Evidence Act 1995, s. 6(4).

The effect of this is not of any great consequence. It simply means that a separate piece of testimony is in principle provided by the witness's statement in addition to the witness's verbal evidence. A judge is not likely to find that it adds greatly to the picture, however, since both pieces of evidence come from the same witness and the consistency shown may be consistency in a lie, just as easily as in the truth.

3.7.1.2   Previous consistent statements

The general rule is that a witness may not be asked in chief whether he has previously made a statement consistent with his testimony. The reason is that such evidence is in the main pointless. To show that a witness told a consistent story may as easily prove consistency in a lie as consistency in the truth, and it adds little to the trier of fact's overall picture of the disputed facts.

The important exception to this rule in civil cases is where a previous consistent statement is admitted to rebut an allegation of recent fabrication by the witness. If it is alleged by the cross-examiner that a witness's story has been recently concocted, then a previous statement concerning the same matter becomes admissible. This is especially the case if the allegation is directly that the witness has collaborated with one of the parties to falsify his evidence. To bring in this rule it is not enough merely to attack the truth of the witness's evidence; there must be a question of time involved, in the nature of 'When did you invent this version?'

The best illustration, albeit in a criminal context, is the case of *R v Oyesiku* (1971) 56 Cr App R 240. The accused was charged with assaulting a policeman. After he had been arrested his wife went to see the family solicitor and described what had occurred, which was to the effect that it was the police who had been the assailants. At the time she made this statement the wife had not been able to see her husband in the cells. At trial the wife was cross-examined to the effect that she had collaborated with her husband to make up her untruthful version. The Court of Appeal held that it would have been proper for the solicitor to have been called to prove that the wife had given him a statement at a time when she could not possibly have colluded with her husband.

In fact this principle most often arises during *re-examination* after the allegation has been put in cross-examination, but it is nonetheless convenient to deal with it here.

Where a previous consistent statement is put in evidence to demonstrate this, by virtue of s. 6 of the Civil Evidence Act 1995, such a statement is evidence of the facts to be taken into account by the trial judge. It obviously has a particular usefulness if the timing of the previous statement demonstrates that the allegation of fabrication is unfounded.

3.7.1.3 Unfavourable and hostile witnesses

When preparing cases, solicitors take a statement in written form from each witness. A good statement taken early in the case will provide a lot of background information. Some of this may be irrelevant, e.g., if a witness is invited to expand on a subject area in the hope of providing new information or new leads. In a personal injury case for example, it may be helpful to let a witness talk at length about the situation in a factory, or the attitude of the management to safety issues generally. When the final witness statement is prepared in its formal shape for exchange, a good deal of this background or inadmissible material may be left out. It sometimes happens that a witness changes his mind about cooperating between giving an initial statement and the trial. It may be difficult to decide whether to risk calling the witness (despite his uncooperative attitude) by a witness summons and hoping that he will give evidence truthfully in accordance with his first statement. The witness may indeed have refused to sign the later formal statement, putting his evidence in admissible form. In that case a copy of his first statement may have to be served. Sometimes even witnesses who have signed the later, formal statement may decide to be uncooperative at trial.

A witness who gives evidence at trial in accordance with a prior statement is said to be 'coming up to proof'. The following paragraphs deal with the situation where a party's own witness lets him down and thus does not 'come up to proof'.

A witness no longer has to be taken laboriously through his evidence and give it all orally. A witness statement will usually now stand as examination-in-chief so the witness will just be asked to give his name and address and to confirm that his written statement is true. In the past, a witness might be unhelpful in a variety of ways. He might, for example, have genuinely forgotten key aspects of his evidence. This should be rare because it is perfectly proper practice to send a witness a copy of his statement shortly before trial and ask him to re-read it and familiarise himself with it.

Now, the fact that a witness is being uncooperative will usually be demonstrated by him saying, when asked to confirm that his written statement is true, that he cannot remember it and wishes to withdraw it; or by saying that it is not and asking to give some directly opposite version; or perhaps in cross-examination coming out with some quite different story. We shall now consider the rules relevant to this difficulty.

(a) *The general common law rule*

The general rule at common law is that a party may not *impeach* his own witness, i.e., he cannot call evidence from another source to show that his own witness is mistaken, forgetful or lying. All he can do is call other witnesses, if he has them, and hope that they will be more favourable and that the judge will prefer those witnesses. Nor, at common law, can a party cross-examine his own witness or attack his own witness's character.

(b) *Types of unhelpful witnesses*

There are two kinds of such witnesses:

(i) An *unfavourable* witness is one who is not 'coming up to proof' and fails to prove some fact in issue or proves the opposite fact. Unfavourable witnesses cannot be cross-examined, attacked as to credit or have their previous inconsistent written statements put to them to show their lack of credibility.

Unfavourable witnesses may be unfavourable because of lapse of time since the incident so that they are forgetful, or are mistaken or foolish. It is when an advocate is confronted with such an unfavourable witness that the bar on leading questions bites the hardest. Often, if the advocate could just prompt his witness with a key fact it might unlock that witness's memory, but he cannot in principle do this.

(ii) A *hostile* witness is one 'not desirous of telling the truth at the instance of the party calling him'. Where an advocate finds that his own witness appears hostile, he should proceed to ask the judge to allow him to treat the witness as hostile. Whether a witness is hostile may in principle be detected by the judge from the witness's demeanour, since hostile witnesses often exhibit a truculent or an awkward attitude, but the witness's previous written statement may also be shown to the judge so that he can see how glaring the inconsistency is from what was written before. The judge must then consider whether the witness is indeed simply foolish, or mistaken or forgetful, or whether he is actually hostile. If the judge allows the witness to be treated as hostile, at common law cross-examination of a party's own witness is then permitted, e.g., by leading questions to test the memory and perception of the witness and by putting the witness's previous inconsistent statement to him.

(c) *Statute*

A statute now governs the matter, namely the Criminal Procedure Act 1865, s. 3, which, despite its title, applies equally to civil proceedings. The statute in effect duplicates the common law. The section reads:

A party producing a witness shall not be allowed to impeach his credit by general evidence of bad character, but he may in case the witness shall, in the opinion of the judge, prove adverse, contradict him by other evidence, or by leave of the judge, prove that he has made at other times a statement inconsistent with his present testimony; but before such last mentioned proof can be given the circumstances of the supposed statement, sufficient to designate the particular occasion, must be mentioned to the witness, and he must be asked whether or not he has made such statement.

Thus the procedure is to invite a hostile witness to consider whether he has ever made a previous statement and, if he denies it, to show it to him and ask him for his explanation of the inconsistency. Thereupon the matter is governed by a further statute, the Civil Evidence Act 1995, s. 6(3), which provides that where a previous inconsistent or contradictory statement is put in evidence under s. 3 of the 1865 Act, *'the statement shall by virtue of this subsection be admissible as evidence of any facts stated therein of which direct oral evidence by [the witness] would be admissible'*. The net effect of this, therefore, is that the trial judge can choose between the two versions and decide which to believe. He can thus take into account any reasons for the change of heart by the witness such as, for example, the suggestion of a grudge having arisen between the witness and the party calling him, or other forms of bias.

3.7.2 Cross-examination

All witnesses are liable to be cross-examined. All parties have a right to cross-examine any witness not called by them. Therefore, if there are several defendants, each has a right to cross-examine the claimant's witnesses and each other's.

There are two objectives in cross-examination, namely:

(a) to elicit information about the facts in issue favourable to the party cross-examining;

(b) to test the truthfulness of, and where necessary cast doubt upon, the evidence given in chief by the witness.

When conducting cross-examination it is an advocate's duty:

(a) to challenge every part of a witness's evidence which is in conflict with his own case;

(b) to put his own case to the witness in so far as the witness is able to say anything relevant about it;

(c) to put to a witness any allegation against the witness which it is proper to put.

If an advocate fails to challenge the evidence-in-chief on any point he may be held to have accepted it and not later be able to call witnesses to contradict it, or to comment upon it adversely in his closing speech.

In cross-examination leading questions may be asked, and indeed are the norm, since the advocate is often putting his own version of the facts to the witness and inviting his agreement. A judge will control cross-examination and disallow questions which become improper, vexatious or oppressive. The usual exclusionary rules of evidence apply to evidence sought to be obtained by cross-examination as much as to evidence-in-chief, so that, for example, the rule against improper evidence of opinion applies.

When framing cross-examination it is vital to bear in mind the objectives mentioned earlier and to ensure that each question, or series of questions, is not merely a ramble around peripheral matters but is directed, however lengthily and persistently, to one or other of the prime objectives of furthering one's own client's case by obtaining evidence from the witness in its favour, or to undo previous adverse evidence from that witness.

The two most important topics in the practice of cross-examination concern:

(a) previous inconsistent statements; and

(b) cross-examination and collateral issues.

3.7.2.1 Previous inconsistent statements

We have already considered the problem of prior inconsistent statements by *one's own witness* and the effect of s. 3 of the Criminal Procedure Act 1865 (see **3.7.1.3**). We are now dealing with the situation where an advocate knows that his opponent's witness has made a previous statement inconsistent with his evidence-in-chief, and the procedure by which one can put this inconsistent statement to him.

The relevant sections are ss. 4 and 5 of the Criminal Procedure Act 1865, both of which apply in civil as well as criminal proceedings.

(a) *Section 4*

This applies to oral previous statements. If a witness is asked during cross-examination about a former statement made by him which is inconsistent with his present testimony, then if he does not admit having made such a statement proof may be given that he did in fact make it by calling a witness who heard him say the words in question. However, before that can be done there must be two other steps, namely:

(i)   the circumstances in which the alleged statement was made must be put to the witness; and

(ii) he must then be asked whether he made such a statement.

(b) *Section 5*

This applies where the previous statement is in writing. A witness can be cross-examined about such a statement without the statement actually being shown to the witness; but if the cross-examiner actually intends to contradict the witness by using the witness statement, he must draw the witness's attention to those parts he intends to use to contradict the witness. Accordingly, if the witness retracts his evidence-in-chief and agrees with his former statement, there may be no need to use the statement itself.

A cross-examiner is not obliged to put the statement in evidence (remembering that to do so makes the whole statement available to the judge and that there may be matters in it that the cross-examiner would prefer him not to see), and this is so even if he shows it to the witness because that is not 'putting it in evidence'. However, the cross-examiner *must* go on to put the statement in evidence if he wishes to use it as a contradictory statement.

The usual procedure is that counsel asks the witness to read the statement to himself and asks him if he wishes to adhere to what he has said in examination-in-chief. If the witness says 'No', counsel has achieved his object. If he says 'Yes', then counsel will need to decide whether and how to use the statement.

The concluding words of s. 5 are confusing in the civil context where there is no jury. The section concludes:

Provided always, that it shall be competent for the judge, at any time during the trial, to require the production of the writing for his inspection, and he may thereupon make such use of it for the purposes of the trial as he may think fit.

From this it would appear that a judge has the right to demand a statement even where counsel does not propose to put it in evidence. Case law in a criminal context, however, would indicate that a judge would never take this direction without the consent of counsel using the statement.

(c) *The use of the statement when admitted*

By virtue of s. 6(1) of the Civil Evidence Act 1995, a contradictory previous statement *is* evidence of the facts in question. It is thus within the judge's power to choose which of the two contradictory versions he prefers to believe. Often the wisest course would be for the judge to conclude that the witness before him is a liar and to disregard the whole of his evidence. It may in some circumstances, however, be right for the judge to prefer the previous statement to the oral evidence, or the latter if an explanation of the change of mind is forthcoming.

3.7.2.2 Cross-examination on collateral issues

As noted earlier, cross-examination should be directed either to the issues in the case or to collateral issues. When it is directed to the issues in the case, what is asked is up to counsel and there is an opportunity for counsel to call evidence in contradiction or rebuttal of what a witness says. There are, however, special rules relating to cross-examination on *collateral* issues, designed to stop a multiplicity of sidetracks being pursued in the interests of saving time.

(a) *The credit of the witness*

The most important collateral issue is the credit of the witness, that is, the question of the extent to which the witness's evidence is trustworthy. The general rule is that a witness's answers in relation to the *issues in the case* can be contradicted by further evidence but that answers relevant *only to the witness's credit* are final.

It must be acknowledged that in marginal cases this is a difficult rule to apply. The best illustration (although from a criminal context) was the old rule (now modified by statute) that in a rape case one could ask the victim whether she had previously had consensual intercourse with the accused and, if she denied it, call evidence to rebut her denial. However, if one went on to ask her whether she had had intercourse with other men and she denied it, no evidence in rebuttal could be called. The reasoning was said to be that the first instance went to the issue (i.e., the likelihood of consent) and the second just to credit (promiscuous reputation), but the dividing line as far as relevance is concerned is highly artificial.

(b) *Exceptions to the general rule*

There are several exceptions to the general rule that answers by a witness as to his credit are final. In the following cases evidence in rebuttal is allowed:

(i) *Evidence of the physical or mental condition of the witness such as to show he is unreliable*

If it is alleged that the witness suffers from some medical condition such that his evidence ought not to be believed and he denies suffering from that condition, evidence of the condition may be called. Thus, for example, if it is suggested that a witness could not possibly have seen a certain incident at the distance claimed because he is chronically short-sighted and he does not wear spectacles, or that the witness suffers a hysterical personality and is prone to fantasise, then such evidence becomes admissible (see *Toohey* v *Metropolitan Police Commissioner* [1965] AC 595).

(ii) *Bias or partiality*

If it is alleged that a witness is biased against a party or partial in a party's favour and the witness denies it, then it may be proper to put in evidence circumstances from which the bias or partiality is said to have arisen. Thus in the case of *R* v *Shaw* (1888) 16 Cox CC 503, where the accused was charged with forgery, the main witness against him was one P who said that he had seen the accused committing the forgery. P was asked whether he did not have a grudge against the accused arising out of an incident some two years before, and he denied this. The defence were then allowed to call a witness to whom P had sworn he would get even with the accused because of the grudge.

(iii) *Previous convictions*

By virtue of the Criminal Procedure Act 1865, s. 6, the witness may be questioned as to whether he has been convicted of any crime. If he denies it, it is in order for the cross-examining party to prove such conviction.

In civil cases this rule is subject to the provisions of the Rehabilitation of Offenders Act 1974. Section 4(1) of that Act forbids the questioning of a person about 'spent' convictions. Convictions become 'spent' under the Act by reference not to the offence charged but to the kind of sentence passed, with certain kinds of sentence becoming 'spent' very quickly and more serious kinds of penalty never becoming spent. Subject to that, however, one can in principle put convictions of any kind to a witness no matter how irrelevant in truth to his credit. It would obviously be fruitless, though, to put to a witness, say, convictions for past driving offences and the like. Convictions for offences denoting lack of credibility, such as perjury, criminal deception, etc., are the most useful. It is also permissible to put to a witness the question of how he pleaded at his trial for the past offence, since it is clearly relevant to credit to show, if it is the case, that he pleaded not guilty but was nonetheless convicted having been disbelieved by the jury.

(iv) *Evidence of general reputation for untruthfulness*

This is an ancient common law rule which provides that after a witness has given evidence the cross-examiner can call evidence that the first witness has a general reputation as a liar and that his evidence should not be believed. This is an exception of limited use in ordinary litigation and it is not sufficient to call a witness simply to say that he would disbelieve the first witness. General reputation in the locality is what matters. See *R* v *Richardson* [1969] 1 QB 299.

3.7.3 Re-examination

In re-examination of one's own witnesses, leading questions may not be asked. Questions should be confined to matters which have arisen out of cross-examination, and thus re-examination cannot be used to supplement defects in an advocate's own examination-in-chief, except where these have been touched on in cross-examination.

A new matter may only be introduced with the permission of the judge, and permission will not easily be given, primarily because if new matter is introduced, the cross-examiner must then be given another opportunity to cross-examine and so the trial will become somewhat undisciplined.

Re-examination is usually an attempt to salvage evidence which has been shaken in cross-examination. It involves counsel asking his own witness, obviously in a more sympathetic manner than that shown by the cross-examiner, to explain or clarify any ambiguities or confusion brought out in cross-examination.

3.7.4 Evidence in rebuttal

All the evidence which the claimant intends to call should be before the court by the end of his own case. New evidence can only be called after the defence case with permission of the judge, and he will only give permission if the evidence relates to a matter which could not reasonably be foreseen. The best examples in case law are from criminal cases, but the rule is the same.

A clear example is *R* v *Day* [1940] 1 All ER 402. In this case the accused was charged with forgery. The prosecution called their evidence and the defence gave evidence denying the forgery. Thereafter the prosecuting counsel applied for leave to call a handwriting expert. The judge permitted this. On appeal the conviction was quashed. The evidence was wrongly admitted as it did not relate to a matter arising unexpectedly; it should have been clear to the prosecution from the outset that they would have needed a handwriting expert. There had thus been a material irregularity.

It seems, however, that a trial judge has a wide discretion to allow the claimant to call further evidence after the close of his case. Such evidence may be allowed, for example, to make good a purely formal omission, as in *R* v *Francis* [1990] 1 WLR 1264 where the prosecution were allowed to recall an inspector in charge of an identification parade to tell the court that it was the appellant who had been identified, that detail having been omitted in error in examination-in-chief.

Although generally more latitude is allowed about evidential matters in civil trials, given that full witness statements are usually served long before trial, a judge may take some persuading that anything has arisen which was so unexpected as to require evidence in rebuttal and which the claimant ought not to have anticipated so as to enable him to bring evidence to meet it in his own part of the case.

3.7.5 The judge's right to call witnesses

It is usually considered an essential part of the adversarial process that the parties themselves decide which witnesses they wish to call and what questions to ask. There is a good deal of case law in a criminal context about the occasions when a judge, without the consent of either party, may call and examine witnesses. In a civil context, however, the general rule is that the judge can call witnesses if he has the consent of all parties.

This situation is now highly unlikely because of the provision for full prior disclosure of witness statements and experts' reports. It is therefore hard to envisage why a judge would wish to call any witness whose evidence had not been put before him in the trial bundle. Of course, the court itself can appoint *expert witnesses*, but that will inevitably occur at an earlier stage than the trial and a report will have been disclosed in advance to both parties.

The judge has a discretion whether or not to permit the parties to cross-examine any witness whom he himself calls, though it will normally be appropriate for him to allow this (although he may restrict it to the subject matter of the witness's testimony).

Civil evidence (2): The Civil Evidence Acts 1995 and 1968

4.1 Hearsay and the Civil Evidence Act 1995

4.1.1 The rule against hearsay

The rule against hearsay was said to be the great rule of evidence underlying much of the common law. The definition of 'hearsay' is the same for civil as for criminal cases although the rule forbidding hearsay is of virtually no significance in civil proceedings following the Civil Evidence Act 1995 ('the 1995 Act').

Section 1(2) of the 1995 Act defines hearsay in the following words:

'hearsay' means a statement made otherwise than by a person while giving oral evidence in the proceedings which is tendered as evidence of the matters stated.

Hearsay is what most laymen would know to be hearsay, that is, where a witness attempts to tell the court what he was told by someone else before the proceedings. Hearsay also includes such things as a written statement (such as a witness statement) to be put before the court as evidence of the facts stated in it, and even includes a witness telling a court what he himself may have said on previous occasions. It is important to understand that it is not always hearsay when a witness wishes to repeat something to the court which has been said to him outside court, or a document of some kind is put before the court. It will not be hearsay at all if it is not 'tendered as evidence of the matters stated'. So, for example, if D says to A that C is a thief and C gets to hear of this, in the defamation proceedings which he might bring against D, he can call A to give evidence of what D said. The point is not to show that the words were *true*, but merely to show that they were *uttered* to demonstrate publication, an essential element in defamation. Likewise, if a document is put before the court not to prove the truth of the contents of what is stated in it but, for example, to demonstrate that it is a forgery or merely to show what terms a contract, or will, or lease contained, that also will not be hearsay.

4.1.2 The death of the rule against hearsay

Section 1(1) of the 1995 Act provides the simple and revolutionary statement that '*In civil proceedings evidence shall not be excluded on the ground that it is hearsay*'.

The effect of this is simple and clear. *All* hearsay is now admissible in English civil proceedings. Moreover, there is no discretion in the court to refuse to admit it, or to consider its weight or usefulness at the stage of admissibility. It simply *must be* admitted before the court and the judge has no discretion to stop it unless the piece of evidence which is hearsay also infringes some quite separate rule (for example, that it is inadmissible evidence of opinion from a layman who is not entitled to give the evidence in question).

Hearsay is therefore generally admissible and s. 1(2)(b) goes on to say that that simple rule includes hearsay of *any degree* and therefore hearsay evidence may be put before the court no matter how many intermediaries it goes through, even though the number of intermediaries may make the end result highly unreliable (as in a Chinese whispers scenario where witness W tells the court what he was told by A who had heard it from B who originally heard it from C who had heard it from D). On the question of *admissibility*, the number of intermediaries is irrelevant though that may be highly relevant when the court comes to decide what *weight* it will attach to the evidence.

It must be stressed therefore that the court cannot exclude evidence simply on the grounds that it is hearsay. This does not, however, deprive the court of the very wide general discretion which it has under CPR 32.1 to control the evidence and in particular 32.1(2), which provides:

the court may use its power under this rule to exclude evidence that would otherwise be admissible . . .

thus the court may exclude evidence if, for example, a witness refused to attend for cross examination which the court had required. So in *Polanski v Conde Nast Publications Ltd* (2005) *The Times*, 11 February 2005 the claimant was unwilling to attend the trial of his own action in the UK because he feared arrest and extradition to the USA on the basis of conviction for sexual offences in the USA many years ago, for which he had not yet been sentenced. The House of Lords held (reversing the Court of Appeal) that it was wrong to deprive the claimant of his claim and that he should be permitted to give evidence by video link, rather than using its powers to compel him to attend in the UK.

4.2 Safeguards in relation to hearsay evidence

Section 2 of the Act provides necessary safeguards, because clearly hearsay evidence, if put before the court by surprise, would be capable of causing great injustice. First, one obviously cannot cross-examine an absent witness to test his truthfulness, and secondly one would have been given no opportunity of investigating the nature of the hearsay in question, for example, by attempting to interview the witness who does not come to court and perhaps calling other evidence to contradict what the hearsay evidence will say. Accordingly, s. 2 provides that a person who wishes to use hearsay evidence must give appropriate notice of that fact and particulars relating to the evidence which are 'reasonable and practicable in the circumstances' so as to enable the opponent who receives the notice 'to deal with any matters arising from its being hearsay'.

This means that if a party, say C, is intending to use hearsay evidence at trial, he must give ample notice of his intentions to D so that D can decide whether he wishes to trace the absent witness and call him as a witness himself, or have him interviewed to check that he really did say the words attributed to him. Although there will be many cases when hearsay involves a witness repeating an oral statement the most common use of hearsay evidence will be where one party wishes simply to put in evidence in court a written statement from an absent witness without calling that person. This will be the main example considered in the rest of the text.

4.2.1 Procedural rules

Section 2(2) specifies that rules are to be made providing for the manner and time at which this notice is to be given. Those rules now appear at CPR, r. 33.2. (see **Chapter 19**)

Section 2(3) goes on to provide that the parties can agree between themselves to waive the notice requirement, which is only an instance of the general principle that the parties in a civil case can, by agreement, waive any of the rules of evidence if they wish.

4.2.2 The sanction for disregarding procedural rules

The issue then remaining is, what is the sanction on a party who has failed, contrary to the rules, to give the appropriate notice and advance information? Since s. 1(1) is in absolute terms and *requires* the court to receive the hearsay evidence, it would not be an appropriate sanction for the trial judge to say that he proposed to punish the party who had not given the appropriate notice by forbidding the use of evidence. The sanction expressed in s. 2(4) is that the court may *'consider the exercise of its powers with respect to the course of proceedings and costs'*. In other words, if surprise hearsay evidence is introduced, it may offer the other party an adjournment so that he can consider how to collect evidence to meet the hearsay on terms that the offending party who has failed to give the notice pays all the costs of the wasted day in court. In addition, the court may take account of the failure to give notice 'as a matter adversely affecting the weight to be given the evidence'. Therefore the judge in effect has a sanction by saying that he will penalise the failure to abide by the rules, whether that resulted from a simple oversight or deliberate sharp practice, by simply disbelieving the piece of evidence put in.

4.2.3 The witness who is not to be called

Section 3 provides that rules of court shall provide that if a party has indicated in advance that he intends to use hearsay evidence, any other party may call the absent witness with the permission of the court and, having called him to court, contrary to the usual rules, may cross-examine him as if he were a witness called by the party who initially indicated an intention to use his evidence in hearsay form. Therefore the decision whether or not to use such evidence must be taken after careful consideration because if one indicates a general intention to use such evidence the other party may call a witness whose evidence, or indeed possibly whose very existence, was unknown to him initially. This will therefore be an important practical and tactical consideration.

The rule now in CPR, r. 33.2, states that if a party intends to rely on hearsay evidence at trial and either:

(a) that evidence is to be given by a witness giving oral evidence; or

(b) that evidence is contained in a witness statement of a person who is not being called to give oral evidence,

that party complies with s. 2(1)(a) of the Civil Evidence Act 1995 by serving a witness statement on the other parties in accordance with the court's order.

When serving that witness statement, the party who intends to rely on the hearsay evidence must inform the other parties that the witness is not being called to give oral evidence and must give the reason why. The party proposing to rely on the hearsay evidence must serve the notice no later than the latest date for serving witness statements. If the hearsay evidence is to be in a document, he must supply a copy to any party who requests him to do so.

So whether the hearsay evidence is to be given orally by a witness who will be called (e.g., so he can recount what some other person not to be called told him out of court) or the hearsay comprises a witness statement from someone who will not be before the court at all, notice must be given. There are no technical requirements as to the form of the notice.

The notice must give a reason why a witness is not being called. It does not matter how good or flimsy the reason is, however, as the court has no power for that alone, to rule the statement inadmissible. The reason for not calling the witness may, however, have a great impact on the separate question of what *weight* the court will give to the hearsay evidence.

4.2.4   Circumstances when notice of intention to rely on hearsay evidence is not required

The rules discussed above apply in the case of evidence to be given at trial, but CPR, r. 33.3, declares that the duty to give notice of intention to adduce hearsay evidence does not apply:

(a) to evidence at hearings other than trials (i.e., interim applications during the course of the case);

(b) to statements allegedly made by the deceased in probate actions; or

(c) where the requirement is excluded by any practice direction.

Rule 33.4 provides that when one party seeks the permission of the court to call someone who has made a statement which the other party has indicated they intend to rely on as hearsay evidence, the application must be made to a district judge not more than 14 days after the day on which a notice of intention to rely on the hearsay evidence was served. Thus a fairly prompt decision will need to be made if one wishes to call such a witness before the court.

It should be noted that Part 33 applies to all hearsay and not merely to the most common instance, which is the witness statement. If, for example, a set of accounts is to be used to prove the matters stated, the requirement to give notice applies.

4.3   Section 4: The weight to be attached to the statement

Section 4 of the 1995 Act is a vitally important section because, as we have seen, s. 1(1) provides simply that all hearsay is admissible before the court. Section 4, however, sets out a number of *essential criteria* to which the court may have regard in deciding whether it will believe the truth of the hearsay adduced. The opening words of s. 4(1) provide that the court can have regard to *'any circumstances from which any inference can reasonably be drawn as to the reliability or otherwise of the evidence'*. This clearly means that the court must have regard to all the common-sense features which might tend to make hearsay evidence less reliable than credible oral testimony before the court. Apart from this general statement, the rest of the section provides some particular matters to which the court will have to have regard. Subsection (2) goes on to say that, in particular, regard can be had to whether:

(a) it would have been reasonable and practicable for the party by whom the evidence was adduced to have produced the maker of the original statement as a witness;

(b) the original statement was made contemporaneously with the occurrence or existence of the matter stated;

(c) whether the evidence involves multiple hearsay;

(d) any person involved had any motive to conceal or misrepresent matters;

(e) the original statement was an edited account or was made in collaboration with another or for a particular purpose;

(f) the circumstances in which the evidence is adduced as hearsay are such as to suggest an attempt to prevent proper evaluation of its weight.

4.3.1 The court's duty to assess the hearsay

In considering these matters the court will therefore want to know why no attempt has been made to produce the original maker of the out-of-court statement to give oral evidence, and if no satisfactory explanation of the witness's absence, e.g., illness, death, absence abroad or other genuine unavailability is advanced, the court may well draw adverse inferences. Likewise, the court will want to see how *contemporaneous* the hearsay statement was with the matters to which the statement was directed. As is well known, witnesses' memories fade very fast indeed, even about quite striking incidents, and therefore if a written statement was taken from a witness, say three days after an incident, and one party wishes to use the statement rather than calling the witness at trial, that statement will have a great deal more weight than one that was taken perhaps a year or more afterwards. Possibly the central features will still be remembered, but witnesses are unlikely then to remember the peripheral details which often help to set the whole picture, for example, if a witness has seen a dramatic road traffic accident although he may remember what happened to the vehicles at the centre of the action, he may not be able to remember such matters as the width of the road, angle of the junction, how other vehicles were parked, or the lighting or traffic conditions.

On the matter of *multiple hearsay*, it is again self-evident that hearsay at only one remove has less risk of being unreliable than hearsay which has been repeated in turn through many mouths before reaching the court and this is simply a matter of common sense. Similarly, if any person involved had a *motive to conceal or misrepresent*, because, for instance, they have a close bond to one or other party to the litigation, or perhaps even some active grudge against a party in the litigation, then due weight will be given to that feature. Thus self-evidently, if there has been a road accident a hearsay statement from a disinterested passer-by is a more valuable piece of evidence than a hearsay statement from a passenger in one of the vehicles, passengers being notoriously inclined to side with their own driver in relation to disputes about responsibility for an accident. Thus if the form of the hearsay were to be a witness statement tendered on behalf of the defendant and the statement came from a bystander, the court would naturally give it more weight than if it came from the defendant's passenger.

If the statement which is to be used is in some way an *edited or collaborative account* it will have less immediate value than one person's own statement in his own words. For example, if what is put forward is an edited account of proceedings before a committee of inquiry, and describes the conclusions they came to about, say, whether commercial fraud had occurred in the activities of a company's management, that will be much less valuable than full factual accounts from each of the people called as witnesses before the committee who may in turn be able to contribute hard facts.

Finally, and here there is clearly some overlap with the first of the criteria, the court will have regard to whether the circumstances indicate an *attempt to prevent proper evaluation* of the evidence by it being tendered in hearsay form rather than by bringing the person who knows the facts at first hand to court. Again a close examination of the reasons for the claimed unavailability of the original witness will be undertaken and if the court is not satisfied as to the genuineness of this unavailability, it will have due regard to that feature in deciding what weight if any to attach to the evidence.

The result of the court having to have regard to all these criteria is that, if it is possible, it will be better in the majority of cases to call the witness to give oral evidence so that he can be suitably cross-examined and the court will have the opportunity of judging his manner and demeanour to assist in assessing his credibility. Using evidence in hearsay form will therefore only be the norm for either relatively uncontroversial evidence, or evidence which is impossible, or perhaps simply inconvenient or too expensive to call. A party would need to consider very carefully whether the advantages of getting in the evidence unchallenged because the absent person cannot be cross-examined is not far outweighed by the fact that the court may then attach little weight to it.

4.3.2   Competence of the absent witness, and attacking his evidence

Section 5 of the 1995 Act can be more briefly dealt with. It provides, which is simply a matter of common sense, that one cannot get round the rules as to competence of witnesses by purporting to submit their evidence in a hearsay statement, so that if the court has reason to believe that the statement is from a child, or someone suffering a mental handicap, it will have to investigate the competence of the original witness who is the source from which the evidence comes.

Moreover, there is the further provision in s. 5(2) which is both common sense and common fairness that since, if hearsay evidence is to be admitted, the opponent is deprived of the opportunity of cross-examining the absent witness to test his evidence, that opponent may adduce any evidence about the credibility of the absent witness that he could have used in cross-examining him had he been present. Thus he may in particular prove that there was a previous inconsistent statement which says something different from that which is in the hearsay statement now adduced, or that the absent witness has a reason for being biased in favour of the party who is using his evidence or has a grudge against the opposite party, or had previous convictions for perjury, or as the case may be. The evidence which one can adduce under this section includes everything on which it would have been proper to cross-examine the absent witness had he been present.

Where one wishes to attack the credibility of an absent witness, notice of that intention must be given by virtue of CPR, r. 33.5(2), not more than 14 days after the day on which a hearsay notice relating to the hearsay evidence was served. No precise form of notice is prescribed by the rules. This is again a relatively short time span in which to consider what may be a very important piece of evidence, obtain one's client's instructions upon it, and see what other evidence is available to attack the credibility of the witness about whose existence one may have been totally unaware. The court will have the general power to extend the time period which it will do, on application, if good reason is shown. As generally, one's opponent can be asked to agree to an extension under CPR, r. 2.11, and the agreement should be in writing in which case no court order is required.

In order to demonstrate the format of a notice and notice in response indicating intention to attack credibility, examples are given at the end of this chapter.

4.4   Section 6: Use of previous statements of witnesses

Section 6 of the 1995 Act provides that if a party has given notice in advance that he intends to use the hearsay statement of a witness, but at trial actually calls that witness, the hearsay statement cannot be used without the leave of the court except for the specific purpose of rebutting a suggestion that the evidence has been fabricated. The purpose of this is simply to save court time by the unnecessary proliferation of multiple accounts of the same thing from the same witness. It is of little evidential value, if a witness is actually called and gives oral evidence then to introduce his previous written statement. This is discussed fully in the context of oral evidence of witnesses at **3.7.1.2**. The rules as to putting previous inconsistent statements of a witness to him, whether he is a hostile or an opposition witness, are preserved by the rest of s. 6. These matters are discussed fully in relation to witnesses who appear at court at **3.7.2.1**. Thus you can use the previous statement to discredit either a hostile witness whom you yourself have called but who lets you down, or opposing witnesses who have said something inconsistent in a previous statement.

Section 6(4) provides that nothing in the Act is to change the rules relating to refreshing of memory, so that witnesses may refer to statements for that purpose without them becoming part of the evidence. This topic is discussed at **3.7.1.1**.

4.5   The effect of the 1995 Act on various common law rules

Section 7 of the 1995 Act is a lengthy and confusingly worded section which preserves various common law rules about the admissibility of certain specific kinds of hearsay evidence which were themselves preserved in the Civil Evidence Act 1968. The most important of these is to provide that evidence of informal admissions made by a party is still admissible. An example of an informal admission would be where one driver gets out of his car after a collision and apologises for causing the accident. Evidence of that admission could be given at trial, after giving notice, whether by the other driver or by a passer-by who overheard it. It is beyond the scope of this text to discuss the precise historical and technical reasons why such a specific provision might have been thought by the draftsman of the 1995 Act to be required, since one could easily have said that the general provision in s. 1(1) as to the admissibility of **all** hearsay would have covered the position. Putting it simply, s. 9 of the Civil Evidence Act 1968 expressly preserved certain common law rules and it might have been thought that the repeal of the 1968 Act might have the effect of repealing those rules unless they were restated explicitly in the 1995 Act. None is of any great practical significance in everyday litigation and all would certainly have been encompassed in the general terms of s. 1(1).

4.6   Sections 8 and 9: Technical methods of proof and definitions

Sections 8 and 9 of the 1995 Act are extremely useful. They are supplemented by s. 13 and together they provide definitions of certain terms and provisions for means of proving hearsay statements.

Section 8 provides that if a statement is contained in a document it can be proved either by production of the document, a copy or a copy of the copy and it is up to the court to decide how the document needs to be authenticated. This useful provision means the death of the old so-called 'best evidence' rule, which at its zenith forbade the reception into evidence of a copy of a document if the original was still in existence. Now carbon copies, photocopies, or printouts, authenticated in such manner as the court may direct, are admissible. Moreover s. 9 goes on to provide that if a document is part of 'the records of a business or public authority' it can be received in evidence without further proof so that there is no need to call a witness to describe the contents and attest to the authenticity of it. In such cases documents are taken to be part of the proper records of a business or public authority if there is a certificate (which could easily be endorsed on the document itself) certifying that it is a true copy of the record signed by an officer of the business or authority. Section 9(4) goes on to provide that the word 'record' means a record in whatever form and thus could include manuscript entries in a ledger, the contents of computer databases, or copies of accounts. The words 'public authority' are said to include any public or statutory undertaking, any government department, and any person holding office under the Crown. The word 'business' is rather oddly defined to include 'any activity regularly carried on over a period of time whether for profit or not by any body (whether corporate or not) or by an individual'. This is a very wide definition indeed and would include all manner of activities which surely would not be viewed as 'businesses' by most people. For example, personal records of an obsessive train-spotter, birdwatcher or collector of statistical material about sporting events and the like would no doubt qualify as 'business records' for these purposes under the definition.

4.7 Miscellaneous

Section 13 of the 1995 Act makes it clear that the provisions of the Act extend beyond mere statements of fact in hearsay form to include statements of opinion. Of course these will only be admissible where the original witness would have been entitled to give a statement of opinion to the court—principally where that witness is an expert in the field concerned.

Section 10 of the Act provides for admissibility in evidence of the Ogden Tables and will have the effect of permitting the court to use higher multipliers in personal injury litigation when computing loss of earnings and continuing care claims (see **1.2.2.3** for discussion).

4.8 Part II of the Civil Evidence Act 1968

4.8.1 Section 11: Admissibility of previous convictions

We now turn to the second part of the Civil Evidence Act 1968 which deals with miscellaneous matters, and particularly to s. 11. The law used to be that a party's conviction for criminal offences was not admissible in civil proceedings. This was so even where the conviction appeared directly relevant to the civil suit, i.e., arose out of the same facts. For example, suppose that a collision occurred between vehicles driven by C and D. The police eventually prosecuted only D who was convicted of the offence of careless driving. Before the coming into force of s. 11 of the Civil Evidence Act 1968, in subsequent civil proceedings between C and D, no reference at all to D's conviction for careless driving could be made, even though the issue in the trial, negligence, is almost exactly the same as the issue which has already been judged in the criminal proceedings, i.e., carelessness. Now, however, by s. 11 of the Act:

In any civil proceedings the fact that a person has been convicted of an offence by a court in the United Kingdom is admissible to prove, where relevant, that he committed that offence and he shall be taken to have committed it unless the contrary is proved.

An early case which very neatly demonstrates the working of the section on reversing the burden of proof is as follows:

Wauchope v *Mordecai* [1970] 1 WLR 317

The claimant was riding his bicycle when the driver of a parked car opened the door suddenly, knocking the claimant off. The defendant was prosecuted before the magistrates' court on the charge of opening a door in such a way as to cause injury and was convicted. The claimant then brought an action in the county court and sought to treat the conviction as admissible evidence. The judge did not know that the Civil Evidence Act 1968 had now come into force. He ignored the conviction altogether and said it was irrelevant. He came to the conclusion on the facts that he could not be sure whom to believe—the claimant, who claimed that the car door had opened suddenly, or the defendant, who claimed that he had opened the car door long before the claimant reached it and that the claimant must have been daydreaming. The judge decided that as he was not sure whom to believe, the whole decision rested on the burden of proof. Accordingly, the claimant had not discharged that burden, and he gave judgment to the defendant. On appeal, the Court of Appeal gave judgment for the claimant. The effect of s. 11 (which was in force) was to make the evidence of conviction admissible and to reverse the burden of proof, so that it was now up to the defendant to show that he had *not* opened the door in such a way as to cause injury. Since the judge had decided matters by reference to the burden of proof, this should have meant that the claimant would succeed.

4.8.1.1   The relevance of the conviction

The clearest use of s. 11 is where the crime and the subsequent civil action are based on the very same facts, e.g., an error of judgment while driving. An example is given above where, after a collision between C and D, the police prosecute only D who is in due course convicted in the magistrates' court of the offence of driving without due care and attention. In the subsequent civil proceedings between the parties, the conviction can be used by C against D and will have the effect of reversing the burden of proof on the issue. In other words, it will now be for D to prove positively, on a balance of probabilities, that he was wrongly convicted, i.e., that he did not drive carelessly at the time of the incident. Here, with the interchange of the words 'careless' and 'negligent', it can be said that the issue in the civil proceedings is precisely the same as that in the criminal proceedings, in so far as it relates to D's conduct.

There is a more difficult case where the crime is not precisely the same as the tort but may or may not be relevant to it. Suppose, for example, that there is a collision between C and D caused by D's brakes failing. D is subsequently charged with, and convicted of, the offence of using a vehicle with defective brakes. There is no doubt that in factual terms, D's vehicle caused the accident, but the question is what use this conviction is to the claimant. For this offence there is strict liability, and therefore if the brakes were in fact defective, this is sufficient to ground a criminal conviction. In the tort of negligence, however, there is no such strict liability, and what must be shown in every case is that there was a breach of the duty of care viewed in terms of the conduct of the reasonable man. Accordingly, one might envisage two different situations. In the first, D does not have his vehicle serviced for many months, even after the need for such servicing becomes apparent. He continues driving the vehicle even after it has become obvious to him that the brakes are very weak indeed, and finally the brakes fail, leading to the collision. If all these facts could be proved there is no doubt that negligence is established and therefore that D will be liable in tort to C. Imagine, however, a situation in which D is scrupulous about having his vehicle properly serviced, and in fact has had the vehicle serviced only an hour before the accident occurs. The braking system was thoroughly overhauled and checked but a mechanic at the servicing garage failed to fit some part properly, with the effect that the brakes fail the first time they are applied at speed, leading to the accident. In this situation, D is certainly still guilty of the criminal offence, which is one of strict liability. There is, however, no element at all of lack of reasonableness in his conduct this time. Therefore, under these circumstances, the conviction would be of no use in proving D's negligence. Any action by C in these circumstances would be better brought against the negligent garage.

Consequently, with offences of strict liability, and which relate to the condition of the vehicle rather than to the manner of its driving, one cannot always immediately see whether a conviction will or will not be relevant. Suppose, for instance, that a vehicle is driven with windscreen wipers which do not work. The criminal offence of driving a vehicle without effective windscreen wipers is certainly established. If an accident occurs to that vehicle, however, then clearly the state of the windscreen wipers is quite irrelevant to the causation of the accident, unless it happens to be raining at the time so that the driver's vision is substantially impaired. If the accident occurs during dry weather, then it is neither here nor there that the windscreen wipers were deficient. In each individual case, therefore, unless the tort is the very same thing as the crime, e.g., cases of dangerous or careless driving, one must look closely at the circumstances to decide how relevant the conviction is.

4.8.1.2   The effect of the conviction

It is important to note that where a conviction is set out in the statement of case, it is not by any means conclusive proof that the person committed the crime concerned. It merely reverses the burden of proof on the issue and requires the convicted person to prove that his conviction was wrong.

This is by no means impossible. Although in principle one would be trying to show that a conviction reached on the standard of proof appropriate in a criminal case, i.e., beyond reasonable doubt, was wrong, there may well be a reason why this is possible. In the case of driving offences particularly, such offences are prosecuted in the magistrates' court. Many people may actually plead guilty by post to relatively trivial driving offences, or may not choose, or be able, to have legal representation when answering such charges because the criminal courts may not grant legal representation for driving offences. Where there is a collision between vehicles, the same incident in criminal terms may be the relatively trivial offence of careless driving, but in the civil action in the High Court, sums of tens of thousands of pounds may be involved. The degree of legal expertise brought to bear on the civil action by the solicitors and barristers on each side and the High Court judge, may lead to a very different conclusion from that reached by three lay magistrates who have received a plea of guilty by letter, made mainly because the person concerned could not afford legal representation or the time off work to attend court, and who thought that conviction was inevitable because of police evidence against him.

4.8.1.3   Procedural requirements for the use of s. 11

Section 11 of the Civil Evidence Act 1968 is implemented by PD 16, para. 10.1, which provides that a party wishing to rely on a conviction must state in his statement of case full particulars of it and the issue to which it is said to be relevant. In response to the allegation the other party may:

(a) *deny* the conviction itself (e.g., say that it does not in fact relate to him); or

(b) allege that the conviction was *erroneous* (e.g., say that he pleaded guilty in ignorance of some fact which could have constituted a defence, or was otherwise wrongly convicted); or

(c) deny that the conviction is *relevant* to any issue (e.g., say that although convicted of using a vehicle with a defective tyre, the state of the tyre did not contribute in any way to the accident).

The use of the section and the operation of s. 11 are illustrated in the following example:

EXAMPLE

Vehicles driven by C and D are involved in a collision. Subsequently the police prosecute D for three offences, on each of which he is convicted:

(a) driving the vehicle without due care and attention;

(b) driving a vehicle with two defective tyres;

(c) driving a vehicle while uninsured.

The claimant's solicitors will obtain a certificate of conviction from the magistrates' court and will then insert in the claimant's particulars of claim details of the relevant convictions. They will introduce convictions only for the offences of driving without due care and attention and driving with defective tyres. Obviously, while it may be relevant to the source from which compensation comes, lack of insurance does not in itself contribute to how an accident occurs, and therefore they will not refer to this third offence.

In his defence, the defendant may well meet this by alleging:

(a) The conviction for driving without due care and attention was erroneous in that he was convicted against the weight of the evidence by the magistrates.

   In that case, the burden of proving this is on the defendant to the civil standard of proof, and it will now be for him to establish at the subsequent trial, on the balance of probabilities, that he was not driving carelessly. Accordingly, if the judge is undecided about the matter, i.e., he cannot make his mind up which version to believe of how the accident occurred, he must find in favour of the claimant, because the defendant now bears the burden of proof on this issue. If it were not for the operation of s. 11, then in that situation he would have to decide in favour of the defendant because it is normally for the claimant to prove every element of his claim. Therefore the effect of s. 11 is simply to reverse the normal burden of proof.

(b) With regard to the conviction for driving with defective tyres, the defendant may admit the conviction and that it was correct, but go on to deny that the conviction is in any way relevant to how the incident occurred, e.g., he may say that the incident arose because of a head-on collision when neither party had the time to brake. Accordingly, the state of the tyres is factually quite irrelevant to how the incident came about. It will then be for the claimant to establish the relevance of this matter.

4.8.1.4 Further points

For completeness, it is worth pointing out that if two motorists are involved in an accident and the police prosecute only one of them who is convicted of driving without due care, then that conviction can be used by the other driver; this does not mean, however, that a driver who was not prosecuted (or was acquitted) must necessarily be held totally free from any liability in tort. The prosecution are not concerned with degrees of blame, only with assessing whether there is sufficient evidence to establish guilt to a criminal standard of proof. Motorists charged with careless driving often try to show that some other driver was partly to blame, but this is no defence to the criminal charge. It may, however, be very important in the civil action because of the effect of a finding of contributory negligence by the claimant. Thus the fact that the police chose not to charge one party is no evidence at all that he bore no proportion of responsibility, and it is open to the other party to seek to show:

(a) that his own conviction was wrong;

(b) that the other party was wholly to blame for the accident; or

(c) even if he cannot establish (a) and (b), that the other party was at least contributorily negligent.

4.8.2 Section 13: Defamation proceedings and convictions

Section 13 of the Civil Evidence Act 1968 provides that for a defamation action a conviction is conclusive evidence that a person committed the offence concerned. This is designed to remedy the difficulties and abuse of a series of cases in the mid 1960s in which convicted criminals, long after their appeals had been dismissed, tried to reopen their cases by civil proceedings. An example is the well-known case of *Hinds* v *Sparks* [1964] Crim LR 717, in which a convicted robber successfully sued the former chief of the Flying Squad who had serialised his memoirs in a Sunday newspaper. In the course of these he discussed the claimant's guilt of a certain armed robbery. The claimant's libel action was successful, because at that time the defendant could not rely on the claimant's conviction. Such a situation could not now happen in the light of s. 13.

4.8.3 Findings in civil cases

We have so far dealt with the result of a conviction in criminal proceedings in subsequent civil actions. It should be noted that findings in *civil cases* are outside the 1968 Act and the general law is:

(a) If the previous case is between the *same parties*, a judgment will create an estoppel between them preventing them denying the facts as found.

(b) If the previous case is between *different parties*, then the finding of the first court is inadmissible in later proceedings.

EXAMPLE

A lorry driven by D leaves the road and crashes into a bus queue, injuring several people. Each issues a separate claim. The case of C1 comes to court, the lorry driver is found to be negligent and damages are awarded. However, when the case of C2 comes to court C2 cannot rely on the previous finding of negligence. He has to prove negligence again. Similarly, if the previous action had ended in a verdict for the defendant on a finding of no negligence, this would not have been of any use to the defendant either in the second action.

4.8.4 Relevance of other conduct

The concept of relevance has been discussed at a number of places in the text. In the context of disclosure reference should be made to **18.3**; in the context of the relevance of convictions reference should be made to **4.8.1.1**. To be **relevant** a piece of evidence must be logically probative of something bearing on the dispute in question. Thus, for example, while one can certainly set out, say, all convictions arising out of a given road accident which caused injury to the claimant which may demonstrate bad driving by the defendant, one is not permitted to refer to the whole of the defendant's record of driving convictions on other (or indeed subsequent) occasions simply to demonstrate that in general terms he is a bad driver. The court would conclude that however gross the driving record it would not be legally relevant to show negligence on the occasion in question. There is, however, a principle of the law of evidence, much more relevant in criminal cases, known as the '*similar fact*' principle whereby if one is able to show that a party has engaged in very similar conduct on another occasion, the court might be persuaded to conclude that, notwithstanding that the occasion may have been months or years before the incident with which the litigation is concerned, the conduct by the other party is in some way relevant. Moreover the conduct by the other party does not have to have ended in a criminal conviction, and one may just wish to show similar behaviour in a commercial context. It is unlikely that this principle would ever be relevant in the context of road traffic accidents though it might conceivably be relevant in, say, factory accidents in order to show a continuing pattern of an unsafe system of work by the employer especially if the machinery or process in question was the same as that which led to the present incident. Here convictions under the Factories Act 1961 or more recently under the Health and Safety at Work etc. Act 1974 might well be of assistance to an injured claimant. It is in the commercial sphere, however, that evidence of past behaviour is more likely to be relevant and if the court concludes that what the other party did on some previous occasion is of sufficient similarity to the conduct now alleged, it may allow evidence of that other incident. So in the leading case of *Mood Music Publishing Co. Ltd* v *De Wolfe Ltd* [1976] Ch 119 the claimants, a songwriter and his publishers, believed that the defendants had published a song which very closely copied one of the claimant's works. The defendants contended that it was a coincidence, but the claimants had reason to believe that the defendants habitually engaged in this kind of activity. Accordingly, they employed someone to approach the defendants pretending to be a songwriter who had recorded a piece of music from the radio in the USA and who asked the defendants if they would help him by making a slight rearrangement of it so that he could pass it off as his own work. When the defendants willingly agreed to this course of conduct the claimants wished to use evidence of their general unscrupulousness in the original proceedings concerning the pirated song and the court held that this was a sufficiently similar course of action on the part of the defendants as to have genuine probative value in the present action.

4.8.5 Miscellaneous further matters

There are miscellaneous further matters contained in the concluding sections of the Civil Evidence Act 1968. Only one is of much general significance, the privilege against self-incrimination. Section 14(1) of the Act expressly preserves the right of a person in civil proceedings to refuse to answer any question on the grounds that to do so might expose that person or his or her spouse to criminal proceedings in the UK. Where such a claim to privilege is taken, either at the stage of disclosure of documents, or at the trial, it will be for the trial judge to assess whether there is a realistic risk of prosecution. See **5.2.1.1**.

4.8.6 Examples of a hearsay notice and notice in reply

IN THE MIDDLEMARCH COUNTY COURT   Case No: MM 006141

BETWEEN: **Felix Holt**   Claimant

and

Harold Transome   Defendant

Notice of Desire to Adduce Hearsay Statement

Take Notice that at the trial of this action the Claimant desires to give in evidence the statement made in the following document, namely the witness statement of Esther Lyon dated 3 November 2006 a copy of which is annexed hereto.

And further take notice that the particulars relating to the said statement are as follows:

(a) It was made by the said Esther Lyon

(b) The said Esther Lyon may not be called to give evidence at the trial because she is a construction works manager currently working on the construction of a new airport at Kuala Lumpur, Malaysia, which project will last until late 2007. It is not possible to fix the trial to coincide with her annual leave because she has not decided when this leave will be nor even whether she will return to the UK during it.

Dated 23 November 2006

To: The Defendant

Dorothea Brooke & Co.
Solicitors for the Claimant

IN THE MIDDLEMARCH COUNTY COURT   Case No: MM 006141

BETWEEN: **Felix Holt**   Claimant

and

Harold Transome   Defendant

Notice of Intention to Attack Credibility of Absent Witness

Take Notice that at the trial of this action the Defendant intends to attack the credibility of Esther Lyon, in respect of whom the Claimant has given notice of intention to adduce hearsay evidence in the following respects:-

(a) The Defendant contends that Esther Lyon is the sister-in-law of the Claimant

(b) Shortly after the accident giving rise to this cause of action Esther Lyon gave a statement to the Defendant's insurers in substantially different terms from the description of the accident contained in the said witness statement of Esther Lyon, but refused to sign the typed statement tendered to her.

Dated 6 December 2006

To: The Claimant

Lydgate & Co.
Solicitors for the Defendant

Civil evidence (3): Evidence of opinion and privilege

5.1 Evidence of opinion

5.1.1 The general rule

The general rule is that a witness may only testify as to matters actually observed by him and may not give his *opinion* about those matters. The drawing of inferences from narrated facts is the whole function of the trier of fact, i.e., in a civil case, the judge.

The distinction between fact and opinion is easy enough to see in cases at both ends of the spectrum. Thus a statement that A was driving on the wrong side of the road is clearly fact; that he was driving negligently is opinion; but statements of how fast someone was driving or, say, as to identity of handwriting are clearly both.

In civil cases in the modern era there is a considerable relaxation of the rule that a witness may not testify as to matters of opinion. Where it is impossible to separate facts from inferences based on them, the law usually permits the witness to narrate both. This is sanctioned by s. 3(2) of the Civil Evidence Act 1972, which states:

It is hereby declared that where a person is called as a witness in any civil proceedings, a statement of opinion by him on any relevant matter on which he is not qualified to give expert evidence, if made as a way of conveying relevant facts personally perceived by him, is admissible as evidence of what he perceived.

The effect of this is that where a witness gives evidence in what is really a compendious way of narrating individual facts, there should be no difficulty. Thus if a witness wishes to say 'X was drunk', while this is a matter of opinion, since the witness could certainly narrate the individual facts on which it is based, e.g., he could say that X staggered, his breath smelt of drink, his speech was slurred, his eyes were glazed, etc., the compendious way of stating this is permitted.

5.1.2 Expert witnesses

To the general rule prohibiting evidence of bare opinion there is one exception, namely, the case of expert witnesses. The most important modern use of experts is that of medical witnesses in personal injury litigation. Other frequent instances are the evidence of consultant engineers, handwriting experts, valuers, and increasingly the evidence of forensic accountants who in the context of, for example, personal injury, loss of future earnings, commercial frauds or tax matters testify about matters involving complex computations.

5.1.2.1 Competence of expert witnesses

It is for the court to accept that a witness is an expert, i.e., to rule on whether he has undergone a sufficient course of study, or is of sufficient experience to qualify. Such evidence is always introduced by a statement of qualifications, although no formal qualifications are necessarily required depending on the nature of the activity about which expert evidence is to be given. Thus, for example, an experienced car mechanic, even one who did not have any formal certificate or diploma, would certainly be an acceptable witness about some matter to do with motor vehicles, e.g., as to whether a given vehicle had been adequately serviced. Of course, for more complex mechanical matters the evidence of a qualified consulting engineer would be preferable.

It is always desirable to ensure that one's choice of expert witness is such that the court will feel confident in relying on their evidence, and this is so whether the expert is to be jointly instructed by both parties or whether it is the kind of case where each will be permitted to have their own expert. So, for example, in personal injury litigation the judge will become used to seeing the same handful of medical consultants, part of whose practices involve a substantial amount of medico-legal work, i.e. the examining of claimants, the preparation of medical reports and the giving of evidence in court cases in respect of such matters as the likely period or degree of incapacity. In each locality there will be a number of such experts having a substantial medico-legal practice on whom solicitors, and judges can rely for full and disinterested opinion evidence, even if in any given case there may be a radical difference between the claimant's and the defendant's experts.

It is vital to remember that the court will control the issue of expert evidence and that permission to call an expert will be needed. In general, the parties will be expected to attempt to co-operate on a choice of a single jointly instructed expert (see **20.2**).

5.1.2.2 The ambit of expert opinion evidence

By s. 3(1) of the Civil Evidence Act 1972 an expert may give his opinion *'on any relevant matter on which he is qualified to give expert evidence'*. In this section 'relevant matter' includes an issue in the proceedings (s. 3(3)).

It therefore follows that an expert may testify about the very matter in question. For example, in a medical negligence case an expert witness may testify as to whether, in his belief, the defendant doctor was negligent in the carrying out of some medical procedure or diagnosis.

5.1.2.3 The content of expert evidence and hearsay

An expert need not have personal knowledge of every relevant matter within the field of his expertise. Once someone qualifies as an expert he is entitled to base his testimony on academic books, or articles, professional publications, research data, etc. from the experiments of others.

See, for example, *H v Schering Chemicals Ltd* [1983] 1 WLR 143, where, in a civil action for damages against a drug company, it was held that an expert witness could properly refer to learned articles, findings of research in his field, etc., and the court would regard references to reputable authority within the expert's field of expertise as supporting any inferences which the expert drew in the case in question. The fact that he was in essence relying on hearsay did not disqualify him from testifying on the relevant matter.

5.1.2.4 Procedural rules governing expert evidence

By virtue of the CPR and in particular Part 35, the calling of expert evidence at trial is subject to the procedural rules which will be considered in greater detail at **Chapter 20**. In general, the court will require an attempt to agree on a choice of expert who can be jointly instructed. If that is not appropriate because of the weight or complexity of the case, each party will be permitted to call its own experts. The court will control this to the point of being required to give permission for named experts to be employed. Where each side is to call its own witness the court will require full prior disclosure of written reports between the parties well in advance of the trial in the interests of saving time and costs. There is a procedure for posing written questions in advance to the opposing expert and for the parties to agree, or the court to order that the experts meet in an attempt to resolve differences in their evidence.

These rules assist with efficiency and fairness so that each side is well aware of what the other side's experts will say and each can in turn obtain its own expert witnesses comments upon the opinion of opposing experts. Thus, if no agreement on the expert evidence is possible, counsel on each side is fully armed at trial with the material on which to cross-examine the opposing expert witness.

It should be noted that the requirement for prior disclosure applies even to a party to an action who wishes to give expert evidence on his own behalf, and also to 'in-house' experts giving evidence on behalf of their employers, as well as to independent experts.

5.2 Privilege

In general, public policy favours the open and frank conduct of legal proceedings. This means one should be able to ask any question at trial and insist upon an answer, and that any material document should be made available to all parties and to the court for inspection. This cannot be an absolute rule, however. There are conflicting interests which must be balanced, and in some circumstances facts or documents which may appear relevant to the fair conduct of a given piece of litigation may be withheld, either in the public interest, or in the exercise of private privilege, i.e., a rule which protects certain kinds of private communication from disclosure. It is now appropriate to consider the doctrine of privilege under its two main heads, private privilege and public interest privilege.

5.2.1 Private privilege

5.2.1.1 Self-incrimination

The Civil Evidence Act 1968, s. 14, provides that no witness can be required in civil proceedings to answer any question or produce any document or thing if to do so would expose that person or that person's spouse to proceedings for any criminal offence in the UK.

Thus in a civil case a witness or party cannot be compelled to answer any question which would, in the opinion of the judge, have a tendency to expose that witness to a criminal charge.

There are some exceptions to this, the most important of which is s. 72 of the Supreme Court Act 1981, which provides that a person shall not be excused from answering relevant questions on the grounds of potential self-incrimination in certain kinds of proceedings, in particular, infringement of rights pertaining to intellectual property or passing off.

5.2.1.2 Legal professional privilege

Privilege arises in a civil case at two stages. One is, of course, the trial itself, and if privilege is properly claimed it entitles a witness to decline to answer certain questions or produce certain documents to the court. The other stage is disclosure, where in pre-trial procedures each party is required to admit the existence of and show to each other all relevant documents. This procedure must be carried out with complete honesty so that a party must show to his opponent all relevant documents, even if one of them is utterly conclusive of liability against the party who has it. The exception to this principle is where a party can claim a privilege for a certain document or class of document, in which case, while the existence of the document in general terms must be revealed, the contents need not.

EXAMPLE

A claimant in a case arising out of a road accident, when his vehicle collided with that of the defendant at unmarked crossroads, obtains a statement from an eye-witness which blames him (the claimant) for the accident. The claimant is obliged to reveal that he has the statement, though he need not name the witness or show the statement to his opponent because it is privileged.

In civil proceedings, communications, oral or written, can be withheld from evidence and inspection by an opponent before trial, if the communication:

(a) was to enable the client to obtain legal advice; or

(b) was made with reference to actual or contemplated litigation; or

(c) was written 'without prejudice'.

5.2.1.3 Lawyer–client communications

The privilege applies whether the communication relates to litigation or not—the important point is said to be that anyone taking legal advice is asking about legal rights which may have to be enforced by litigation, however unlikely litigation may seem. The communication must arise out of the lawyer–client relationship in some way, so that casual conversations between friends who also happen to be solicitor and client are not within the privilege. The privilege extends to all forms of communication, written, oral, fax, e-mail, etc.

5.2.1.4 Communications with third parties for the purpose of actual or contemplated litigation

For this privilege to apply there must be a definite prospect of litigation but it is not necessary that proceedings should have started, or even that the cause of action should have arisen. The communication must have been made, or the document brought into existence, for the purpose of enabling the legal adviser to act or advise with regard to litigation. The most common examples of the privilege are therefore advice from counsel to solicitor on conduct of the claim; and statements taken from witnesses, or experts' reports obtained by the solicitor for litigation.

5.2.1.5 Documents having a dual purpose

The main problem that has arisen and been the subject of much case law concerns a document which has come into being for more than one purpose. Suppose, for example, that after a factory accident a witness fills in an accident report form for his employer which may partially be for the safety officer to consider improvements to factory procedures. If the injured person sues, is this report privileged, i.e., in the course of disclosure can the claimant see it in advance?

In *Waugh* v *British Railways Board* [1980] AC 521, a report prepared for an internal enquiry after a fatal rail accident, headed 'For the information of the Board's Solicitor', was basically prepared:

(a) so that the enquiry could establish future safety measures; and

(b) to enable the Board's solicitor to advise for the purpose of the litigation that was bound to ensue.

The Board resisted disclosure on the grounds of legal privilege.

The House of Lords held that public interest in the proper administration of justice required disclosure of such a vital item of evidence, thus privilege could only be claimed where the preparation for the purpose of litigation was shown to be '*the dominant purpose*' for the preparation of the report. It was always open to a court to investigate which was the dominant purpose. It was not conclusive that the document purported on the face of it to have been prepared for such a purpose. On the facts, as the document appeared to have two equal purposes the document was not privileged and had to be disclosed.

5.2.1.6 Without prejudice communications

No privilege attaches to communications *between* the parties or their advisers. Thus letters written by the other side can always be produced in evidence, e.g., to establish admissions or to use for cross-examination on the basis of inconsistency in versions of facts given. The exception to this is the case of 'without prejudice' correspondence.

Where correspondence is entered into with a view to attempting to settle a dispute, whether or not actual litigation has yet begun, letters are often marked 'without prejudice' or contain those words within the text. The use of these words confers a joint privilege on both writer and recipient so that the letters may not be put in evidence without both parties' consent. Frequently admissions, or partial admissions, are made in such correspondence in an effort to compromise, which is why the privilege is required to protect the person making the admission or other tactical concession. There may also be without prejudice meetings or telephone conversations in which what is said is privileged and may not be repeated.

So long as correspondence is directed at a bona fide attempt to compromise an action, it is not in fact necessary that the words 'without prejudice' be marked on the correspondence at all. Likewise, the mere marking of correspondence with the words 'without prejudice' will not protect it if it is not in fact bona fide written for the purpose of negotiations. Thus to mark a letter 'without prejudice' would not protect it if it was in fact defamatory.

Although, therefore, it is not strictly necessary to employ the words 'without prejudice', it is better, and likely to save potential disputes as to the status of the correspondence, always to use those words where that is the intention. Exceptionally, if a person wishes to keep open the right to refer to matters in court despite the letter being written in an attempt to negotiate a compromise, he must stipulate expressly that the correspondence is 'open' for this purpose.

The dangers of being unclear about this are well demonstrated by the case of *Dixons Stores Group Ltd* v *Thames Television plc* [1993] 1 All ER 349 where, in substantial litigation, long-running correspondence between the parties' solicitors which had been at times on a without prejudice basis and at other times open, left the parties unclear about whether certain letters which they had exchanged were without prejudice or not, an issue which had to go as far as the Court of Appeal to be resolved.

The privilege conferred by the without prejudice status of the correspondence is discharged when the correspondence does lead to an agreement. Thus if, say, D writes to C offering to pay £10,000 in full and final settlement, marking the letter 'without prejudice', and C then writes to D accepting the offer, this has the effect of 'opening' the correspondence so that if D does not pay the money, P may sue on the agreement contained in the letters.

5.2.1.7   Exceptions to the rule

Even though legal professional privilege prima facie applies, the general principle may be affected by the following exceptions:

(a) Waiver by the client—the privilege belongs to the client not the solicitor, and thus a client may waive it.

(b) Communications to facilitate crime or fraud (see *R* v *Cox* (1884) 14 QBD 153)— a document which is prepared to facilitate fraud does not attract legal professional privilege. If a lawyer participates in the fraud, he ceases to act as a lawyer. If he is himself innocent of any fraud, the privilege is still lost if the clients have the criminal purpose, for example as in the case of *Cox*, where they sought advice about fraudulently backdating a document.

5.2.1.8   Inadvertent disclosure of privileged documents

A difficult question is, is the privilege lost if the privileged document falls into the hands of someone else, e.g., one's opponent, by accident? The rule is that where this happens, in principle the privilege is usually lost and the opponent can use the document. Thus if an opponent produces the privileged document or a copy of it at trial, nothing can be done to prevent this. However, if one finds out *in advance* that an opponent has such a document, it may be possible to obtain an injunction to prevent the use of the privileged document by that opponent.

The precise working out of the principle is unclear, in particular because it seems from other authorities on improperly obtained evidence generally (see **5.3**) that there is little discretion in the trial judge to prevent the use of improperly obtained evidence at trial. Thus whether or not an injunction can be obtained depends upon whether the party whose privilege is about to be breached realises in time that the other party has the document so that a separate action can be launched for an injunction. In *Goddard* v *Nationwide Building Society* [1987] QB 670, where the claimants contended that a note in the hands of the defendant was privileged and applied for an injunction restraining the defendant from using it, the Court of Appeal granted the injunction requiring the defendant to deliver up the note and restraining him from disclosure or making any use of the information contained therein. A similar result occurred in *English and American Insurance Co. Ltd* v *Herbert Smith & Co.* (1987) *The Times*, 22 January 1987, where a barrister's clerk mistakenly returned documents to the wrong solicitor. The court again held that it was undesirable that the security that one normally had in obtaining legal advice should be threatened by mischance and granted an injunction restraining the use of the material thus obtained.

This matter is now dealt with in the *Guide to the Professional Conduct of Solicitors*, 8th edn., 16.06, which states that a solicitor is usually under a duty to pass on to the client and use all information which is material to the client's business, regardless of the source of that information, but goes on to acknowledge exceptional circumstances, including the position where a solicitor comes into possession of inadvertently disclosed privileged information. The principle now is that where it is obvious that privileged documents have been mistakenly disclosed, the solicitor should immediately cease to read the document if he has started doing so, inform the other side and return the documents.

If it is not obvious that they have been mistakenly disclosed, which may often be the case because it may not be clear, until one has read through to the conclusion, what the tenor of the whole document is, then the matter is governed by CPR, r. 31.20, which says:

> Where a party inadvertently allows a privileged document to be inspected, the party who has inspected the document may use it or its contents only with the permission of the court.

Unfortunately although a plain enough statement, this rule is not mentioned at all in the accompanying Practice Direction to Part 31. It gives no guidance as to the circumstances in which the court would give permission to use the inadvertently disclosed document. It is probably best to assume that no change in the exercise of the court's discretion provided by the previous case law is intended. This seems to be confirmed by the case of *Breeze* v *John Stacey and Sons Ltd* (1999) *The Times*, 8 July 1999.

5.2.1.9 Privilege and other professions

There is no professional privilege for other professions in general, even those such as accountants who may give quasi legal advice. There are, however, certain quasi exceptions two examples of which are:

(a) By virtue of the Copyright Designs and Patents Act 1988, ss. 280 and 284, in civil proceedings a privilege may be claimed in respect of communications between a person and his patent agent or trademark agent made for the purpose of pending or contemplating proceedings.

(b) By s. 10 of the Contempt of Court Act 1981:

> No court may require a person to disclose, nor is any person guilty of contempt of court for refusing to disclose, the source of information contained in a publication for which he is responsible, unless it be established to the satisfaction of the court that disclosure is necessary in the interests of justice or national security or for the prevention of disorder or crime.

This section creates a limited privilege in respect of sources of journalists and others, reversing previous case law which had held that journalists had no privilege whatsoever to refuse to answer relevant questions.

5.2.2 Public interest privilege

Where evidence is excluded because of some public interest in withholding it which outweighs the usual public interest in open litigation, it is usually called 'public interest privilege', or 'public interest immunity'. The right to claim the privilege is by no means restricted to the government or the Crown—it may be claimed by bodies such as local authorities, quangos, the police and the like.

5.2.2.1 The principle

The principle is that whoever makes the claim to privilege, the court may demand to see the document and will then rule on whether the greater public interest lies in open and frank disclosure in litigation or in confidentiality. So in *Burmah Oil Co. Ltd* v *Bank of England* [1980] AC 1090, disclosure was sought of various memoranda of meetings attended by government ministers, and other documents which would have revealed the inner workings of high level government. The House of Lords held that it was going too far to lay down that no document in any particular category should ever in any circumstances be produced, even when they were high-level documents to do with government. The nature of the litigation and the apparent importance to it of the documents in question might in extreme cases demand production even of the most sensitive communications at the highest level (see, for example, *Nixon* v *United States* (1974) 418 US 683 relating to the disclosure of Presidential papers). The courts will always bear in mind that it is in the public interest that justice should be done and should be publicly recognised as having been done.

The House of Lords in *Burmah Oil Co. Ltd* v *Bank of England* subsequently found that some of the documents in question were likely to reveal the attitude of the Bank of England to the transactions the subject of the litigation, and so these could be inspected. Once the House of Lords had inspected them, however, the House held that the documents did not contain material which was 'necessary for fairly disposing of the case' and on that ground upheld the objection to disclosure, i.e., on the basis that disclosure would not have assisted the party seeking it.

As the speeches in this important case and many others make clear, the court is essentially engaged in a balancing exercise between the claimed public interest, giving due weight to the ministers' views, and the desirability of open litigation.

The court must always have regard to the overriding objective of the Civil Procedure Rules (see **Chapter 10**), and particularly, in the context of disclosure, to considerations of efficiency, economy and proportionality.

5.2.2.2   Types of document covered by public interest privilege

It is quite impossible to attempt closely to categorise the types of public document where exclusion is likely to be ordered. Most confusingly, even cases involving essentially the same type of document have ended in conflicting decisions. This is most apparent in a series of cases which dealt with the problem of enquiries into police conduct under s. 49 of the Police Act 1964. The question later arose in each case as to whether the statements given for the purpose of complaints against the police should be liable to disclosure in civil proceedings, e.g., proceedings brought by persons alleging false imprisonment or wrongful arrest. It was difficult to see any coherent line arising from the case law and differently constituted Courts of Appeal took different decisions on relatively similar facts. See for example *Peach* v *Metropolitan Police Commissioner* [1986] QB 1064; *Neilson* v *Laugharne* [1981] QB 736; *R* v *Metropolitan Police Commissioner, ex parte Hart-Leverton* [1990] COD 240; *Evans* v *Chief Constable of Surrey* [1988] QB 588; *Makanjuola* v *Metropolitan Police Commissioner* [1992] 3 All ER 617 (a particularly strange case because the complainant sought disclosure of *her own* earlier statement but it was still refused). The specific problem in those cases was eventually resolved by the House of Lords ruling authoritatively on the matter in *R* v *Chief Constable of West Midlands Police, ex parte Wiley* [1995] 1 AC 274. However, further difficulty has been caused by *Taylor* v *Anderton* [1995] 1 WLR 447 where the Court of Appeal held that investigating officers' reports, as distinct from police complaints statements, would be accorded public interest immunity.

These cases indicate the difficulty that the court will often have in deciding on a matter of public interest immunity and whether it can properly override a certificate from the relevant Secretary of State. The capacity for public interest immunity to be abused by ministers of the Crown or, in effect, their civil servants, is obvious and is what of course led to the Scott inquiry into the circumstances in which, having given approval for the export of armaments to Iraq, several ministers of the Crown successively signed public interest immunity certificates when relevant documents were called for by defendants who were prosecuted for being involved in those self-same exports.

5.2.2.3   The court's decision on where the public interest lies

The decision as to where the public interest lies is in the end one for the court. It has been held in some recent cases that the court may even take the point of public interest immunity where it is not claimed by either of the parties.

For an indication of how nicely balanced the point may be, the following two cases can be compared:

D v *National Society for the Prevention of Cruelty to Children* [1978] AC 171

The NSPCC sought help from members of the public in giving information concerning child abuse and offered a guarantee of confidentiality. A malicious informant falsely told the NSPCC that the claimant's daughter had been ill treated. In due course the claimant brought an action for damages against the society alleging negligence, contending that insufficient care had been exercised in investigating the complaint before sending an inspector to see the child. The claimant sought discovery of the identity of the malicious informant. The House of Lords held that the identity should not be disclosed because the public interest required that people with genuine suspicions of child abuse should feel free to communicate those suspicions without being put in fear of defamation proceedings. That was so even though the effect of the ruling in the present case was to protect a malicious person.

Campbell v *Tameside Metropolitan Borough Council* [1982] QB 1065

The claimant was a schoolteacher who had been attacked in the class by a violent pupil. She brought an action against the education authority contending that it should have known that the pupil had a violent disposition and that he should have been educated in a special unit. She sought preliminary disclosure of reports maintained by the authority which were believed to contain material which would have demonstrated the authority's knowledge of the pupil's tendencies. The Court of Appeal held that in the present case, while there was some merit in the defendant's argument that the writing up of teachers' and educational psychologists' reports on children might be made less candid if the writers thought they might be used in subsequent litigation, this should be overriden by the need for open litigation.

This case indicates that the burden of justifying non-disclosure is always upon the party seeking it and not the converse. The more low level the document is the more difficult will it be to justify withholding it.

The Human Rights Act 1998, which was brought into force in October 2000, is likely to have a dramatic effect on the concept and use of public interest immunity. It will undoubtedly be contended in many cases that claimants (or possibly defendants) cannot have a fair trial as guaranteed under Article 6 of the European Convention on Human Rights and Fundamental Freedoms where disclosure of obviously relevant and possibly essential information which would have assisted them with the preparation of their cases, is refused. This might, for example, have led to a different outcome in the case of *D* v *NSPCC*, above.

The fact that information generally is more readily in the public arena is not necessarily relevant here. Legal privilege overrides any requirement to disclose information under either the Data Protection Act 1998 or the Freedom of Information Act 2000.

5.3 Improperly obtained evidence

The rule in civil cases in essence is that evidence, if relevant, is admissible no matter how it was obtained. Thus even in the case of a privileged document, if it is obtained by, say, subterfuge, or even theft, the document can be used in court. However, the court does have the power to prevent abuse of process of the court, which it sometimes interprets so as to prevent a party using in some way or adducing in court a document wrongly obtained, or improperly using a document properly obtained. Everything appears to depend upon whether the party whose document it was gets wind of the situation in advance of trial. If so, and a request for the return of the document and an undertaking that it will not be used is refused, then on the general principles previously discussed it would appear that a separate action will lie for an injunction requiring the return of the document. If, however, the document is simply produced at trial in the instant case, it will then be too late to seek an injunction.

The law in this area remains unsettled. In *Riddick* v *Thames Board Mills Ltd* [1977] QB 881, in proceedings between the claimant and the defendant concerning the claimant's employment, a memorandum was revealed which contained passages which were allegedly defamatory of the claimant. It was held that a party was entitled to be protected against the improper use of materials disclosed, for purposes other than the litigation for which they were disclosed. Accordingly, the claimant was not entitled to use the memorandum as the basis for an action in defamation. (For further discussion of this principle see **18.10**.)

This case appears to assume that the court has a discretion to exclude evidence on grounds of policy, as does the case of *ITC Film Distributors* v *Video Exchange Ltd* [1982] Ch 436. There, the defendant, during the trial of an action for breach of copyright, obtained by a trick certain papers which the claimant's solicitors had brought to court for the trial. Since the papers were undoubtedly relevant and apparently admissible the defendant sought to put them in evidence. Warner J held that despite the general rule that the court had no power to exclude relevant evidence, the public interest in the due administration of justice required the parties to be free to bring papers into court without fear that they might be filched during the trial. This consideration outweighed even the competing public interest that the court should receive all available evidence. The matter was one of public policy.

In this case the misconduct in obtaining the papers might also have amounted to contempt of court. It is not clear whether Warner J was ruling the evidence inadmissible (which it was surely not), or creating a new discretion to exclude in such cases. In the subsequent case of *Goddard* v *Nationwide Building Society* [1987] QB 670 Nourse LJ indicated clearly that Warner J's decision should not be regarded as one under some inherent discretion but as one based on public policy.

There is little doubt that the court's wide-ranging case management powers and overriding objective to do justice and to be fair (see **Chapter 10**) now confer the power to exclude evidence. Its general powers under CPR, r. 32.1, permit the court to control the evidence to be used in proceedings by giving directions about:

(a) the issues on which it requires evidence;

(b) the nature of the evidence which it requires to decide those issues; and

(c) the way in which the evidence is to be placed before the court.

Moreover, and crucially, under r. 32.1(2):

The court may use its powers under this rule to exclude evidence that would otherwise be admissible.

In principle, therefore, and on the assumption that the CPR are never challenged so as to call into question whether or not they are *ultra vires*, these provisions amend the substantive law of evidence so as to provide that the court can exclude material, even if it is in principle admissible under the strict rules of evidence.

Civil evidence (4): Preparation of civil evidence

6.1 Practical considerations: Introduction

As has previously been observed, except for those rare cases where the entire case is on admitted facts and the dispute turns on a matter of law or construction of documents, it is not sufficient to have a good case. A party must always consider at every stage whether he has sufficient admissible evidence to prove his case, and this is relevant not just to issues of liability but to every matter of quantum.

The CPR require a spirit of cooperation so that items of evidence should be agreed if possible; it is too early to say with certainty to what extent the new atmosphere encouraged by the CPR will have effect in bringing about early settlements, but the initial indications are that the settlement rate is higher than it used to be. Moreover, since only about 3 per cent of all cases went to trial under the previous regime, the real importance of the CPR is that many cases should be settled relatively early in their life rather than close to trial, because the process is 'front-end loaded', that is, the timescale imposed, taken together with the requirement for a spirit of cooperation, means the parties are fully aware of each other's cases relatively early on. In particular, the requirement, where possible, for joint instruction of a single expert means that both parties know precisely what the expert evidence is as soon as the report is received and any questions on it raised, rather than, as might previously have been the case, waiting to go to trial to see whether the trial judge prefers one side's expert to the other.

The fact that there is a very high settlement rate is all the more reason for approaching each case thoroughly from the outset. One should begin collecting evidence as soon as one has seen the client for the first time and this is of course particularly the case where one of the *pre-action protocols* applies (see **Chapter 9**).

There is a substantial tactical advantage in approaching every case as though it will go all the way to trial. By keeping thoroughly on top of every detail in the case from start to finish, a solicitor immeasurably increases his own confidence in the outcome and his negotiating position with defendants. Moreover, it is wrong to consider that this is providing some 'Rolls Royce' version of litigation as opposed to what is the norm. To approach litigation in this way *should be* the norm and is what every client consulting a solicitor in a litigation matter is entitled to expect.

It must, however, be borne in mind that the costs that can be recovered are likely to be 'proportionate' to the amounts involved and also that the court will only allocate relatively short times for trial (e.g., for trials involving less than £15,000 only one working day will be allocated unless the factors are unusual). There must therefore always be some element of reasonableness in the amount of work expended in preparing a case for trial.

6.2 Evidence of facts

6.2.1 Statements from the client

Obviously a thorough statement should be taken from the client at the outset. It is in the nature of things, however, that a client's case may develop as the litigation rolls on. This is especially so if there is any continuing element in quantum, especially in personal injury cases. It must be remembered that a client's statement must also be exchanged at the relevant time and it is vital that this be as comprehensive as possible. The initial statement, as with that of other witnesses, should include any material, even if legally inadmissible, which might be helpful.

The eventual statement for exchange must not contain such inadmissible material, but should nonetheless, especially in personal injury cases, deal thoroughly with every aspect of quantum as well as liability, and in this regard it is as well to have a checklist to put to a client. Although round-sum figures may well be awarded for such matters as 'loss of amenity', so that, for example, one claimant who has suffered a common type of injury, say a broken ankle, is prima facie likely to obtain much the same as every other claimant, these figures can be adjusted to take into account specific aspects of a person's interests or lifestyle. Thus if one can substantiate that the claimant is a very keen sportsman so that his enjoyment of life has been considerably impaired by the injury, as opposed to someone who had a sedentary hobby, that may be reflected in damages. Similarly in the case of more serious or permanent injuries, it is always important for the claimant to describe his whole lifestyle to show how he is now affected. For example, if he commonly did a lot of DIY, painting and decorating, or looked after his own large garden, then the fact that he is no longer able to do these things will be reflected in monetary terms in reimbursement for the outside assistance which he has to employ. A client must set out his evidence on *every* material matter.

Likewise, a client should describe in detail any injuries or pain he is suffering, even if he might tend to make light of it. If he continues to suffer sleepless nights or throbbing pains, then these should be reflected in his statement and he should not be encouraged to adopt a stoic attitude towards them. The same applies in other kinds of litigation, e.g., about commercial or contractual matters. A claimant's statement should always carefully detail every element of quantum as well as matters relevant to liability because if he does not put these matters in his statement for exchange he may either be refused the right to give any evidence about them at all later; or possibly an adjournment may be awarded to the opposing party to call evidence to meet the client's allegations, and the cost of that adjournment will inevitably be paid by the party who is to blame.

6.2.2 Interviewing potential witnesses of fact

It is vitally important to interview potential witnesses of fact as soon as possible after receiving instructions. Any delay in obtaining this evidence will substantially impair its quality. Even where a witness has seen a very spectacular incident, e.g., a very bad road accident, memory of vital details soon fades, such as approximate distances from the kerb, the line of manoeuvre taken by one of the vehicles, the number of other vehicles in the vicinity, the lighting conditions and so on. It is therefore important to interview all material witnesses as soon as possible, and as thoroughly as possible to obtain comprehensive statements.

Having taken the statement one must of course remain alive to what the witness has said throughout the litigation. For example, when the defence is received it may be that there are matters in it on which the witness has not commented but on which he should be given the chance to give his version. Important new facts may emerge. At that time the witness may be re-interviewed, with the defence or other document which contains new facts to hand.

The statement should initially be taken as earlier described in as full a form as possible. Thus it may include hearsay, opinion, speculation, or indeed details of a previous similar instance, e.g., after a factory accident where a description of previous incidents might show continuing lack of regard for employees' safety. This information is for the purpose of the party's solicitor being able to consider lines of enquiry and other sources of information. It therefore forms a vital function in the early stages of investigation. However, in the more formal witness statements which are to be exchanged and put before the judge at trial, inadmissible material such as opinion must not appear. Solicitors are usually perfectly competent to judge what is or is not admissible, but in cases of difficulty counsel's opinion on evidence may be taken before exchange, and indeed in exceptional cases counsel may assist in drafting the witness statement. The final form of statement for exchange, taken from the witness's original full proof of evidence, needs to be prepared in typed and paragraphed form and must contain a statement of truth, then sent to the witness for signature in preparation for exchange.

6.2.3 Statements from the defendant or defence witnesses

If acting for the defendant, taking statements from the defendant or defence witnesses requires quite as much skill as when acting for the claimant, although in the nature of things one has to make less of the running. In particular, it will not usually be relevant for defence witnesses at this stage to comment on matters of quantum, although if, for example, the case concerns an accident at work then evidence about such matters as the claimant's pay and future prospects will clearly be within the knowledge of the personnel department of the defendant company.

Again, it is as well to obtain a thorough proof of evidence at an early stage, notwithstanding that the hard factual information on which it might be based may appear to remain readily available. For example, the claimant's immediate superior may have particular views about the claimant's actual competence as a worker. It is as well to have these committed to paper as soon as possible in case, for example, the superior leaves, dies, or in some way becomes disenchanted with the firm, e.g., by himself being refused a promotion or being made redundant so that his sympathies may change and his view of the claimant might materially improve!

6.2.4 Witness statements and the rules of evidence

In **Chapter 19** some aspects of the drafting of witness statements for exchange are considered.

It may be that witness statements can be *agreed* between the parties. This applies not only to witness statements which are wholly uncontroversial, but possibly to at least some parts of the more contentious evidence too. This will have the useful effect of limiting the issues at trial. Where statements are agreed, they can be put before the judge without calling the witnesses who made them.

6.2.5   Witnesses of fact: Summary

(a) It is generally best if witnesses of fact attend to give oral evidence at trial if they are available. A judge prefers to see a witness, even though the observation of demeanour is generally recognised as being a highly fallible guide to finding the truth. Thus if a party has a witness, whether as to liability or to quantum, it is as well to call the witness unless his statement has been agreed in advance.

(b) If the witness is uncontroversial, or unavailable for some good reason then one can serve a copy of his evidence on the defendant, give the Civil Evidence Act notice and put the hearsay statement in at trial. It must always be remembered that the trial judge will apply the criteria in s. 4 of the Civil Evidence Act 1995 in deciding what weight he will attach to the evidence of the absent witness. He will in particular ask why the witness has not attended and may draw adverse inferences from absence.

(c) Notices to admit facts. We have already considered the nature of admissions procured by a notice to admit facts (see **3.5.2.2**). This is a useful alternative means of proving facts which are expensive or inconvenient to prove by oral evidence. It may be that the statements of one or several witnesses can be wholly dispensed with by the timely service of a notice to admit facts which achieves a successful response.

6.3   Documentary evidence

6.3.1   The authenticity of documents

When producing documents to the court it is necessary to demonstrate their authenticity.

As is discussed in **Chapter 18**, there is a procedure known as *disclosure* in most claims, in which each party is required to serve on his opponent a list of documents which are in his possession and which are relevant to the action. Where this happens then by virtue of CPR, r. 32.19(1), the party receiving that list is deemed to admit the authenticity of the document unless he serves a notice that he wishes it to be formally proved at trial. By r. 32.19(2) a notice requiring a disclosed document to be proved at trial must be served:

(a) by the latest date for serving witness statements; or

(b) within seven days of disclosure of the document,

whichever is the later.

Accordingly if no such notice is served, it will be taken that the opponent admits that the documents are authentic. If there is an active dispute as to the authenticity of the document, then the party who disclosed it must formally prove it at trial, which will involve calling evidence about how the document came into being. So, if it is the authenticity of a will which is in dispute, the solicitor who drafted it and witnessed its execution may need to be called (with consequent expense).

If a party inappropriately challenges the authenticity of a document then there are likely to be costs consequences under r. 44.3(5), which provides that when deciding on issues of costs, the court's discretion allows it to have regard to the conduct of all the parties including: *'whether it was reasonable for a party to raise, pursue or contest a particular allegation or issue'*.

Accordingly, to the extent that an unnecessary challenge to authenticity prolonged the trial or involved the calling of extra witnesses, the costs of that part of the proceedings may be ordered to be borne by the party responsible, even if he wins the trial generally.

This procedure has only to do with the *authenticity* of a document. It is quite a different thing to challenge the *truthfulness* of a document's contents. The distinction can be seen in the following example.

EXAMPLE

Suppose that after some incident which occurred in 2003 and is now the subject of litigation, the claimant produces a purported witness statement which he says was typed out and signed by a colleague of his who saw the incident. That person died in 2005. If the defendant wished to challenge the *authenticity* of the document (for example, to say that the statement had been fabricated by the claimant and the witness's signature forged) then he would need to give the notice referred to above. If, however, the defendant conceded that the statement was genuine, it would still be open to him to challenge the *truthfulness* of what was set out in it by the deceased witness and no notice would be necessary. The witness statement would subsequently be put in as a hearsay statement and its *credibility* should then be challenged.

Passivity by a party who receives a *notice to admit facts* indicates that he *does not* admit the facts. Inaction, however, by a person who receives copies of documents on disclosure will indicate that the person *does not dispute* authenticity and if he wishes to do so he must take positive action to serve the notice.

Chapters 7 to 13

We have now completed a discussion of the academic or semi-academic matters which underlie the civil litigation process. We shall now continue by discussing civil litigation in a practical way. The order of chapters attempts to follow, where possible, matters as they arise in the course of mainstream litigation, though at each stage possible sidetracks and alternatives are indicated which can be picked up in the later chapters. Most cases will still end early by compromise, default judgment, or the court itself striking out one or other party's case. Whilst these may be mentioned briefly as the discussion proceeds, in order not to lose the narrative thread these ways in which cases may be brought to an early end are discussed more thoroughly in **Chapter 26**.

For a through understanding of **Chapter 7**, it will be necessary to re-read the chapter after the usual course of a civil claim has been studied because there are some references within the text to the Civil Procedure Rules and to the way in which various developments in a case may impact on costs considerations. Clearly, however, the financing of civil litigation is a preliminary matter which must be considered at the outset. For that reason there is no alternative to the topic being considered generally at this early stage, even though it means that some of the concepts referred to within the chapter will not have been studied.

Funding civil litigation and costs

7.1 Financing civil litigation

7.1.1 Introduction

In this chapter we shall consider the crucial matter of the way in which a solicitor is re-munerated in litigation work and the extent to which all or any part of the charges which a client incurs for litigation work may be recovered eventually from an opponent. We shall also consider how the grant of public funding to one or other party may affect the general position. This chapter should be considered in conjunction with **Chapter 33**, which deals with the process by which the court assesses solicitors' and barristers' fees where they cannot be agreed.

It is vital at the outset of a litigation matter to ensure that one's client has a clear picture of the various possible outcomes of the litigation in terms of costs. If a client comes to see a solicitor in connection with a non-contentious matter such as conveyancing, then he is usually under no illusion that anyone will be paying the solicitor's fees except himself. Parties intent on embarking on litigation will need to have explained to them the full range of possibilities about funding and have any misconceptions that they may have dispelled.

It is vital to establish a proper professional relationship with the client (see further **8.6**). A solicitor's relationship with a client is governed primarily by the law of contract, in par-ticular, implied duties as to payment and the exercise of proper professional competence. The law of tort may also be relevant, e.g., since breach of the implied term to use proper professional competence will also amount to the tort of negligence. It may sometimes be worthwhile framing actions against a negligent solicitor alternatively in tort and contract because the rules as to limitation, and remoteness and quantum of damages may be dif-ferent. These obligations are also tempered by the rules of professional conduct, which often have a bearing on matters to do with how a solicitor may charge a client.

For the businesslike conduct of litigation it is usually essential to ensure that the source of finance is clearly established at the start. Substantial payments on account from the client are usually required, and in order to ensure that payments in advance continue throughout the course of the litigation so that the solicitor is always, so to speak, 'ahead' of his own bills in terms of the money he is holding, these payments will be topped up or repeated from time to time. When money on account of costs is received it will be paid into the firm's client account.

7.1.2 Method of charging

Fees for work in litigation matters are worked out on the basis of actual time spent in the conduct of the client's case. Thus time spent, for example, interviewing in the office, collecting evidence, whether inside or outside the office, researching the law, perusing documents, conducting negotiations with the opponent, and travelling to and attending court for interim applications or the trial is all charged on an hourly basis.

The rates chargeable may depend upon the type of activity, so that something which requires minimal mental input, such as driving from the office to court, may be charged at one rate, whereas something that requires a high degree of concentration and skill, such as advocacy or perusing documents obtained on disclosure or researching the law, will be charged at a different rate. Arguably this is not entirely logical, because time spent driving to court on a client's business is time that could have been spent on another client's business, possibly at a higher rate. Nonetheless, this method of charging is common. Likewise, firms will of course have different rates of charging depending on the level of the personnel involved on the case, so that a firm will be entitled to charge more for the time of a senior partner than for that of a junior employee, say a trainee solicitor, who is engaged on some of the more mundane tasks in a case. These basic charging rates, computed by the hour, may be adjusted further to take into account aspects of the case itself, as indicated in the next paragraph.

7.1.3 Factors other than time when deciding what to charge

The matters to take into account when deciding what to charge include the following:

(a) the amount or value of any property involved;

(b) the importance of the matter to all the parties;

(c) the particular complexity of the matter or the difficulty or novelty of the questions raised;

(d) the skill, effort, specialised knowledge and responsibility involved;

(e) the time spent on the case;

(f) the place where and the circumstances in which the work or any part of it was done.

These matters are listed in CPR, r. 44.5(3), as factors to which the court must have regard when it assesses costs.

Thus, for instance, if a matter is both weighty, in the sense of the amount of money involved, and urgent, perhaps because an injunction is immediately needed, so that two or three employees of the firm have to cancel their diary engagements on the day instructions are received to give all their attention to the urgent matter, then naturally a higher charge can be made than for a purely routine case. Most firms have a time-recording system which ensures that every minute spent on a client's business is billed. In some cases the billing is done through time-recording sheets which each fee earner has to fill in for the working day showing what time has been spent on which client's file. More sophisticated systems permit a fee earner to key into a central computerised accounts record the time spent on a case, direct from his desk top.

7.1.4 Interim billing

Efficient firms prepare accounts for the client, usually on a quarterly basis, and thus send the client every three months an account of the work they have done in the preceding quarter. Once the bill has been delivered the firm is in principle entitled to transfer the money which they hold from their client account to the firm's office account (i.e., the money now becomes the firm's own money). If this exhausts the money being held, then further payments on account should be sought. This continues until the end of the case.

By the end of the case a solicitor will ensure that he has been paid in full in advance. After the trial (subject to any appeal) the solicitor can bring the matter to an end and send the final bill. If the client has been successful in the claim, since the loser is usually ordered to pay the bulk of the winner's costs in litigation, the solicitor will now have the task of setting about recovering as large a proportion of the costs as possible for the client, in order to reimburse the client for as much as possible of what he has paid out.

7.1.5 Definition of 'costs'

It is important to note that the term 'costs' has two distinct meanings in litigation. In general speech the word 'costs' usually refers to the total of a solicitor's bill. However, this bill will in fact comprise three distinct elements. The first of these is the solicitor's firm's own fees for the only thing which the firm has to sell, namely its time and expertise. The correct term for these fees is '*profit costs*' but confusingly the term 'costs' is sometimes used to mean simply this element.

The second element on the bill is money paid out by the solicitor in the conduct of litigation on the client's behalf. This will include such things as court fees, travelling and accommodation expenses if part of the work has to be carried out at some distance from the solicitor's office, counsel's fees, fees to expert witnesses for reports and attending at trial, etc. The proper term for these payments is '*disbursements*'.

The third element is VAT on the whole of the profit costs and most of the disbursements (but not court fees).

The general term 'costs' thus usually includes profit costs, disbursements and VAT.

7.1.6 Relations with the client

It is a vital part of running a successful litigation practice to ensure that one's clients are satisfied. This involves giving clients a full account of the progress of their case, and in particular trying to give an honest idea of how long a case will last. Nothing is more unsettling for a client than to have the impression that his case can be dealt with in a matter of weeks, only to find that it lasts some years because of procedural matters which are so familiar to the solicitor that he has overlooked the need to explain them to the client.

One part of keeping clients happy is to make the position as to costs very clear at the outset. Information must be given to the client about the firm's method of charging in terms of the hourly rate, and it must be made clear that there is no litigation matter in which an accurate estimate of the hours involved can be made, although some general idea may be possible. The basis of charging, and the practice of interim billing and of payment on account must be carefully explained to the client so that he knows precisely what outlay he is likely to have and at what intervals. It can, of course, be explained to the client that costs will normally 'follow the event', i.e., that a successful party will generally be able to recover costs from the loser, but that this is within the discretion of the court. (The client must also, of course, be warned that if he loses, he will become liable for his opponent's costs as well as yours.) It must also be made clear that what can be recovered from the loser may very well not involve the whole of the costs in the case and that, anyway, there may be no guarantee that the loser is able to pay.

A solicitor must comply with the Solicitors' Cost Information and Client Care Code 1999 in giving his client full information. This may involve a solicitor considering in particular whether the client would be entitled to apply for help under the Community Legal Service; whether there should be an option of funding the claim under a conditional fee agreement; whether there is any insurance which may cover the position; or whether legal costs can be met from any other source, such as a trade union.

The client should also be told the special rules applicable to litigation against persons who are funded by the Community Legal Service which, generally speaking, impose limitations on the costs that can be recovered against them (see **7.5.7.1**).

The practices described above, particularly at **7.1.1**, are those primarily applicable to cases where the client is paying for his own litigation in the traditional way. There are, however, a number of alternatives to that way of funding litigation, some of which have only come into existence within the very recent past, and it is now appropriate to consider alternative methods of funding litigation.

7.2 Trade union or similar funding

Trade unions very commonly provide a range of benefits for their members apart from the traditional ones of involvement in industrial disputes. In a litigation context they usually provide financial support for trade union members in at least two fields of litigation, namely, personal injuries arising out of work, and employment law disputes. Some trade unions provide a range of other benefits and some provide a form of 'legal expenses insurance cover' generally so that a member may obtain financial assistance across the whole range of personal problems, including even matrimonial disputes. More usually, however, a trade union member will be entitled to free legal advice and assistance in pursuing a claim against his employers only. The trade union will usually require the claim to be submitted for consideration by some trade union official, or small panel, and thereafter will send it out to the trade union's own nominated solicitors who, if they agree that the case appears well founded, will then carry on with the litigation, if necessary, to trial. Trade unions usually require some system of reporting back and for the solicitor from time to time to certify what the running costs of the litigation are and whether it remains the case that there appear to be reasonable prospects of success. A great volume of litigation is funded in this way and there are several large firms of solicitors specialising in litigation on behalf of trade union members.

Some other bodies have somewhat similar schemes for the benefit of their membership such as, for example, the AA and the RAC. However, assistance from nationwide organisations such as those is generally subsumed into what is really legal expenses insurance to which we now come.

7.3 Legal expenses insurance

Legal expenses insurance arises out of an insurance policy which confers, amongst any other benefits which it provides, the right for the policyholder to receive legal advice about a whole range of legal matters and, if the facts appear to indicate that successful litigation could be maintained in respect of the problem, to fund that litigation. The most basic form of legal expenses insurance is that which is included in all motor insurance policies which, as a bare minimum, provide that the insurance company will defend any proceedings brought against the insured in respect of a claim of negligence.

The insurer will thus not only pay the damages, but pay the solicitor's costs of defending the action as well as the opponent's costs if the opponent is successful. Everyone who has motor insurance has legal expenses insurance in this limited form.

What we are mainly concerned with here, however, is legal expenses insurance which would cover the legal expense of bringing a claim, as well as defending claims. It is currently estimated that there may be as many as 17 million insurance policies which provide for legal expenses insurance in one or other form. A very large number of these will be the motor insurance policies referred to above. Similarly many household insurance policies contain provision for legal expenses insurance, at least in the context of what the household policy covers, for example, defending claims brought by a person injured by a slate falling from your roof. Many such policies, however, are remarkably widely worded and cover the householder to enable him not merely to *defend* litigation, but also to *bring* it, arising not just out of incidents connected with the house but generally. Indeed, both with household insurance and some other forms of insurance, the insurance cover may extend to all members of the policyholder's family and for that reason it is suggested that in fact the majority of the population may already have some form of legal expenses insurance, whether they appreciate it or not.

There are many other more general forms of legal expenses insurance which provide for legal advice, assistance and payment of the costs of litigation, however the litigation may arise. These policies are often provided at very modest cost and sometimes at no cost at all as a sort of bonus add-on to existing policies. Sometimes they are offered as a bonus element in other commercial relationships entirely. For example, many banks offer legal expenses insurance to the holders of certain kinds of accounts or credit cards.

7.3.1 Nature of legal expenses insurance

If one has a legal expenses insurance policy then the first port of call is usually to report on a prescribed form the matter about which one wishes to have advice, or eventually to litigate. This will usually be passed on to one of a panel of lawyers for preliminary approval, although the precise administrative arrangements vary. The policyholder is in principle entitled, once cover has been approved, to instruct his own lawyer, but that lawyer will then have the duty of reporting faithfully on whether or not the claim is viable and remains viable once proceedings have started. Most insurance policies exclude support for litigation in certain fields, for example, defamation. Most will not of course cover litigation where the cause of action arose before the policy commenced (although see below).

The result of this is that if the majority of the population have legal expenses insurance, the bulk of litigation in future may well be brought by one party who has this form of insurance against another. Insurers will therefore have to become even more adept than they are at present in anticipating litigation risks and the costs and benefits of bringing or resisting litigation. Also increasingly it may be that the same insurer is in effect funding both parties to the litigation if they both happen to have legal expenses policies with it. There is nothing new about this, of course, because that may well have been the position sometimes in the past, as where two motorists collide and are badly injured and both happened to be insured with the same company.

It follows therefore that decisions about the conduct of litigation will increasingly be taken on a commercial basis. Legal expenses insurers are most unlikely to fund difficult test cases or cases where the cost of the proceedings may hugely outweigh the damages available, even in the event of total success.

We have briefly described the nature of legal expenses insurance above, but a new and possibly surprising development is the rise of so-called 'after the event' insurance. This involves a policy covering a cause of action which arose before the policy was obtained and may actually now be a free-standing form of insurance, although at correspondingly higher premiums. It is simply a way of funding litigation. Where this will be particularly material is as an ingredient in conditional fee agreements, as to which see **7.4**.

7.4 Conditional fee agreements

Conditional fee agreements are permitted under the Courts and Legal Services Act 1990 as amended by the Access to Justice Act 1999.

The nature of such an agreement is that it provides that the lawyer's costs, or some part of them, are payable only in the event of the success in the litigation. In further discussion of conditional fees we will concentrate for the moment on conditional fees when acting for the claimant, although such fees are possible when acting for a defendant, as will be discussed at the very end.

A conditional fee agreement must be in writing and comply with any regulations presently or to be prescribed by the Lord Chancellor, the current requirements being set out in the Conditional Fee Agreements Regulations 2000 (SI 2000/692) as amended by The Conditional Fee Agreements (Miscellaneous Amendments) (No.2) Regulations 2003 (SI 2003/3344). A conditional fee may now be used in all types of civil litigation other than family proceedings. It may also be used in any other kind of proceedings which resolve disputes, for example, arbitration or mediation, and it is not limited to formal litigation.

7.4.1 Nature of conditional fees

In a conditional fee case, if the client is successful, the solicitor will obtain any costs which are awarded against the losing opponent. A conditional fee agreement involves a 'success fee' in such cases, whereby on top of whatever costs are recovered from the losing opponent, a further amount up to an agreed percentage, which cannot be more than 100 per cent of the original costs, may be recovered from the successful party out of his damages. Thus a solicitor has a personal stake in the success of the litigation. The success fee in principle must be related to the risks involved in the litigation. For example, a passenger in a car who has been badly injured in a collision and who sues both drivers involved is highly unlikely to lose outright, so it is arguable that if he is represented under a conditional fee agreement, the success fee should be nothing like 100 per cent and might indeed be very modest. The way in which this might be subject to the court's scrutiny is discussed in **7.4.2**. Moreover, under the Law Society's model form of agreement a success fee cannot be more than 25 per cent of the total damages recovered. It must be stressed that at the time of writing this is simply in the nature of a recommendation and is not a binding rule. It is, however, something to which the court might have regard if the success fee were ever challenged, whether by the client or by the other party (as to which see **7.4.2** and **7.4.4**).

Thus to take a simple example, suppose that a client apparently has a cause of action but success is far from certain. His solicitor demands a success fee of 100 per cent and the client agrees. The litigation is wholly successful so that the client receives damages of £20,000. The amount of costs obtained from the defendant is £4,000. The conditional fee which initially will be recovered out of the client's damages is a further £4,000. Thus the client will receive £16,000 and the lawyer has made a further 'profit' on the litigation of £4,000 on top of the £4,000 costs which had been recovered from the defendant. It will be observed that on these figures the success fee is within the 25 per cent in the Law Society's model agreement.

The above figures are a simplistic example which requires some further explanation. In fact what the solicitor seeks to recover in total is:

(a) 'the basic costs' of the litigation;

(b) any shortfall in the 'basic costs' recovered from the paying party; and

(c) the agreed success fee.

'Basic costs' means the amount of costs which can probably be recovered on the standard basis of assessment from the loser in the litigation. Although in successful, well-conducted litigation that amount will wholly be payable by the losing party, there will of course be cases where there is a shortfall in that figure. Suppose, for example, that the costs of some interim stages had been awarded against the otherwise successful claimant and these were offset from the costs recoverable from the defendant, so that, for example, only £3,000 was recovered from the defendant towards a basic costs figure of £4,000. That does not have the effect of reducing the claimant's liability to his own solicitor for costs. In those circumstances the claimant would be liable to pay the shortfall between the solicitor's proper charge for the case and the amount actually recovered from the defendant (i.e., a further £1,000 towards basic costs), but in addition the success fee would still be based on the full figure of £4,000.

Conditional fee agreements may also be entered into by barristers who may thus have their own fees enhanced by up to 100 per cent.

7.4.2 Challenging the success fee

It is perfectly possible for a client in any case to challenge his or her own solicitor's bill. The basis of this, and the procedure for doing so, are briefly described at 33.1 in the general chapter on costs which appears towards the end of this book. A client can, as part of that challenge, if appropriate, challenge all or part of the success fees even if the client freely entered into the agreement. It liable for these fees, even though, as 7.4.4 explains, one hopes eventually to recover all of them from one's opponent.

There may nonetheless be a shortfall between costs due to the solicitor and costs recovered from the opponent, as explained above in 7.4.1. Alternatively the court may only award a success fee against the opponent at, say, 70% whereas the agreement signed by the client allows for 100%. In principle the solicitor is then entitled to obtain the remaining 30% from the client.

It ought to be said that many solicitors feel morally obliged to waive the last 30% in such circumstances and accept only what they can recover from the opponent, whatever their strict entitlement may be. Indeed, many of the better firms expressly advertise this, with phrases such as "we deduct nothing from your damages whatever the outcome" or similar. However, if a solicitor wishes to insist on his or her entitlement to recover the difference between what he or she can get from an opponent, and what appears strictly due under the Conditional Fee Agreement signed by the client, then the client does have the right to ask the court to adjudicate on this matter.

These provisions were intended to help allay a considerable anxiety that was felt about the whole business of conditional fees, which is the possibly distasteful appearance of a solicitor being seen to negotiate about fees, perhaps with a badly injured client who is unintelligent and may have little idea about alternative sources of funding or about his prospects of success. It was felt necessary to insert these provisions so as to enable a client to have the court consider at least the appropriateness of the 'uplift' represented by the success fee. Thus at its simplest, if the client's prospects of success were very good indeed, as in the example of the car passenger referred to earlier, the court would give close scrutiny to a success fee of say 100 per cent and would expect a much more modest uplift in those circumstances, though one taking into account that no litigation is certain and that the solicitor is giving up his right to require payments on account and disbursements as the litigation progresses.

In dealing with assessment of these matters, the costs judge must have regard to all relevant factors as they reasonably appeared to the solicitor or counsel when the conditional fee agreement was entered into. The client is required to set out in advance the reasons why the percentage increase should be reduced and indicate what he believes the percentage increase should be.

7.4.3   When should a solicitor enter into a conditional fee agreement?

All firms are likely to have their own policies in relation to this. Except in the very simplest case, a firm which commonly offers conditional fee agreements will need to do at least some work investigating the merits of the case, beyond the terms of the client's first statement before it can decide whether it will enter into a conditional fee agreement or not. Most firms will provide a procedure whereby the risk assessment is carried out by a senior member of staff once preliminary facts have been investigated. Some firms appear to have a policy of applying a blanket success fee, in those cases which they take on, of 100 per cent. It is highly unlikely that this would survive scrutiny on a costs assessment, should the client be disgruntled. However, for the reason we are now going on to describe it is unlikely to be the client who is disgruntled in a case where he succeeds and there is a success fee.

7.4.4   Claiming the success fee from the losing party

The Access to Justice Act 1999, s. 27, brought in a new s. 58A to the Courts and Legal Services Act 1990, which provides that costs orders may include provision requiring the paying party to pay the success fee as well as the ordinary costs of the winning party. Thus at the end of the case, it will be open to the court to order costs as it does now (and indeed if it is a fast track case to go on to assess them summarily), but then to consider any application for the losing party to pay the success fee so that the winning party in effect receives his damages untouched (subject to there being any shortfall in respect of the 'basic costs' as described above). It will therefore be open to the losing party to make submissions about why the success fee should not be ordered against his client. If it is ordered, as it now usually will be, then it will be open to the losing party to raise questions about whether the amount of the success fee claimed was appropriate given the criteria already described as to the chances of success generally, just as in the case where the success fee can be challenged by the original client himself.

7.4.5   After-the-event insurance

It is not enough to allay a client's fears about costs of litigation which he cannot fund simply to provide a conditional fee agreement, so that his own solicitor does not require to be put in funds as the case proceeds. A further vital factor is to consider what is to happen if the client loses. In a conditional fee agreement a client's own solicitor, as we have explained, has a large stake in the litigation and will get no fees at all if the client loses. There is nothing in this, however, that will absolve the client from himself being subject to a potentially ruinous costs order obtained by the successful opponent. For this reason, conditional fee agreements almost always go hand in hand with a form of after-the-event insurance policy which covers the client for any costs awarded to his opponent. There are now very numerous after-the-event insurers who have entered this market and who are apparently finding it profitable. They find it profitable because they can be reasonably confident that if a solicitor is willing to put thousands of pounds worth of work into a case for which he will not be paid at all in the event of failure, that solicitor will only take cases with good prospects of success. Some insurers are thus happy to provide insurance for a one-off premium provided that the claimant's solicitor demonstrates that there is a conditional fee agreement in existence and that his evidence seems to indicate a good prospect of success. Other insurers are more demanding, and in particular may require, for example, in personal injury cases, that the solicitor must be a member of the Law Society's Personal Injury Panel or have other specialist qualifications.

By virtue of the Access to Justice Act 1999, s. 27, the one-off insurance premium can be recovered also as part of the client's costs. It is impossible to indicate what exactly these premiums are. Whereas until recently they were very much standard figures depending on the type of litigation, insurers are now much more awake to the need to assess claims individually. They are likely to be in a band of approximately £250–£1,000. In difficult, potentially very expensive litigation, the premium may be very much more.

The issues surrounding claiming the success fee and the insurance premium from the losing party led to much first instance litigation in 2001/2002. A test case reached the House of Lords in May 2002. The case is *Callery* v *Gray* [2002] UKHL 28. The outcome is unfortunately rather inconclusive, the House of Lords declining to give very precise guidelines and suggesting that the lower courts need to assess what success fee is appropriate in the circumstances of each case. A more technical discussion is beyond the scope of this book.

7.4.6   Defendants and conditional fees

For obvious reasons most conditional fee agreements hitherto have been entered into by claimants because it has been necessary that there should be an eventual fund of money from which the success fee can be paid. However, now that success fees may be recovered from the losing party, subject to objections and to the court's assessment procedures, it may be increasingly common for defendants to use them. What will be difficult will be to decide when the defendant has won. It may, for example, be that the success fee relates not to whether liability is won or lost, but whether damages are reduced below a certain level. Thus, if a defendant is willing to concede liability at the outset, but the litigation will still be lengthy and expensive because of disputes about quantum, a conditional fee might still be possible. The issue of success might then turn on whether, say, damages can be reduced below a certain figure and, if so, by how much. The issue of whether a claimant can be pressured into accepting a Part 36 offer (see **Chapter 25**) may also be material. The definition of success may therefore differ and be rather more subtle in many cases and need to be carefully defined in the conditional fee agreement.

At the time of writing, at least in the field of personal injury litigation, there is no indication that insurance companies are showing particular interest in attempting to force solicitors who are on their panels to enter into such agreements.

7.5 'Legal aid' or public funding

Although the term 'legal aid' will undoubtedly live on in the popular consciousness for many years, with effect from April 2000 the proper term is 'public funding' or 'funding under the Community Legal Service'. This has the effect of replacing legal aid as previously administered under the Legal Aid Act 1988 with a different basis of funding, although in some respects the provisions are similar.

7.5.1 Community Legal Service

Section 4 of the Access to Justice Act 1999 set up the Legal Services Commission, which is required to establish, maintain and develop the Community Legal Service to provide legal services to individuals. The object is that individuals should, subject to public resources generally, have access to legal services that effectively meet their needs. The Commission has now published a Funding Code which defines its approach to funding civil cases. Although it is envisaged that funding may be available to bodies or individuals other than qualified lawyers for some purposes, for example, Citizens Advice Bureaux and other such agencies, we will concentrate entirely on funding through solicitors and counsel.

7.5.2 Franchising and contracting

Generally speaking, in order to be publicly funded, a solicitor must have a franchise. The franchise, introduced in respect of legal aid several years ago, is a type of quality assurance. A franchise is granted to a firm of solicitors following audits carried out at their offices by officials, formerly of the Legal Aid Board and now of the Legal Services Commission. Franchises are granted for prescribed areas of work, such as housing, personal injury, clinical negligence disputes, debt claims and the like. In order to obtain a franchise a solicitor's firm must undergo an investigation of office systems and client care, followed by a check on the way in which randomly chosen individual files have been dealt with in the recent past, to ensure the competence of, and appropriate level of supervision for, the staff dealing with the files. When a franchise is granted, the firm concerned is monitored by audits which usually take place annually.

Funding by the Legal Services Commission is by *contracting* and the Courts and Legal Services Act 1990 allows for remuneration to be arranged by direct negotiation by fixing standard rates or local rates. The exact way that this works and the mechanism by which national or local budgets are to be fixed is beyond the scope of this work, but it is important to know that there will undoubtedly be limits on hourly rates, the number of cases which a solicitor may take, and the like, and that when acting for the publicly funded litigant, one is unlikely to be able to charge the same rates as in the case of a privately paying client.

One aspect of a franchise is that it enables a solicitor, within reason, to decide personally which cases should be taken on with public funding.

7.5.3 Levels of service

There are several levels of legal service provided under the Community Legal Service scheme and we shall now consider each of these in turn. They are:

(a) legal help;

(b) help at court;

(c) legal representation, consisting of:

(i)   investigative help; and

(ii) full representation.

(d) support funding which may include:

(i)   investigation support; or

(ii) litigation support;

(e) other services.

7.5.3.1   Legal help

Legal help is a system for giving advice about law or procedure in the solicitor's office. It might include undertaking some correspondence on behalf of a client and even trying to assist him to negotiate the outcome of some dispute. It would certainly cover advice on documents. It does not cover advocacy or issuing or conducting court proceedings, but it could include assisting a client who is acting in person, for example, by helping him draft his witness statement or preparing legal submissions for him.

The general criteria for the grant of legal help are:

(a) Is there sufficient benefit to the client having regard to the circumstance of the matter, including the personal circumstances of the client, to justify work being carried out?

(b) Is it reasonable for the matter to be funded out of the Community Legal Service Fund having regard to any other potential sources of funding?

7.5.3.2   Help at court

Help at court involves the legal representative acting for the purposes of a particular hearing only, but without formally coming on the record as the client's lawyer for the whole proceedings. It is intended to be a quick and informal way of helping clients who need someone to speak for them at court and might involve, for example, a case where a district judge adjourns a hearing because it seems to him that one of the parties needs advice in connection with some aspect of the case and perhaps even advocacy for one further limited part of the case. It is, for example, quite common for this form of help to be given to unrepresented defendants in housing possession cases where everything that needs to be said for them can probably be said at one short hearing to enable them to avoid a possession order being obtained against them.

The criteria for help at court are:

(a) There must be sufficient benefit to the client having regard to the circumstances, including his personal circumstances.

(b) It must be reasonable for the matter to be funded out of the Community Legal Service Fund, having regard to other potential sources of funding.

(c) Are the nature of the proceedings and the circumstance of the hearing and of the client such that representation is appropriate and will be of real benefit to the client?

(d) Help at court may not be given if the contested nature of the hearing is such that it is more appropriate that it should be given through some other level of legal representation (see **7.5.3.3** and **7.5.3.4**).

7.5.3.3 Legal representation

Legal representation involves the provision of legal assistance for a party to existing legal proceedings or someone who is contemplating bringing proceedings. It includes litigation services, advocacy and, generally speaking, all the legal assistance that is usually given by a person providing representation in civil proceedings, including preliminary steps and steps to negotiate a compromise. It may take two particular forms:

(a) *Investigative help*. This form of funding is limited to the preliminary investigation of the strength of a proposed claim. It can include permitting a solicitor to obtain witness statements, visit the scene of an accident, and even obtain expert advice. It can include court proceedings, perhaps limited to, for example, applying for early disclosure of documents or the opportunity to inspect premises. It is appropriate for cases that may need a good deal of work before the proper prospects of success can be assessed. There are cost benefit considerations as well, including the necessity that damages recovered should exceed the small claims track limit (see **Chapter 17**), unless there is some competing feature such as a wider public interest. It is also necessary that the cost benefit analysis would satisfy the criteria for full representation (see below).

The criteria for granting this include the important feature that it should be refused if there are other funding arrangements possible; it should be refused, in particular, if funding should be limited to *investigative support* (see **7.5.3.4**). It should be granted only where the prospects of success are uncertain and substantial investigative work is required to be done.

(b) *Full representation*. This is public funding for the full running of a case up to its conclusion and enforcement of judgment. It will only be considered if it is clear that there are reasonable prospects of success and there must generally be a demanding investigation of the merits of the case.

Full representation will be refused if there are other potential sources of funding, including conditional fee agreements, which will of course often be the case where the client's success seems probable to a level which would justify full representation anyway. It will be refused if the prospects of success are unclear or borderline, and there is no significant wider public interest or the case is not of overwhelming importance to the client. It may be refused generally on cost–benefit grounds.

7.5.3.4 Support funding

Support funding authorises the same services as legal representation (see **7.5.3.3**), but is limited to either *partial* public funding of the claim, leaving the balance to be privately funded, or to public funding for initial investigation of a claim with a view to its being pursued under a conditional fee agreement. Support funding is intended primarily for difficult personal injuries cases which may have high commencement or investigative costs and which would otherwise be difficult to bring because the lawyer would be reluctant to enter into a conditional fee agreement. There are two levels of support funding:

(a) *Investigative support.* This is a kind of funding limited to the investigation of the strength of a proposed claim with a view to a conditional fee agreement. It is limited to relatively high-cost cases which are likely to involve initial costs of over £1,000 in disbursements and counsel's fees or £3,000 in solicitor's costs at prescribed rates. It will be refused unless damages are likely to exceed £5,000. Investigative support will be granted only if there are reasonable grounds for believing that when the investigations are completed, the case will be strong enough to justify proceeding on a private basis, with litigation support if appropriate.

(b) *Litigation support.* This is any type of support funding other than investigative support and is intended to provide partial funding for high-cost litigation which will eventually, or in part, be supported by a conditional fee agreement. It is likely to be limited to cases with very high start-up costs which are likely to exceed £5,000 in disbursements or counsel's fees or £15,000 in solicitor's costs at prescribed rates. Litigation support will be refused if the prospects of success are uncertain (in which case investigative support should be considered), borderline or poor. It may be refused also on cost–benefit grounds.

In the case of litigation support, the conditional fee agreement proposed must comply with requirements of the Funding Code and satisfactory insurance for the client's payment costs must be available.

7.5.3.5 Other services

Levels of service other than those referred to above *may* be funded by the Community Legal Service, but only if a specific order or direction is made by the Lord Chancellor. It is envisaged that other levels may eventually be prescribed to fill in gaps in the existing levels or to provide for a new category entirely.

7.5.4 The cost–benefit analysis

A full cost–benefit analysis must be undertaken where full representation or litigation support is applied for. Putting it crudely, if the benefit expected to be obtained does not justify the level of costs, public funding will be refused. Thus, an exact as possible estimate of the likely total costs should be made through to the end of proceedings using such standard remuneration rates as may be prescribed by the Commission. A realistic estimate must be made of the amount of money sought from the other side, taking into account any likely deductions for contributory negligence or the like. It will also have to be demonstrated that the defendant is in a position to pay.

Moreover, costs are capped at £70 per hour for solicitors, £90 per hour for senior counsel and £50 per hour for junior counsel. The apparent basis for this is that once cases get to this level, the lawyers should also take some risks of losing by having their public funding rates (i.e., the rates that they could claim from public funds if the case were lost) reduced. There is nothing to stop them charging normal private client rates when claiming costs from the other party if they win the case.

Unless there is some wider public interest, full representation or litigation support will be refused in the following circumstances:

(a) if the prospects of success are *very good* (80 per cent or more), *but* the likely damages do not exceed the likely costs;

(b) if the prospects of success are *good* (60–80 per cent), *but* the likely damages do not exceed the likely costs by a ratio of 2 : 1; or

(c) if the prospects of success are *moderate* (50–60 per cent), *but* the likely damages do not exceed the likely costs by a ratio of 4 : 1.

In claims which are not for money, but have no wider public interest, full representation or litigation support will be refused unless the likely benefits from the proceedings justify the likely costs, such that a 'reasonable private paying client' would be prepared to litigate. This is also the test in cases where the applicant for funding is the defendant.

The matter will have to be considered more generally in claims which have a wider public interest.

7.5.5 Other criteria for funding

(a) An application may be refused if there is alternative funding available to the client through insurance or otherwise (this does not mean, however, that an application is excluded just because there might be the possibility of a conditional fee agreement).

(b) An application may be refused if there are complaint systems, ombudsman schemes or forms of alternative dispute resolution which should be tried before litigation.

(c) An application may be refused if it appears premature.

(d) An application may be refused if it appears more appropriate for the client to be assisted by some other level of service.

(e) An application may be refused if it appears unreasonable to fund the case, for example, in the light of the existence of other proceedings or the interests of other parties.

(f) An application will be refused if the claim has been or is likely to be allocated to the small claims track (because in principle the costs recovered on that track are very limited, see **Chapter 17**).

7.5.6 Financial eligibility

Public funding will of course only be available to those who are financially eligible under regulations. The regulations provide for income and other assets to be taken into account and for the setting off of assets in various forms so that, for example, the value of the family home is usually left out of account initially. There are certain permitted deductions for dependants and the like. There are also detailed regulations about assessment of the income of self-employed persons. A person may be expected to bear part of the costs personally by contribution if his means are above a certain minimum. It is beyond the scope of this work to set out the detailed figures, which are usually changed annually.

7.5.7 Miscellaneous further matters

7.5.7.1 Costs against a publicly funded individual

There are several restrictions which vary the usual position in relation to costs where one of the parties is publicly funded. If a party is publicly funded and loses the case, then generally speaking his own costs will need to be assessed by the court for payment by public funds. This may be unnecessary if costs are below a certain figure because they are payable at prescribed rates, in which case application can be made direct to the Legal Services Commission. In larger cases, however, the court will be involved in the assessment process.

We now need to consider a variation in the usual rules where someone who has received public funding loses and his opponent seeks a costs order against him. By s. 11 of the Access to Justice Act 1999 the costs against an individual in relation to any proceedings or part of proceedings funded for him shall not exceed the amount (if any) which is a reasonable one for him to pay, having regard to all the circumstances including:

(a) the financial resources of all the parties to the proceedings; and

(b) their conduct in relation with the dispute to which the proceedings relate.

Regulations have been made specifying the principles to be applied in determining the amount of any costs awarded against a party and may also require payment of any costs awarded in those cases by the Community Legal Service directly (s. 11(4)(d)). These are the Community Legal Services (Cost Protection) Regulations 2000 (as amended by subsequent regulation). See **7.5.7.2**.

The net effect of this is that one must take carefully into account, when advising the opponent of a publicly funded party that the usual costs consequences may not apply. This will also be material, for example, when entering into a conditional fee agreement against a publicly funded party or when making disclosure to insurers who may be funding such litigation. It is difficult at present to know how the court will interpret the provisions which restrict costs against publicly funded parties. The wording of the relevant part of s. 11 of the 1999 Act is in similar terms to a previous provision in s. 17 of the Legal Aid Act 1988.

Quite a sophisticated body of case law arose under the 1988 Act which to some extent defined the circumstances in which costs could be awarded against publicly funded parties. The following general propositions emerged:

(a) The court would investigate the financial resources of all the parties, including the person who is not publicly funded. Because a party receives public funding, it does not mean that he is virtually destitute. The value of his home is left out of account in computing his assets; it may well therefore be possible, either at the end of the litigation or at some time in the future for proper costs orders to be enforced.

(b) One could also have regard to the conduct of the parties in the litigation. Thus if it becomes clear at trial that the publicly funded party has substantially misrepresented his case and his evidence is disbelieved, it may be that the court will take a more robust attitude to ordering costs against him.

(c) If there are interim costs orders, in favour of the legally aided party, it may be perfectly proper to offset the successful non-publicly funded party's eventual costs against those orders. It is for this reason that summary assessment of costs cannot be ordered in favour of a publicly funded party (although it can be ordered against him).

A costs order may of course be made against a publicly funded person who has in principle 'won' the litigation, for example, where he has recovered some amount of money, but has failed to beat a Part 36 payment in (see **Chapter 25**). In that situation it may be perfectly proper to allow the usual costs order to 'bite' so that the opponent's costs from the time when the offer was rejected are paid out of the damages awarded, which will be represented by part of the money presumably paid into court.

7.5.7.2 Costs against the Legal Services Commission

As a long stop, it may be possible to apply for costs direct from the Legal Services Commission (LSC). This is provided by s. 11(4)(d) of the 1999 Act and the Regulations under it. The conditions which must be satisfied are as follows.

(a) The proceedings must have been finally decided in favour of the non-publicly funded litigant.

(b) The non-publicly funded litigant must make the application for costs order against the LSC within three months of the making of a costs order against the publicly funded litigant (which should have been applied for under the provisions mentioned in the previous paragraphs).

(c) The court must be satisfied that it is *just and equitable* in the circumstances that provision for the costs should be made out of public funds.

(d) The proceedings must have been *instituted by* the publicly funded litigant (i.e., only a successful *defendant* can apply for such a costs order).

(e) It must be shown that the non-publicly funded litigant will suffer *severe financial hardship* if the order is not made.

It is important to note that when one is acting for a successful defendant against a publicly funded claimant, *all* these conditions must apply. The personal liability of the publicly funded claimant must have been considered by the court, although it is irrelevant whether any order was or was not made. The words 'just and equitable' tend to mean that the successful defendant should have behaved reasonably throughout the case, including making any proper admissions and concessions, and should have won on the merits rather than on a technicality. The term 'severe financial hardship', it has been said of the same phrase in s. 18 of the Legal Aid Act 1988 in the case of *Stewart* v *Stewart* [1974] 1 WLR 877, should be given a liberal interpretation so as to exclude only large companies, insured persons and the really wealthy. Even an apparently prosperous professional person may not be outside the scope of the section given that such a person's commitments and outgoings may well be commensurate with his or her income. The wealth of an applicant's spouse should be taken into account only to a limited extent (see *Adams* v *Reilly* [1988] QB 372).

There are detailed provisions for the time when such an application should be made. The application should be made at any time within three months of the end of the trial and should be accompanied by the successful defendant's bill of costs, a statement of resources (to demonstrate that the defendant will suffer hardship) and a notice to the effect that a costs order is being sought against the Commission. These documents must be served on the unsuccessfully funded party and the Regional Director of the LSC. Determination of the issue may then be dealt with by a District Judge and the Regional Director of the LSC may appear at the hearing, instruct counsel to appear on his behalf, or may instead rely on a written statement to be served and filed before the hearing.

It should be noted lastly that the requirement to show that the defendant will suffer severe financial hardship unless an order is made applies only in proceedings at first instance. On appeal the court can consider the justice of the situation generally. Indeed, under the identically worded provision of the Legal Aid Act 1988 on appeals, costs of even substantial companies, building societies and a police force have been ordered to be paid by the predecessor of the LSC.

7.5.7.3 Excluded categories of work

There are certain categories of work for which public funding is not available at all. These are set out in sch. 2 to the 1999 Act. The most important excluded categories are:

(a) allegations of negligently caused injury, death or damage to property, apart from allegations relating to clinical negligence (the effect of this is, of course, to exclude all personal injury claims; however personal injury claim by *children* may still be eligible for public funding);

(b) disputes about land, including conveyancing. boundary disputes;

(c) wills and trusts;

(d) defamation or malicious falsehood;

(e) matters of company or partnership law or *'other matters arising out of the carrying on of a business'*, a category which may also include much litigation, for example, that of small traders pursuing trade debts.

7.5.8 Summary

By whatever means litigation is funded, a client is still entitled to the same level of client care and costs information. In the case of a privately paying client, it is not just the method of charging and the eventual likely cost of the case that should be indicated where possible, but the firm's own system for receiving money on account of costs and interim billing. Full advice should also be given about possible alternative methods of funding and about liability for an opponent's costs, both of the case as a whole and of interim stages. In principle, at the stage of each interim application, the client should be told about the possible costs consequences when his instructions are taken.

It is always appropriate to investigate whether a client has legal expenses insurance, even if the firm in question does not operate conditional fee agreements. If conditional fee agreements are used by the firm, it is suggested that proper consideration must be given to the appropriate level of success fee and it is inappropriate to fix a global 100 per cent fee in cases with little litigation risk attached, bearing in mind that the fee may be subject to scrutiny by the courts, either at the instigation of a client or of the losing opponent.

If the client is publicly funded, consideration must be given to a case plan so that applications for the appropriate levels of funding are made at the right time.

7.6 Costs during the case

It is important to remember that under the CPR, applications in the course of a claim should be infrequent. The court's interventionist procedure, which will enable it to give comprehensive directions without the parties attending at an early stage in a case, ought to mean that only in unusual circumstances, or where one of the parties does not comply with what has been ordered by the court, will there need to be any hearing to deal with the unusual situation, or to enforce compliance. The whole host of routine applications which used to be the norm should now be entirely avoided. In most cases where an application is made to the court, it will be because something unexpected has arisen or because of non-compliance with an existing order. At the end of each such hearing it is important to ensure that some order for costs is made. If costs are not dealt with, the presumption is that there is *no order for costs*—that neither party is to obtain from the other any costs at all related not just to that hearing, but to the preparation for it. Examples of common orders for costs are as follows. (Reference should also be made to **21.9** and **Chapter 33**.)

7.6.1 'Costs in the case'

This means in effect that whoever wins the eventual trial will also recover from his opponent the costs of that particular application, including not merely the attendance at court for the application itself (which may have taken only a few minutes), but also the necessary preparation and drafting of documents for it, attendances on the client or witnesses in connection with it, etc. This order is appropriate in purely routine applications which have progressed the case procedurally to the advantage of both sides, or the merit of which is unclear until the eventual outcome is known. While formerly the most common form of order, this is likely to be used less in future, as routine applications should be unnecessary if the court gives comprehensive case management directions.

7.6.2 'Claimant's (or defendant's) costs in any event'

This order is different from costs in the case. It means that regardless of who succeeds at the trial, the named person will nevertheless recover the costs of this application. It inevitably implies some criticism of the conduct of the other party. It would, for example, be appropriate where the other party has refused to give disclosure of some document which should have been disclosed, or has failed to comply with some step in time or at all, which was ordered by the court.

Where this is ordered there will usually be a *summary assessment* of costs and the party who hopes to obtain an order in this form should have served on his opponent not later than 24 hours before the hearing, and filed a copy at court, a schedule showing what costs he is seeking, describing briefly the work done, the rates charged and so on. The district judge who makes the order will then assess the costs straightaway and, in general, they will be ordered to be paid within 14 days. It should be noted that a summary assessment of costs cannot be undertaken where the *successful* party is legally aided. For further discussion of summary assessment see **33.6**.

7.6.3 'Claimant's (or defendant's) costs in the case'

This is the midway stage between the first and the second orders. It implies a more modest criticism of the conduct adopted by the party who has lost the interim application. An order in this form means that the successful party will obtain his costs of this stage if he wins at trial. But if he loses at trial, then although he will not get his costs of this stage neither will the opponent who does win at trial, whose slowness or inappropriate conduct has led to the necessity for this application and hearing. Summary assessment will again be appropriate, as it will in both the next two kinds of order.

7.6.4 'Costs thrown away'

An order for costs in this form covers costs which have been wasted in some way due to the default of a party. An example is where a default judgment has been obtained by the claimant after the defendant, by some oversight, fails to return his acknowledgement of service to the court in time. If the defendant can show some merit in defending the case, or some excuse for having returned his acknowledgement of service late, he may be able to get the judgment set aside and be able to go on to defend, but will inevitably be ordered to pay the costs thrown away, i.e., the cost of the claimant having gone to the trouble of obtaining judgment in default and also of attending on the summons to oppose the application to set it aside.

7.6.5   'Costs of and caused by'

This is where, for example, the court makes an order permitting a party to amend a statement of case. The party in whose favour the costs order is made is entitled to the costs of preparing for and attending the application and the costs of any consequential amendments that need to be made to his own statement of case.

7.6.6   'Costs reserved'

In essence this means the same as costs in the case (see **7.6.1**), so that the winner of the eventual trial will receive the costs of the interim stage. The difference here is that the matter may be reopened before the trial judge if the circumstances require it. Accordingly, if the eventual outcome of the trial makes the court take a quite different view of the appropriateness of an earlier procedural stage, the decision on the costs of that stage can be reviewed. If the matter is not reopened at trial, or no different or further order is made, then the term means precisely the same as costs in the case.

Managing a civil litigation practice

8

To acquire mastery of the rules of civil procedure requires constant practice and constant effort in keeping up to date. The Civil Procedure Rules 1998 (CPR), introduced in April 1999, made enormous changes to civil procedure and a series of cases have already indicated that generally speaking authorities dealing with the interpretation of the previous rules have little use for interpreting the CPR. This is so even where the previous rule was almost the same as the present rule, simply because, whatever the rules themselves say, the underlying approach required by the CPR is substantially different.

It is important to keep up to date and for this *The Times* remains a particularly useful source, many cases on procedure only being reported there. Likewise electronic sources are invaluable. The Lord Chancellor's Department have a website for the CPR; and there is a daily update by the Lawtel service.

8.1 Files

The file is the record of a client matter, and without the proper file it would be impossible to deal with most cases. Merely keeping a cardboard file with the papers within it is not sufficient, however. For the efficient conduct of the action to which each file relates, the file must be logically arranged and properly maintained. A cardboard folder with an ill-assorted jumble of papers is unlikely to be a comprehensive record; letters may be filed out of sequence or lost and important documents such as statements of case, medical reports or original receipts may go astray amongst the copy correspondence. A good file keeps together relevant records so that once obtained and placed in the file, the same information does not have to be sought again elsewhere and can easily be found.

Each file should contain an information sheet at the beginning, containing, first, the essential details required by the office as a central record. These are sometimes obtained by the use of standard client questionnaires and include the client's personal details, address, telephone number, method of contact and the like. The second part should provide for the insertion of additional useful information, such as the limitation period dates, time limits for service, hearing dates, availability of witnesses, etc. A correspondence file should be distinct from items of evidence and draft documents. In a civil case a further division of the file may be necessary into those documents which must be, and those which need not be, disclosed to your opponent. If the file becomes too bulky it should be divided into separate folders, preferably in such a way that when you are dealing with routine correspondence and telephone calls the file needed contains the current correspondence file only, with the addition of current draft documents. The use of ring

binder files or box files with coloured dividers is often an essential aid to proper organisation. Proper management of the file will prevent the papers from becoming dog-eared
and being mislaid, as well as being more convenient for instant access.

The importance of the diary and an effective reminder system is discussed in **8.2**
below but any such system should be complemented by regular and systematic review
of all the current files. It is essential that accurate records are kept of everything that
happens in the file. This must include the date of and time spent on every attendance
and the content of that attendance; every telephone call, together with an indication
of what it was about; all the time spent considering the case, both before and after seeing the client (indicating briefly the nature of the discussion and any required follow-up
action). Most of us have imperfect memories, and thus each item of work should be
recorded separately as it is completed. The note should say exactly how long each item
took and, if some special factor made it take longer than expected, why that was. This
kind of note serves several purposes. Apart from being a useful reminder of just what
was dealt with at the relevant stage, it may be of vital assistance in substantiating costs
claimed from opponents or for justifying a bill to your own client. In addition, and all
litigation lawyers have to face this, there will be cases that are lost. When you have a
combination of a lost case and a client with a difficult personality, it is the experience
of every litigation lawyer sooner or later to face allegations that he conducted a case
incompetently. The lawyer may therefore need to justify to the client, or to professional negligence insurers, just what he did, when, and how, to defend such an allegation.

Information should therefore not be kept only in someone's head, however reliable
their memory; files should be interchangeable and information kept in a uniform way
within an office so that any person in the firm taking over the conduct of the case for
any reason is able to tell from the file exactly what has happened to date. It must be
borne in mind in litigation matters that problems may arise unexpectedly, and even
someone who thoroughly briefs other members of the firm before going on his annual
holiday may not have covered every conceivable contingency.

Keeping good memoranda on the file is also an aid to billing and provides the foundation of the claim to costs, as indicated earlier. Even if full time sheets are maintained, it
is still necessary for memoranda to appear on the file as well. Attendance notes
filed in support of a bill on assessment of costs must explain what was done as well as
indicate the time taken.

8.2 Use of a diary

The necessity for an office diary is obvious, namely to ensure attendance at the right
place at the right time and to avoid the requirement to be in two places at once. A diary
should be more than a mere list of appointments, however. It can be both an essential
safeguard, and a weapon. It serves as a safeguard when used to note important time
limits, not merely the Limitation Act date for the issue of proceedings but also other
key dates, e.g., for compliance with case management directions. Missing time limits
where time is of the essence is a frequent source of negligence actions against solicitors.
In the conduct of civil litigation it will assist case management by noting forward each
time limit which applies and ensuring that the opponent complies with them and, if
necessary, making application to the court where the opponent is in default. This is of
vital assistance in negotiation tactics in the way explained later (**9.6.3**).

Many solicitors use wall charts and information technology to supplement diaries, but whichever method is used it is essential that your secretary is briefed on the need to act as a further longstop in entering reminders and key dates.

8.3 Time management

A further and important use of the diary is for managing a workload. Work on each matter should be planned and prioritised, with time allocated to it in the diary. It is always tempting to put off something which you find difficult or boring or time-consuming in favour of other, less important work. Most solicitors who have at some stage lapsed into bad practices are very aware of the temptation to deal with quick, satisfying matters that arrive on their desks, while worrying or difficult tasks are post-poned, initially from day to day but eventually from week to week. One example which many civil litigators dislike is the task of computing special damages in heavy-weight cases and the preparation of schedules in the appropriate form. The temptation to put this off is exacerbated if you know that your own files are in a mess and that finding and collating the necessary receipts, letters from employers and the like will in itself take some time. Most litigation lawyers would say, however, that however much they dislike this task, when they do eventually buckle down to it, it always proves less difficult than feared.

When contributing to discussions about your own workload, whether as a new employee talking with the supervising partner, or eventually as a partner delegating work to others, it is always vital to have a general idea of how much of your working day is likely to be spent outside the office, to the obvious detriment of your ability to cope with a great deal of paper work. If you like to do your own advocacy in chambers, or possibly even, eventually, at trial, then you will need back-up staff to help cope with the more mundane aspects of civil litigation practice such as taking statements, draft-ing lists of documents and the like. Even if you do not go to court a great deal but have a practice which involves a lot of time out of the office visiting, e.g., the site of factory accidents, or if you are a lawyer engaged in construction disputes and a great deal of your time is spent visiting buildings with expert witnesses, much the same applies. Civil litigation lawyers are thus often to be found organised into 'teams' or 'groups' for the proper sharing of caseloads.

8.4 Use of information technology

Even if you have a mixed civil litigation practice comprising not only personal injury cases but a variety of other kinds, most civil claims necessitate the writing of similar letters at certain stages. Thus letters to employers, witnesses, the court office and opponents involve commonly used precedents. Such letters are often kept as drafts on word processor disks, with blank spaces for the insertion of the particulars relevant to the case. Use of standard letters and precedents keeps the routine work to a minimum, leaving the solicitor and the secretary free to concentrate on the more important work. In the solicitor's case this involves concentrating on the decision-making aspects of the file and not on the routine administration. Precedents can likewise be used for lists of documents, common forms of claims, defences and applications where one has a practice which involves similar types of action, e.g., factory accidents or debt collecting.

Apart from these basic uses of information technology in civil litigation particularly, many larger firms have litigation support systems which, with the use of computers and word processors, assist in the back-up work for litigation. This may involve the employment of document analysts who assist fee-earners by organising documentation in cases where there are vast amounts of it, e.g., pharmaceutical product claims or other major commercial actions. Data can be organised for quick analysis and retrieval and comparison purposes on custom-designed databases. Automation and office technology are thus important components in case management in such cases. At present, however, the cost of such systems is prohibitive except for the larger firms, but inevitably their use will become more common.

8.5   Time costing

8.5.1   The need for time costing

Solicitors' charges cannot be based simply on the amount of time spent. We have already considered some of the relevant factors governing the way in which a solicitor may charge clients, or eventually have part of his clients' bill paid by his opponent. It is important for a firm, in deciding how much to charge, to know how much it costs it to do the work in the first place. Time costing is not therefore a method of billing but a method of establishing what each fee earner needs to charge each hour to cover the true cost of running the firm, and what should be charged, therefore, on each matter to cover the cost of carrying out the work which has been done. How much will eventually be charged for each hour of the fee earner's time to the client is a quite different question. The extra element over and above what it costs to do the work in the first place represents the profit to the firm, i.e., the income of the partners. So time costing is used to establish the cost of running the firm, by which is meant keeping the firm open for each hour of the day.

8.5.2   Method of calculation

The method of calculation is to attribute to each fee earner the amount of his own salary plus other incidental expenses attributable to him (e.g., the employer's national insurance contribution and pension contribution), together with any support staff exclusively devoted to that fee earner (e.g., his own secretary) and then a due proportion of all the other expenses of the firm including rent, business rate, provision of office technology and salaries of every individual who does not directly earn fees for the firm. The effect is thus to produce an annual sum required to be earned by each fee earner as his notional share towards the true cost of running the office. Thus if, for example, the annual sum for an assistant solicitor, taking into account his own salary and the cost of other expenses attributable to him together with a contribution towards more general overheads, is, say, £88,000, an hourly expense rate for him can then be calculated.

The Law Society publish a booklet called *The Expense of Time* which demonstrates how this calculation should be made. That booklet suggests that it is fair to assume that most fee earners do 1,100 hours of chargeable work per year, taking into account non-fee-earning time at weekends, holidays, sickness, continuing education and, of course, the amount of time which fee earners must expend in some form of administration which is not directly billable to any given client. The rate applicable to the solicitor in the above example will thus be £80 per hour. £80 per hour, then, is what it costs the firm to provide his services to the client for that hour, and that forms the basic element of what the client is to be charged. To that figure has to be added whatever proportion the firm thinks appropriate in order to provide a reasonable rate of profit for the partners. Thus from the base of £80 per hour it is possible that the time of that assistant solicitor would in fact be billed at, say, £130 per hour, though the latter figure will depend in part on the urgency and complexity of the case, the amount involved and the responsibility.

8.5.3   Time sheets

The *Expense of Time* exercise can only be effectively carried out if proper daily time sheets are maintained by individual fee earners. Information recorded on these time sheets will then be collated to calculate the amount of chargeable time spent on an individual client's file by all fee earners who have worked on it. The result will show what it has cost the firm for whatever work has been done on each separate matter.

Time records will show the length of time, though it is still essential to keep notes on the file showing how the time was spent, with an explanation of what was achieved in the time so as to help the costs draftsmen when the time comes to prepare the bill. If you know that you have spent 30 hours on a matter but can in fact justify only 10 of them, this will not be helpful in satisfying the costs judge who considers your bill on assessment.

It is appropriate to mention that in certain cases which have come before the High Court where the Law Society's booklet *The Expense of Time* has been considered, the booklet's methodology has been severely criticised as unscientific. See, for example, *Johnson* v *Reed Corrugated Cases Ltd* [1992] 1 All ER 169. Nonetheless, it may be a useful first method for a firm to calculate its overhead rates.

8.6   Client care

Many complaints about solicitors arise because the client feels, whether rightly or not, that his lawyer is not taking a sufficiently active and personal interest in the case. You may lose a client no matter how well you have dealt with his affairs unless he is kept fully informed and treated as an important member of the team working on his own case. This is the best way to establish sufficient rapport to enable the client to communicate his problems to you fully and for you to understand them at each stage of the case. You must, of course, remain sufficiently detached despite this closeness of contact to provide the objective and independent advice required. Few things are more embarrassing than litigating against an opposing solicitor who so identifies with his client's case that his emotions are involved and a most unprofessional atmosphere is created between the solicitors.

Rules of professional practice require that certain general information be given to clients and that every firm should operate a complaints handling procedure, resolving problems with clients by virtue of the Solicitors' Practice Rules 1990, r. 15. This rule and the Solicitors' Costs Information and Client Care Code 1999 require a client to be given a good deal of specific information.

Any information given about costs must be accurate, given clearly and in a way and at a level which is appropriate for the particular client. There should be a proper explanation of any technical terms with which a client may be unfamiliar, for example, the word 'disbursement'. Any information given orally should be confirmed in writing and information should be updated at appropriate stages throughout the case. What is required is that the client should be told how the firm's fees are calculated and should be given the best information possible about the eventual cost of the case. There should also be a discussion of how and when the client is to pay costs, taking into account any other necessary factors, for example, the availability of insurance, public funding and the like.

Apart from this, the client should be made aware of the firm's complaints handling procedure, which should be in writing. The client should be told the name of the person with whom any problems should be raised and a copy of the complaints procedure should be provided on request.

9

Pre-action and general considerations

We have already considered the financing of civil litigation and the important topic of case and file management. We shall now consider matters relevant to gathering evidence. Most of the early part of this chapter will be concerned with personal injury litigation but many of the points made are of general relevance to any kind of action. We shall then go on to consider specifically matters which one might need to consider in a contract or commercial case.

9.1 Personal injury litigation

The steps which we shall describe ought to be taken by a prudent solicitor before issuing proceedings. That is not to say, of course, that some of those steps cannot be postponed until after issuing a claim, and if, for example, the claimant has consulted you in the last week of the limitation period they will almost all have to be postponed until after the issuing of the claim. However, it is as well to remember that full particulars of claim (see **Chapter 11**) will need to be served within a very short time after the claim has been served. Regard must now be had to the duties of cooperation between the parties in every case and, specifically in personal injury cases, to compliance with the spirit and letter of the pre-action protocol. It is still best to collect all the evidence one can on all relevant matters available at the outset of the case, so as to be better able to negotiate the successful settlement which is, after all, the main objective of litigation. The evidence should be kept in an organised and orderly manner (as described in **Chapter 8**) and you should ensure that you are always on top of all the facts.

Nonetheless, to suggest that all the following steps are essential, even in cases where they could be applicable, is a counsel of perfection. An example of this is that while a client really should never be told that he has a cast-iron case on liability, there are many cases where the solicitor can make that judgment for himself. Thus if the client is a passenger in a vehicle which has been involved in a collision, then it is overwhelmingly probable that his solicitor will manage to establish negligence against one or other of the drivers involved. Thus, where the merits of the claim are very obvious, e.g., where it is clear that unsafe working practices have led to a factory accident, or where the client is knocked down on a zebra crossing by a vehicle which is manifestly on the wrong side of the road at the time, a solicitor might well omit some of the following stages. It is always as well, however, to bear in mind that if liability is ultimately denied in a personal injury case, it may prove awkward, and even impossible, to collect evidence on liability too late in the day. The solicitor should therefore be seeking the very earliest indication from the defendants that liability is not seriously in issue, whatever point they try to maintain by their defence, before omitting early steps, e.g., the collection of evidence from eye-witnesses while their memories are fresh. It should always be remembered that that work will be paid for in the end and that the client is entitled to a thorough professional service and not to have his solicitor cut corners.

In the following paragraphs we consider a number of important aspects of early work in personal injury cases and other routine litigation.

9.1.1 The first interview with the client

In some personal injury cases a solicitor may well be contacted within a few days of even a major accident, possibly by the anxious relatives of the victim. In other cases the victim does not begin to apply his mind to compensation until he has left hospital or is considerably recovered. In any event, at the first meeting the solicitor must obtain some basic information in order to advise the client generally about his prospects; it should be remembered that the question of costs and funding the action must be thoroughly discussed (see **8.5**).

9.1.1.1 Funding

It is important to establish the basis on which the litigation will be funded, whether by legal expenses insurance, conditional fees or public funding (see **Chapter 7**).

9.1.1.2 Taking statements

The initial statement should begin with basic details, including full name, date of birth, address, telephone number, national insurance number, marital status, children, education where relevant, employer's name and address and any works reference.

Techniques of taking clients' statements vary considerably. Clients are often poor at deciding what is relevant and what is irrelevant to their case, even on liability, still more on quantum. Even to describe how an accident happened on the road or the workings of factory machinery is very difficult for a lay person. It is sometimes a good idea to get the client to draw an approximate plan of a road junction and to use toy vehicles to enable him to show who did what, how and when. You should in due course visit the road junction for the purpose of taking photographs, and where necessary have professional plans prepared showing precise dimensions, angle, curvature and so on to check this early account. In the case of factory accidents involving complicated machinery, all that can be done at the early stage is to obtain as much information from the client as possible. An early inspection of the factory machinery will then be required, the procedure for which is described at **9.1.2.5** below.

When interviewing the client in a personal injury case, you should attempt to obtain as much information as possible, even if some of it seems of marginal relevance at the time. Because clients are not skilled at sifting the relevant from the irrelevant, it may appear that a good deal of time is wasted, but in fact, if you let a client talk on, sometimes the most crucial detail of all comes out, the importance of which had been unappreciated by the client. This is sometimes so on liability but is even more likely to be the case on quantum. By letting a client describe all the ways in which his life has been affected by the injury, extra elements of the claim can often emerge which would not have been discovered simply by taking questions on a formal questionnaire by reference to nature of lost earnings, bonuses, promotion opportunities, pension arrangements, perks and so on. The client's account of his whole life may be needed here, so that if, for example, it suddenly emerges that the client was a keen do-it-yourself enthusiast but has now been incapacitated so that he will never be able to do that again, a very worthwhile sum can be added to the claim for the cost of employing professional decorators, carpenters and the like over the rest of his lifetime. In industrial disease cases particularly, where the client may need to describe his whole work record going back perhaps some decades, the client should be encouraged to talk freely even if a great deal of irrelevance emerges.

The method of actually taking the statement varies. Many prefer to jot notes while the client is talking and then to dictate a full statement immediately after the client has left, sending it to him for him to make any necessary additions or amendments. In due course we shall consider the procedure by virtue of which in all cases witness statements, including those of the parties, have to be exchanged substantially in advance of trial. It is imperative that all the evidence which will go in that statement is obtained as soon as possible. However, the information in the statement now under discussion should not be confined to the things which it will be necessary or prudent to put in the statement for exchange. The client's initial statement should contain everything he can think of that seems relevant, including matters which will not be admissible in evidence and therefore will not appear in the later formal statement for exchange. For example, the client may wish to describe other incidents or bad practices at the factory concerned or put a good deal of opinion evidence in the statement, things which it will not strictly be proper to include in the formal statement for exchange. At this stage, however, you are collecting evidence not for the trial judge but for your own conduct of the case, and collecting this kind of information may provide useful lines of enquiry.

The statement should be signed by the client. This is not so that it can be used if the client should later die (because the statement would in fact be admissible anyway under the Civil Evidence Act 1995). The reason is to protect the solicitor himself. It is important in litigation more than in almost any other field of work (except perhaps those involving taxation or financial advice) for a solicitor continually to keep proper records of advice given so as to protect himself against any later suggestion of negligence. For example, if at trial matters come out in a very different way from the client's version as put in the statement of case, and the client is put in difficulties in cross-examination, he may well allege that his own solicitor misinterpreted, or even distorted, his version of what occurred. Naturally one would not then use the proof of evidence to discredit the client at trial, but should any subsequent allegation of negligence in taking the statement be made, the signed copy will be useful. For the same reason it is best to send statements to the client at home to consider at leisure to avoid any suggestion that he simply signed what was put in front of him without reading it in the office.

9.1.1.3   Timescale

Apart from taking the client's own statement at first interview, it will be important to give him a rough timescale for future action indicating the stages at which you will wish to see him to review the case or to comment on evidence collected from other parties. In the early stages a fair degree of frequency of contact is often best (see **8.5**). It reassures the client that early action is being taken on his case and can usually be justified on assessment of costs. The client should certainly be told that, except for the simplest case, it is unlikely that any progress towards settlement will be made in less than several months. There will of course be exceptions to this, where the injuries were minor or there has been a complete recovery, in which case it may well be possible that the case will be settled during the carrying out of the procedures under the pre-action protocols.

9.1.2   Collecting evidence on liability

9.1.2.1   The police accident report

A copy of the police accident report book should usually be obtained if the police were involved at the scene. The chief constable of the force in whose area the accident occurred should be contacted by letter, giving the date and place of the incident and sending the appropriate fee. In due course an extract from a police accident report book will be sent. In some places police forces are very slow to deal with this request. In any event, the accident report will not be sent until any criminal proceedings have been concluded, although at least insurance details will be sent if the rest of the report is not available. A substantial fee is payable.

The police accident report is an extremely useful source of information about a number of matters. It comprises at the very least the names and addresses of the people involved; the insurance particulars of any vehicles involved; witnesses' names and addresses and some-times brief statements; details of vehicle damage; a plan or scale drawing prepared by a policeman at the scene showing the layout of any junction and the position of vehicles; and details of whether there has been a prosecution and its result. If the police consider that some aspect of the condition of a vehicle may have caused the accident there may be an examination at a police garage by a police vehicle examiner.

At the early stage of investigation this can save a good deal of legwork. It may be necessary to reinterview the witnesses, however, because the statements taken were principally for the purpose of establishing criminal liability against just one driver and the witnesses may not have been given a full opportunity to comment on the relative culpability of others involved in the incident, whom the police were not interested in charging. The statements are sometimes extremely brief.

9.1.2.2   Interviewing witnesses

The police accident report and the client's own account are likely to give details of witnesses. Witnesses should be interviewed at length in the same way as the client himself. Clearly they will have nothing to say relevant to quantum, and in a road accident case they may simply be describing an incident which took only a matter of seconds to happen and their statements will not be long. In a factory accident case, however, it may be that the claimant's workmates are in a position to give a great deal of detail about matters which may become relevant in relation to a system of work at the factory, including descriptions of past incidents and so on.

Such witness statements should be taken in the long form at this stage, including matter which may be strictly inadmissible in evidence, though when the statements are prepared for service they will need to be trimmed to the appropriate form and sent back to the witness for re-signing. It is always important to interview witnesses as soon as possible. As indicated above, some solicitors are inclined to cut corners at this stage since it may appear pointless to interview witnesses as to liability when liability seems overwhelmingly clear and it is believed that it will be conceded early in negotiations. Nonetheless, that approach can cause difficulties and it is far better to interview witnesses as soon as possible. No matter how dramatic an incident, witnesses' memories fade remarkably quickly. If the statement is not taken for some months it will be much vaguer–perhaps not on central matters, but on peripheral things such as the precise line taken by a vehicle, how close to the kerb it was, or how a relevant manoeuvre was started.

9.1.2.3   Inspecting the scene

If the accident occurred locally it is often worthwhile for the solicitor to go to see the layout of the road and to attempt to visualise how things must have occurred. Photographs should be taken, especially if there is any risk that the layout of the scene might be changed, e.g., by the introduction of a mini roundabout, or by the demolition of a building which may have obscured the view from one angle across a junction. It is often advisable to meet the client at the scene so that he can point out again just where the vehicles were on the road at the relevant time. Going back to the scene of the accident may also jog the client's memory about some vital detail. In due course, if the matter goes to trial, a good plan of the junction will be required.

9.1.2.4   Road accident cases: Examining the vehicle

If instructions are received early enough so that the defendant's vehicle is still in the state in which it was at the time of the accident, it may be worthwhile attempting to examine it. It may be, of course, that it is difficult to discover its whereabouts, although the police may be able to let you know this. This is because the initial letter to the defendant's insurance company often takes some weeks to receive attention. There is probably no rule of etiquette which prevents you telephoning the potential defendant directly at home and asking when the vehicle can be inspected. Some would consider this to be sharp practice, however. Nonetheless, a certain amount of speed is certainly going to be required since, unless the vehicle is a total write-off, the defendant will want to have it repaired as swiftly as possible.

If inspection is possible then a layman's inspection (i.e., by the solicitor personally) can at least show whether the tyres are in good condition, and perhaps whether the lights were working and the nature of any bodywork damage. It may be worth taking photographs of such damage. For example, if the claimant is a pedestrian knocked down by the defendant, it may subsequently be alleged that the claim is exaggerated and that there was only slight contact. If on an inspection of the vehicle it is discovered that there is a very substantial dent in the wing, this will be a vital piece of evidence. If on a preliminary inspection there is any suggestion that the condition of the vehicle in some way contributed to the happening of the accident (e.g., that it had been inadequately maintained), it may be desirable to have an expert witness attend promptly. A consultant engineer may be able to ascertain problems with the braking or steering system which pre-dated the accident.

9.1.2.5   Accidents at work

The collection of early evidence about this can be rather more difficult than in the case of road accidents. It may be difficult to visualise the precise nature of the claimant's job. Of course, if a particular solicitor acts often in relation to accidents at the same factory, or for the same group of trade unionists or employees, technical terms will rapidly become second nature, but it can be difficult for a non-technically minded lawyer to visualise what is involved where a layman is describing some system involving flanges, pulleys, sprockets, bogies and the like. It can be a good idea to ask the client to draw the relevant piece of machinery, or, if he is back at work or has willing former workmates, to ask one of them to take a camera into work and photograph the relevant things. In due course a formal inspection of the site of the accident may be necessary. The client should be asked whether there have been any proposals made, whether in consequence of his accident or otherwise, for changes at the workplace, e.g., in layout, fencing or replacement of obsolete machinery. If that is the case then very swift action may be needed to ensure that the nature and layout of the machinery or work process is recorded in some permanent form, e.g., by a video under the procedures for obtaining *pre-action inspection* mentioned below.

If you are instructed by a trade union on behalf of one of its members, it should be asked to cooperate in assisting with interviews with the shop steward or safety representatives. Even if you are not instructed by the trade union, those persons are likely to be perfectly willing to assist in relation to accidents to a workmate. Under health and safety regulations brought in in 1993, employers are required to carry out 'risk assessments' to examine every area of their premises and activities and to formulate plans for dealing with potential problems. A great deal of documentation must therefore inevitably be created by employers who comply with these important provisions and this naturally gives scope for demands to see such documents. An employer who has not carried out any of these exercises is clearly unlikely to be able to impress the court as having a safe system of work. There may be other documents which you will want to see in due course such as the records of proceedings of any safety committee or details of the notification of the accident to some other body, e.g., the local authority or the Health and Safety Executive. It is also worth writing to the Health and Safety Executive to ask whether it has looked into the circumstances of the accident and made records or taken photographs. It can also be asked whether it had ever visited the premises prior to the accident and what recommendations were made or notices served.

If the case seems to be one of urgency, the defendants or their insurers should be asked for immediate facilities for an inspection by a consulting engineer. They should in any event be asked to give an undertaking to preserve any piece of machinery or other relevant equipment *in situ* pending full inspection and trial. If there is non-cooperation it may be necessary to make an immediate application to the court for an order permitting inspection and videoing, and requiring the retention of property which may become a matter of evidence in subsequent proceedings. Naturally, an attempt should be made to agree the identity of an engineer with the defendant and to instruct him jointly.

The duties of cooperation imposed on defendants under the CPR and the pre-action protocols ought to mean that it is possible to progress these matters without the need to apply to the court.

9.1.2.6   Tripping cases

In the case of clients who have fallen on broken or uneven pavements the claim is usually to be made under s. 41 of the Highways Act 1980. It may also be possible, or advisable, to join whoever created the danger, e.g., the electricity company whose subterranean works nearby may have caused the problem.

In this case above all others it is vital to collect evidence before notifying the defendants of the problem. Whatever the funding problems that local authorities have in relation to their operations generally, they are notoriously swift, on the intimation of any claim in relation to a tripping accident, at getting their operatives round to knock the offending pavement flat or replace the broken stone. Cynical solicitors believe that their speed in this is so great that they must have a helicopter on standby, because often it is done on the very day that the complaint is received. This may, of course, be in the interest of preventing future accidents at the point, though many contend it is in the hope of destroying the evidence in case the solicitor notifying the claim has been sufficiently incompetent not to have taken a photograph or exact measurements of the precise location. Photographs should be taken of the 'trip' where paving stones have become raised or lowered from their neighbours, showing the precise measurement against a ruler. The client will have to attend with you at the time of taking the photographs in order to ensure that the paving stone is correctly identified.

9.1.2.7   Occupier's liability accidents

It is difficult to generalise about the procedures in occupier's liability accident cases. If, for example, the potential defendant is a neighbour or friend of the claimant, over whose frayed or badly laid stair carpet the claimant has tripped, perhaps with serious consequences, then often the claimant will be in something of a quandary. The claimant himself may be reluctant, even in the case of serious injuries, to sue his friend, relative or neighbour. The claimant's mind can be set at rest, however, that very often the ultimate compensating party will be an insurance company and that the claimant need feel no worse than in the case of his being a passenger in a friend's car and wishing to claim in those circumstances. Investigation of the insurance position should be made. Even if the potential defendant does not have a specific occupier's liability policy, compensation for this kind of accident is often included as a term of the insurance arranged by building society mortgagees. Only if the potential defendant is uninsured need the claimant then make the difficult decision of whether to seek proper compensation or not.

In collecting evidence in relation to such claims one must tread a difficult line. A solicitor should be reluctant to compromise the potential defendant too much by interviewing him and obtaining admissions because such conduct on the defendant's part may breach the terms of the policy so that his insurers are entitled to repudiate. In such cases it may be best simply to ask if the claimant can photograph the offending piece of carpet or floor and then intimate the claim direct to the insurance company before seeking formal facilities for inspection of the place in question. In other kinds of occupier's liability cases, e.g., a fall on slippery floors or staircases in department stores, there is no need to feel such compunction about obtaining evidence. There would be no reason not to photograph the area in question, prepare plans and so on, including obtaining details of the type of any floor tiling so that an engineer may in due course advise.

9.1.2.8   Attending criminal proceedings or inquests

If the client is a claimant in civil proceedings arising out of a road traffic accident there will usually have been some consideration given to criminal prosecution. Criminal cases come to court very much more swiftly than civil cases, sometimes within a matter of weeks of the incident concerned. If funding has already been arranged for a case, it may be worthwhile to attend criminal proceedings. If your client has been charged along with the other party with careless driving or some other motoring offence, then you may well be there as an advocate anyway. In that situation it will obviously be desirable (although far from conclusive for civil purposes) to obtain the acquittal of your client. On the assumption, however, that your client is simply a victim, it can be equally important to see what happens in relation to the potential opponent. Naturally you have no *locus standi* to intervene in these proceedings and are simply an observer.

You will be able to obtain full details of the eventual outcome and should also take notes of evidence. The defendant is likely to be represented at the expense of his insurance company in most cases. It may be that some useful admission is made by the defendant in the course of the hearing which can be noted for future use. It may also be possible to save time by taking statements for the civil proceedings from prosecution witnesses who are waiting for the case to start. It can also be useful to observe the demeanour and apparent credibility of the defendant. If he appears shifty and evasive this is likely to be useful information should the civil proceedings be defended.

If your clients are the personal representatives or dependants of a person who has been killed in an accident it can be vital to attend an inquest. An inquest is an inquiry into the cause of death in order to ascertain into which of the several categories of finding available to a coroner the case falls. The solicitor is not entitled as of right to cross-examine witnesses about how an incident occurred, nor to attempt to attribute civil liability. The coroner has the discretion to permit cross-examination and will usually allow this fairly liberally, although the cross-examination will not be in quite the same style as in an ordinary civil court. Nonetheless, it is often possible to obtain useful evidence and lines of enquiry, and equally to observe the demeanour of witnesses for future purposes.

9.1.2.9   Instructing experts

In some cases everything at trial will turn upon the nature and quality of expert evidence on liability. Experts on matters relevant to *quantum* need perhaps not be instructed quite so swiftly. It can, however, be vital to instruct an expert witness on matters relevant to liability at a very early stage. Chiefly for this purpose you will be considering instructing a consulting engineer to examine, say, a vehicle, factory machinery, the type of flooring in premises where a slipping accident occurred and so on. If there is open access to the item or area in question the defendant need not be consulted nor his permission obtained. If, however, it is a case of factory machinery, then the defendant will have to be asked for permission, and at the same time it is usual to seek an undertaking that the machinery will be preserved in its present state. If there is no positive response to this fairly swiftly, it may be necessary to apply to the court for inspection, the procedure for which is considered below at **9.1.4.2**.

Regard must of course be had to the pre-action protocol and the duty to cooperate in choice of experts (see below). Sometimes, however, if one does not move fast to obtain expert evidence, it will be lost for ever, for example, where the defendant proposes to have his vehicle scrapped or repaired very shortly and the defendant's insurers have not responded swiftly to the initial letter under the pre-action protocol. A difficult decision may then need to be made about whether to risk losing the expense of instructing the engineer or risk losing an opportunity to inspect the evidence. If there is good reason for wanting to inspect the vehicle, and the defendants are too slow, or uncooperative, then it is unlikely that a court would subsequently disallow the costs of instructing an engineer.

In road traffic accidents the question of cause and effect is often easier to see. Nevertheless, specialist road traffic accident reconstruction experts may be useful and their employment, at least in big cases, is common. They are expert at reconstructing and interpreting the precise angle of impact, distances, and speed.

Other experts who may be of use in establishing liability include consultant surveyors in cases involving bad building design or maintenance; and ergonomics experts in relation to such matters as work routines, workloads, and especially in repetitive strain injury cases.

In all these cases it is vital to give consideration to the duty of cooperation between the parties and the provisions of Part 35 of the CPR which are discussed at length in **Chapter 20**. In modest cases serious effort should be made to agree on the appointment of a jointly instructed expert on every issue. Part of the duties of cooperation will involve going to some lengths to see if that can be achieved. A party who rushes to appoint his own choice of expert without giving proper consideration to what the court might require from him by way of cooperation may well find that the expert's report is not acceptable to the court and it orders a jointly instructed different expert. The claimant will not recover the costs of appointing the unnecessary expert from his opponent. Despite this there will be many cases where the amount involved means that each party will be entitled to have its own expert, or indeed where the solicitor needs to consult an expert at an early stage to decide whether or not the client has a case worth pursuing.

9.1.3 Collecting evidence relevant to quantum

We have already considered the question of quantum of damages generally in **1.2**. It may be that there is some element of each of those heads of damage in a client's claim. It is vital to begin collecting evidence on quantum at the earliest stage. At the outset one must tell the client to pass over, and keep carefully in future, all receipts for items connected with this claim no matter how trivial. For example, if a client needs to attend hospital as an outpatient for many weeks, it will usually be considered reasonable for him to go by taxi if he is unable to drive, and receipts should be obtained for each excursion. Likewise, receipts should be obtained for such things as dry-cleaning clothes after the accident, or for the purchase of replacement items, to say nothing of the larger disbursements such as car repair and car hire accounts.

If realistic negotiations with an insurance company can be opened early, then some idea of relevant figures will be needed in case settlement can be achieved even before the issue of proceedings. It may be that this is possible even in cases of serious injury, especially if there is no claim for future loss of earnings and an immediate and accurate prognosis is obtainable. In any event, for the good tactical reasons previously described, the claimant is likely to have an early monopoly of material relevant to quantum. This must of course be disclosed promptly and fully to the defendant in compliance with the spirit of cooperation and the protocols. If, however, as the case progresses information on quantum is kept in a thorough, constantly updated, and professional manner, the claimant's solicitor will be better informed than the defendant about the key elements of the claim and this can often lead to a defendant admitting that he is in no position to challenge given items and conceding aspects of the claim.

9.1.3.1 Obtaining medical evidence

Writing to the client's GP for a medical report on the claimant is of no use save in the case of the most minor accidents. Similarly, obtaining a report from the casualty officer at the hospital where the client was admitted is not of much use for the trial itself. However, in both cases they can provide vital information to the claimant's solicitor. You should always ensure that you obtain a copy of your client's GP's notes. Clients, even with highly meritorious cases, may often be tempted to over-egg the pudding and may claim, for example, that their favourite hobby was an active sport. If you have obtained the client's GP's notes and find that in the recent past there have been prolonged periods of incapacity due to back pain, it is as well for you to know this so that the client can be gently discouraged from exaggerating the degree of his sporting enthusiasms. The defendants' solicitors, if they are competent, will certainly obtain copies of a claimant's GP's notes in due course, so it is better for you to obtain them before any exaggerated claims are made which may affect the client's credibility generally.

An early report is often helpful. It may take some months to obtain an appointment with a suitable consultant and the steps to obtain this should be put in hand immediately. The need to cooperate with the defendant and where possible to obtain agreement to the choice of expert must always be considered. This will cause some difficulty in making rapid progress with the claim given the time which must be allowed for the defendant's insurers to consider the position under the pre-action protocol, discussed in **9.4**. In most accident cases, orthopaedic injuries will play at least some, and usually the major, part. If it is the kind of case where each party will obtain its own medical evidence, a consultant with a substantial medico-legal practice should be instructed. When instructing him, send a copy of the client's statement, although indicating that it is undesirable that any reference to the precise causation of the accident appears in the final form of the report. However, it is important for the specialist to know just what is said about how the accident occurred, because in giving a prognosis it can make a great deal of difference to know whether, for example, a broken ankle occurred because of an impact from the side by a vehicle, or, say, by falling. The orthopaedic specialist should be asked to recommend other specialisms which merit separate investigation. For example, it may not be clear whether some kinds of pain have an orthopaedic or a neurological origin. The consultant should be asked to give any prognosis that is possible at the time, and in particular to indicate at what interval it would be desirable to re-examine the claimant. If, as is common, there will be a delay of many months in obtaining this report, it is sometimes worthwhile to obtain a report from the hospital where the client has been treated and ask them to make any necessary recommendations for other specialists.

When writing to the specialist with instructions it is vital to ask all proper questions which may touch on quantum of damages. Thus one should ask not simply about when the claimant will be able to return to work (he may have an entirely sedentary job) but, if it is the case, when the claimant will be fit to resume his hobby or sporting activities, as appropriate.

When instructing the specialist it is important to remember that in a report submitted for consideration to the court the specialist will have to formally acknowledge that he appreciates that it is his duty to assist the court objectively. He will also be required to summarise his instructions and he should be instructed in clear, professional and objective language, not with an implicit request to come to the most favourable conclusion possible.

The pre-action protocol is primarily aimed at fast track cases, i.e., those with a value of under £15,000. While the protocol in principle requires cooperation in the joint instruction of experts, the delay caused by that, and by the fact that it takes some months to obtain an appointment with a busy consultant, has led to a new feature in civil litigation. This is the setting up of small groups of doctors, usually only offering their services for modest personal injury cases, particularly whiplash accidents, who undertake to carry out reports on claimants within a very short time of being instructed. Some claimant solicitors who handle a substantial caseload of such accidents are going to these specialist groups of doctors to obtain reports without consulting defendants and are then inviting the defendants to agree the report. This puts the defendant's solicitors in something of a quandary, because if the claim is modest they are unlikely to want the expense of a further report of their own. If they dispute what has been done they are often faced with the answer that speed was important, that the claim is a modest one and that any extra information they might need they can obtain by posing questions to the doctor concerned. In those circumstances many defendants, especially if liability is not in dispute, currently take the line of least resistance. This is now a common feature of personal injury litigation in some areas, but the procedure adopted is on the face of it in breach of the spirit of the protocol, at least if there is reasonably prompt cooperation from the defendant's insurers or solicitors.

Although the amounts may only be modest, in principle the defendant is entitled to have some input into the choice of experts and if objection were to be taken it is suggested it would be likely that the court would refuse to permit the evidence from the previously instructed doctor and would require joint instruction of a new expert.

9.1.3.2   Writing to employers

When writing to employers the nature and complexity of the information required obviously depend upon the type of job and the severity of the injury. At the very least it is usual to send the employer a schedule of the previous 26 weeks before the accident for the employers to fill in, giving details of the client's gross and net earnings. Such a long period is usually chosen in order to obtain a true average in case of fluctuating bonuses or overtime.

In the letter it may be necessary to ask other more detailed questions. For example, if the injury is one of considerable severity and the claimant is unlikely to return to work for a long time, or ever, a great deal of help from the employers will be needed to build up a pattern of the claimant's career so as to maximise the claim. If the claimant is relatively young and has only just started out in his career, and this is perhaps his first job, then the information to be obtained from the employers may prove to be the most vital element in the case in maximising the damages. Thus questions should be asked about the client's prospects within the firm or in his profession generally; about what earning levels might have been achieved for an average person, and for an above-average person at, say, five-yearly intervals for the rest of his working life; what assessments had been made by the personnel department as to the future prospects of the claimant; and, if any formal assessments have been carried out (e.g., annual reviews), the employer should be asked to provide copies of them. If the claimant may return to work, questions must be asked about his status in the firm and loss of promotion opportunities; if he is viewed as a less valued employee because of the nature of his disability (e.g., he has lost a limb, or has been facially disfigured in a job where appearances are important), this information should also be obtained. One must bear in mind of course that employers may be cautious before committing themselves to a view of the claimant's employability in the light of his injury given the protection available to employees under the Disability Discrimination Act 1995. A copy of the client's contract of employment should also be sought.

It may be necessary to supplement this letter with an interview in due course with the employers' personnel officer, or the claimant's immediate superior. If the employers are not also the defendants (e.g., in road accident cases) they are likely to take a positive and upbeat view of the claimant's previous prospects since they will have no interest in depressing the level of his claim. If, on the other hand, the employers are also the defendants (e.g., a factory accident) it may prove more difficult to obtain useful information. If there is no cooperation at all on these matters then one may end up having to collect evidence about the claimant's prospects from every other source that is available, e.g., workmates who may be willing to say that he was viewed as a high-flyer amongst his contemporaries, or from employment consultants or the various government agencies which are able to supply details of average earnings for many occupations at many stages of a career. This evidence will assist in fixing the *multiplicand* described in **1.2.2.3**. It must be remembered that this figure is not necessarily the claimant's *current* earnings but is a figure which takes into account his prospects.

9.1.3.3   The self-employed claimant

A good deal of work will need to be done here and sometimes a forensic accountant will in the end have to be consulted, as indeed in many cases involving substantial loss of earnings from whatever source. The accounts of the claimant's business will need to be perused and it is often best to have an independent accountant who has experience in giving evidence to do this, rather than the firm which may have prepared the claimant's accounts. This is because, for obvious and perfectly legitimate reasons, the accounts hitherto will have been prepared with the probable objective of minimising his apparent income and thus avoiding tax. If the position is that he has been badly injured and will not work again or will not work for some considerable time, it will now be in his interests to *maximise* his apparent income for the purpose of his claim. It will prove impossible to do this if one uses the same accountants who drew up the original accounts. Underlying trends must be analysed to see whether the business was genuinely improving even though net profits may not have increased in the recent past. It should also be ascertained what extra benefits in non-taxable form the claimant was able to obtain by virtue of being self-employed, e.g., running what was in essence a private car on the firm, entertaining expenses and the like. These pieces of information can all be used in due course to maximise the claim.

9.1.3.4   Maximising benefits

Experienced personal injury lawyers treat it as part of their job to ensure that an injured claimant obtains all necessary benefits due to him, and in the case of those assisted by their trade union this may indeed include representation at the various benefits appeal tribunals which exist where an unsatisfactory initial assessment of benefit has been made. In due course, as we have seen, credit for these benefits will have to be given and they will in essence have to be repaid out of compensation to the Compensation Recovery Unit of the DSS. Nonetheless, it will assist the claimant's morale and standard of living to obtain as much as he can at present in the way of such benefits. The law, however, is that failure to claim such benefits is not treated as improper failure to mitigate damages (*Eley* v *Bedford* [1972] 1 QB 155).

9.1.4   Applications to the court

We have so far considered the various ways of collecting evidence on liability and quantum *informally*, i.e., without the need to involve the court. We now consider two kinds of preliminary application to the court which may be useful in obtaining evidence at a very early stage, especially in cases where the evidence is vital to ascertain liability, or where there is any risk of the evidence being lost or destroyed.

In personal injury cases and clinical negligence cases there should be strict adherence to the protocols (see **9.7**). However, even in cases where those protocols do not apply, such as commercial actions, the parties are instructed to have regard to the *spirit* of them and the overriding point of the protocols is to encourage cooperation and full disclosure of information between the parties. It ought to be the case that both parties will cooperate with each other when supplying copies of documentation and permitting inspection of the factory where the accident occurred, the machinery in question, or the goods whose quality or value is in dispute. Sometimes, though it may be impossible to see the documents or objects required due to difficulty in getting instructions from the client or obstructiveness on the part of the parties. Where that is the case, the court has power to make orders permitting a potential party to a claim (clearly, this will usually, though not invariably, be the claimant rather than the defendant) to apply to the court under CPR, r. 25.1, for an *interim remedy*. Various interim remedies are set out in r. 25.1, but the kind with which we are currently concerned are those under r. 25.1(1)(i) and (c) under which applications to the court can be made for:

(a) pre-action disclosure and inspection of a document; and

(b) application for pre-action inspection of objects or places.

9.1.4.1 Application for pre-action disclosure of documents

The general provision as to interim remedies is in CPR, r. 25.1, but the specific rule concerning disclosure before proceedings start is set out at r. 31.16.

Where a potential party to a claim believes that another potential party has some vital document in his possession which the first party must see before the claim starts, then he may apply to the court for an order granting him sight of the document. In the nature of things this is more likely to be the potential claimant seeking documents in the potential defendant's possession, but it is possible to think of instances where a defendant, having been warned of the claimant's intention to start proceedings and in compliance with the spirit of the pre-action protocols, decides to seek documents from a potential claimant which he is unwilling to disclose, thus prompting an application by the potential defendant.

The application is made to the court and must be supported by evidence (that is, a written statement by the potential claimant or defendant). It must show that the applicant for the order and respondent to the application are likely to be parties to subsequent proceedings and that if proceedings had already started, the respondent's duty by way of standard disclosure of documents would extend to this document or class of documents.

The application must also specify the documents which the respondent is said to have and should indicate why they are important and why it is relevant for the claimant to see them before the action commences.

The matters which the district judge must consider when deciding on the application are set out in r. 31.16(3), which requires the judge to be satisfied that:

(a) the applicant and respondent are likely to be parties to subsequent proceedings;

(b) if proceedings had started the respondent's duty would extend to disclosing the documents in question; and

(c) disclosure before proceedings have started is desirable in order:

    (i) to dispose fairly of the anticipated proceedings;

    (ii) to assist the dispute to be resolved without proceedings; or

    (iii) to save costs.

The most important criterion therefore involves the district judge being satisfied that there is some particular point in ordering the documents to be disclosed before a claim is started. If he concludes that the documents, while clearly relevant and of interest in such claim as may be started, do not contain anything which 'makes it desirable' that they should be disclosed in advance of commencing the claim, he will refuse the order. Applications for routine documents therefore are likely to fail. A good example of a case where pre-action disclosure will be ordered is where it is essential for a potential claimant to see the document to decide whether or not he has a case at all. This sometimes occurs in clinical negligence cases where the potential defendant has a monopoly of the relevant information. In factory accidents, complaints or accident reports about factory procedures or risk assessment procedures, which employers should have carried out, might be another example. In non-personal injury cases, where the pre-action protocols do not strictly apply, relevant documents might include the manufacturer's specification for allegedly defective goods which have been sold by a retailer to a customer.

9.1.4.2   Pre-action inspection of objects or places

Part 25 of the CPR provides for a wide variety of interim remedies, including, by r. 25.1(1)(c), order for:

(a) detention, custody or preservation of relevant property;

(b) the inspection of relevant property;

(c) the taking of samples of relevant property;

(d) the carrying out of experiments on or with relevant property;

and, under r. 25.1(1)(d), an order to be made authorising a person to enter any land or building in the possession of a party to the proceedings for the purposes of carrying out an order under sub-paragraph (c). In addition, under r. 25.1(1)(i), the court may order, pursuant to s. 33 of the Supreme Court Act 1981 or s. 52 of the County Courts Act 1984, inspection of property before a claim has been brought.

Rule 25.2 specifically permits the making of an order for an interim remedy before a claim has been made if the matter is urgent or it is otherwise desirable to do so in the interests of justice.

The court may make an order on the application of either potential party to a claim. The object in question need not be the subject matter of the claim (e.g., the goods that have been sold). It is sufficient that *some issue may arise* in relation to the object or place in question, that there is some evidential significance. Under these provisions the court could, for example, make orders in the following instances:

(a) if following a road traffic accident, if the condition of the vehicle is alleged to have substantially contributed to it, an order that the defendant produces the vehicle for inspection by an engineer appointed by the potential claimant;

(b) an order permitting a potential claimant to inspect a factory where an accident occurred with an engineer and to take videos of layout, or moving machinery;

(c) where it is said that perishable goods lack satisfactory quality (for example, imported fruit), an order permitting a sample of the fruit to be taken for inspection;

(d) if it becomes known to one party that another party is about to market a new brand of goods which he claims will infringe his patent or trademark, an order permitting him to have a sample of those goods to have laboratory tests carried out on them to see to what extent they infringe his patent or are of sufficient similarity to his own goods to infringe his trademark.

The feature common to all of these cases is urgency, the presumed feature being that the potential defendant, having had the potential claim intimated to him, has declined to cooperate in giving inspection of the thing or place voluntarily. Showing that feature will assist the court to conclude that it is 'desirable' to order the remedy before an action starts. When ordering any of the remedies under r. 25.1 the court *may* go on to order that the potential claimant commence the claim within a certain time. The word 'may' acknowledges that the potential claimant, having obtained the information, may conclude that he has no cause of action and there may be no further action between the parties.

9.1.4.3 Costs orders in the case of pre-commencement disclosure and inspection of objects or places

By CPR, r. 48.1, there is a presumption that where an order for pre-commencement disclosure of documents and inspection of property is made, the court will award the person against whom the order is sought his costs:

(a) of the application; and

(b) of complying with any order made on the application.

This recognises that it is a burden for someone who is not yet formally a party to proceedings, to have to attend court, deal with the application and perhaps go to some expense, for example, in a search for relevant documents, to comply with it.

However, the court may make a different order by virtue of r. 48.1(3) having regard to all the circumstances, including:

(a) the extent to which it was reasonable for the person against whom the order was sought to oppose the application; and

(b) whether the parties to the application have complied with any relevant pre-action protocol.

In personal injury or clinical negligence cases, where a potential defendant is dragging his heels in providing documents or facilities for inspection which he should have given voluntarily, not only is he likely to be deprived of an order for costs, but he may well have to pay those of the potential claimant. This is a powerful incentive for compliance with the protocol. In cases where protocols do not strictly apply, the court may have regard to the desirability of parties complying with the spirit of them. If there is something relatively speculative about the application, an order that the respondent should receive the costs involved should be made. Complying with the spirit of the protocols does not, of course, oblige every potential defendant to deal with every request for information or documents, especially where these may be vexatious or frivolous.

If, however the court concludes on a balanced view that the potential claimant's claim is brought in good faith and the documents would be relevant and the potential defendant could easily supply them or permit the object to be inspected, it may, for example, order each party to bear their own costs or penalise the potential defendant for any perceived obstructiveness by making him pay the applicant's costs.

9.1.5 Motor insurance

A claimant who suffers personal injuries in a road traffic accident can sue the defendant in the tort of negligence. The existence or absence of motor insurance makes no difference whatsoever to the actual prosecution of a claim under the CPR. It does, however, have enormous practical significance, particularly on the vital question of whether the claimant is going to receive any damages which he is awarded by the court. Claimants are often very confused about their rights and/or liabilities in relation to motor insurance. The position is much simpler than it may appear.

If the claimant was a pedestrian at the time, matters are considerably simplified. His own insurance position is irrelevant, and even if he had a personal accident insurance policy which paid him an enormous sum it would not be taken into account in computing the damages due from the defendant. If the claimant was himself a driver at the time of the incident, then, however clear-cut liability seems, he must be advised to notify his own insurers at once if he has not already done so, since there will inevitably be a term under the policy requiring him to do this within some fairly brief period.

Until 2003 the action was always brought against the motorist who was allegedly liable and not against the insurer. This could lead to difficulties if, for example, their insured did not cooperate with them. Fortunately, the position has now been considerably simplified.

By virtue of the European Communities (Rights Against Insurers) Regulations 2002 SI 2002/3061, a claimant who wishes to sue in relation to an accident which occurred on a road or public place caused by the use of a vehicle which is insured with a policy which satisfies s. 145 of the Road Traffic Act 1988, can now sue the insurance company directly. The Regulations provide that the insurer 'shall be directly liable to the entitled party, to the extent that he is liable to the insured person'.

In other words one can dispense with serving proceedings on the driver who is liable at all, and proceed straight away against the insurance company. Insurance companies always use a panel of firms of solicitors in any given area who handle all their road traffic litigation and who will be notably competent and experienced.

A central register of insurance details is to be kept, called the Motor Insurers Information Centre which will be searchable on payment of a modest fee and the centre will have a duty to cooperate with the person seeking to find the identity of the insurer of the named vehicle.

It is still important to consider certain technical matters to do with motor insurance, which are as follows:

9.1.5.1 'Road Traffic Act insurance'

Road Traffic Act insurance is the most basic insurance that can be obtained in respect of a motor vehicle. Such policies are actually quite rare and are often issued only (at correspondingly high premiums) to those drivers who are a very bad risk, e.g., drivers with recent drink-driving convictions, so that no insurance company will sell them more extensive cover. Such a policy implies that the person insured is covered *only* in respect of those risks for which insurance is compulsory under ss. 143 and 145 of the Road Traffic Act 1988. Under these sections it is an offence to use or permit the use of a vehicle on the road unless the driver is insured in respect of legal liability for the following three matters, namely:

(a) personal injury or death to any other person;

(b) the cost of emergency hospital treatment;

(c) damage to property (other than the insured vehicle itself and goods in it carried for hire or reward) up to a value of £250,000 in each claim.

Consequently, where the defendant has this kind of insurance a claimant will be covered for damages for personal injuries and loss of earnings, and for damage to his own property caused in the accident, e.g., to his motor car and its contents.

9.1.5.2 'Third party fire and theft'

This is a wider type of liability than the last. The person who has this kind of insurance cover will not only be covered for personal injury and damage to some other person's property including his own passengers, but, in addition, will be protected against theft of or fire damage to *his own* vehicle, so that if the vehicle is stolen and never recovered he will be paid the market value.

9.1.5.3 'Comprehensive insurance'

Under this type of cover an insured driver will be indemnified in respect of personal injury damage or property damage to any other person, and in addition will be covered in respect of damage to or loss of his own vehicle. This is so whether or not he was himself to blame for any incident in which his vehicle was damaged or destroyed. The premiums for this sort of cover are naturally considerably higher than for 'third party fire and theft' liability.

A comprehensively insured motorist who is to blame for an accident and suffers personal injuries will have no claim under his own vehicle insurance policy in respect of those personal injuries, though he may be covered by a quite separate personal accident policy, but he will be covered for damage to his vehicle.

9.1.5.4 Subrogation

An insurance company which has paid a claim by the person insured (e.g., someone comprehensively insured who has had his vehicle damage paid for by his own insurance company) may exercise its rights of subrogation by using the insured person's name to bring proceedings against anyone else involved who is alleged to be negligent in the action. This right will be expressly reserved in the insurance policy.

9.1.5.5 'No-claims bonus'

A no-claims bonus is a discretionary bonus awarded by way of a discount on future premiums for years in which no claim has been brought under a policy of motor insurance. The bonus increases year by year, usually up to a maximum of about 65 per cent. After several years, therefore, this may be a very substantial benefit, reducing the annual premium for a policy from, say, £1,000 to £350. If any claim at all is brought against the policy the bonus is lost, even though the insured motorist was not himself to blame for the incident (for example, if his car was rammed by a hit-and-run driver who left the scene of the incident before he could be identified). It is possible to take out, for an additional premium, a type of policy where the no-claims bonus is 'protected' so that the bonus is retained provided there is no more than, say, one claim within any two-year period.

9.1.5.6 'Excess' in comprehensive insurance

This involves the motorist agreeing to bear a so-called 'excess', i.e., the first part of any claim. This may be a small figure, such as £50, and will avoid the insurance company having to be bothered with very trivial claims, e.g., for scratches to paintwork, loss of a wing mirror, etc. It may be that the insured can obtain a reduction on premium if he is willing to have an excess of a rather larger figure, e.g., £250. In many cases he would be well advised to agree to this, especially if his no-claims bonus is anyway worth more to him than £250 a year. In that event he would not trouble the insurance company at all with a claim for minor accident damage up to this figure and his no-claims bonus would be preserved. Should a claim be made involving a higher figure than this he would bear the first £250 of it which is the nature of the 'excess'.

9.1.5.7 'Knock for knock' agreement

If two vehicles which are both comprehensively insured are damaged in an accident, the insurance companies involved may well decide to each settle their own insured motorist's claim. They will do this if they have a pre-existing 'knock for knock', agreement as insurance companies often have. It saves them a good deal of time and trouble, and possibly litigation costs, in establishing the exact cause of an accident. Motor insurance companies doubtless consider that the matter is one of 'swings and roundabouts', i.e., that taking into account the saving on investigation and litigation costs over any given year they will lose nothing by the arrangement and may well gain.

The problem for a motorist who finds himself involved in this arrangement is that liability may seem perfectly clear. He would normally have expected his insurance company to have attempted to negotiate full settlement of his claim by the other insurance company but may now find matters settled to his disadvantage because he will immediately lose the amount of his excess and indeed his no-claims bonus. In such a situation it will usually be worthwhile for the motorist who considers he was the innocent party in the incident to bring an action against the other motorist for his uninsured losses, i.e., the loss of his no-claims bonus and excess. Since it is actually somewhat difficult to establish the amount of a no-claims bonus, which may be cumulative over some years, it is probably better in such a case if the client takes legal advice in time, to advise him not to claim on his own insurance policy but to try to pay for the accident damage himself and meanwhile to bring proceedings against the other driver for the whole amount involved. Alternatively, if his own insurers have already paid, there is no reason why he should still not sue for the whole amount involved provided that if he is successful he then reimburses his own insurers with the amount which they have already paid him in settlement of the claim. They will then reinstate his no-claims bonus. A knock for knock agreement between insurers naturally does not bind the insured person himself not to proceed in the way previously described.

Recently, knock for knock agreements have lost their popularity with major motor insurers and are now considerably less common.

So far we have been concerned with a *client's own* insurance policy. It is now vital to consider problems to do with the opponent's insurance, or lack of it.

9.1.6   The opponent's motor insurance policy

If a claimant obtains judgment against a defendant for personal injuries and consequential loss, the claimant may enforce that part of the judgment against the defendant's insurers even though the insurers themselves may have been entitled to avoid or cancel the defendant's policy, or indeed may already have done so. This is by virtue of ss. 151 and 152 of the Road Traffic Act 1988.

Insurance contracts are contracts *uberrimae fidei*, i.e., of utmost good faith. A vital ingredient of this is that a person taking out an insurance policy must disclose all material matters to the insurer. Suppose that a person obtained a policy of motor insurance without disclosing to the insurers that he had previous accident claims against him, or driving convictions. Under the basic law of insurance the insurers, if they discover these matters, would be entitled to repudiate the policy and thus not to pay any claims on it. The effect of ss. 151 and 152 of the Road Traffic Act 1988 will generally be to stop the insurers repudiating, at least to the extent that they are obliged to compensate some other party for compulsorily insurable damages, i.e., the damages which must be insured under ss. 143 and 145 of the Act (see **9.1.5.1**).

A claimant can use s. 152 to ensure this payment if *before or within seven days* after the *commencement of proceedings* (i.e., the issue of the claim) he gave proper notice of his intention to commence proceedings to the insurers. It is therefore important to remember in every case to give a potential defendant's insurers notice of intention to commence proceedings. The initial letter of claim used to start the procedure under the pre-action protocol should contain the relevant notice and the claimant would then be covered for the purposes of s. 152. If, having commenced proceedings, the need to add further defendants becomes apparent, it is prudent to write a further s. 152 letter to each of them.

It is always sensible to give written notice so there is no possibility for dispute. Perhaps surprisingly, however, recent cases have held that even oral notice over the telephone to the defendant's insurance company or its solicitors will suffice.

9.1.7 The Motor Insurers' Bureau

The Motor Insurers' Bureau (MIB) is a body set up and financed by motor insurance companies. There are two distinct agreements made between the MIB and the former Ministry of Transport (now the Department of the Environment, Transport and the Regions).

9.1.7.1 Uninsured drivers

Where it is apparent that a driver is *uninsured*, i.e., that there is no policy at all in force in relation to the motor vehicle in question (as compared to the position described in **9.1.6** in relation to s. 152 of the Road Traffic Act 1988 where there is such a policy but the insurance company had the right to repudiate it), one might expect a claimant to be without a remedy, i.e., that while he could sue the uninsured motorist he might have considerable difficulty in enforcing any judgment obtained. The effect of the MIB agreement is to mitigate this problem.

Where a potential opponent is found to be uninsured, this should be brought to the attention of the MIB. They will then appoint a local insurance company to act as their agent for the purpose of negotiating the claim. Of course it must be proved that the uninsured driver was negligent. The mere fact that he was uninsured is not in itself grounds for bringing a claim. The insurance company appointed to negotiate on behalf of the MIB will have the power to settle matters without proceedings being issued. However, if liability and compensation cannot be agreed, then a claim must be issued against the uninsured driver.

Under the Motor Insurers Bureau (Compensation of Victims of Uninsured Drivers) Agreement 1999, the claimant has to satisfy a number of conditions in order for the MIB to pay an award of damages in respect of an uninsured driver. Compliance with the conditions must be strict and solicitors need to familiarise themselves thoroughly with the various requirements.

In an MIB case, notice of commencement of proceedings must be sent to the MIB (or its identified insurer acting as agent) not later than 14 days after commencement of proceedings and must be accompanied by a copy of the sealed claim form, particulars of claim, schedule of losses, and medical reports and other relevant documents. The Motor Insurers' Bureau is at Linford Wood House, 6–12 Capital Drive, Milton Keynes, MK14 6XT, Fax 01908 671681.

The MIB has the power to waive non-compliance with this requirement, or late compliance, but their policy is not to do so. The claim then proceeds normally, except that the MIB has the right to be added as a party. Alternatively, it will merely treat itself as if it was the insurance company of the uninsured driver and arrange for representation on his behalf. Naturally it can take any defences open to the uninsured person, or, e.g., make allegations of contributory negligence just as in the case of any other defendant. When judgment is obtained, if it remains unpaid by the defendant for seven days (as it presumably will be) the MIB will pay the judgment and will also pay the normal assessed costs. The judgment must then be assigned to the MIB so that it is subrogated to the rights of the claimant and may attempt to recoup money it has paid out from the uninsured motorist. In fact it is rarely worth its while attempting to do this. In the nature of things, a person who did not have the means or inclination to insure his vehicle is unlikely to have substantial assets. It must be noted that the agreement applies only to claims in respect of which insurance was compulsory under ss. 143 and 145 of the 1988 Act (see **9.1.5.1**).

9.1.7.2   Untraced drivers

A separate agreement, the latest version of which is dated 1996, applies in the case of *untraced* drivers (i.e., hit-and-run drivers). However, this agreement only applies in the case of personal injury and death claims. Here, of course, proceedings cannot be issued at all against an unknown defendant. Accordingly there is no need to make application to the court at all, but the MIB must be notified within the usual limitation period, i.e., three years of the accident, by letter. It will then arrange for the case to be investigated and must be satisfied that the untraced driver was negligent and that the death or injury was not caused deliberately by him, i.e., that he did not use the motor vehicle as a weapon. If he did then any claim should be directed to the Criminal Injuries Compensation Authority, which compensates the victims of crimes of violence. The MIB then makes an award on a voluntary basis, assessed in the same way as that in which a court would have assessed damages at common law, i.e., it will include the usual items of pain, suffering, loss of amenity, loss of future earnings. However, damage to property is *not* recoverable, and thus a claimant cannot recover from the MIB if a hit-and-run driver collides with his parked car and makes off.

If the amount of the award is not agreed or the refusal to make any award is not accepted, there is an appeals procedure by way of arbitration by one of a panel of Queen's Counsel. There is also an accelerated procedure in the case of claims up to a total of £50,000 which allows the parties to settle the application without a full investigation. In this case there is no right of appeal.

In the case of untraced drivers the MIB is under no obligation to pay legal costs. In fact the MIB pays a standard fee together with certain acceptable disbursements, in particular, the cost of a police accident report and medical reports.

9.2   Contract and commercial cases

9.2.1   Collecting and assessing documentation

Naturally pre-action considerations in commercial cases are determined by the type of dispute, the nature of the parties and the things in dispute. It may sometimes be that such disputes depend just as much on factual evidence and even eye-witness accounts as a personal injury case, in which instance it would be important to collect evidence as previously described (see **9.1.2**).

The most common type of contract or commercial case is a straightforward debt-collecting claim. In such a case it is important to ensure that all relevant documentation has been obtained from the client. Thus the written contract or terms of trade, if any, should be obtained and perused. It may sometimes be the case, for example, that a client's version of what his contractual terms are is not borne out by inspection of the documents themselves; a client's terms of trade may not have been updated for many years. This may be the time to persuade the client to let you redraft the documents or do other commercially based work for him. This kind of approach is somewhat pompously called 'client education' by the Law Society, but the opportunities it gives for marketing one's practice should not be overlooked. For example, a recent survey showed that fewer than half of all small and medium-sized businesses had written terms of trade requiring interest in the event of late payment of invoices. Indeed an astonishingly high proportion, over a third, were said to have no written terms of trade at all.

Even where there is a term of trade apparently importing interest in the event of late payment, you may be disappointed to find that the client has for some reason incorporated this into the form of invoice itself rather than the order form. In this instance, of course, as a simple matter of contract law, the term for interest will be of no effect since an invoice does not form part of the documents which create the contract.

9.2.2   Acting for a purchaser

Naturally you may also be called upon to advise on the import of a contract or terms of trade from the opposing party's point of view, where a disgruntled purchaser may be sued for the price of the goods.

If instructed by the purchaser the claim may be for a total refund of the purchase price, or for a refund of part of a price already paid to compensate for deficiencies for the goods supplied. It may well be that there are additional claims for damages for inconvenience, disappointment, distress, repairs, hire of replacements, and even for personal injuries caused by some defective article. In this kind of personal injury case it is by no means certain that an insurance company will be involved, thus, for example, where a defective appliance (say an electrical item) has been purchased from a small shop and the item has caused injuries, you may need to look further afield than the shopkeeper to the protection afforded under the Consumer Protection Act 1987 against the manufacturer or importer. In contract and commercial cases regard must always be had to ensuring that all proper defendants are brought into the action, especially with a view to seeing that the potential defendant has the ability to pay the damages and/or debt.

9.2.3   Enforcement of judgment

The topic of enforcement of judgment is dealt with in detail in **Chapter 34**. It must always be borne in mind that there are only limited means of enforcing judgments. Thus a claimant who has obtained judgment in a debt case is often disgruntled to find that where the defendant fails to pay he can often do this with impunity and that there is, for example, no realistic possibility whatsoever of getting a person committed to prison for non-payment of a civil debt. It is vital to advise a client early on, therefore, that good money should not be thrown after bad in pursuing expensive litigation against someone who does not have the ability to pay a judgment when obtained. Money spent at an early stage on obtaining an enquiry agent's report into the financial status of a potential defendant, both in a debt case and in other forms of commercial disputes, may well be worthwhile. An essential part of protecting one's own position is thereafter to confirm in writing advice given to the client that there may be difficulties in enforcing judgment.

9.2.4   Timescale

One feature of commercial contract disputes which is perhaps different from personal injury cases is the speed at which they proceed. If the client is intending to sue for a substantial debt, he will want to progress as rapidly as possible. In personal injury cases there are likely to be all manner of necessary delays, indeed a certain amount of delay is actually required in complying with the pre-action protocols. Some kinds of commercial cases may need to be pursued at key stages with even more swiftness than a client requires in a debt-collecting case, however. For example, we have considered above in the context of remedies the nature of interim injunctions (see **1.7.4**). If a client consults a solicitor in connection with an urgent, business-related situation, the solicitor will have to ensure that he acts both swiftly and expertly because a procedural or evidential mistake made in this kind of litigation can have fatal consequences to the client's business position.

9.2.5   Evidence and interim injunctions

When one needs to apply for an interim injunction the basic position is that comprehensive evidence will have to be put forward about the merits of a client's claim. The basic test to be satisfied is the *American Cyanamid* test referred to at **1.7.4.1** above. In order to ensure that all the various elements of this test are satisfied, the client and, if it is a business organisation, possibly several of the client's managerial personnel involved in the matter, will need to swear affidavits which are often very lengthy, setting out the background to the case, the present position and justifying the harm that is likely to be caused unless an injunction is granted. It may be that lines of enquiry will have to be pursued very urgently and commercial inquiry agents instructed to investigate such matters as, for example, attempts by former employees to poach contacts and customers, the misuse of trade secrets and the like. Statements will have to be obtained and rapidly put into the form of evidence which can be brought before the court (see **19.5** and **19.8**). Counsel may need to be involved urgently at this stage, both in terms of ensuring his availability for a very early hearing and to see that he approves the evidence to be used. Conferences with counsel may need to be called involving the client, and it may be that whole days have to be set aside for this and all other work postponed.

It may be a vital matter also to ensure judge availability for an early application. In principle, an application for an interim injunction should be made immediately after a claim has been issued and served, by application to a Judge. However, applications may be made much more urgently than this, e.g., an application for an injunction to be made even before a claim has been issued. In extreme cases it is possible to apply orally for an injunction without any documentation, and even to see a judge out of court hours for this purpose. Such applications are relatively rare save in specialised commercial work, however. Where injunctions are obtained without notice they are usually limited in time (e.g., to last for only seven days) and thereafter the claimant must make a formal application for the injunction to be renewed with full documentation and on proper notice before it lapses.

9.2.6   Experts' reports

It may be that the nature of the action involves experts' reports just as much as a personal injury case might do. It may be, for example, that a consultant engineer is called upon to advise that a piece of machinery sold is inadequate for its purpose or has certain malfunctions which led to other undesirable consequences. Accountants may need to be employed, in particular to justify loss of profits or loss of earnings claims.

9.2.7   Pre-action protocols

The pre-action protocols in personal injury and clinical negligence cases are discussed below at **9.4**. The spirit of these protocols should be observed even in cases to which they do not strictly apply. The court would always therefore expect to see some reasonable intimation of claim and an opportunity given to investigate and negotiate. This cannot of course be taken too far in simple debt cases, which do after all provide the majority of all litigation and where one party will almost inevitably be unrepresented. It would not be suggested, for example, that three months leeway should be given to a debtor to investigate whether or not a debt was due. On the other hand, a reasonable period should be allowed to a potential defendant in a seriously defended commercial case. In every case it will be for the court to consider what it thinks reasonable, that is, what would have been in accordance with the overriding objective on the facts of the case, if issues relating to reasonableness in costs are raised arising out of the claimant's pre-action approach.

9.3   The letter of claim

9.3.1   In contract and commercial cases

Having obtained sufficient information from a client, it is normal to start matters moving by writing a letter of claim. In a debt case this is perfectly straightforward and will consist of a terse demand for the payment in full of the debt within a relatively brief period, on the basis that invoices and reminders from the client have presumably been ignored for some time. Such a letter should always insist that the amount is paid in full to the solicitor direct and specify a date upon which proceedings will be issued if payment is not received. It is vital, to ensure credibility with the potential defendant, that if payment is not made proceedings are indeed issued on the day in question and that this is in no sense a bluff.

If the litigation is of some other kind, e.g., on behalf of a disgruntled purchaser seeking compensation in respect of a defective item, then no doubt some greater length of explanation is necessary in the letter detailing the defects complained of and making a demand for what it is that the client wants, e.g., return of the purchase price in full in exchange for the goods, or the cost of repairs necessary to make the goods of merchantable quality.

9.3.2   Personal injury cases

Because of the need now to comply with the pre-action protocols, which are discussed in **9.4**, there is a general requirement on claimants to set out the detailed basis of their case.

If properly worded, a letter of claim sent to the insurer will be sufficient to satisfy ss. 151 and 152 of the Road Traffic Act 1988 (see **9.1.6**). Letters should not, when written direct to a defendant, solicit a direct reply but should include the instruction to pass it on to the insurer. Any reply, especially one admitting liability, may well compromise the validity of his insurance policy. The letter before action should be an open letter and not one written 'without prejudice' (see **5.2.1.5**).

9.4   Pre-action protocols

The purpose of *pre-action protocols*, by which is meant a system of procedural requirements that the parties are required to carry out before issue of proceedings, is:

(a) to focus the attention of litigants on the desirability of resolving disputes without litigation;

(b) to enable them to obtain the information they reasonably need in order to enter into an appropriate settlement;

(c) to enable them to make an appropriate offer (of a kind which can have costs consequences if litigation ensues); and

(d) if a pre-action settlement is not achievable, to lay the ground for expeditious conduct of proceedings.

The approach is that disputes should where possible be resolved without litigation. If litigation is unavoidable, the purpose of pre-action protocols is to make both parties well informed at the outset. The objectives can be achieved only if the court itself takes more account of pre-litigation activity, which is described below.

Although it was hoped that pre-action protocols would be developed from many areas of litigation, in fact only eight have been formulated at the time of writing. These are the protocols for personal injury claims; clinical negligence claims, construction and engineering disputes; professional negligence claims, defamation actions, housing disrepair claims against landlords, industrial disease claims, and judicial review proceedings. Many others are in the course of consultation or drafting. These include in particular a number of protocols aimed at subdivisions of personal injury litigation, including specialist protocols for road traffic claims, and actions against the police. Consultation usually takes place between specialist bodies such as the Association of Personal Injury Lawyers and representatives of the insurance industry in the relevant field. It is not known when any of these protocols is likely to be brought into effect.

A very important paragraph in the general Practice Direction on the pre-action protocols now provides that in every case the parties must consider alternatives to litigation befoe proceeding. (See **Chapter 35**.)

The most important two protocols are those for personal injury claims and the resolution of clinical disputes. The main part of the personal injury protocol appears at the end of this chapter. It is worth reading through. It is rather like a statement of best practice with the object of encouraging greater contact between the parties at the earliest opportunity, exchange of full information and pre-action investigation with the main objective of putting the parties in a position to settle cases fairly and early without resorting to litigation at all.

9.4.1   The effect of non-compliance with the protocols

A practice direction, PD Protocols, has been issued, which applies to the present protocols and any others that may subsequently come into existence. The practice direction sets out the objectives. It then goes on to consider the crucial issue of compliance with the protocols and notes that the court will expect all parties to have complied in substance with the terms of an approved protocol. The court will take into account compliance and non-compliance when giving directions for the management of proceedings under CPR, rr. 3.1(4) and (5) and 3.9(e), and when making orders for costs. In particular para. 2.3 of the practice direction provides that if in the opinion of the court non-compliance with the protocol has led to the commencement of proceedings which might otherwise not have been needed or has led to costs being incurred that should not have been, the orders the court may make include:

(a) an order that the party at fault pay the costs of the proceedings or part of them;

(b) an order that the party at fault pay those costs on an indemnity basis;

(c) if the party at fault is a claimant in whose favour an order for the payment of damages or some specified sum is subsequently made, an order depriving that party of interest on such sums for such period as may be specified or awarding interest at a lower rate;

(d) if the party at fault is a defendant, an order awarding interest on any damages awarded to the claimant at a higher rate (not exceeding 10 per cent above base rate) (see also CPR, r. 36.21(2)) than the rate at which interest would otherwise have been awarded.

The practice direction goes on to give examples of culpable failure to comply with the protocol, which in the case of a claimant includes not providing sufficient information or not following the procedures required; and in the case of a defendant, not making a preliminary response to the letter of claim in time (21 days under the personal injury protocol, 14 days under the clinical negligence protocol); or not making a full response within three months of the letter of claim or not disclosing documents.

Where there has been non-compliance with the protocol then by para. 2.4 of PD Protocols the court will exercise its powers with the object of placing the innocent party in no worse a position than he would have been in if the protocol had been complied with. The question of sanctions is further discussed in **9.4.2.2**.

9.4.2 The spirit of the protocols applies generally

The general importance of the new spirit of cooperation underpinning the protocols is further stressed by para. 4 of PD Protocols. This provides that the court will expect the parties, *even in cases not covered by any approved protocol*, to act reasonably in exchanging information and documents and generally try to avoid the necessity for the start of proceedings. Thus unless one can demonstrate genuine urgency, a claimant in any type of case will be expected to have attempted to resolve matters with the defendant and failing that, to have obtained and exchanged information about the claim. Thus commencing proceedings unless there is great urgency, without at least a letter of claim, is likely to be frowned on.

The above cannot be taken too far in every case. The majority of all litigation is in fact nothing more than debt collecting and where a debtor fails to respond to reasonable correspondence, including reminders and final reminders, it is not suggested that anything more than a last letter before action is required. However, every case will turn on its own facts.

It is worth considering the following practical points:

9.4.2.1 Costs generally

By CPR, r. 44.3(4), in deciding what order to make about costs the court must have regard to all the circumstances including the conduct of all the parties. Rule 44.3(5) then goes on:

The conduct of the parties includes—

(a) conduct before, as well as during, the proceedings and in particular the extent to which the parties followed any relevant pre-action protocol.

This applies both in relation to orders made during the case and at the conclusion.

9.4.2.2   Other sanctions generally

By r. 3.8, where a party has failed to comply with a rule, practice direction or court order, the court may impose a sanction which will take effect unless the party in default applies for and obtains relief from that sanction. When deciding whether to grant relief under r. 3.9, the court will have regard to a number of factors, but in particular under r. 3.9(1)(e):

the extent to which the party in default has complied with other rules, practice directions, court orders and any relevant pre-action protocol.

Thus, failure to abide by the protocol can lead to a sanction immediately. Even if no sanction is imposed, the failure can be taken into account generally when considering the party's conduct at later stages in the litigation.

The sanctions that might be imposed include the following:

(a) if the claimant is in default, a stay of proceedings to allow the defendant to collect its information and, so to speak, 'catch up';

(b) costs (which can be ordered to be paid forthwith);

(c) an order forbidding permission to call evidence from an expert who has been instructed by one or other party without compliance with the protocols (see **9.4.4** below);

(d) under r. 3.1(5), the court may order a party to pay a sum of money into court if that party has without good reason failed to comply with any rule, practice direction or relevant pre-action protocol. Thus, this seems to be a general sanction and if applied against a claimant could in effect amount to having to give security for costs or for costs at some future stage, such as the joint instruction of an expert; and as applied against a defendant might be to order him to pay the whole amount of the claim or some part of it into court.

9.4.3   The pre-action protocol on personal injury claims

As will be noted from the notes of guidance, the personal injury protocol is primarily designed for road traffic, tripping and slipping and accidents at work cases, which include an element of personal injury with a value of less than £15,000 and which are likely to be allocated to the fast track. This is because matters move swiftly once proceedings are issued. The notes of guidance do acknowledge that some flexibility in the timescale of the protocol may be necessary. Paragraph 2.4 goes on to note, however, that the approach advocated by the protocol may well be appropriate to some higher-valued claims and suggests that the spirit, if not the letter, of the protocol should still be followed for claims which would end up on the multi-track.

The protocol applies to claims which *include a claim for personal injury*, and then to the entirety of those claims. This may cause difficulties, for example, where the personal injury element of a claim is modest and may be easily resolved, but there are expensive vehicle repairs. The claimant may wish to move very swiftly to have the vehicle examined and repaired, if repairable, or scrapped and replaced if not. Despite the terms of the protocol as to instruction of experts, it is suggested that it would be considered reasonable for a claimant to give the defendant's insurers less notice of his intentions in relation to the vehicle and to insist that they have it inspected, if they wish to do so, more swiftly than the timescale in the protocol might indicate. A claimant should not be put in the position of wondering whether a defendant's dilatory insurer will or will not accept his own assessment of the vehicle and garage estimates, especially when a defendant may well mount arguments about the length of period of alternative vehicle hire. Common sense will have to allow for some variations of the timetables in the protocol about such matters.

9.4.4   The problem of expert witnesses

The question of instruction of expert witnesses is more fully discussed in **Chapter 20**. There are some difficulties, however, with knowing what is the proper procedure because of apparent discrepancies in the protocol. The guidance notes at para. 2.11, while acknowledging the need for joint selection of experts, say that 'The protocol promotes the practice of the claimant obtaining a medical report, disclosing it to the defendant who then asks questions and/or agrees it and does not obtain his own report'. In fact, the wording of the protocol suggests at para. 3.14, quite properly, that before any party instructs an expert, he should give the other party a list of the names of one or more experts in the relevant speciality whom he considers suitable. A frequent problem is that the claimant may have needed treatment, and may choose to go to the specialist who has treated him for his medical report. This should not happen in future under the protocol. Although there are advantages to the claimant in using the doctor who has actually treated him, the court may well conclude that the expert is less objective, both because he will have established a relationship with his patient and because he will naturally conclude that being the treating doctor, his own views as to prognosis, etc. cannot be challenged. It is preferable for the procedure as to joint instruction of experts canvassed from paras 3.14 to 3.18 to be followed so that a mutually acceptable expert can be instructed. A claimant who goes ahead and instructs his own expert unilaterally may well find that the court subsequently refuses permission to call that expert and insists that an expert be jointly instructed. This will leave the claimant to bear the irrecoverable costs of the first expert, whatever the outcome of the case.

9.4.5   Protocols and the small claims track

It will be seen in due course in **Chapter 13** that for a case to be allocated to the small claims track the personal injury element must be less than £1,000. Although the spirit of the protocol ought to be honoured to the point of giving some reasonable opportunity to compromise the claim, where there is a limited fixed costs regime as on the small claims track, the court would not be too prescriptive in criticising the actions of a claimant's lawyer who simply wished to get on with the case as economically as possible once it was clear that liability would not be accepted. It is suggested that only the most flagrant disregard of the spirit of cooperation provided for in the protocols would lead to a costs sanction and a finding of unreasonableness on the small claims track. See also **Chapter 17**.

9.4.6 The protocols and expiry of the limitation period

If a claimant first instructs his solicitor very late in the limitation period then, as indicated at para. 2.8 in the notes of guidance, the solicitor should give as much notice of intention to issue proceedings as is practical and the party should consider whether the court might be invited to extend time for service of the claimant's supporting documents and the service of any defence or, alternatively, to stay the proceedings while the recommended steps in the protocol are followed.

9.5 The use of counsel in litigation

9.5.1 Barristers

Until 1994 barristers enjoyed a monopoly of rights of audience in open court in the High Court and above. Since 1994, however, solicitors who have sufficient experience of advocacy in the courts in which solicitors have hitherto been able to appear may apply for a qualification entitling them to appear as advocates in the higher courts. For those with substantial judicial experience (e.g., as recorders) or those who actually have advocacy experience before higher courts (e.g., in the case of some solicitors who formerly were barristers) the qualifications may be granted on their experience hitherto. For those not in this category there is a qualification procedure, involving assessment, interview, and attendance at an approved advocacy training course. Despite this, for the foreseeable future, such solicitor advocates will be few in number and most firms of solicitors will be obliged to employ members of the Bar to conduct High Court trials, although all solicitors have right of audience in county court trials.

The lack of a right of audience in the High Court is, frankly, now of very little importance. Only a tiny proportion of claims go to trial in the High Court because the financial jurisdiction of the county court is itself unlimited. Thus very substantial claims indeed remain in the county court throughout their life and only the very largest of personal injury and commercial claims tend to be issued in the High Court. Moreover, even if they are issued in the High Court, it does not ensure that they will remain there right through to trial and certainly the trial itself will only be before a High Court Judge in cases of very substantial amounts, novel points of law, or where the case concerned is something of a test case.

Because of the sums of money involved and because counsel are specialists in trial advocacy, whereas solicitors usually have more general practices, it is common to use counsel who will appear at trial to assist throughout the case. It is a somewhat over-worked analogy but a reasonably accurate one to say that counsel's position vis-à-vis the solicitor corresponds approximately to that in medicine of a consultant and a general practitioner. The specific advantages are that counsel is usually free to concentrate his own mind on one case until he has completed the task associated with it. Solicitors, however, may well be running some hundreds of files at any one time, and in any given working day may have to apply their minds to some aspect of work in relation to 20, 30 or more of such files. Counsel may have many sets of instructions sitting on his shelves but he does not have to keep them continuously under review in the way that a solicitor does.

In essence counsel receives a set of instructions from a solicitor requesting him to do a certain task, some examples of which are described below. He then completes that task having done any necessary legal research, something which solicitors rarely have the time to do given their workload, and then returns the whole set of instructions together with his own completed work on the matter to the solicitor. He does not keep any running file on a case, nor indeed usually any copy of the piece of work he has himself done on the case. He does not follow it up or have direct contact with the client or witnesses, and it may be that the matter is settled and he never sees that set of instructions or that client's case again. On the other hand, the papers may be sent back to him for further work to be done on the case at intervals, often several months apart. Thus counsel does not have the same kind of continuity of involvement as a solicitor does, which allows him to concentrate his mind on each task in hand and to retain a more objective and detached view of the legal problems affecting a client whom, unless the case is one of the small minority which comes to court or where there is a conference with the client, he may never see.

9.5.2 Solicitors

Solicitors do of course have rights of audience in all the lower courts including the county court (whose financial jurisdiction in tort and contract cases is now unlimited in amount) and in other courts where important civil matters are dealt with, in particular the employment tribunal. Nonetheless, because of counsel's specialist expertise, in that he is engaged day to day in advocacy, it is usual to brief counsel in many of the courts where a solicitor does have a right of audience. It is also, paradoxically, often cheaper for the client to have a specialist counsel represent him, because a barrister's fees for a day in court may well be less than those of a solicitor would have been, because a solicitor has to charge, in the main, by the hour. When a barrister is briefed, in many cases there is no need for anyone from the solicitor's firm to accompany him. In other cases it is possible simply to send some junior member of the office staff to sit with him in court. In more complex matters it may, of course, be necessary for a senior representative, or even several representatives of the solicitor's firm, to accompany counsel.

9.5.3 The particular uses of counsel

9.5.3.1 To give advice in writing

Both before and after proceedings are issued counsel may be asked to give advice in claiming about such matters as *liability* (e.g., does he think the facts disclose a cause of action and does he think that the defendant is liable); *quantum of damages* (e.g., does he think on the facts that the offer put forward by the defendant is a reasonable one and should be accepted); *practical steps* (i.e., how does he think evidence should be collected and presented to maximise a claim in a large case); *procedural tactics* (e.g., does he think that an application for pre-action disclosure or summary judgment would be likely to succeed on the basis of the facts as known); *evidence* (e.g., what witnesses need to be called to prove which part of a claimant's case and what documentary evidence needs to be brought to court and what procedural action needs to be taken).

To obtain counsel's advice on these kinds of matter one simply drafts a set of instructions to him. All material documents of any relevance, e.g., witness statements, police accident reports, computation of damages, etc., are enclosed and in the text of the 'brief' a solicitor sets out his commentary on the matters involved, usually now in a ring-binder file with the solicitor's instructions first, followed by accompanying documents neatly and coherently supplied in an appropriate order separated by dividers. Subsequent sets of instructions in the same matter can then be added at the front. Papers in this format are easier for counsel to work on.

Many instructions to counsel are astonishingly brief. Often instructions say something like, 'Here are the instructions and counsel will see the nature of the problem'. Instructions should, however, be thorough and professional. The first time he gets a set of instructions in relation to a case counsel will know nothing about the history of the matter, and he should be taken through the background; there should be a commentary on each of the documents supplied; and, if possible, the solicitor should summarise his own view of the law involved and give his own provisional views on the question on which he is seeking counsel's advice. The solicitor should then pose the questions on which counsel's advice is sought.

These papers are then delivered to counsel's chambers and in due course counsel will supply written advice in which he sets out his views on the questions put. Instructions should be full and self-contained in every case. Even if counsel has dealt with some aspect of the case before, this may have been many months ago and in the interim counsel may have been involved in many other similar cases, so his memory will need to be refreshed about this one.

9.5.3.2   To advise in conference

Sometimes the questions to be considered are so complex, or the position in the case at present so nebulous, that it is more satisfactory to have a so-called 'conference' with counsel in his chambers. 'Conference' is a somewhat grandiose term for an informal discussion about the case, but it is particularly useful in the early stages of complex or very large cases so that counsel may indicate to the solicitor what lines of approach he may recommend. Counsel's advice may indeed become as specific as recommending named expert witnesses, or the way in which an approach to a large loss of earnings claim should be formulated.

Instructions as previously described should still usually be drafted and sent to counsel, if possible well in advance of the conference so that he can do some preliminary research on the case and give it his mature consideration. Such conferences are often in the late afternoon after counsel has finished in court for the day. It is not uncommon, especially in the later stages of litigation which it seems will go to trial, for the client to attend this conference. This is likely to be the first occasion on which a barrister, even if he has advised many times about a case as it went on, will have seen the client face to face. It is designed to give the client confidence in the barrister of the solicitor's choice. Conversely, however, it tends to increase the client's disappointment if the named barrister is unavailable for the trial itself, a problem with which all solicitors have to contend. In such a case, if the client had never seen his barrister it would presumably make little difference to him which barrister appeared at the trial. At such conferences counsel will often take the client through his version of events, sometimes in a fairly testing manner in order to see how he performs as a witness. This may well affect the ultimate advice that counsel gives. For example, if under searching questioning clear implausibilities or inconsistencies come out, or even if the client unfortunately has a shifty and evasive manner, the barrister may form the view that as he will make a poor witness some offer of compromise which has been put forward ought to be accepted.

Until 1995 the rules of etiquette of the Bar forbade barristers to meet witnesses of fact other than their clients before the trial, but they may now do so if necessary. They may, also, see expert witnesses in conference, and if there are difficult matters of expert evidence which have not been resolved between the experts, it is increasingly common for there to be a round-table meeting with the experts, the barrister and the solicitor to attempt to progress matters further. The object of this meeting is so that the expert witnesses are able to give the barrister all the necessary ammunition with which to cross-examine the opposing expert and to explain differences of opinion between themselves and the opposing expert. In substantial cases it is now not uncommon for conferences to take the form of negotiation meetings with the other side with both parties' solicitors, barristers and even experts present.

9.5.3.3 To draft statements of case

Counsel may be employed as a specialist draftsman in a number of fields. In non-contentious work counsel may draft, for example, trust deeds, partnership agreements or wills. In litigation counsel is generally used for drafting statements of case. Drafting is a specialist art form, and while a solicitor may well draft straightforward statements of case, usually drafting more complex case statements of case in personal injury or commercial actions will be left to counsel. It may, of course, be that a solicitor does such a specialised form of work (e.g., deals only with factory accidents for trade union members who work in a particular type of factory) that he becomes very expert in the field and has an ample collection of precedents from previous cases. In such a case the solicitor may well feel able to draft the statement of case himself. Nonetheless, this aspect demonstrates a useful background role for counsel which is that of longstop for professional negligence. Whilst the case law shows that in fact a solicitor is meant to bring his own independent scrutiny to every aspect of every case, and will still be negligent if relying on counsel's advice or drafting which was manifestly in error, it can be a useful back-up, if professional negligence is ever alleged, for a solicitor to show that he instructed experienced counsel and reasonably relied on what counsel drafted or advised.

In instructing counsel to draft documents, it is particularly vital to send all necessary papers and give a full narrative of the matter. Drafting inevitably leads to delay in litigation. Although drafting a fairly straightforward statement of case ought to take a barrister not much more than an hour, and often a lot less if he has ample precedents on which to draw, excessive workloads and typing difficulties in barristers' chambers may mean that the draft document and accompanying instructions are not returned within weeks, or even months, although the story of the solicitor who sent his set of instructions a birthday card to celebrate their being with the barrister for a year is doubtless apocryphal! One should ensure by means of a continuing relationship with the counsel of one's choice and his clerk that sets of instructions requiring the drafting of documents for court are returned promptly. It is the delay in getting drafting returned that is likely to lead to a request for an extension of time in particular.

Counsel have generally adapted well to changes brought about by the CPR so that drafting is done rather more swiftly than previously. Most counsel now are adept in the use of information technology and will be able to word process their own drafts from precedents. Sometimes, however, the involvement of counsel to draft documents may lead to some slippage in case management timetables, although the overall timetable must not be prejudiced by it.

9.5.3.4 As advocate

(a) *In open court*

Subject to the exception indicated in **9.5.1**, counsel has exclusive rights of audience in contested matters in the High Court, Court of Appeal and House of Lords. It is usually considered preferable to brief counsel in the county court as well for the reasons previously outlined. We shall return to the question of the contents and preparation of a brief at a later stage.

(b) *In pre-trial applications*

A solicitor has a right of audience in all pre-trial applications before a district judge, or a circuit judge or a High Court judge in chambers. A competent solicitor will usually appear in such applications even on matters of some substance, such as summary judgment or interim payment applications. The solicitor will have the whole file at his fingertips and will be experienced in such applications. There is hardly ever cross-examination of witnesses in such matters, as proceedings are on written evidence alone, and the solicitor will be perfectly competent to deal with the law, practice and facts. If a solicitor is less experienced, or perhaps due to pressure of work unavailable for such hearings, it may be appropriate to brief counsel to attend on important applications. It would not be normal to brief counsel on purely routine or procedural matters such as attendance at a case management conference, although on larger multi-track cases that may happen. The costs of counsel appearing on a pre-trial application can be claimed if one is successful in the litigation. If there is to be a summary assessment of costs then the district judge will deal with the issue of whether it was reasonable to employ counsel at the time when making his summary assessment.

9.5.4 Counsel's clerk and the organisation of chambers

9.5.4.1 The organisation of chambers

The Bar is divided into two kinds of barrister—Queen's Counsel and junior counsel. Queen's Counsel comprise about 10 per cent of the practising Bar. They are practitioners of considerable seniority and eminence who in the main are used only in the most serious criminal trials and the most weighty civil litigation. Their fees are correspondingly higher. Queen's Counsel do not usually draft statements of case and their whole work is giving advice, in writing or orally (a conference with a Queen's Counsel is called a 'consultation'), and appearing as advocates. When appearing as advocates Queen's Counsel are often accompanied by junior counsel to assist them, although the rule which formerly required this in every case has been abrogated.

The remaining 90 per cent of barristers are known as the Junior Bar. Most junior barristers never become Queen's Counsel and remain junior barristers until they retire. They may undertake any work whatsoever, and a great deal of their time in civil cases is often given over to drafting.

Barristers are self-employed and may not practise in partnership. Nonetheless, they organise themselves into groups called 'sets of chambers' for the purpose of providing office accommodation economically and sharing of common facilities such as secretarial staff, telephones, fax machines and the like. In addition, each set of chambers will employ one or more clerks. Although they may not practise in partnership, and to some extent each member of a set of chambers could be considered a business rival of his colleagues, most sets of chambers do develop a group ethos and a good deal of 'team spirit' and members will go to great lengths to assist each other with informal advice about difficult cases, which are sometimes discussed collectively, and senior members of chambers will go to great lengths to promote the careers of more junior members. Some chambers also develop considerable rivalries with other chambers.

9.5.4.2   The barrister's clerk

A barrister's clerk's relationship with his barristers is somewhat like that of a theatrical agent and his actor clients. That is, it is his function to keep his barristers fully employed, to negotiate fees for the work which they do, to ensure that they do not have two important cases coming up in different courts on the same day, and so on.

Barrister's clerks until recently were usually remunerated by way of a percentage of the fee of each barrister in their chambers for each piece of work done, whether drafting, advising or advocacy. Typically this proportion was 10 per cent of the net fee, and thus it is easy to see that if a barrister's clerk was running a chambers of say some 25 barristers, his income being 10 per cent of each barrister's total fees was likely to exceed the income of almost every barrister in his chambers. Barrister's clerks exercise an inordinate power in chambers because although solicitors usually direct their work to a named barrister, in case of unavailability of that barrister the clerk is the ultimate distributor of such work (called 'returns'). The clerk thus has a considerable power to make or break a barrister's career, particularly in the early years where few barristers will receive work directed to them personally and will be reliant on work which more senior members of chambers are unable to accommodate.

Barrister's clerks come from a variety of backgrounds, but usually do not have formal, legal qualifications. Most chambers now have departed from the principle of remunerating their clerk on a commission basis. Increasingly fixed salaries, although of a weight to reflect the very demanding nature of the work involved and possibly with a much more modest commission element or bonus, are being employed. In addition, many chambers now also employ so called 'practice managers' who often do have formal accountancy or management qualifications and will be able to deal with aspects of the increasing complexity of a barrister's life involving, as it commonly does now, information technology systems, computerised accounts and so on. Such practice managers often have marketing functions as well as purely administrative ones so that, for example, part of their job will be to keep the profile of the members of chambers high with solicitors, to keep contact with solicitors and to explore new areas of legal work in which members of chambers can develop specialisms.

Typically, therefore, a successful chambers would have someone still described as a 'senior clerk' and would also employ several 'junior clerks' who themselves would probably take responsibility for several of the members of chambers and for some or other aspect of chambers administration. There might then be a 'practice manager' responsible for the functions mentioned above.

One previously important aspect of a barrister's clerk's work which has in part been taken out of their hands for civil cases, is the process of listing. Previously the barrister's clerk would virtually have the ultimate say on the time at which, within a given few weeks, a case would come up for trial. Now the listing function is undertaken by the courts themselves. In principle a fast track trial will be listed on the day that suits the court and the witnesses and the parties will generally speaking be expected to change counsel if their original choice is unavailable, although the availability of counsel is one of the factors that can be put forward for consideration when listing is first considered. All this practically means to a barrister's chambers, however, is that the clerk in chambers will move mountains to ensure that even if the original choice of a barrister is unavailable, a comparable barrister from chambers can be provided.

If the clerk has been unable to ensure that the chosen barrister does not have a competing engagement, he will reallocate the work to some unoccupied member of chambers. A solicitor, of course, is perfectly entitled to reject this and take a brief back and instruct a barrister from another chambers, but in most cases solicitors develop a good working relationship with certain chambers and will know the replacement well. Solicitors often prefer the matter to remain with the same chambers, perhaps in the belief that the barrister originally instructed, who may well have done a good deal of preparatory work on the brief by now which will in principle be wasted and unremunerated, will be more cooperative in coaching the late substitute in any problems involved than he would for a member of another chambers. Sometimes solicitors have a touching faith in the ability of the barrister's clerk to nominate an alleged expert in his chambers in the field of law in question.

9.6   Negotiations

9.6.1   Introduction

The purpose of negotiations is to set in motion a process which will, one hopes, resolve a conflict or disagreement between the parties. In the case of a claimant it is hoped that the process of negotiation will lead to the early acceptance of liability and an offer of compensation at the best obtainable figure, or to some other remedy which is sought, such as an agreement to pull down a wall blocking a right of way, to avoid the necessity to go to trial to seek an injunction. In the case of a defendant, at its best one hopes the negotiation process will convince the claimant that he has no cause of action and that he will withdraw. Short of this, the defendant hopes to escape from the litigation as cheaply or successfully as possible by buying off the claim for considerably less than the maximum which the court might eventually order him to pay.

Negotiations in litigation are usually conducted on a 'without prejudice' basis so that the contents of letters, and what is said in face-to-face or telephone conversations, cannot be repeated to the court. This is because in the course of negotiations concessions, and even admissions, are often made for the sake of moving the negotiation process along, with each party reserving the right to withdraw those concessions or admissions should the case go to trial.

In the litigation process there may be no negotiation at all. It may become apparent to both sides at the very outset that the parties are completely in conflict and the matter can only be resolved by the court. Such cases would, however, be extremely rare. Where negotiation takes place it may be that there is no more than one single meeting or discussion in an attempt to achieve settlement; more commonly the negotiating process may go on from before proceed-ings are even issued right through to, and during, the trial itself. It is by no means unknown for cases to be compromised part-way through a trial, usually after the day's business has been concluded, by meetings between solicitors or counsel involved. Where that happens, in a sense there has been at least a partial failure of the negotiating process, the main aim of which should be to identify the terms on which an agreement can be achieved as early as possible in the interests of saving legal costs, an approach which now permeates the CPR.

9.6.2   Negotiation techniques

There is a great deal of literature written about negotiations and the various tactics and techniques to be employed. Most of this literature is from the business field and in essence deals with techniques of salesmanship. These techniques are not to be scoffed at or ignored. In the non-contentious areas—as, for example, where the parties and their lawyers sit down to negotiate the terms upon which one company will merge with or acquire another; or where a potential tenant is negotiating for the terms of a business lease with a landlord; or even where an individual is in negotiation about the price of a house—these techniques have a part to play. The difference between those situations and litigation, however, is that in the end, in those situations, if the parties cannot agree there need be no falling out personally between them and they will simply walk away and probably never meet again. With litigation the crucial difference is that this is not possible. With litigation, if negotiation cannot achieve an outcome, the matter will go on and someone else, i.e., the court or arbitrator, will decide the rights of the parties. The sort of literature which suggests of negotiation that 'the aim is for both sides to feel good about the outcome: it is not a duel: there does not have to be a winner and a loser' has, perhaps, a limited application to the field of litigation. In the main it is not necessary for the parties to feel well disposed to each other by the end of the negotiations; probably in personal injury litigation the claimant will never again have any contact with the defendant; even in other forms of litigation it is generally not a feature of the process to ensure that the parties remain happy in each other's company. There are, of course, exceptions to this; where businesses fall out about one particular past contract, it may be possible for them to commence litigation (or more commonly *arbitration*) while attempting to preserve their relationship for other contracts and the future. Negotiations in that context may need to be carried out in a somewhat different and more conciliatory manner than is the case in litigation generally.

9.6.2.1   The aggressive approach

A solicitor should always act with the client's interests in mind, but, particularly if the parties have fallen out personally, that does not need to be reflected in the solicitor's behaviour. Whilst one may share the sense of injustice felt by a claimant with what seems to be an excellent case, especially one who is litigating against some large and intransigent organisation, it is important to ensure that the litigation never becomes personalised between the solicitors. The best solution in litigation is usually obtained by courtesy allied to firmness. This approach is also consistent with the overriding objective in the CPR. It is an obvious fact of human nature that if a solicitor feels that he is personally belittled and badly treated by his opponent, he is likely to try all the harder to 'get his own back' and may take every procedural or tactical point which can make life difficult for the person who has annoyed him.

Any inclination to be aggressive must always be tempered by reasonable conduct and in the light of the cooperative approach under the CPR, it must be the case at every stage that an opponent is given reasonable time to respond. This is especially so in cases where the aggressive approach was formerly at its peak, namely, in personal injury actions where now, because of the need to comply with the pre-action protocol, such steps as immediately instructing a favourable specialist of one's own choice in every field, giving an opponent only seven days to respond, can no longer form part of good litigation practice.

9.6.2.2   Disparity of bargaining power

A feature often experienced when acting for claimants, and not only in personal injury matters, is that there is often a great disparity of bargaining power between the parties. Thus if you are suing a local authority, a government department, or especially one of the privatised utilities, you are involved in litigation where the outcome may matter hardly at all to the defendant. Indeed, often the claimant's sense of frustration is measurably increased in such a case by the fact that the decision to resist his claim has manifestly been taken by a low-level employee, and the decision to support that employee's decision has been cavalierly under-taken simply because of the possibility of facing down the claimant to the point where he will have to risk significant sums to enforce his rights. This is pre-eminently the case where the litigation involves less than £5,000 and the claimant is unlikely to obtain a proper order for costs. The most striking aspect of this disparity in bargaining power, however, is in personal injury litigation where often the claimant, a lone individual who may have been injured in circumstances which have had a traumatic effect on him personally, and in effect ruined his life in both personal and financial terms, is facing a huge insurance company so that the outcome of the litigation means everything to the claimant but will be a mere pinprick to the defendants.

Although the overriding objective in the CPR refers to a court attempting to ensure that parties are on an equal footing as much as possible, this cannot be literally carried through in every aspect of every case. Certainly procedurally, attempts will be made to ensure equality, but the difference in importance of the eventual outcome is something which the courts cannot really address. Since the disparity in bargaining power is often a crucial advantage to the defendant, it is the duty of the claimant's solicitor to counteract this by doing everything reasonably within his power to obtain and keep the initiative.

Personalities of successful negotiators differ widely. Aggressive and truculent behaviour may sometimes prove successful, at least with opponents who are easily intimidated; likewise personal charm and courtesy may achieve much the same outcome. When acting for a claimant with a good case, however, matters of personality should take second place to the crucial feature in preparation for successful negotiation, which is thorough groundwork.

9.6.3   Preparing for negotiation

Nothing matters more than thorough preparation. When a solicitor is negotiating on behalf of a claimant, since he can dictate the timing of the start of the claim, it is essential that he has all his material in scrupulous order. The law should have been thoroughly researched so that it can, if necessary, be cited in negotiations; and all evidence and documents should be thoroughly prepared, collated and available.

Receipts, vouchers and other necessary documents to prove every head of claim should always be kept in good order, and computations of quantum should be constantly updated so that at any discussion about the case the claimant's solicitor has at his fingertips the relevant items of detail and a good idea of what the case is worth to settle.

Although the court will itself generally fix the timescale for the action, the claimant's solicitor can at least ensure that he is always ready to comply with the time limits and that, if the defendant does not observe those limits, prompt approaches to the defendant are made, followed up by immediate applications to the court. Without being unreasonable some pressure can always be kept on defendants procedurally by considering moving the case along swiftly on liability even if there are difficult areas of quantum, by applications for a split trial (see **1.4.2**). Proper applications for interim payments (see **22.5**) can also help to concentrate the defendant's mind on whether a claim is really worth defending on liability.

9.6.4 Commencing negotiations with insurers

In personal injury cases negotiations commonly start with the defendant's insurers, whether it be a road, factory, or occupier's liability accident. Insurers employ usually fairly competent claims staff who, while they may have no legal qualification, rapidly become fairly expert in the law and practice relevant to personal injury litigation. These claims staff usually have a considerable incentive to see if the claim can be reasonably settled because, if it can, then sending the file to the insurance company's chosen solicitors is avoided with the consequent saving on costs since everything will have been dealt with in-house. If proceedings are issued, then insurance companies usually send the file immediately to their solicitors.

However, increasingly some large insurance companies employ in-house solicitors who will actually conduct litigation, at least on the fast track and small claims track, themselves. These companies are no doubt very well aware of the statistics which indicate that for every £1 in compensation that an insurance company pays out, it pays out a further 80 pence, or thereabouts, in legal costs. They therefore have a high cost-benefit incentive to deal with the cases in-house and if possible to deal with them early and reasonably, which is very much in keeping with the spirit of the CPR. Certainly most insurers respond appropriately to the initial letter under the pre-action protocols and whilst it remains unclear whether the settlement rate pre-action is any higher, parties are certainly better prepared to settle actions which do commence, much earlier in their life. In particular insurers who have a hopeless case seem much more inclined to concede liability at the outset and even to pay reasonable amounts immediately, for example, to tender the amount necessary to enable the claimant to have his car repaired so that a claim for continuing hire can be brought to an end.

9.6.5 Early settlement and costs

Where in negotiations, even before a claim is issued in court, the parties are able to settle the claim for an agreed sum, or on other terms such as a defendant agreeing to desist from some activity to which the potential claimant objects, it is usual for the party offering the compromise to agree to pay reasonable legal costs. Even though no proceedings have been issued, if the parties can agree everything else, but cannot agree what the reasonable costs should be, it is open to the person who would have been the claimant to apply to the court under CPR 44.12A to assess the costs, even though no action has been commenced. This matter will be further discussed at para **26.9**.

9.7 The pre-action protocol for personal injury claims

The text of the main part of the protocol is set out below.

9.7.1 Introduction

1.1 Lord Woolf in his final Access to Justice Report of July 1996 recommended the development of pre-action protocols:

To build on and increase the benefits of early but well informed settlement which genuinely satisfy both parties to dispute.

1.2 The aims of pre-action protocols are:

- more pre-action contact between the parties;
- better and earlier exchange of information;
- better pre-action investigation by both sides;
- to put the parties in a position where they may be able to settle cases fairly and early without litigation;
- to enable proceedings to run to the court's timetable and efficiently, if litigation does become necessary;
- to promote the provision of medical or rehabilitation treatment (not just in high value cases) to address the needs of the claimant.

1.3 The concept of protocols is relevant to a range of initiatives for good litigation and prelitigation practice, especially:

- predictability in the time needed for steps pre-proceedings;
- standardisation of relevant information, including documents to be disclosed.

1.4 The courts will be able to treat the standards set in protocols as the normal reasonable approach to pre-action conduct. If proceedings are issued, it will be for the court to decide whether non-compliance with a protocol should merit adverse consequences. Guidance on the court's likely approach will be given from time to time in practice directions.

1.5 If the court has to consider the question of compliance after proceedings have begun, it will not be concerned with minor infringements, e.g. failure by a short period to provide relevant information. One minor breach will not exempt the 'innocent' party from following the protocol. The court will look at the effect of non-compliance on the other party when deciding whether to impose sanctions.

9.7.2 Notes of guidance

2.1 The protocol has been kept deliberately simple to promote ease of use and general acceptability. The notes of guidance which follow relate particularly to issues which arose during the piloting of the protocol.

Scope of the protocol

2.2 This protocol is intended to apply to all claims which include a claim for personal injury (except those claims covered by the Clinical Disputes and Disease and Illness protocols) and to the entirety of those claims: not only to the personal injury element of a claim which also includes, for instance, property damage.

2.3 This protocol is primarily designed for those road traffic, tripping and slipping and accident at work cases which include an element of personal injury with a value of less than £15,000 which are likely to be allocated to the fast track. This is because time will be of the essence, after proceedings are issued, especially for the defendant, if a case is to be ready for trial within 30 weeks of allocation. Also, proportionality of work and costs to the value of what is in dispute is particularly important in lower value claims. For some claims within the value 'scope' of the fast track some flexibility in the timescale of the protocol may be necessary; see also paragraph 3.8.

2.4 However, the 'cards on the table' approach advocated by the protocol is equally appropriate to higher value claims. The spirit, if not the letter of the protocol, should still be followed for multi-track type claims. In accordance with the sense of the civil justice reforms, the court will expect to see the spirit of reasonable pre-action behaviour applied in all cases, regardless of the existence of a specific protocol. In particular with regard to personal injury cases worth more than £15,000, with a view to avoiding the necessity of proceedings parties are expected to comply with the protocol as far as possible e.g., in respect of letters before action, exchanging information and documents and agreeing experts.

2.5 The timetable and the arrangements for disclosing documents and obtaining expert evidence may need to be varied to suit the circumstances of the case. Where one or both parties consider the detail of the protocol is not appropriate to the case, and proceedings are subsequently issued, the court will expect an explanation as to why the protocol has not been followed, or has been varied.

Early notification

2.6 The claimant's legal representative may wish to notify the defendant and/or his insurer as soon as they know a claim is likely to be made, but before they are able to send a detailed letter of claim, particularly for instance, when the defendant has no or limited knowledge of the incident giving rise to the claim or where the claimant is incurring significant expenditure as a result of the accident which he hopes the defendant might pay for, in whole or in part. If the claimant's representative chooses to do this, it will not start the timetable for responding.

The letter of claim

2.7 The specimen letter of claim at Annex A will usually be sent to the individual defendant. In practice, he/she may have no personal financial interest in the financial outcome of the claim/dispute because he/she is insured. Court-imposed sanctions for non-compliance with the protocol may be ineffective against an insured. This is why the protocol emphasises the importance of passing the letter of claim to the insurer and the possibility that the insurance cover might be affected. If an insurer receives the letter of claim only after some delay by the insured, it would not be unreasonable for the insurer to ask the claimant for additional time to respond.

2.8 In road traffic cases, the letter of claim should always contain the name and address of the hospital where the claimant was treated and, where available, the claimant's hospital reference number.

2.9 The priority at letter of claim stage is for the claimant to provide sufficient information for the defendant to assess liability. Sufficient information should also be provided to enable the defendant to estimate the likely size of the claim.

2.10 Once the claimant has sent the letter of claim no further investigation on liability should normally be carried out until a response is received from the defendant indicating whether liability is disputed.

Reasons for early issue

2.11 The protocol recommends that a defendant be given three months to investigate and respond to a claim before proceedings are issued. This may not always be possible, particularly where a claimant only consults a solicitor close to the end of any relevant limitation period. In these circumstances, the claimant's solicitor should give as much notice of the intention to issue proceedings as is practicable and the parties should consider whether the court might be invited to extend time for service of the claimant's supporting documents and for service of any defence, or alternatively, to stay the proceedings while the recommended steps in the protocol are followed.

Status of letters of claim and response

2.12   Letters of claim and response are not intended to have the same status as a statement of case in proceedings. Matters may come to light as a result of investigation after the letter of claim has been sent, or after the defendant has responded, particularly if disclosure of documents takes place outside the recommended three-month period. These circumstances could mean that the 'pleaded' case of one or both parties is presented slightly differently than in the letter of claim and response. It would not be consistent with the spirit of the protocol for a party to 'take a point' on this in the proceedings, provided that there was no obvious intention by the party who changed their position to mislead the other party.

Disclosure of documents

2.13   The aim of the early disclosure of documents by the defendant is not to encourage 'fishing expeditions' by the claimant, but to promote an early exchange of relevant information to help in clarifying or resolving issues in dispute. The claimant's solicitor can assist by identifying in the letter of claim or in a subsequent letter the particular categories of documents which they consider are relevant.

Experts

2.14   The protocol encourages joint selection of, and access to, experts. The report produced is not a joint report for the purposes of CPR Part 35. Most frequently this will apply to the medical expert, but on occasions also to liability experts, e.g. engineers. The protocol promotes the practice of the claimant obtaining a medical report, disclosing it to the defendant who then asks questions and/or agrees it and does not obtain his own report. The protocol provides for nomination of the expert by the claimant in personal injury claims because of the early stage of the proceedings and the particular nature of such claims. If proceedings have to be issued, a medical report must be attached to these proceedings. However, if necessary after proceedings have commenced and with the permission of the court, the parties may obtain further expert reports. It would be for the court to decide whether the costs of more than one expert's report should be recoverable.

2.15   Some solicitors choose to obtain medical reports through medical agencies, rather than directly from a specific doctor or hospital. The defendant's prior consent to the action should be sought and, if the defendant so requests, the agency should be asked to provide in advance the names of the doctor(s) whom they are considering instructing.

Alternative dispute resolution

2.16   The parties should consider whether some form of alternative dispute resolution procedure would be more suitable than litigation, and if so, endeavour to agree which form to adopt. Both the claimant and defendant may be required by the court to provide evidence that alternative means of resolving their dispute were considered. The courts take the view that litigation should be a last resort, and that claims should not be issued prematurely when a settlement is still actively being explored. Parties are warned that if the protocol is not followed (including this paragraph) then the court must have regard to such conduct when determining costs.

2.17 It is not practicable in this protocol to address in detail how the parties might decide which method to adopt to resolve their particular dispute. However, summarised below are some of the options for resolving disputes without litigation:

- Discussion and negotiation

- Early neutral evaluation by an independent third party (for example, a lawyer experienced in the field of personal injury or an individual experienced in the subject matter of the claim)

- Mediation—a form of facilitated negotiation assisted by an independent neutral party.

2.18 The Legal Services Commission has published a booklet on 'Alternatives to Court', CLS Direct Information Leaflet 23 (www.clsdirect.org.uk/legalhelp/leaflet23.jsp), which lists a number of organisations that provide alternative dispute resolution services.

2.19 *It is expressly recognised that no party can or should be forced to mediate or enter into any form of ADR.*

Stocktake

2.20 Where a claim is not resolved when the protocol has been followed, the parties might wish to carry out a 'stocktake' of the issues in dispute, and the evidence that the court is likely to need to decide those issues, before proceedings are started. Where the defendant is insured and the pre-action steps have been conducted by the insurer, the insurer would normally be expected to nominate solicitors to act in the proceedings and the claimant's solicitor is recommended to invite the insurer to nominate solicitors to act in the proceedings and do so seven to 14 days before the intended issue date.

9.7.3 The protocol

Letter of claim

3.1 The claimant shall send to the proposed defendant two copies of a letter of claim immediately sufficient information is available to substantiate a realistic claim, and before issues of quantum are addressed in detail. One copy of the letter is for the defendant, the second for passing on to his insurers.

3.2 The letter shall contain **a clear summary of the facts** on which the claim is based together with an indication of the **nature of any injuries** suffered and of **any financial loss incurred**. In cases of road traffic accidents, the letter should provide the name and address of the hospital where treatment has been obtained and the claimant's hospital reference number. Where the case is funded by a conditional fee agreement (or collective conditional fee agreement), notification should be given of the existence of the agreement and where appropriate, that there is a success fee and/or insurance premium, although not the level of the success fee or premium.

3.3 Solicitors are recommended to use a **standard format** for such a letter—an example is at Annex A: this can be amended to suit the particular case.

3.4 The letter should ask for **details of the insurer** and that a copy—be sent by the proposed defendant to the insurer where appropriate. If the insurer is known, a copy shall be sent directly to the insurer. Details of the claimant's National

Insurance number and date of birth should be supplied to the defendant's insurer once the defendant has responded to the letter of claim and confirmed the identity of the insurer. This information should not be supplied in the letter of claim.

3.5 **Sufficient information** should be given in order to enable the defendant's insurer/solicitor to commence investigations and at least put a broad valuation on the 'risk'.

3.6 The **defendant should reply within 21 calendar days** of the date of posting of the letter identifying the insurer (if any) and, if necessary, identifying specifically any significant omissions from the letter of claim. If there has been no reply by the defendant or insurer within 21 days, the claimant will be entitled to issue proceedings.

3.7 The defendant ('s insurers) will have a **maximum of three months** from the date of acknowledgment of the claim **to investigate**. No later than the end of that period the defendant (insurer) shall reply, stating whether liability is denied and, if so, giving reasons for their denial of liability including any alternative version of events relied upon.

3.8 Where the accident occurred outside England and Wales and/or where the defendant is outside the jurisdiction, the time periods of 21 days and three months should normally be extended up to 42 days and six months.

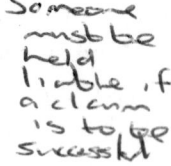

3.9 Where **liability is admitted**, the presumption is that the defendant will be bound by this admission for all claims with a total value of up to £15,000. Where the claimant's investigation indicates that the value of the claim has increased to more than £15,000 since the letter of claim, the claimant should notify the defendant as soon as possible.

Documents

3.10 If the **defendant denies liability**, he should enclose with the letter of reply, **documents** in his possession which are **material to the issues** between the parties, and which would be likely to be ordered to be disclosed by the court, either on an application for pre-action disclosure, or on disclosure during proceedings.

3.11 Attached at Annex B are specimen, but non-exhaustive, **lists** of documents likely to be material in different types of claim. Where the claimant's investigation of the case is well advanced, the letter of claim could indicate which classes of documents are considered relevant for early disclosure. Alternatively these could be identified at a later stage.

3.12 Where the defendant admits primary liability, but alleges contributory negligence by the claimant, the defendant should give reasons supporting those allegations and disclose those documents from Annex B which are relevant to the issues in dispute. The claimant should respond to the allegations of contributory negligence before proceedings are issued.

3.13 No charge will be made for providing copy documents under the protocol.

Special damages

3.14 The claimant will send to the defendant as soon as practicable a Schedule of Special Damages with supporting documents, particularly where the defendant has admitted liability.

Experts

3.15 Before any party instructs an expert he should give the other party a list of the **name**(s) of **one or more experts** in the relevant speciality whom he considers are suitable to instruct.

3.16 Where a medical expert is to be instructed the claimant's solicitor will organise access to relevant medical records—see specimen letter of instruction at Annex C.

3.17 **Within 14 days** the other party may indicate **an objection** to one or more of the named experts. The first party should then instruct a mutually acceptable expert (which is not the same as a joint expert). It must be emphasised that if the claimant nominates an expert in the original letter of claim, the defendant has 14 days to object to one or more of the named experts after expiration of the period of 21 days within which he has to reply to the letter of claim, as set out in paragraph 3.6.

3.18 If the second party objects to all the listed experts, the parties may then instruct **experts of their own choice**. It would be for the court to decide subsequently, if proceedings are issued, whether either party had acted unreasonably.

3.19 If the **second party does not object to an expert nominated**, he shall not be entitled to rely on his own expert evidence within that particular speciality unless:

(a) the first party agrees;

(b) the court so directs; or

(c) the first party's expert report has been amended and the first party is not prepared to disclose the original report.

3.20 **Either party may send to an agreed expert written questions** on the report, relevant to the issues, via the first party's solicitors. The expert should send answers to the questions separately and directly to each party.

3.21 The cost of a report from an agreed expert will usually be paid by the instructing first party: the costs of the expert replying to questions will usually be borne by the party which asks the questions.

9.7.4 Rehabilitation

4.1 The claimant or the defendant or both shall consider as early as possible whether the claimant has reasonable needs that could be met by rehabilitation treatment or other measures.

4.2 The parties shall consider, in such cases, how those needs might be addressed. The Rehabilitation Code (which is attached at Annex D) may be helpful in considering how to identify the claimant's needs and how to address the cost of providing for those needs.

4.3 The time limit set out in paragraph 3.7 *of this protocol* shall not be shortened, except by consent to allow these issues to be addressed.

4.4 The provision of any report obtained for the purposes of assessment of provision of a party's rehabilitation needs shall not be used in any litigation arising out of the accident, the subject of the claim, save by consent and shall in any event be exempt from the provisions of paragraphs 3.15 to 3.21 inclusive of this protocol.

9.7.5 Resolution of issues

5.1 Where the defendant admits liability in whole or in part, before proceedings are issued, any medical reports obtained under this protocol on which a party relies should be disclosed to the other party. The claimant should delay issuing proceedings for 21 days from disclosure of the report (unless such delay would cause his claim to become time-barred), to enable the parties to consider whether the claim is capable of settlement.

5.2   The Civil Procedure Rules Part 36 permit claimants and defendants to make offers to settle pre-proceedings. Parties should always consider before issuing if it is appropriate to make Part 36 Offer. If such an offer is made, the party making the offer must always supply sufficient evidence and/or information to enable the offer to be properly considered.

5.3   Where the defendant has admitted liability, the claimant should send to the defendant schedules of special damages and loss at least 21 days before proceedings are issued (unless that would cause the claimant's claim to become time-barred).

A   Letter of claim

To

Defendant

Dear Sirs

Re: Claimant's full name

Claimant's full address

Claimant's clock or works number

Claimant's employer (name and address)

We are instructed by the above named to claim damages in connection with an **accident at work/road traffic accident/tripping accident** on   day   of   *(year)* at *(place of accident which must be sufficiently detailed to establish location)*.

Please confirm the identity of your insurers. Please note that the insurers will need to see this letter as soon as possible and it may affect your insurance cover and/or the conduct of any subsequent legal proceedings if you do not send this letter to them.

The circumstances of the accident are:-

(brief outline).

The reason why we are alleging fault is:

(simple explanation, e.g., defective machine, broken ground).

A description of our client's injuries is as follows:-

(brief outline)

(In cases of road traffic accidents)

Our client (state hospital reference number) received treatment for the injuries at (name and address of hospital).

Our client is still suffering from the effects of his/her injury. We invite you to participate with us in addressing his/her immediate needs by use of rehabilitation.

He is employed as *(occupation)* and has had the following time off work *(dates of absence)*.

His approximate weekly income is (insert if known).

If you are our client's employers, please provide us with the usual earnings details which will enable us to calculate his financial loss.

We are obtaining a police report and will let you have a copy of the same upon your undertaking to meet half the fee.

We have also sent a letter of claim to *(name and address)* and a copy of that letter is attached.

We understand their insurers are *(name, address and claims number if known)*.

At this stage of our enquiries we would expect the documents contained in parts *(insert appropriate parts of standard disclosure list)* to be relevant to this action.

Please note that we have entered into a conditional fee agreement with our client dated   in relation to this claim which provides for a success fee within the meaning of section 58(2) of the Courts and Legal Services Act 1990. Our client has taken out an insurance policy with [name of insurance company] of [address of insurance company] to which section 29 of the Access to Justice Act 1999 applies. The policy number is   and the policy is dated   . Where the funding arrangement is an insurance policy, the party must state the name and address of the insurer, the policy number and the date of the policy, and must identify the claim or claims to which it relates (including Part 20 claims if any).

A copy of this letter is attached for you to send to your insurers. Finally, we expect an acknowledgment of this letter within 21 days by yourselves or your insurers.

Yours faithfully

Jurisdiction and the Civil Procedure Rules

10.1 The High Court

There are three divisions of the High Court, namely, the Queen's Bench Division, the Chancery Division and the Family Division. The jurisdiction of the Family Division does not concern us. The jurisdiction of the Chancery Division and that of the Queen's Bench Division overlap to a small extent but in the main their work is quite different.

Proceedings are allocated to the Chancery Division by s. 61 of the Supreme Court Act 1981 and para. 1 of sch. 1 to that Act. In particular, matters to do with mortgages; trusts; the administration of estates; bankruptcy; partnership; patents, trademarks and copyright; and the sale, exchange or partition of land are dealt with there. Whilst perhaps as recently as 15 years ago the daily work of the Chancery Division was seen as being dull, rarely involving interesting disputes of fact, since then it has, so to speak, spread its tentacles into a number of areas of purely commercial law work. This, together with the fact that proceedings for urgent interim relief, in particular injunctions of various kinds, often form part of the day-to-day work, has led to the situation where the Chancery Division now has a much higher profile. In this text, however, we shall be concerned mainly with the work of the Queen's Bench Division, which deals with almost all cases brought in tort and contract.

The Queen's Bench Division of the High Court consists of the Central Office, that is, the office of the High Court contained in the Royal Courts of Justice building in the Strand, London, and also the District Registries which are the offices of the High Court outside London. The personnel of the Queen's Bench Division with whom we are concerned are as follows.

10.1.1 Masters of the Queen's Bench Division

Masters are the judges who deal with almost all matters of an administrative or a judicial nature in a High Court action in the Central Office in London up to the stage of the trial itself.

The only form of application with which we are concerned which will not be dealt with by a master but by a High Court judge is an application for an injunction. Save in very limited circumstances—in particular, where an injunction is to be granted by agreement between the parties—a master has no jurisdiction to grant an injunction.

10.1.2 District Judges

District Judges are the equivalent of Queen's Bench Division masters in the district registries. The district registries are the offices of the High Court outside London and there are about 100 of such registries in towns throughout England and Wales. A district judge also has powers in relation to the work of the other two divisions of the High Court and will also deal with the assessment of bills of costs, which in London is dealt with by a specialist costs judge. Thus the work of district judges is somewhat less specialised than that of the Queen's Bench Division masters.

10.1.3 High Court judges

High Court judges sit to hear the actual trial of cases on the multi-track in open court. They are likely only to be involved in the trial of cases either of great importance, because they are test cases, or of considerable substance. As a very rough guide when deciding whether to list a case for hearing before a circuit judge, or a High Court judge in some courts, the test is whether the case is worth £250,000 or more. High Court judges also form one appeal tier and hear appeals from some decisions of district judges and circuit judges (see **Chapter 36**).

10.2 The county court

The constitution of the county court is governed by the County Courts Act 1984. The county court now has no upper financial limit to its jurisdiction in matters involving tort and contract. There are about 230 county courts in England and Wales. There is thus likely to be a registry of the county court in quite small towns in rural areas while there may be no district registry of the High Court for many miles. In large towns, almost always the same building is both the local district registry of the High Court of Justice and the county court registry. In large towns there may be as many as 15 or more district judges. In some smaller courts there may be only one.

10.2.1 The district judge

The equivalent of the High Court district judge is called the county court district judge. Where the district registry of the High Court and the county court are in the same town, the same person will be both district judge of the High Court and district judge of the county court. The jurisdiction of such a district judge is to try any undefended case (even on the multi-track) or any case on the fast track; and in addition the district judge will deal with pre-trial applications in precisely the same way in which a district judge of the High Court does.

When sitting as a district judge of the county court the district judge has wide powers to grant interim and final injunctions even though a district judge of the High Court may not.

10.2.2 Circuit judges

The judge who will hear trials in the county court is likely to be a circuit judge whose work will consist of alternatively trying civil county court actions on his circuit (i.e., local group of county courts), dealing with family cases, particularly disputes relating to children, and periods in the Crown Court sitting in criminal cases.

Circuit judges are full-time judges, but their jurisdiction is exercised in addition by *recorders* (i.e., practising solicitors or barristers appointed to sit part-time for a pre-scribed number of days a year on rota).

10.2.3 The court manager

The court manager is in charge of all administrative matters in a county court. In addi-tion, although not himself a solicitor or barrister, or even necessarily having any form of legal qualification, the court manager increasingly has some minor judicial func-tions. In particular he or she deals with some matters to do with the rate of instalments by which a judgment debtor is required to pay judgments at a stage called a 'disposal' and also with attachments of earnings (see **Chapter 34** below).

10.2.4 The bailiff

The High Court employs nobody for the purposes of service of documents or enforce-ment of judgments. The High Court enforcement officer may be called upon to help enforce judgments but he is not an employee of the High Court. In the county court, however, there is an officer called a bailiff who is employed for personal service of claims and other applications and court orders; and for some of the steps in enforcing judgment, particularly by a so-called *warrant of execution* where the judgment debtor's goods are seized and sold at auction to realise the amount of the judgment (see **34.3.1.2**).

10.3 The Civil Procedure Rules 1998

Since 26 April 1999 all litigation has been conducted under the Civil Procedure Rules 1998 (CPR). These are very lengthy, currently running to over 1,000 pages when one includes the schedules and practice directions which accompany them. The rules were drafted not only to provide an entirely new framework for civil litigation, but to attempt to impose a new culture in which speed, efficiency and encouraging an atmosphere of cooperation between the parties would be the objectives. They were put in place in the light of the findings of a national survey conducted by Lord Woolf between 1994 and 1996, which found that excessive cost, delay and the difficulty and obscurity of the former rules were serious impediments to justice.

At the time of writing this text the rules have been in force for just over five years and it is quite apparent that, with some few qualifications, they have been entirely success-ful in bringing about the change in litigation culture. It is not proposed to say any more about the former rules. Indeed, a series of cases in the Court of Appeal since 1999 has emphasised that even where terms and concepts appear similar under the CPR to the former rules, courts are not obliged to take into account or apply authorities on the former rules and that 26 April 1999 represented an entirely 'new start' in the civil litigation process.

10.3.1 The Civil Procedure Rules

The CPR comprise a number of Parts, each of them subdivided into a number of rules, dealing with different aspects of civil procedure. Each Part is supplemented by a practice direction (PD), which assists in fleshing out the rules and indicating what the appropriate requirements are. For example, Part 32 deals with evidence at court hearings and is relatively brief in itself, running to just over two pages. It is, however, supplemented by a practice direction which is about three times longer and sets out with more precision what should be presented to the court and what considerations the court will bear in mind.

Apart from the Parts and practice directions there are a number of prescribed forms which should be used at appropriate stages of the action, for example:

(a) the *claim form* which commences an action;

(b) the *application notice* by which a party wishing to apply to a judge for some order about how the case should proceed, makes his application;

(c) *allocation questionnaire*, which in most cases the parties are required to complete and return to the court after the defendant has filed his defence to the claimant's claim and which will allow the court to give directions for how the case is to proceed.

10.3.2 The overriding objective

The rules commence with an important statement in Part 1 which:

(a) sets out the *overriding objective*;

(b) indicates that the court must always give effect to that objective;

(c) imposes upon the parties the duty of assisting the court in that objective; and

(d) sets out the court's *duty* (not just *power*) to manage cases.

Part 1 is of such fundamental importance when considering every other aspect of the rules that it is now set out in full.

The overriding objective

1.1 (1) These Rules are a new procedural code with the overriding objective of enabling the court to deal with cases justly.

(2) Dealing with a case justly includes, so far as is practicable—

(a) ensuring that the parties are on an equal footing;

(b) saving expense;

(c) dealing with the case in ways which are proportionate—

(i) to the amount of money involved;

(ii) to the importance of the case;

(iii) to the complexity of the issues; and

(iv) to the financial position of each party;

(d) ensuring that it is dealt with expeditiously and fairly; and

(e) allotting to it an appropriate share of the court's resources, while taking into account the need to allot resources to other cases.

Application by the court of the overriding objective

1.2 The court must seek to give effect to the overriding objective when it—

(a) exercises any power given to it by the Rules; or

(b) interprets any rule.

Duty of the parties

1.3 The parties are required to help the court to further the overriding objective.

Court's duty to manage cases

1.4 (1) The court must further the overriding objective by actively managing cases.

(2) Active case management includes—

(a) encouraging the parties to co-operate with each other in the conduct of the proceedings;

(b) identifying the issues at an early stage;

(c) deciding promptly which issues need full investigation and trial and accordingly disposing summarily of the others;

(d) deciding the order in which issues are to be resolved;

(e) encouraging the parties to use an alternative dispute resolution procedure if the court considers that appropriate and facilitating the use of such procedure;

(f) helping the parties to settle the whole or part of the case;

(g) fixing timetables or otherwise controlling the progress of the case;

(h) considering whether the likely benefits of taking a particular step justify the cost of taking it;

(i) dealing with as many aspects of the case as it can on the same occasion;

(j) dealing with the case without the parties needing to attend at court;

(k) making use of technology; and

(l) giving directions to ensure that the trial of a case proceeds quickly and efficiently.

It is quite clear that the stated objectives are not a mere pious exhortation to do one's best. They are to be rigorously applied. In r. 1.1 it must be carefully noted that 'dealing with cases justly' includes aspects designed to ensure that one party cannot take advantage of the other by his superior bargaining position caused by inequality of resources. The court is obliged to ensure that cases are deal with *expeditiously* as well as fairly and that an appropriate share of the court's resources is allotted to each case, thus making clear that the court will have the power to run the case to a tight timetable and with an economical method of disposing of it (for example, by limiting the amount of evidence or expert witnesses which each party can call, requiring written rather than oral evidence, or even fixing a time limit for speeches at the trial itself). Aspects of the court's duty to manage cases under r. 1.4 further reinforce this provision. Each of them contains some reference to cooperation, limiting of issues, speed or assisting the parties to settle the case or progress it economically.

10.3.3 The court's case management powers

Part 1 of the CPR sets out the court's duties and these are supplemented by detailed provisions in Part 3 which sets out the court's case management powers. Again, because of their importance it is appropriate to set out rr. 3.1 to 3.4 in full.

The court's general powers of management

3.1 (1) The list of powers in this rule is in addition to any powers given to the court by any other rule or practice direction or by any other enactment or any powers it may otherwise have.

(2) Except where these Rules provide otherwise, the court may—

(a) extend or shorten the time for compliance with any rule, practice direction or court order (even if an application for extension is made after the time for compliance has expired);

      (b) adjourn or bring forward a hearing;

      (c) require a party or a party's legal representative to attend the court;

      (d) hold a hearing and receive evidence by telephone or by using any other method of direct oral communication;

      (e) direct that part of any proceedings (such as a counter claim) be dealt with as separate proceedings;

      (f) stay the whole or part of any proceedings or judgment either generally or until a specified date or event;

      (g) consolidate proceedings;

      (h) try two or more claims on the same occasion;

      (i) direct a separate trial of any issue;

      (j) decide the order in which issues are to be tried;

      (k) exclude an issue from consideration;

      (l) dismiss or give judgment on a claim after a decision on a preliminary issue;

      (m) take any other step or make any other order for the purpose of managing the case and furthering the overriding objective.

(3) When the court makes an order, it may—

      (a) make it subject to conditions, including a condition to pay a sum of money into court; and

      (b) specify the consequence of failure to comply with the order or a condition.

(4) Where the court gives directions it may take into account whether or not a party has complied with any relevant pre-action protocol.

(5) The court may order a party to pay a sum of money into court if that party has, without good reason, failed to comply with a rule, practice direction or a relevant pre-action protocol.

(6) When exercising its power under paragraph (5) the court must have regard to—

      (a) the amount in dispute; and

      (b) the costs which the parties have incurred or which they may incur.

(6A) Where a party pays money into court following an order under paragraph (3) or (5), the money shall be security for any sum payable by that party to any other party in the proceedings, subject to the right of a defendant under rule 37.2 to treat all or part of any money paid into court as a Part 36 payment.

      (Rule 36.2 explains what is meant by a Part 36 payment)

(7) A power of the court under these Rules to make an order includes a power to vary or revoke the order.

Court officer's power to refer to a judge

3.2 Where a step is to be taken by a court officer—

      (a) the court officer may consult a judge before taking that step;

      (b) the step may be taken by a judge instead of the court officer.

Court's power to make order of its own initiative

3.3 (1) Except where a rule or some other enactment provides otherwise, the court may exercise its powers on an application or of its own initiative.

      (Part 23 sets out the procedure for making an application)

    (2) Where the court proposes to make an order of its own initiative—

      (a) it may give any person likely to be affected by the order an opportunity to make representations; and

      (b) where it does so it must specify the time by and the manner in which the representations must be made.

(3) Where the court proposes—

    (a) to make an order of its own initiative; and

    (b) to hold a hearing to decide whether to make the order,

it must give each party likely to be affected by the order at least 3 days' notice of the hearing.

(4) The court may make an order of its own initiative, without hearing the parties or giving them an opportunity to make representations.

(5) Where the court has made an order under paragraph (4)—

    (a) a party affected by the order may apply to have it set aside, varied or stayed; and

    (b) the order must contain a statement of the right to make such an application.

(6) An application under paragraph (5)(a) must be made—

    (a) within such period as may be specified by the court; or

    (b) if the court does not specify a period, not more than 7 days after the date on which the order was served on the party making the application.

Power to strike out a statement of case

3.4 (1) In this rule and rule 3.5, reference to a statement of case includes reference to part of a statement of case.

(2) The court may strike out a statement of case if it appears to the court—

    (a) that the statement of case discloses no reasonable grounds for bringing or defending the claim;

    (b) that the statement of case is an abuse of the court's process or is otherwise likely to obstruct the just disposal of the proceedings; or

    (c) that there has been a failure to comply with a rule, practice direction or court order.

(3) When the court strikes out a statement of case it may make any consequential order it considers appropriate.

(4) Where—

    (a) the court has struck out a claimant's statement of case;

    (b) the claimant has been ordered to pay costs to the defendant; and

    (c) before the claimant pays those costs, he starts another claim against the same defendant, arising out of facts which are the same or substantially the same as those relating to the claim in which the statement of case was struck out,

the court may, on the application of the defendant, stay that other claim until the costs of the first claim have been paid.

(5) Paragraph (2) does not limit any other power of the court to strike out a statement of case.

While reading these at one sitting is heavy going, it will be important to refer back to them when considering practical and tactical possibilities at each individual stage.

Rule 3.1 describes the court's general powers of management and provides that it is up to the court to decide what time limits will be imposed on the parties, what procedural directions will be given and indeed, generally, under r. 3.1(2)(m), *'take any other step or make any other order for the purpose of managing the case and furthering the overriding objective'*.

Rule 3.3 should also be carefully noted. The court does not need the parties to have made some application which brings them before it before the court begins to case manage on its own initiative. It may do so with or without offering the parties the opportunity to make representations, although if no such opportunity to make representations has been given, by r. 3.3(5) the party affected may apply to have the order set aside, varied or stayed and there will then be a hearing on the issue.

10.3.3.1   The power to strike out a statement of case

A 'statement of case', which will be discussed below, is the document comprising the written case of each party, claimant or defendant. When the judge considers the case file, he has the power to strike out the claimant's claim or the defendant's defence, if:

(a) neither appear to disclose reasonable grounds for bringing or defending the claim;

(b) the statement of case is an abuse of process likely to obstruct the just disposal of the proceedings; or

(c) there has been a failure to comply with a rule, practice direction or court order.

This is an extremely draconian power, which will assist in disposing of a very large number of cases. It is unlikely that a party with competent legal representation would not manage to put his case sufficiently well on paper to avoid problems at this stage. However, a very large amount of litigation, as has been previously stated, is simple debt collecting by banks, finance institutions, clothing catalogue companies, and the private electricity, gas and water companies. In such cases the 'defence' when it is received will often not in reality be a defence at all, but simply a claim that the defendant is unable to pay. To dispose of those cases at an early stage will save a significant amount of the court's time. Where the court does take the initiative in this way it will be noted that the party affected has (under r. 3.6) the right to apply to set the judgment aside and ask for a hearing on the merits. This may occur because the litigant in person has set out his statement of case badly, overlooking vital facts which, if included, would have demonstrated that striking out in such a peremptory fashion was inappropriate.

EXAMPLE

In a simple road traffic accident case involving only vehicle damage the claimant's form of claim indicates that the defendant was to blame. The defendant simply files at court a brief statement saying, 'This is not my problem because I passed on the details to the insurance company'. (This defence might not be as obstructive as it may appear, many laymen having no real idea of the legal consequences of insurance.) Accordingly, the judge might well strike out this defence as disclosing no basis to defend the claim.

10.3.4   Who exercises the court's powers?

The court's powers are exercised by a 'procedural judge', which is simply the name given to any judge exercising procedural functions. In most cases case management will be undertaken by a master in the High Court in London, or a district judge in the High Court outside London or in a county court. Exceptionally in heavyweight or complex cases, matters may be referred to a circuit judge or even a High Court judge for him to consider what direction should be given for how the case is to proceed. For example, a High Court judge might be asked to make an important procedural ruling on how one case, which is perhaps a test case for hundreds of other claimants, should proceed. In routine litigation, however, all these matters will fall to be decided by a district judge.

10.3.5 The schedules

While the CPR repeal and replace wholesale the previous rules which governed litigation in the High Court and county court, there are two lengthy schedules to the Rules as it was impractical in the time available to rewrite every single rule. Some of the previous rules therefore survive in these schedules. They will not be of great concern in mainstream litigation because many of them concern very specialist provisions which are of no general effect. One very significant exception is that part of the rules on enforcement of judgments remains subject to the previous rules and is still contained in the schedules to the CPR. The reason for this is that there has been a review of the law relating to enforcement of judgments and at this time it has been possible to bring only part of the changes made in consequence of that review into effect as new rules within the CPR. See **Chapter 34**.

10.3.6 Specialist lists

The text, and the rules on which we shall mainly be concentrating are those for routine civil litigation, particularly personal injury and contract and commercial cases. There are also specialist courts in England and Wales, which, because of the nature of the litigation conducted there, have developed their own procedures which, have been entirely different from that in the ordinary courts. The underlying law is of course the same so that, for example, the law of evidence is common across all courts, but practical and procedural features may be very different. The CPR specifically permit the 'specialist lists' to operate such variations of the procedures. This is, for example, applicable to:

(a) the Commercial Court (properly titled the 'Commercial list of the Queen's Bench Division');

(b) Mercantile Courts (which exist in a number of large provincial centres such as Birmingham, Manchester, Leeds and Bristol); and

(c) the Technology and Construction Court (which operates in London and a number of large provincial centres and, as its name indicates, deals particularly with disputes in the construction industry and other cases where technical expertise is required);

(d) the Administrative Court (formerly the Divisional Court of the Queen's Bench Division) where proceedings for judicial review are now governed by CPR, Part 54.

We shall now go on to describe the procedure to bring and defend a claim in the ordinary courts under the Civil Procedure Rules 1998.

10.4 Outline of a claim under the Civil Procedure Rules

Stage 1

The potential parties to a claim must be aware of their duties to cooperate and to explore settlement before the issue of litigation and to treat litigation as a last resort, rather than an inevitable step; they must observe the *pre-action protocols* in cases where there are such protocols; and ought to observe the spirit of the protocols where possible in other forms of litigation.

Stage 2

The claimant issues at court his claim form setting out his claim, supported by particulars of claim explaining his case in detail. The particulars of claim and claim form are verified by a 'statement of truth' signed by the claimant. Having been issued at court the claim is *served* on the defendant, accompanied by a 'Response Pack' provided by the court.

Stage 3

The defendant files at court his defence within 14 days of receiving the claimant's claim form and particulars of claim (which together are called his *statement of case*). If the defendant needs more time to respond, he can file an acknowledgement of service indicating that he intends to defend; he must then within 28 days of receiving the claim form file his defence at court and it will be served on the claimant.

Stage 4

The court will send out allocation questionnaires to each party which require certain information from them.

Stage 5

When the allocation questionnaires are both returned the district judge will review them and allocate the case. If they are not all returned or are inadequately completed, he may convene an allocation hearing at very short notice for the information to be given orally, and then allocate the case to a given track which will be either:

(a) small claims—for cases in general worth less than £5,000;

(b) fast track—for cases worth less than £15,000 where the trial may be anticipated to take less than a day; or

(c) multi-track—for cases which are larger, longer or more complex than those appropriate for fast track. There is no upper limit.

Whichever track he allocates to he will attempt to give comprehensive written directions telling the parties what to do and with what timetable, which they must abide by.

Stage 6

(a) *Small claims track*—There are various standard forms of directions depending on the type of case, e.g., holiday disappointment claims; road traffic accident claims; contract debt claims; landlord and tenant disputes. There are also standard directions which can be added to manually to accommodate the problems of any particular case. In essence the parties will be given a timetable for the various necessary steps and the case will then be given a hearing date, sufficiently far in the future to enable the parties to comply with the steps required of them.

(b) *Fast track*—Directions will be given on the fast track mainly for:

(i) disclosure of documents;

(ii) exchange of witness statements;

(iii) agreement and exchange of expert evidence on the principle that no oral expert evidence will be allowed at the trial.

In addition, on the fast track a hearing date will be fixed either to a specified date or within a 'window' of no more than three weeks, which will be no later than 30 weeks in the future. The trial will take place within that period. Well before the trial listing questionnaires will be sent out to the parties for them to confirm that the case is still live and has not been settled, and to give the court information, to assist it in listing the case, as to how long it will last (bearing in mind that if it is to last more than one court day, i.e., five hours, fast track trial may no longer be appropriate).

(c) *Multi-track*—Where the case is proceeding on the multi-track more comprehensive directions will be given. The court will acknowledge that it may be impossible to issue set directions in an appropriate form without consulting the parties and may list a 'case management conference', which the parties must attend with responsible representatives so that the court can hear more details about the case and decide how it is to proceed. Certain standard directions may be given to the parties to be carried out in advance of the case management conference to make this more fruitful. These may include provisions for disclosure of documents and exchange of expert evidence and even witness statements.

Stage 7—Trial

The respective cases on whatever track will come for trial. The trial judge has wide case management powers during the hearing including the right:

(a) to restrict evidence;

(b) to limit the length of submissions;

(c) to decide on what issues he wishes to hear evidence first; and

(d) to determine the general order of proceedings.

OVERVIEW OF CLAIM

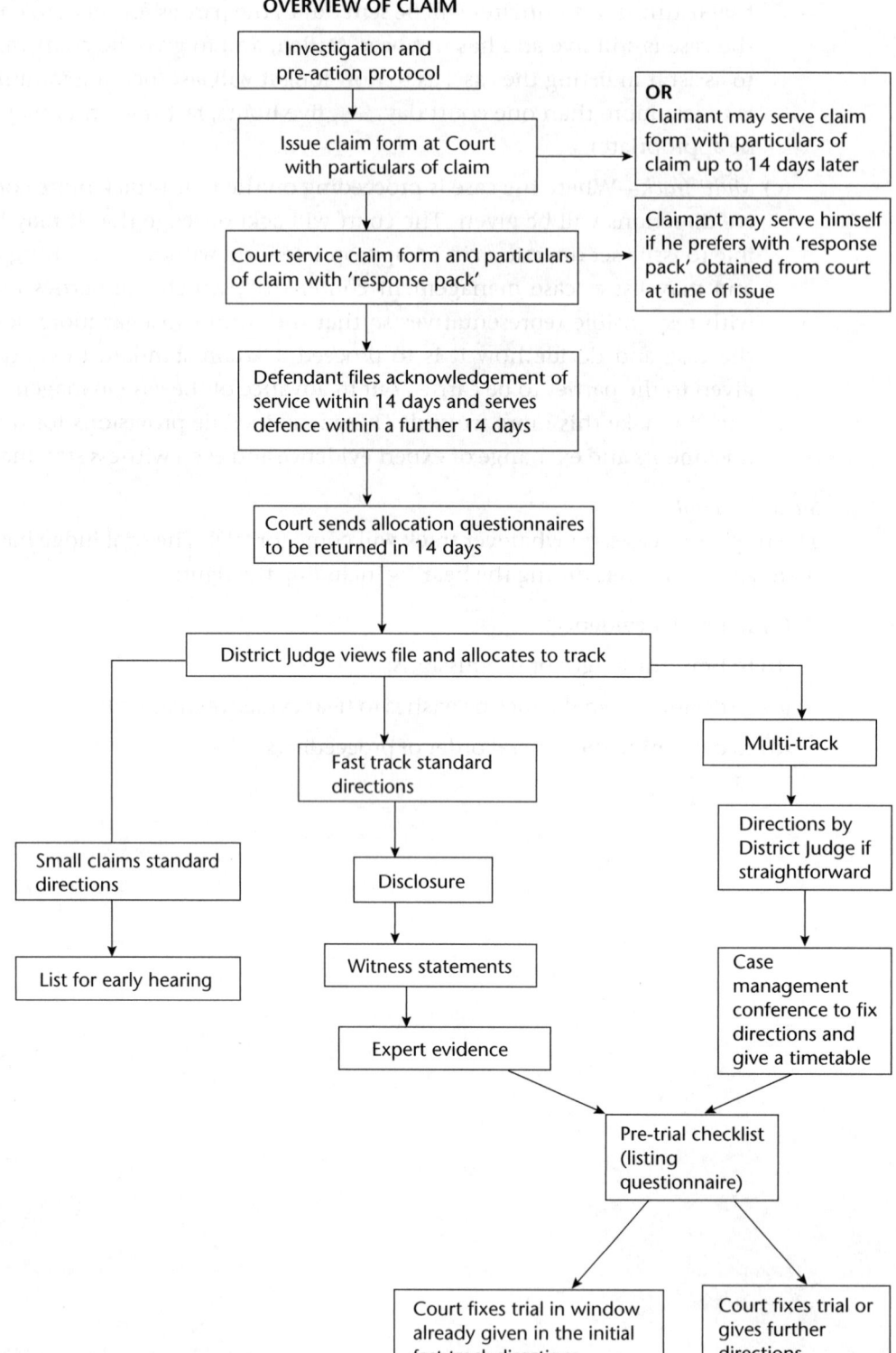

Commencing a claim

11.1 Joinder of parties and causes of action

11.1.1 Introduction

The court is concerned, in the furtherance of the overriding objective, with ensuring that all available parties and causes of action are before the court in the one set of proceedings so as to minimise costs and delay and to increase the efficiency of the litigation process. The statutory basis for this approach was set out 24 years ago in the Supreme Court Act 1981, s. 49(2), of which requires the court to exercise its discretion so as to ensure that:

> as far as possible, all matters in dispute between the parties are completely and finally determined, and all multiplicity of legal proceedings with respect to any of those matters is avoided.

The CPR absolutely reflect this viewpoint. Under r. 3.1(2)(g) and (h) the court has powers to *consolidate* proceedings and to try two or more claims on the same occasion.

11.1.2 Joinder of parties

In r. 7.3 it is provided that a single claim form may be used to start all claims which can conveniently be disposed of in the same proceedings and all parties jointly entitled to a remedy must be joined as joint claimants (r. 19.2). In r. 19.1(2) the court is empowered to add a party where it is desirable:

(a) to enable it to resolve all the matters in dispute in the proceedings; or

(b) to resolve a matter between an existing party and a proposed new party which is connected with an issue in the claim.

Likewise the court has the power to 'tidy up' proceedings under r. 19.1(3) by removing a party where it is not desirable for him to remain a party to the claim.

To take a common example: if one driver should leave the road and knock down several people standing in a bus queue all the potential claimants can combine together to issue just one claim form against the driver, because their actions arise out of the same facts. There is no *obligation* to do so and indeed in many cases it might be tactically or procedurally inconvenient. In that case each could issue a separate claim form.

Where there is more than one claimant on the same claim they must all use the same solicitor and counsel and may not generally make allegations of fact which are inconsistent with each other's cases. Thus, if some or all of the persons in the bus queue happened to know each other or be related, they might well combine to issue one form of claim. If, however, they were strangers, each might prefer to issue separate proceedings using his own choice of solicitor and counsel.

Similarly, if the cause of a motorway accident seems to be the negligence of two or more drivers, e.g., where there is a crash involving several vehicles in fog, and it may be impossible for an injured person initially to judge which of several other drivers may have been to blame, the claimant can (and would usually be wise to) sue all possible defendants in the same proceedings. If there is more than one *defendant*, each is entitled to his own individual choice of solicitor and counsel—there is no compulsion to use the same one as there is likely to be a conflict of interest in such cases as each defendant attempts to blame the others.

11.1.3   Joinder of causes of action

In terms of joinder of causes of action there is nothing to stop a claimant who has a number of causes of action against the same defendant or defendants suing for all of them in the same proceedings, even if there is no factual connection between them. For example, if a claimant is owed money by a defendant and in the course of discussions the argument becomes heated and the defendant assaults the claimant, there is nothing to stop the claimant including both causes of action on the same claim form. Whether it would be tactically wise to do so would be another matter, and indeed it might be in such a case that the court would think it convenient to dispose of the two issues by allocating them to different tracks so that they end up being dealt with separately, (see **13.2**), but the right to start proceedings in this way exists.

11.1.4   Joinder of issues by the defendant: Counter claim

If a defendant has one or more claims against a claimant, he may raise them in the same proceedings by way of a counterclaim under Part 20 of the CPR. This is known as a 'Part 20 claim'. The nature of his cause of action against the claimant need not in any way be factually related to the claimant's claim against him. Thus if, for example, the defendant allegedly owed the claimant a sum of money and after a meeting to discuss financial matters at the claimant's offices, the defendant tripped on frayed carpeting and fell down the stairs breaking his leg, he would be perfectly entitled to counterclaim for his injuries in any action brought by the claimant for the debt. Alternatively, he could issue separate proceedings of his own.

Part 20 claims are discussed separately in **Chapter 27**.

11.1.5   Consolidation

Under the court's case management powers, it has a power of its own initiative (or on the application of any party) to *consolidate* actions to save costs and time. It might do this where there are several claims by separate claimants arising out of the same incident, for example, a specific spoiled holiday or an accident which involved several victims. However, to return to the bus queue example, while it would be *convenient* to consolidate their actions, there is no mechanism by which the court will be informed of how many potential claimants there are, if they all have separate solicitors and propose to issue proceedings at their own time and pace (within the Limitation Act period), and indeed in courts at different ends of the country. Although one might think it would be very much in a defendant's interests to have all the cases consolidated to proceed together in the one court, that may not be the case. It often suits defendants to have claimants suing in separate proceedings and to use different tactics against each. Moreover, attractive though the prospect of consolidating the claims of say, 10 claimants might be, circumstances may vary between claimants with minor injuries, who wish to proceed on the small claims or fast track, and those with major injuries who wish to hold back their claims until detailed medical and other evidence has been collected and who may not even issue proceedings until relatively late in the limitation period. Subject to these sorts of problems, however, consolidation of actions will often be an attractive option for the court in applying the overriding objective and basic case management principles.

11.2 Bringing a claim

It is first necessary to explain the term 'statement of case'. By CPR, r. 2.3(1), 'statement of case' means a claim form, particulars of claim where these are not included in the claim form, defence, Part 20 claim, or reply to defence.

An action is commenced by a claim form in a prescribed form called N1 which is included at the end of this chapter. The following must be stated on the form:

(a) The *court* in which the claimant wishes to issue the claim. This may be either the county court of his choice, the High Court in London or a district registry. If it is the High Court, the division should be specified.

(b) The *parties*, namely claimant and defendant, and, if either is sued in a representative capacity (e.g., as personal representative of an estate), that fact must be stated. Full names must be given where possible.

(c) The *addresses* of all parties. If there is more than one defendant a separate claim form must be prepared for each, giving their name in the relevant box. On the assumption the claimant is employing a solicitor, the solicitor's office should be given as the address for service on page 1. The address must include postcode.

(d) There must then be brief *details of the claim* (CPR, r. 16.2(a)).

EXAMPLE 1

The claimant's claim is for damages for personal injury and loss caused by the defendant's negligence in a motor accident at London Road, Middlemarch on 5 September 2006.

EXAMPLE 2

The claimant's claim is for the sum of £12,531 being the amount outstanding on invoices delivered in respect of goods supplied to the defendant between March and May 2006.

Much fuller and more precise details of the allegations will be contained in the particulars of claim which will be issued and served usually at the same time as the claim form, although they may be served up to 14 days after the claim form is served.

(e) Each claim form must also specify the *remedy* which is sought. This must be contained within the brief details of claim, hence the references to damages and debt above in the examples; if an injunction is claimed that should also be set out. However, it is important to note that by virtue of r. 16.2(5) if one fails to specify a particular remedy on the claim form that does not prohibit a court from granting such a remedy if the claimant later establishes that he is entitled to it.

(f) *Statement of value.* If the claimant is claiming money, the claim form must contain a statement of its value (CPR, r. 16.2(1)(c)). The relevant provisions of Part 16 and Part 7 ought to be followed and in particular PD 7. The statement of value must specify:

(i)   the amount of money being claimed if it is an exact sum;

(ii) if a precise sum is not being claimed, as in damages for personal injury, the claimant should indicate the maximum that he seeks and it is also of help if he specifies the minimum he considers he is likely to get to assist the court in allocating to track. For example, one might specify that one expects to get 'damages between £5,000 and £15,000' so the court will know that this is potentially a fast track case; or damages 'exceeding £15,000, but not more than £50,000' which will be multi-track.

(iii) The claimant may say that he cannot state how much he expects to recover. This might well be the case, for example, where it is one of the rare cases tried by a civil jury as would be the case in a false imprisonment, defamation or a malicious prosecution claim.

A claimant must state whether the amount he expects to recover is more than £1,000 for pain and suffering in a personal injury case as even if the value of the claim as a whole is under £5,000 in such a case it cannot be allocated to the small claims track (see **17.2.2**). There is a similar provision in respect of housing disrepair claims which is also discussed at **17.2.2**.

11.3 High Court or county court?

This is still a matter of choice for the parties *except where a statute allocates proceedings exclusively to one or the other,* as is the case with most landlord and tenant matters, and claims under the Consumer Credit Act 1974, all of which are allocated to the county court only. If a claim is to be issued in the High Court the claim form must explain why it is being filed there and, to comply with the rules, must state:

(a) that the claimant expects to recover more than £15,000 (if he cannot state this, the case cannot be issued in the High Court);

(b) that some other enactment provides that the claim may be commenced only in the High Court, and name the enactment;

(c) if the claim is one for personal injury that the claimant expects to recover £50,000 or more (this being a quite independent limitation on the right to issue in the High Court in personal injury cases);

(d) that the claim needs to be in one of the specialist High Court lists, stating which list (e.g., the Commercial Court; the Admiralty list, etc.).

As noted earlier at paragraph 9.5.1 the county court has an unlimited jurisdiction. Accordingly, unless the case is very large indeed, or there are real complexities of law, or the case is a test case in some way, most solicitors will issue all personal injury cases, and most commercial cases in the county court. The only major class of exception to this is where the claimant wishes to issue his claim in one of the specialist High Court lists, such as that of the Commercial Court or Admiralty, as mentioned above. Even issuing a claim in the High Court is no guarantee that at some stage it will not be transferred to a county court; and even if it remains in the High Court it does not follow that a High Court Judge will be appointed to deal with the trial. The Lord Chancellor has power to elevate Circuit Judges to High Court status to conduct any trial he thinks within their capabilities and is increasingly willing to do so in cases which do not truly merit a High Court Judge.

11.3.1 Computation of values

Under CPR, r. 16.3(6), where a value has to be stated, the value should be stated honestly, although, given how early in the case the statement has to be prepared, a good deal of latitude is likely to be allowed so long as the value was given in good faith in the state of knowledge at the time. In personal injury cases in particular, there may be uncertainty for sometime about the extent of the claimant's injuries and how potential damages, especially a continuing loss of earnings claim, may be computed. The following matters must be *disregarded* in stating the value:

(a) interest;

(b) costs;

(c) any potential finding of contributory negligence which may reduce the value;

(d) any potential counterclaim or defence of set-off (see **Chapter 27**);

(e) any payments that the defendant may have to make in a personal injury case to the Compensation Recovery Unit out of the gross amount of damages due to the claimant.

11.3.2 Statement of truth

Under the CPR a claim form, or any other statement of case, must be verified by a statement of truth. This is a statement in the following terms:

I believe that the facts stated in this (*name of document*) are true.

It is undoubtedly preferable that this should be signed by the party in person. It is, however, possible for the legal representative of the party to make a statement of truth, in which case the wording is:

The claimant/defendant believes that the facts stated in this (*name of document*) are true.

It is important to note that if a statement of truth is made by a legal representative, it must be signed by a named individual whose name is clearly shown in print next to the signature. It must not be signed simply in the name of the solicitor's firm.

In the case of a company or other corporation the statement of truth must be signed by one of the senior personnel listed in PD 22, giving his or her position in the organisation (chairman, director, treasurer, etc.). If the claimant is a partnership, any of the partners may sign.

11.3.3 Consequences of making a statement of truth

Any person who makes a false statement in a document verified by a statement of truth, or who causes such a statement to be made without an honest belief in its truth, is guilty of contempt of court. It is for this reason that it is highly desirable that such statements be signed by the party in question. If a statement is signed by a legal adviser its contents and the consequences of signing it are deemed by virtue of the signature to have been explained to the party and the signature will be taken by the court as meaning that the party has authorised a representative to sign (PD 22, para. 3.8). A solicitor must therefore always ensure that he has received specific full instructions on the contents of documents signed by him.

11.3.4 Particulars of claim

In the majority of cases the claim form will be supplemented by a full form of *particulars of claim* which will usually be served together. If they are not, the claim form must contain a statement that particulars of claim will follow and they must be served within 14 days after service of the claim form. Particulars of claim must include:

(a) A *concise statement of the facts* on which the claimant relies. The word 'concise' should not be taken too literally and it is desirable that a clear indication of precisely what the case is about should be given. In fact increasingly there is quite a full narrative in the particulars of claim to the extent even of setting out matters of evidence. Although prolixity is to be deplored generally, giving a full picture at this stage may assist in the early resolution of the case.

Thus, for example, if the claim is in respect of an accident which caused personal injuries at the factory of the claimant's employers, the particulars of claim will set out details of the way in which the accident occurred, a series of allegations of the ways in which the defendant employers were in breach of proper health and safety procedures; a description of the injuries suffered by the claimant; and a description of the financial consequences flowing from the claimed injuries. These will generally be in the form of a schedule attached to the particulars of claim, which must be signed, with a statement of truth, though if they were very brief they might be set out in the body of the particulars of claim itself.

The particulars of claim will then go on to claim the appropriate relief, namely, damages.

If the case concerned a breach of contract, the particulars of claim would normally describe the terms of the contract and the way in which it came about; and then go on to explain what breach was claimed and indicating what loss it had caused the claimant. The particulars would then end with a formal claim to damages, either in a specified amount, if it were capable of quantification, or general damages.

(b) Details of any *interest* claimed including an explanation of whether it is claimed under some contract with particulars, or under a statute. If the claim is for a specified sum of money, the particulars of claim should state the percentage rate of interest claimed and give the computation of interest due as at the date of issue of proceedings together with the daily rate of interest accruing after that date.

(c) If either *aggravated or exemplary damages* are being claimed, a statement to that effect, together with the grounds on which they are claimed.

(d) If *provisional damages* are being claimed in a personal injury case, a statement to that effect, together with the grounds on which they are claimed.

(e) If the claim is to enforce a right to recover *possession of goods*, a statement showing the value of the goods.

(f) If the claim is based upon a *written agreement*, a copy of the contract or contractual documents must be attached to or served with the particulars of claim.

(g) If the claim is based upon an oral agreement or an agreement by conduct, full particulars of the words spoken or the conduct relied upon.

There are a number of other specific matters raised by Part 16 which must be dealt with if the case concerns them. These include:

(a) allegations of fraud;

(b) illegality;

(c) misrepresentation;

(d) breach of trust;

(e) notice or knowledge of the fact;

(f) details of unsoundness of mind or undue influence;

(g) wilful default;

(h) any facts relating to mitigation of loss or damage.

In addition, there are specialised requirements in a number of other claims for information which must be supplied. Reference to PD 16 should be made in such cases. The most important of these, however, relates to personal injury claims in which there are specific matters to be included in the particulars of claim or served with it. In particular:

(a) the claimant's date of birth;

(b) brief details of the personal injuries;

(c) a schedule of details of any past and future expenses and losses claimed;

(d) a report from a doctor about the injuries must be attached if the claimant is relying on a doctor's evidence;

(e) a statement claiming provisional damages (if applicable), together with a statement that there is a chance that in the future the claimant may develop some serious disease or deterioration and specify what that is.

11.3.5 Issue of the claimant's statement of case

The claim is issued by the claimant's solicitor or a member of his staff attending at the county court or District Registry with the appropriate forms and fee. Alternatively the claim can be issued by post. The relevant number of copies of the claim form must be produced and the court fee paid. Cheques are payable to Her Majesty's Court Service.

The court fee depends on the amount for which the claim is issued on a sliding scale from £30 for claims of up to £300, to £1,700 for claims of £300,000 or over. Those on low income or benefits may claim a fee exemption. When the claim is issued, the court seal is attached to the claim form, which indicates the date of issue. If the court is to serve the claim, it then posts it to the defendant at the address given for the defendant on the claim form, together with a 'response pack' of documents, which is discussed in chapter 12.

11.4 Issue, filing and service of proceedings and other documents

It is perhaps important to clarify technical terms in relation to what is done with documents in the course of proceedings.

(a) *Issue* indicates that something is taken to or sent to the court to be processed by the court usually on payment of a fee, whereupon the court will affix its seal on the form and will initiate the proceedings or some step in them.

(b) *Filing* is defined as 'delivering a document by post or otherwise to the court office', which indicates that the document then goes into the court file and will remain there as part of the official record of proceedings. Most important documents generated in the course of a claim have to be filed at court and eventually, when the case is prepared for trial before a judge, it will be up to the claimant to file at court (or 'lodge' to use an alternative term) a 'trial bundle' of the relevant documents. The judge will wish to read all the documents in advance of the case, including not merely the statements of case of each party, but all the witness statements, experts' reports and other documents disclosed between the parties during proceedings which it is thought important for the judge to see (including in some cases a great deal of correspondence between the parties and between their solicitors).

(c) *Service* indicates the process of bringing a document to the attention of the opposite party by delivering it to him personally, or by post or by some other approved method.

11.4.1   Service of documents

Service of any document which the court has issued or prepared (remembering that the court itself may generate documents on its own initiative) may be effected either by the court or the party who put in motion the stage of proceedings which led to the document being created. It is up to the party concerned initially to choose how a document is to be served. This applies not just to the claim form, but to application notices, court orders and other documents.

11.4.2   Service by the court

If a party wishes the court to serve a document, he must file an extra copy at the court which will then decide which method of service to use (CPR, r. 6.3(2)). This will usually be done by first-class post and the court will then notify the claimant that the claim form has been served, and what was the deemed date of service (in the case of first-class post, the second day after it was posted: CPR, r. 6.7). If for any reason the court has been unable to effect service, it will notify the party concerned indicating what method was attempted (e.g., if the letter was returned marked 'not known at this address'). Self-evidently the court will have sent out notice of deemed service by the time they receive the information that the document was not in fact served. Once the court has failed to effect service, it is up to the party concerned to try to effect service (PD 6, para. 8.2).

11.4.3   Service of claim form, etc. by a party

Many practitioners prefer to serve documents themselves for greater certainty. This is particularly the case where they think that the defendant is likely to be evasive or where absolute certainty of service is required for the proceedings, as is often the case in debt-collecting litigation. A party which intends to effect service itself must notify the court of that (CPR, r. 6.3(1)(b)). Where the claimant's solicitors effect service of the claim form they must file a certificate of service within seven days and give the date of service.

11.4.4   Methods of service

A number of methods of service are possible under the CPR r. 6.2.

11.4.4.1   Personal service

(a) *On an individual*

Personal service, involves giving it to him individually. If it is delivered by hand to him and he will not accept it, it is sufficient to leave it near him (e.g., at his feet) informing him what it is.

(b) *On a limited company* (see also **30.1.2**)

Personal service is achieved by leaving a document with a person holding a senior position (e.g., director, treasurer, secretary, chief executive, manager or other officer) within the company (CPR, r. 6.4(4)).

(c) *On a partnership* (see also **30.6.4**)

A document is served personally by leaving it with any one of the partners or with a person (who need not be a partner) having, at the time of service, management of the partnership business at the firm's principal place of business.

11.4.4.2   Postal service

This must be carried out by first-class post to an address which the claimant bona fide believes is that of the defendant or at which he is bound to receive the document. The defendant is then deemed to have received it on the second day after posting. It is the claimant's risk if he adopts any other address than the one where he bona fide believes the defendant to reside. (For example, if the defendant's address is actually unknown, but it is well known that he has a particular friend or relative at a certain address, posting the documents to him there will be successful if he acknowledges them and responds, but if he fails to do so it may be an onerous task for the claimant to satisfy the court that he really had them and it is certainly unlikely that the court will assume he had them from the second day after posting.)

If the person is served as the proprietor of a business (i.e., a sole trader) he may be served by post either at his usual or last known residence or at a place of business or last known place of business.

11.4.4.3   Service on a nominated solicitor

Service may be made at the office of a nominated solicitor and obviously postal service will suffice for this. It must be the case that the solicitor is properly appointed to accept service for the present proceedings. A party can not simply serve documents on a solicitor who happened to have previously represented the defendant, say on a conveyancing transaction. Specific authority is required for every case. Postal service on a solicitor will of course be the norm now in cases where the parties are observing the protocols or the spirit of the protocols because it is assumed that both will be legally represented from the outset.

Where a defendant nominates a solicitor for service of proceedings before proceedings are issued, the claimant must serve the proceedings on that solicitor and does not then have the option for serving the defendant direct.

11.4.4.4   Service via document exchange

There are detailed requirements in PD 6, paras 2 and 3.

Service via document exchange is permitted where the party's address for service or its headed notepaper includes a DX address, provided it has not already specifically indicated that it would not accept service by DX.

The document exchange is an alternative network for delivery purposes which is a cheap method of transmitting documents between businesses, including solicitors' firms and barristers' chambers.

11.4.4.5   Service by fax or other electronic method

Service by fax or e-mail may be effected only where the party or its legal representative has indicated in writing willingness to accept service by the method being used. It is best in practical terms also to send a hard copy of a document by post. The rules do not specifically require this, but where the other party claims not to have received the document by fax, e-mail or other electronic method, the court may take account of the fact that a hard copy was not sent. It should be noted that whereas fax may be used by and on an unrepresented party, service by e-mail or other electronic methods may only take place where both parties are legally represented and the document is served at the legal representative's address, and he has previously specifically expressed his willingness to accept service as indicated above. Merely indicating an e-mail address on notepaper will not suffice.

11.4.4.6   Service on limited companies

Under s. 725 of the Companies Act 1985 a company may be served at its registered office. The deemed date of service is two working days after posting by first-class post and four working days if by second-class post. Overseas companies having a place of business or a branch office in Great Britain must provide the Registrar of Companies with the names and addresses of persons resident in Great Britain authorised to accept service.

In addition to those statutory methods, the address for service of a company by virtue of CPR r. 6.5(6) is not its registered office, but either its principal office (i.e., its main place of business) or any place within the jurisdiction which has a real connection with the claim. So if one is embarking on litigation against, say, a large supermarket chain about an accident which occurred at a certain branch, the company may be served either at its registered office, its principal office, or at the location where the accident occurred.

11.4.4.7   Service of documents other than the claim form and particulars of claim

There are obvious reasons why there are likely to be more difficulties and technicalities attached to service of the document which initiates proceedings. An evasive defendant may seek to defeat proceedings entirely by making himself scarce so that the forms cannot be delivered to him by any of the approved methods. Once a claim has started, however, and has been validly served then most of the technicalities of service no longer matter. When responding to the claim form, the defendant is required to give an address for service. If he is going to be legally represented, from that point on everything for him can be posted to his solicitor or faxed, if appropriate. If he is not going to be represented, then he is bound by whatever address for service he has given in his response to the claim form. If he declines to respond to the claim form then in principle there will be no need to serve any other documents on him and the matter will proceed to a judgment in default and assessment of damages and the next time he will be involved is when the claimant goes about enforcing whatever judgment has been obtained.

Service of documents on the claimant will provide no difficulties because he must give an address for service, which will be his solicitors' if he is legally represented, on the claim form.

Usually, after the commencement of proceedings documents in the case will simply be exchanged between the solicitors. In the case of non-urgent documents they may very well have recourse to DX.

11.4.4.8 Contractual provision for service of claim form

Where there is a contract between the parties it may well provide for how documents are to be served between them in the event of disputes and give addresses. This is not uncommon particularly in the construction industry where huge companies may be involved and it will be inconvenient to have documents, which have a short time limit for response, sent simply to the company's head office. There may be a specific provision inserted that it be served by post to a nominated individual in some department of the company which deals with contractual disputes or with the contract in question such as on-site management, in the case of a buiding company.

The rules on method of service and details to be certified and the deemed date of service are in CPR, rr. 6.7 and 6.10, which provide:

6.7   Deemed service

(1) A document which is served in accordance with these rules or any relevant practice direction shall be deemed to be served on the day shown in the following table.

Method of service	Deemed day of service
First class post	The second day after it was posted.
Document exchange	The second day after it was left at the document exchange.
Delivering the document to or leaving it at a permitted address	The day after it was delivered to or left at the permitted address.
Fax	• If it is transmitted on a business day before 4 pm, on that day; or • In any other case, on the business day after the day on which it is transmitted.
Other electronic method	The second day after the day on which it is transmitted.

(2) If a document (other than a claim form) is served after 5 p.m. on a business day, or at any time on a Saturday, Sunday or a bank holiday, the document shall be treated as having been served on the next business day.

(3) In this rule—

'business day' means any day except Saturday, Sunday or a bank holiday;

And

'bank holiday' includes Christmas Day and Good Friday.

6.10   Certificate of service

Where a rule, practice direction or court order requires a certificate of service, the certificate must state—

(a) that the document has not been returned undelivered; and

(b) the details set out in the following table—

Method of service	Details to be certified
Post	Date of posting
Personal	Date of personal service
Document exchange	Date of delivery to the document exchange
Delivery of document to or leaving it at a permitted place	Date when the document was delivered to or left at the permitted place
Fax	Date and time of transmission
Other electronic means	Date of transmission and the means used
Alternative method permitted by the court	As required by the court

11.5 The time for service of a claim form

The general rule is that a claim form must be served within four months of the *date of issue*. This is the date of the court's seal which is also the relevant date for determining whether it has been issued within the limitation period. If the claim form is to be served out of the jurisdiction, then the period for service is six months.

In the spirit of making speedy progress and conducting litigation efficiently, it might be thought that four or six months is plenty of time in which to serve a claim and that one would not have issued proceedings if one did not intend to get on with the claim promptly. Sometimes, however, the claim form is not served promptly. There may be good reasons—such as that the defendant is proving evasive and cannot be found, or because negotiations have suddenly reached a peak of activity and it might be possible to settle the case without proceedings being progressed; or it may be due to sloppiness.

The court has the power to extend the four or six months for service, but if this is not done, the claim form's validity lapses at the expiry date. If the case is still within the limitation period, that causes no particular difficulty, although the court fee on issue will be lost. One can simply reissue proceedings in the same form. If, however, the four or six months also span the end of the limitation period so that the claim is now out of time, then in principle the claimant has lost his opportunity to bring his case and will presumably turn his attention to pursuing his solicitors under their negligence insurance.

If the claim form cannot be served in time then an application to extend the period should be made while the claim form is still valid; if the time has already expired the court may still extend the time for service, but may only do so by virtue of CPR, r. 7.6(3), if:

(a) the court has been unable to serve the claim form;

(b) the claimant has taken all reasonable steps to serve the claim form, but has been unable to do so; or

(c) in either case the claimant has acted promptly in making the application.

An application for an order to extend the time of service must be supported by evidence. It may be made without notice to the potential defendant (indeed this will usually be the case because the defendant has not yet been served with the claim form and is not yet involved).

Generally speaking the courts require a very high standard of diligence to be shown before they will extend the 'life' of a claim form. The court will want to be shown that the proper efforts have been made to locate and serve the defendant early in the life of the claim form and that the claimant's solicitors have not left things until late in the four months before finding themselves in difficulties. Generally speaking, extension will only be allowed where the defendant is proving evasive, despite all reasonable efforts to trace him being shown.

There have now been many authorities on this point. See, for example, *Vinos* v *Marks and Spencer plc* (2000) *Independent,* 17 July 2000 and *Smith* v *Probyn* (2000) *The Times,* 29 March 2000. It will therefore be important for someone applying to extend the period to demonstrate by written evidence, with a chronology attached, just what has been done where, when and how to attempt to serve the claim form promptly after its issue.

A copy of the claim form appears on the next two pages. An example of a claimant's statement of case which would accompany or be served subsequently appears at the end of **Chapter 12** in sequence with a copy defence arising out of the same case.

Claim Form

In the	

		for court use only
Claim No.		
Issue date		

Claimant

SEAL

Defendant(s)

Brief details of claim

Value

Defendant's name and address			£	
		Amount claimed	
		Court fee	
		Solicitor's costs	
		Total amount	

The court office at

is open between 10 am and 4 pm Monday to Friday. When corresponding with the court, please address forms or letters to the Court Manager and quote the claim number.

N1 Claim form (CPR Part 7) (01.02)   *Printed on behalf of The Court Service*

	Claim No.	

Does, or will, your claim include any issues under the Human Rights Act 1998? ☐ Yes ☐ No

Particulars of Claim (attached)(to follow)

Statement of Truth
*(I believe)(The Claimant believes) that the facts stated in these particulars of claim are true.
* I am duly authorised by the claimant to sign this statement

Full name _____

Name of claimant's solicitor's firm _____

signed _____ position or office held_____
*(Claimant)(Litigation friend)(Claimant's solicitor)   (if signing on behalf of firm or company)

*delete as appropriate

Claimant's or claimant's solicitor's address to which documents or payments should be sent if different from overleaf including (if appropriate) details of DX, fax or e-mail.

Defending the claim; statements of case

12.1 Introduction

Once the claim form and particulars of claim (that is, the claimant's 'statement of case') have been conveyed by one or other of the approved methods to the defendant, he has to respond. If he wishes to defend all or part of the claim he must file a 'defence', and if he does not do so default judgment will be given on application by the claimant (see **Chapter 26**). A copy of the defence filed must be served on every other party at the address for service given in the claim form.

When the claim form is issued by the court, the copy for service on the defendant is accompanied by a 'response pack' which is a series of forms known as N9 which are illustrated at the end of this chapter. This pack contains an acknowledgement of service form, together with forms (and explanatory notes as to how to complete them) which indicate how the defendant should respond depending on which option he chooses to adopt, as between admitting the claim, partially admitting the claim and defending and/or counterclaiming. The question of admissions and partial admissions, and the course which the case will take if the claim or any part of it is admitted, is discussed at **26.5**.

The forms illustrated are those appropriate for a case for unspecified amounts of monies such as a claim for damages in tort. A slightly different set of forms is sent out in the case of claims for a specified amount of money, such as a debt.

In practice, if the defendant has solicitors they will use the acknowledgement of service form from the 'response pack'. If the defendant proposes to admit all or part of the claim he may also use those forms, although they would usually be accompanied by an attempt to negotiate direct with the claimant's solicitors without involving the court. If, however, a defendant intends to defend, the solicitors will generally discard the form and prepare a full defence on ordinary plain paper.

12.2 Timescale for filing a defence

Generally speaking, a defence must be filed within 14 days of service of the particulars of claim. The particulars of claim normally accompany the claim form, but may be served up to 14 days later. If the claim form does not include the particulars of claim in its body and no particulars of claim are served, the claim will be so defective that it is likely to be referred by the court staff to a district judge to consider striking it out on the court's own initiative.

Alternatively, if no particulars of claim at all are forthcoming, the defendant should write to the claimant seeking them and, if there is no response within a reasonable time, may apply to the court to strike out the claim.

As was noted above, the defendant has the option of filling in an acknowledgement of service giving notice of his intention to defend the case, instead of immediately serving a full defence. Where he does this his time for filing the defence is extended to 28 days after service of the particulars of claim (r. 15.4(1)(b)).

In addition to this a defendant can obtain the claimant's agreement to a further extension (see **12.2.1**).

Different provisions apply where the claim form is served out of the jurisdiction; moreover, if the claim form is served on the agent of a principal who is out of the jurisdiction, the court will state what the period for responding is (r. 6.16(4)).

12.2.1   No response from the defendant

If the defendant does not file an acknowledgement of service, or if having done so he does not then file a defence within the appropriate time, the claimant may proceed to obtain a default judgment from the court. This will bring the case to an end either wholly or in part. The procedure is dealt with in CPR, Part 12. See **Chapter 26**.

The claimant may agree to give the defendant a further period of extension for filing a defence, which can be up to a further 28 days. The defendant must notify the court of this in writing (r. 15.5(2)). In principle, this is the maximum extension which may be granted.

If no defence is filed and at least six months have expired since the end of the period for filing a defence, and no defendant has served or filed a defence and the claimant has not entered or applied for default judgment under CPR, Part 12, or summary judgment under Part 24, the court will *stay* the claim. This means that no further steps are permitted to be taken on it, although the court may permit the stay to be lifted on application by either party explaining the reason for the delay.

12.3   The contents of the defence

This is dealt with by CPR, r. 16.5. In his defence the defendant must state:

(a) which of the allegations in the particulars of claim he *denies*;

(b) which allegations he is unable to admit or deny, but which he *requires* the *claimant to prove*; and

(c) which allegations he *admits*.

If he denies any allegation he must state his reasons for doing so and if he intends to put forward a different version of events from that given by the claimant, he must state his own version. If he fails to deal with an allegation, he is taken to admit that allegation. This is subject to a certain amount of latitude in two instances, by r. 16.5(3), where a defendant fails to deal with an allegation but:

(a) if he has set out in his defence the nature of his case and it is different to the allegation then he is taken to require the allegation to be proved; and

(b) if the claim includes a money claim, the claimant is required to prove the amount of money claimed unless there is an express admission.

We shall now consider these matters in somewhat more depth.

The defence is a response to the allegations in the particulars of claim and in principle should deal with each one of them. It must deal with them in one of three ways:

(a) If an allegation is *admitted* the claimant is relieved of the burden of proving the matter at trial and it is taken to be established. If in a personal injury case he is prepared to agree that an accident happened (which is usually set out as paragraph 1 of the particulars of claim) the defendant would probably admit that this was so even though going on to deny the claimant's subsequent allegations that the cause was the defendant's negligence.

(b) He may *deny* an allegation. This normally implies that he will put up a positive case to the contrary. Under r. 16.5(2) if a defendant does deny an allegation he must state his reason for doing so. If he intends to put forward a different version of events he must state his version. If by any chance a defendant fails specifically to answer an allegation, so long as he sets up some opposite case somewhere in his defence, he is taken to deny it.

(c) The defendant may say that he is *unable to admit or deny* a given allegation, but requires the claimant to prove it.

This is different from denying. One example is where it is alleged in the particulars of claim that the claimant has suffered certain injuries and has been caused a substantial loss of earnings because of them. Whilst there may by this stage be sufficient medical evidence for the defendant to admit that the injuries were caused in the accident (while perhaps denying responsibility for the accident at all), he would probably be rash to admit the full claim for loss of earnings because he is unlikely yet to have had the opportunity to investigate it properly. He will therefore require the claimant formally to prove these matters by proper evidence at trial.

12.4 Specific matters relevant to the defence

Statement of value
The claim form is required to contain a statement of value, which will be of assistance at certain stages, in particular, on allocation. If the defendant states that he disputes this valuation of the claim (even on the assumption that liability could be estab-lished), he must say why and give his own statement of value. Thus if, say, the claimant claimed damages which were to be 'more than £15,000 but less than £100,000' (the object of which would be to attempt to persuade the court to put the matter into the multi-track) and the defendant considered this highly exaggerated, it would be open to him to say that he disputed the statement of value and that he considered that even on full liability the claimant's claim was worth less than £15,000.

Representative capacity
If the defendant is defending in a representative capacity (e.g., as executor of an estate) he must state that fact.

Personal injury claims
If a defendant in a personal injury claim has received a copy of the medical report with the particulars of claim, he should state specifically whether he agrees with it or disputes it, in which case he should give his reasons for doing so (PD 16, para. 14.1(2)) and

if he has already obtained his own medical report, it should be attached to his defence.

If he is not in a position to do either because he has no knowledge of the matter then he should state that. In such a case, clearly he will also want to have intimated to the claimant direct if he wishes to raise questions to the claimant's expert; or agree facilities to instruct his own; or to apply to the court for directions about appointment of experts.

Obviously a defendant will be in difficulties disputing the claimant's medical report unless he has already obtained his own evidence. However, there may be an issue as to why there has not been compliance with the pre-action protocols and an attempt to agree the appointment of an expert at the start. If the claimant has gone ahead without attempting to comply with the protocols, then an early application by the defendant to the court can be expected to disallow the claimant's medical evidence and to invite the court's assistance in the selection of an expert for joint instruction.

Schedule of expenses

If the claimant has attached a schedule of past and future expenses, the defence must attach a counter-schedule stating which items are agreed or which are disputed and why. If individual items can neither be agreed nor disputed because the defendant lacks the knowledge at this stage, then that statement should appear. If the defendant is in a position to contend for specific alternative figures, they should also be given.

If it is too early in the case for the defendant to have formed his own view as to the appropriate figures, then it is likely that one of the directions to be given subsequently will involve him doing so.

Limitation Act defence

A defendant who relies on the expiry of any limitation period must give in his defence details of the date on which it is alleged that the relevant period expired (PD 16, para. 16.1).

Set-off

If a defendant wishes to rely wholly or in part on the defence of set-off, he may include this in the defence (see **27.2.2**).

Date of birth

The defendant is now also (From 6 April 2006) required to notify the court of his date of birth. This is to make enforcement of any judgment more efficient if the claimant wins.

Statement of truth

The defendant is required to verify his defence by a statement of truth signed by himself (preferably) or by his solicitor in the terms 'I believe/the defendant believes that the facts stated in the defence are true'.

12.4.1   What happens next?

Upon filing and service of the defence the court will send out *allocation questionnaires* to the parties which have to be returned within 14 days so that the file can then be put before a district judge for him to consider allocation to track and case management directions.

12.5   Reply

Normally the filing of defence will be the last of the 'statements of case'. However, it is possible for the claimant to file a further document in response to the defence (and in some few instances it is in fact necessary to do so, for example, in defamation cases where a defence of qualified privilege has been raised, the claimant will need to serve a reply claiming malice, if that is what he contends).

Generally, however, a reply is not required and r. 16.7(1) specifically says that:

> A claimant who does not file a reply to the defence shall not be taken to admit the matters raised in the defence.

In the interests of establishing the matters in dispute, however, it may sometimes be appropriate for a claimant to file a reply. There is potentially also a costs penalty to consider when filing a reply because by r. 16.7(2) a claimant who files a reply to a defence, but fails to deal with any matter raised in the defence, shall be taken to require that matter to be proved. If at trial the court concludes that something should have been formally conceded in the reply so that time has been wasted in the defendant having to prove it, there will be costs consequences.

It is now necessary to deal briefly with two further matters relevant to statements of case, namely, amendment and requests for further information.

12.6 Amendment of statement of case

This is dealt with by Part 17 (and Part 19) of the CPR.

It might be imagined that by the time negotiations had broken down and a party was ready to serve a claim form, that party would have a fairly comprehensive factual picture of how he says the incident in question arose, his cause of action and the facts necessary to plead in support of it. Certainly it might be imagined that a party would know who his opponents should be! In a surprising number of cases, however, vital information may come to light only after (and sometimes well after) a claim form has been issued. It is now necessary to consider the topic of amendment.

The rules are as follows. Under r. 17.1 a party may amend his statement of case at any time *before* it has been served on any other party, but if his statement of case has been served, a party may amend it only with:

(a) the written consent of all other parties; or

(b) the permission of the court.

We shall first discuss amendment in general and then the particular rules relevant to amendment as to *parties*.

It will be remembered that *statements of case*, that is, the claim form, particulars of claim, defence and reply are verified by a statement of truth and it is important for a party to state honestly what he believes the facts to be and not to indulge in what used to be called 'the sporting theory of justice'. Previously, a party could allege any number of alternative and even inconsistent versions of the same facts, proceeding at trial only on those he chose then to adopt. Because a claimant or defendant will have had to state that he honestly believes the facts in his statement of case to be true, it will now often be difficult for him to later state that a different version is true without causing embarrassment at trial and opening himself up to obvious cross-examination on inconsistencies. However, it may be that he is not changing or abandoning anything said in his statement of case, but is simply inserting new material based on recently acquired knowledge. The first version of a document that has a statement of truth attached to it is of course important, but if new facts do come to light which may not only entitle, but actually oblige a party to change his statement, then he should not hesitate to do so. So long as the original version was given honestly in the state of knowledge he had at the time, there should not be any great difficulty.

12.6.1 Method of application

If the opponent's consent to the amendment cannot be obtained, then the applicant should file at court:

(a) an application notice; and

(b) a copy of the statement of case showing the proposed amendments.

There will then be a hearing and if permission to amend is given, the applicant should within 14 days of the date of the order or such other period as the court may direct, file with the court the amended statement of case re-verified by a statement of truth. An amended statement of case and the court copy of it should be endorsed as indicated in PD 17, e.g., headed:

'Amended Particulars of Claim . . . by order of District Judge Fox dated 14 November 2005 . . .'

If the court's permission was not required, e.g., because of consent of the parties, the heading should be:

'Amended Particulars of Claim under CPR, r. 17.1(2)(a).'

The practicalities of amendment require the party amending to retype the statement of case. Generally speaking, if the amendment is simply to delete something which was in the original statement of case and to put in new material, the retyped statement of case should not show the original text, but if the court thinks it desirable both for the original text and the amendment to be shown, the court may direct that the original text remain. This might be necessary because the court thinks it important for the trial judge to see the change of allegation or what was abandoned. Where that happens, in order to make the document comprehensible, the court will direct that the amendments should be shown in a different coloured ink or by use of a numerical code. The order of colours to be used for successive amendments should there be more than one (although this would now be extremely unusual) is red; green; violet; yellow. Any text which is to be deleted should be struck through in the relevant colour in a way that leaves it legible, and any text replacing it should be inserted or underlined in the same colour.

12.6.2 Amendment as to parties

As indicated in the introduction to **12.6** one really might think that by the time one gets round to issuing a claim form one would have ascertained who one's opponent was. The circumstances where there might be difficulties and this might not apply, however, include cases where a pedestrian has sued one particular motorist and the defendant's defence is that he struck the pedestrian in the course of taking avoiding action because of a car negligently driven by some other person. The claimant in that case might well find it prudent to bring in the other driver to the proceedings as an alternative defendant.

Similarly a feature quite commonly encountered in employment cases, especially in the building industry, is that accidents may be caused or contributed to by a variety of people. Indeed in the building industry a remarkable number of claimants seem not to be entirely sure who their employers are or even if they are self-employed at any given time. In such cases it may not be until quite late in the proceedings that facts emerge to show that the person truly responsible, say, for a building site accident was not the subcontractor from whom the claimant believed he was receiving instructions on what to do, but the head contractor or some other subcontractor on site. Similarly, when one has investigated the true employment position it may be that one needs to add further allegations as well as adding further parties.

In cases where there is a change of parties, Part 17 is supplemented by Part 19. Under Part 19 the court is given wide powers to order a person to be added as a new party if:

(a) it is desirable to add the new party so that the court can resolve all the matters in dispute in the proceedings; or

(b) there is an issue involving the new party and an existing party which is connected to the matters in dispute in the proceedings and it is desirable to add the new party so that the court can resolve that issue.

In addition, the court may order any person to cease to be a party if it is not desirable for that person to be a party to the proceedings.

Further, the court may order a new party to be substituted for an existing one (rather than simply being added as an extra) if:

(a) the existing party's interest or liability has passed to the new party; and

(b) it is desirable to substitute the new party so that the court can resolve the matters in dispute in the proceedings.

These provisions are set out in CPR, r. 19.1. They clearly give the court very wide powers to ensure that all the correct parties are before it so that justice can be done. If the court takes the initiative it will direct how matters are to proceed. If an application is made for permission to remove, add or substitute a party, that may be made either by an existing party or by the person who wishes to become a party. A very common example is where a claim is being brought against an uninsured driver and notice is given to the Motor Insurers' Bureau. The Bureau will usually seek to be added as a party to enable them to be represented in the proceedings and contest the claim since it is likely that the uninsured driver will take little action in the proceedings.

Any application for removal, addition or substitution must be served on all parties to the proceedings and any other person affected by the order. It is important to note that nobody may be added or substituted as a *claimant* unless his written consent is filed at court. While it may be open to the claimant to drag in extra *defendants* to ensure that justice can be done, nobody can be compelled to become a claimant who is unwilling to participate.

Once a new party is added, the court will give further directions as to filing and serving the claim form on any new defendant, serving other relevant documents, and the management of the proceedings.

12.6.3   Adding new parties after the end of a relevant limitation period

This is one of the most difficult problems in civil procedure. It may well come about (as in the building site case referred to above) where a claimant, having instructed solicitors late in the day who have done their best to investigate the claim under the protocol and get proceedings issued in time, find well after the three-year limitation period has expired that some other party should be added to the proceedings as a potential defendant. The interrelationship between CPR, r. 19.4, and s. 35 of the Limitation Act 1980 is a very difficult one. In personal injury cases, matters may be less difficult because of the court's general power to disapply the Limitation Act period under s. 33 of the 1980 Act. In contract cases, however, where there is no such general power, great difficulty is caused in the interpretation of these provisions. A detailed discussion of this subject is beyond the scope of this text.

12.6.4 The court's approach to amendment generally

The court's approach to amendment generally is subject to the general principles in the CPR. No particular principles, tests or criteria are set out under Part 17 for allowing amendments and therefore regard must be had primarily to the overriding objective in Part 1 and the court's case management powers in Part 3. Thus, for example, a late amendment which might cause delay or postponement of a trial, perhaps because it introduced new material in respect of which further disclosure and witness statements would be required, would be unlikely to be permitted. Having regard to the interests of justice, however, the court should be cautious before it debars a party from being heard on an important matter by virtue of a failure to set it out fully in a statement of case. The importance of Article 6 of the European Convention on Human Rights, which guarantees the right to a fair trial, must also be considered. This topic is more particularly dealt with in **Chapter 37**.

It will also be borne in mind that because a statement of case must be verified by a statement of truth, a party who wishes to amend by deleting one version and inserting another entirely different one, as opposed to merely introducing new material, would clearly have some explaining to do in the application and be subject to cross-examination as to credibility at trial.

12.7   Requests for further information: Part 18

When one receives a statement of case from one's opponent there should be enough in it to make clear what case a party has to meet. It may, however, sometimes be the position that a party receiving a statement of case needs more information about it in order for him to decide how to respond, or how to progress his case generally. There is a very general provision in Part 18 of the CPR which permits a party to seek further information or clarification.

It should first be noted that Part 18 is very brief and provides essentially that under r. 18.1(1) the court may at any time order a party:

(a) to clarify any matter which is in dispute in the proceedings; or

(b) to give additional information in relation to any such matter, whether or not the matter is contained or referred to in a statement of case.

Where the court makes an order, the party against whom it is made must file his response and serve it on the other parties within the time stipulated in the order and the response must be verified by a statement of truth.

It is important to note the scope of this provision. Although we are presently discussing it in the context of a statement of case, there is nothing to stop it being used about any other matter which arises. The procedure can be used to seek further information or clarification, for example, about witness statements or experts' reports.

12.7.1 The procedure

The procedure for requesting further information in relation to a statement of case is set out in the Practice Direction to Part 18, which provides the following:

Preliminary request

There must be a preliminary request for clarification or information made in written form between the parties. It should ask for the information by a certain date which must be a reasonable time in the future. The request should be concise and strictly confined to matters which are reasonably necessary and proportionate to enable the party requesting the information to prepare his own case or understand the case he has to meet. Such a request must be in a single comprehensive document and not piecemeal (e.g., not dotted around in a series of different letters).

Ideally, the request should be made in a separate, formal document and not a letter unless the request is a simple one.

Format of the request

By PD 18, para. 1.5, the request must:

(a) be headed with the name of court and the title and number of the claim;

(b) state that it is a request under Part 18 and state the date on which it is made;

(c) set out in a separate numbered paragraph each request for information or clarification;

(d) if the request relates to a document, specify the paragraph or words to which it relates;

(e) state the date by which the first party expects a response to the request.

Responding to a request

If the other party agrees to respond, then the response should be formally set out with the name of court, title and number of claim and identify itself as a response. It should then go on to repeat the texts of each separate paragraph of the request and under it (or along-side it if it is set out in 'half page' format which will often be convenient) should set out the response. The response should be verified by a statement of truth.

If the party from whom further clarification or information was sought has refused to give it, or has given it in an unsatisfactory form, the first party may apply to the court by application notice, setting out what it is he seeks and attaching to it the text of the order sought. There will then be a hearing before the court, at which the court will have to consider the request and any objections to it. In general, the party from whom the information is sought may rely on one of four principal grounds for objection, namely that:

(a) the request for information or clarification is unnecessary, irrelevant or improper;

(b) he is unable to provide the information or clarification;

(c) insufficient time has been given to him to formulate his response;

(d) the request can only be complied with at an expense which is disproportionate to the claim.

Where any of these responses is put forward, the court will have to consider the appropriateness of the request and whether it is necessary to compel the party concerned to respond as originally requested or whether the request is inappropriate in the light of the overriding objective.

EXAMPLE

An example of a request and response would be as follows:

REQUEST
Of paragraph 3 of the claimant's particulars of claim and the allegation that the defendants operated an unsafe system of work, state in detail each and every fact relied on in support of that allegation.

CLAIMANT'S RESPONSE
The claimant will contend that the defendants operated an unsafe system of work in the following respects:

(a) By failing to ensure that all relevant employees had proper training in the use of the model X123 mechanical hoist operated by the defendants at their premises.

(b) By continuing to employ one Calum Thomas, notwithstanding that the said Calum Thomas had been involved in previous incidents of horseplay on the equipment, as a result of which other employees had narrowly escaped injury in the months of June and August immediately preceding the incident giving rise to this cause of action.

(c) By failing to supply the workforce with steel cap industrial boots.

(d) By failing to ensure that there were sufficient employees on duty in the workshop so as to ensure that the lifting processes could be carried out properly. The makers' specification for the said X123 hoist recommends that no fewer than four employees be engaged in its operation, but at the relevant time the defendants employed only three persons in the said workshop.

(e) Given that the three workmen in the workshop at the time of the incident giving rise to this cause of action were respectively aged 17, 18 and 19, failing to ensure that the said workers were supervised by a more senior employee.

I believe that the contents of the response to this request for further information are true.

Peter Brown

Peter Brown, Claimant

12.7.2 Conclusion

It has been appropriate to consider all these aspects of statements of case here. Some of the matters mentioned, however, if they arise at all, will arise after the court has begun to consider case management which normally will commence when the defendant, or the first of the defendants if there are more than one, has filed and served his defence and the parties have responded to allocation questionnaires.

12.8 Example of a personal injury claim

We shall now briefly consider the statements of case of a claimant and a defendant in a substantial personal injury claim. Statements of case are set out below, together with a commentary on the nature and effect of what is alleged by each party.

IN THE MIDDLEMARCH COUNTY COURT   Case No:—MM 060131

BETWEEN   Mary Ann Evans   <u>Claimant</u>

and

George Eliot   <u>Defendant</u>

Particulars of Claim

---

1. On 3 January 2006 the Claimant was a passenger in the Defendant's motor car registration number C418 AND which was being driven by the Defendant along Stoney Road, Middlemarch when the said car left the road and collided with a concrete bus stop post.

2. The collision was caused by the negligence of the Defendant.

Particulars of Negligence

The Defendant was negligent in that he

    (a) drove too fast

    (b) failed to keep any, or any adequate lookout

    (c) drove the car, or allowed the same to travel off the carriageway of the road on to the pavement adjacent thereto and into collision with the bus stop

    (d) drove when his ability to do so was impaired by the consumption of alcohol

    (e) failed to slow down, brake, steer or otherwise manoeuvre his car so as to avoid the collision which by the exercise of proper driving skill and care he could have avoided.

3. The Claimafnt will rely on the happening of the accident as evidence in itself of the negligence of the Defendant.

4. The Claimant will rely on the conviction of the Defendant at Middlemarch Magistrates' Court on 16 May 2006 on a charge of driving a motor vehicle while having a concentration of alcohol in the blood in excess of the prescribed limit as relevant to the issue of negligence.

5. By reason of the accident the Claimant whose date of birth is 3rd September 1955 sustained pain and injury loss and damage.

Particulars of Injury

The Claimant sustained a closed fracture of the midshaft of the left humerus and a compound fracture of the left forearm with considerable damage to the soft tissue. The left forearm developed gas gangrene necessitating amputation at the level of the elbow and subsequently at five inches above the elbow joint. She also sustained facial laceration and crushing of the upper lip, the loss of two teeth and injury to the right eye. Full particulars are set out in the medical reports respectively of Mr Charles Ramadhin dated 7 May 2006; and Dr John Valentine dated 13 May 2006 served herewith.

By reason of the personal injuries the Claimant has suffered pain, discomfort and severe nervous shock, and has been considerably disabled by the amputation. She works as a freelance engineering systems designer and is considerably handicapped in such work despite the fitting of a prosthesis. She will be unable to cope with site visits and in office work has great difficulty in coping with the management of instruments. Although she regularly worked up to 60 hours a week before the date of the said collision she is now able to manage only 30 hours. Her chances of advancement in her profession have been severely curtailed. She may be unable to fulfil contracts and thus may cease to be able to work on a freelance basis. She has been seriously disabled in the labour market and will always be at risk in this respect. A schedule of past and future losses is attached.

6. In respect of damages awarded to her the Claimant is entitled to interest pursuant to section 69 of the County Courts Act 1984 for such period and at such rates as to the Court shall seem just.

    And the Claimant claims

    (1) Damages exceeding £100,000

    (2) Under paragraph 6 hereof interest pursuant to statute for such period and at such rates as to the Court shall seem just.

    Margaret Tulliver

I believe that the facts stated in this particulars of claim are true.

MAEvans

....

Mary Ann Evans

Filed 15 July 2006 by Dorothea Brooke and Co. of 9 Railway Cuttings, Middlemarch, Loamshire. Solicitors for the claimant.

12.8.1 Particulars of claim

From the particulars of claim it will be observed that the action is brought by a passenger in a car which collided with a concrete bus stop. The claim alleges negligence in failing to manage the vehicle so as to avoid the collision. The claimant gives five different explanations which may have contributed to the accident. The form of words of sub-particular (e), which is a general one common in road traffic cases, in effect invites the court to consider every aspect of the defendant's driving.

In paragraph 3 the claimant indicates that she is relying on the maxim *res ipsa loquitur*. In fact it is not necessary to set this out since *res ipsa loquitur* is merely a way of looking at evidence, but it is very common to do so in accidents when no other vehicle is involved. In reality it adds little to the statement of case.

At paragraph 4 it will be noted the claimant is in the fortunate position of being able to rely on a conviction of the defendant. Had this conviction been for careless or dangerous driving, the claimant would have been in an extremely strong position. The conviction unfortunately was for having excess alcohol in the blood, and while this is of course a much more serious offence than careless driving, it is less useful as a means of demonstrating negligence because it is self-evident that a driver may in fact drive competently notwithstanding having drunk to excess. It is certainly worth including, however, and will be a relevant extra factor at trial in the assessment of the whole of the defendant's driving conduct.

Thereafter the particulars of claim give particulars of injury and of the ways in which the claimant's career will be affected. It indicates that a full set of medical reports is served with the particulars of claim, as the rules require, and also that a schedule of past and future losses is supplied. The method of drafting this schedule varies. Some solicitors continue to put in the text of the particulars of claim itself 'one-off' items of special damages such as damaged clothing, private medical treatment and the like, while serving a separate schedule dealing with loss of earnings, future loss of earnings, loss of pension rights, etc. We will assume that in this instance this claimant has put all her particulars of special damage, including the smaller items, in that schedule.

The particulars of claim concludes with a claim to damages and interest.

This looks like an open and shut case so that the defendant has little hope of escaping or even reducing his liability. However, even in such an unpromising situation it may be possible for a defendant, while not in any sense making false statements, to keep issues alive in the hope of negotiating a better settlement.

12.8.2 Defence

IN THE MIDDLEMARCH COUNTY COURT   Case No: MM 060131

BETWEEN   Mary Ann Evans   Claimant

and

George Eliot   Defendant

_____

Defence

_____

1. Paragraph 1 of the Particulars of Claim is admitted.

2. The defendant makes no further admissions as to any of the allegations contained in the Particulars of Claim and in particular denies that he was negligent, either as alleged or at all.

3. The defendant does not admit the extent of the claimed injury, loss or damage or the cause of any such injury, loss or damage. The defendant will obtain his own medical evidence and, after disclosure of documents, serve a counter-schedule of loss and damage.

4. The accident in question was not due to any negligence on the part of the defendant, but was caused by the sudden and unexpected deflation of the rear nearside tyre of the vehicle, which resulted in the defendant being temporarily deprived of his ability to control the vehicle properly.

5. The defendant further denies the relevance of his conviction referred to in paragraph 4 of the Particulars of Claim. Moreover, whilst maintaining that denial, if the accident was in any way due to alcohol, which the defendant admits having consumed, the defendant will contend that the claimant in accepting a lift when she knew that the defendant had been drinking was herself guilty of contributory negligence since she knew, or should have known, that his ability properly to control the vehicle might be impaired.

6. Moreover, any injury which the claimant sustained in consequence of the accident was caused wholly or in part by her own negligence in failing to wear or make any proper use of the seat belt with which the vehicle was equipped.

Adam Bede

I believe that the facts stated in this defence are true.

George Eliot

....
George Eliot

Filed 29 July 2006 by Deronda & Co. of 10 King Street, Middlemarch. Solicitors for the Defendant.

12.8.3 The defence

In the defence it will be observed that the defendant agrees that an accident occurred, but denies negligence in any respect. The defendant makes no admissions as to the extent of the injuries suffered by the claimant or damage because, of course, the defendant has no direct proof of these matters at this stage.

The defendant then goes on to make the best of what is obviously a fairly weak case, since he collided with a bus stop with no other vehicle involved, by three different allegations.

First, in paragraph 4, the defendant raises so-called 'inevitable accident' as a defence, saying that the vehicle left the road because of a sudden tyre burst. If this can be shown then the defendant will escape liability, there being no 'fault', and the claimant, notwithstanding her terrible injuries, will receive no compensation. Even if this tyre burst is demonstrated (the burden of proof being on the defendant), it may of course still be possible for the judge to conclude that the defendant's consumption of alcohol affected his ability to manage the skid into which the vehicle went.

In paragraph 5 the defendant denies the *relevance* of his conviction, in other words suggests that his ability to manage the car was not affected by the alcohol which he agrees he had consumed. This denial requires the claimant to establish relevance. In some instances, if something wholly irrelevant was contended by a claimant, a defendant would be well advised to apply to strike out the offending allegation from the particulars of claim and have that matter determined by a district judge before trial. Thus, for example, if the claimant pleaded some ancient, unconnected conviction, perhaps as a way of attempting to show that the defendant was habitually a bad driver, that would be the case. In the present instance, however, the matter of relevance would be left for the judge at trial to decide. On the face of it it is unlikely that the judge will find that there is *no* relevance in the fact that the defendant had drunk to excess.

The defendant then goes on to raise the contributory negligence of the claimant in allowing herself to be carried by a driver whom she knew to have drunk to excess. The case law establishes that in such an instance there may well be a substantial discount on damages (perhaps up to 25 per cent) to reflect the claimant's degree of blameworthiness for her injuries.

Lastly, the defendant seeks further reduction for contributory negligence by the allegation that the claimant was not wearing a seat belt. As is also well-known, on the case law, this may likewise lead to a reduction in damages for up to 25 per cent, provided that the claimant's injuries would in fact have been reduced or avoided by the wearing of a seat belt.

By the end of the defence, therefore, the defendant has at least succeeded in putting into issue enough allegations to make it quite certain that the claimant will not be able to obtain summary judgment (see **26.6**). In addition, there are now sufficient 'balls in the air' for the claimant's lawyers to be left with some uncertainty about the outcome of the case, so that the defendant at least has something to negotiate with in what is obviously, given the claimant's future career impairment, a very large claim indeed.

(In fact the claimant's solicitors in the actual case on which this is based were able by the delivery of a request for further information, to establish that the defendant had not kept the tyre which had allegedly burst, and thus he was going to be unable to establish that at trial. The evidence, moreover, that the claimant had been in a separate room from the defendant at the party where they had both been before the defendant gave the claimant a lift home was very strong, and as the defendant appeared to have had only four or five pints of beer and was well used to drink, although over the limit, there were no indications in his behaviour that he had drunk to excess. Also the impact which caused the most damage was from the side, the car having swerved into the bus stop, and although it was true that the claimant was, foolishly, not wearing a seat belt, most of the injuries would not have been saved by such a seat belt and in negotiation no discount was given for contributory negligence for failure to wear a seat belt.)

Response Pack

You should read the 'notes for defendant' attached to the claim form which will tell you when and where to send the forms

Included in this pack are:

- either **Admission Form N9A**
  (if the claim is for a specified amount)
  or **Admission Form N9C**
  (if the claim is for an unspecified amount
  or is not a claim for money)

- either **Defence and Counterclaim Form
  N9B** (if the claim is for a specified amount)
  or **Defence and Counterclaim Form N9D**
  (if the claim is for an unspecified amount
  or is not a claim for money)

- **Acknowledgment of service**
  (see below)

Complete

If you admit the claim or the amount claimed and/or you want time to pay ▶	the admission form
If you admit part of the claim ▶	the admission form and the defence form
If you dispute the whole claim or wish to make a claim (a counterclaim) against the claimant ▶	the defence form
If you need 28 days (rather than 14) from the date of service to prepare your defence, or wish to contest the court's jurisdiction ▶	the acknowledgement of service
If you do nothing, judgment may be entered against you	

Acknowledgement of Service

Defendant's full name if different from the name given on the claim form

In the

Claim No	
Claimant	
Defendant	

Address to which documents about this claim should be sent (including reference if appropriate)

	if applicable
fax no.	
DX no.	
Ref. no.	
e-mail	

Tel. no.   Postcode

Tick the appropriate box

1. I intend to defend all of this claim ☐

2. I intend to defend part of this claim ☐

3. I intend to contest jurisdiction ☐

If you file an acknowledgement of service but do not file a defence within 28 days of the date of service of the claim form, or particulars of claim if served separately, judgment may be entered against you.

If you do not file an application within 28 days of the date of service of the claim form, or particulars of claim if served separately, it will be assumed that you accept the court's jurisdiction and judgment may be entered against you.

Signed _____
(Defendant)(Defendant's solicitor)
(Litigation friend)

Position or office held
(if signing on behalf of firm or company)

_____

Date

The court office at

is open between 10 am and 4 pm Monday to Friday. When corresponding with the court, please address forms or letters to the Court Manager and quote the claim number.

N9 Response Pack (5.02)   *Printed on behalf of The Court Service*

Admission (unspecified amount, non-money and return of goods claims)

In the	
Claim No.	
Claimant (including ref.)	
Defendant	

- Before completing this form please read the notes for guidance attached to the claim form. If necessary provide details on a separate sheet, add the claim number and attach it to this form.
- If you are not an individual, you should ensure that you provide sufficient details about the assets and liabilities of your firm, company or corporation to support any offer of payment made.

In non-money claims only

☐ I admit liability for the whole claim
(Complete section 11)

In return of goods cases only

Are the goods still in your possession?
☐ Yes   ☐ No

Part A Response to claim (tick one box only)

☐ I admit liability for the whole claim but want the court to decide the amount I should pay / value of the goods
OR
☐ I admit liability for the claim and offer to pay £ [____] in satisfaction of the claim
(Complete part B and sections 1 - 11)

Part B How are you going to pay the amount you have admitted? (tick one box only)

☐ I offer to pay on (date) [____]

OR

☐ I cannot pay the amount immediately because (state reason)

[____]

AND

I offer to pay by instalments of £ [____]
per (week)(month)
starting (date) [____]

1   Personal details

Surname [____]

Forename [____]

☐ Mr   ☐ Mrs   ☐ Miss   ☐ Ms

☐ Married   ☐ Single   ☐ Other (specify) [____]

Age [____]

Address [____]

Postcode [____]

Tel. no. [____]

2   Dependants   (people you look after financially)

Number of children in each age group

under 11 [____]   11-15 [____]   16-17 [____]   18 & over [____]

Other dependants (give details) [____]

3   Employment

☐ I am employed as a [____]
My employer is [____]

Jobs other than main job (give details) [____]

☐ I am self employed as a [____]

Annual turnover is............................ £ [____]

☐ **I am not** in arrears with my national insurance contributions, income tax and VAT

☐ **I am** in arrears and I owe........... £ [____]

Give details of:
(a) contracts and other work in hand
(b) any sums due for work done
[____]

☐ I have been unemployed for [years] [months]

☐ I am a pensioner

4   Bank account and savings

☐ I have a bank account

☐ The account is in credit by........ £ [____]

☐ The account is overdrawn by.... £ [____]

☐ I have a savings or building society account

The amount in the account is.......... £ [____]

5   Residence

I live in
☐ my own property   ☐ lodgings
☐ jointly owned house   ☐ rented property
☐ council accommodation

6   Income

My usual take home pay *(including overtime, commission, bonuses etc)*	£		per
Income support	£		per
Child benefit(s)	£		per
Other state benefit(s)	£		per
My pension(s)	£		per
Others living in my home give me	£		per
Other income *(give details below)*			
	£		per
	£		per
	£		per
Total income	**£**		**per**

7   Expenses

(Do not include any payments made by other members of the household out of their own income)

I have regular expenses as follows:

Mortgate *(including second mortgage)*	£		per
Rent	£		per
Council tax	£		per
Gas	£		per
Electricity	£		per
Water charges	£		per
TV rental and licence	£		per
HP repayments	£		per
Mail order	£		per
Housekeeping, food, school meals	£		per
Travelling expenses	£		per
Children's clothing	£		per
Maintenance payments	£		per
Others *(not court orders or credit debts listed in sections 9 and 10)*			
	£		per
	£		per
	£		per
Total expenses	**£**		**per**

8   Priority debts

(This section is for arrears only. Do not include regular expenses listed in section 7)

Rent arrears	£		per
Mortgage arrears	£		per
Council tax/Community Charge arrears	£		per
Water charges arrears	£		per
Fuel debts: Gas	£		per
Electricity	£		per
Other	£		per
Maintenance arrears	£		per
Others *(give details below)*			
	£		per
	£		per
Total priority debts	**£**		**per**

9   Court orders

Court	Claim No.	£	per

Total court order instalments	**£**	**per**

Of the payments above, I am behind with payments to *(please list)*

10   Credit debts

Loans and credit card debts *(please list)*

£		per
£		per
£		per

Of the payments above, I am behind with payments to *(please list)*

11   Declaration

I declare that the details I have given above are true to the best of my knowledge

Signed

Date

Position or office held *(if signing on behalf of firm or company)*

Defence and Counterclaim
(unspecified amount, non-money and return of goods claims)

In the

Claim No.	
Claimant (including ref.)	
Defendant	

- Fill in this form if you wish to dispute all or part of the claim and/or make a claim against the claimant (a counterclaim)
- You have a limited number of days to complete and return this form to the court.
- Before completing this form, please read the notes for guidance attached to the claim form.
- Please ensure that all the boxes at the top right of this form are completed. You can obtain the correct names and number from the claim form. The court cannot trace your case without this information.

How to fill in this form
- Set out your defence in section 1. If necessary continue on a separate piece of paper making sure that the claim number is clearly shown on it. In your defence you must state which allegations in the particulars of claim you deny and your reasons for doing so. **If you fail to deny an allegation it may be taken that you admit it.**
- If you dispute only some of the allegations you must
  - specify which you admit and which you deny; and
  - give your own version of events if different from the claimant's.

- If the claim is for money and you dispute the claimant's statement of value, you must say why and if possible give your own statement of value.
- If you wish to make a claim against the claimant (a counterclaim) complete section 2.
- Complete and sign section 3 before returning this form.

Where to send this form
- send or take this form immediately to the court at the address given on the claim form.
- Keep a copy of the claim form and the defence form.

Community Legal Service Fund (CLSF)
You may qualify for assistance from the CLSF (this used to be called 'legal aid') to meet some or all of your legal costs. Ask about the CLSF at any county court office or any information or help point which displays this logo.

Community Legal Service

1. Defence

Defence (continued)   Claim No. [   ]

2. If you wish to make a claim against the claimant (a counterclaim)

If your claim is for a specific sum of
money, how much are you claiming?   £ [   ]

I enclose the counterclaim fee of   £ [   ]

My claim is for *(please specify)*

[   ]

- To start your counterclaim, you will have to pay a fee. Court staff can tell you how much you have to pay.

- You may not be able to make a counterclaim where the claimant is the Crown (e.g. a Government Department). Ask at your local county court office for further information.

What are your reasons for making the counterclaim?
If you need to continue on a separate sheet put the claim number in the top right hand corner

[   ]

3. Signed

(To be signed by you or by your solicitor or litigation friend*)*

*(I believe)(The defendant believes) that the facts stated in this form are true. *I am duly authorised by the defendant to sign this statement

delete as appropriate

Position or office held (if signing on behalf of firm or company)

Date [   ]

Give an address to which notices about this case can be sent to you

Postcode

Tel. no. [   ]

if applicable

fax no.	
DX no.	
e-mail	

Case management

The central feature of the CPR is that in every case the court will manage the litigation and do so in accordance with its overriding objective by using its case management powers (see **Chapter 10**). Moreover, the parties are required to carry out their part of the adversarial procedure in a spirit of procedural co-operation.

13.1 Key features

The key features of case management are as follows:

13.1.1 Allocation

There are three different 'tracks' for cases, the choice of which is almost entirely dictated by the value of the case. A case will initially therefore be allocated to one of those three tracks which are respectively:

(a) The small claims track—for cases worth less than £5,000.

(b) The fast track—for cases worth between £5,000 and £15,000.

(c) The multi-track—for cases worth more than £15,000.

13.1.2 Case management

When the court allocates a case to a track, it will try to order how that case is to proceed by standard-form directions adapted to take into account what the court knows about the case concerned. The directions will, roughly speaking, reflect the value of the claim in terms of the formality or complication of the procedures to be followed so that, for example:

(a) On the small claims track, generally speaking, the parties will be sent a set of procedural directions that they must carry out. There will be a fixed date of hearing, usually less than six months after the action commenced, and usually with a hearing time of no more than two hours and often rather less.

(b) On the fast track, matters will proceed with fairly standardised directions to a hearing which will take place no more than nine months after the case commenced and will last no more than one day.

(c) On the multi-track a more complex procedure will be adopted, depending on what seem to be the features of the case. There will be greater flexibility on the multi-track and cases will generally be allowed considerably longer for the necessary procedures to be followed.

13.1.3 Case management conferences

The objective of giving directions which are appropriate for the case concerned and which must be scrupulously carried out in accordance with the timetable, telling both parties everything that they need to do so that expensive hearings are avoided, is to attempt to achieve a situation where the parties never need attend before the court from commencement of the case until the trial and simply follow the directions given to them. Accordingly, only if some new feature appears in the case which is not provided for in the standard directions given, or if one party disobeys the directions and needs to be brought before the court by the other party to ensure compliance, need there be any hearing between commencement and trial.

If this cannot be achieved, perhaps because at the stage of allocating the case and giving initial directions there is some uncertainty as to some issues, then the court will usually give such directions as it can at the outset, but require the parties to attend before it for a 'case management conference' at some fixed date in the future. By this time it will expect the parties to have carried out the directions it has already given and to be in a position to give the court full information so as to enable the court to give final, further directions to lead the case on to trial.

Case management conferences are mainly of importance on the multi-track, where the amount involved may mean that the litigation is more complex. There will, however, often be cases on the fast track where the standardised directions are inappropriate, or even where the court does not have sufficient information from the parties to give proper directions without such a conference. On the small claims track there are no 'case management conferences' as such, although one of the orders which the court may make is to call the parties before it for a preliminary hearing, as to which see **Chapter 17**.

The above is a bare outline of the process of allocation and case management, but it is now necessary to develop it in considerably more detail.

13.2 Allocation questionnaires and allocation

When a defendant files a defence the court will generally serve an allocation questionnaire on each party. This will not be done if the court considers it already has sufficient information and can proceed without questionnaires, for example, where the amount involved is clearly such that the case is destined for the small claims track (e.g., in a simple contractual dispute, or a road traffic accident with no personal injuries involved, where there is simply a claim for car repairs of a modest figure).

The allocation questionnaire is in a set form and contains the date by which it must be returned (14 days after the date when each party receives it). The allocation questionnaire requires each party to fill in a good deal of information about the case—indeed the parties are instructed to cooperate with each other in attempting to fill in their questionnaires, though this provision (set out in PD 26) seems rarely observed. A form of allocation questionnaire is illustrated at the end of this chapter.

When returning his questionnaire unless the claim is for less than £1,000 the claimant must pay a further court fee. This is £100 for all claims above £1,000. If he succeeds in his claim, the court fees can of course be recovered by the claimant as part of his legitimate outgoings, whether or not he employed solicitors.

13.2.1 What if the parties do not return the allocation questionnaires?

If the parties do not comply with the requirement to file the allocation questionnaire, the court has a wide variety of sanctions. The likely outcomes are described below. It should be borne in mind that this is probably going to be the first time at which the *procedural judge*, who will be the district judge, will have seen the case file, as hitherto the file has been dealt with by the office staff at court. Files will then be sent up to a district judge automatically on the day after the date on which the allocation questionnaires should have been returned. At this stage the district judge may think that he has sufficient information to enable him to allocate the case to track without the need for the questionnaires, in which case he will do so. It should be noted that this will not absolve the claimant from paying the allocation fee. If he does not pay it, the claim will be struck out. A claimant will have to recommence the claim, paying a new fee, to start the proceedings again.

If the district judge does not feel he has sufficient information simply from the statements of case to allocate to track and give early directions, then:

(a) if both parties are in default of filing the allocation questionnaire, he may make an order that unless questionnaires are filed within a given time after the date of the order, both the claimant's statement of case and the defendant's will be struck out;

(b) if only the claimant has failed to file an allocation questionnaire, he may order that the claim will be struck out on a given date after the order unless the questionnaire is filed;

(c) if only the defendant has failed to file a questionnaire, he will probably proceed on the basis of the information contained on the claimant's questionnaire, so that whatever proposals the defendant might have wished to put forward for procedural steps cannot be taken into account;

(d) alternatively to any of the above, he may call an *allocation hearing*. This is likely to be within a very short timescale, possibly within only four or five days. Both parties will be instructed to attend by responsible representatives (which they are likely to find highly disruptive to their workloads at such short notice) and it will almost certainly be the case that any party in default of returning the allocation questionnaire will not receive any order for the costs of attending and may well have to pay the costs of any opponent who has filed the questionnaire. Any party who does not attend is likely to find further sanctions applied including, if it is the claimant, his case being struck out.

Although the above are the sanctions for failing to file an allocation questionnaire, an allocation hearing may also be fixed for other reasons, where the court feels it needs more information, for example, because what is said in the two allocation questionnaires is substantially in conflict or because the information given is inadequate. If there needs to be an allocation hearing because of inadequate information, then again any party who completed the questionnaire inadequately is likely to be refused any order for costs of attending court.

Finally it should be noted that there might well have been some action or hearing before this time in the case. For example, there may have been an application for an urgent interim injunction (see **22.6**) or for summary judgment (see **26.6**). At the end of those hearings, if the hearing did not bring the litigation to an end, the court will have gone on to give further directions including allocation to track.

13.2.2   The contents of the questionnaire

As will be noted from the forms (see end of chapter) the parties are requested to respond to a number of matters and it is perhaps appropriate to comment briefly on these now.

(a) The parties are required to indicate to which track they think the case should be allocated. This is merely meant to assist the district judge and even if they are unanimous in their choice, it does not bind the court, which should form its own view.

(b) The parties are asked whether they would like a *stay* for settlement. If they both would, or if the court forms the view that a stay would be useful, then a direction may be made staying the proceedings for one month (r. 26.4(2)) which the court has power to extend for such further period as it thinks appropriate (r. 26.4(3)) which will usually be the case if either party subsequently writes in requesting that extension. The court will not let this become an occasion for stringing things out for vague negotiations and will usually require the parties to give a detailed account of what steps have been taken to attempt to settle the case.

In any event, it is suggested that requesting a stay is only likely to be appropriate if there is a genuine prospect of early settlement and the parties may already be quite close to it. If that is not the position then a further month is unlikely to make much difference and there is of course nothing to stop the parties continuing to negotiate while carrying out some of the early steps in the continuing litigation.

(c) The rest of the information required in the allocation questionnaire is to help the court decide what directions to give and to confirm which is the most suitable track. Information needs to be given about witnesses to be called and on which issues and, most importantly, about the state of the expert evidence and the possibility of agreement about it. At the end each party is requested to say how long their own case will take to present.

13.2.3   The allocation to track

When the court has sufficient information to proceed, it will consider allocation. The primary feature is the financial value of the claim, but it is important to note here that it is for the court to form its own view (so far as it can) of that value. For example, particulars of claim put forward by unrepresented litigants which claim exaggerated amounts or claim for heads of damage which are not available in law, will be scrutinised by the court which will attribute its own value so far as it can on the information available. In deciding on the value of the claim what matters is the amount still in dispute. Any sum for which the defendant does not admit liability counts as being 'in dispute', but the court can disregard, by virtue of PD 26, para. 7.1:

(a) sums for which summary judgment on a part of a claim have been entered;

(b) any distinct items in the claim for which the defendant has admitted liability; and

(c) any distinct items in the claim which have been agreed between the parties.

Accordingly, even if the initial dispute concerned a figure of £100,000, if the defendant is admitting all but £10,000 of it then it will be safe to allocate the claim to the fast track. It must be clearly noted, however, that if the defendant is disputing *liability in principle* then it is the gross value of the claim which counts.

EXAMPLE

The claimant is claiming £100,000. The defendant disputes any liability at all, but the parties have been able to negotiate on what would be the appropriate quantum if the defendant were liable and the defendant is prepared to offer £96,000 if he is found liable. This does not mean that because only £4,000 is in dispute the case can go to the small claims track. Since liability is in dispute as well as a minor aspect of quantum, the case will have to go to the multi-track in view of the total value of the claim.

We shall now go on to consider features in deciding on allocation.

13.3 The small claims track

The small claims track is meant to provide an economical and straightforward procedure for cases such as modest road traffic and other accident claims, consumer disputes, simple landlord and tenant cases, etc. **Chapter 17** describes the small claims procedure in detail. Here we are only concerned with the features which lead to a case being allocated to the small claims track initially.

The following kinds of claim will *not* be allocated to the small claims track even if they have a value under £5,000:

(a) Personal injury cases where the value of the claim for pain, suffering and loss of amenity exceeds £1,000 (r. 26.6(1)(a)).

(b) Housing disrepair claims where tenants of residential property seek orders compelling their landlords to carry out repairs and also generally speaking seek damages for breach of covenant caused by their having to live for a time in the unfit housing until the repairs are carried out. Where either of these heads of damages amount to more than £1,000 the case will not be dealt with on the small claims track even though the gross value of the claim remains under £5,000.

(c) Claims by residential tenants seeking damages against their landlords for harassment or unlawful eviction (r. 26.7(4)).

(d) Claims involving a disputed allegation of dishonesty (PD 26, para. 8.1(1)).

It is open to the parties to agree that a case proceeds on the small claims track even if the value is more than £5,000; however, the parties' unanimous agreement is not conclusive and the court may impose its own view. In principle, a case should not go on the small claims track if the hearing is likely to take more than one day.

Several features of the small claims track are different from litigation on the other tracks and for that reason small claims are discussed separately in **Chapter 17**. About 80 per cent of all litigation will be in the small claims track and because of the upper limit now being £5,000 (despite the restrictions on recovery of costs discussed in **Chapter 17**) a substantial minority of litigants will be legally represented. Indeed, it has been said many times that for most people a claim of up to £5,000 would most certainly not be viewed as a 'small claim'.

One feature of the small claims track, however, is that most parties will not be legally represented and this will involve the court in practical problems such as obtaining compliance with rules and directions to ensure the efficient progress of litigation. This is most apparent in the matter of the allocation questionnaire. Where it is clear to the court staff that the claim will proceed on the small claims track there is a briefer, simpler form of allocation questionnaire that they may send out. If the staff are unsure they will send out the general form. Although relatively straightforward to complete and despite the fact that the form is accompanied by some notes for guidance, difficulties have been experienced in getting it back, properly and fully completed, from litigants in person and some, who have already paid a court fee of £60 or more to start their litigation for modest amounts, receive a significant shock when (in cases of over £1,000) the further £80 allocation fee is demanded so early in the case. In fact district judges, responding sensibly and flexibly to the spirit of the new rules, are often managing to take decisions about allocation without requiring a great deal of information from unrepresented parties, on the basis simply of the amount involved and the type of claim. A hearing of most cases on the small claims track typically takes no more than about one to two hours and no great problems in relation to disclosure of documents etc. generally arise. When the court sends out written directions after allocation to the small claims track, it is almost always sufficient to enable the case to be properly disposed of at the first substantive hearing, generally no more than about six months after the case was started.

Before going on to discuss the tracks, it is important to deal with one other matter relevant to how, when and where a case will proceed and that is the subject of transfer.

13.4   Transfer of proceedings

This is dealt with in CPR, Part 30, and PD 30.

Putting it simply, a claim can be issued in any court which has jurisdiction to hear it and generally speaking there need be no local connection between the claim and the court. Many bodies, for example, insurance companies and trade unions, channel most of their work to a given firm of solicitors who are likely to issue proceedings in the local court no matter where the parties live and wherever the cause of action arose. The place of issue, however, does not determine where the case will ultimately proceed and the following are the basic rules.

13.4.1   Automatic transfer

If the claim is for a specified sum of money against a defendant who is an individual, when a defence is filed the claim will be transferred to the individual's home court. If there is more than one defendant who is an individual and they have different home courts, the claim will be transferred to the home court of the first to file a defence (r. 26.2(5)).

The 'defendant's home court' is defined by r. 2.3(1) to mean the court for the district in which the defendant's address for service is situated and this may therefore be the court nearest to his solicitor's address rather than his own.

If someone is suing an individual defendant for a debt, or even for what should be general damages, but the claimant has chosen to specify a sum of money, the case will be transferred to the defendant's home court. If the defendant is a limited company this will not occur. The provision can also be avoided by claimants not claiming a specified sum of money. This is easy enough to do in a personal injury claim where a claimant would probably be foolish to fix on a given sum. Claimants' solicitors often get round this rule even in cases which do appear to relate to a specific sum (for example, after a road traffic accident where there have been no personal injuries so that the entire claim is for car repairs) by also claiming an unspecified sum as general damages for inconvenience and loss of use of the vehicle. If properly claimed this will defeat automatic transfer to the defendant's home court.

13.4.2 Two special cases

It should be noted that if the defence is that the money has been paid or there is a partial admission, there will be no automatic transfer at that stage. A notice is sent to the claimant of what the defendant says and only if he rejects the defendant's contention and requests that the case proceed, will it be transferred to the defendant's home court.

13.4.3 Other transfer

The court has a wide discretion under CPR, Part 30, to order transfer between the High Court and county courts and between different county courts. In particular, if a claim is to be allocated to the multi-track it is likely to be transferred to a civil trial centre although that is not inevitable. A trial centre is likely to be in a large town and will usually have a combined court building with several courtrooms and a number of district judges and circuit judges there all the time with a High Court judge there from time to time. A district judge may in such a case transfer the case to a civil trial centre straightaway or give case management directions himself and then transfer. In fact it seems that there are substantial local variations as to what is to happen where a case is commenced in a small county court. Whether case management in multi-track cases remains in the county court, is transferred to a larger court, or has part of the case management carried out in the small court before transfer depends on location.

One of the main objectives of the CPR was to erode the differences between High Court and county court. There is now very little practical importance in whether a case is transferred between the High Court and the county court or vice versa. The only distinction is the level of judge who may ultimately try the case, though even that may be subject to the trial being switched at a late stage, to whichever level of judge is convenient or available.

The factors under CPR, r. 30.3(1) and (2), which govern a court's general decision to order transfer are as follows:

(a) the financial value of the claim and the amount in dispute if different;

(b) whether it would be more convenient or fair for hearings (including the trial) to be held in some other court;

(c) the availability of a judge specialising in the type of claim in question;

(d) whether the facts, legal issues, remedies or procedures involved are simple or complex;

(e) the importance of the claim to the public in general;

(f) the facilities available at the court where the claim is being dealt with and whether they may be inadequate because of any disability to the party or potential witness.

13.4.4 Transfer from one county court to another

The power to transfer may be exercised either upon application by any party or by a court acting on its own initiative. The powers are very wide-ranging. In its most common-sense application the court is likely to see whether there is in fact any local connection with the case and the issue of transfer will become a matter of geography. A common scenario follows:

EXAMPLE

XYZ are a legal expenses insurer who channel most of their work to a firm of solicitors in Middlemarch. One particular case involves a claimant, C, who lives in Exeter and suffered a road accident there, 200 miles from Middlemarch. The claim is issued in Middlemarch and is worth about £10,000. The defendant also lives in Exeter. Because of the court in which the claim is issued, the defendant's insurers decide to use the solicitor on their panel who is also based in Middlemarch and a defence is filed. At the point when the court is considering allocation directions, either party will be asked to give reasons why the case should proceed in any particular court. They may contend that it should continue in Middlemarch for the convenience of the solicitors. In that case the court is likely to:

(a) transfer the case immediately to Exeter County Court so that all case management directions can be given there since that is the most sensible place for a trial involving parties and witnesses who live in Exeter; or

(b) let the case proceed in Middlemarch for the convenience of the solicitors, but send it for trial to Exeter at some later stage. In fact arrangements for doing this are now quite flexible. If the case were to proceed on the fast track, telephone contact is made with Exeter immediately to ensure that a suitable 'window' for the trial is allocated there at the appropriate time while other directions continue in Middlemarch.

One powerful incentive to send the case to Exeter is that in a straightforward fast track case there need be no further hearings between allocation and trial, so it may not matter very much that the solicitors are in Middlemarch. Should there be such hearings, however, the costs of attending them from Middlemarch would be considerable. In principle the parties should send to each hearing responsible representatives who are familiar with the file. It may not be adequate for the Middlemarch solicitors simply to instruct solicitor agents in Exeter to attend such hearings. The court will weigh all the factors for each case.

13.5 Specialist lists

In cases on a specialist list (such as the commercial list of the Queen's Bench Division) automatic transfer does not happen and there are particular provisions relating to such cases (PD 26, para. 10.2(2)).

Allocation questionnaire

To be completed by, or on behalf of,

In the

Claim No.

Last date for filing
with court office

who is [1ˢᵗ][2ⁿᵈ][3ʳᵈ][   ][Claimant][Defendant]
[Part 20 claimant] in this claim

Please read the notes on page five before completing the questionnaire.

You should note the date by which it must be returned and the name of the court it should be returned to since this may be different from the court where the proceedings were issued.

If you have settled this claim (or if you settle it on a future date) and do not need to have it heard or tried, you must let the court know immediately.

Have you sent a copy of this completed form to the other party(ies)?   ☐ Yes   ☐ No

A Settlement

Do you wish there to be a one month stay to attempt to settle the claim, either by informal discussion or by alternative dispute resolution?   ☐ Yes   ☐ No

B Location of trial

Is there any reason why your claim needs to be heard at a particular court?   ☐ Yes   ☐ No

If Yes, say which court and why?

C Pre-action protocols

If an approved pre-action protocol applies to this claim, complete **Part 1** only. If not, complete **Part 2** only. If you answer 'No' to the question in either Part 1 or 2, please explain the reasons why on a separate sheet and attach it to this questionnaire.

Part 1

please say which protocol

The* _____ protocol applies to this claim.

Have you complied with it?   ☐ Yes   ☐ No

Part 2

No pre-action protocol applies to this claim.

Have you exchanged information and/or documents (evidence) with the other party in order to assist in settling the claim?   ☐ Yes   ☐ No

D Case management information

What amount of the claim is in dispute?   £ [   ]

Applications

Have you made any application(s) in this claim?   ☐ Yes   ☐ No

If Yes, what for?   [   ]   For hearing on [   ]
(e.g. summary judgment,
add another party)

Witnesses

So far as you know at this stage, what witnesses of fact do you intend to call at the trial or final hearing including, if appropriate, yourself?

Witness name	Witness to which facts

Experts

Do you wish to use expert evidence at the trial or final hearing?   ☐ Yes   ☐ No

Have you already copied any experts' report(s) to the   ☐ None yet   ☐ Yes   ☐ No
other party(ies)?   obtained

Do you consider the case suitable for a single joint expert in any field?   ☐ Yes   ☐ No

Please list any single joint experts you propose to use and any other experts you wish to rely on. Identify single joint experts with the initials 'SJ' after their name(s).

Expert's name	Field of expertise (e.g. orthopaedic surgeon, surveyor, engineer)

Do you want your expert(s) to give evidence orally at the trial or final hearing?   ☐ Yes   ☐ No

If Yes, give the reasons why you think oral evidence is necessary:

continue over ⫸

Track

Which track do you consider is most suitable for your claim? Tick one box

☐ small claims track   ☐ fast track   ☐ multi-track

If you have indicated a track which would not be the normal track for the claim, please give brief reasons for your choice

---

E   Trial or final hearing

How long do you estimate the trial or final hearing will take?

_____ days _____ hours _____ minutes

Are there any days when you, an expert or an essential witness will not be able to attend court for the trial or final hearing?

☐ Yes   ☐ No

If Yes, please give details

Name	Dates not available

F   Proposed directions (Parties should agree directions wherever possible)

Have you attached a list of the directions you think appropriate for the management of the claim?

☐ Yes   ☐ No

If Yes, have they been agreed with the other party(ies)?

☐ Yes   ☐ No

G   Costs

*Do **not** complete this section if you have suggested your case is suitable for the small claims track **or** you have suggested one of the other tracks and you do not have a solicitor acting for you.*

What is your estimate of your costs incurred to date?

£ _____

What do you estimate your overall costs are likely to be?

£ _____

In substantial cases these questions should be answered in compliance with CPR Part 43

H Other information

Have you attached documents to this questionnaire?   ☐ Yes   ☐ No

Have you sent these documents to the other party(ies)?   ☐ Yes   ☐ No

If Yes, when did they receive them?

Do you intend to make any applications in the immediate future?   ☐ Yes   ☐ No

If Yes, what for?

In the space below, set out any other information you consider will help the judge to manage the claim.

Signed   Date

[Counsel][Solicitor][for the][1st][2nd][3rd][   ]
[Claimant][Defendant][Part 20 claimant]

Please enter your firm's name, reference number and full postal address including (if appropriate) details of DX, fax or e-mail

		if applicable
	fax no.	
	DX no.	
Tel. no. Postcode	e-mail	
Your reference no.		

Notes for completing an allocation questionnaire

- If the claim is not settled, a judge must allocate it to an appropriate case management track. To help the judge choose the most just and cost-effective track, you must now complete the attached questionnaire.
- If you fail to return the allocation questionnaire by the date given, the judge may make an order which leads to your claim or defence being struck out, or hold an allocation hearing. If there is an allocation hearing the judge may order any party who has not filed their questionnaire to pay, immediately, the costs of that hearing.
- Use a separate sheet if you need more space for your answers marking clearly which section the information refers to. You should write the claim number on it, and on any other documents you send with your allocation questionnaire. Please ensure they are firmly attached to it.
- The letters below refer to the sections of the questionnaire and tell you what information is needed.

A Settlement

If you think that you and the other party may be able to negotiate a settlement you should tick the 'Yes' box. The court may order a stay, whether or not all the other parties to the claim agree. You should still complete the rest of the questionnaire, even if you are requesting a stay. Where a stay is granted it will be for an initial period of one month. You may settle the claim either by informal discussion with the other party or by alternative dispute resolution (ADR). ADR covers a range of different processes which can help settle disputes. More information is available in the booklet 'Resolving Disputes Without Going To Court' available from every county court office.

B Location of trial

High Court cases are usually heard at the Royal Courts of Justice or certain Civil Trial Centres. Fast or multi-track trials may be dealt with at a Civil Trial Centre or at the court where the claim is proceeding. Small claim cases are usually heard at the court in which they are proceeding.

C Pre-action protocols

Before any claim is started, the court expects you to have exchanged information and documents relevant to the claim, to assist in settling it. For some types of claim e.g. personal injury, there are approved protocols that should have been followed.

D Case management information

Applications

It is important for the court to know if you have already made any applications in the claim, what they are for and when they will be heard. The outcome of the applications may affect the case management directions the court gives.

Witnesses

Remember to include yourself as a witness of fact, if you will be giving evidence.

Experts

Oral or written expert evidence will only be allowed at the trial or final hearing with the court's permission. The judge will decide what permission it seems appropriate to give when the claim is allocated to track. Permission in small claims track cases will only be given exceptionally.

Track

The basic guide by which claims are normally allocated to a track is the amount in dispute, although other factors such as the complexity of the case will also be considered. A leaflet available from the court office explains the limits in greater detail.

Small Claims track	Disputes valued at not more than £5,000 except · those including a claim for personal injuries worth over £1,000 and · those for housing disrepair where either the cost of repairs or other work exceeds £1,000 or any other claim for damages exceeds £1,000
Fast track	Disputes valued at more than £5,000 but not more than £15,000
Multi-track	Disputes over £15,000

E Trial or final hearing

You should enter only those dates when you, your expert(s) or essential witness(es) will not be able to attend court because of holiday or other commitments.

F Proposed directions

Attach the list of directions, if any, you believe will be appropriate to be given for the management of the claim. Agreed directions on fast and multi-track cases should be based on the forms of standard directions set out in the practice direction to CPR Part 28 and form PF52.

G Costs

Only complete this section if you are a solicitor and have suggested the claim is suitable for allocation to the fast or multi-track.

H Other Information

Answer the questions in this section. Decide if there is any other information you consider will help the judge to manage the claim. Give details in the space provided referring to any documents you have attached to support what you are saying.

Chapters 14 to 17

It is now appropriate to explain the way in which the following chapters are organised. As has already been noted there are three tracks, the small claims track, the fast track and the multi-track. In order to continue the theme of 'case management', the next chapter deals with the fast track, because it is the track on which case management is likely to be most important. Thereafter there is a chapter on the multi-track, and after that a short chapter on sanctions for disobedience to procedural orders. Lastly, in this section there is a chapter on the small claims track. The reason why the chapter on the small claims track is last is that, although litigation on it is subject to case management in the general sense, because of the high proportion of unrepresented litigants and the special rules relevant to procedures and particularly recoverable costs, the small claims track is very much a separate kind of litigation, and it would break the thread of a discussion of case management to put it before discussion of the other tracks and sanctions. The sanctions referred to in the short chapter will of course be available on the small claims track also but, rightly or wrongly, a district judge is likely to be rather more indulgent of litigants in person than he might be of lawyers.

THE FAST TRACK

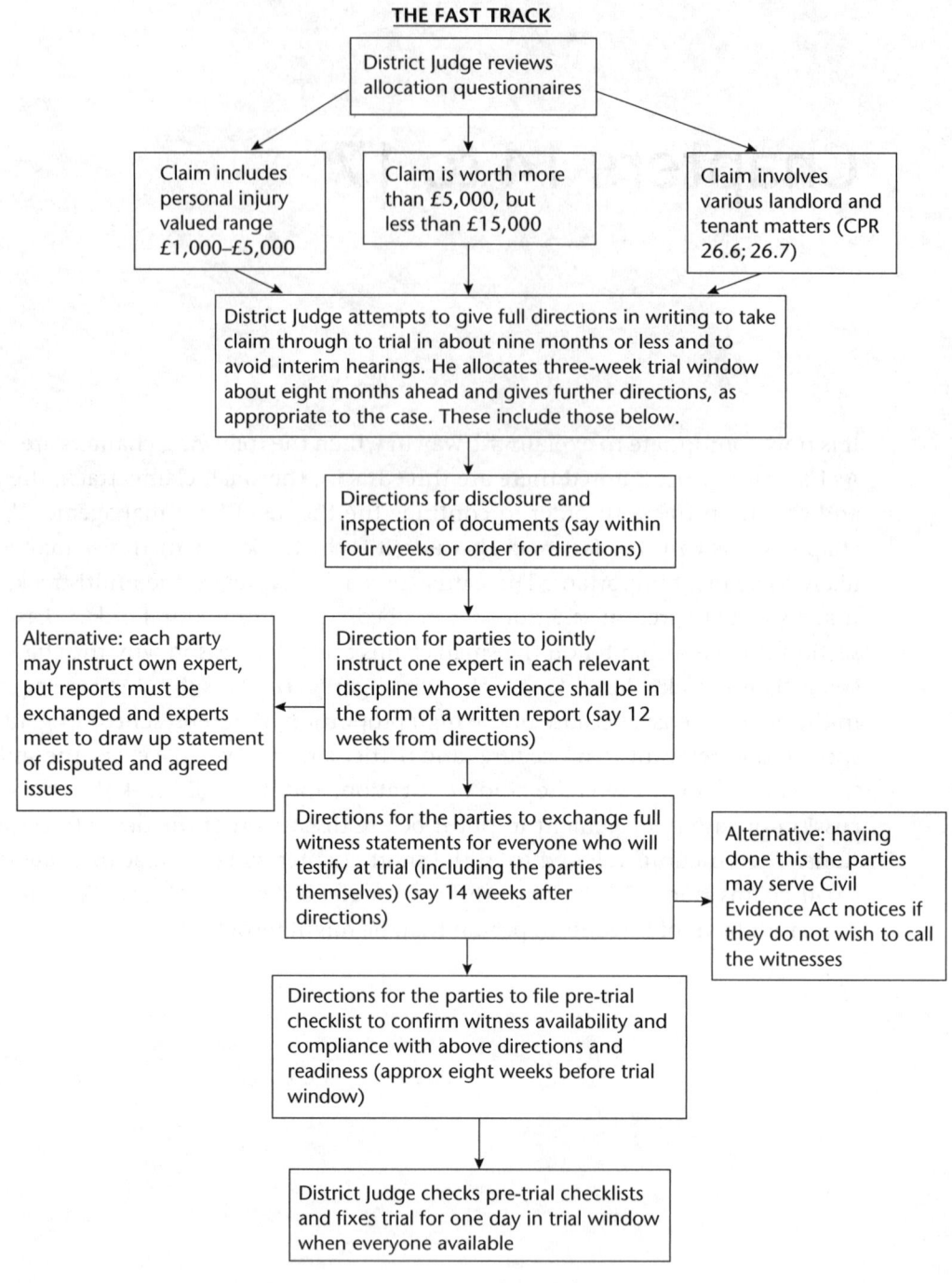

District Judge reviews allocation questionnaires

Claim includes personal injury valued range £1,000–£5,000

Claim is worth more than £5,000, but less than £15,000

Claim involves various landlord and tenant matters (CPR 26.6; 26.7)

District Judge attempts to give full directions in writing to take claim through to trial in about nine months or less and to avoid interim hearings. He allocates three-week trial window about eight months ahead and gives further directions, as appropriate to the case. These include those below.

Directions for disclosure and inspection of documents (say within four weeks or order for directions)

Alternative: each party may instruct own expert, but reports must be exchanged and experts meet to draw up statement of disputed and agreed issues

Direction for parties to jointly instruct one expert in each relevant discipline whose evidence shall be in the form of a written report (say 12 weeks from directions)

Directions for the parties to exchange full witness statements for everyone who will testify at trial (including the parties themselves) (say 14 weeks after directions)

Alternative: having done this the parties may serve Civil Evidence Act notices if they do not wish to call the witnesses

Directions for the parties to file pre-trial checklist to confirm witness availability and compliance with above directions and readiness (approx eight weeks before trial window)

District Judge checks pre-trial checklists and fixes trial for one day in trial window when everyone available

The fast track: CPR, Part 28

14.1 Allocation to the fast track

The fast track is the track for cases falling into the £5,000–£15,000 range and which can be disposed of by a trial which lasts less than five court hours.

With cases in this range a very high proportion of the parties will have legal representation and therefore the allocation questionnaires should be thoroughly completed. Although the allocation questionnaires are sent out at an early stage in the case, if there has been compliance with the pre-action protocols in personal injury and clinical negligence cases, and the spirit of the protocols in other cases, there should have been ample time for the parties to have cooperated to the point where the allocation questionnaires can be fully completed. In principle, the trial must last no more than a day and oral expert evidence must be limited to no more than two expert fields and to one expert per field.

The decision as to track is made early in the case and further factors may arise which change the view of whether the case can be accommodated in one working day. If that happens, there is flexibility in the rules which permit change of track and reallocation at any stage. It must also be remembered that different issues can be dealt with separately so that, for example, if the medical prognosis is unclear and will remain so for say 18 months, the court can order that the issue of liability be tried first on the fast track in a hearing lasting less than a day, leaving the issue of quantum to be decided later, which can also be on the fast claims track if the hearing will last less than a day. This flexibility does not extend to the court forcing cases on to the fast track if they appear to exceed £15,000 in value. Cases above this value can be put on the fast track only if all parties agree.

EXAMPLE

There is an apparently simple contractual dispute involving a sum of £16,000 and both parties agree that the hearing need last only two hours, there being only one witness of fact on either side. Despite this, the case will have to be allocated to the multi-track because of its value, unless both parties agree to the fast track. If one of the parties will not agree, for example, because he contends that there is a difficult point of law involved, or is simply an obstructive litigant in person, the court has no power to force the action on to the fast track.

Of course the court seeks to ensure a spirit of cooperation and is likely to ask some searching questions, and to impose some pressure on the parties to agree to the case being dealt with on the fast track. It is not out of the question that the court could even suggest that the case be dealt with on the small claims track for even greater speed and efficiency, but the parties' consent is essential.

14.2 Procedure on the fast track

When claims are allocated to the fast track, further directions will be given in writing setting out a timetable to be followed between the parties, and giving a fixed trial date, or a 'window' of no more than three weeks for the time when the trial will take place leaving the exact date to be fixed. In either case, the trial date will be no later than 30 weeks after allocation. Although 30 weeks might sound a long time, it is in fact not very long to collect evidence on all the issues, correspond with one's opponent and see what can be agreed and what remains in contention, bearing in mind that whatever evidence is forthcoming will have to be compressed into a five-hour trial timetable. One particular difficulty may be that by the time of allocation one or both parties may well still await experts' reports on some aspect of the case. Simply obtaining the report may take a matter of several weeks and it will then need to be discussed with the client and sent to the other side for agreement. The other side may need to send it to their expert for his comments and when the parties are undertaking this for each field of expertise, this feature alone will cause the parties some anxiety as to whether everything can be prepared within 30 weeks. Moreover, very good cause indeed will need to be shown for adjourning the trial from the date or period fixed. This is part of the objective of the rules so as to avoid the parties going to excessive lengths and taking steps which are disproportionate to the value of the claim.

In claims worth £15,000 or less, the court will generally speaking be very reluctant to permit the parties to have separate experts and is likely to insist on a jointly commissioned report. Although the pre-action protocols apply at present only to certain kinds of claim, the spirit of those protocols should be honoured where possible in other cases. There will eventually be relatively few cases where the parties do not instruct a joint expert.

It is for this reason that claimants, who will still have the initiative at the outset, will want to prepare their cases as thoroughly as possible before proceedings are even issued. Defendants will also have to investigate every claim that is intimated to them and in the personal injury field, and particularly with road traffic accidents, this will cause insurance companies serious difficulties in adapting their practices to the litigation timetable.

14.3 Directions

The case management directions issued on allocation are meant to be comprehensive and to provide for every eventuality in the case under consideration. The objective is to reduce costs and court time by giving the parties every instruction they will need to prepare mainstream cases for trial so that there will be no need for any hearings. The rules do not of course forbid the parties making applications to the court before the trial and in due course we shall consider the procedure for making such applications. Generally applications will deal with the following matters, namely:

(a) for further directions or rulings by the court on matters which the standard directions hitherto issued do not cover and on which the parties need a ruling; or

(b) by one party where the other party is in breach of the directions already ordered by the court so that the innocent party cannot properly prepare his case for trial until the other party is forced to comply. This might, for example, be the case where one or other party has not given disclosure of documents adequately or has declined to exchange witness statements or experts' reports or indeed to respond to correspondence seeking agreement about matters.

For applications of the first kind, where some matter has arisen which is not dealt with in the standard form of directions issued so that the parties need a ruling on it, probably no issue of fault by either party will arise and the order for costs will be 'costs in the case'. With the second kind, however, the court will need to consider imposing a sanction on the party whose refusal to comply with the orders already made may be causing grave difficulties to the other party to the point where they may not be able to prepare their case for trial and there is a risk that the trial date may have to be adjourned. Various sanctions are available to the court and these are discussed in **Chapter 16**.

The directions then will be given upon allocation and will to whatever extent is possible, on the basis simply of written information, be tailored by the district judge to the needs of the case. It is possible, and indeed ought to be done in cases with any complications, for the parties to correspond to see whether a set of agreed directions can be put before the court with the allocation questionnaires. If that is done and they are acceptable to the court (which is not bound by any agreement between the parties) then directions in that form can be given. If for any reason there has been an allocation hearing, whether because one or other of the parties has not filed the allocation questionnaire in time, or because the court considers that further information is needed, then at the allocation hearing the court can give rather more 'customised' directions to accommodate information that the district judge has been given verbally about the case. In the majority of cases, however, directions will only need to deal with the following matters:

(a) Disclosure of documents.

(b) Service of witness statements.

(c) Expert evidence.

(d) Fixing the date of trial or the 'window', that is, the period of no more than three weeks within which the trial must take place, and the location of that trial.

14.3.1 Disclosure

This important subject is dealt with fully in **Chapter 18**. The district judge may take the view that no disclosure of documents is likely to be necessary at all given the nature of the case, or he may direct *standard disclosure* or if he has sufficient information may specify an individual kind of document in respect of which disclosure should take place. (See generally on this CPR, r. 28.3, and PD 28.) An order for standard disclosure will tell the parties that they must exchange lists of documents by a given date. Where the court directs the parties to do some act, the order itself will state a calendar date rather than a period (e.g., it will say that something is to be done by 24 September 2006 rather than 'within four weeks of this order'). The standard period for disclosure will probably be fixed at a date four weeks after the date on which the parties should receive the order giving notice of allocation and directions.

14.3.2 Witness statements

The subject of exchange of witness statements and what should go in them is further considered at **Chapter 19**. The parties will be required to exchange full witness statements verified by statements of truth from all the witnesses whom they intend to call at trial. The period for this will be after the date for disclosure of documents because it is sometimes necessary to have the parties comment on documents obtained from the other side. A typical order would provide for a date about 10 weeks after the notice of allocation was sent out. The statements must be full and should not be mere outlines. In view of the fact that the final hearing will last less than five hours in all, it is almost inevitable that the judge taking the trial will insist that there be no evidence-in-chief and that each witness merely confirms on oath that his witness statement is true, before being cross-examined.

14.3.3 Expert evidence

Ideally, the court prefers that the parties cooperate to instruct jointly a single expert in each relevant field and there is a very heavy presumption in favour of this in a fast track case. That expert's report, supplemented by the replies to any written questions that either party wishes to put to him, could then go in at the trial and the expert would not be called as a witness, thus substantially shortening the process. Some of the difficulties for a potential claimant in respect of this have been mentioned earlier (see **Chapter 9**) and will be discussed again in **Chapter 20**. By CPR, r. 26.6(5), expert evidence at trial on the fast track is limited to one expert per party in each expert field and to no more than two fields of expertise. Potentially, therefore, there could be four experts testifying at trial though that would be only in the most unusual of cases. Even if four experts are called, the oral procedures in relation to them are likely to involve only a modest amount of cross-examination because their reports can and ought to be supplemented by their answers to written questions posed in advance of trial by the opposing party under CPR, r. 35.6. A party who disagrees with an opponent's expert should have posed in advance most of the questions which would otherwise have been asked in cross-examination. At trial it is open to the court to impose on a party a time limit for questioning any given witness and one can well envisage a judge restricting cross-examination to say half an hour per expert to deal only with the areas still in disagreement between the experts. It must also be noted that under r. 35.12 the court has the power to direct a discussion between the experts with a view to producing an agreed statement of the issues on which they agree and disagree. If on the fast track a case throws up these features, it is most unlikely that the initial order for directions given on allocation will cover all eventualities and further directions may be needed in such a case. If the court concludes that there is any risk of the difficulties between the experts leading to the trial overrunning one day, it may be reallocated to the multi-track.

The basic direction that the court will give is usually that expert evidence should be exchanged about three months after the notice of allocation (PD 28, para. 3.12). There are a number of different possibilities in relation to expert evidence and the options provided within standard directions are:

(a) *Joint instruction of a single expert.* This will be the preferred option unless either party can put up (in his allocation questionnaire or hearing) a good argument why this is inappropriate. For the procedure on choosing the expert and instructing him see **Chapter 20**.

(b) *Simultaneous exchange of reports.* This ought to be the norm although it is important to remember that by this stage the parties will have needed to put up a good case as to why they should each have their own expert. If they have already obtained their own expert's report before allocation, they should have exchanged them voluntarily so that the court could give a meaningful direction after seeing to what extent the experts disagreed.

(c) *Sequential service of experts' reports.* This may well be because the claimant has already obtained and served his.

(d) *Discussions.* The court can order discussions between experts within a short time after service of experts' reports and the filing of a joint statement of agreed issues and those in dispute.

(e) *Order for no expert evidence.* This is necessary and refusing both parties permission to call any expert evidence at trial.

(f) *Order for expert evidence in written form.* This orders that expert evidence is permissible at trial, but must be in written form.

(g) *Deferring the decision* on whether oral expert evidence at trial is permissible until some later stage, say, at the time of the case being listed for trial.

14.4 Pre-trial checklist

Standard fast track directions will provide for all parties to file completed pre-trial checklist, also called 'listing questionnaires,' by a certain date. This is a standard court form, used also on the multi-track. In order to be useful this date will have to be at least eight weeks before the trial date or the beginning of the trial 'window' period. At the same time each party must file an estimate of costs in a standard form. A further substantial court fee is payable on filing a pre-trial checklist. This is a vital document which indicates to the court what has happened since directions were given, what evidence is agreed and updates the court on the parties' beliefs as to how long the trial will take, what the costs are and what witnesses will be called. When these checklists are received, it will be vital for the district judge to review them thoroughly to see whether there is anything in them which indicates that the potential trial date is likely to be abortive, for example:

(a) the fact that either side is unprepared;

(b) that the trial will now clearly take more than five hours; or

(c) that the court is now informed that a key witness will be unavailable at the time of the potential trial.

This is an opportunity for the district judge, in collaboration with the listing officer at the trial centre where the case will actually be heard (which may be different to the county court where it was started), to ensure that a trial date which will be effective can be given. Information in the listing questionnaire may indicate a need to reallocate to a different track and it may be necessary to call the parties before the court for that to be considered.

14.4.1 Listing for trial

On receipt of the pre-trial checklist the district judge will:

(a) fix the date of trial unless that has already been done;

(b) give any further directions for the trial that seem called for by the checklists, including a timetable for any further steps that need to be taken;

(c) give directions about the course of the trial. It is open to the court to give fixed times for cross-examination, the putting of the whole of each party's case and for submissions. This is a discretionary matter and many district judges will be reluctant to tie the hands of the trial judge in this way unless they know that they will be the trial judge. If the court decides to set such a timetable it must consult with the parties (CPR, r. 39.4). The court may go beyond the standard form of directions and name individual witnesses indicating how long is to be allowed for each of them. It is unusual for this to be done on the listing directions, though it may well be that the trial judge on the morning of the case in consultation with the advocates may fix a timetable for the day.

14.4.2 Trial bundles

The claimant must lodge a paginated and indexed bundle of documents at court seven days before the hearing so that the judge may have the opportunity of reading it at least on the morning of the case, if not earlier. This will ensure that the trial is efficient and that all the parties are referring to the same documents at the same time and place. Identical bundles must be given to the opponent and a further bundle kept to be used by witnesses.

The court may direct that a *case summary*, which should not exceed 250 words, should also be filed, which will direct the trial judge to the key issues. Where it refers to documents it should give the page numbers. This document should indicate what issues are now agreed and whether, for example, certain heads of damages can be conceded in agreed figures, so as to focus the trial judge's mind on the relevant parts of the trial bundle.

14.5 The trial

This is likely to take place in the county court most convenient to the parties, which will probably be where the case has been proceeding (as long as that county court has a trial hearing room). Flexibility is intended in the use of county court facilities and cases may be switched for trial between nearby county courts, depending on availability of accommodation and judges. Although the CPR were designed to encourage early settlement of cases, it remains the position that a fair proportion of cases will be settled only shortly before trial, thus freeing up extra courtrooms and judges who had been 'booked' at a relatively late stage. In a large conurbation, such as Birmingham or Manchester, there may be 20 or more courtrooms within a radius of about 10 miles. To facilitate maximum flexible use of the accommodation, a case which has been proceeding in one court may be switched for the trial itself to another court nearby.

In view of the directions which ought to have been carried out and the trial bundle, the judge will almost certainly not need opening speeches and may set a trial timetable if none has been set before. A trial judge will almost certainly order witness statements to stand as evidence-in-chief and may limit the length and scope of cross-examination and submissions.

Although the trial must last less than five hours, it does not follow that it will all be completed on the same day—a judge might be listed to hear a two-hour case for part of the morning before starting a full-day case which may overrun into the second day. If by any chance the reason for a case overrunning is due to an underestimate of time, the judge will normally try to sit on the following day to complete it. If it cannot be dealt with the following day, the judge will attempt to have it re-listed in the very early future so that all issues are fresh in his mind. If a substantial underestimate of time has been given, the judge may impose costs sanctions on whoever is to blame.

14.6 Costs on the fast track

The general rule is that at the end of a fast track trial, unless any of the parties is publicly funded or is a child or mental patient, the court will make a summary assessment of the costs of the whole claim immediately after giving judgment. For this purpose the parties are required to file and serve (not less than 24 hours before the trial) signed statements of their costs in the appropriate form, setting out:

(a) the number of hours claimed;

(b) the hourly rate by reference to the status of the fee earner, whether partner, assistant solicitor, legal executive, etc.;

(c) the amount and nature of all disbursements, counsel's fees and VAT.

Any failure to file or serve that statement of costs will be taken into account and the court may well refuse any order for costs if none has been filed, although that might be an extreme sanction. It may be possible that the parties can agree the amounts of costs dependent on the outcome. There will, however, be some sanction if no schedule of costs has been served until so late in the day that the party on whom it has been served has very little time to consider it or get proper instructions on it, since there may be serious injustice caused in the summary assessment of costs procedure, especially as the amount of costs may well be as great as, or more than, the amount of the claim itself. In such a situation the summary assessment of costs may have to be adjourned to a future date and the party who was guilty of late service of the schedule, thus necessitating the adjournment, is likely to have to pay all the costs of the adjourned hearing.

It is worth noting that one of the central planks of the proposals for fast track cases was that there would be a fixed limit on the amount of *all* the costs that could be recovered from one's opponent. Unfortunately, lengthy consultation about how these limits should be fixed led to a great deal of dissent and pilot programmes indicated wide disagreements even within the judiciary about what might be considered fair levels of overall costs for running even quite routine cases. Although the proposal that the costs payable by a losing opponent should be capped in this way remains under discussion, it is not in force and is unlikely to be for a long time to come, although the issue of capping fast track costs is said to remain 'at the top of the Lord Chancellor's agenda'. However, the costs of the trial itself *are* fixed by virtue of Part 46. These are the costs of attending on the day whether or not a barrister is used. They are in essence, an advocate's trial fees and are limited to the following amounts which may be recovered from the losing opponent.

Value of claim up to £3,000	£350.00
Between £3,000 and £10,000	£500.00
Claim for non-money remedies	£500.00
Claim over £10,000	£750.00
Additional fee for solicitor attending trial with counsel	£250.00

For a successful claimant the value of the claim for the purpose of these provisions is fixed at the amount of the judgment excluding interest, costs and any reduction for contributory negligence. If the defendant is successful, the amount is fixed by reference to the amount claimed on the claim form.

The solicitor's attendance fee with counsel is not automatic and the court must be satisfied that it was necessary (r. 46.3(2)).

If a fast track claim settles before the start of the trial (and there are still many that settle on the morning of the hearing) the amount can be the same as the above, but may not be more. In deciding on a fair amount to be allowed to the advocate for abortive preparation, the court will take into account the stage at which the claim was settled and when the court was notified of that fact.

If there are split trials on liability and quantum so that there are in effect two fast track trials, the first one may be up to the maxima specified above, but the second should not exceed two-thirds of that figure, subject to a minimum amount of £350.00 (r. 45.3(3)).

Lastly, if the court concluded that the trial was in any sense prolonged by improper behaviour of the successful party (e.g., calling unnecessary evidence or making unnecessarily lengthy submissions) it may reduce the amounts; if such behaviour came from the losing party the amounts may be correspondingly increased to be paid to the successful party.

Example of directions on fast track case

The claimant John Leigh is injured in a road traffic accident on 15 November 2005 caused, he claims, by the defendant Simon Broomhead, whose lorry collided with John Leigh's car. John Leigh has suffered soft tissue injuries to his spine and neck in a typical 'whiplash' accident, where damages are likely to be less than £5,000 for personal injuries. The claimant has a medical report from an orthopaedic consultant, Farida Akhtar, dated 3 May 2006, which recommends re-examination some six months later. John Leigh's loss of earnings, vehicle damage, hire of alternative vehicle, etc. amount to about £3,000.

A claim is issued in September 2006 and a defence is filed disputing liability, but without making any counter claim because Simon Broomhead's lorry suffered no significant damage in the collision with John Leigh's car.

The court sends out allocation questionnaires in October 2006 and these are returned by the parties fully completed with the appropriate details on the basis of which the district judge is able to give full directions through to trial without needing to call the parties before him for a case management conference.

Although the standard timetable for fast track directions runs for about nine months between allocation and trial, if it seems that the case will be ready for hearing rather earlier, the court can and usually does shorten the timetable slightly as it has in the following case. The court will have considered whether to order a split trial, that is, to have liability tried first and issues of quantum on some subsequent date if the claimant succeeds, but in a straightforward case like this will probably not order that. This is because if the claimant does succeed, it means there will be two separate trials with a consequent increase in preparation and advocate's fees. Everything can certainly comfortably be dealt with within one working court day in a straightforward case like this. When estimating the length of hearing, the court will take into account the estimates that both parties are obliged to provide on their allocation questionnaires, the number of witnesses which each have said they will call and also the fact that in such a case there will not be any oral expert evidence, the expert's evidence being given only in the form of written reports.

IN THE MIDDLEMARCH COUNTY COURT   Case No: 6MM14793

BETWEEN   John Leigh   Claimant

and

Simon Broomhead   Defendant

DIRECTIONS

---

1. The claim is allocated to the fast track. The trial window is from 1–22 April 2007. The estimated length of trial is four hours.

2. Each party shall give standard disclosure to every other party by list. The latest date for delivery of the lists is 30 November 2006. The latest date for service of any request to inspect or for a copy of a document is 6 December 2006.

3. Each party shall serve on every other party the witness statements of all witnesses of fact on whom he intends to rely. There should be simultaneous exchange of such statements no later than 6 February 2007.

4. The claimant may rely on the expert evidence of Farida Akhtar, orthopaedic consultant, in the form of the report dated 3 May 2006, already served; and an updated report to be served no later than 6 December 2006.

     The time for service of any questions addressed to the expert shall be no later than 14 days after service of the expert's further report. Any such questions shall be answered within 14 days of service of a question.

5. Pre-trial checklists shall be filed no later than 20 February 2007.

6. The claimant shall lodge an indexed bundle of documents contained in a ring binder and with each page clearly numbered at the court no more than seven days and not less that three days before the start of the trial.

7. Each party must inform the party immediately if the claim is settled, whether or not it is then possible to file a draft consent order to give effect to their agreement.

9 November 2006
District Judge Ross

Listing questionnaire
(Pre-trial checklist)

To be completed by, or on behalf of,

| |
| |

who is [1ˢᵗ][2ⁿᵈ][3ʳᵈ][   ][Claimant][Defendant]
[Part 20 claimant][Part 20 defendant] in this claim

In the	
Claim No.	
Last date for filing with court office	
Date(s) fixed for trial or trial period	

| This form must be **completed** and **returned** to the court no later than the date given above. If not, your statement of case may be struck out or some other sanction imposed. | If the claim has settled, or settles before the trial date, you must let the court know immediately. | **Legal representatives only:** You must **attach** estimates of costs incurred to date, and of your likely overall costs. In substantial cases, these should be provided in compliance with CPR Part 43. | For multi-track claims only, you must also **attach** a proposed timetable for the trial itself. |

A Confirmation of compliance with directions

1. I confirm that I have complied with those directions already given which require action by me.

☐Yes ☐No

If you are unable to give confirmation, state which directions you have still to comply with and the date by which this will be done.

Directions	Date

2. I believe that additional directions are necessary before the trial takes place.

☐Yes ☐No

If Yes, you should attach an application and a draft order.

*Include in your application all directions needed to enable the claim **to be tried on the date, or within the trial period, already fixed.** These should include any issues relating to experts and their evidence, and any orders needed in respect of directions still requiring action by any other party.*

3. Have you agreed the additional directions you are seeking with the other party(ies)?

☐Yes ☐No

B Witnesses

1. How many witnesses (including yourself) will be giving evidence on your behalf at the trial? *(Do not include experts - see Section C)*

Continued over ⇗

N170 Listing questionnaire (Pre-trial checklist) (12.02)   *Printed on behalf of The Court Service*   1 of 3

Witnesses continued

2. If the trial date is not yet fixed, are there any days within the trial period you or
your witnesses would wish to avoid if possible? *(Do not include experts - see Section C)*

Please give details

Name of witness	Dates to be avoided, if possible	Reason

Please specify any special facilities or arrangements needed at court for the
party or any witness (e.g. witness with a disability).

3. Will you be providing an interpreter for any of your witnesses?   ☐Yes ☐No

C Experts

*You are reminded that you may not use an expert's report or have your expert give oral evidence unless the court has given
permission. If you do not have permission, you must make an application (see section A2 above)*

1. Please give the information requested for your expert(s)

Name	Field of expertise	Joint expert?	Is report agreed?	Has permission been given for oral evidence?
		☐Yes ☐No	☐Yes ☐No	☐Yes ☐No
		☐Yes ☐No	☐Yes ☐No	☐Yes ☐No
		☐Yes ☐No	☐Yes ☐No	☐Yes ☐No

2. Has there been discussion between experts?   ☐Yes ☐No

3. Have the experts signed a joint statement?   ☐Yes ☐No

4. If your expert is giving oral evidence and the trial date is not yet fixed, is
there any day within the trial period which the expert would wish to avoid,
if possible?   ☐Yes ☐No

If Yes, please give details

Name	Dates to be avoided, if possible	Reason

D Legal representation

1. Who will be presenting your case at the trial?   ☐ You   ☐ Solicitor   ☐ Counsel

2. If the trial date is not yet fixed, is there any day within the trial period that the person presenting your case would wish to avoid, if possible?   ☐Yes ☐No

If Yes, please give details

Name	Dates to be avoided, if possible	Reason

E The trial

1. Has the estimate of the time needed for trial changed?   ☐Yes ☐No

If Yes, say how long you estimate the whole trial will take, including both parties' cross-examination and closing arguments   ☐days ☐hours ☐minutes

2. If different from original estimate have you agreed with the other party(ies) that this is now the **total** time needed?   ☐Yes ☐No

3. Is the timetable for trial you have attached agreed with the other party(ies)?   ☐Yes ☐No

Fast track cases only
The court will normally give you 3 weeks notice of the date fixed for a fast track trial unless, in exceptional circumstances, the court directs that shorter notice will be given.

Would you be prepared to accept shorter notice of the date fixed for trial?   ☐Yes ☐No

F Document and fee checklist
Tick as appropriate

I attach to this questionnaire -

☐An application and fee for additional directions   ☐A proposed timetable for trial

☐A draft order   ☐An estimate of costs

☐Listing fee

Signed	Please enter your [firm's] name, reference number and full postal address including (if appropriate) details of DX, fax or e-mail
[Counsel][Solicitor][for the][1st][2nd][3rd][ ] [Claimant][Defendant] [Part 20 claimant][Part 20 defendant]	
Date	Postcode

Tel. no.		DX no.		E-mail	
Fax no.		Ref. no.			

3 of 3

The multi-track: CPR, Part 29

15.1 Introduction

As its name implies, the multi-track allows many options as to how a case will proceed from allocation to trial. Unless the parties both consent, the court cannot force a claim worth more than £15,000 on to the fast track. This, however, means that sometimes straightforward disputes in contract and tort, where the length of trial may be no more than a couple of hours with simply the claimant's word against the defendant's and no other witnesses, will be on the multi-track. Even though for the parties to fail to agree to allocation down to the fast track in such a case might appear contrary to the overriding objective, if one or both of the parties maintains its opposition to such transfer, the court has no power to impose it. The multi-track thus ranges from modest cases to cases involving claims for catastrophic injuries, quantified in the millions, and multi-million-pound commercial disputes. Case management on the multi-track must therefore reflect the flexibility that will be necessary to ensure that each case is dealt with in accordance with the overriding objective, particularly in terms of speed and allocation of an appropriate proportion of the court's resources. In larger and more complex disputes, to some extent the court will have to be guided by the parties and their assessment of appropriate procedures and timescales. The court may, by skilful use of the provision to order that separate issues be tried at separate times, attempt to break up the case into smaller segments where possible.

Cases on the multi-track in London will be dealt with usually in the Royal Courts of Justice. Outside London the trials will take place either at one of the major trial centres, e.g., Birmingham, Bristol, Manchester, or may very well end up being tried at any county court which happens to have a courtroom available. This is particularly the case where the proceedings are relatively straightforward and likely to last only one or two days, even if the amount involved is above £15,000.

Very heavyweight cases may well be transferred to the local civil trial 'centre', i.e., the court in the nearest large town or city, i.e., for further case management there, and this will certainly be so for cases involving very large sums or multiple parties. Although one of the main objectives of the CPR was to stamp out local variations in practice so that a uniform system might be applied, case management of multi-track cases in some areas seems to remain in the smaller courts ('feeder courts'), whereas in others such cases are transferred at a very early stage to a major trial centre.

15.2 Directions

The allocation decision is made after return of the allocation questionnaires. What happens next will depend largely on how full the information is in the allocation questionnaires and, crucially, whether the parties have cooperated to the extent of trying to agree directions. It will be very much in the parties' interest to attempt to agree directions because solicitors will still prefer, as far as possible, to run cases on a timetable they consider realistic rather than leaving this to a district judge who may not be aware of all the features of the case and may initially impose directions which prove to be unworkable. If the parties do submit joint directions the court will always scrutinise them and is certainly not bound to accept them, but if the parties have considered that they need a given length of time to carry out a certain stage, the court may be reluctant to impose a different view. As well as the information in the allocation questionnaires, the parties may file other documents at court, but by virtue of PD 26, para. 2.2, the parties should, when submitting further documents:

(a) confirm that all parties have agreed that the information is correct and that it should be put before the court; or

(b) confirm that the party who has sent the document to the court has delivered a copy to all the other parties.

Examples are given in PD 26 of material which will assist the court, for example:

(a) a party's intention to apply for summary judgment or some other order that may dispose of the case or some of the issues in it;

(b) a party's intention to issue a Part 20 claim or add another party (see **12.6.2** and **Chapter 27**);

(c) the steps the parties have taken in the preparation of evidence, in particular, expert evidence and the steps they intend to take;

(d) any directions the party believes will be appropriate;

(e) any particular facts that may affect the timetable; or

(f) any fact which may make it desirable for the court to fix an allocation hearing or a hearing at which case management directions will be given.

The practice direction reiterates the necessity for cooperation between the parties, particularly at this early stage.

If the court considers it does not have sufficient information to give comprehensive directions that will take the case from allocation to trial it will call a case management conference. It may call that immediately or it may direct that certain basic procedural steps which are likely to be material in every kind of case be carried out in advance so that at the case management conference everyone is better informed. Examples of such stages would be to direct that parties undertake disclosure of documents and possibly exchange witness statements and expert evidence. The court may then list a case management conference after the final date by which those directions were to be carried out. As an extra incentive to thorough preparation for the case management conference it may specify a trial period. It is suggested that unless the case is very straightforward there is probably little point in doing this as one of the purposes of the case management conference is to assess the future of the case. There is little point in fixing unrealistic trial periods which may need to be vacated, though undoubtedly just specifying a trial period will assist in concentrating the parties' minds wonderfully!

15.3 Case management conferences

The court has a discretion whether to call such a conference and in straightforward cases and particularly those where the parties have agreed directions which seem to the court comprehensive and realistic, there is little point in doing so since one of the objectives of the rules is to avoid multiplicity of hearings. If the court contemplates ordering evidence on a particular issue to be given by a single expert then PD 29, para. 4.13, provides that a case management conference must be held unless the parties have consented to the order in writing. The limiting of expert evidence in large cases is likely to be one of the most difficult areas where, however robust the court's own approach would be, in the interests of justice it is obliged to listen to what the parties have to say.

It is vital to note that each party must be represented by someone who has authority to make procedural concessions and who is familiar with the file and evidence. If inadequate representatives are sent and the case management conference needs to be adjourned, the court will normally order that the party in default pay the costs. This is likely to involve a wasted costs order against the solicitor personally (see **33.8**).

At the case management conference the court will:

(a) review what has been done so far; and

(b) decide on directions that are needed to push the action on to trial in accordance with the overriding objective; and

(c) attempt to ensure that reasonable agreements are made between the parties for the future conduct of the action; and

(d) record any agreements or concessions reached.

If the case is complex then directions may be given for either party (though usually the claimant) to file a *case summary* of up to 500 words so that the court can understand the principal issues, if these are not clear by the documents already filed. This is intended to be a non-contentious document, recording in a neutral fashion what the issues are. Its contents should, where possible, be agreed between all the parties.

At the case management conference, on the assumption that a number of basic directions have been carried out so far, it should be possible for the court to focus on outstanding issues. It is likely to consider:

(a) whether further information should be provided from each party either by clarification of statements of case or further witness statements;

(b) whether the procedure between the parties in relation to expert evidence has been satisfactory, if orders are needed for questions to be put to opposing experts and if meetings of experts should be ordered;

(c) whether it would be appropriate to have split trials on any issues, for example, to have a disputed Limitation Act issue tried early or separate trials of liability and quantum;

(d) when there should be another case management conference and who should undertake it. Further case management will often be by the same district judge. Very large or complex cases may be sent for case management to be undertaken from the start by a circuit judge or even a High Court judge;

(e) whether there should be a pre-trial review. The difference between a case management conference and a pre-trial review is that the latter is conducted by the judge who will hear the trial. He will consider the case sufficiently far in advance of trial to enable him to give worthwhile further directions as to how the case should be prepared and presented;

(f) whether it is possible to fix a date for the trial or to give a 'window'. This is likely to be a more difficult matter on the multi-track because several witnesses and even several expert witnesses may need to attend. The need to accommodate witness availability, particularly over popular holiday periods, is likely to mean that the court dare not give a fixed date for trial, but is likely to provide some mechanism for the parties to confirm dates of availability while allocating the trial to a given period in the future. It will also be necessary for there to be a realistic estimate so far as possible of how long the trial will take, since a good deal of skill in allocating the court's resources is required. It may not be until it is seen how much of the evidence is agreed that a realistic estimate of length of trial can take place.

15.4 Pre-trial checklist

If it is possible to fix a period for trial, the court will give written notice to the parties and specify a date by which the parties must file Pre-trial checklist (CPR, r. 29.2(3)). Pre-trial checklists are in the prescribed form which has already been discussed in connection with the fast track and they should be filed at court not less than eight weeks before the trial date or window. Each party is obliged to return the completed checklist together with a costs statement, indicating the costs so far, and the claimant has to pay a listing fee. Once all the checklists have been received or the time for returning them has expired, the procedural judge will make directions or, in cases of complexity, will call a listing hearing if there needs to be a discussion about such matters as agreement of evidence or length of trial.

15.5 Directions at other hearings

We have described the way in which complex cases will proceed and the hearings that will manage the case. It is important to note, however, that where the parties are before the court for any purpose the court will consider how case management generally may be undertaken. For that reason, the hearings should always be attended by responsible representatives who are familiar with the file.

15.6 Variation of the case management timetable

If any party wishes to vary the timetable then an application should be made to the court. However, the parties are often able to vary times by agreement in so far as they relate to the carrying out of actions directly between themselves. They may not, however, without an application to the court, vary any directions which would have the effect of changing any of the following:

(a) a date fixed for holding a case management conference;

(b) a date fixed for holding a pre-trial review;

(c) a date fixed for the return of pre-trial checklists; or

(d) a date fixed for trial or trial window.

This is perhaps one of the most dramatic changes introduced by the CPR. The previous practice, whereby if the parties were willing to adjourn some aspect of the case the court would usually endorse it without enquiry, has disappeared. The essential parts of the case management timetable may *not* be changed by consent between the parties without a specific application to the court. The court is likely to be very reluctant to permit such variations and certainly very reluctant to adjourn or vacate the trial date. It should be noted that even if other dates in the timetable are varied by agreement, the parties are required to apply for a consent order and file a draft of that order and an agreed statement of the reasons why the variation is sought (PD 29, para. 6.5(2)). The file will then be put before a district judge and he will normally endorse the agreement. If, however, he considers that the agreement imperils one of the other important dates, for example, because it allows too little time between the carrying out of some stage which the parties have agreed to defer and the trial itself, then he may refuse to do so and call the parties before him for a hearing to explain the position and confirm that they will be able to honour the court's timetable.

Example of directions on the multi-track

This claim is brought by Barry Tarrant, who claims that on 3 January 2005, whilst shopping in Middlemarch Superstore, he slipped on a spillage of yoghurt or cream near the dairy counter. Mr Tarrant is a self-employed roofer and claims that he twisted his knee very badly in the accident, as a result of which he has not been able to work since the accident and will never again be able to work in a physically demanding job such as roofing. He has no other skills and does not think it will be easy to find a sedentary job. He is therefore claiming a lifetime future loss of earnings as a roofer, though he concedes he may be able to find some employment at some stage doing something else, which will inevitably be less well-paid than his previous occupation. His business has of course had to be closed.

He also claims to have been a very active sportsman before the incident and now to be unable to enjoy those pastimes.

The defendants have carefully investigated the matter and do not believe that the incident happened at all. Nothing was reported at the time to any member of staff, and the claim was made only several weeks after the date of the alleged accident, by which time the CCTV footage from 3 January, showing the dairy counter, had been erased. The defendants say there are other suspicious features, including that Mr Tarrant did not go to casualty at the local hospital at the time, but only reported matters to his GP 10 days after the incident. They say that the facts are quite consistent with Mr Tarrant, if he suffered any accident at all, having suffered it at work or somewhere else and seeking now to make a fabricated claim.

The parties have co-operated before the issue of proceedings in choice of experts, and the claim was issued on 4 November 2005. By this time the claimant had been examined by an orthopaedic consultant, Jane Davies; and because he claims that he suffers from serious depression caused by his injury and his inability to work, by a consultant psychiatrist, Calum Simons.

The defendants have had the claimant examined by their own choice of orthopaedic consultant, Mr Paul Massey, who has indicated in his first report that he is unable to find any physical causes for the symptoms which the claimant contends that he has. The report suggests the likelihood of fabrication. On the basis of that report the defendant has commissioned a private investigator to carry out a video surveillance of the claimant and the investigator has filmed the claimant playing football in his garden with his teenaged son; and up a ladder doing physically demanding repairs at his own house; and apparently participating in a 'fun run' at the local park. The video and a witness statement supporting it have been served on the claimant's solicitors. The claimant's explanation is that on the days in question he was trying to 'battle through the pain' and make the best of it, but that after each bout of activity he suffered a significant relapse.

The defendant now also wishes to commission a report from a psychiatrist, but it has not yet obtained that report.

After service of the particulars of claim and defence, allocation questionnaires are sent out by the court, fully completed by the parties and sent back to court. Each party has also submitted draft directions which they consider appropriate and in this case the district judge has decided it would be better to call the parties before him for a case management conference in an attempt to progress the case as efficiently and economically as possible towards trial. It is clearly a significant case involving, on the claimant's version, hundreds of thousands of pounds in terms of lost earnings. The court will therefore have no objection to each side having its own expert witnesses and if necessary, for those expert witnesses to give oral evidence at trial, expensive though that may be.

When the court sends out notice to the parties to attend the case management conference, the claimant takes advantage of that hearing to issue an application to be dealt with at the same time, asking the court to rule the video surveillance inadmissible because of breach of the claimant's right to privacy under Article 8 of the European Convention on Human Rights.

As will be observed, the district judge dismissed that application, holding, as is the usual outcome for such applications, that the defendant's right to a fair trial and to defend itself overrides the obvious apparent breach of the claimant's privacy by being filmed in his own garden.

Whilst it is possible that the court would set a timetable ending with a further case management conference, in this case the court has set a timetable through to trial without calling the parties back before it. If anything happened which would throw the timetable out, or any new matters arise, the parties can of course apply to vary the timetable at some later stage. It will be noted that the court has not in this case ordered a split trial of the issues of liability and quantum, largely because the medical evidence will be essential on the issue of liability as well as quantum, i.e., is the claimant fabricating the whole incident?

The order for directions might look like this:

IN THE MIDDLEMARCH COUNTY COURT   **Claim No: 5MM 33971**

BETWEEN   Barry Tarrant   <u>Claimant</u>

and

Middlemarch Superstores plc   <u>Defendant</u>

Upon hearing the solicitor for the claimant and the solicitor for the defendant.

_____

DIRECTIONS

_____

1. The claim is allocated to the multi-track.

2. The claimant's application that the evidence of private investigators instructed by the defendant and the video surveillance film taken by them be ruled inadmissible at trial is dismissed.

3. Each party shall give standard disclosure to every other party by list. The latest date for delivery of the lists is 8 March 2006; the latest date for service of any request to inspect or for a copy of the document is 22 March 2006.

4. Each party shall serve on every other party the witness statements of all witnesses of fact on whom he intends to rely. There shall be simultaneous exchange of such statements no later than 10 May 2006.

5. The parties have permission to rely at trial on expert evidence as follows:
    The claimant: Ms Jane Davies FRCS, orthopaedic consultant, Mr Calum Simons, consultant psychiatrist.
    The defendant: Mr Paul Massey FRCS, orthopaedic consultant, Dr Suzanne Marsland, psychiatrist.
    The parties may rely on the reports of Ms Davies, Mr Simons and Mr Massey already served. The report of Dr Marsland shall be served no later than 9 April 2006.
    The time for service on another party of any questions addressed to an expert instructed by that party is not later than 3 May 2006. Any such question shall be answered within 14 days of service.

6. No later than 31 May 2006 there shall be a without prejudice discussion between the relevant experts in each discipline, to identify the outstanding issues between them and to reach agreement if possible. The experts shall prepare for the court a statement of the issues on which they agree and on which they disagree with a summary of their reasons and that statement shall be filed with the court no later than 14 June 2006. The court will decide whether oral evidence from the experts shall be permitted on filing of pre-trial checklists.

7. The claimant shall serve an updated schedule of loss no later than 14 July 2006. The defendant shall serve a counter schedule by no later than 28 July 2006.

8. The parties shall file pre-trial checklists no later than 18 August 2006, accompanied by copies of all experts reports and questions and responses to questions and the schedule of loss and counter schedule. The parties shall co-operate in an attempt to agree an estimated length of hearing to be communicated to the court with the pre-trial checklists.

9. The trial of this case will take place on a date to be fixed in the period 1 October to 30 November 2006, with a present estimated length of hearing of two days.

10. The claimant shall lodge an indexed bundle of documents contained in a ring binder and with each page clearly numbered at the court not more than seven days and not less than three days before the start of the trial.

11. Costs in the case
    24 February 2006
    District Judge Keeley

16

Sanctions

It is now appropriate to consider what sanctions are available for non-compliance with the court's directions. In principle, these sanctions are available on all three tracks but perhaps are more likely to be material on the fast claims track where the parties will be under considerable time pressure to carry out each of the steps. On the multi-track, more latitude in terms of length of time will clearly have to be allowed in bigger cases, but non-compliance is likely to be penalised for the simple reason that where one party fails to carry out what they need to do, it will inevitably postpone the next stage; for example, if one party delays giving proper disclosure of documents the innocent party may not be able to prepare his witness statements or instruct his expert. We therefore need to consider the sanctions that may be imposed for breach of court orders generally.

The court intends that its case management will have teeth. In cases of serious non-compliance with court orders, this will lead in effect to the end of the case of the party in default, and in others will involve restrictions on the way in which that party may conduct its case in future, including restrictions on the evidence which it may call at trial. It remains to be seen whether these sanctions in their most draconian form will survive examination under the Human Rights Act 1998 and whether they breach Article 6 of the European Convention on Human Rights, which guarantees a fair trial. For fuller consideration see **Chapter 37**. The most common sanctions which a court may impose are as follows:

16.1 Striking out

The court may strike out a statement of case of either party if it appears that there has been a failure to comply with a rule, practice direction or court order (CPR, r. 3.4(2)(c)).

This is undoubtedly the most drastic power and will be reserved for wholesale default or repeated breach of court orders which have put the whole case management time table at risk. The court may strike out a part of the statement of case rather than the whole of it so that if, for example, a party repeatedly failed to give proper disclosure of documents which supported some aspect of a damages claim, the court might strike out those heads of damage from the particulars of claim.

The court may impose this penalty on its own initiative or may do so on application by another party. It is important to note here that where an 'innocent' party meets default by an opponent he has to follow the procedure in PD 28, para. 5, and PD 29, para. 7, for fast track and multi-track respectively. The innocent party must write to the party in default warning that if the situation is not rectified immediately, he will apply for an order to enforce it. The innocent party must then apply for such an order without delay. In the spirit of cooperation required by the rules, if the default is not very significant (for example, missing a key date for disclosure by a few days), the innocent party will be expected to let the party in default put this right as long as the 'key dates' in case management are not put at risk. If the default means that other dates become unrealistic, the innocent party should apply to the court for a new timetable and request that the defaulting party pay the costs of the further application. It is important to note, however, that when considering the effect of defaults which have put the case management timetable at risk, by virtue of PD 28 and PD 29:

(a) The court will not allow a failure to comply with directions to lead to the postponement of the trial unless the circumstances are exceptional.

(b) If practical, the court will exercise its powers in a manner that enables the case to come for trial on the dates or within the dates previously set.

(c) The court will reassess what steps each party now needs to take to prepare for trial, direct that they do so in the shortest practicable time and impose a sanction for non-compliance. The most likely sanctions late on in the case will be that the party who fails to comply will be refused the right to raise or contest issues, for example, a party may be refused the right to call expert witnesses.

(d) If it appears that the delay means that the trial as a whole cannot proceed fairly, the court may direct that the trial can proceed on the issues which are ready at the time. Extra costs caused by the need to reconvene the trial to resolve outstanding issues will be paid by the party in default.

(e) If there is no option but to postpone the trial, any adjournment will be for the shortest possible period.

16.2   Debarring evidence

The court may order that a party in default be debarred from adducing evidence on a particular issue or from a particular witness, lay or expert.

This is likely to be a very drastic sanction to be imposed probably where there has been more than one failure to disclose a key piece of evidence in time.

EXAMPLE

The claimant's claim arising out of a road accident includes a large element for loss of profits of his business. An early case management direction is made for disclosure of his business accounts so that his claim for loss of profits can be justified. The claimant has failed to give disclosure. An early application to compel compliance with the previous order by the defendant has led to an order that unless the claimant discloses the accounts by a given date, he will be debarred from calling that evidence.

If the claimant still does not disclose his business accounts within the time fixed by the court order, he will not be permitted to include his claim for loss of profits at trial and will be confined to his other heads of claim.

However drastic the form of order imposed, it is still possible for the court to grant relief from sanctions. It might do this if the accounts were eventually disclosed late, but in time to permit the defendant to investigate the position thoroughly and decide what evidence of his own he wished to call about the matter. The defaulting party would be very much thrown on the court's mercy and would need to demonstrate that there was no prejudice to the defendant in this situation. The court's indulgence could certainly not be relied upon (see **16.8.**).

16.3 Disallowing expert's evidence

By CPR, r. 35.13, a party who fails to disclose an expert's report may not use the report at the trial or call the expert to give oral evidence unless the court gives permission.

The regime in relation to expert evidence is now viewed as a matter of such importance in limiting costs that it would be almost inconceivable that the court would permit a party to call an expert witness at trial whose report had not previously been disclosed (see **Chapter 20**).

16.4 Non-compliance with Practice Direction, Part 32

PD 32, para. 25, provides that if an affidavit, witness statement or exhibit does not comply with the formal requirements of CPR, Part 32 or PD 32, the court may refuse to admit it as evidence and may refuse to allow the costs arising from its preparation (see **Chapter 19**).

16.5 Ordering payment of a sum of money into court

A court may order a party in default to pay a sum of money into court where that party has without good reason failed to comply with a rule, practice direction or a relevant pre-action protocol (CPR, r. 3.1(5)).

When exercising its power under this rule, the court must have regard to the amount in dispute and the costs which the parties have incurred or which they may incur.

This therefore might be an appropriate sanction if the court forms the view that either party is deliberately dragging its heels. The amount ordered to be paid in should clearly not exceed the amount involved in the case and the nature of this sanction is unclear. It presumably intends the party in default to give security either for the amount in dispute, or for the costs incurred or particularly incurred by the default in compliance with directions. The rule gives no guidance at all to the circumstances in which it is considered appropriate to impose this, as distinct from any other, sanction. There is still no reported case setting out any principle for applying this sanction.

16.6 Costs

This is likely to be the most appropriate sanction in routine cases. The court may always order costs and indeed may assess them and order them to be paid immediately by the defaulting party. This is likely to be the most realistic form of sanction and the one most generally imposed. Thus, if, for example, a party has failed to comply with an order to disclose certain documents and there has subsequently, after some correspondence about the matter, been an application by the other party to enforce that order, the court when hearing that application will order the defaulting party to pay the costs of the wasted work done and is quite likely to order them to be paid on the indemnity basis and to be summarily assessed and payable within 14 days. This may well be a significant figure and will bring home to the party at fault the consequences of non-cooperation. If the party against whom costs have been ordered does not pay them, however, that is not a further ground for striking out the action, neither is it a contempt of court. The party who has been awarded the costs must enforce them in the same way as any other judgment.

For fuller discussion of costs at interim hearings see **Chapter 33**.

16.7 Non-compliance with an order imposing a sanction

If a party fails to comply with a rule, practice direction or order imposing a sanction, the sanction takes effect unless the defaulting party applies for, and obtains relief from, the sanction (CPR, r. 3.8). Extensions of time in relation to sanctions cannot be agreed between the parties.

16.8 Applications for relief from a sanction

A party in breach of a rule may apply for relief from the sanction imposed by issuing an application notice supported by evidence, that is, a statement or witness statement by the solicitor or party in default. Rule 3.9 provides that the court will then consider all the circumstances and sets out a number of factors to be considered when deciding what the consequences will be for non-compliance with the original order and whether the sanction should be imposed. Under r. 3.9, these features are:

(a) the interests of the administration of justice;

(b) whether the application for relief has been made promptly;

(c) whether the failure to comply was intentional;

(d) whether there is a good explanation for the failure;

(e) the extent to which the party in default has complied with other rules, practice directions, court orders and any relevant pre-action protocol;

(f) whether the failure to comply was caused by the party or his legal representative;

(g) whether the trial date can still be met if relief is granted, the effect which any failure to comply had on each party and the effect which the granting of relief would have on each party.

All of these features ought to be considered where a party applies for relief from a sanction which the court has imposed (such as striking out of a statement of case or disallowing the right to call a witness). It is obviously important that the courts are seen to be applying the rules rigorously, but this must always be tempered by the justice of the individual case. It is suggested that the courts will rapidly acknowledge that the timescale for carrying out some actions under the new rules is relatively brief and if a party can show a good reason for what may appear to be continued failure to comply with a court order, the court may temper the sanction. Sometimes default can be explained by difficulties of communication, for example, if the claimant has been transferred overseas for some weeks because of his job, or key documents cannot be found. If it is clear that the non-compliance with the court order was not intentional and contemptuous, the court may give relief so long as the other party has not been prejudiced (which is unlikely in the case of modest delays) and the case management timetable can also be preserved.

16.9   Non-compliance with pre-action protocols

In cases where protocols apply, the court has a further express sanction (although it is suggested that this is anyway implicit in the range of discretionary costs orders that could be made). In particular, PD Protocols, para. 2.3, sets out orders that the court may make where it concludes that failure to observe a protocol has led to the commencement of proceedings which might otherwise not have been needed or led to extra costs being incurred. In such cases the court may:

(a) order the party at fault to pay the costs of the proceedings or part of those other costs of the other party;

(b) order that the party at fault pay the costs on an indemnity basis (see **Chapter 33**);

(c) if the party at fault is a claimant who is eventually successful, order that he be deprived of interest on such sum over such a period as may be specified or that interest be awarded at a lower rate;

(d) if the party at fault is a defendant and the claimant succeeds, make an order awarding the claimant interest at a higher rate on the damages or part of the damages for such period as the court may order, the rate not to exceed 10 per cent above bank base rate.

The overriding objective described under para. 2.4 of PD Protocols is that in exercising its powers, the court wishes to place the innocent party in no worse a position than he would have been if the protocol had been complied with.

Other sanctions that can be imposed where there is non-compliance include fixing the case management timetable in such a way as to ensure cooperation and exchange of information, and if it is the claimant who has not observed the protocols and failed to give the defendant adequate opportunity to investigate, staying proceedings to enable the defendant to 'catch up' before requiring him to progress the case.

Small claims: CPR, Part 27

17.1 Introduction

It will be recalled that an important objective of the CPR is that, under r. 1.1(2), the court should seek to:

(b) [save] expense;

(c) [deal] with the case in ways which are proportionate—
   (i) to the amount of money involved;
   (ii) to the importance of the case;
   (iii) to the complexity of the issues; and
   (iv) to the financial position of each party.

In carrying out this objective a separate regime is set up for the small claims track. The term 'small claims' is unfortunate given that the upper limit of the financial jurisdiction (£5,000) represents a sum which many would consider large.

17.2 The small claims jurisdiction—venue and level

When a claim is commenced and a defence is filed the first matter to be dealt with will be a consideration of whether it should stay in the court where it was issued. Under CPR, r. 26.2(1), if the defendant is an *individual* and the claim is for a specified amount of money and was not commenced in the defendant's home court, the court will transfer the proceedings there. If there are two or more defendants, the court will transfer to the home court of the first defendant to file his defence. There is no automatic transfer if the defendant is a company, or partnership.

There are two other complications here: where the defence is either that the money claimed has already been paid; or there is a partial admission by the defendant. In either case, the claimant is sent notice of what is being said and asked whether he wishes to proceed further. If he says he does, transfer will then be dealt with.

The phrase 'specified amount of money' is obviously apt to describe simple debt claims. However, it is also open to a litigant, and clearly this is only likely to be done by litigants in person, to state the amount of money he thinks the claim is worth, even where it is in essence a claim for unliquidated damages such as personal injury or a holiday disappointment claim. The advantage of him doing so is that if the defendant takes no action, he can then obtain judgment in default for the amount of his claim and there will be no judicial investigation as to quantum. If the defendant then applies successfully to set aside the judgment, quantum will of course remain at large when the proceedings continue. The disadvantage of claiming a specified sum of money rather than damages limited to some upper figure is that on the filing of a defence the case will be transferred to the defendant's home court. If the claim is not for a specified amount of money, on the face of it the case will remain in the court of issue. The court anyway has a discretionary power to transfer proceedings to another county court, or to the High Court or list if it considers it appropriate to do so before allocating a claim to a track (r. 26.3).

When completing the allocation questionnaire, as we have seen, a party may request the proceedings to be *stayed* while the parties try to settle the case by alternative dispute resolution or other means. In modest claims this is unlikely to involve a formal alternative dispute resolution procedure though it may include such things as participation in an arbitration system within a given industry (as with holiday claims). It may merely amount to an indication of a desire to negotiate. If all parties request a stay or the court of its own initiative considers that such a stay would be appropriate, it will direct that the proceedings are stayed for one month (r. 26.4(2)) or for such longer period as it considers appropriate. If the claim is in fact settled the claimant must tell the court. If he does not notify the court that the claim is settled then the court will give such directions as to the management of the case as are appropriate. At the expiry of whatever period is allowed the court will give further directions about the case.

17.2.1   Pre-allocation procedures: The possibility of summary judgment

It is not inevitable that a case where the claim is for £5,000 or less will be allocated to the small claims track. The case may end before allocation. It is open to a claimant immediately upon receiving an acknowledgement of service or defence to apply for *summary judgment* (see **26.6**). There are two reasons why this may well prove to be a means of disposing of a proportion of small claims. The first is the upper limit of £5,000 which means that there are likely to be more substantial disputes within the system.

The second is the need where such an application is made for a defendant to satisfy the demanding test of showing that he has a real prospect of successfully defending the claim. It is also possible for a defendant to apply for summary judgment against a claimant to dispose of a hopeless claim on the same test. Where one or other party successfully takes this early initiative, the case will be disposed of there and then with the consequence that it has never been allocated to any track. In that situation the successful party can apply for costs in the ordinary way and is not subject to the rule providing for only modest fixed costs on small claims which is discussed below. Where a case does end early by summary judgment, the court will undoubtedly undertake a summary assessment of costs there and then.

We shall now go on to discuss the position of cases which are allocated to the small claims track.

17.2.2   The small claims track

By CPR, r. 26.6(1), the small claims track is the normal track for:

(a) any claim which has a financial value of not more than £5,000;

(b) any claim for personal injuries where:

    (i)   the financial value of the whole claim is not more than £5,000; and

    (ii) the financial value of any claim for damages for personal injuries is not more than £1,000.

NB: By r. 26.6(2) 'damages for personal injuries' are defined to include only pain and suffering and loss of amenity. Thus special damages in any form, even loss of earnings, are not taken into account in fixing the value of a personal injury claim below £1,000. Thus if there is a minor injury, say to the finger of a professional musician which incapacitates him for a short period, causing him to lose a lucrative booking, if the general damages would be under £1,000 the extra special damages will not bring the claim outside the small claims limit, unless the whole claim would then exceed £5,000.

    (c) any claim which includes a claim by a tenant of residential premises against his landlord where:

        (i)   the tenant is seeking an order requiring the landlord to carry out repairs or other work to the premises (whether or not he also seeks some other remedy);

        (ii)   the cost of the repairs or other work to the premises is estimated to be not more than £1,000; and

        (iii) the financial value of any other claim for damages is not more than £1,000.

It would seem therefore that in housing disrepair cases, which are typically brought against local authorities, for the case to be allocated to the small claims track there is now an artificial limit of £2,000 to the whole claim, given that the cost of repairs must be under £1,000 and the cost of any other general damages claim has a similar limit.

17.2.3 A specific exception

By r. 26.7(4) the small claims track is *not* the normal track for a claim which includes a claim by a tenant of residential premises against his landlord for damages for harassment or unlawful eviction, even if the amount of damages sought is under £5,000.

17.2.4 Remedies and the small claims track

There is no restriction on the nature of remedies which can be granted on the small claims track. Thus injunctions, possession, restitution, specific performance and the like are available to the same extent that they are available on the other tracks. Exceptions are, however, that by s. 7 of the Civil Procedure Act 1997 jurisdiction to grant freezing injunctions and search orders is restricted to the High Court.

17.3 Important differences between the small claims and other tracks

The important differences between small claims and the other tracks are:

    (a) a number of other rules and procedures have no application on the small claims track;

    (b) the procedures after allocation;

    (c) the procedure at the hearing;

    (d) costs provisions.

17.3.1 Restriction on application of other rules (r. 27.2)

In the small claims jurisdiction the following Parts of the CPR do not apply:

    (a) Part 25 (interim remedies except as it relates to interim injunctions);

(b) Part 31 (disclosure and inspection);

(c) Part 32 (evidence) except r. 32.1 which contains the power of the court to control evidence generally;

(d) Part 33 (miscellaneous rules about evidence);

(e) Part 35 (experts and assessors) except r. 35.1 which empowers the court and provides a duty for the court to restrict expert evidence and sets out the expert's overriding duty to the court (r. 35.3); and the rules (35.7 and 35.8) which deal with instructions to joint experts.

(f) Part 18 (request for further information);

(g) Part 36 (offers to settle and payments into court);

(h) Part 39 (hearings except r. 39.2—general rule that hearings are to be in public).

In principle, the other parts of the rules apply to small claims except to the extent that any rule limits such application.

17.4 Procedure after allocation to the small claims track (r. 27.4)

Once the case has been allocated to the small claims track the court will give standard directions in one of several forms depending on the type of case. These forms of directions are set out at the end of PD 27, and the relevant one will be sent out by the court as an official court form. There are a variety of ways in which the case may proceed and we shall now examine the alternatives.

This text is of course written for the benefit of those who will be the legal representatives of parties. However, much litigation in the small claims track is between two parties, neither of whom have lawyers, including disputes between neighbours, and between consumers and the providers of goods and services. A substantial amount of small claims litigation consists of disputes between householders and tradesmen.

However, an understanding of procedure on the small claims track is likely to be of importance to most litigation solicitors (outside firms which deal exclusively with major litigation). This is largely because of the existence of legal expenses insurance. It has been estimated that there may be as many as 17 million insurance policies which cover legal expenses, including not merely the obvious category of motor insurance, but also a wide variety of other types of policies. This is likely to mean that in fact the majority of the population, since some of these policies will cover all members of the policyholder's family, may have the advantage of legal expenses insurance for some types of claim and these may include quite modest consumer disputes. It is a feature of the average district judge's small claims hearings list that one or both parties is likely to be legally represented at some stage of the case, although it may well be that the legal representatives do not attend the eventual trial. Moreover, parties may receive assistance under the Legal Help scheme for drafting documents or responding to court orders, and may anyway take legal advice about the early stages of such a claim, even though that advice, if there is no insurance policy covering legal costs, is bound to conclude that it is likely to be unremunerative for the party to be legally represented for the full hearing. In addition, there is a considerable category of litigants, including large companies, local authorities and the like, who will employ solicitors in their litigation department who will certainly have to handle small claims cases on a regular basis, especially given the percentage of small claims litigation which is, in effect, merely disputed debt collecting.

Indeed, litigation in the small claims track may be the place where early advocacy experience is obtained. At best, such cases may be run relatively formally between skilled litigators, but litigators will also have to have, or develop, the skill of running proceedings efficiently against an unrepresented party who is either unwilling or even unable to understand what is required of him in the way of compliance with court orders, and to whom the courts extend a certain amount of indulgence which they might not extend to those with professional representation. We shall go on in this text to consider the options available to the court and the outcomes and responses which the legal representative of a party might have to consider.

17.4.1 Option 1

The court may simply give standard directions and fix a date for the final hearing.

The form of standard directions differs depending on the type of case. If no other form of directions is specified then the basic standard directions contain a direction:

(a) for service of copies of any documents on which a party intends to rely no later than 14 days before the hearing;

(b) for the original documents to be brought to the hearing;

(c) for notice of hearing date and time; and

(d) an instruction to the parties to inform the court immediately if the case is settled by agreement.

District judges' experience of the small claims jurisdiction will usually enable them to give a reasonable estimate of the length of hearing for routine cases. Experience of small claims shows a very high rate of late settlement or simply 'no show' by the parties even for consumer disputes which hitherto appear to have been litigated with enthusiasm, or even personal animosity between the parties. This feature has enabled the courts generally to adopt 'back-to-back' small claims case listings, so that for example two or more district judges are jointly listed to hear many hours' worth of cases whose litigants are all instructed to attend court at 10.00 a.m. or 2.00 p.m. Experience shows that it is usually safe for the court to list twice or even three times the number of cases that could in fact be properly dealt with if all were effective. The upper limit of the small claims jurisdiction will mean that there are more cases where the litigants most certainly will appear and take longer to present their cases because the amounts involved are more significant. Conversely, the standard directions for certain types of cases (see below) to exchange witness statements and for the claimant to prepare other documents for use of the court ought to assist in identifying the issues and resolving them more swiftly. The Practice Direction at 27 PD 2.5 now requires the court to consider carefully whether ordering witness statements is appropriate in the particular case. Most district judges consider it is usually advantageous to order them. Having said that it is true that litigants in person, even well educated ones, often have difficulty drafting witness statements and differentiating between relevant and irrelevant facts. Where one party is legally represented and the other is not, a lawyer may find it frustrating to be confronted with manifestly inadequate witness statements which will need to be amplified by lengthy oral evidence at the hearing when he himself has gone to some trouble to put his client's version into a full and thorough statement. However, apart from encouraging the court to make more drastic orders there is perhaps not a great deal that can be done. Without a series of preliminary appointments (which will be time consuming, expensive and may delay things unacceptably) it may be difficult to extract a full detailed witness statement from unintelligent litigants and the court will have to rely on obtaining information through questioning by the district judge at the hearing.

The other standard directions take into account the different features for:

(a) road traffic cases;

(b) building disputes;

(c) vehicle repairs and similar claims;

(d) disputes between landlord and tenant (including claims for return of deposit or in respect of damage by tenants);

(e) breach of duty cases, e.g., negligence, deficient professional services, etc.

These are adapted to the peculiarities of the respective type of case, and generally impose a certain level of formality of procedure on the parties which will assist in clarifying the issues and shortening the hearing.

Although, as noted above, many of the formalities of cases on other tracks do not apply to the small claims track, in order to make the hearing efficient many district judges will usually give fairly formal directions, especially if both parties are legally represented. For example, a direction that the parties file full witness statements which can stand as evidence in chief makes the hearing shorter, more efficient and may encourage settlement. District judges have a discretion to add this kind of direction whenever it seems appropriate. There may also be cases in which ordering formal disclosure of documents rather than ordering it in the rather modified form normal on the small claims track seems appropriate.

The court has a general power under r. 27.7 to add to, vary, or revoke directions.

17.4.2   Option 2

The court can give *special directions* and consider what further directions are to be given no later than 28 days after this date.

A common example where such directions are useful in practice is where both the claimant's statement of case and the defence are wholly inadequate to convey to the court just what the issues are. For example, the claimant may simply refer to an unpaid invoice for a large sum; and the defendant may simply deny any liability at all. The court is then presented with two short documents which might not even indicate the types of goods or materials supplied and the reason why payment is disputed. Often such cases are between parties who have had a continuing contractual relationship, e.g., builders' merchant and builder, where large sums of money have been paid over the years but internal accounting procedures have not always been very satisfactory at allocating payments to given invoices, and some long-running discrepancy is now being sued for and challenged. To resolve this kind of case almost always requires a preliminary appointment but it is useful to send out directions to require the parties to go to some effort to clarify matters for the court.

Special directions will usually be appropriate where the issues need to be clarified in some way, particularly by the disclosure of documents between the parties and to the court. After further documents setting out the parties' positions and their legal entitlement (and sometimes whether the correct parties have been involved hitherto) the court should be in a position to decide how to proceed, which will be either for listing, giving yet further directions, or perhaps calling the parties before it for a preliminary hearing under r. 27.6 (see **17.4.4.1**).

17.4.3 Option 3

The court may give *special directions* and fix a date for the final hearing. This will be appropriate where there is some issue which can be clarified which falls outside the usual run of standard directions, but it seems unlikely that a further hearing or supplementary directions will be necessary.

17.4.4 Option 4

The court may fix a date for a *preliminary* hearing under r. 27.6.

17.4.4.1 The preliminary hearing

Rule 27.6 provides that the court may hold a preliminary hearing, which is a very limited form of case management hearing, for the consideration of the claim *only* in one of three situations, namely:

(1) Where it considers that special directions under r. 27.4 are needed to ensure a fair hearing *and* it appears necessary for a party to attend court to ensure understanding of what must be done to comply with the special directions.

(2) To enable the court to dispose of the claim on the basis that one of the parties has no real prospect of success.

(3) To enable it to strike out a statement of case or part of it on the basis that the statement of case or the part to be struck out discloses no reasonable grounds for bringing or defending the claim.

The circumstances therefore where a preliminary hearing will be held are quite tightly defined. Under r. 27.6(2) the court must also have regard to limiting the expenses of the parties attending court and therefore considerations not merely of proportionality to the amounts involved, but whether or not either party is legally represented and even travelling distances should be considered. If one is acting for a party against an opponent who is also legally represented, it really should be possible for the solicitors to agree what directions are necessary to avoid the unwelcome extra expense of this hearing, which will generally speaking be irrecoverable from the other party. If one is litigating against an unrepresented opponent, it may frankly be best to send one's client along with written instructions on what to ask for as a means of saving costs (unless the client is specifically willing to pay) as attending on the client's behalf will undoubtedly take at least an hour of the solicitor's time from leaving the office to return.

The three separate circumstances therefore involve the following alternatives:

(a) Cases where the court thinks, perhaps from the content or appearance of the documents so far received, that one or other of the parties may not fully have understood what was needed. It may be necessary to get the parties before the court to ensure that they understand what is necessary so that the case can progress properly and efficiently. Special directions may need to be considered and it would be inappropriate simply for the district judge to draft these and send them to the parties without hearing representations about them or inviting the parties to clarify some aspect which further special directions may help with.

(b) The second basis for a preliminary hearing is where it is apparent from the documents that one or other party has no chance of success. Examples might be an action on a dishonoured cheque where the defence makes some complaint about the quality of the goods supplied; where a claimant is basing his case on no cause of action known to English law; or where the reality of the 'defence' simply amounts to an allegation of inability to pay. Preliminary hearings will usually be given short appointment times of, say, 15 minutes. It will assist both the court (for future listing) and the parties involved to remove such hopeless cases.

(c) The third provision is supplementary to the second. Clearly if the failure to disclose cause of action or defence is a result of lay drafting, an opportunity should be given to correct that, but if on examination it seems the case is hopeless, this is in effect a specific variant of the previous power to bring the claim or defence, or some part of it, to an end.

Under r. 27.6(4), at the preliminary hearing the court may treat the hearing as final if all the parties agree. It is unlikely that this will apply unless the point is a very short one, because the court is unlikely to have fixed very long for a preliminary appointment. It is self-defeating if a preliminary appointment is given the same length of time as a substantive hearing. If there is one short point and the parties agree to it resolving the issue, it can be dealt with by the court. Otherwise after the preliminary hearing the court will fix the date of the final hearing and inform the parties of the amount of time allowed and give other appropriate directions.

17.4.5   Option 5

17.4.5.1   Proceeding without a hearing (r. 27.10)

The court may, *if all parties agree*, deal with the claim without a hearing. The court cannot impose this on the parties without agreement due to the effect of the Human Rights Act 1998 which came into force in October 2000, as a result of which the right to a fair trial might well have been infringed by such an order. This is an excellent example of the way in which the European Convention has already influenced civil procedure. See further **Chapter 37**. No such difficulty applies of course where the parties consent. In such a case a lawyer will usually want to deliver written submissions on behalf of his client as well as written evidence.

17.5   Conduct of the final hearing (r. 27.8)

The final hearing will normally be before a district judge, but there is a specific provision in PD 27 that it may be before a circuit judge. It is suggested that this would be highly unlikely, because it makes for extreme difficulty in the question of appeals, which are heard before a judge of the next higher level.

17.5.1   Representation

Under PD 27 the parties may present their own case at the hearing or it may be presented by a lawyer (i.e., barrister, solicitor or legal executive employed by a solicitor) or by a lay representative. A lay representative may only appear if the party is present or if he is that party's employee or if the court gives permission. Any officer or employee may represent a corporate party.

17.5.2 Public/private hearing

The hearing will be in public. However, the judge may decide to hold it in private if:

(a) the parties agree; or

(b) a ground mentioned in CPR, r. 39.2(3), applies.

Under r. 39.2(3) the court is entitled to take into account a variety of factors in directing that a hearing or any part of it may be in private. This includes where:

(a) publicity would defeat the object of the hearing;

(b) there are matters of national security (unlikely in a small claims context!);

(c) publicity would damage confidentiality of information including information relating to personal financial matters (a provision which arguably may often apply in small claims cases); or

(d) the court considers it to be necessary in the interests of justice.

PD 27 goes on to say at para. 4.2 that a hearing that takes place at the court will generally be in the judge's room, but it may take place in a courtroom.

Under CPR, r. 39.2, the general rule that all hearings are to be in public is partly qualified because it says that '*The requirement for a hearing to be in public does not require the court to make special arrangements for accommodating members of the public*'.

District judges' private rooms will usually accommodate no more than about six to eight people. If there are two parties, especially if either or both are legally represented, and there are one or two witnesses (who will usually be present throughout small claims hearings), there are unlikely to be more than one or two chairs available for members of the public. Such hearings would rarely, if ever, generate much interest for casual passers-by, and there are so many small claims hearings that they will almost always be conducted in the district judge's room because open court accommodation is simply not available. It remains to be seen if this is sufficient to comply with the European Convention on Human Rights and Fundamental Freedoms, Article 6 of which requires a public hearing in civil cases. In *R (on the application of Pelling)* v *Bow County Court* (2000) *The Times*, 19 October 2000, the Administrative Court dismissed an argument that the practice of hearing small claims trials behind outer security doors fitted with locks meant that it was not a public hearing.

17.5.3 Method of proceeding

Rule 27.8 of the CPR allows the court to adopt any method of proceeding that it considers to be fair, and to limit cross-examination. PD 27, para. 4.3, provides also that the judge may:

(a) ask questions of any witness himself before allowing any other person to do so;

(b) ask questions of all or any of the witnesses himself before allowing any other person to ask questions of any witnesses;

(c) refuse to allow cross-examination of any witness until all the witnesses have given evidence-in-chief;

(d) limit cross-examination of a witness to a fixed time or to a particular subject or issue or both.

It will therefore be up to the district judge hearing the case to decide how to proceed. If both parties are unrepresented he is likely to explain to them the order of events—he will take the evidence of each of them uninterrupted by the other party, but may then allow questions to be put or may himself try to extract necessary information by questions. He will try, generally speaking, to put both parties at their ease. The extent to which he will be prepared to involve himself in what is still, after all, meant to be an adversarial process will vary from case to case. He must be sure on the one hand not to appear to be favouring either party by helping them to supplement the deficiencies in their case, but equally to do justice he will have to ensure that everything necessary is brought out. If both parties are legally represented, matters may proceed more efficiently with some degree of formality so that events mirror an open court trial, e.g., opening speeches, formal evidence given in chief (although in such cases provision for witness statements to stand as evidence-in-chief may be useful), cross-examination and re-examination, and closing speeches. With unrepresented litigants, the district judge will assess the situation and the parties and decide what he needs to hear in order both to do justice and ensure that the parties feel that, within reason, they have had their say. Although a district judge may control cross-examination by the parties, it is suggested that it is not appropriate to forbid cross-examination entirely (*Chilton* v *Saga Holidays plc* [1986] 1 All ER 841).

17.5.4 Recording evidence and the giving of reasons

By PD 27, para. 5, the judge may direct that all or part of the proceedings will be tape-recorded and this is now usually the case, and a party may thereafter obtain a transcript on payment of the proper charges.

The judge will make a note of the central points of the oral evidence, although the whole case is tape-recorded (para. 5.3). By paras 5.4 and 5.5 he will make a note of the central reasons for his judgment, unless it is given orally and tape-recorded by the court. The judge is expressly permitted to give his reasons 'as briefly and simply as the nature of the case allows' and he will normally do so orally at the hearing, but he may give them later either in writing or at a hearing fixed for him to do so.

Where the judge decides the case without a hearing under r. 27.10, or a party who has given notice under r. 27.9(1) does not attend the hearing, the judge will prepare a note of his reasons and the court will send a copy to each party.

17.5.5 Non-attendance of the parties at the final hearing (r. 27.9)

It is very common for one or both of the parties to fail to attend the final hearing, sometimes with no explanation, or sometimes having written or faxed some explanation for their absence. The district judge has the options described below: if you represent a party and the opponent does not appear, clearly you will attempt to persuade the district judge to proceed with the matter. The rules are as follows:

(a) If a party who does not attend a final hearing has given the court written notice *at least seven days before* the date that he will not attend and requested the court to decide the claim in his absence, the court will take into account his statement of case and other documents he has filed.

(b) If a *claimant* does not attend or give that notice then the court *may* strike out the claim.

It will be appreciated that the word 'may' gives the court some discretion. A party who has misunderstood the requirement to give seven days' notice and perhaps sends in a fax on the morning of the hearing, requesting the court to deal with the case on the basis of his written statements, will no doubt be given some latitude. If the opposing party can demonstrate any prejudice caused by the lack of notice of the other party's non-appearance, an adjournment may be permitted. This might be because the party who is present needed to cross-examine the absent party about some feature of his case which would have demonstrated that a piece of evidence was false or that a certain document was not authentic. One party may need the other to attend in order to establish quantum, e.g., claims by former employees to commission payments based on sales. Generally speaking, a party who attends is likely to do better than a party who does not.

(c) If a *defendant* does not attend a hearing or give the notice referred to and the claimant does, the court may decide the claim on the basis of the claimant's evidence only.

(d) If *both parties* do not attend and do not give notice, the court may strike out the claim and any defence and counterclaim.

Nothing in these provisions affects the general power of the court to adjourn a hearing for good reason, e.g., where a party who wishes to attend cannot do so for reasons such as illness.

17.6 Setting judgment aside and rehearing (r. 27.11)

A party who was neither present nor represented at the hearing of the claim, and who did not give written notice to the court under CPR, r. 27.9(1), may apply for an order that a judgment shall be set aside and the claim reheard.

Application must be made not more than 14 days after the day on which notice of the judgment was served on that party. The court may then by r. 27.11(3) grant an application *only* if the applicant:

(a) had a good reason for not attending or being represented at the hearing or giving written notice to the court under r. 27.9(1); *and*

(b) has a reasonable prospect of success at the hearing.

Moreover, a party may not apply to set judgment aside under this rule if the court dealt with the claim without a hearing under r. 27.10 (i.e., by order of the court with the consent of the parties dispensing with the hearing).

This provides a twofold test for someone who did not appear at the hearing and who seeks to reopen the case. The court will first require the application to be made within 14 days of the party in question receiving notice; the application to set aside will itself be on notice to the other party; and the party applying will have to show a good reason for not having attended, been represented or having given written notice to proceed in his absence. It will be for the court to decide what form of proof is required, but the burden is clearly on the applicant. The court is likely to be sceptical of alleged postal failures, sudden unspecific illnesses or urgent work commitments. The case of *Shocked v Goldschmidt (1994)* [1998] 1 All ER 372 indicates the proper approach. If a party deliberately absents himself from court without proper reason he has no right to have the case reheard, however strong his case. If the court concludes that there is good reason to proceed, then there is still an obligation on the party applying to show a *reasonable prospect of success*. This will obviously go beyond consideration of whatever documents have been filed or provided and may lead to the court asking for an affidavit or further documentary proof.

17.6.1 If judgment is set aside

By r. 27.11(4), if judgment is set aside the court must fix a new hearing date. The hearing may take place immediately after the hearing of the application to set aside the judgment and may be dealt with by the judge who set aside the judgment. It is most unlikely that the court will in fact proceed to hear the case fully after an application to set judgment aside. The court would have been reluctant to allocate sufficient time to such an application because experience shows that a fair proportion of people who apply to set aside a judgment which was obtained against them in their absence, do not trouble to attend on the application to set it aside either!

17.7 Right of appeal on the small claims track

There is a right of appeal against the decision of the court on a small claims hearing. This will not take the form of a rehearing but is subject to the usual procedure and restrictions on appeal, as to which see **Chapter 36**.

17.8 Costs on the small claims track (r. 27.14)

17.8.1 Costs after allocation

There are considerable restrictions on costs orders between the parties. In principle by CPR, r. 27.14(2), the court may not order a party to pay a sum to another party for that other party's costs except:

(a) the *fixed costs* payable under Part 45 attributable to issuing the claim. (These are on a very modest sliding scale going up to a maximum of only £80 for solicitors' fees, to which the court fees will be added.)

(b) in proceedings which include a claim for injunction or specific performance, an amount to be specified in a practice direction for legal advice and assistance relating to that claim. Currently, PD 27 provides for an amount not exceeding £260.00.

(c) costs assessed by the summary procedure in relation to an appeal under r. 27.12;

(d) such further costs as the court may assess by the summary procedure and order to be paid by a party who has behaved unreasonably.

In addition, the court may also order a party to pay:

(a) all or part of any court fees paid by another party;

(b) expenses which a party or witness has reasonably incurred in travel and subsistence for a hearing;

(c) any loss of earnings (up to an amount specified in the practice direction, currently £50.00) for attending a hearing;

(d) an expert's fees up to an amount not exceeding that specified in a practice direction (currently £200.00 per expert).

By virtue of r. 27.5, no expert may give evidence whether written or oral at a hearing without the permission of the court.

This is a vital restriction on recoverable costs. The costs to be awarded are decidedly modest and will be a serious disincentive to employing a lawyer for those parties who do not have the benefit of legal expenses insurance guaranteeing them such representation (this remains common in road traffic accident claims).

17.8.2   What is 'behaving unreasonably'?

Cases dealing with the word 'unreasonably' tend to show that an objective test should be applied. Matters which may be considered unreasonable in this context are, for example:

(a) making a claim which the court has found to be wholly false (although the court should be wary of coming to the conclusion that a claim is wholly false merely because it has in the end preferred one party's evidence to another's);

(b) failure to inform of non-attendance of a witness;

(c) deliberate delay in dealing with an undeniable claim so as to force a party to issue proceedings;

(d) filing a spurious defence and then not attending the final hearing;

(e) paying the claim in full just before the final hearing; and

(f) making unnecessary procedural applications.

A material factor may be that the rules on payments into court and offers to settle have no application in these proceedings. It remains to be seen whether despite this, the court will treat a reasonable offer to compromise which has been refused as relevant to reasonableness generally when awarding costs. For that reason it is important to put any such offer in written form, heading it 'without prejudice save as to costs', which means that the letter is privileged from production, but can be produced after the hearing as evidence of reasonableness.

The court is required, where it concludes that a party has behaved unreasonably, to assess the costs by the summary procedure (see **33.6**). It will thus be important for a party which anticipates being able successfully to press a claim for costs to have completed and be able to justify the 'statement of costs' form. This is to be used on summary assessments of costs and indicates the status of fee earner, time claimed for attendances, correspondence, documents and other work.

17.8.3   Reallocation from the small claims track (r. 26.15)

For any case reallocated from the small claims track to another track the costs provisions cease to apply after the claim has been reallocated and the fast track or multi-track rules will thereafter apply.

17.8.4   Costs in exceptional cases (r. 27.14(5))

Where the parties have consented to a claim being allocated to the small claims track from some other track even though the financial value of the claim exceeds the limit for the small claims track for costs purposes, the claim is to be treated as if it were proceeding on the fast track. Trial costs are at the discretion of the court and shall not exceed the amount set out for the value of the claim if it were a fast track case.

In addition, by r. 27.15, if a claim is allocated to the small claims track and subsequently reallocated to another track the costs limits in r. 27.15 will cease to apply after reallocation and the fast track or multi-track rules will thereafter apply.

17.8.5   Allocation of assessments of damages and disposals

Cases may come into the small claims track on issues of quantum only, after liability has been determined elsewhere, whether by trial of a preliminary issue, judgment in default or summary judgment. Where such cases are referred to the small claims track, the limitation on costs in respect of the small claims hearing will apply, although costs of earlier stages will be based on the sums available on the track concerned. In principle, it is likely that at the conclusion of any hearing, after which proceedings are to be transferred to the small claims track, the court will have undertaken a summary assessment of costs of the proceedings.

Chapters 18 to 20

Chapters 18 to 20 consider in detail three particular aspects of civil evidence. By the case management stage the court will be concerned to give definite directions in the interests of encouraging openness between the parties and, particularly, in the interests of limiting costs and proceeding efficiently towards trial in a manner proportionate to the issues involved in the case.

When it gives case management directions, whether at allocation or later, the court will be anxious to see it has as much information as possible in order to assess what directions should be given for each of the following matters. If little information is provided in the allocation questionnaire, no doubt the court will give fairly standardised directions in what seems to be a modest value or routine case. In more complex cases, it will be vital for the parties to convey as much information as possible to the court so that the directions can be adapted to the particular kind of case.

The next three chapters therefore deal in turn with:

Chapter 18   Disclosure of documents;
Chapter 19   Exchange of witness evidence;
Chapter 20   Expert witnesses.

Disclosure of documents:
CPR, Part 31

18.1 Introduction

Disclosure of documents is the stage of an action at which one party reveals to the other what relevant documents are, or have been, in its possession and provides an opportunity for that other party to inspect and take copies of those documents. A party will be entitled to refuse inspection of documents only by claiming that they are irrelevant or there is some privilege attaching to them. The substantive law of privilege is discussed at **Chapter 5**.

Disclosure of documents takes place in almost every case. In major commercial actions, perhaps between multiple parties, it can take a long time and involve many thousands of documents recording business transactions going back many years. Even in simple cases such as road traffic accidents, however, there will usually be some documents. The defendant will probably not have any, but the claimant will at least have car repair invoices as well as documents to substantiate any other damages claimed: for example, loss of earnings claims by reference to wage slips, or a letter from his employer.

Part 31 of the CPR provides rules about disclosure and inspection of documents and these apply to all claims except those on the small claims track. In every case an order of the court is necessary unless the parties agree to undertake the procedure voluntarily.

18.1.1 The principle (CPR, r. 31.2)

A party *discloses* a document by stating that the document exists or has existed. This then gives a right of inspection under r. 31.3 to the opposing party except where:

    (a) the document is no longer in the control of the party who disclosed it; or

    (b) the party disclosing the document has a right to withhold inspection of it; or

    (c) where a party contends that it would be *disproportionate* to the issues in the case to permit inspection of certain documents (see **18.8**).

18.1.2 What is a 'document'?

By r. 31.4, a document is defined as *'anything in which information of any description is recorded'*. A copy is defined as *'anything onto which information recorded in the document has been copied, by whatever means and whether directly or indirectly'*. Thus document is not confined to paper and includes disks, audio cassettes, video cassettes, and computer programs.

18.2   The usual rule—disclosure limited to 'standard disclosure'

By CPR, r. 31.5(1), a party is not required to give more than *standard disclosure* unless:

(a) the court orders otherwise;

(b) the court dispenses with or limits standard disclosure; and

(c) the parties agree in writing to dispense with or limit standard disclosure.

Rule 28.3(2) provides that on the fast track the court may decide not to direct standard disclosure, but may direct that no disclosure takes place or specify the documents or classes of documents which the parties must disclose. This is likely to occur, if in pursuance of the pre-action protocols there has already been substantial or total disclosure at some earlier stage. On the multi-track r. 29.2 deals with case management generally and disclosure will be ordered in almost every case.

The court when exercising its case management powers, therefore, having scrutinised the statements of case and allocation questionnaires, may decide to limit standard disclosure to what it perceives to be the relevant issues. For example, where the statements of case make it clear that the whole litigation turns on whether a written contract was or was not subsequently varied by agreement between the parties, the court may limit disclosure 'to the issue as to whether or not the contract dated 25 February 2002 was varied in the course of correspondence between the parties, between 15 April and 7 May 2002'.

18.2.1   Time for disclosure on the fast track

One of the first matters that the district judge is likely to consider, having read the statements of case and the allocation questionnaires, is what disclosure appears to be necessary. He will then give appropriate directions. It is of course possible for the parties when returning their allocation questionnaires to submit drafts of directions they consider appropriate and where possible these should be agreed in advance between them. If the parties have identified what disclosure they want, then it is unlikely that the court will impose its own view.

18.2.2   The nature of standard disclosure (r. 31.6)

By r. 31.6, standard disclosure requires a party to disclose *only*:

(a) the documents on which he relies;

(b) the documents which could:
   (i)   adversely affect his own case;
   (ii)   adversely affect another party's case; or
   (iii) support another party's case;

(c) the documents which he is required to disclose by any practice direction.

This requires the disclosing party to admit the existence of, and subsequently grant inspection of, all documents on which he proposes to rely. In addition, he must disclose those which could adversely affect his own case or support another party's case. There is a requirement of absolute honesty in undertaking disclosure.

This duty of honesty may lead the court to restate the duties already expressed to exist in relation to solicitors, namely, that they should give their clients full and early advice about the duty to preserve documents as in *Rockwell Machine Tool Co. Ltd* v *E.E. Barrus (Concessionaires) Ltd* [1968] 2 All ER 68. The duty to advise a client might well now extend to advising them to make an early and thorough search for relevant documents. The best advice that one can give a client is to submit all documents that might be conceivably relevant, leaving the solicitor to sift through them to see if he thinks they are legally relevant to the case and to see whether privilege can be asserted for any of them.

It is not unknown at this stage for a client to produce a document which is adverse to his case and insist that the solicitor does not disclose it to the opponent. Where this happens and the client cannot be persuaded otherwise, a solicitor must withdraw from the case. It is a vitally important part of a solicitor's duty to the court that he should never be party to dishonesty on disclosure.

18.3   The duty of disclosure (r. 31.8)

By CPR, r. 31.8(1), there is only a duty to disclose documents which are now or have been previously *within one's contro*l. A document is in a party's control if:

(a) it is or was in his physical possession;

(b) he has or has had a right to possession of it; or

(c) he has or has had a right to inspect or take copies of it.

Disclosure therefore is the process of revealing the existence of documents, whether one has or has not access to them at present. If one has parted with the only copy of a document, disclosure must nonetheless be undertaken under this principle because it may be open to the opposing party to force the disclosing party to recover it or copies of it. A party who no longer has documents may still be required to give disclosure (and eventually inspection) if he has the right to control the documents personally in the capacity in which he is sued. This is not necessary if his control of documents is in another capacity, e.g., as director of a company (*B* v *B* (*Matrimonial Proceedings: Discovery*) [1978] Fam 181). There will always be questions of fact as to the nature of control, e.g., whether the documents of a subsidiary company are within the power of its parent company; or whether the documents of a company are in the power of its majority shareholder.

18.3.1   Disclosure of copies (r. 31.9)

A party need only disclose one copy of a document. However, a copy should be treated as a separate document if it has a modification, obliteration or other marking or feature on which a party intends to rely or which adversely affects his own case, another party's case or supports another party's case. If, for example, several copies of a memorandum have been sent out by someone who later becomes a party to litigation in which the memorandum is material, and some have been returned to the originator with other people's comments written upon them, which might be useful to one's opponent in litigation, these other copies must be disclosed.

18.3.2   The duty of search (r. 31.7)

Rule 31.7 provides a specific duty, although one already implicit in the essence of the rule, which is that when giving standard disclosure a party is required to make a reasonable search for documents falling within r. 31.6(b) or (c). This reinforces the duty of honesty in the process. Should the issue of reasonableness of the search be called into question, then there is a further sub-definition which involves considerations of cost and proportionality in the proceedings.

Specifically, the rule provides that in deciding the reasonableness of a search the factors *include* the following (i.e., these are not exhaustive):

(a) the number of documents involved;

(b) the nature and complexity of the proceedings;

(c) the ease and expense of retrieval of any particular documents; and

(d) the significance of any document which is likely to be located during the search.

There is a specific provision that if a party has not searched for a category or class of document on the grounds that to do so would be unreasonable he must state this in his disclosure statement and identify the category or class of document (r. 31.7(3)). This is a difficult provision because on the face of it this only matters if the documents in question would have been disclosable and of some relevance to the litigation. It will presumably apply where the documents have been last seen so long ago that a search is most unlikely to be successful. This is unlikely to apply to a private individual as any documents he is likely to have would be at home or at his workplace but it may well apply in the case of a large organisation which keeps voluminous archives where the search for the document would take an unreasonable amount of time compared to its potential importance. Disputes under this provision will inevitably turn on their own facts.

The rule is supplemented by para. 2 of PD 31, which re-stresses the overriding principle of *proportionality* and suggests that in some cases it may be reasonable to decide not to search for documents which came into existence before a particular date or to limit the search to documents in a particular place or documents in particular categories.

18.3.3 The procedure for standard disclosure (r. 31.10)

Each party must make and serve on every other party a list of documents in form N265. In order to make the process efficient the rule provides that the list must:

(a) satisfactorily identify the documents in a convenient order and manner and as concisely as possible; *and*

(b) indicate which documents are no longer in the party's control and what has happened to them.

Under para. 3.2 of PD 31 it is suggested that if a large number of documents fall into a particular category the disclosing party may list the documents as a category rather than individually, e.g., '50 bank statements relating to account number 31336 at London Bank between 1998 and 2002'.

There must also be 'a disclosure statement' (r. 31.10(5)). A disclosure statement is a statement made by the party disclosing the documents which:

(a) sets out the extent of the search that has been made to locate documents;

(b) certifies that he understands the duty to disclose documents; and

(c) certifies that to the best of his knowledge he has carried out that duty (r. 31.10(6)).

By virtue of PD 31, the form of disclosure statement must also expressly state that the disclosing party believes the extent of the search to have been reasonable in all the circumstances; and in setting out the extent of the search should draw attention to any particular limitations on the extent of the search which were adopted for proportionality reasons and give the reason why those limitations were adopted, e.g., difficulty or expense.

Should the party not be an individual then the company, firm, association or other organisation involved must also identify the person who makes the statement and explain why he is considered an appropriate person to make the statement.

The parties may agree in writing to disclose documents without making a formal list and without making a disclosure statement (r. 31.10(8)). Any such written agreement should be lodged with the court.

18.3.4   The duty to disclose is a continuing one (r. 31.11)

The duty of honest disclosure continues until the proceedings are concluded. Thus if new documents are created which are not privileged, or if documents are found or come to light at any time during the proceedings, that party has a continuing obligation to notify the other parties.

18.4   Dissatisfaction with opponent's disclosure

Suppose that when disclosure is undertaken there is a document or class of document whose existence had been anticipated and which is believed to be relevant to the issues, but the opponent does not include it in his list? The first step with this, as with all such queries, is simply to raise the matter in letter form and see what the response is. The responses might clarify the matter but there may then be slippage in the case management timetable. For example, although the solicitor for the opponent may be conducting matters efficiently, he may say that he is awaiting information from the client so that it appears that it is the client who is dragging his heels.

In view of the tight time limits, particularly on the fast track, a party faced with this sort of response cannot wait very long before launching an application to the court. How courts organise themselves in terms of listing applications which are urgent is a matter of local practice, but it is certainly unlikely that one could get a hearing even for a 20-minute application in much under a month. Vital time will have been lost. Moreover, other stages of the case may be affected if disclosure is not undertaken fully. Some of the documents may be needed to instruct an expert witness properly, or for other witnesses to comment upon in their witness statements. Faced with this situation, if an unsatisfactory response or no response is received a party should apply for specific disclosure of the documents in question under r. 31.12. The court may make an order for *specific disclosure* ordering a party to do one or more of the following:

(a) disclose documents or classes of documents specified in the order;

(b) carry out a search to the extent stated in the order;

(c) disclose any documents located as a result of that search.

An order for *specific inspection* is an order that a party permit inspection of a document named in the order.

Any application for an order under this paragraph must be made by application notice, specify the order that the applicant intends to ask the court to make and must be supported by evidence. The rules do not provide what this evidence should contain, but it is suggested that the statement should explain the nature of the dispute, the stage reached in the proceedings, and the factors which lead one to conclude that the documents sought exist, are relevant, and are within the control of the opposing party.

The rules do not say in what form compliance with any order for specific disclosure should be undertaken. It is likely, however, that the form of order will require the party against whom it is made to file evidence or certify in some form whether the documents exist and the extent of any search made. The court will of course have regard to the overriding principles of proportionality and reasonableness.

18.5   Inspection and copying of documents (r. 31.15)

Where a party has a right to inspect a document then he must give the party who disclosed the document written notice of his wish to inspect it and must be permitted to inspect it not more than seven days after the date of receipt of that notice. A party may, instead of physical inspection, request a copy of the document and if he also undertakes to pay reasonable copying costs, the party who disclosed the document must supply him with a copy no later than seven days after the date of receipt of request.

Generally speaking, obtaining a copy of a document is sufficient unless there is any reason to think that physical examination of the original would be of importance in the litigation, for example, to see what condition the document is in, look closely at amendments on the face of the document and the like. In one case of which the writer is aware the whole litigation changed when, on inspection of documents, an original was found to have two small staple holes in the top indicating that another document had at one time been attached to it. When this other document was called for and inspected, it was found to be vital to the outcome of the litigation. If in that case the party had been content merely to ask for photocopies the staple holes would not of course have been seen.

It is important to note that once a document has been disclosed and inspected a party in possession of it is deemed automatically to be on notice to produce the document at trial. Moreover, the party who receives disclosure is deemed to admit that the document is authentic in the sense of being what it appears to be without formal evidence needing to be called to prove the document (see further **23.4**).

18.6   Pre-action and non-party disclosure (rr. 31.16 and 31.17)

Pre-action disclosure has already been thoroughly dealt with at **9.1.4.1**.

18.6.1   Non-party disclosure (r. 31.17)

It is possible to obtain an order requiring someone who is not a party to a claim to disclose documents relevant to it. This procedure may be used in any claim. Situations where non-party disclosure may be required are, for instance, where an important document has passed into the possession of some other person not concerned with the litigation who will not permit a party to see it. Another example occurs sometimes in personal injury cases if the claimant was formerly employed by a small firm which is not the defendant but which simply will not respond to letters requesting information about the claimant's loss of earnings and job prospects, it may be necessary to apply to inspect the wages records.

An application for non-party disclosure must be supported by evidence and an order will be made only where the documents of which disclosure is sought are likely to support the case of the applicant or adversely affect the case of another party and disclosure is 'necessary in order to dispose fairly of the claim or to save costs'.

An application must specify the relevant documents and the evidence in support must explain how they are within the text mentioned above. The application requires the respondent, when making disclosure, to specify what documents he no longer controls or for which he claims the right to withhold inspection.

18.6.2 When the order may be made

By r. 31.17(3) the court may make an order only in the circumstances indicated above. The party seeking the documents will have to satisfy the court of the importance of the documents in question. The application notice should be served on the non-party together with the evidence in support.

When deciding on whether to grant the order the court will always have to decide if it is necessary for the party to see the document in advance of trial. If it is not then a witness summons for the person in possession of the document to bring it to the trial may suffice. Few documents, however, will be so simple that they can be adequately digested, by both parties, on the morning of the hearing and without them appearing in the trial bundle for pre-trial reading.

Nothing in the provisions as to pre-action or non-party disclosure prevents the party in question claiming to withhold inspection of the document on the basis of privilege, or claiming that the documents could only be discovered after a search which would be considered unreasonable in the circumstances. The court will have to consider the merits of those objections in the same way as in the case of disclosure generally.

18.6.3 The costs of non-party disclosure applications

By r. 48.1(2) and (3) there is a presumption that the court will award the non-party the costs of the application and of complying with any order made on the application. There is a saving provision allowing the court to make a different order to bear in mind the reasonableness of the non-party's opposition to the application.

18.7 Claim to withhold inspection or disclosure of a document

The law of privilege, which is part of the substantive law of evidence, is not changed in any respect by the CPR. There may be disputes about disclosure or inspection for many reasons, for example:

(a) factual disputes about the relevance or existence of the document;

(b) factual disputes about whether the document has ever been under the party's control;

(c) a claim to withhold disclosure on the basis of public interest immunity;

(d) a claim to withhold inspection on the basis of private privilege, i.e., professional legal privilege, litigation privilege, or the privilege against self-incrimination;

(e) a claim by a person that it would be 'disproportionate' to the issues in the case to permit inspection of documents under r. 31.3(2).

Nothing further need be said about factual disputes as to the existence of documents or their relevance. If these matters are in issue the court will simply have to decide whom it believes. If it is denied that a document *exists*, it will be very difficult for the court to come to any other conclusion than that the party who asserts that is telling the truth. Where, however, it is denied that a document is *relevant*, it is always open to the court to insist on seeing the document.

It is now necessary to discuss the issue of privilege. By r. 31.19 it is open to 'a person' to seek to withhold disclosure of a document. Use of the words 'a person' rather than 'a party' indicates that it is open to non-parties who have received an application for non-party disclosure to make applications to withhold disclosure of the documents in question. The rules apply in turn to public interest immunity and private privilege.

18.7.1 Public interest immunity

A person may apply *without notice* for an order permitting him to withhold disclosure of a document on the ground that disclosure would damage the public interest.

Unless the court otherwise orders, an order of the court under r. 31.19(1) must not be served on any other person or be open to inspection by any other person.

This provides a procedure in respect of documents claimed to be subject to public interest immunity where the other side are not informed of the application. It will involve the court in a weighing exercise, bearing in mind that evidence, and submissions are from one party only. Under r. 31.19(6) the court may ask the persons seeking to withhold disclosure to produce the document to the court and invite any person, whether or not a party, to make representations. Where appropriate, therefore, the court can convert the without notice procedure into proceedings on notice to the other party. Rule 31.19(7) expressly declares that nothing in Part 31 generally affects any rule of law permitting or requiring a document to be withheld from disclosure or inspection on the ground of public interest. The concept of public interest immunity is discussed more fully in **Chapter 5**.

18.7.2 Private privilege

There is a separate provision in relation to 'private' privilege. Under r. 31.19(3), a person who wishes to claim that he has a right or a duty to withhold inspection of a document or part of a document must state in writing that he has such a right and the grounds on which he claims that right or duty. By r. 31.19(4) that claim must be in the list in which the document is disclosed, or, if there has been no list, in a formal notice to the person wishing to inspect the document.

A party may then apply to the court to decide whether a claim made under that paragraph should be upheld. A party may take the initiative to claim privilege in their own documents and seek an order of the court to that effect; or the opposing party from whom disclosure is withheld may make that application. It is suggested in PD 31, para. 6.1, that a claim to withhold inspection of a document does not require an application to the court so the party who wishes to challenge that claim must apply to the court. Although this is applicable in the case of disputes about private privilege, in the case of public interest immunity the 'without notice' procedure referred to above is likely to be the norm initially. In disputes about private privilege the court may require the persons seeking to withhold inspection of a document to produce it to the court and invite any person, whether or not a party, to make representations. See also **Chapter 5**.

18.7.3 Restriction on use of an inadvertently disclosed privileged document (r. 31.20)

This rule provides that where a person inadvertently allows a privileged document to be inspected, the party who has inspected the document may use it or its contents only with the consent of the court. This provision and the case law which preceded it is discussed fully at **5.2.1.8**. It is considered that the rule introduces no change in practice.

18.8 Disproportionality (r. 31.3(2))

Under r. 31.3(2), where a party considers that it would be *disproportionate* to the issues in the case to permit inspection of documents within a category or class of document of which he has given standard disclosure under r. 31.6(6), he is not required to permit inspection of documents but must state in his disclosure statement that inspection of those documents will not be permitted.

This is quite a new basis for withholding inspection of a document whose relevance and existence appear to be admitted. The concept of proportionality is an important one in considering the new rules purposively, although it is in fact only alluded to expressly at this point in the rule about disclosure. It imports considerations not merely of technical relevance to the litigation, but of how expensive or time-consuming the carrying out of inspection is likely to be. Given that by this time the party having the documents will have presumably found them and identified them so that any search is likely to have been successful, this would seem to focus the court's attention on the cost of carrying out inspection and presumably on the fact that, e.g., the time to be taken in view of the number of documents would be excessive, or that inspection would need to be in some distant place.

This is a very difficult concept because, the first party having concluded that the documents are of sufficient technical relevance to fall within the proper bounds of standard disclosure, what basis is used to determine that the costs of the opposite party inspecting them will be disproportionate? If the first party has done their job properly under the rules and searched for and sifted the documents as to relevance, the cost of physical inspection of the documents would seem likely to be only a small proportion of the cost of finding and identifying them in the first place. If the documents were not sufficiently relevant, they should not have been disclosed at all. The test will presumably focus on the question of how peripheral to the litigation the documents are and the cost of inspecting them. On the face of it one might think that whether or not to incur the cost should initially be a matter for the inspecting party, no further costs to the disclosing party being involved, save those of permitting the inspecting party access to the documents. Early guidance from the higher courts on the concept of 'proportionality' is likely to be forthcoming.

18.9   Consequences of failure to disclose (r. 31.1)

A party may not rely on any document which he fails to disclose or for which he fails to permit inspection unless the court permits.

It is difficult to see why a court should grant any latitude to a party who, having failed to give proper disclosure and inspection, then seeks to use the document at trial. The key issue will of course be prejudice to the other party, though, given the first party's obvious default, the court may not be inclined to inquire too nicely into this matter. The rule will give the court some residual discretion which may perhaps be more liberally exercised in the case of accidental non-disclosure, especially by unrepresented parties. Solicitors will need to protect themselves by writing comprehensively to clients about the nature of duties of disclosure in order to protect themselves from potential wasted costs orders.

18.10   Subsequent use of disclosed documents (r. 31.22)

Where documents are disclosed for the purpose of an action the general principle is that they must be used by the other party solely for that action. It is quite wrong, and indeed a contempt of court, for a party who gets copies of an opponent's documents obtained in litigation to circulate them to others, pass them to the press, or even use them himself for purposes unrelated to the litigation (for example, to poach the other party's customers). The previous case law, which undoubtedly still applies, shows that the court will treat it as a serious contempt of court even in extreme cases such as where one party obtains disclosure of documents in litigation which show that the other party has been committing tax frauds. To send the documents to the Inland Revenue is still a serious contempt, though one might think that the court would be slow to protect those guilty of tax fraud. However, complete honesty in the disclosure process must be encouraged and nothing must be permitted which would affect that principle. This is now reflected in r. 31.22. By r. 31.22(1) a party to whom a document has been disclosed may use it only for the purpose of the proceedings in which it is disclosed except where:

(a) the document has been read to or by the court or referred to at a hearing which has been held in public; or

(b) the court gives permission; or

(c) the party who disclosed the document and the person to whom the document belongs agree.

The court may make an order restricting or prohibiting the use of a document which has been disclosed even where the document has been read to or by the court.

An application for such an order may be made by a party or by any person to whom the document belongs.

Thus the previous principle remains. If the document is used in court then the restriction on subsequent use of it is lifted. There is of course some difficulty in the words 'referred to' at a hearing. Suppose that a document has merely been briefly referred to and not read out? Does that mean that it is now sufficiently in the public arena that anybody can use it for other purposes or publish it further? The issue is unresolved.

An order may in any event be made by the court permitting a party to use a document for other purposes in its general discretion. One example is *Apple Corps Ltd* v *Apple Computer Inc* [1992] 1 CMLR 969, where documents, which had been disclosed in English proceedings, were required for the purposes of parallel proceedings before the European Commission, which constituted a cogent reason why the documents were permitted by the court to be used outside the English proceedings.

Witness statements and witness evidence at trial and other hearings

19.1 Introduction

Chapter 18 considered documents and documentary evidence and the way in which it must be disclosed in preparation for trial. We are now going to consider the still more important topic of the evidence of witnesses and the use of written statements taken from them, either at trial or in interim hearings. It will be important to consider the provisions of **Chapter 4** in conjunction with this chapter.

19.1.1 The court's power to control evidence (CPR, r. 32.1)

It is provided that the court may control the evidence by giving directions as to:

(a) the issues on which it requires evidence;

(b) the nature of the evidence which it requires to decide those issues; and

(c) the way in which the evidence is to be placed before the court.

Moreover, and most importantly, under CPR, r. 32.1(2):

The court may use its power under this rule to exclude evidence that would otherwise be admissible.

These provisions take to its highest point the principle of 'court control'. They allow the court to override the wishes of the parties as to how they would like to conduct their case, whether on liability, quantum or remedies sought, and to impose the court's own robust discretion as to the evidence that would be appropriate in order to allow the parties fairly to demonstrate their cases. They allow the court to identify the order of issues with which it wishes to deal and to restrict the ways in which evidence about those issues can be given as between oral, written, hearsay or other evidence.

Rule 32.1 is the dominant rule which will enable the court to restrict the number of witnesses that either party may call, whether they are witnesses of fact or experts. Most importantly, the provision that the court may exclude evidence which would otherwise be admissible is an extraordinary extension of the court's powers because evidence is only ever admissible if it is 'relevant', and this enables the court to impose its own view of what is 'relevant' on the parties. This power may be used at a pre-trial stage or at the start of, or during, the trial itself. It will be a strong-minded procedural judge who in the face of objection by either or both parties decides to restrict the evidence in advance of trial in any draconian way although it will be commonly used in aid of the identification of preliminary issues under other rules (e.g., as to split trials of liability and quantum). It is suggested that this power will be more commonly used during a trial by a judge who has the full trial bundles and considers that some of the evidence intended to be adduced would not assist him because it is peripheral, irrelevant or repetitive.

19.2   The general rule about witness evidence (r. 32.2)

Rule 32.2 of the CPR provides that any fact which needs to be proved is to be proved at trial by *oral evidence in public* and at any other hearing by *evidence in writing*. This is subject to any provision to the contrary in the rules or any order of the court.

Accordingly, evidence at trial is to be given in general by oral evidence. This is subject in turn to r. 32.5(2) which provides that a witness statement will stand as evidence-in-chief unless the court orders otherwise. This is why it is vital to draft witness statements as thoroughly as possible because the judge may well refuse to let the witness expand on his statement at trial. If some vital matter has been missed out, he may be unable to call evidence to deal with it. The witness must nonetheless attend and be open to cross-examination to satisfy the requirement for 'oral evidence given in public'.

At pre-trial hearings of whatever kind written evidence is to be the norm. Thus on interim applications of any kind, even very substantial ones such as for interim injunctions or summary judgment, oral evidence will be rare. The court does have the power to permit oral evidence in exceptional circumstances.

19.2.1   Evidence by video link or other means (r. 32.3)

To reflect the use of new technology and in the interests of saving time and costs the CPR permit a witness to give evidence by video link, for example, if a witness is abroad and cannot or will not return. If his evidence is of sufficient importance, rather than simply serving his witness statement under the Civil Evidence Act 1995, a party may tender him for cross-examination by video link. An order in advance of trial for this must be obtained and the other parties' views taken into account. It will remain highly exceptional.

The case of *Polanski* v *Conde Nast Publications Ltd* has already been discussed at paragraph **4.2.4** above. In this case the claimant who had sued for defamation did not wish to attend the trial due to the fact that he was wanted in the USA for sentencing in relation to a sexual offence and would be arrested and extradited on his arrival in the UK. He sought to give evidence from France by video link and the Court of Appeal in its discretion refused this because of its disapproval of the claimant escaping the proper process of the criminal law. The House of Lords however reversed this holding it to be an irrelevant matter and permitted the claimant to give evidence by video-link.

19.3   Requirement to serve witness statements for use at trial (r. 32.4)

Rule 32.4 of the CPR defines a witness statement as '*a written statement signed by a person which contains the evidence which that person would be allowed to give orally*'.

The court will order the parties to serve witness statements of the evidence on which they intend to rely at trial. The court may give directions as to the order in which witness statements are to be served and whether or not the witness statement is to be filed in court.

This is one of the most important matters which the district judge will have to consider on giving directions on allocation or subsequently at a case management conference. It is hard to envisage any circumstance in which an order for prior disclosure of witness statements would not now be made. The usual order will be that they be served within a relatively short time of the giving of directions, typically about 10 weeks after that stage. Solicitors will have to be thoroughly prepared for this relatively early in the case. The statements, as indicated on a number of occasions previously, must be full and must incorporate everything which the witness might have wished to say in evidence-in-chief.

The court will give directions as to the order in which witness statements are to be served. The normal principle would be that these should be simultaneous unless there is some reason why sequential service might be appropriate. Such reasons may exist, for example, where one party may not know fully what case he has to meet until he sees it set out in his opponent's witness statement, perhaps in a case where requests for further information under Part 18 have been unsuccessful. One party may in such circumstances be ordered to serve his witness statements first, or at least that of the claimant. Such circumstances may arise in cases such as *Kirkup* v *British Rail Engineering Ltd* [1983] 1 WLR 1165 where, in an industrial deafness claim arising out of facts which occurred many years before, the defendant could not truly identify some of the issues until the claimant's statement was served.

19.3.1 Use at trial of witness statements which have been served (r. 32.5)

Subject to CPR, r. 32.6 (see below), if a party who has served a witness statement wishes to rely on the evidence of the witness at trial, he must nonetheless call the witness to give oral evidence unless the court orders otherwise or he puts the statement in as hearsay evidence.

Section 1 of the Civil Evidence Act 1995 makes all hearsay admissible without discrimination; no permission of the court is necessary nor is there any discretionary power in the court to exclude hearsay evidence. A party may serve a Civil Evidence Act notice in relation to a witness statement if he does not propose to call the witness. Apart from this provision the court may 'order otherwise' in any event (i.e., permit a person to use a written statement anyway) although it is difficult to see why the court should be inclined to do so if a person does not serve a Civil Evidence Act notice. A party will know whether he wishes to rely on the facts set out in the statement and will either call the witness to comply with r. 32.5 or alternatively have served a Civil Evidence Act notice. Presumably the rule is to govern matters at trial where the witness is found to be unavailable or does not appear on the day of the trial. The rule will supplement the provisions in the Civil Evidence Act 1995, although by virtue of s. 2(4) failure to serve a Civil Evidence Act notice does not affect the *admissibility* of the statement in any way. The court may, however, take this into account in considering the exercise of its powers for the course of proceedings and costs. For example, it may adjourn the proceedings so that the witness can be called at the cost of the party in question, or may treat it as a matter adversely affecting the weight to be given to the evidence of the absent witness.

A witness may with the permission of the court amplify his witness statement or give evidence in relation to new matters which have arisen since the witness statement was served on the other parties (r. 32.5(3)). It remains to be seen when the court will give such permission. It is only likely to do so if the matter left out of the witness statement is material and there is some good reason for not having included it and no prejudice to the opponent is caused at trial. The court has, as we have seen, a very general and wide-ranging power to control evidence under r. 32.1. If new matter has arisen, or the deficiencies of the original witness statement have been perceived some time in advance of trial, it may well be better to seek permission to serve supplementary witness statements rather than relying on the discretion of the trial judge to permit a witness in evidence-in-chief to go outside his witness statement.

19.3.2   Cross-examining on the statement

The provisions of r. 32.5(3) discussed in **19.3.1** refer only to the question of whether *the party who calls the witness* can have him amplify it with oral evidence. The opposite party when cross-examining is free to range as widely as he wishes, within the general test of relevance. It would of course be foolish by ill-judged cross-examination to allow a witness to bring in evidence matters favourable to the case of the party who called him which were not already set out in his witness statement.

19.3.3   What if a party serves a witness statement but does not then call the witness?

If a party who has served a witness statement does not call the witness, or previously serve a notice that he intends to use the witness statement as hearsay evidence, any other party may put in the witness statement as hearsay evidence (r. 32.5(5)). Thus, if at trial for the first time it became clear that the opposing party did not intend to call a certain witness whose statement had been served, the court would clearly be entitled to use its discretion to permit the statement to be used by the opponent, notwithstanding the understandable failure of the opponent to serve a Civil Evidence Act notice.

19.4   Evidence in proceedings other than at trial (r. 32.6)

Rule 32.6 of the CPR deals with hearings other than the trial itself, such as interim applications or hearings relating to enforcement of judgment. The general rule is that evidence at such hearings is to be by witness statement unless the court or any practice direction or enactment requires otherwise. Oral evidence will remain highly exceptional. In such proceedings a party can rely on matters set out in his statement of case or his application if either is verified by a statement of truth.

19.4.1   Evidence by affidavit

Unless a statement supported by a statement of truth is given honestly it will be a contempt of court. Until the CPR evidence at such hearings had to be given by a document that was actually sworn on oath called an *affidavit*. Dishonestly swearing an affidavit constituted the crime of perjury. By changing from affidavits to the simpler witness statements with statements of truth, it was intended to simplify the formalities of preparing written evidence for proceedings, while preserving a criminal sanction to indicate the importance which the court attaches to truthfulness. However, affidavits are expressly preserved for certain purposes and in particular by PD 32, paras 1.4 to 1.6, in the following circumstances:

(a) where *sworn* evidence is required by any enactment, statutory instrument, rule, order or practice direction;

(b) in any application for a search order, a freezing injunction, or an order requiring an occupier to permit another to enter his land; and

(c) in any application for an order against anyone for alleged contempt of court.

Thus it will be observed that in any proceedings against someone for contempt of court for having given a false statement of truth, the evidence has to be provided on affidavit.

19.4.2   Order for cross-examination at an interim hearing (r. 32.7)

Where at a hearing *other than the trial* evidence is to be given in writing, any party may apply to the court for permission to cross-examine the person giving the evidence. If the court gives permission, but the person does not attend as required, his evidence may not be used unless the court permits.

A separate application to the court for permission for the attendance of witnesses at pre-trial hearings is therefore required. It is anticipated that in the interests of economy such applications will rarely be made or succeed. The court will have to be sure that in order to do justice on some interim issue there must be a thorough investigation of evidence. The court will have the power to restrict the issue narrowly and to restrict what evidence it will hear (r. 32.1). To call evidence at most interim applications is usually self-defeating. Under the provisions relating to summary judgment (Part 24) or interim payments (Part 25), it is doubtful that the applicant will succeed if, to establish his case, he needs permission to cross-examine the defendant. Conversely, it may well be a useful tactic for a defendant opposing such applications to seek an order for cross-examination of the claimant. In the interests of efficient case management, it is unlikely that the court will permit this other than in exceptional cases.

19.5   The form of witness statements (r. 32.8)

PD Part 32, paras 17.1 to 22.2, describes the formalities of preparing witness statements. They must be set out with the full heading of the claim and at the top right of the first page there should be clearly written:

(a) the party on whose behalf the statement is made;

(b) the initials and surname of the witness;

(c) the number of the statement in relation to that witness (i.e., if there has been more than one statement);

(d) the identifying initials and number of any exhibit to the statement referred to;

(e) the date the statement was made.

The statement should be expressed in the first person and in the witness's own words so far as possible. It should give full name, address, occupation and state that he is a party to the proceedings or is the employee of such a party if that is the case.

A witness must also indicate clearly what statements are made from his own knowledge and what are merely matters of information or belief and give the source of that information or belief.

Other formalities are prescribed including that the statement should be divided into numbered paragraphs; the pages should also be numbered; and any numbers referred to in the statement including dates should be expressed in figures not words.

The suggestion in PD 32 that the witness statement should be expressed in the witness's own words should not be taken literally. If one really left witnesses to give their own version of events and did not re-draft it in some slightly more formal way, some witness statements would look very strange indeed. Thus no doubt solicitors will continue to change the statement of a witness who, for example, says:

'When he jumped the red it done me bleeding head in'

to the slightly more formal:

'I was quite perturbed when he disregarded the traffic signal'.

It is certainly true, however, that solicitors should not put words into the witness's mouth or improve on a witness's evidence to the extent that the witness does not recognise what he has said. Such procedures may well be ruthlessly exposed in cross-examination and there may be cost penalties or other professional consequences for a solicitor who has imposed too enthusiastically his own version of what the witness said.

19.5.1 What if a witness is uncooperative or untraceable?

By r. 32.9 a party who is required to serve a witness statement for use at trial, but is unable to obtain one, can apply *without notice* for permission to serve a 'witness summary' instead.

A witness summary is a summary of the evidence, if known, which would otherwise be included in the witness statement, or if it is not known the matters about which the party serving the summary will question the witness (r. 32.9(2)).

This provision deals with the situation where either the witness's whereabouts are known so that he can effectively be called at trial, but the witness has been uncooperative; or where the witness is untraceable. Clearly it is tactically undesirable to call an uncooperative witness who refuses to give a witness statement at all. This position sometimes arises in cases such as those between former employees and employers, whether personal injury or other, where the claimant anticipates that people still working for the employer could give useful evidence, but are inhibited by their unwillingness to compromise their prospects by appearing to side with the former employee. Although the risks are obvious, the only way of getting the evidence to trial is therefore likely to be a witness summons and it will be necessary to attempt to serve a 'gist' statement summarising what the witness would say. Clearly it will often be impossible to do that in very much detail. There will sometimes be circumstances where, for example, a witness has initially given a verbal statement but declined to sign the written version. In that case his evidence will be available in virtually its full form.

Initially there is a 'without notice' procedure in which the court, acting on evidence itself in witness statement form from the party, will be asked to make an order permitting a witness summary. There will usually be a statement from the solicitor explaining how the witness has proved uncooperative or is now untraceable. If satisfactory evidence is put forward, there is no reason why the court should decline to make the order sought. The only consideration would be whether the procedure seems to be in some way an abuse of process.

Unless the court orders otherwise, a witness summary, when served, must include the name and address of the intended witness and must be served within the period in which a statement would have had to be served (r. 32.9(4)).

19.6 Consequences of failing to serve a statement (r. 32.10)

This rule more than almost any other must be enforced vigorously if it is to be effective in achieving early mutual disclosure of the parties' full cases with the objective of encouraging compromise and avoiding trial, or alternatively making the trial efficient. The relevant rule, r. 32.10, is briefly expressed and simply provides that if a witness statement or summary for use at trial is not served within the time specified by the court then the witness may not be called to give oral evidence unless the court permits.

The court, in order to show that the rules have teeth, is likely to be very sparing in the use of its discretion to permit a party to call witnesses where the evidence was not disclosed, either at all or at the right time. Late applications for permission to call witnesses are likely to be unsuccessful. It remains to be seen to what extent the court will really be prepared to see substantial injustice done in a case where the fault is entirely that of the legal advisers in failing to identify the issues so as to collect evidence properly and serve it at the right time. The issue of prejudice to an opposing party will be relevant, but is unlikely to be conclusive. Litigants may therefore be left to their own devices against their advisers where there has been such failure, whether it has been as a consequence of an honest oversight, tactical misjudgment or simple incompetence. As with all serious sanctions, the court will have to be mindful of the requirement to provide a fair trial under Article 6 of the European Convention on Human Rights (for further discussion see **Chapter 37**).

19.6.1 What if one's opponent does not serve his statements?

Witness statements will usually be served simultaneously either on a date which the court fixes in the order or at any time up to and including a date fixed in the order. In either case practitioners usually contact their opponent to ensure an agreement that each parties' statements will be put in the post or DX on a given date, so neither party has the advantage of seeing the other side's statements in advance. The advantages of seeing one's opponent's witness statements in advance are obvious. It is not suggested that solicitors would get their witnesses to adapt their evidence to meet whatever is set out in the opponent's statements, but seeing the opponent's statements is a useful way of identifying the issues, e.g., it might occur to you that your witnesses had completely overlooked the need to deal with something referred to in the opponent's statements and further paragraphs could then be inserted.

Suppose that as the day approaches you have contacted your opponent for a firm agreement to put the witness statements in a DX on a given date and there is simply no reply. What should one do? Some send their own documents anyway. Others, however, mindful of the advantage this might give an opponent will prefer to apply to the court for a sanction to be imposed. The normal form of application would be for an order that unless the opponent does now agree to a date for exchange, he will be refused the right to call any evidence at all at trial. It will be necessary to ask the court to give a very early hearing date for that application for it to have any useful effect.

If making the application does not provoke the opponent into complying with the order for exchange, then at the hearing the court is virtually certain to grant an order debarring the party in default from calling any witness evidence at all unless it is exchanged within some further short period, possibly no more than seven days after the hearing. Naturally, the party in default will also be ordered to pay the costs which are likely to be summarily assessed and payable forthwith.

19.6.2   What if new evidence arises or is discovered late?

If a party realises that he has material evidence which has not been served, he will need to apply immediately for leave to call it. It would be extremely risky to make that application only at trial. An attempt to serve it, even without permission, should be made at the earliest moment so as at least to minimise prejudice to the opponent. The court's discretion is more likely to be used for witnesses who have only recently been traced or identified where reasonable competence has been shown.

19.7   Sanction for false statements (r. 32.14)

As has been noted in **11.3.3**, by CPR, r. 32.14(1), a party is guilty of contempt of court if he makes, or causes to be made, a false statement in a document verified by a statement of truth without an honest belief in its truth.

Proceedings for contempt of court in relation to a statement of truth may only be brought by the Attorney-General or by anyone else with the permission of the court (r. 32.14(3)).

This part of the rule specifically creates an offence in relation to false evidence, thus avoiding the need to bring it within the scope of more nebulous crimes such as attempts to pervert the course of justice. False evidence on oath, whether by affidavit or in the course of the trial, will of course amount to perjury as before.

19.8   Evidence by affidavit (rr. 32.15 to 32.17)

Affidavit evidence can be given instead of, or in addition to, a witness statement when required by the court, or by a provision contained in any other rule, practice direction or other enactment. (See earlier **19.4.1**.) However, a witness is expressly permitted to give evidence by affidavit if he chooses to do so at any hearing other than a trial, in which case the rules relating to the filing and service of the affidavit apply as if it were a witness statement. Affidavits must comply with requirements set out in PD 32. Affidavits must largely be in the same format as witness statements but in addition, they commence by a statement in which the *deponent* (as the person swearing an affidavit is known) commences by giving his full name and address and saying that the evidence is stated on oath.

At the end of the affidavit there is then a so-called 'jurat' which authenticates the affidavit and is signed before a person entitled to take oaths, which includes commissioners for oaths, practising solicitors, and some members of the court staff.

Unless a rule or practice direction requires it, there is little point in putting evidence into affidavit form because a witness statement will do just as well and the expense of swearing the affidavit is saved. The rules specifically provide that if evidence is given in affidavit form where a witness statement would have been sufficient, the additional costs of making it cannot be recovered from the other party unless the court orders otherwise.

19.9 Notice to admit facts (r. 32.18)

This procedure has already been described at **3.5.2.2**. By CPR, r. 32.18, a party may serve notice on another party requiring them to admit facts or the part of the case specified in the notice. Notice must be served no later than 21 days before the trial.

If the notice attracts an admission, it may only be used in the proceedings in question and by the party who served the notice. Where a party is able to identify a severable fact or series of facts which he thinks he can prove irrespective of the outcome of the litigation as a whole, he may attempt to obtain an admission by this procedure. If a fact is admitted then the cost of proving it is saved. If the fact is not admitted, but the person tendering the notice succeeds in proving those facts at trial, whatever the outcome, then he should be awarded the costs of proving them.

This provision as to costs is under r. 44.3 and in particular the court's powers to have regard to the conduct of the parties and their reasonableness under r. 44.3(5)(b).

19.10 Summary of the procedure for witness evidence at trial

(a) The court will, when giving directions upon allocation, or subsequently in the exercise of its case management powers, always order that the statements of any witnesses which the parties wish to call at trial be put in written form and exchanged well in advance of trial, and on the fast track usually no later than 10 weeks after allocation.

(b) The initial statements which the parties will have taken usually in a more discursive form should then be put into admissible form and prepared in the format required by PD 32.

(c) A specific date and procedure for exchange should be agreed and the witness statements will then be exchanged and will stand at trial as the witnesses' evidence-in-chief.

(d) If a party does not comply with the requirement to serve witness statements, the other party should apply immediately to enforce the court's order. It will usually be successful both in obtaining a sanction that if the other party does not serve the statement within some further short time, that party be debarred from calling evidence at trial and that the party in default will also be ordered to pay the costs of the application.

EXPERT EVIDENCE

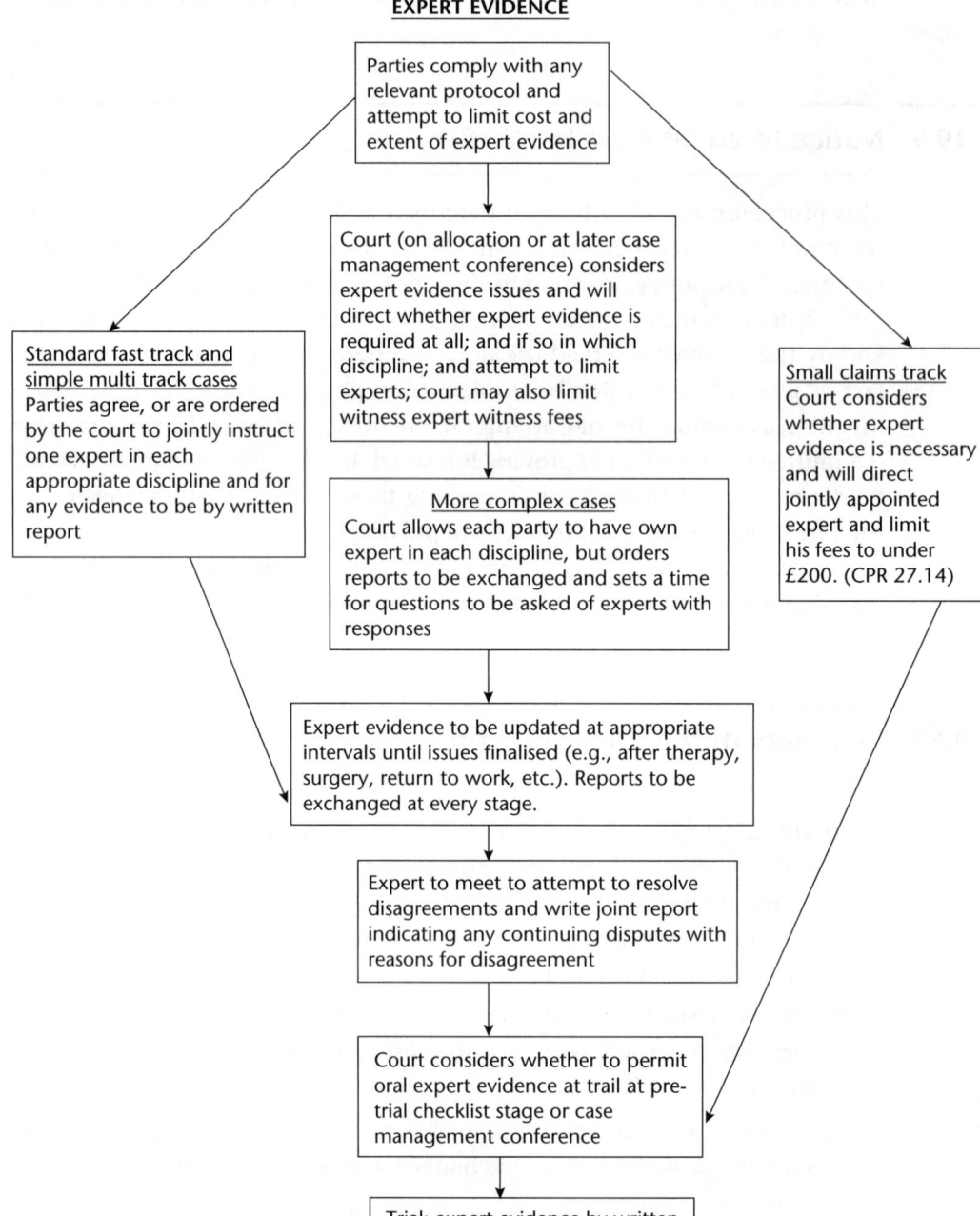

Parties comply with any relevant protocol and attempt to limit cost and extent of expert evidence

Court (on allocation or at later case management conference) considers expert evidence issues and will direct whether expert evidence is required at all; and if so in which discipline; and attempt to limit experts; court may also limit witness expert witness fees

Standard fast track and simple multi track cases
Parties agree, or are ordered by the court to jointly instruct one expert in each appropriate discipline and for any evidence to be by written report

Small claims track
Court considers whether expert evidence is necessary and will direct jointly appointed expert and limit his fees to under £200. (CPR 27.14)

More complex cases
Court allows each party to have own expert in each discipline, but orders reports to be exchanged and sets a time for questions to be asked of experts with responses

Expert evidence to be updated at appropriate intervals until issues finalised (e.g., after therapy, surgery, return to work, etc.). Reports to be exchanged at every stage.

Expert to meet to attempt to resolve disagreements and write joint report indicating any continuing disputes with reasons for disagreement

Court considers whether to permit oral expert evidence at trail at pre-trial checklist stage or case management conference

Trial: expert evidence by written report or orally

Expert witnesses: CPR, Part 35

20.1 Introduction

A major objective of the CPR was to cut down the proliferation of expert evidence which was seen as being a cause of great delay and expense under the previous system.

Part 35 of the CPR contains the provisions on expert witnesses.

Part 35 commences with three specific provisions to which the rest are subject. These are:

Rule 35.1—expert evidence shall be restricted to that which is reasonably required to resolve the proceedings.

Rule 35.3—it is the duty of an expert (that is, one who has been instructed to give or prepare evidence for the purpose of court proceedings) to help the court on the matters within his expertise. That duty overrides any obligation to the person from whom he has received instructions, or by whom he is paid.

Rule 35.4:

(1) No party may call an expert or put in evidence an expert's report without the court's permission.

(2) When a party applies for permission under this rule, he must identify—
   (a) the field in which he wishes to rely on expert evidence; and
   (b) where practicable, the expert in that field on whose evidence he wishes to rely.

(3) If permission is granted under this rule it shall be in relation only to the expert named or the field identified under paragraph (2).

(4) The court may limit the amount of the expert's fees and expenses that the party who wishes to rely on the expert may recover from any other party.

It will therefore first be the task of the court to decide whether it needs expert evidence at all. Under general principles of evidence, expert evidence is *only* admissible where the matters in question fall outside the court's experience.

This rule therefore permits the court when giving directions about expert evidence to identify the expert from whom such evidence will be received and to specify an upper limit on his fees, quite apart from the general powers which the court would have to restrict them anyway at the time of the detailed assessment of costs under Part 44.

There is not only a detailed Practice Direction to Part 35 but also a protocol for the instruction of experts, issued in June 2005.

20.2 Directions about experts

The stage at which the court will usually first be required to give directions about expert evidence will be upon allocation. If a case is allocated to the fast track, directions will be tailored to the needs of the case in the light of the information which the parties have provided in their allocation questionnaires. It is possible, and indeed desirable for the parties to correspond between themselves to attempt to agree directions which can then be submitted to the court for approval (see PD 28, para. 3.6).

Ideally these will include a direction for the parties to choose jointly, and instruct a single expert in each discipline.

On the multi-track there are similar provisions.

The court has specific power to direct:

(a) a single joint expert on any appropriate issue *unless there is good reason not to do so* (thus indicating that it will be for the parties to establish to the court's satisfaction that a single expert will not suffice);

(b) disclosure of experts' reports by way of simultaneous exchange on issues where a single joint expert is not directed;

(c) if experts' reports are not agreed, a discussion between experts for the purposes set out in r. 35.12 (see **20.6.2**);

(d) if it appears that expert evidence will be required on both liability and quantum, the exchange of reports on liability simultaneously, but that those relating to the amount of damages be exchanged sequentially.

20.2.1   What if a party has already instructed his own expert?

This problem has been briefly considered in **Chapter 9**.

In principle, a party who instructs his own expert without attempting to agree the choice of a joint expert with his opponent will be at risk as to costs. The pre-action protocols (where they are relevant) generally presuppose a jointly instructed expert (although the provisions are not without some ambiguity—see **9.4.4**). Even in actions where the protocols do not strictly apply the parties are required to observe the spirit of them. A party who, wishing to embark on litigation, instructs his own expert will therefore be subject to the following potential problems:

(a) the court may not give permission for that expert's report to be used so that the party concerned loses the costs of instructing him;

(b) the opposing party may attempt to insist upon a jointly instructed expert so that the costs of the first expert are wasted;

(c) if the first party wishes to attempt to persuade the opponent to use his expert's report as the only report in the case, he will obviously have to disclose it at an earlier stage than that ordered by the court and the opponent might still not agree to its use.

As against that, there may sometimes be powerful considerations where one party will wish to obtain its own report. These include:

(a) in cases with a technical element a claimant may not be sure that he has a case at all until an expert's report has been obtained;

(b) there may be such lengthy waiting lists to get a report from the chosen expert that the claimant needs to initiate these procedures as soon as he instructs solicitors;

(c) in straightforward cases and given that he will disclose the letter of instructions, if the expert he has instructed is well known and accepted as reputable by the opponent, time may be saved and the report may be accepted, perhaps subject to further questions being put by the opponent under r. 35.6.

In general, however, it is undoubtedly better to approach one's opponent in an attempt to agree a jointly instructed expert, whether specifically under the protocols where they apply, or in the spirit of them where they do not.

20.3 The expert's report (r. 35.5)

By r. 35.5, expert evidence is to be given in a *written report* unless the court directs otherwise. If a claim is on the fast track, the court will *not* direct an expert to attend a hearing to give oral evidence unless it is necessary to do so in the interests of justice.

There is thus a strong presumption in favour of the evidence being given in written form with the consequent saving of witness fees. On the fast track the presumption is that the order will debar oral evidence. There are further directions about the form of the expert's report, the questions to be answered and the issue of instructions to the expert to which we shall come in due course.

20.3.1 Putting questions to jointly instructed or opposing experts (r. 35.6)

By r. 35.6(1) a party may put to:

(a) an expert instructed by another party; or

(b) a single joint expert instructed under r. 35.7 (see **20.4**)

written questions about his report.

Such questions may be put by virtue of sub-paragraph (2) once only; must be put within 28 days of service of the expert's report; and must be for the purpose only of clarification of the report, unless in any case the court gives permission or the other party agrees. Thereafter, an expert's answers to those questions shall be treated as part of the expert's report.

20.3.2 What if the expert does not reply?

By r. 35.6(4) if an expert who has received such questions does not answer, the court may make one or both of the following orders in relation to the party who instructed the expert, namely: that the party may not rely on the evidence of that expert or recover the fees and expenses of that expert from any other party. This provides a general procedure to replace any cross-examination on the assumption that the expert evidence will be in written form only. Where an expert's report is received from an opponent questions can now be put which require comment on supplementary material, or put an opposing viewpoint. There is a 28-day prima facie time limit for undertaking this procedure and litigators will need to act promptly. Although experienced litigators will no doubt be able to formulate many questions themselves, in substantial litigation a party will probably want to confer with his own expert about the opponent's report and obtain assistance in drafting technical questions. Sometimes, counsel's assistance will be required in drafting the questions where the need to challenge or clarify aspects of the expert's report is substantial or may even determine the litigation.

The sanctions for failure to reply set out in r. 35.6(4) are not exhaustive. Clearly the most aggressive approach would be an application that the evidence of the expert who has failed to respond should be disallowed entirely and it may well be that that order will be made unless some reason for non-reply can be shown. If that order is not made then it will of course be open to the trial judge to disregard the evidence as the expert has not responded to legitimate questions, and if there is an opposing report, to prefer that report. Naturally in any application for sanctions in respect of non-reply to the questions the appropriateness of the questions themselves may be investigated so that inappropriate questions may be 'disallowed' in that the court may decline to direct that the expert who is failing to reply should have his report disregarded. In all these applications the primary objectives set out in CPR, Part 1 must always be borne in mind. The court will always seek solutions which are proportionate in time and cost to the issues and which should reflect an attitude of cooperation between the lawyers.

20.4   Court's power to direct that evidence be given by a single joint expert (r. 35.7)

By CPR, r. 35.7, where two or more parties wish to submit expert evidence on a particular issue, the court may direct that the evidence is to be given by one expert only. In that case the parties wishing to submit the expert evidence, 'the instructing parties', should attempt to agree who the expert should be, reflecting the attitude of cooperation enjoined by CPR, Part 1. If they cannot do so, by r. 35.7(3) the court may:

(a) select the expert from a list prepared or identified by the instructing parties; or

(b) direct that the expert be selected in such other manner as the court may decide.

The good sense and simplicity of this procedure is obvious. It is to be hoped that in most litigation, applications to the court to appoint an expert will prove unnecessary. The court is likely to be critical of parties who decline to cooperate, to the point of imposing costs sanctions. Given the attitude of impartiality and objective assistance to the court, urged upon the expert himself by the rule, there should be few cases in which solicitors cannot agree upon an expert.

20.4.1   Instructions to a single joint expert (r. 35.8)

By r. 35.8 where the court gives directions under r. 35.7 for a single joint expert to be used, each instructing party may give instructions to the expert but must at the same time send a copy of their instructions to the other party.

The court may give directions about the payment of the expert's fees and expenses and any inspection, examination or experiments which the expert wishes to carry out.

In other words the court may arbitrate on identifying the questions and issues on which the expert is to give advice where that involves inspection, examination or experiments, either in the interests of limiting costs, accelerating the procedure, or identifying what is reasonable in the circumstances of the case.

The court may, before an expert is instructed, by r. 35.8(4)(a) limit the amount that can be paid by way of fees and expenses to the expert and direct that the instructing parties pay that amount into court. Unless the court otherwise directs, the instructing parties are jointly and severally liable for the payment of the expert's fees and expenses, even if the court has not directed them to be paid into court.

By this means the court can ensure that the expert's fees are known fully in advance to both parties and that they can proceed with certainty and bear in mind also the likely costs. No doubt experts will initially be asked to confirm that they will be available and are willing to be instructed and invited to indicate the likely level of their fees.

20.4.2 Is a single expert's report binding on the parties?

Generally speaking, the parties will be expected to accept the evidence of the jointly instructed expert. In a possibly surprising development, however, in *Daniels* v *Walker* [2000] 1 WLR 1382, a Court of Appeal headed by the Master of the Rolls, Lord Woolf, decided that if one of the parties who had agreed to instruct jointly a single expert was unhappy with that expert's report, then, subject to the court's discretion, he should be allowed to obtain and if appropriate rely on a report from another expert. Before he could do so, however, he would have to demonstrate that his reasons for wanting a separate expert were not fanciful and that he genuinely wished to obtain further information before making a decision as to whether to accept part or the whole of the previous expert's report.

The court suggested that it was appropriate to regard the instruction of a joint expert as a first step in obtaining expert evidence on a particular issue and that in the majority of cases that should not only be the first step, but the last step. The court also observed that where there was only a modest sum involved a court might take a more rigorous approach because it might be disproportionate to obtain a second report and what should happen should be that questions should be put to the original expert. A different approach might be taken in a more substantial case.

Interestingly also, the court went on to observe in strong terms that arguments based on Article 6 of the European Convention on Human Rights and the Human Rights Act 1998 were quite inappropriate and that counsel should take a responsible attitude to raising human rights points (see further **Chapter 37**).

20.5 The contents of the expert's report (r. 35.10)

Rule 35.10 of the CPR sets out the duties of an expert. It provides in particular that the report must comply with the requirements set out in PD 35, which has recently (Spring 2002) been rewritten in an extended form. It is important to note that the expert's report should be addressed to the court and not to the party from whom the expert has received his instructions. At the end of the report there must be a statement that the expert understands and has complied with his duty to the court and the report must be verified by a statement of truth with the following wording:

I believe that the facts I have stated in this report are true and that the opinions I have expressed are correct.

The report must state the substance of all material instructions, whether written or oral, on the basis of which the report was written. It is important that a chosen expert should be sent full and honest instructions and no attempt to persuade him to be partial or to favour any particular view should be included in the letter of instructions. The actual letters of instructions are not, generally speaking, privileged from inspection, but the court will be slow to order that they be produced to the other side unless there is reason to believe they are inaccurate or incomplete. In the case of a jointly instructed expert the letters of instruction must be sent to the other side.

Experts who are frequently instructed in litigation will of course be thoroughly familiar with their duties under Part 35. It is nonetheless important to set out in the letter of instruction an indication of the duties of the witness to give the court objective unbiased testimony. It is also worth pointing out to the expert his duties under PD 35, para. 1.1, because these are often ignored. In particular, it is important to remind the expert that if there is a range of opinion on the matters dealt with in his report, he should summarise that range of opinion and give reasons for his own.

20.6 Separate experts

It is desirable to at least consider the joint instruction of a single expert in every kind of case. It must be conceded, however, that there will be cases which are so complex, due to the amounts involved, or the way in which pre-action negotiations have proceeded, where it is obvious that each side ought to be permitted to have their own experts. In such cases even the most robust court will not attempt to insist on the instruction of a single joint expert. Each party can obtain an expert's report on his own behalf, but observance of r. 35.3 ought to mean that expert evidence is given with the genuine objective of assisting the court to form a fair view and that the expert should not be a 'hired gun' for the party instructing him.

20.6.1 Use by one party of expert's report disclosed by another (r. 35.11)

By r. 35.11 where a party has disclosed an expert's report, any party may use it as evidence at the trial. Where both parties have been permitted to use competing experts and the report of one party's expert has been disclosed but that party decides not to rely on it at trial, the opposing party may do so.

It is not unknown that an expert instructed by one party, say the defendant, delivers a report which comes to substantially similar conclusions to that delivered by the claimant. The defendant may serve the report, but then conclude that there is little point in calling his witness and agree with the claimant's evidence. In that situation there is nothing to stop the claimant using the defendant's report to supplement the evidence of his own witness and put both reports before the court to show, say, the unanimity of medical opinion.

20.6.2 Discussions between experts (r. 35.12)

Where each side has their own competing experts who disagree, a useful procedure is provided by r. 35.12 to attempt to shorten the trial and limit the areas on which there is disagreement.

Rule 35.12 provides that the court may at any stage direct a discussion between experts for the purpose of requiring them to identify the issues in the proceedings and where possible reach agreement on issues. The Protocol requires the court to consider issues of cost and proportionality before directing such discussions which are usually by telephone rather than face-to-face. The court may specify the issues which the experts must discuss and may direct that, following a discussion, they must prepare a statement for the court showing the issues on which they agree and disagree and a summary of their reasons for disagreeing. It is suggested that on the multi-track an order in this form is likely to be very common (see PD 29, para. 4.10(6)).

The contents of the discussion remain private and are not to be referred to at trial unless both parties agree (r. 35.12(4)).

This represents the last stage of an attempt to confine the areas of expert evidence. The stages through which the parties will move in relation to contested issues of expert evidence are usually as follows:

(a) Each party will exchange experts' reports and will ask their own expert to comment upon the report obtained from the opponent.

(b) In the light of those comments, which will need to be sought fairly swiftly, the parties may put questions under r. 35.6 to the opposing expert. The replies to those questions will then need to be carefully considered and perhaps referred back to one's own expert for his views.

(c) In the light of any continuing areas of disagreement, at a subsequent case management conference the court will consider giving a direction for the experts to meet and discuss their differences in the hope of preparing a joint report which indicates any issues on which they are able to agree and highlights the remaining issues on which they are unable to agree. Alternatively, the parties may have undertaken this voluntarily. The issues at trial can then focus entirely on the areas of disagreement. At such a meeting it is possible that the experts may be able to agree everything that was previously in dispute between them so that there is no need to call them at trial. For example, issues such as whether the claimant is or is not able to go back to work may depend upon the trial judge forming a view of the claimant's credibility as a witness and are not really medical matters at all.

Whatever the conclusion of the meeting of experts it will then be for the parties to consider what expert evidence they wish to present to the court and to give clear information about the amount of time which will be taken up at trial.

20.6.3   What if one fails to disclose an expert's report?

Rule 35.13 provides that a party who fails to disclose an expert's report may not use the report at the trial or call the expert to give evidence orally, unless the court gives permission.

This rule to an extent states the obvious given that r. 35.4 provides a general power for the court to restrict expert evidence. It is difficult to conceive of circumstances in which the court would permit oral or written evidence from an expert at trial which had not previously been disclosed, unless perhaps in a case where remarkable latitude was being given to an unrepresented litigant, the point was simple and could be dealt with without surprise or prejudice by the opponent and the costs of adjourning would be substantial.

Applications for interim orders: CPR, Part 23

21.1 Introduction

In principle, case management by the court ought to mean that the court gives directions for what the parties are to do at each stage, and the case should progress from commencement to trial without the parties needing to attend court at all. In more complicated cases where at the initial stage of giving directions the court cannot adequately foresee how it will develop in terms of expert evidence or how long the trial will take, the court may decide to call the parties before it for a *case management conference*. This will usually happen at some advanced stage of the case after other directions have been issued which are to be carried out between the parties, but if either of the parties has failed to return an allocation questionnaire, or perhaps if the information given in it is inadequate, the court may call the parties before it for an *allocation hearing* when, as well as allocation to track, other case management directions are likely to be given.

We now have to consider applications by the parties for interim orders. The term 'interim orders' refers to orders made by the court at any stage between commencement and trial. We are now concerned with applications by the parties for such orders rather than orders made by the court of its own initiative.

The most common kind of applications are where one party:

(a) wants some interim order or remedy and has attempted to obtain the other party's agreement to this, but that agreement is refused;

(b) is in default of some step which ought to have been taken under case management directions and the innocent opponent needs to ensure that the step is taken promptly so as to preserve the case management timetable.

21.2 The procedure

This is governed by Part 23 of the CPR. A party wishing to make application to the court does so by an 'application notice', which means a document in which the applicant states his intention to seek a court order. The application is of course made to the court where the case is proceeding. The application notice must state what order is sought and why the applicant is seeking it. The application notice must be signed and will have at the top of it the title of the claim, its reference number and the full name of the applicant. If the applicant wants the matter to be dealt with at a hearing, that must be stated (PD 23, para. 2.1). Normally an application should be supported by written evidence (that is, a witness statement from the party concerned) setting out the facts entitling him to whatever he is seeking. If the application is of a purely procedural nature, e.g., to enforce some step which case management directions have already required the opponent to take, but which has not been taken, this can be set out on the face of the application notice, in which case the application notice itself can be verified by a statement of truth. A prescribed form of application, form N244, is included at the end of this chapter.

There is space on the back of the application notice for a brief statement to be set out and this is often used in routine matters; on more substantial applications a separate full statement will be needed.

The notice should be filed at court and the court will usually insert the date and time of hearing on it or it may notify the parties that it proposes to consider the application without a hearing.

21.2.1   Service of the application

The normal rule is that the court will serve the application notice and any documents in support by first-class post. If the applicant notifies the court that he wishes to effect service for greater certainty, he may do so himself. In this case further copies must be filed at court.

Service must be effected as soon as possible after the application is issued and in any event not less than three clear days before it is to be heard. The phrase 'three clear days' means that three ordinary working days must intervene between the date on which the application is served and the date of hearing.

EXAMPLE

If an application is to be heard on a Friday it must be served no later than the preceding Monday to give three clear days; if the application is to be heard on a Monday it must be served no later than the preceding Tuesday to give three clear working days.

The court does have power to abridge time under r. 23.7(4) 'if in the circumstances of the case sufficient notice has been given'. Accordingly, if the application is one that can be briefly disposed of on a purely procedural point and let us say the court was able to give a very early hearing date soon after issue, but because of a postal delay the application was only served with two clear days' notice, it would be open to the court to conclude that no possible prejudice had been caused by the lack of a third clear day and agree to abridge the time.

The documents to be served are the application notice itself, copies of any written evidence in support and a copy of any draft order which the applicant has attached to his application setting out the terms of what he is seeking.

21.3   Applications which may be dealt with without a hearing

Under CPR, r. 23.8, the court may deal with an application without a hearing if:

(a) the parties agree the terms of the order sought (for example, a marginal variation of the timetable for case management directions or the addition of some extra relatively uncontroversial provision to those directions already given);

(b) the parties agree that the court should dispose of the application without a hearing (for example, where the issue is straightforward and perhaps the only point of contention is simply how much extra time a defaulting party should be allowed for taking some further step); or

(c) the court does not consider that a hearing would be appropriate.

By virtue of PD 23, para. 2.1, the application notice should contain either a request for a hearing or a request that the application be dealt with without a hearing. If there is a request for a hearing the court staff will endorse the time and date of the hearing without reference to a district judge. If there is a request that it be dealt with without a hearing, the file will be given to a district judge for him to decide whether the application is suitable for consideration without a hearing. If he agrees, the court may still inform both the applicant for the order and the *respondent* (which is the technical term for the party against whom an application is made) and may give directions for the filing of evidence or further evidence. If the district judge does not accept that he can adequately deal with things in written format and requires a hearing, the hearing date will be fixed.

21.4 When should an application be made?

Paragraph 2.7 of PD 23 is important and it provides that 'Every application should be made as soon as it becomes apparent that it is necessary or desirable to make it'.

In other words, the parties must at every stage thoroughly review their case for the foreseeable future, not only in terms of whether they have complied with the court's directions and are able to do so for the next stages, but also in terms of how they should prepare their cases generally. Paragraph 2.8 goes on to suggest that wherever possible applications should be made at a time when parties are already before the court, to save hearings. If a case management conference has been fixed, and a party wants a specific order to be made and has perhaps canvassed this with the opponent who does not agree, that party should make a specific application so that the court is aware of what will be asked for in advance of the hearing. Paragraph 2.9 reminds the parties that at every hearing the court may wish to review the conduct of the case as a whole and give further case management directions. The parties must be ready to assist the court in doing this and it will again be essential that the person attending is someone with full knowledge of the file.

21.5 Applications made without service of application notice

Self-evidently, to comply with the rules of natural justice, applications should usually be made on notice to the other party so that they can respond and put their own viewpoint. That is the general rule (CPR, r. 23.4(1)).

There are a number of exceptions under specific rules where application is made to the court direct usually for permission to take some other preliminary step, e.g., to extend the time for serving a claim form under r. 7.6(4). Quite apart from where a specific rule permits it, para. 3 of PD 23 sets out six circumstances in which the court will allow an applicant to proceed without serving an application notice on his opponent, namely:

(a) where there is exceptional urgency;

(b) where the overriding objective is best furthered by doing so;

(c) by consent of all parties;

(d) with the express permission of the court;

(e) where a date for a hearing has already been fixed for some other matter and the party wishes to make an application, but does not have sufficient time to serve an application notice. In this situation the applicant should then inform the other party and the court as soon as he can of the nature of the application and the reason for it and make the application orally; or

(f) where a court order, rule or practice direction permits.

The second of these provisions offers a very wide and general test. It must also be remembered that some potential aspects of dealing with a case justly may be in conflict with each other. Thus a party may contend that it will assist to dispose of matters swiftly and economically by permitting an application without notice; but it is possible to respond to that by suggesting that it will not be possible to deal with something justly where the other party is either not informed at all or not informed in sufficient time to voice his objections adequately.

If proper notice cannot be given under the rules then informal notice should be given as soon as possible, however late in the day that may be. The exception would be where the application depends for its effectiveness on some element of surprise or secrecy such as applications for freezing injunctions and search orders (discussed at **22.2.4** and **22.2.5**).

21.5.1 Procedure following an application without notice

If the court refuses an application made without notice to one's opponent then no procedural problem arises. The court might refuse such an application either on its merits, because the case for whatever was sought was not made out, or might simply consider it inappropriate to proceed without notice because there was insufficient urgency and no particular circumstances which required that procedure. The court will then direct the party to apply by the proper method on notice to the opponent.

If, however, the court accedes to the application and grants the order sought, then it must be served on the respondent together with the application notice and any evidence used in support. The order when made must (under r. 23.9(3)) contain a specific statement to the effect that the respondent has a right to apply to set aside or vary the order within seven clear days of it being served. In principle, if the opponent then decides to make that application, the matter should go back before the original judge who granted the order.

Consequently, where an application without notice has been granted, the opponent has the right to have the matter reviewed and of course to adduce any further evidence he wishes, for example, to show that the evidence upon which the original application was based is misleading or incomplete and to put his side of the case. Pending the hearing of that application, which the court will treat as urgent and list for very early hearing, he must preserve the status quo so far as possible. If the order was a freezing injunction directing him to retain his assets without disposing of them, he must obey it. In the case of more routine procedural orders, for example, an order permitting the claimant to renew the claim form so as to extend the time for service beyond the initial four-month period, it will be open to the respondent to put his case before the court. A defendant may contend that the evidence on which the claimant's application was based, which, for example, alleged that he had been evading service, was completely untrue, and he might wish to show that he had always resided at the same address and had made no attempt to evade service.

21.6 Consent orders

The court may deal with an application without a hearing if the parties agree on the terms of the order sought. The parties may want some particular direction, in which case the application notice and the consent order should be lodged at court to be reviewed by the court. A 'hostile' application may have been issued, but in the period between issue and the hearing of the application the parties may have come to an agreement.

EXAMPLE

The claimant contends that the disclosure of documents offered by the defendant is inadequate and, after an exchange of correspondence, decides to issue an application to the court to attempt to compel the defendant to disclose further documents. The defendant's solicitor reviews the matter with his client and they conclude on reconsideration that some of the documents which the claimant seeks are relevant, though they maintain their refusal in respect of others. The claimant's solicitor decides to accept this offer to compromise the issue and progress the litigation. The parties may then either draw up a consent order indicating what documents the defendant has agreed to disclose or might in fact dispose of the matter simply by the application being withdrawn and the parties cooperating in relation to the new disclosure.

In either case the parties should ensure that they agree what costs order is involved and preferably should agree a figure for costs to be inserted in the consent order or agree that there should be no order for costs (PD 44, para. 4.4(3)). If a consent order is required it must be drafted by the parties.

It should be noted that the court has the power to refuse to approve a consent order. In routine cases it is unlikely to do so unless the order is so badly drafted that it makes no sense. It is not open to the parties to agree to vary key dates in the case management timetable and consent orders in that form will be refused unless the parties are able to make out a strong case in accompanying documentation for that variation, so that the court will approve it.

21.7 Hearing of the interim application

The hearing will usually be in public unless secrecy is absolutely required or confidential information about the financial position of a party will be given. Although the European Convention on Human Rights and Fundamental Freedoms requires public hearings, those who drafted the CPR have provided (at r. 39.2) that the court is not required to change its sitting arrangements so as to accommodate the public if it is impractical. Most hearings will be held in district judges' private rooms which can usually only accommodate about six to eight people. Thus if the application is attended only by a lawyer for each of two parties, there may in fact be room to accommodate a few members of the public. The parties may of course wish to attend applications of any importance and would then have the right to bring friends or supporters with them.

It is considered unlikely that the general public will have any interest in seeing the huge majority of routine interim applications and if casual observers attended, for example, a busy court where there are say six district judges sitting, the list in the public area would give them little guidance as to which if any hearings were likely to raise matters of any interest to the general public.

Attendance at such hearings may of course be considered useful experience for law students. The court staff, or even the judges if asked in advance, will assist in indicating to them which applications are of more substance or interest, although since more substantial hearings are usually conducted by reference to a good deal of documentation, which will not be available to the public, even the more substantial applications, such as those for summary judgment or an interim payment, may not mean much to the audience.

21.7.1   Hearings by telephone

The overriding objective requires the court to have regard to using technology. In future, video link hearings with the parties' solicitors not having to leave their offices may become common. Indeed, there have been provisions for such hearings (although relatively little used) for some years. A few courts and some solicitors' offices and sets of barristers' chambers already have the technology in place for this. The rules presently provide in particular for *telephone conference calls* under r. 3.1(2)(d). This enables the court to hold a hearing by telephone or any other method of direct oral communication. If the court decides to hold such a hearing it will allocate a time and give suitable directions. PD 23, para. 5, contains detailed provisions for setting up and paying for telephone hearings. The position as from autumn 2006 is that telephone hearings will be the norm for most interim hearings up to an hour long, including case management conferences. They will not be used for final hearings on any track, nor application for summary judgment (see **26.6**), infant settlement hearings (see **31.5**) or various other kinds of hearings. They are also unsuitable if both parents are litigants in person, or where there are numerous parties.

21.8   Costs at the end of interim hearings

If an interim hearing has been brought about through no fault of either party, but simply because the court is to be invited to exercise its case management powers because of some development in the case, it would be wrong to penalise either party with the costs of the hearing.

Suppose, for example, in what seemed a routine personal injury case that the claimant has suddenly developed severe symptoms so that further medical evidence is now needed, and that the claim will be considerably larger than had been expected. The directions already given may be inadequate, and the court may need to approve the appointment of other experts and to set back the case management timetable that has already been fixed, by months or even years.

In this situation obviously the parties will be expected to cooperate in attempting to agree how the case should proceed. Even if they reach an agreement they will have to come before the court so that the court can exercise its case management powers to fix a new timetable (assuming that it accepts that the original timetable will no longer suffice).

Suppose therefore in that situation the parties come before the court for another half hour's appointment for further directions. The likely outcome in terms of costs would be 'costs in the case' since neither party is blameworthy. Costs in the case will also of course be the usual order at ordinary case management conferences so that the costs will depend upon the eventual outcome of the whole litigation.

Many interim applications, however, will involve one party in effect complaining about the other's conduct, in particular, that the other has defaulted in carrying out some previous direction of the court, or has failed to be reasonable about some procedural matter. In that case where an interim application is disposed of in less than a day (and this will apply to the majority of all such applications) and provided that neither party is a person under a disability and the successful party is not legally aided, the court will usually go on to make a summary assessment of costs. This will usually be an order that the unsuccessful party at the application pay the other party's costs, usually within 14 days.

To assist with this process, the PD on costs requires the parties to serve on each other, not less than 24 hours before the interim hearing, signed statements of their costs in a prescribed form, setting out in brief the work done, the hourly rate charged and the number of hours claimed. Any failure to file at court or serve this statement of costs without good excuse will be taken into account and if the party who succeeds on the application has failed to do it the court will take that as an indication that no costs are sought. The form for statement of costs is illustrated at the end of this chapter.

Three further points should be noted:

(a) It is of course open to the parties to agree each other's costs in advance dependent upon the outcome of the application and the court will usually endorse any figure that is put forward without enquiry.

(b) It will be important for the unsuccessful party to attempt to ensure that the work done was reasonable and relates entirely to the application. Thus, for example, if the application is to do with a dispute concerning disclosure of documents generally, the unsuccessful party should ensure that the other party is not 'loading' on to the costs claimed some costs of work that would have had to be undertaken in any event.

(c) An order for summary assessment of costs cannot be made in favour of a publicly funded party because that party's costs will need to be reviewed by the court as a whole at the end of the case. It can, however, be made *against* a publicly funded party. The order should not be that the publicly funded party pays the costs within 14 days, but rather that the determination of whether or not they are to be paid should be deferred to the end of the case or that they should only be payable by way of set-off from any other costs or damages to which the publicly funded party is, or becomes, entitled. Thus, for example, it would be possible for the court which concluded that a publicly funded party was culpable in some procedural matter to summarily assess costs against him in the sum of say £500. If, however, the publicly funded person eventually won the litigation as a whole, this figure would then be deducted from any general order for costs in his favour.

21.9 Evidence at interim applications

This topic is fully considered at **19.4**.

Application Notice

You should provide this information for listing the application

1. How do you wish to have your application dealt with

   a) at a hearing? ☐
   b) at a telephone conference? ☐ } *complete all questions below*

   c) without a hearing? ☐ *complete Qs 5 and 6 below*

2. Give a time estimate for the hearing/conference
   _____(hours)_____(mins)

3. Is this agreed by all parties? ☐ Yes ☐ No

4. Give dates of any trial period or fixed trial date _____

5. Level of judge _____

6. Parties to be served _____

In the	
Claim no.	
Warrant no. (If applicable)	
Claimant (including ref.)	
Defendant(s) (including ref.)	
Date	

Note You must complete Parts A **and** B, **and** Part C if applicable. Send any relevant fee and the completed application to the court with any draft order, witness statement or other evidence; and sufficient copies for service on each respondent.

Part A

1. Enter your full name, or name of solicitor

I (We)[1]   (on behalf of)(the claimant)(the defendant)

2. State clearly what order you are seeking and if possible attach a draft

intend to apply for an order (a draft of which is attached) that[2]

3. Briefly set out why you are seeking the order. Include the material facts on which you rely identifying any rule or statutory provision

because[3]

Part B

I (We) wish to rely on: *tick one box*

the attached (witness statement)(affidavit) ☐   my statement of case ☐

4. If you are not already a party to the proceedings, you must provide an address for service of documents

evidence in Part C in support of my application ☐

Signed _____   **Position or office held** _____

(Applicant)('s Solicitor)('s litigation friend)   (if signing on behalf of firm or company)

Address to which documents about this claim should be sent (including reference if appropriate)[4]

	if applicable	
	fax no.	
	DX no.	
Tel. no. Postcode	e-mail	

The court office at

is open from 10am to 4pm Monday to Friday. When corresponding with the court please address forms or letters to the Court Manager and quote the claim number.

Part C   Claim No.

I (We) wish to rely on the following evidence in support of this application:

Statement of Truth

*(I believe) *(The applicant believes) that the facts stated in Part C are true
delete as appropriate

Signed

(Applicant)('s Solicitor)('s litigation friend)

Position or office held

(if signing on behalf of firm or company)

Date

Statement of Costs
(summary assessment)

In the	
	Court
Case Reference	

Judge/Master

Case Title

[Party]'s Statement of Costs for the hearing on *(date)*   **(interim application/fast track trial)**

Description of fee earners*
  (a)   *(name) (grade) (hourly rate claimed)*
  (b)   *(name) (grade) (hourly rate claimed)*

Attendances on   *(party)*

(a) *(number)*	hours at £		£	0.00
(b) *(number)*	hours at £		£	0.00

Attendances on opponents

(a) *(number)*	hours at £		£	0.00
(b) *(number)*	hours at £		£	0.00

Attendance on others

(a) *(number)*	hours at £		£	0.00
(b) *(number)*	hours at £		£	0.00

Site inspections etc

(a) *(number)*	hours at £		£	0.00
(b) *(number)*	hours at £		£	0.00

Work done on negotiations

(a) *(number)*	hours at £		£	0.00
(b) *(number)*	hours at £		£	0.00

Other work, not covered above

(a) *(number)*	hours at £		£	0.00
(b) *(number)*	hours at £		£	0.00

Work done on documents

(a) *(number)*	hours at £		£	0.00
(b) *(number)*	hours at £		£	0.00

Attendance at hearing

(a) *(number)*	hours at £		£	0.00
(b) *(number)*	hours at £		£	0.00
(a) *(number)*	hours travel and waiting at £		£	0.00
(b) *(number)*	hours travel and waiting at £		£	0.00

Sub Total £   0.00

	Brought forward £		0.00

Counsel's fees *(name) (year of call)*

Fee for [advice/conference/documents]   £

Fee for hearing   £

Other expenses

[court fees]   £

Others   £

(give brief description)

Total   £   0.00

Amount of VAT claimed

on solicitors and counsel's fees   £

on other expenses   £

Grand Total   £   0.00

The costs estimated above do not exceed the costs which the *(party)*
is liable to pay in respect of the work which this estimate covers.

Dated

Signed

Name of firm of solicitors
[partner] for the *(party)*

---

* 3 grades of fee earner are suggested: (1) Solicitors with over 4 years post qualification experience (2) Other solicitors and legal executives and fee earners of equivalent experience (3) Trainee solicitors and fee earners of equivalent experience. 'Legal Executive' means a Fellow of the Institute of Legal Executives. Those who are not Fellows of the Institute are not entitled to call themselves legal executives and in principle are therefore not entitled to the same hourly rate as a legal executive. In respect of each fee earner communications should be treated as attendances and routine communications should be claimed at one tenth of the hourly rate.

Interim remedies: CPR, Part 25

22.1 Introduction

In all claims the claimant will be seeking a certain remedy. Usually this will be an award of money in the form of damages or payment of a debt. In some claims something more complex than an order for simple payment of money is required. A claimant may want, for example, an injunction, an order for specific performance, rescission of a contract, the taking of accounts, or the dissolution of a partnership. As a claim proceeds on one or other of the tracks through to a trial there may be case management conferences and applications by one or other side for various orders of a procedural nature: e.g., to compel the other party to comply with directions already issued; to extend time limits for taking some step; or to rule on some matter in dispute between the parties (e.g., the disallowing of some item of evidence or the instruction of an expert).

What we are now about to consider are applications to the court in advance of trial for something that is more than a merely procedural order. The common feature of the matters mentioned below is that each involves the court awarding what amounts to a *remedy* in some form or other. Sometimes these interim remedies may involve the court awarding in part, or on a temporary basis, the same remedy that the claimant is seeking at the eventual trial. This is true, for instance, of applications for an interim injunction to prevent the defendant taking a step until the full claim is heard; or for an interim payment which is a part payment of debt or damages being made on account, pending final determination of matters at trial. Other forms of interim remedy are applications for the court to assist by requiring one or other party to preserve evidence until trial, or to make evidence in the form of physical objects or documents available for inspection at a certain stage. It is first appropriate to list the interim remedies which a court may grant under Part 25 of the CPR. These include the orders listed in r. 25.1(1), which are:

(a) an interim injunction;

(b) an interim declaration;

(c) an order for detention, custody, preservation, inspection, taking samples from, carrying out experiments on relevant property; sale of relevant property which is of a perishable nature or which for some other reason it is desirable to sell quickly and for the payment of income from relevant property until a claim is decided;

(d) an order authorising a person to enter any land or building in the possession of a party to the proceedings for the purpose of carrying out an order of the kind previously mentioned;

(e) an order under s. 4 of the Torts (Interference with Goods) Act 1977 to deliver goods;

(f) a 'freezing injunction', which used to be called a *Mareva* injunction;

(g) an order directing a party to provide information about the location of relevant property or assets or to provide information about relevant property or assets which are or may be the subject of an application for a freezing injunction;

(h) a 'search order' under s. 7 of the Civil Procedure Act 1997 (which used to be called an *Anton Piller* order);

(i) an order for disclosure of documents for inspection of property before a claim has been made under s. 33 of the Supreme Court Act 1981 or s. 52 of the County Courts Act 1984;

(j) an order under s. 34 of the Supreme Court Act 1981 or s. 53 of the County Courts Act 1984 for disclosure of documents or inspection of property against a non-party;

(k) an order for interim payment;

(l) an order for a specified fund to be paid into court or otherwise secured where there is a dispute over a party's right to the fund;

(m) an order permitting a party seeking to recover personal property to pay money into court pending the outcome of the proceedings and directing that if he does so, the property should be given up to him; and

(n) an order directing a party to prepare and file accounts relating to the dispute.

(o) an order directing accounts and inquiries by the court.

(p) orders relating to enforcement of intellectual property rights.

It is important to note that although this is a long and apparently exhaustive list, by virtue of r. 25.1(3), the fact that a particular kind of interim remedy is not listed in r. 25.1(1) does not affect any power that the court may have to grant that remedy. A court may grant an interim remedy whether or not there is a claim for a final remedy of that kind. The court has a very wide power in this regard.

22.2 Types of interim remedy

We have already discussed in the text some aspects of interim remedies, including the material on interim injunctions (see **1.7.4**) and orders for disclosure of documents or for inspection of property before a claim has been made (see **9.1.4.2**). Because of its importance, there is a specific treatment of the question of *interim payments* below, but it is now perhaps appropriate to discuss briefly the other forms of interim remedy, for which application may be made.

Although most of the following forms of remedy are relevant mainly in larger commercial actions and therefore unlikely to be within the scope of what a trainee will deal with in routine litigation, in fact they can arise even in quite mundane circumstances. For example, disputes between relatives or former cohabitees about who is the true owner of a given motor car and cases where one party needs an order urgently to ensure that evidence is preserved pending trial or is made available for inspection by him before trial.

22.2.1 Interim declarations

Some proceedings seek only a *declaration* of parties' legal entitlements (for example, as to where a boundary may be between adjoining landowners). The form of an interim declaration therefore would be to make a provisional ruling on the matter in question, perhaps to preserve the status quo and in effect prevent one party removing fences erected by the other, or building walls of his own.

22.2.2 An order for detention, custody, etc.

This useful and wide-ranging provision permits a party to apply for an order that items which are either the subject matter of the whole action (e.g., goods whose title is in dispute) or simply items as to which some dispute may arise should be preserved, provided for inspection, etc. in certain forms. It allows, in particular, for the court to order that a party make the objects in question available for inspection by the other party so that he can obtain his own expert evidence on them. It would also extend to permitting inspection, for example, of the scene of a factory accident. In relation to perishable goods, it permits an order for sale even though the title to the goods may be in dispute: for example, if there was a dispute concerning a consignment of fruit which had a shelf life of only a few weeks the title to which was in dispute. The court could then order the sale of the fruit at the best price with the proceeds to be paid into court pending the resolution of the litigation.

The supplementary provision permitting a court to authorise a person to enter land for carrying out any of the above is obviously a practical and useful ancillary remedy.

22.2.3 An order under s. 4 of the Torts (Interference with Goods) Act 1977

This statute enables the court at trial to make an order for delivery of goods whose title is in dispute from one party to another. This particular provision permits this to be ordered on a temporary basis. It might apply, for example, in the case of a motor car whose title for some reason is in dispute and where the claimant contends that he is likely to suffer great hardship by being deprived of it pending the outcome of the action. It enables the court to order the return of the car to him on a temporary basis pending final resolution.

22.2.4 A freezing injunction

A freezing injunction permits a claimant to apply to the court to seize and freeze some or all of the assets of a defendant because he fears that the defendant will take steps to remove his assets from the jurisdiction or otherwise dispose of them to defeat the purpose of any judgment which the claimant might obtain. Its most common use is in substantial commercial litigation involving a defendant with an overseas connection, but it is certainly not confined to that. It was, for example, used in one particular case where a fatal accident was caused by a Nigerian company which had no relevant insurance in the UK but did have one asset here, namely, an aeroplane. The High Court permitted the aeroplane to be seized as security for any eventual award of damages to the claimant.

It should be noted that before such a draconian order can be made the claimant must satisfy a number of conditions. The order can in any event only be made by a High Court judge. Evidence for this kind of application must also be by *affidavit*, i.e. a sworn witness statement.

The supplemental provision to a freezing injunction may be an order which directs a party to provide information about the location of property or assets so that they can be effectively seized (e.g., bank accounts, the whereabouts of property or vehicles). A full discussion of freezing injunctions is beyond the scope of this text.

22.2.5 A search order

This is also a draconian form of remedy which can only be granted by a High Court judge and which requires affidavit evidence. It is again mainly used in commercial cases, in particular, in intellectual property disputes where there are claimed breaches of trademarks or illicit copying of materials such as video cassettes, DVDs and CDs. It is an order permitting a claimant (or more usually a *potential* claimant because this particular form of relief is often applied for before proceedings are even issued) to enter the property of the defendant and search it for evidence of illicitly made copies of copyright material, lists of suppliers and customers.

There are very detailed provisions as to the basis on which such an application can be made, the precise mechanisms by which the order, if granted, can be carried out and the way in which a report back to the court which authorised the process must be made.

22.2.6 An order under s. 34 of the Supreme Court Act 1981 for disclosure of documents, etc. against a non-party

This is discussed at **18.6.1**.

22.2.7 An order for a specified fund to be paid into court

The usefulness of this is obvious. If ownership of a fund is in dispute a party may seek an order that it be paid into court pending the resolution of the dispute. Clearly it will be necessary to show something more than that the fund is in dispute. It is also usually necessary to show that the fund may in some way be at risk if retained by the person who now has it.

22.2.8 An order permitting a party seeking to recover personal property to pay money into court . . . and directing that the property should be given up to him

This is a useful adjunct to the court's general powers. If there is a dispute about ownership or possession of personal property such as a motor car, it enables the party who wishes the property to be returned to him to obtain an order that it be returned to him provided that he pays a given sum of money (usually the value of the object or at least the value of the use of the object, such as an equivalent to hire charges), pending the outcome of the dispute into court.

22.2.9 An order directing a party to prepare and file accounts

This may commonly be made even in quite mundane litigation. It does not necessarily refer to something as complex as company or partnership accounts and may simply be an account of the dealings between the parties—a series of invoices between say a builders' merchant and a small builder where it is unclear what has been paid and when for each invoice. It is quite a common procedural order in routine litigation.

22.3 Time when an order for an interim remedy may be made

An order may be made at any time including both before proceedings are started and after judgment has been given, but subject to any rule, practice direction or enactment which provides otherwise. Moreover, by virtue of CPR, r. 25.2(2)(b), the court may grant an interim remedy before a claim has been issued *only* if the matter is urgent or it is otherwise desirable to do so in the interests of justice. In these circumstances where the court grants an interim remedy before a claim has even been issued it may, although it does not have to, give directions requiring a claim to be commenced. This will obviously be appropriate where an order for an interim injunction has been made because it would be most unfair to permit the successful party to sit back with the benefit of its interim injunction and never begin proceedings. In other cases, however, this may not be appropriate. So, for example, where there is an application for pre-action disclosure of documents, the whole point of which is to enable a potential claimant to decide whether he wishes to issue proceedings at all, there may be no such order.

22.3.1 Method of application

An application for an interim remedy is made on an application notice. The notice will of course usually be served on the other party, but by r. 25.3, the court has the power to make the order without giving the other party notice if it appears that there is good reason. This is common where both urgency and secrecy are required as part of the purpose of obtaining the order. Applications for freezing orders to restrain a potential defendant from removing assets from the jurisdiction or disposing of them are almost always made without notice being given, so the potential defendant does not have a chance to defeat the object of the proceedings. The same applies to applications for search orders for the same reasons.

Other forms of application, however, may require neither urgency nor secrecy and normally should be on notice. An application for an interim remedy must be supported by evidence unless the court orders otherwise.

22.4 Jurisdiction and level of judiciary

As indicated above, freezing injunctions and search orders may only be granted by High Court judges or any other judge duly authorised for that purpose. In relation to other interim injunctions, an injunction can only be granted by any judge who has jurisdiction to conduct the trial of the action. So, as district judges have jurisdiction to deal with fast track trials (i.e., up to £15,000, or above with the consent of the parties), a district judge has the power to grant an injunction at trial, or an interim injunction before it, in a case up to that limit.

With regard to all other interim remedies a district judge has jurisdiction to grant them on whichever track or whatever the amount of the claim involved.

We shall now go on to consider interim payments.

22.5 Interim payments

22.5.1 Nature and availability of interim payments

An interim payment is a payment in advance on account of any eventual award of damages which a claimant might receive. Interim payments are available in claims for debt, or for damages whether in tort, contract or under any other principle of law. Interim payments are also available in certain other limited circumstances which we discuss below.

It is undoubtedly in the case of personal injury actions that interim payments are most important and we shall commence with a discussion of interim payments in that context before going on to other kinds of case.

22.5.2 Interim payments in personal injury actions

As has already been mentioned (**1.4**), except in those cases in which the possibility of an award of provisional damages or periodical payments exist, an award of damages is a once and for all matter. Therefore, a claimant's solicitor would usually not be wise to hurry a case to trial too quickly if the claimant has suffered personal injuries of any seriousness. It will be important to see how the claimant's medical condition stabilises so that a proper judgment can be made as to how the quality of his life, and particularly his potential earning power, has been affected. Even if it were procedurally possible, therefore, to get substantial personal injury cases to trial within a few months, it would, generally speaking, be highly undesirable to do so.

In the normal case, once an award of damages has been made the claimant cannot go back to court for more if his condition deteriorates or his improvement does not reach the levels expected by his medical advisers. On the assumption, therefore, that the claimant himself has some interest in a degree of delay in bringing his case to trial, the psychological effect on the claimant of this delay must be considered. As has previously been noted, the reality of personal injury litigation is that an individual is litigating against a huge insurance company. Even in cases where the individual has no worries about his own legal expenses (e.g., where he is supported by a trade union or legal expenses insurer) he is aware of the importance of the success of his claim to his and his family's financial future. The insurance company, while no doubt usually guided by proper commercial principles so that they will not wish to incur large sums in wasted legal costs fighting hopeless cases, will also be aware that there are tactical advantages for them in delaying matters and thus bringing pressure upon the claimant to accept the smallest sum that they can escape with paying. It would be foolish to pretend that the psychological pressures imposed by litigation on an insurance company are anything like the pressure on an injured individual. The degree of anxiety that the individual may feel will, of course, be exacerbated if he is now so disabled as to be virtually housebound and may have little on which to exercise his mind for much of the day apart from the prospects of his claim. Litigation in those circumstances must seem virtually interminable. It is easy to imagine the pressure upon any such individual, but the pressures will be increased still further if the individual is also suffering financial hardship as a consequence of the injury. For example, if he had previously been a highly paid employee and is reduced to living on benefits, he will not only see the quality of his life substantially diminished but also have the worries of mortgage arrears and other debts accumulating.

In such a case the possibility of an application for an interim payment may be vitally important, both to relieve immediate financial pressure upon the claimant and to improve his morale and make him more optimistic about the eventual success of his claim.

In fast track cases the considerations referred to above are unlikely to apply because in essence the case should proceed to trial in well under a year from commencement. Even if a longer period than this is required to resolve matters entirely, say because of some uncertainty about the claimant's medical condition, the court is quite likely to bring the case on for trial on the preliminary issue of liability only on the usual time table and the claimant, if he succeeds on liability, can then be awarded an interim payment. Multi-track cases involving larger sums and perhaps more difficult issues on liability will inevitably proceed at a slower pace, however robust the court's case management, and again the court will be alert to see whether the issue of liability can be tried early. In future, in personal injury cases anyway, the need for applications for interim payments may be reduced by the greater speed of the litigation process, but we will proceed to describe the procedural aspects first for personal injury cases.

22.5.3   The grounds for an interim payment

An application can be made to the court on one of the grounds set out in CPR, r. 25.7(1) which reads as follows:

The court may only make an order for an interim payment where any of the following conditions are satisfied:

(a) The defendant against whom the order is sought has admitted liability to pay damages or some other sum of money to the claimant;

(b) The claimant has obtained judgment against that defendant for damages to be assessed or for a sum of money (other than costs) to be assessed;

(c) It is satisfied that, if the claim went to trial, the claimant would obtain judgment for a substantial amount of money (other than costs) against the defendant from whom he is seeking an order for interim payment, whether or not that defendant is the only defendant or one of a number of defendants to the claim; or

(d) The following conditions are satisfied:

(i) the claimant is seeking an order for possession of land (whether or not any other order is also sought) and

(ii) the court is satisfied that if the case went to trial, the defendant would be held liable (even if the claim for possession fails) to pay the claimant a sum of money for the defendant's occupation and use of the land while the claim for possession was pending;

(e) In a claim in which there are two or more defendants the order is sought against any one or more of those defendants, the following conditions are satisfied:

(i) The court is satisfied that if the claim went to trial, the claimant would obtain judgment for a substantial amount of money (other than costs) against at least one of the defendants (but the court cannot determine which); and

(ii) all the defendants are either

(a) a defendant that is insured in respect of the claim;

(b) a defendant whose liability will be met by an insurer under section 151 of the Road Traffic Act 1988 or an insurer acting under the Motor Insurers Bureau Agreement or the Motor Insurers Bureau, where it is acting itself; or

(c) a defendant is a public body . . .

(4) The court must not order an interim payment of more than a reasonable proportion of the likely amount of the final judgment.

(5) The court must take into account

(a) contributory negligence; and

(b) any relevant set of or counter claim.

These provisions appear complex, but are not really so. The main complexity is in relation to personal injury claims, under 27(1)(e) it will be noted that an interim payment can only be ordered if the defendant is either:

(a) insured in respect of the claim (that is, any liability will be met by an insurer or the Motor Insurers' Bureau); or

(b) a public body.

The reasons for this provision are to ensure that applications for interim payments are not made pointlessly against parties who cannot pay them. In the huge majority of personal injury cases the defendant will be insured. This is bound to be so for employer's liability accidents and road traffic accidents, and these account for more than 90 per cent of all personal injury claims. There may be other cases however, where there is no insurance, for example, occupiers' liability cases or injuries caused by animals. In road traffic accident cases, even if there is insurance which could be avoided by the insurer, or there is no insurance at all, an application for an interim payment may still be made because eventual damages will be met either by the insurer concerned (s. 151 of the Road Traffic Act 1988) or by the Motor Insurers' Bureau.

The reason why a claim may still be brought if the defendant is not insured but is a public body is that certain public bodies are not required to have insurance, but may, so to speak, act as their own insurer, as many local authorities do.

In relation to the three basic grounds for obtaining an interim payment, there is clearly no problem with the first and second which imply that the case has come to an end on the issue of liability, either because the defendant has already admitted it or because the claimant has already obtained judgment on the issue of liability (e.g., in consequence of a split trial or by summary judgment). It is the third ground that will naturally cause difficulty because it requires a district judge, at a time when the defendant is still prima facie defending, to arrive at some assessment of who is likely to win the case and whether or not (assuming that it is the claimant) he is likely to receive 'substantial damages'. In this case the district judge will not consider himself bound by the contents of the defendant's defence, even though it is verified by a statement of truth, but will look to see what serious issues arise and whether the defendant is merely trying to keep the issue of liability 'alive' for tactical reasons.

22.5.4 The application under Part 25

To apply, the claimant is required by PD 25B, para. 2.1, to issue an application notice supported by evidence dealing with the following:

(a) the sum of money sought by way of interim payment;

(b) the items or matters for which the interim payment is sought;

(c) the sum of money for which final judgment is likely to be given;

(d) the reasons for believing that the conditions set out in r. 25.7 are satisfied;

(e) any other relevant matters;

(f) in personal injury claims, details of special damages and past and future loss.

In a personal injury case the claimant should attempt to indicate what sum he seeks and the amount he hopes eventually to recover at trial. If the interim payment is meant to be a payment on account for specific items (for example, vehicle repairs or loss of earnings to date) that information should be given. The requirement to satisfy r. 25.7 clearly invites the claimant to demonstrate by further evidence why he is sure that he will obtain substantial damages and thus to indicate what evidence he intends to put forward (for example, proof of the defendant's conviction for dangerous driving arising out of the incident concerned or witness statements of bystanders).

Any documents in support of the application should be exhibited and, in personal injury claims particularly, all medical reports should be supplied. Likewise letters from employers giving details of loss of earnings and other documentary evidence, such as the receipted account for vehicle repairs, should be included.

22.5.5   Demonstrating the need for an interim payment

There is actually no requirement in the rules for the application to be made only in a case of hardship so that it is open even to a wealthy claimant to make an application. Indeed many solicitors commonly make routine applications for interim payments to ensure that the pressure is kept on defendants to save costs by admitting liability if they have not done so already. As PD 25 requires the claimant to identify the items or matters for which the interim payment is sought, it would naturally be appropriate for him to give some explanation in support of these—to demonstrate that his loss of earnings to date because of the accident has caused him difficulty with mortgage arrears, or that he would like to have private medical treatment which he cannot afford unless an interim payment is made.

The application may not be issued until the end of the period for filing an acknowledgement of service and when issued must be served with the accompanying evidence at least 14 days before the hearing. If the respondent to the application wishes to rely on written evidence, he must file the written evidence and serve copies on every other party at least seven days before the hearing. If the applicant wishes to respond to that, he must file and serve his evidence at least three days before the hearing.

22.5.6   The court's decision

When the case comes before the district judge he will decide whether he considers liability is sufficiently clearly established to enable him to make an interim payment order. The wording in r. 25.7(1)(c) indicates that he must be satisfied that 'the claimant *would* obtain judgment'. Case law on similar wording in the old rules showed that it was not enough simply to show that the claimant was likely to succeed on a balance of probabilities. A very high degree of probability was required in a case where liability was still in dispute. Indeed in one case, which was probably an overstatement, the court suggested that what was necessary was for the claimant to show that he *will* succeed which, taken literally, implies a standard of proof equivalent to virtual certainty. It is nonetheless suggested that a high degree of probability will be required.

22.5.6.1   Multiple defendants?

Suppose that in a claim the claimant is suing two or more parties and does not really know which of them is likely to be held ultimately liable. Straightforward examples might be where two cars collide and one then bounces on to the pavement injuring a claimant; or where the claimant is working on a building site and scaffolding collapses. He may initially sue his own employer, but that person may be only a small subcontractor and may contend that the management of the whole site is the responsibility of the main contractor; the main contractor in turn may say that the responsibility should be that of the subcontractor who erected the scaffolding in question; and the scaffolder may in turn contend that the scaffolding when erected was perfectly safe, but because of inadequate security provided by the site owner that vandals had tampered with the scaffolding joints overnight, which was something beyond his control. The injured workman may therefore eventually feel it prudent to add all these people as alternative defendants. Can he then get an interim payment?

The answer might at first sight appear to be no, in that one might think that given the degree of probability required to establish the grounds to obtain an interim payment, it is not enough to show that he would succeed only against *somebody* without identifying that person. However, r. 25.7(1)(e) provides that an interim payment order can be made against any defendant provided all the defendants are insured and the court is satisfied that the claim will succeed against somebody. This is a sensible and virtually risk-free rule. In personal injury litigation where all defendants are insured, any interim payments improperly awarded against a defendant who is ultimately exonerated can be compensated for at the final determination of the case by an order that the defendant who is ultimately found liable repay the innocent defendant the interim payment and interest on it. The provision applies also in non-personal injury cases provided *all* defendants have insurance or are public bodies. See also **22.5.9**.

22.5.6.2   How much should be awarded?

Having decided whether an award will be made at all, the court must go on to consider what amount should be awarded. By r. 25.7(4) and (5) the court may only order a *reasonable proportion* of the likely amount of any final judgment taking into account any contributory negligence or set-off or counterclaim. It is important to note in personal injury cases, by virtue of PD 25B, paras 4.1 to 4.4, that the defendant will need to obtain a certificate of recoverable benefits which will have to be taken into account in the ultimate distribution of the interim payment.

The test of what will be a reasonable proportion of damages is very much a matter of judgment on the facts of any given case. A rule of thumb that used to be suggested was to award the claimant the whole of his loss of earnings and other special damages incurred to the date of the application, together with a reasonable proportion of the approximate level of general damages taking a conservative view. This may still be a good guideline in many cases.

It should be noted that it is open to the court under r. 25.6(7) to require payment of an interim payment by instalments. In such a case the order must set out the total amount of the interim payment and the amounts and dates of each instalment. In personal injury cases this is unlikely to be necessary. It is open to a claimant to make more than one application for an interim payment and if any interim payment is made to relieve hardship and the case later takes longer than expected to reach trial, a second application can be made in due course for further sums. A second application can even be made if the first application failed, say if new evidence has emerged enabling the court to take a different view on liability.

22.5.7   Case management

On any application for an interim payment, whether the application succeeds or fails, the district judge may go on to give further case management directions. If application for the interim payment was made early, this would also be a convenient moment to deal with allocation.

22.5.8 Voluntary interim payments

Because of the availability of interim payments, it will be a sensible part of negotiation to see if the defendant will agree to make a voluntary interim payment. Insurance companies are sometimes willing to make voluntary interim payments even before proceedings have been issued if liability seems clear. Indeed, where a defendant is not proposing to contest liability, he may as well offer an interim payment since it avoids the costs of an application to the court. One particular use of an interim payment may be for private medical treatment which will enable an injured claimant to be treated more quickly than if he had to wait for NHS treatment. This may benefit both parties because it may hasten the claimant's recovery and return to work, thus reducing his loss of earnings claim.

Likewise, many insurance companies are now alert to the fact that in road traffic cases tendering the amount necessary for vehicle repairs to the claimant at a very early stage will enable him to have those repairs done and stop the need for expensive car hire.

In personal injury cases where correspondence with the defendant or his insurers will have been undertaken in compliance with the protocol, clearly an attempt to agree liability and obtain a voluntary interim payment will have been made. As with any other kind of application, if one launches a formal application to the court without having previously explored the possibility of obtaining an interim payment voluntarily, the claimant might well be penalised in costs, even if an interim payment was awarded.

22.5.9 Interim payments in non-personal injury cases

The illustrations and commentary above largely concern personal injury cases. However, an interim payment may be awarded in any kind of case which is within r. 25.7. These would include situations where there are claims in contract and payments are often used to improve a claimant's cash flow. It should be borne in mind in contract cases that if the grounds are sufficiently clear-cut to enable a party to obtain an interim payment, they will usually be sufficiently clear-cut to enable him to obtain summary judgment, on liability at least, under Part 24.

Other cases where interim payments are useful are where an order has already been obtained for an *account to be taken* as between claimant and defendant, for instance, where a partnership has been dissolved and until the drawing up of accounts the precise liability of the defendant to the claimant cannot be known. An interim payment can be made on account while the accounts are being drawn up. Likewise in claims for possession of land an interim payment application may be made. See **25.7**(1)(d). This can arise, for instance, where the claimant is undeniably the owner of the land and the defendant is said to be wrongfully in occupation. An interim payment application in these circumstances may be used to compel the defendant to pay sums equivalent to rent whilst the claim carries on to trial. It is necessary to obtain an award from the court in such cases because it is probably unsafe for the claimant to accept voluntary interim payments as a matter of law, since this may be deemed to be waiver of breaches of covenant or the like or acceptance of the defendant's tenancy.

In non-personal injury cases, it is not sufficient for the claimant to show that he will succeed against *someone* unless r. 25.7(1)(e) applies. If any of the defendants are *not* insured or public bodies he must also show that he will recover against the *particular defendant* from whom an interim payment is sought. Previous case law indicated, and this is probably still applicable, that interim payment applications are not appropriate where the factual issues are complicated or where difficult points of law arise which may take many hours to argue (see *Schott Kem Ltd* v *Bentley* [1991] 1 QB 61).

Preparing for trial

In this chapter we consider the last stages of preparation for trial and some of the tactical and procedural steps that need to be taken by a party to ensure that he is ready and that his case is well prepared.

23.1 Complying with court orders

Orders for progress to trial may have been obtained at various stages. In a fast track case there may well never have been an attendance before the court and full directions will have been sent by post at the time of allocation. In multi-track cases and fast track cases where some complications have arisen, there will have been a case management conference (in bigger cases there may have been more than one) and also a pre-trial hearing involving the judge who will eventually take the trial. Whatever has happened hitherto, it is vital for the parties to comply fully with all directions given and to bear in mind that the court will not permit the case management timetable to be varied by consent if that would lead to postponement of the date of trial. The date of trial or at least a 'window' of three weeks, during which the trial will fall, will have been known for many months and the parties will have had every opportunity to ensure availability of witnesses, expert witnesses and the counsel of their choice.

It is the main function of the pre-trial checklist, which is usually ordered to be filed about eight weeks before the likely trial date, to confirm to the court that all directions have been completed and to update the court on the parties' estimate of the length of trial, now that all the evidence is known and the true matters in issue can be identified.

In trials which are likely to be lengthy (say three days or more) and particularly those where it is sought to have a High Court judge, probably application will have been made for a fixed date of trial many months in advance. This will assist also with ensuring availability of witnesses, particularly expert witnesses who may have many calls on their time.

Although evidence of witnesses as to the facts ought to have been exchanged some considerable time before, it is possible that issues in relation to expert evidence remain in dispute also. Provided that the order permits oral expert evidence at trial, this will cause no difficulty, but there are likely to have been orders requiring the experts to meet to discuss outstanding disagreements and it is important to ensure that those meetings have taken place and that the outcome of them is known.

23.2 Evidence

The importance of ensuring that a party can prove his case by admissible evidence has been constantly stressed. It is customary, in more substantial cases, to ask counsel formally to advise on evidence.

Counsel will be the person presenting the case at trial, and even if he has advised on the merits of the case once or more often, it is usual to send the papers back to him at this relatively late stage for him to consider just what appears to be outstanding, in the light of what has been conceded or agreed so far, and what evidence he thinks appropriate to prove each given point outstanding, and by what method. A full set of instructions should thus be drafted for counsel explaining all the outstanding matters, the progress of the case so far, and asking for his advice in a series of specific questions. The solicitor himself should go through the relevant matters and give his own views on the points at issue. Copies of all relevant documents should be enclosed. It may also be necessary to indicate to counsel matters that do not appear in documentary form, e.g., the contents of telephone negotiations with an opponent. Counsel will review the evidence in the whole case on both liability and quantum, thus the instruction should deal fully with matters of medical evidence, details of loss of earnings and other special damages.

It is usually appropriate to ask for counsel's advice in written form rather than at a conference, although it is also customary to have a conference with counsel at a slightly later stage, to which we shall come in due course.

When advice is received from counsel it should, of course, be implemented immediately.

23.2.1 Evidence of the facts

One must consider how each relevant item of evidence will be put before the court. There are three main possibilities:

23.2.1.1 Hearsay evidence

If it is intended to adduce hearsay evidence under the Civil Evidence Act 1995, one should ensure that the appropriate notices have been given.

23.2.1.2 Notice to admit facts

This is a useful alternative to calling witnesses to give oral evidence, particularly in cases where the evidence in question will be inconvenient or expensive to adduce. The nature and purpose of the notice to admit facts has been described earlier at **3.5.2.2**.

A notice to admit facts must be thoroughly drafted to cover with precision the points on which agreement is sought. The notice should be served no later than 21 days before trial. The consequence, as we have seen, is that if the opposite party fails to admit a fact which he should have admitted, he will bear the costs of proving the fact at trial whatever the outcome of the trial.

If the opposing party admits the facts in question then a copy of the document containing the admission will be included in the evidence for trial.

23.2.1.3 Witnesses

It is wise to issue and serve a witness summons on all lay witnesses, even members of the claimant's family or close friends who have promised their co-operation in attending trial. It is always disappointing to find that witnesses may well put their own concerns (such as going on holiday) before a party's justifiable entitlement to insist that they turn up to testify at trial. Witnesses should be told that this witness summons does not represent any slight on their reliability but is merely a matter of formality. The reason for doing this is that if a witness summons has not been served and a key witness does not attend at trial, then either the judge may not permit an adjournment at all (in which case the claim may well be lost), or, if he does permit an adjournment, it will inevitably be at the cost of the party requesting it. On the other hand, if a witness summons has been served but the witness still does not attend, the judge will agree that there is no fault in the party requiring the adjournment and it will therefore usually be allowed without penalty.

A witness summons may either:

(a) require the witness to attend court for the purpose of giving verbal testimony and this would be appropriate to ensure the attendance of an eyewitness; or

(b) require a witness to attend court to produce, and if necessary prove, the authenticity of some document or thing. For example, it may be necessary to issue a witness summons to compel a claimant's employer to attend court to bring wages and salary records with him. It may be that no other evidence from the employer is needed except to prove the authenticity of these wages records.

The method of obtaining a witness summons is to prepare two copies for each witness in the prescribed form N20 and attend the court counter where the court will seal a copy for service. A judge is not involved and no permission from the court is needed except in two circumstances, namely:

(a) if one seeks to have the witness summons issued less than seven days before trial;

(b) if the witness summons is for a witness to attend court for any hearing except a trial (such as an interim application).

If permission is needed then applications should be made without notice to a district judge. In principle, the file will be taken to him straightaway, if an urgent decision is needed.

Once the witness summons is issued by sealing, in principle it will be served by the court, usually by post. If a party wishes to serve it himself for greater certainty, it will be returned to him. If it is to be sealed by the court then the party on whose behalf the witness summons is issued must deposit in the court office the money that has to be paid or offered to the witness.

The witness summons must be served on a witness no later than seven days before trial to be binding.

Money to be paid to a witness

By r. 34.7, at the time of service of a witness summons the witness must be offered or paid a sum 'reasonably sufficient to cover his expenses in travelling to and from the court' together with such sum by way of compensation for loss of time, as may be specified in a practice direction. PD 34 actually says that the sum referred to is based on the same sums payable to witnesses who attend the Crown Court in criminal trials and which are fixed presently by the Costs in Criminal Cases (General) Regulations 1986.

23.2.1.4   Witness summonses and expert witnesses

It is now increasingly common to serve a witness summons on expert witnesses. Popular expert witnesses may become double or treble booked for their various commitments and may even be summonsed for different trials in different locations on the same day. Although oral evidence from expert witnesses is very much the exception in fast track cases, if such evidence is needed, the window for trial should have been known for many months before, and in multi-track cases the witnesses' availability will have been one of the factors in listing the case for trial. It is still important to serve a witness summons on an expert, who can then justifiably claim that that is his primary commitment on the day in question. If he then gets a witness summons for a different case on the same day, he will be able in good faith to tell the solicitors in the second case that he is unavailable and the second trial will have to be rearranged if he is to attend.

23.2.1.5   The trial date

If a fixed date of trial is known at the time of issue of the witness summons, that date should be inserted in the summons. However, if one is to issue and serve the summons early in the case, all that will be known is that the trial will be listed in a 'window' of three weeks. In a case where the witness summons does not specify the date of trial it still binds the witness, and the solicitor concerned will 'activate' the summons for a particular date by telephoning or writing to the witness.

23.3   Production of original documents

If a party is in possession of an original document, then that original should be produced at trial. Such a document's inclusion in a list of documents on disclosure requires the other party to give positive notice if he does not admit its authenticity, and thus the dispute about that matter can be determined before the trial. If the opposing party possesses the document, notice to produce the document should be given. If there is non-compliance with that notice the other party may prove the contents of the document by secondary means, e.g., carbon copies, photostats, or even a verbal account of what it contained.

If somebody other than one of the parties is in possession of an original document required for the trial, a witness summons should be served on that person requiring him to bring it. Under CPR, r. 31.7, one has the power to make an application for non-party disclosure, requiring the party to produce a document for inspection. Even after it has been inspected it may still be needed for trial unless the other party is willing to accept its authenticity so that photocopies can be produced without needing the original in court.

By virtue of PD 32 (para. 27.2), all documents contained in agreed bundles at trial shall be admissible at the hearing as evidence of their contents unless the court orders otherwise, or a party gives written notice of objections to the admissibility of a particular document. It is important, therefore, to bear this in mind when 'agreeing' documents.

23.4   Computations in damages claims

In larger personal injury cases a considerable amount of the judge's time is likely to be taken up with investigations of complex figures for loss of earnings, cost of future care, etc. The same will apply in some kinds of commercial actions where, for example, a party is claiming loss of profits over a considerable period. In order to cut down the amount of the judge's time at trial taken up with investigating difficult arithmetical matters, the parties will inevitably have been given directions about how to prepare, either at the case management conference or later.

In such cases the usual form of direction will be that the claimant prepare a schedule showing the computation of the amounts for which he contends, explaining, with reasons, the justification for each figure in some convenient format. The order will not simply permit the defendant to turn up at trial and dispute each item. The defendant in turn will be required at some appropriate stage to serve a *counter schedule*, setting out his opposing contentions for each item and the reasons for them. Both schedule and counter-schedule must now be signed and contain a statement of truth. Sometimes it will be convenient to order that these are set out on the same page in a document which used to be known as a 'Scott schedule' whereby disputed items are listed usually in five or more columns, showing:

(a) the figure for which the claimant contends for a particular item or rate of loss;

(b) his brief arguments in support of it;

(c) the figure which the defendant contends for and his arguments in support of it;

(d) possibly a further column for the claimant's reply to the defendant's contentions; and

(e) a blank column for completion by the trial judge in the course of hearing the evidence.

This form of schedule is particularly useful in clarifying the issues in building and construction disputes where there may be many hundreds of items, the nature and value of which are each disputed. It is probably not appropriate in personal injury claims where, although the disputes may be very substantial, there are only a few items in dispute, e.g., the rate of pay which the claimant would have had had he been able to return to work and achieved certain promotions, or the rates of pay the claimant can now earn in some job that pays less well than his former occupation, or the period for which it was appropriate for the claimant to have remained off work.

These documents should be prepared in a user-friendly form for the trial judge so that he can clearly see the issues in arithmetical terms.

23.5 Listing of cases

We have already considered the primary rules in relation to listing of cases which provide that on both fast track and multi-track a fixed date of trial or a trial window will be given very substantially in advance. A pre-trial checklist will be completed in both kinds of case—several weeks before the intended trial. When these are returned containing up-to-date information they will, amongst other things:

(a) show what issues are agreed and what remain outstanding;

(b) give the numbers of witnesses to be called; and

(c) give each party's estimate of the length of trial.

Often on the multi-track the parties will be ordered to file an agreed case summary to assist. At this stage the case will be listed by the combined efforts of the listing officer of the relevant court and possibly the judge who is likely to hear the case. In multi-track cases a trial may last days or weeks and in those cases further listing arrangements will have been put in place at a much earlier stage to ensure availability of both judge and court.

23.6   Trial timetables

The court must, in consultation with the parties, set a timetable for the trial unless it considers that it would be inappropriate to do so (CPR, rr. 28.6 and 29.8). In multi-track cases the trial timetable is likely to be set at a pre-trial review, but in other cases it will be done on paper perhaps following requests for information in writing from the court to the parties. When parties file their pre-trial checklists, they should make any appropriate representations. Among the matters which need to be considered are:

(a) whether any opening speeches are required and if so how long will be permitted;

(b) how much time will be required for evidence-in-chief and whether the witness statements can simply be ordered to stand as the evidence-in-chief or whether time will be permitted for witnesses to amplify them;

(c) what time should be permitted for the cross-examination of each witness and what parts of the witness's evidence could be agreed;

(d) what expert evidence is to be given and how much time will be needed to cross-examine the experts;

(e) the order in which witnesses should be called;

(f) the time to be permitted for closing speeches.

If a timetable is fixed it is important that it is realistic and that it is kept to. One of the issues which the court will want to address is likely to be that of expert evidence where opposing experts are to be called. While normally the claimant presents his case to its end and then the defendant presents his, with expert evidence it will usually be convenient for the experts to attend on the same day so they can hear each other's evidence. That may mean interrupting the normal order of events and a direction that they attend at the same time and give evidence one after the other is likely to become the norm. When that will be in the trial is also a matter for judgment. Clearly, if they are both commenting on the state of health of the claimant, it is desirable that their evidence be given after his and it may even be desirable that they are in court while he gives his evidence. These, among others, are some of the complications which will need to be considered when the trial timetable is fixed.

In order to assist with the fixing of the trial timetable, the parties may be requested to file a *statement of issues* and a case summary to focus on what is really important in the case.

23.7   Trial bundles

At the trial the judge will want the documents in convenient form for reference. He will not want to go hunting back through the court's case file in which a great variety of documents may have been filed, some of them duplicating each other, and many of them irrelevant to the trial itself. The trial bundle contains the relevant documents for the trial so that if, for example, liability has been determined in advance, the trial bundle will contain only the documents relating to quantum. If the issue for the trial is liability only with quantum to be decided later, then the converse will be the case.

In pursuit of the principles of economy and proportionality, it is expected that while the trial bundle must be complete so that no delay is caused by the need to locate other documents during the trial, it contains only what is really of significance for the trial. It used to be common, for example, for solicitors to include in the bundle virtually the whole of the correspondence between themselves since the case commenced, which might have added hundreds of pages to the bundle. This is almost certainly unnecessary and is likely to be frowned on since the judge will probably scrutinise the bundle in advance of trial and if he gives over many hours to reading documents which prove to be totally irrelevant, he is likely to be displeased. Certainly the costs of preparing multiple copies of superfluous material will be disallowed.

As much as possible of the documentary evidence should be 'agreed' between the parties. In this sense 'agreed' has the special meaning of 'agreed as authentic and relevant to the trial'. It does not indicate that the *contents* of such documents are agreed. It thus has a very different meaning from the context in which the word is used of, say, expert reports, where the term 'agreed' means 'agreed as to substance and truth'.

EXAMPLE

It may be that there has been a great deal of correspondence between the parties about the dispute before solicitors were ever instructed. In such correspondence, each party may have asserted, increasingly strongly, the justice of their own position and their complaints about the other party's conduct. This correspondence will be highly relevant at trial to show what was being said at the earlier stages and how the argument developed. It must therefore be put before the court. It does not, however, of course follow that each party 'agrees' with the contents of what is asserted in the other party's correspondence. What is agreed is that the correspondence is authentic and relevant and should be before the court for that reason.

It is usual for the claimant to indicate to the defendant what documents he considers material for the trial bundle and to supply a copy index; the defendant then should make any counter proposals for other material to be added to the bundle or, for example, if he considers that irrelevant and even inadmissible material has been included in the claimant's proposal to put forward his suggestions for the exclusion of such evidence from the bundle. At least four bundles are likely to be necessary for the average trial, there being one bundle for each party, one bundle for the judge, and one to be provided to any witness in the witness box for comment during the course of his testimony.

The rules on the multi-track require a bundle to be lodged not more than seven or less than three days before trial by virtue of CPR, r. 39.5(2). Somewhat oddly, standard fast track directions in PD 28 provide that trial bundles should be lodged at least seven days before trial.

23.7.1   Contents of the trial bundle

Essentially the bundle should contain copies of:

(a) the claim form and all statements of case;

(b) a case summary and/or chronology where appropriate;

(c) all requests for further information and the answers;

(d) all witness statements and summaries to be relied upon;

(e) any hearsay notices;

(f) any notices of intention to rely on plans or photographs;

(g) all experts' reports and written responses to questions;

(h) any order giving trial directions; and

(i) any other necessary documents (e.g., relevant correspondence and original documents).

The bundles should be continuously paginated throughout and indexed with a description of each document with its page number. If any documents are in manuscript and likely to be difficult to read then a typed transcript should follow immediately after the document. If the bundle exceeds 100 pages, numbered dividers should be used between groups of documents. The documents should normally be contained in lever-arch or ring-binder files. If there are a lot of documents, it may be helpful to separate them into different coloured files for ease of reference by the judge and any witnesses who need to refer to them when giving evidence.

23.8 Skeleton arguments

In a case of any complexity the parties will be ordered to exchange and file 'skeleton arguments' identifying the true issues, the propositions to be advanced, the authorities to be cited and if appropriate a chronology of events. These will not be required, of course, in a routine case or one turning entirely on factual evidence. Sometimes also (especially in commercial disputes), a detailed chronology—for example, reciting the different stages of changes of shareholding or directorships in a web of interlocking companies—can be invaluable in enabling a judge to see the issues clearly. Naturally counsel's assistance in drafting the skeleton is required to identify the issues involved and the propositions of law and the authorities which he proposes to cite, and so if any such order has been made at the case management conference one will have to stay closely in touch with counsel about this at the relevant stage.

23.9 Final negotiations

As the case approaches its final stage it will become clearer whether or not it is indeed going to be seriously defended. Of course, insisting on the strength of your defence and leaving offers or further offers until very late in the day is an obvious tactic in negotiations. A defendant must weigh up the mounting costs of this 'last ditch' bluff against his knowledge of the probably rising anxiety of a claimant whose (in personal injury cases, and sometimes in business disputes) whole quality of future life will depend on the outcome. As we have already remarked, this is what gives defendants a tremendous psychological advantage in personal injury cases since the real defendant, being a large insurance company, does not have anything like as personal a stake in the outcome of such cases. Nonetheless, the defendant's insurer's solicitors will have to consider to what degree the costs are rising in proportion to the amount at stake in the claim itself.

In very large claims substantial amounts can be risked on bluffing until the very last stage in order to take advantage of any faltering in the claimant's determination. In more modest claims the costs of going to trial represent a very considerable proportion of the global costs of settlement, and therefore defendants are likely to put in their true final offer somewhat earlier. As we shall see in **Chapter 25**, payments into court under Part 36 can still be made, and take effect, even very late in a case; and although by then the point of a gamble is rather less pressing on a claimant, if the trial is likely to be long, or expensive in terms of the number of expert witnesses, any payment in is not a matter lightly to be disregarded. Negotiations direct between the parties may therefore become particularly intense in the immediate pre-trial stage.

It may be that after a meeting of experts a round table meeting will be arranged. It may even be the case that counsel is involved in these meetings. Even if counsel is not formally involved there may be some interchanges between him and his opponent in the immediate pre-trial stage about the way in which the case is to be formally presented for convenience between them, and at which possible offers of settlement could be discussed. This may be particularly important if, as is regrettably sometimes the case, the solicitors for the claimant and defendant appear to be no longer taking a detached view of the case, so that the interposition of a more objective viewpoint helps the true issues to emerge. The negotiation position may also change because of new evidence coming out very late in the case. The exchange of witness statements in particular will already have been an important point at which one or other party sees that his case is somewhat weaker than he has supposed. Similarly, the precision with which a claimant can prepare and serve a schedule of past and future losses may make the defendant see that the apparently outrageous figures being claimed in earlier negotiations can perhaps be substantiated at trial by hard factual evidence.

When negotiating for a claimant at a late stage, it is naturally imperative to give the impression that he is now happy to press on with the trial and let the court decide. Any appearance of hesitancy is likely to be seized on by the defendant. In the case of a defendant, then, ideally a payment into court under Part 36 which is relatively close to the likely award should have been made at the earliest stage, thus putting the claimant at risk for as much as possible in the way of continuing costs. If new evidence has emerged which makes the claimant's claim seem stronger or bigger than had previously been thought, it is as well to make a further payment in late on if the defendant hopes to get out of the action without the costs of trial. An alternative, albeit brinkmanship, tactic (as is well known) is to wait to make that final offer at the courtroom door, when the claimant's nervousness at the ordeal of giving evidence, as well as at the gamble involved, may be at its peak.

23.10 Using counsel

23.10.1 Conference with counsel

It will commonly be the case that a conference with counsel will be arranged not long before the trial. Usually, in civil litigation, a client will not have seen his own barrister until this late stage, all other matters having passed between barrister and solicitor in written form. If the facts remain seriously in dispute on either liability or quantum, it is common to arrange a conference with the client present. The barrister will probe the contested parts of his client's story, suggesting to him the way in which he will be cross-examined about it and looking for his response to likely questions. He may want to explain to the claimant why he gave written advice at earlier stages to refuse offers or payments into court, and answer questions from the client about the possible difficulties to be faced and the prospects of success.

Quite often such a conference is in two parts, the first with the client present and the second with the solicitor alone, the client usually having been told there are legal matters to be discussed which would bore him. Once the client has left the barrister may then give the solicitor further advice about the client's prospects, e.g., if the client, under close questioning, has seemed to be evasive, or clearly gaping holes or improbabilities have appeared in his account of what happened. It may be that in the light of seeing how the client has performed as a witness, even in the limited context of a conference in a private room, the barrister will firmly urge the solicitor to accept some offer that has been made, or to see whether any improved offer can be obtained before the delivery of briefs for trial.

23.10.2   Conferences with expert witnesses

Until 1995 barristers were not permitted to see witnesses of fact before trial in order, supposedly, to preserve their detachment. Following a change in the rules of professional conduct, barristers are now permitted to see witnesses of fact, although cases in which barristers will request to see witnesses of fact before the trial will probably remain rare. Barristers have, however, always been permitted to see *expert witnesses* and it may well be helpful to arrange a conference with expert witnesses if there are substantial disputes concerning expert evidence.

The expert in the case normally attends the barrister's chambers for the conference, although increasingly such conferences can take place in the solicitor's offices where sometimes the accommodation is rather better. The purpose of the conference is for counsel to ask detailed questions about the expert's views, e.g., in a personal injury case about the prognosis of the claimant, or to seek clarification of the matters in the consultant's or his opponent's report and ask for ammunition from the consultant about lines of cross-examination to take with the opposing expert.

23.10.3   Briefing counsel

23.10.3.1   Delivering the brief

The solicitor should prepare a brief for the counsel who has been involved in the case hitherto. A brief should generally be delivered not so late that counsel cannot prepare the case thoroughly, nor so early that the brief cannot take account of new developments, e.g., offers made at a late stage. When a solicitor chooses to deliver a brief is very much a matter of feel but in a substantial action at least a month before the date of trial is thought to be the minimum. Counsel's clerk should be contacted very much earlier than this, however, to be told to expect the brief and to confirm counsel's availability; he may then be involved in using his powers of persuasion with the listing officer to ensure that within its 'window' the case comes into the list at a time convenient for the counsel concerned. The other side should be notified that one is about to deliver a brief because the brief fee becomes payable upon its delivery, even if the case is settled immediately thereafter. This is therefore a powerful final incentive to the opposing party to consider settling since a very heavy disbursement is about to be incurred on the claimant's side for which the defendant will be liable if he loses or settles later. In fact, despite this rule, if the case is settled shortly after delivery of the brief and before counsel has commenced work on it, it is usual to negotiate a reduction in the brief fee with counsel's clerk.

23.10.3.2   Contents of the brief

One thing a brief should not be is brief. A solicitor should not trust to the fact that a barrister is already familiar with the case from having drafted the statement of case or given advice in connection with it. A good brief should set out in coherent, chronological order a discussion of all relevant issues of fact, evidence and law, and supply copies of all necessary documents including proofs of evidence, computations of special damages, the statement of case, procedural orders, accounts of negotiations with the opponents and so on.

If a skeleton argument has been required, the papers should have been sent to counsel well in advance of the trial to enable him to draft the skeleton argument for filing at court and service on the opponent. In that case, counsel will already have all the papers and need only be updated by a so-called 'back page brief' perhaps indicating to him any last-minute telephone negotiations before trial, since he will already have all the other documents.

Counsel should be given a copy of the court bundle so as to correspond with the bundle which the judge will have for ease of cross-reference in opening speech, cross-examination, or argument.

The brief should deal with any relevant issues of law, including the solicitor's own views about any given matter. This may be a considerable help to counsel and it is far better for the client to have two independent minds brought to bear on legal problems in this way rather than the solicitor feeling that he must inevitably defer to counsel's greater abilities in research and legal knowledge.

23.10.4   Where the counsel of choice is unavailable

If the counsel of one's choice, who has been involved in the case hitherto, is unavailable, perhaps because he is involved in an overrunning case elsewhere, then the solicitor should insist on a counsel of comparable seniority from the same chambers; and if no such counsel is available, he should go to other chambers. Clerks are usually very reluctant to let a brief go 'out of chambers' and will devise all manner of imaginative arguments about why somebody far junior to the counsel of first choice is competent to deal with it, but unless a solicitor has independent knowledge of the competence of the suggested substitute, he should not hesitate to take the brief elsewhere.

23.10.5   Counsel's fee

When the brief is delivered no fee will be marked on it initially but counsel's clerk will assess what he considers the 'weight' of it to be, and may well discuss it with the barrister concerned. Barristers increasingly take an interest in the amount of their fees and are less inclined to leave every such matter to their clerks. The fee suggested will be based on a variety of factors, including the apparent importance of the case, length of trial, amount involved, seniority and popularity of the barrister concerned, and greed. After some negotiation it is usually possible to agree on a fee but if it is not then the solicitor must ask for the brief to be returned.

The brief fee is for the work involved in preparing the case and for the first day in court, and that is why in principle the brief fee becomes payable immediately because counsel may immediately start doing substantial research on it even though the trial does not commence for some weeks. It is also necessary to agree a so-called 'refresher' fee, i.e., a fee for the second day in court and subsequent days. This fee is typically only a fraction of the brief fee itself. In a publicly funded case there is no need to agree a fee. Counsel's clerk will in due course put forward a fee note in the sum he suggests, which will be considered at assessment of costs by the district judge.

It will be recalled that in fast track cases the advocate's fee for the trial is fixed (see **14.6**), accordingly in a fast track case the brief fee agreed by the solicitor is likely to be only the same as this amount. There is of course nothing to stop counsel from insisting on a higher fee, if he can get it from the solicitor, although the client's approval will be needed because the client will need to be told that even in the event of total success only the fixed fee will be recoverable from the losing opponent and therefore the client will be bearing part of the barrister's fee himself. Agreement of fees above the fixed rate is very unusual.

23.10.6   The last conference

It is common to have a last 'conference' at court on the morning when the case is due to start. For this purpose the solicitor usually arrives well before the start of the trial to meet counsel with the client for the last time. This is because late concessions, or even further offers, may have come in, often as late as the night before the trial. In addition, counsel may well have received approaches direct from his opposite number and there may be further matters to discuss. However, this 'conference' must clearly be distinguished from the earlier conference to which we have referred. The morning of the trial is no time for a first thorough review of matters with a client, and it is imperative that that conference comes about well in advance of the trial.

24

The trial

In this chapter we consider the course of the trial itself. We discuss the immediate preliminaries to the trial and the tasks of the solicitor in organising witnesses and evidence at the trial itself; the order of events at the trial and some aspects of professional conduct; and the importance of making all necessary and appropriate applications at the conclusion of the trial, whether one has acted for the successful or the unsuccessful party.

24.1 Preliminary matters

In the High Court solicitors do not have a general right of audience in open court except those few who have obtained the Higher Courts Right of Audience Qualification, and therefore a barrister will have to be briefed.

The principle under the CPR is that the Court Service is determined that trial dates will be honoured. Great flexibility in listing, and indeed in relocating the place of trial even very late in the day, will assist in this. As has been pointed out in **14.5**, a large conurbation such as Birmingham, Manchester or Bristol may well have 20 or more civil courtrooms available for use on any given day within a short radius and therefore where the judge who it was originally intended would hear the case is unavailable, for example, due to a previous case overrunning, cases may be switched at the last minute to another judge in a different court. This is obviously undesirable if the case management has taken into account that a certain judge will hear the case, but it may be better than the alternatives which may be an adjournment of indefinite length until the judge in question has a free day in his calendar.

24.2 The day of the trial

On arrival at court (which should be at least an hour before the trial is listed to start) there may well be further contact with the other side. As suggested in **23.9**, further offers may be made and even if these do not dispose of the case entirely it may be possible at this late stage to agree some matters which will shorten the trial, for example, by agreeing computations of loss of earnings subject to liability. At the start of the trial the judge will expect the advocates to identify the main issues to let him know what is no longer in dispute.

24.3 The trial and case management

We have already discussed the setting of a trial timetable. The judge has very wide powers to direct the course of proceedings and may dispense with speeches and even refuse to hear certain witnesses, even though their evidence is admissible in law. A judge will seek to shorten the trial so far as is consistent with justice by directing that the witness statements exchanged stand as evidence-in-chief and that the length of oral submissions and the time allowed for examination and cross-examination are limited. He may also require written submissions to be made in advance or instead of final speeches. He will usually only require this where the end of the evidence is reached in the afternoon to give the parties the opportunity to draft the written submissions overnight.

24.4 The course of the trial

24.4.1 Counsel for the claimant's opening speech

If the judge requires an opening speech, which is now not common since there will often have been skeleton arguments submitted in writing, then the trial will commence with it. In the speech, counsel will introduce the nature of the case, indicate what propositions of law he needs to rely on, if any, and set out the facts which support his case and indicate which witnesses he will call to prove them.

24.4.2 The evidence of the claimant and witnesses

The order of calling witnesses is entirely up to the claimant's counsel, but it is usual for the claimant to testify before his witnesses. All the witnesses are usually present in court in a civil case, although if for any reason an advocate contends that there is any risk of collusion, the judge may order a given witness to sit outside until his time comes.

It will be remembered from **23.6** that as part of efficient trial management, if there are expensive expert witnesses, the court may well direct that they give their evidence consecutively instead of in the usual order, so that the defendants' expert may well testify immediately after the claimant's expert, rather than in the course of the defendant's general evidence.

A witness will take the oath, identify his witness statement and confirm that it is true and then be tendered for cross-examination. It remains to be seen to what extent judges will permit witnesses to amplify their witness statements. In principle, a witness statement should be a full account of everything the witness wishes to say and it would be rash to rely on the judge permitting witnesses to amplify their statements at all, except perhaps to deal with any new matters which have arisen since the statement was signed. Even in such a case it might be preferable for an application to be made before trial for permission to put in an updated written witness statement.

After the witness has confirmed his witness statement and given such other evidence as he is permitted to do he can be cross-examined by any party who did not call him. If there are two or more defendants, and indeed parties added under the Part 20 procedure (see **Chapter 27**), the claimant and his witnesses may be cross-examined by several counsel.

24.4.3   Submission of 'no case to answer'

At the conclusion of the claimant's case the advocate for the defendant may make a submission of no case to answer. This is relatively rare in civil cases, but if it is made it is decided upon the same principles as apply in criminal cases. Thus it should succeed if either the evidence adduced so far has not established some necessary element in the claimant's case, or if his evidence has been so discredited in cross-examination or is so manifestly unreliable that no reasonable court could find in his favour.

These procedures really mattered and were devised at the time when most civil trials were before a jury. In other words, after a judge had ruled against a defendant's submission the matter would then be left to the jury, each party making a further closing speech. Where trials are before a judge alone the procedure is of less significance. Exceptionally it may be that some vital ingredient in the claimant's case has not been made out, so that even if all the facts given in evidence are accepted there is no basis for finding liability against the defendant, and in that situation such a submission may be appropriate.

24.4.4   The defence and closing speeches

Thereafter counsel for the defendant may make an opening speech in principle, although this will be subject to the judge's discretion. It is more likely that the judge will have invited defence counsel to amplify his skeleton argument immediately after the claimant's opening speech. He will then call his client and witnesses, and they will be cross-examined on behalf of every other party and re-examined as appropriate. There follows a closing speech by the advocate for the defendant and then a closing speech by the advocate for the claimant. If the defendant has called no evidence, however, the order of closing speeches is reversed.

24.4.5   Parties added under the Part 20 procedure

If there is another party joined by the present defendant in an additional claim under the Part 20 procedure (see **Chapter 27**), the trial will usually be between all the parties in the interests of economy and consistency. The further party may take such part as the judge decides to allow and will usually be allowed to cross-examine the claimant and his witnesses as well as introducing his own evidence relevant to the claimant's claim against the defend-ant. If he defeats the claimant's claim against the defendant, there can be no further issue (about that matter anyway) between the defendant and him. The trial may still continue between defendant and the further party about any other matter for which the defendant is claiming against him. How the trial will be conducted in these cases depends very much on the issues and the trial judge's view of what will be convenient. It may be convenient, for example, for the judge to deal entirely with the claimant's case against the defendant and rule on it before going on to hear, virtually separately, the proceedings between the defendant and the further party. Unless the claimant has amended his case to join in the further party as an additional defendant a claimant will of course have no interest in this.

24.4.6   Judgment

Even in cases of considerable complexity, judgment is usually given on the final day of the trial. Occasionally, it may be reserved to some future date. The judgment in full will consist of a review of the facts and evidence, together with the judge's specific findings in relation to the matters in issue. If rulings on points of law are required it is more likely to be the case that judgment will be reserved. The judge will review the authorities, give his decision and his reasoning and indicate the amount of his award or the terms of any other remedy granted.

The solicitor should take as full a note as possible of the evidence during the case so that he may assist counsel there and then should any matter arise, e.g., the need to know precisely what was said by a witness who testified earlier in the day. Likewise, both counsel and solicitors should take as full a note as possible of the judgment (in case of an appeal), because even though recording equipment is in use it has been known to fail.

24.5 Further applications

At the conclusion of the case when the judge has given his judgment, a number of applications may be necessary.

24.5.1 Interest on damages

If the claimant has won he will ask for final judgment to be entered and make an application for interest on damages. In a case of some complexity, e.g., a large personal injury case with many items of special damages, where differing rates of interest are due over differing periods, calculators will be needed and there may need to be an adjournment so the parties can attempt to agree a computation of interest and save the judge's time. The parties should have attempted to agree special damage computations, subject to liability, before the trial as part of the process of exchanging schedules and counter schedules and in compliance with the overriding obligation to cooperate and narrow down the areas of dispute so far as possible.

If the case is not a personal injury case, so that there are no absolute, clear guidelines in the case law and the claimant is, for example, seeking some rate of interest which is higher than the norm, e.g., interest at a true commercial rate on a large sum of money, or interest equivalent to a rate which he has himself had to pay on borrowed money, then there may need to be argument, and even evidence, on this matter. The court has the power to award compound interest and thus computations may well take some time. Thereafter the judge will make his award of interest.

24.5.2 Where there has been a Part 36 payment into court or offer

If there has been a Part 36 payment into court or offer by the defendant (see **Chapter 25**), the question will be whether or not the judgment has 'beaten' it. In the case of a payment into court this is a simple matter of arithmetical calculation. The court may need to go on to consider a written offer for some other remedy, such as the terms upon which a defendant would submit to an injunction. There may need to be further arguments about whether the net effect of the judgment just delivered has been a better outcome for the claimant or not. If the ingredients in the making of an offer are complicated, for example, in a defamation case to make an apology in certain given terms, plus an undertaking that the libel will never be repeated, plus a payment into court, the issue of whether or not the claimant has done better may be the subject of lengthy submission.

If the court decides that the claimant has done better than the offer, then the usual costs consequences will ensue. If it decides that he has not then in principle the award of costs will be adjusted from 21 days after the offer was communicated.

In the case of a Part 36 offer by the claimant, the court will again need to consider whether the claimant has done better than his offer or not. If he has the court ought to go on to make the awards for interest and costs as discussed in **Chapter 25**.

24.5.3 Interim payments and the recoupment of damages

If there has been an interim payment this needs to be communicated to the judge so that it can be taken into account in the final form of judgment. Similarly, if any money can legitimately be withheld from the award in a personal injury case by the defendant under the recoupment provisions for onward transmission to the CRU (see **1.2.1.4**), the figures must be available and communicated to the judge.

24.5.4 Costs

There will need to be an application for costs. An application will be made by the successful party for costs to be assessed. In a fast track trial lasting less than one day it is probable that the court will proceed to a summary assessment of costs. The necessary costs statements should have been exchanged in advance of the case. Even at the time of writing, however, seven years after the Civil Procedure Rules came into effect, it has been noted by many that circuit judges in particular are very uncomfortable with dealing with summary assessment of costs. Counsel are often uncomfortable with presenting arguments about them for the very good reason that under the previous regime neither circuit judges nor, usually, barristers ever had any experience of dealing with costs and arguments in relation to them. In many cases, there is already a tendency to decline to carry out summary assessment of costs and order a detailed assessment. This may well appear a fairer procedure if, as is not uncommon, the costs claimed by a successful party exceeds the amount at stake in the action. In cases that are not on the fast track, detailed assessment will be the norm and an order for it will be made at the end of the trial.

24.5.4.1 Miscellaneous matters

Orders will need to be made also for assessment of the costs if one of the parties is publicly funded. If that party has lost, the court may have to consider applications for costs against that party and the relevant criteria under the Access to Justice Act 1999.

It is normal for the court to deal with assessment of costs at the end of the hearing of interim applications, and in principle to assess them summarily then and there. Sometimes costs are reserved, however, if it is not clear until some future event on whose side the merits of the application lay.

If the conduct of the opponent's legal representatives has given cause for complaint, it may be that this is the occasion when an application for wasted costs should be made. The trial judge may make an appropriate order if he has seen sufficient evidence of what occurred at the trial, but more usually he will adjourn the question either back to himself after the legal representative has had the opportunity to consider what representations to make, or he may refer it to the district judge who assesses the costs.

24.5.5 Stay of execution

If judgment has been given against the defendant, it may be that the defendant wishes immediately to ask for a stay of execution. This may arise in two situations:

(a) *Pending appeal.* The mere giving of notice of appeal does not in itself stay a judgment, and a winning party would be perfectly entitled to go ahead to enforce that judgment pending appeal. Therefore there has to be a specific application to the trial judge at the time, or subsequently to the Court of Appeal, to stay execution on the judgment.

(b) *If the judgment debtor does not have the means for immediate payment.* Application can then be made to the trial judge for an order staying enforcement of the judgment, usually on terms that it is paid by instalments. This will naturally not be relevant in cases where the defendant is insured. If the defendant has not asked for a stay of execution at the trial, he may apply at any time thereafter by application to a district judge with a full statement of means and there will then be a further hearing.

24.6 Drawing up the judgment

Normally the judgment after trial will be drawn up by the court itself (CPR, r. 40.3) although the court may order a party to draw it up, or a party may agree to do so with the court's permission. If drawn up by a party, sufficient copies must be filed for service on all parties and the draft will be checked by the court from the judge's handwritten note before it is sealed.

A judgment takes effect immediately it is pronounced and it is not necessary to wait until it has been sealed and served. A judgment for the payment of money must be complied with within 14 days unless the court specifies some other date, for example, where the court has made an order for payment by instalments.

Although a judgment takes effect immediately it is pronounced, the time within which an appeal must be lodged usually runs from the day when the order is formally sealed by the court.

A county court judgment is notified to the Register of Judgments, Orders and Fines, which keeps a register of county court and High Court judgments which is used as the basis for credit enquiries by those in the finance industry.

Chapters 25 and 26: Bringing a case to an early conclusion

Up to now, we have described mainstream procedures for bringing a case from before commencement through to judgment. It is now appropriate to consider ways in which a case may be brought to an end before trial, as the huge majority of cases are. We shall first consider a tactic open to both parties, though undoubtedly of particular use to a defendant, whereby a party may bring a particular kind of pressure to bear on the other to settle a case on agreed terms, under the rules in **Part 36** of the CPR. There then follows a more general chapter dealing with all the ways in which a case may be brought to an end before trial. The chapters are:

Chapter 25   Payments into court and offers to settle: CPR, Part 36
Chapter 26   Termination without trial.

Payments into court and offers to settle: CPR, Part 36

25.1 Introduction

We now come to an important provision which permits one party to bring pressure on the other party to make him give serious consideration to an offer to compromise litigation. The full extent of this possibility will be explained in detail below. Students often consider this a very complicated set of rules, but in fact there is less to this than meets the eye. Put crudely, because the spirit of the CPR is to urge compromise, if someone wishes to make a reasonable offer of settlement, the other party dare not refuse it without seriously considering that the court may well impose costs penalties if litigation which should have been settled at an earlier stage has been unnecessarily prolonged. In its main use this permits the defendant to put pressure on a claimant to consider a reasonable offer; but there is also a slightly different form of procedure, which permits a claimant who is eager to settle for a sum which he thinks reasonable to put similar pressure on a defendant. The nature of the pressure, as indicated above, is that there may be very serious consequences because any costs that flow from unreasonableness in prolonging the litigation may be ordered against the party who did not give reasonable consideration to an offer to compromise at an earlier stage.

25.1.1 Explanation

In this chapter we are going to consider a procedural device available principally to a defendant to help him attempt to force a compromise on a claimant. This is by way of *a payment into court* or *offer to settle* on terms. These are the most powerful tactics available to a defendant.

There is also a variant of the procedure under which the *claimant* may make a formal offer to the defendant of the terms upon which he will settle. Where he does this, some limited pressure can also be put upon the defendant in a way which is described later in the chapter.

It should be remembered that the most likely way of all in which a case may end without a trial is by some form of negotiation leading to compromise between the parties. The system of making payments into court or offers to settle under Part 36 of the CPR is an important and formal part of the procedure of negotiation.

In litigation, the parties will generally commence negotiations even before the claim has started and they will continue through the course of the pre-trial procedures in correspondence, meetings and telephone conversations between the parties' solicitors and even during the trial itself. Some trials are compromised during one of the breaks, whether at lunchtime or, if the trial lasts for more than one day, in further negotiations at the end of the day or before the start of the following day. The system of 'Part 36 payments and offers', as it is known, is a powerful weapon in the defendant's armoury and is usually used when informal negotiations seem to have broken down. As we will see, however, the earlier in a case that the Part 36 payment or offer is made the more effective it will be in bringing pressure to bear on the claimant. This is not to say that such a payment or offer finally represents the end of any other attempts to settle the matter—indeed, negotiations may be picked up long after a Part 36 payment has been made and refused. However, Part 36 payments and offers does represent a formal offer which brings home to the claimant the risks he is taking in refusing it.

A Part 36 payment or offer is not always made by a defendant who necessarily feels that he is certain to lose. It may be made by a defendant who realises that it is uneconomic to carry on litigation, or where there are other features such as the desire to avoid the publicity of a trial which might cause the defendant commercial damage.

25.1.2   Procedure for paying money into court

To make a Part 36 payment into court the defendant completes a formal Part 36 payment notice in the prescribed form and sends it to the Court Funds Office in London (*not* the court where the claim is proceeding) with a cheque for the amount in question payable to the Accountant General of the Supreme Court. A sealed copy of the claim form must also be sent. A payment notice should then be served on the person to whom the offer is made and a copy of that notice and a completed certificate of service then filed at the court where the action is proceeding.

The claimant has, in principle, 21 days from the date of service of the notice of payment to consider the defendant's payment into court. It must be noted that a payment into court is *not* an admission of liability. It represents an attempt by the defendant to compromise a case on terms which, as indicated above, might be for reasons other than that the defendant feels certain he will lose the trial.

25.2   The consequences of a payment into court

A Part 36 payment puts pressure on the claimant in the following way: if he does not accept the payment and at the trial the judge (from whom all matters relating to a Part 36 payment in must be kept secret until after he has decided all aspects of liability and quantum) awards a sum *only equal to or less than* the payment into court, he will go on to make a so called 'split' order on costs, that is:

(a) the defendant must pay the claimant's costs on the standard basis from the date of the cause of action arising until 21 days after notice of the payment into court was received; but

(b) the claimant must pay the defendant's costs on the standard basis from 21 days after the notice was received until the end of the trial.

It will be seen that the earlier in the course of proceedings a payment into court is made, the more drastic will the consequences be for a claimant who is not awarded a sum greater than the amount paid in. There are of course two other possible outcomes:

(a) If the judge decides in the *defendant's favour entirely*, then the payment into court is irrelevant. The claimant will usually be ordered to pay the defendant's costs of the whole action on the standard basis.

(b) If the judge awards the claimant *more than the payment into court* then again it is irrelevant. The claimant will be awarded his costs of the whole action on the standard basis.

Obtaining a higher award from the judge than the amount paid into court is called 'beating the payment in'. A claimant who fails to 'beat' the payment in where this has been made at an early stage will be penalised very heavily. Although litigation is somewhat more 'front-end loaded' than it used to be, so that a good deal of preparatory work will have to be done early in every case in order to ensure that one can comply with tight timetables, at least on the fast track, the very heavy costs will still be incurred at the later stages, particularly at and just before trial, in particular, for counsel's brief fees and refreshers, solicitors' fees and expert witness fees for attending trial. The consequence for a claimant failing to beat a payment in are that from the relevant date he is not only having to bear *his opponent's* costs on the standard basis, but also will have to pay his *own solicitor's costs in full* because no one else will be bearing them. An example of the consequences of failure to beat a payment into court is as follows:

EXAMPLE

There is an accident on 3 May 2005. The claimant instructs solicitors on 12 May 2005 and from then on costs start running. Proceedings are issued and served and negotiations are unsuccessful. In January 2006 the defendant makes an informal without prejudice offer of £50,000 plus costs in full and final settlement. The claimant considers this, but refuses it and then on 21 January 2006 the defendant pays £50,000 (plus interest) into court and gives the claimant notice of this. The claimant does not accept the payment into court. The trial takes place over three days in October 2006 and at the end of it the judge awards the claimant total damages of £49,000. The effect on costs would be as follows:

(a) The defendant will pay the claimant's costs on the standard basis up to the last day for the claimant to have considered acceptance of the offer, which is 21 days after it is received. Let us say for the sake of argument that the figure for these costs would be £4,000.

(b) The claimant will have to pay the defendant's costs on the standard basis from the last date for acceptance of the offer until the end of the case (for the sake of argument let us say that this sum is likely to be of the order of £12,000).

(c) Moreover, the claimant will in addition have to bear his own costs for this later period (say a further £14,000).

From his damages of £49,000 the claimant has in effect lost the figure of £26,000 in respect of his own costs plus the defendant's costs from 21 days after the notice of the Part 36 payment was given to him.

If on the same facts the judge at trial had awarded the claimant say £50,001 then the Part 36 payment would have had no effect at all and the claimant would have got his costs on the standard basis for the whole period in the normal way.

This is a simple account of the procedure in a money claim. We shall now go on to consider some refinements to the procedure, looking at matters first entirely from the viewpoint of the defendant and the way in which he might wish to try and bring pressure to bear on the claimant to settle.

25.3 Offers to settle before commencement of proceedings (r. 36.10)

Before proceedings have commenced, there is no possibility of making a payment into court because there is no claim to which it can relate. However, even at this stage a defendant has the tactical opportunity to bring pressure to bear on a claimant.

Before proceedings are issued the defendant may make a formal offer under CPR, r. 36.10, as to the terms on which he is inviting settlement of the litigation. The offer must be expressed to be open for at least 21 days after the date it was made and if made by the defendant must offer to pay the claimant's costs up to a date 21 days after the date the offer was made. The consequences are as follows:

(a) If the offer is accepted then the matter is concluded and all that will be required is for the defendant to fulfil his offer. He will do this by paying the amount which he offered to the potential claimant, or carrying out whatever other promises he indicated in the offer if there were things other than money involved (for example, the defendant offered to refrain from committing further breaches of copyright) and to pay the costs to be assessed by the court if agreement on costs could not be reached.

(b) If a pre-action offer is *not* accepted, then the litigation will commence. By r. 36.10(3) if it is a money claim the defendant must then make a Part 36 payment into court within 14 days of service of the claim form in not less than the sum offered before proceedings began. Thereafter the court at the conclusion of the litigation will take the pre-action offer into account when making any order as to costs. Thus, if at trial a claimant who refused a reasonable offer made before proceedings were started, and did not accept the money when paid into court after the start of proceedings, recovers less than the defendant initially offered, the claimant will usually be called on to pay all the costs of the litigation from its very start. In other words the making of a reasonable pre-action offer starts the time running for the 'gamble' at an earlier stage than the later payment into court. If in such a case a payment into court is made *later* in the litigation then strictly speaking the special rule in r. 36.10 about pre-action offers is not brought into play and the court will focus instead on the date 21 days after notice of the payment in is received for the purpose of considering 'split' orders.

If the litigation is more complex in terms of remedies so that it is not simply a money claim, and the claimant succeeds on some issues in obtaining more than the defendant was offering, but perhaps not on others, the court will have to analyse the overall reasonableness of the parties and the extent to which litigation could have been avoided. This is part of the tendency under the CPR for the court to be flexible to make costs orders which are 'issue based' reflecting each party's conduct in relation to individual aspects of a claim, rather than treating the whole as an 'all or nothing' situation.

25.4 Payments into court and offers after issue of proceedings

After issue of proceedings the defendant may make a formal Part 36 payment into court indicating the amount he will pay in respect of the claimant's claim: if what is sought by the claimant is something other than money, e.g., an injunction, the defendant may offer to submit to an injunction on certain terms which he will set out in his offer.

If the claimant's claim is entirely for money then, in order to make an effective offer, the defendant must usually make a Part 36 payment by actually coming up with the money and paying it into court funds. In a money case usually nothing else will be effective and therefore, unfortunately for him, it is not open to an impecunious defendant to offer to settle the claim by payments in instalments or payments at some future date, such as when he has raised loan finance. If he does not have the money then he is unable to make a Part 36 payment. In fact the court does have a residual discretionary power under r. 36.1(2) to take offers to pay into account, but on the basis of case law from the previous rules (which closely resemble the present rules in this respect) it is most unlikely that a court would accept that a claimant should have compromised his claim merely because a defendant made a written offer to pay money at some future time.

However, despite the principles set out above, the court will be flexible and may give consideration to informal offers. In *Amber* v *Stacey*, LTL, 15 November 2000, CA, the Court held that there were compelling reasons of principle and policy why those prepared to make genuine offers of monetary settlement should do so by way of payment into court, rather than written offer, because of the obvious features of genuineness and ability to pay. Nevertheless, in the case before it, where the defendant made a written offer that did not comply with Part 36 but which was more generous than the award eventually made by the Court, the Court awarded him half of his costs from a period of 21 days after the offer. Similarly, in *Crouch* v *Kings Healthcare NHS Trust and Murry* v *Blackburn NHS Trust* [2004] All ER(D) 189 the Court of Appeal held that offers of settlement could be taken into account even if not accompanied by actual payment into court at least by defendants who were definitely good for the money.

In a claim which is not one for money at all, such as for an injunction or the taking of accounts, a defendant who wishes to settle on certain terms may put those into a formalised offer which is written on terms 'without prejudice except as to costs'. This is a privileged document and is kept secret from the trial judge so that he does not know what terms have been proposed by the defendant, but the defendant may refer to the document when all issues of liability and the form of any remedy awarded have been decided by the judge. If such an offer is refused and at trial the claimant fails to obtain a judgment which is more advantageous to him than the offer, the court will order the claimant to pay the defendant's costs incurred since the latest date on which the offer could have been accepted without the court's permission, unless this would be unjust (r. 36.20).

EXAMPLE

The defendant runs a public house near the claimant's house and has indicated that on Friday, Saturday and Sunday nights he intends to obtain extensions of licensing hours to run a disco in his function room until 2.00 a.m. The claimant immediately applies for an injunction to prevent this contending that the noise and traffic to that time will be excessive and amount to actionable nuisance.

After proceedings have started, the defendant writes a letter of offer expressed to be a Part 36 offer 'without prejudice save as to costs' to the claimant offering to change his plans so as to drop entirely the idea of holding a disco on Sunday evenings; and to limit the disco hours so that they end at 1.00 a.m. on Friday and Saturday nights and to pay for sound proofing to the claimant's house.

If at trial the claimant rejects this offer and after hearing evidence the judge either refuses an injunction at all, or grants it but in less restrictive terms than those asked for by the claimant, for example, permitting the disco to run to 1.00 a.m on Fridays, Saturdays and Sundays, then the defendant may refer to his offer and demonstrate the claimant's unreasonableness in not accepting it, which will lead to the costs consequences referred to above.

If there is a claim for both monetary relief and non-monetary relief (as is commonly the case in actions for nuisance and defamation, where both damages and injunctions are usually sought), the defendant wishing to use the procedure must make a Part 36 payment for the money claim and a separate written Part 36 offer for the non-monetary relief. At the end of the case the court will then have to consider the sufficiency of both in terms of what it has ordered. The court will be flexible in the costs consequences if the outcomes are in some way mixed and will have regard to the question of who is the real winner if the litigation had continued. Thus if, for example, the court awarded slightly less in damages than the amount paid into court, but granted an injunction in far more onerous terms than those to which the defendant indicated he would submit, the court would probably conclude that the claimant was reasonable in proceeding with the case generally, and award the claimant all the costs.

25.4.1 The formalities of Part 36 payments and offers

When serving notice on the claimant of the payment into court (which must be in the prescribed form) the defendant must notify him whether or not the payment is for all the causes of action for which the claimant's claim is brought. If there is only one cause of action on a claim form this is no problem. If, however, the claimant had sued the defendant in the same proceedings for, say, a breach of contract, and defamation on a separate occasion, the defendant's notice will have specified to which of the two causes of action the payment related or indicated that it was for both. The form of the notice is prescribed by PD 36.

In non-money claims the offer must state that it is a Part 36 offer and make it clear to which parts of the proceedings it applies and what precisely is being offered.

25.4.2 Counterclaims

The offer must state whether it takes into account any counterclaim. In cases where the defendant has a counterclaim he must make it clear whether he is offering a global settlement, i.e., deducting the amount at which he values his own counterclaim from what he is offering so that he is offering only the difference; or offering to settle the claimant's claim while proceeding with his counterclaim in full.

25.4.3 The defendant's tactics: How much should he pay in?

In a straightforward contract case it would be reasonably clear how much a defendant should pay in to obtain the tactical advantages of the procedure. Thus if, for instance, the claimant is a supplier of goods who is suing a disgruntled consumer who is unwilling to pay more than a proportion of the price because of some alleged major defect, it may be a simple enough matter to quantify the value of the supposed defect (e.g., the repair costs necessary to put the thing into the state in which it should have been at the time of sale). In such a case a defendant will be paying in (or indeed might earlier have tendered voluntarily to the claimant) the exact amount which in his view represents the value of the goods.

In personal injury litigation no such precise quantification is possible. Even if all the medical evidence is agreed and all the details about the claimant's loss of future earnings or career prospects may be easy to obtain, opinions, even of very experienced practitioners, may well differ markedly as to the value of a claim. Although by reference to the authorities fairly precise figures can be discovered for what, say, the loss of an eye represents in money terms, there are always matters of detail personal to the claimant which may be argued in favour of increasing, or sometimes decreasing, the prima facie figure. In serious accident cases injuries can never really be pushed entirely into one, straightforward category. A claimant who has, for instance, been in an accident serious enough to cause him the loss of an eye, is unlikely to have escaped without facial scarring of some kind and/or broken bones. If there is a substantial future loss of earnings claim with uncertainty about the claimant's future prospects and the stage at which he may return to work, if at all, the area of potential dispute may be greatly increased.

The scope for educated guesswork in arriving at the eventual total award of damages in such cases is considerable. Even very experienced counsel may sometimes differ by many thousands of pounds in the view they take of a case. Consequently the defendant will be trying to aim to pay into court the minimum figure which he can get away with, i.e., the minimum figure which the claimant dare not refuse. Each side will have obtained advice from counsel on the eventual quantum of damages, each predicting what the final award by the judge will be within a certain bracket. This bracket may be expressed in very wide terms, for example in a band of £5,000, so that counsel may have advised that the claimant may recover anything between £20,000 and £25,000 for general damages depending on the view the judge takes (and indeed sometimes depending on who the judge is). In such a case, if a payment into court of £20,000 is made, the claimant will have to think long and hard about the risks of pressing on in the hope of getting a judge who will give an award nearer the top of the bracket which counsel has advised as likely.

There is also, of course, as in most forms of negotiation, an element of bluff. Thus when a defendant's counsel has advised that the claimant will obtain an award in the range of £20,000–£25,000, the defendant's insurance company may decide to authorise the payment into court of only, say, £18,000 in the hope that the claimant's barrister may have been more pessimistic in his predictions and that this will actually represent a figure within the claimant's counsel's bracket which the claimant dare not refuse. In any event, this is not necessarily the last word for the defendant, because if the payment into court is refused it can be increased at any time, and therefore it is still open to the defendant at a later stage to put more pressure on the claimant by paying in, say, a further £2,000 or £3,000 to top it up. (We consider the consequences of this at **25.5.1** below.)

25.4.4   Interest and the payment into court

When making a Part 36 payment into court in any case in which the claimant is likely to be awarded interest (and therefore in contract actions and in personal injury actions of any kind), the defendant must compute the amount of interest which he thinks will be awarded and add this to the amount of the payment in.

EXAMPLE

On the defendant's figures he considers it likely that the claimant may be awarded a sum of £10,000. This is the figure which he wishes to pay into court to put pressure on the claimant. In order to do so he ought to pay into court not just the £10,000 but the interest that would be awarded on that sum computed to 21 days after the date of payment into court. Thus let us say that the interest at the date of payment into court works out at about £970. A prudent defendant will generally round up the amount to the nearest convenient figure, say in the present case £1,000, and will thus pay into court a total of £11,000.

At trial the judge (from whom the payment in has, of course, been kept secret) decides that the case is indeed worth £10,000 (as the substantive award, leaving interest out of account) and gives judgment for that amount accordingly. There then needs to be an enquiry as to whether the claimant has beaten the payment in. The amount of £11,000 paid into court is now examined

> and it will be observed that allowing for interest at the proper rates the defendant actually paid into court slightly more than the judge's award. Accordingly the claimant has not beaten the payment in and will suffer the consequences of a split order on costs. Suppose, however, that the defendant had not troubled to work out and pay in the interest and had only paid the sum of £10,000. Because a payment into court should carry interest up to the date of payment in, the court would have had to enquire what the actual figure paid in represented. If the total paid in had only been £10,000, the court would have had to address its mind to what this figure was and would have come to the conclusion that it represented only just over £9,000 together with the interest on that sum. Accordingly, on the same facts, the claimant would have beaten the payment in because the trial judge had awarded him a final figure of £10,000 plus interest.

Interest on damages does, of course, continue after the date of payment into court until the end of the trial. However, interest for that latter period is excluded from computation when working out whether or not a claimant has beaten the payment into court. The trial judge will make a separate finding of how much interest will be paid from the date of payment into court to the end of the trial and award that figure to the claimant in any event.

25.4.5   Interim payments

If an interim payment has already been made, it must be made clear to what extent this is taken into account. Thus, if the claimant has already obtained an interim payment of £5,000 and the defendant thinks the claim as a whole is worth £15,000, he will pay into court £10,000 stating that he takes the prior interim payment into account.

25.4.6   Payment into court and the compensation recovery unit

In a personal injury case where a defendant makes a Part 36 payment in respect of a claim where benefits have been paid to the claimant for which the defendant is liable to reimburse the Compensation Recovery Unit, the defendant should obtain a certificate of recoverable benefit and file the certificate with the Part 36 payment notice (PD 36, para. 10.1).

The Part 36 payment notice should state the total amount represented by the payment (the gross compensation) and that the defendant has reduced the sum by the recoverable benefits and withheld them for onward payment to the CRU if the claimant accepts.

If the claimant then accepts the Part 36 payment, he will recover the net sum and the balance representing the recoverable benefits will thereupon be paid by the defendant to the CRU.

25.4.7   Periodical payments of damages and Part 36 (see also 1.4.4)

Making offers under Part 36 will be a more complicated business where there is some possibility of periodical payments of damages. There is a new rule 36.2 in effect from April 2005. It permits a defendant who wishes to make an offer to express it either as a lump sum or an offer of periodical payments or a combination of the two. If there is a lump sum offer, there must be an actual payment into court. Periodical payments can however be expressed by way of a simple offer. Any such offer if properly formulated can only be accepted in its entirety and it will be for the defendant to make it crystal clear just what he is offering.

Consequent amendments to rr. 36.20 and 36.21 provide that the claimant who receives such an offer can 'beat' it by obtaining a judgment which is more advantageous. Self-evidently there may well be argument about whether, where the interrelationship of the lump sum and periodical payments is difficult or contingent the claimant has 'beaten' any given offer or not for the costs consequences.

25.4.8 Acceptance by the claimant of a Part 36 payment into court

If the claimant wishes to accept a defendant's Part 36 payment within the 21 days, notice of acceptance is sent to the defendant and filed with the court (PD 36, para. 7.6). The notice must state the claim number and title of the proceedings and payment will be sent out to the solicitor within a very short time.

Where the claimant does accept the amount paid into court, these are the consequences:

(a) All relevant causes of action are *stayed*, i.e., no further action can be taken in respect of them. In other words it is the end of the case except for the assessment of the claimant's costs.

(b) The claimant will then be entitled to have his costs assessed on the standard basis up to the date of acceptance. It will often be possible to agree costs with the defendant. A claimant is entitled to incur reasonable costs on the standard basis within the 21-day period for acceptance, in order to assist him to decide whether to accept. Thus further investigative work by his solicitor, a conference with counsel, or even a further expert's report if there is time to obtain it, will be justifiable.

25.4.9 Acceptance of Part 36 offers

If the claim is not for money, and an offer of acceptable terms to compromise the litigation has been put forward in writing, a claimant must send notice of acceptance to the defendant and file that with the court. The notice must likewise state the claim number and title of the proceedings, identify the written offer and be signed by the claimant or his legal representative. If this disposes of the whole claim then again the claim is stayed and the claimant will be entitled to his costs of the proceedings up to the date on which he served notice of acceptance of the offer on the standard basis. It may be necessary to agree a form of consent order for the court to approve what has been agreed (e.g., the terms of an injunction). See 26.2.

25.5 Procedural matters

We have discussed above the basic procedures and practice in respect of Part 36 payments and offers by the defendant. Before going on to discuss the possibility of the *claimant* making a Part 36 offer, it is important to discuss a number of other procedural possibilities which sometimes arise, namely:

(a) 'topping up' the payment in;

(b) where a claimant having refused a payment in changes his mind and wishes to accept it later than the 21-day period;

(c) where the payment in or offer is made less than 21 days before trial; and

(d) the position if there are two or more defendants.

25.5.1   Topping up the payment in to court or offer

Just as in other forms of negotiation, for example, buying a house or car, the first offer put forward is unlikely to be the final amount which a person is prepared to pay to secure what he wants. The same applies in the litigation process. A defendant may, relatively cynically, make a very small offer initially in the hope that a claimant is unusually nervous at the prospects of litigation or is receiving incompetent advice. Defendants are often gratified to find that some of these initial offers are accepted. As the litigation proceeds the defendant may continue to try to keep pressure on the defendant by increasing the offer from time to time to see the stage at which he is tempted, without ever coming up to anything like the figure that the defendant knows is the real value of the litigation until perhaps just before trial. Although settling the case late in the day will be expensive for a defendant in terms of costs, experience does seem to show insurance companies that the number of claimants who can be scared off, worn down or pressured to compromise early by inadequate payments makes this form of gamble worthwhile.

One aspect of this is that a defendant is perfectly entitled to add to a payment in he has made at any time. The time for acceptance for the whole amount is reopened by this and a further 21-day period is allowed for the claimant to accept the full figure. An example appears below.

EXAMPLE

The claimant's case has some risks attached to it, but on a full liability basis would be worth £50,000. Quite early in the case the defendant pays into court £15,000 in the hope that the claimant, appreciating the risks, will prefer the 'bird in the hand' approach. The claimant does not accept and some months on the defendant pays a further £15,000 into court. Still the claimant does not accept and just before trial the defendant pays a further £10,000 into court bringing the figure to £40,000. This time the claimant accepts.

In the above example if the claimant had refused, then the stage at which the payment into court would have 'bitten' would depend upon what was awarded. If, for example, the claimant had only been awarded, say, £12,000 then he would have ended up paying the defendant's costs as from 21 days after notice of the first payment in; if he had only been awarded £25,000 he would have paid the costs from 21 days after the second payment in; if he had only been awarded £39,000 he would have paid the costs from 21 days after the third payment in.

It is often suggested that defendants or at least insurance companies are motivated by cynical tactics in deciding what to offer. Though this is no doubt sometimes the case, the change in attitude brought about by the CPR has to some extent led to a change in the culture of negotiation. It is also fair to say that in many cases a defendant does not know what is the proper figure until the medical or other evidence has developed, often quite late in the day, so payments in may be 'topped up' in the light of the defendant's increasing knowledge of the case rather than because of cynical motives.

25.5.2   Acceptance out of time

Suppose that a payment in was made more than 21 days before and the claimant now wishes to accept it. What is the position?

This can arise in a variety of cases. It may be that the claimant is only marginally out of time, perhaps because he has been away on holiday for part of the period and needed to discuss the claim with his solicitor. Alternatively it may be that the payment in was made many months before and that the claimant has changed his mind about the prospects of success or otherwise, and wishes to accept what was on offer.

The first step is for the claimant to approach the defendant and see what can be negotiated. If the claimant is only just outside the 21-day period and no great costs have been incurred meanwhile, the defendant may still agree to pay the claimant's costs even up to the date of acceptance. This may indeed even be negotiated if many months have passed. The payment into court may merely be one in a series of offers which the defendant had intended, and if settlement on that basis can still be achieved, the defendant may be prepared to bear the extra costs. It is not unknown for a claimant to decide on the evening of the trial that he would rather accept a payment into court made long before. Even in such cases, it is not unknown for the defendant to offer to pay the costs. After all, the defendant's assessment of his own prospects might have changed for the worse as the case progressed.

In principle, however, a claimant can *only* accept a defendant's Part 36 payment or offer without the court's permission if the parties agree the liability for costs. In that case a consent order for payment of the money should be lodged. If the parties do not agree what the liability for costs should be then the court's permission is required. Application on notice for the court's permission will be made and at the hearing the court will decide whether to permit it and on the costs consequences.

It is important to note that the court may not permit the claimant to accept the payment in *at all*. For example, suppose that as the evidence has developed, the defendant now has fairly clear proof that the whole or part of the claim is fabricated and he is sure that he will win at trial. The defendant may even be given permission to *withdraw* the money he previously paid into court, although it will obviously be greatly to his advantage to leave it there so that he has the benefit of the 'costs gamble' even though the court has refused the claimant permission to accept the money.

Even if the case does not fall into this category and the court will permit the claimant to accept the money, it will usually only do so on condition that he pays the defendant's costs from the date 21 days after he received notice of the payment in. He will, of course, obtain an order for his own costs up to that date. Usually the court will order that these figures be set off against each other, but if there is some risk that the amount owed to the defendant for costs will be greater than the amount owed to the claimant for costs, the court may order that all or part of the money should stay in court funds as security until the costs position has been clarified by detailed assessment of costs.

25.5.3 What if the defendant's Part 36 payment or offer is less than 21 days before trial?

In this situation there is a particular problem, because the claimant will not have had 21 days to consider the matter before the trial starts. Accordingly by r. 36.5(7) an offer made less than 21 days before trial can only be accepted if:

(a) the parties agree the liability for costs; or

(b) permission of the court is obtained.

If, for example, the defendant makes a Part 36 payment in only 15 days before trial, which the claimant wishes to accept, there ought in principle to be no problem. All that is required is that the parties agree the *liability* for costs not the specific amounts. If the defendant concedes, as he obviously will, that he must pay the claimant's costs up to the date of acceptance of the offer there should be no difficulty.

A more serious problem arises where the 21 days which the claimant has to think about the matter spans the start of a trial. There is no problem if the trial is going to be a short one, but if it is likely to last several days or weeks what should a claimant do who wishes to accept during the course of the trial, but still within the 21-day period? It is still open to him to accept without the court's permission if the parties agree liability for costs and it is possible, in the light of the way in which the evidence has developed so far, that the defendant will agree to this. If he will not agree, permission should be sought from the trial judge. There are, however, serious practical difficulties in this because of the rule that the fact and amount of any payment in must be kept secret from the trial judge until all issues of liability and quantum have been decided.

25.5.3.1   What would be the situation therefore if the judge refused permission?

In principle it is likely that the case would be over anyway, since the terms on which he would grant permission would relate only to costs and not to the issues. It is possible to foresee cases where there will be difficulties, for example, where there are two or more issues in a case and a payment in has been made for only one of them, but the issues are in some way intertwined. Of course it may be that the evidence has come out so disastrously for the claimant that the judge is not inclined to let him accept at all. Each case will depend on its own facts. There was provision under the pre-CPR rules for acceptance actually during the course of the trial and those rules in fact gave rise to remarkably little case law, so it may be that the point will only very rarely arise.

25.5.4   Multiple defendants

If there is more than one defendant then by r. 36.17 if they all join in the payment or offer there is no problem and the usual rules apply. Problems arise if only, say, one of two defendants makes the offer or payment in. The position then is:

(a) If the defendants were sued *jointly or in the alternative*, the claimant can accept the offer or payment without needing the permission of the court if he does so within 21 days, provided that:

   (i)   he discontinues his claim against those defendants who have not made the offer or payment; and

   (ii) those defendants give written consent to the acceptance of the offer or payment.

(b) If the claimant alleges the defendants have a *several* liability, then the claimant may accept the offer and continue with his claims against the other defendants without the court's permission.

If the other defendants in (a) above do not consent to the acceptance of the offer then there will need to be an application to the court for permission to accept the offer. At that hearing the court will make whatever orders appear appropriate, including what is to happen to the costs of the other defendants who did not join in the payment in, but against whom the case has been concluded.

25.5.4.1   What costs orders will be made in such cases?

Applying case law from the former rules which are very similar to the present ones, the answer is that in all such cases the court will look to see who are the real winners and losers in the litigation and make an appropriate order for costs. In the case of *Hodgson* v *Guardall Ltd* [1991] 3 All ER 823, the claimant sued four defendants in a personal injury case and all the defendants blamed each other. Eventually only one of them made a payment in to court which the claimant wished to accept. The court permitted this. The issue then was not only who should pay for the costs of the time spent on those aspects of the claimant's case that were brought against the three 'innocent' defendants, but also who should pay the costs of those 'innocent' defendants. The court concluded that it was fair, as all the defendants had blamed each other and the claimant had acted reasonably, to make the 'guilty' defendant who made the payment into court pay the extra costs of all concerned.

In more complicated commercial cases such an easy solution may not be appropriate. The court will have to investigate the reasonableness of each party's conduct and who are the real winners and losers in the litigation and whether in particular the claimant has acted reasonably in joining the other parties in the state of his knowledge at the time.

25.6 Part 36 offer by the claimant

The culture of the CPR is intended to require both parties to cooperate reasonably, both on procedural matters and on the substance of the case. Accordingly, whilst the system described above is a way for defendants to bring pressure on claimants, the CPR also provide a way in which a *claimant* can indicate to the defendant the terms on which he would be prepared to settle a case.

We have already seen that by r. 36.10 a defendant can make an offer to settle before proceedings have begun and this will have an impact on costs. The provision also applies to claimants who can make such an offer to defendants. Similarly at any time after proceedings have commenced, the claimant may make a written offer setting out the terms on which he would accept settlement of the claim and may do so in either a monetary or a non-monetary case. This offer, if reasonably made in the light of what the court eventually decides at trial, will also have a potentially dramatic effect on the party who unreasonably declined it by imposing a penalty not only for costs, but also for damages in the way described hereafter.

25.6.1 The claimant's Part 36 offer

We have already seen that by r. 36.10 either party may make an offer to settle *before* proceedings have begun, and this will have an impact on costs. At any time *after* proceedings have commenced, the claimant may make an offer setting out the terms on which he would accept settlement of the claim. This may be made in either a monetary or a non-monetary case.

If the defendant accepts within 21 days, then by rr. 36.12 and 36.14 the claimant will be entitled to his costs of the proceedings up to the date upon which the defendant serves notice of acceptance. The defendant must then fulfil his promise and pay over the money or do what he undertook to do, and the case is then over except for issues of assessment of costs.

Accordingly, it is open to a claimant in a money case to indicate that he will accept, say, £20,000 (and the figure should also indicate that interest is included in this sum). In a non-monetary case he may set out the terms of an undertaking that he would accept in place of an injunction (say, that the defendant agrees to curb his activities in future which caused the nuisance about which the claimant complained).

If there is more than one cause of action it is open to a claimant to make an offer for one issue only, in the hope of at least taking that out of contention and the case would then go on for the remaining matters.

25.6.2 What if the claimant's offer is not accepted?

What are the consequences where the claimant does better at trial than he proposed in his Part 36 offer?

The rule is that if at trial a defendant is held liable to pay more by way of damages than the claimant proposed, or the judgment against a defendant is more advantageous to the claimant than the proposals, the consequences are as follows:

(a) The court may order interest on the whole or part of any sum of money (excluding interest) awarded to the claimant at a rate not exceeding *10 per cent above bank base rate* for some or all of the period starting with the latest date on which the defendant could have accepted the offer without needing the permission of the court (i.e., 21 days). Bank base rate is currently 4.5 per cent.

(b) The court may also order that the claimant is entitled to:

(i) his costs on the indemnity basis from the latest date when the defendant could have accepted the offer without needing the permission of the court; and

(ii) interest on those costs at a rate not exceeding 10 per cent above base rate.

Although the terms of r. 36.21 appear to give the court a wide discretion, by virtue of r. 36.21(4) where the rule applies 'the court *will* make the orders referred to . . . unless it considers it unjust to do so'. In other words, in the usual situation the order for the relatively penal rates of interest and indemnity basis costs will normally be made where a defendant unreasonably refused a claimant's offer.

25.6.3 Tactics for a claimant

There was nothing in the previous rules to stop a claimant making offers for amounts he would accept or terms upon which he would compromise an action. There was no penalty, however, on a defendant for failing to agree except of course the inherent penalty of the defendant having gone to trial and still lost. Now there is a considerable extra incentive on a defendant to give serious consideration to offers made by a claimant. The 'base rate' is at the moment 4.5 per cent and therefore if the court imposes the inter-est rate referred to, interest at 14.5 per cent on damages will be awarded. Although there is a reference in the rule to the court having the discretion to award that for part only of the period, in principle it is likely to award it over the whole of the relevant per-iod unless it is unjust to do so. The provision for costs is even more punitive, providing not merely that they be on an indemnity basis so that any doubts are resolved infavour of the claimant, but also for interest on them at a similar rate. In high value cases therefore these provisions will give a defendant pause for thought.

25.7 Refusal of Part 36 payments or offers

In the text above we have given examples of the consequences of acceptance or refusal. If a party intends to refuse the opposite party's offer or payment, there is no formal requirement as to how this is to be done. Some solicitors indeed simply acknowledge notice of the payment in or offer and then decline to refer to it further as if it was so far beneath what is an appropriate settlement suggestion as to be outside serious consideration. The party who made it can thus treat the expiry of the 21 days as being sufficient indication of refusal. Others prefer to give firm indication of positive refusal at the earliest appropriate moment, but there are no rules about how this needs to be done. Of course, one Part 36 offer may now lead to a counter offer.

25.8 Compromising procedural applications

In a sense this is an entirely separate matter from the procedure set out above to achieve a substantive compromise of the claim. However, it does rely upon a tactical device which is reflected in Part 36 of the CPR and which was also available under the previous rules. This is the device of a letter written 'without prejudice save as to costs'—one that cannot be referred to during the course of a hearing until the judge has given his decision, but can thereafter be put before him to show whether or not one of the parties was adopting a reasonable position in offering a compromise.

This can also be used for procedural applications to influence the costs outcome.

EXAMPLE

The defendant's solicitors have been uncooperative on matters of disclosure of documents to the point where the claimant, having received no satisfactory response about a document which he considers should clearly have been disclosed, makes an application to the court for an order for specific disclosure. The application is issued in October 2006 and the hearing date fixed for the first week of December 2006. Correspondence continues between the parties about what documents are disclosable and what are not and eventually the defendant's solicitor sends copies of all those documents he thinks should be disclosed, while refusing to give disclosure of, say, two others on the basis that they are irrelevant or privileged. He also writes a letter expressed to be 'without prejudice save as to costs' saying that he has now disclosed all necessary documents, but accepts that the application was properly issued and agrees to pay all the costs up to date on the basis that the application is withdrawn.

The claimant's solicitor does not accept and presses on to the hearing because he wants to get disclosure of the other two documents. At the hearing, however, the defendant's solicitor successfully persuades the judge that the documents in question are irrelevant, or privileged, and disclosure is refused. The defendant's solicitor can then produce his letter. The normal consequence would be that the court will order the defendant to pay the claimant's costs for issuing the application and the subsequent correspondence up to the date the reasonable offer was made; but thereafter the costs, including the costs of the hearing, would be paid by the claimant to the defendant. The judge will then of course proceed summarily to assess both parties' costs and no doubt set off the smaller amount against the larger, requiring the balance to be paid forthwith.

The above example demonstrates that one can impose a costs risk on the other party by the device of a 'without prejudice' letter for interim procedures as well as the trial itself. In all such hearings the court will be concerned to see who has behaved reasonably when deciding on the costs.

Example of order after trial where there have been Part 36 payments into court by the defendant and a Part 36 offer by the claimant

This dispute is between Middlemarch Garden Centres Limited and Middlemarch Construction Limited. The garden centre employed the construction company to landscape two fields which it had acquired behind its existing business and to do substantial alterations so as to extend its car park. It appreciated that this would lead to the closing off of access to the car park, and instructed the construction company to do this during a quiet period in early January 2005. Unfortunately, the construction company, due to manpower problems and other features, was late in commencing work and did not begin the work until March 2005. The closure of the garden centre's car park at a relatively busy period in the spring led to a large loss of business and a good deal of disruption, and the garden centre purported to rescind the contract and instruct a different company to complete the work, particularly in urgently restoring full access to the car park. The garden centre has claimed damages for loss of profits, disruption and the extra cost of employing the second construction company, totalling £140,000. The defendant defends on the merits of the claim, contending that time was never of the essence in the contract and that the garden centre rescinded the contract prematurely. The parties have negotiated, but negotiations have broken down and the claim is issued on 4 November 2005 for £140,000.

As procedural directions are given and the claim is allocated to the multi-track, further negotiations ensue which prove unsuccessful and, accepting that there are significant weaknesses in its case, but believing the claim to be highly exaggerated, on 3 March 2006 the defendant pays into court the sum of £35,000 and notifies the claimant that it has done so. This gives the claimant 21 days to accept, but before 24 March 2006 the claimant's solicitors notify the defendant's solicitors that they are not intending to accept.

The litigation progresses, and on 1 June 2006, since by now there has been full disclosure of documents and service of witness statements (which leads the defendant to take a more pessimistic view of its case), the defendant pays into court a further £40,000, giving notice to the claimant that the amount in court is now £75,000. The claimant now has a further 21 days, until 22 June 2006, to consider its position and if it chooses to, to accept the money in court after which it would also be entitled to have a detailed assessment of all its costs. The claimant instructs its solicitors not to accept; however, after a further meeting with its solicitors, the claimant instructs them to put forward to the defendant a Part 36 offer that it will accept £90,000 in full and final settlement. If this offer had been accepted the claimant would also be entitled to detailed assessment of all its costs. That offer is made in the proper form on 4 July 2006, giving the defendant 21 days from that date to consider the matter and to offer the payment. The defendant decides that this is an overvaluation of the claim and declines to pay this amount.

The claim finally comes for trial in November 2006 and after a hearing lasting three days, much of which is given over to a consideration of the detailed financial information by which the claimant hopes to demonstrate its true loss of profits, the judge awards the claimant £62,000.

The consequences are these:

(i)   The claimant has done better than the defendant's first payment into court on 3 March 2006.

(ii)   The claimant has not, however, beaten the total in court as topped up by the payment in of the further £40,000 (making £75,000 in total) on 1 June 2006.

(iii)   The claimant's own Part 36 offer is irrelevant because the award by the judge has not equalled or exceeded it. If it had, and the judge had, for example, awarded £91,000, then the consequence would be that the claimant would also obtain costs on the indemnity basis; and interest on damages and interest on costs at enhanced rates as from the time of the Part 36 offer by it.

The final form of order therefore is shown below.

IN THE MIDDLEMARCH COUNTY COURT		**<u>Claim No: 5MM43191</u>**

BETWEEN   Middlemarch Garden Centre Ltd   <u>Claimant</u>

and

Middlemarch Construction Ltd   <u>Defendant</u>

JUDGMENT

---

1.   There will be judgment for the claimant in the sum of £62,000.

2.   The defendant shall pay the claimant's costs up to and including 22 June 2006 on the standard basis to be ascertained by detailed assessment.

3.   The claimant shall pay the defendants costs after 23 June 2006 to be ascertained by detailed assessment on the standard basis.

4.   The said sums be set off against each other and any balance due to be paid no later than 14 days after the conclusion of both detailed assessments.

5.   The sum of £62,000 currently in court funds to be paid out to the claimant's solicitors forthwith. The balance of £13,000 in court, together with all interest thereon to be paid out to the defendant's solicitors forthwith.

8 November 2006

His Honour Judge Grout

TERMINATION WITHOUT TRIAL (1)

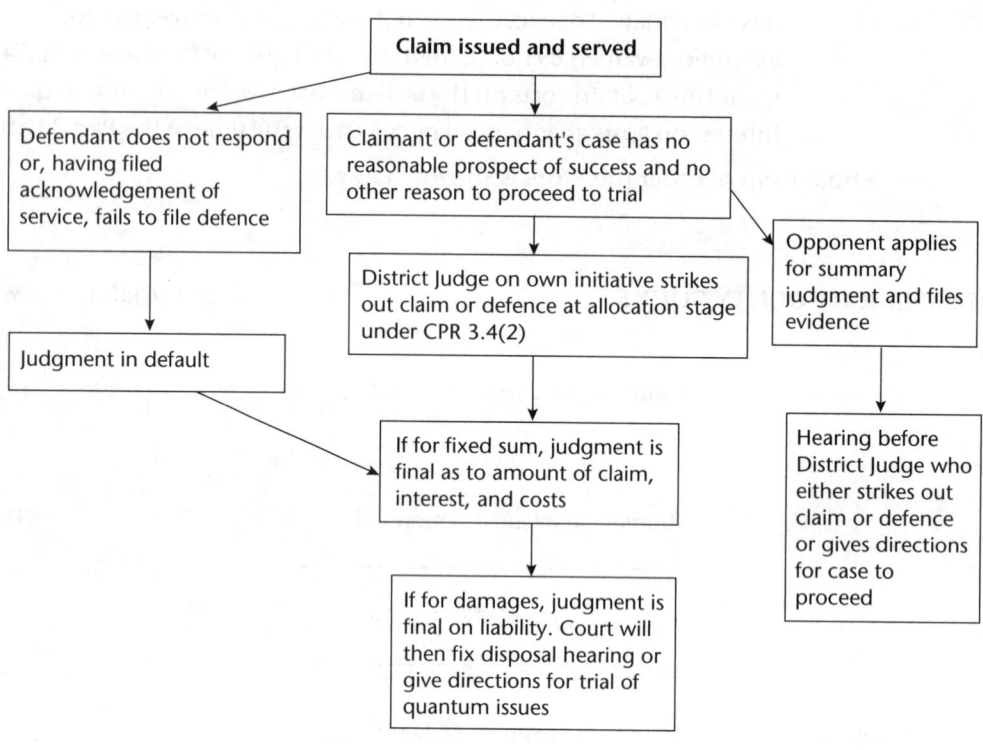

TERMINATION WITHOUT TRIAL (2)

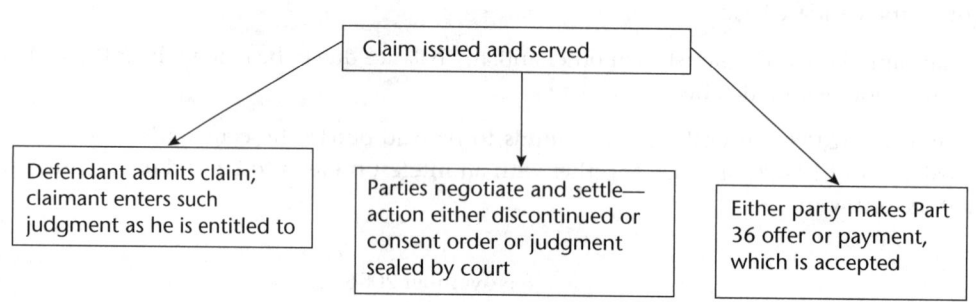

Termination without trial

26.1 Introduction

We have discussed aspects of the course of a claim from commencement to trial considering various other matters along the way including practical, tactical and evidential questions. The case that goes to trial is one of a tiny minority. The vast majority of civil claims do not reach trial, but are negotiated to a settlement at some earlier stage. The negotiation may be informal between the parties, or may end in a Part 36 payment or offer by one or other party, which is accepted by the opponent, thus concluding the claim.

The CPR are, so to speak, 'front loaded' in that solicitors will have to do a great deal of preparatory work early in the case to ensure that they can meet court timetables. This ought to focus their minds on the true issues at an earlier stage. The existence of the pre-action protocols likewise has meant that a higher proportion of personal injury and clinical negligence cases are settled even before the issue of proceedings (bearing in mind the costs sanctions available, where reasonable offers to compromise proceedings before issue are refused).

The effect of the widened scope of Part 36 offers, the sanctions for costs and for delay generally, and the court's powers to stay proceedings while alternative dispute resolution is attempted, ought to mean that fewer cases than ever get to trial. Figures show that no more than about 2,500 multi-track cases per year will ever reach trial. On the fast track, the elimination of irrelevancy and the concentration of the trial process into less than one day with the restrictions that accompany it, also mean that only a tiny proportion of cases which are started in the £5,000 to £15,000 range reach trial.

With small claims prediction is rather less easy. Certainly the procedures available, including those described below in this chapter, ought to mean that a significant number are disposed of without progressing to a hearing, but where two unrepresented litigants are opposing each other, their capacity for negotiation and their procedural knowledge may be limited, so they often turn up for their day in court. However, it would certainly be the experience of most district judges that if a day is fixed for the hearing of several small claims cases, a remarkable proportion of them do not proceed to an effective trial, but are either settled very shortly before the trial or because one or other party fails to attend.

We shall now go on to consider the ways in which cases may end before trial.

26.2 By negotiation, compromise or acceptance of a Part 36 offer or payment

A solicitor has authority to compromise a claim on behalf of a client once a claim has begun: counsel has power to compromise during the trial. However, these implied authorities should never be relied on: the client's express authority to compromise the claim should be obtained in each case. Because, as indicated earlier, negotiations proceed throughout the course of the litigation, an acceptable resolution may be achieved at any time. Provided there is agreement as to costs (that they will be agreed or assessed in default of agreement), the claim may be resolved by the defendant simply making a payment of the agreed amount to the claimant.

If the parties conclude a compromise, any rights of action they had will be replaced by rights under the *contract of compromise*. However, there is a positive requirement on the parties to notify the court of any settlement so that any hearing date can be vacated and the time re-used for some other case. This should be done at the earliest moment that settlement has been achieved, without necessarily waiting for the full terms of a consent order to be drawn up. If some court order is required to implement the agreement, there is provision under CPR, r. 40.3, for obtaining consent orders from the court without attendance by sending in the text of the order required with the consent of both parties endorsed. There is then no need to attend court.

26.2.1 'Tomlin orders'

If the terms of the compromise provide for something other than a simple payment of money, a stay in the form of a *Tomlin order* might be made, i.e., a stay of the action on terms set out in a schedule to the order, with liberty to restore if necessary for the purpose of carrying such terms into effect. The phrase 'liberty to restore' means that if either party considers that the other is not carrying out his side of the agreement, he may restore the matter for the court's further consideration. This method of compromise is commonly used where there are complex terms to be carried out, for example where a defendant undertakes to do certain scheduled work such as building repairs, and the claimant then undertakes to pay for it at certain agreed rates. This kind of compromise would be inappropriate for setting out in a formal court judgment because the court would not have the mechanism to supervise the way in which the work was carried out and thus enforce the terms.

A Tomlin order is not the same as a money judgment, even where it requires payment of a sum of money, thus it cannot be enforced without further application to the court, and does not carry interest unless provided for in the order. If any costs are to be assessed, the order should deal with costs, providing for assessment if that is what is agreed between the parties.

26.2.2 Compromise of the claim of a person under a disability

In any action in which money is claimed by or on behalf of a child or mental patient, no settlement, compromise or payment, and no acceptance of a Part 36 payment into court is valid without the approval of the court. The procedure for obtaining such approval is discussed at **31.3**.

26.3 The court's case management powers

Under CPR, r. 3.3, a court has powers to make orders of its own initiative and may indeed make them without notice to the parties, although in each such case, by r. 3.3(5), any party affected who is dissatisfied may apply to have the order set aside.

Under r. 3.4(2) the court may strike out a statement of case or part of a statement of case if it appears to the court that:

(a) it discloses no reasonable grounds for bringing or defending the claim; or

(b) it is an abuse of the court's process or is otherwise likely to obstruct the just disposal of the proceedings; or

(c) there has been a failure to comply with a rule, practice direction or court order.

Where, therefore, on a review of the proceedings at any stage, the court considers that there is no case for bringing the claim or part of it, or defending the claim or part of it, the court may strike out the claim, the defence or part of either. This may well happen when the court is considering the parties' statements of case at the time of deciding upon allocation.

While this should only happen in the clearest case of the court's own initiative, it does provide the first possibility whereby a case will end early.

Naturally it would be a very robust court that would seek to end proceedings in this way against a party whose case has been professionally prepared. This is far more likely to be of use against litigants in person where their claims are misguided or even vexatious, or where defences disclose no reasonable basis for defending (e.g., the defence is quite incoherent, or perhaps pleads merely an inability to pay rather than disputing the legal basis of the claim).

Striking out is also one of the options open to a court in the general exercise of its case management powers. The court may use this in order to bring proceedings to an end as, for example, a sanction for serious, or repeated disobedience of court orders.

26.4 Judgment in default (CPR, Part 12)

If a defendant fails to respond to proceedings at an early stage, the claimant can bring proceedings to an end without the matter needing to proceed to trial. If a defendant fails to file either an acknowledgement of service or a defence within the time limits laid down in the rules, the claimant can enter judgment in default. Exceptionally, a judgment in default cannot be entered in the following kinds of cases because there always needs to be some form of hearing on the merits. Cases where judgment in default may **not** be entered are:

(a) on a claim where the Part 8 procedure has been used (see **Chapter 32**);

(b) on a claim for delivery of goods subject to an agreement regulated by the Consumer Credit Act 1974;

(c) on a mortgage possession claim;

(d) in certain specialist proceedings including Admiralty proceedings.

In cases other than the above, a claimant can obtain judgment in default where the defendant has either not filed an acknowledgement of service or, having filed it, does not go on to file the defence within the relevant time.

26.4.1 The procedure under Part 12

There are two mechanisms under the CPR for entering a judgment in default and the method used depends upon the remedies sought. If the claim is simply for money, whether for a specified sum (as in a debt) or unquantified damages (as in personal injury cases) judgment is simply entered by a clerk in the court office without the need to attend before a judge. There is a form of request for default judgment which should be lodged at the court counter, or by post.

If the claim includes a claim for a remedy apart from money (for example, for an injunction), an application for judgment must be made on a formal application to the court. There needs to be a hearing in such cases so that the court can give 'such judgment as it appears to the court that the claimant is entitled to on his statement of case' (r. 12.11(1)). The court will therefore have to consider the merits of the claim after hearing evidence, for example, to assess the type of injunction which should be awarded, its duration and conditions.

It should be noted that a claimant may *not* apply for a default judgment in certain circumstances if:

(a) the defendant has applied for *summary judgment* against the claimant under Part 24 (see below) and that application is outstanding; or

(b) the defendant has satisfied the whole claim including any claim for costs for which the claimant seeks judgment; or

(c) the claimant is seeking judgment on a claim for money and the defendant has filed or served on the claimant an admission of the amount due with requests for time to pay.

26.4.2 The application for default judgment

On any request for default judgment, whether 'over the counter' or before a judge, the court must be satisfied that:

(a) the particulars of claim have been served on the defendant;

(b) the defendant has not filed either an acknowledgement of service or a defence and that in either case the relevant period for doing so has expired;

(c) the defendant has not satisfied the claim; and

(d) the defendant has not returned an admission to the claimant under r. 14.4 or filed an admission with the court under r. 14.6 (PD 12, para. 4.1).

26.4.3 The form of the judgment

The form of the judgment is dealt with under r. 12.5.

26.4.3.1 Claim for a specified sum

The form of request for judgment is form N205A or N255. The court will give judgment for the amount mentioned in the claim form plus a figure for fixed costs and for interest accrued up to the date on which default judgment is entered provided that:

(a) full particulars of interest were set out in the particulars of claim;

(b) if the claim is for interest under statute, the rate sought is no higher than that on judgment debts (currently 8 per cent); and

(c) the request for judgment sets out a calculation of the interest claimed between the date to which interest has been calculated in the claim form and the date of the request for judgment.

If the claimant is not satisfied with interest at the rate applicable to judgment debts, then judgment can be entered for the principal amount of the claim. There will need to be a hearing before the court to assess interest after hearing any argument about the rate that should be applied. If interest is claimed under a contractual provision (that is, where the contract between the parties out of which the claim arises fixes the rate of interest in the event of non-payment of sums under the contract) then interest may be computed in accordance with the rate fixed in the contract and there does not need to be a hearing to assess it.

26.4.3.2   Claim for an unspecified sum

If the claim is for an unspecified sum, such as personal injury damages, the form for request of judgment is form N225B or N227 and judgment will then be given on the issue of liability, but no figure will be fixed. When the court gives judgment in this way the file will be referred to a district judge for him to give directions for the hearing at which the amount to be paid will be assessed and when giving those directions he may allocate the case to a track.

Full directions may be necessary before the court is able to assess damages and thus there may be directions for disclosure and production of documents, expert evidence and for the calling of witnesses.

26.4.4   Judgment in default on application to a judge

In cases where some judicial decision is required, such as a claim for an injunction, notice of application in accordance with Part 23 must be filed and notice must be given to the defendant of the hearing even if he has failed to participate in the proceedings in any way by failing to file an acknowledgement. Evidence in support of the application, however, need not be served on a defendant who has failed to file an acknowledgement of service.

26.4.5   Claims against more than one defendant

By r. 12.8, a claimant may obtain a default judgment on a claim for money or a claim for delivery of goods against one of two or more defendants and proceed with his claim against the other. In this situation a district judge will review the matter to decide whether the claim should be dealt with separately from the claim against the other defendants. If he decides that it should not, he will not enter default judgment against the defendant in default but rather will give directions as to how the case is to proceed. Alternatively, it is open to the court to enter a default judgment against one defendant and allow the proceedings to continue against the others. It may be that the claimant is happy to enter default judgment against one defendant only, because he has every prospect of successfully enforcing that judgment either in full or substantially, and on the basis of that he may decide to negotiate with the other defendant or discontinue his claim.

26.4.6 Subsequent procedure where judgment is not final

Where the judgment entered is final on all issues of liability and amount, for example where the claimant is suing for a debt and interest due under a contract, judgment will be complete when it is entered for the amount of the debt, interest and fixed costs. The judgment can be enforced by using the methods described in **Chapter 34**.

If, however, the claim is not for a specified amount of money, but is for damages generally, judgment will only be entered on *liability* and the amount of damages will need to be decided at a later stage by the court. PD 26, para. 12.1(1), deals with the situation of judgments or orders that require:

(a) the assessment of damages;

(b) the assessment of interest;

(c) the taking of an account (as, for example, in actions arising out of a dissolution of a partnership where the claimant is unsure exactly how much he is owed); or

(d) the making of an enquiry as to any sum due (as, for example, in disputes about non-payment of royalties claimed by an author from a publisher where an investigation of sales figures is required); or

(e) the assessment of costs payable under a contract other than a contract between a solicitor and client for legal services.

In these cases the court will need to go on to decide how these amounts are to be assessed. There are two methods of proceeding. The court will either list the matter for a 'disposal hearing' or give directions for the hearing of an assessment of damages or other directions, or stay the action to enable the parties to try to settle the case using alternative dispute resolution or other means.

It is important to understand the difference between a 'disposal hearing' and an 'assessment of damages'.

26.4.7 Disposal hearing

A *disposal hearing* will not normally last more than 30 minutes and there will be no oral evidence. Any evidence should be in writing and served upon the other party at least three days before the hearing. This will therefore be appropriate for very modest claims or for larger claims where there is only one simple issue of principle. One must bear in mind that a very large number of cases come to an end because the defendant plays no part in the proceedings whatsoever. This is certainly the case in many kinds of small claims. Where it is a claim by a tradesman or supplier of goods against a customer who will not pay, there needs to be neither a disposal nor an assessment of damages because once the defendant does not defend the claimant can obtain judgment for the fixed amount. It is usually therefore proceedings between a consumer claimant and a tradesman or supplier defendant which lead to a disposal, because the consumer is not only asking for his money back or part of it, but may also want damages, for example, for having unsatisfactory work done properly by another tradesmen or for disappointment or inconvenience caused by the defendant's incompetence. Damages in those kind of cases can normally be assessed fairly simply on the basis of the claimant's written statement supported by receipts for expenditure and the like. Oral evidence is not permitted and the matter can be dealt with by disposal.

If by any chance the defendant does appear at the hearing (probably having ignored directions from the court to file any evidence in written form well before the disposal), the court will have to consider what to do and whether the justice of the situation requires the court to press on with the hearing, in effect ignoring the defendant's participation, or whether it should give him an adjournment so as to be able to put his challenge to the figures which the claimant claims, in more appropriate form. It is entirely within the discretion of the court, but the court will not be eager to waste the claimant's time, the court time allocated to the hearing, or to give the defendant further indulgence if he has not participated at all in the proceedings hitherto. Everything will depend upon the justice of the situation however.

26.4.8   Assessment of damages

If the assessment of the amount due is likely to be more complex, for example in more substantial personal injury cases or in cases arising out of a need to take accounts between the parties, or in large consumer claims, proper case management may be needed with full directions. This may even be so if the defendant is still not participating in the proceedings as sometimes happens even in substantial personal injury cases. The court will then allocate the case to a track, but it should be noted that even if it is allocated to the multi-track, a master or district judge is able to deal with it and has jurisdiction to do so irrespective of the amount in dispute (PD 26 para. 12.10). However, in very substantial cases the court may give other directions, for example about the need for expert evidence and the final hearing may be listed before a circuit judge or High Court judge.

26.4.9   Setting aside default judgment (CPR, Part 13)

It will be open to a claimant to enter default judgment 'over the counter' or even on application to the court under Part 23 (see 26.4.4 above) very early in the case. Entering judgment 'over the counter' may take place immediately after the 14-day period for filing an acknowledgement of service or defence has expired. As might be expected, there could be a host of reasons, good, bad or indifferent, why a defendant might not have filed an acknowledgement of service. Such possibilities include error by the claimant as where, either in good faith or otherwise, he caused the proceedings to be posted to an address at which the defendant no longer resides; or where the defendant was away from his address on holiday or business for a period longer than the 14 days; or where a defendant while having a perfectly valid defence, has simply not got round to drafting it or instructing a solicitor in the time available. To accommodate these situations there is a procedure for default judgment to be set aside under CPR, Part 13.

26.4.10   Duty of claimant to set aside default judgment

There is a specific duty imposed upon a claimant to apply to set aside the default judgment which he himself has obtained if he discovers it has been entered wrongly, for example, if he finds out that the claim form did not reach the defendant before judgment was entered. The claimant is then obliged to file a request for the judgment to be set aside or apply for directions and must not enforce the judgment meanwhile (CPR, r. 13.5).

26.4.11 Application by the defendant

A defendant can apply for a judgment in default to be varied or set aside by an application under Part 23. If the judgment has been wrongly entered, for example, because the claim form was never served on him at all or the time had not expired for acknowledgement of service or filing defence when the judgment was entered, or the whole of the claim had been satisfied before judgment was entered, the court *must* set aside the judgment.

In every other case the court *may* set aside or vary the judgment if:

(a) the defendant has a real prospect of successfully defending the claim; or

(b) it appears to the court that there is some other good reason why:
   (i)   the judgment should be set aside or varied; or
   (ii) the defendant should be allowed to defend the claim.

In considering these matters the court must have regard amongst other things to whether the person seeking to set aside judgment made an application to do so promptly.

The rules make a distinction between cases where the court *must* set aside the judgment, that is, where it was wrongly entered because of some irregularity, and those where the court *may* set it aside. In deciding whether the judgment should be set aside, the important test is 'whether the defendant has a real prospect of successfully defending the claim'. This is a restatement of the principle in case law which preceded the CPR under the leading case of *Alpine Bulk Transport Co. Inc. v Saudi Eagle Shipping Co. Inc.* [1986] 2 Lloyd's Rep 221. Under this test the court has to form a provisional view of the likely outcome of the litigation.

Accordingly, a defendant who seeks to set aside a judgment which was properly obtained will himself have to file evidence to persuade the court that there are serious issues which provide a real prospect of him successfully defending the claim, by putting forward arguments based on law or facts. The evidence filed must of course be verified by a statement of truth explaining the background (for example, why time passed without him responding properly to the claim form) and setting out his case in sufficient detail to satisfy the test. On receipt of that evidence, it will be open to the claimant to amplify his own statement of case by further written evidence (for example, to demonstrate that the defendant's evidence lacks any credibility or to produce material which undermines it, such as contemporary documents). A lengthy hearing may be necessary and indeed, at the first hearing of the application to set aside judgment, further directions for a full hearing may be given. Previous case law on the *Saudi Eagle* test indicated that the courts were reluctant to let applications to set aside judgment proceed as a 'mini trial' and pointed to the difficulty of a district judge deciding such applications, based on written evidence only. In the exercise of its case management powers the court may be more robust in getting to the bottom of the basis of the purported defence.

26.4.12 Transfer after default judgment

If the claim is for a specified amount of money and a judgment was obtained in a court which was not the defendant's home court and the defendant is an individual, on receiving an application to set aside judgment the court will transfer the application to the defendant's home court, that is, the county court for the district in which his address for service (which may, of course, be the address of his solicitor) is located. This reflects the general rule that where a defence is filed in such a case there is automatic transfer to the defendant's home court (see **13.4**). If the claim is not for a specified amount of money, but for damages to be decided by the court, then it will remain in the court where proceedings have started, unless the court decides to transfer it under its more general powers.

Accordingly, while it is open to a claimant to fix his claim at a specific sum of money, even in those cases where in principle the court should decide the amount (such as personal injury cases), this will then entitle the defendant to have proceedings transferred to his home court. This is likely to increase the costs for the claimant and to cause his solicitors more inconvenience than if matters proceeded in the court of their choice.

26.5 Judgment on admissions (CPR, Part 14)

Part 14 of the CPR sets out a procedure whereby a party may admit the truth of the whole or any part of another's case. This must be done by giving notice in writing and may occur at any stage of the proceedings. The admission may be in a statement of case or more informally, for example, by letter. If a defendant makes an admission, the claimant is then entitled to apply for judgment (r. 14.3(1)). The court will enter such judgment as it appears that the applicant is entitled to.

However, there is a specific procedure where a defendant wishes to make an admission of money claim within 14 days of service of the particulars of claim which will now be considered.

If a defendant wants to bring proceedings to an end by admission of the whole or part of a claim against him, there is a procedure whereby he may do so and attempt to limit his liability for costs. These provisions are in the main to be used by individuals against whom ordinary debt cases are brought by banks, finance companies or the providers of utilities but are available in any debt action. There are four possible situations, namely, where the defendant admits:

(a) the whole of a claim for a specified sum (r. 14.4);

(b) part of a claim for a specified sum (r. 14.5);

(c) liability to pay the whole of a claim for an unspecified amount of money (r. 14.6); and

(d) liability to pay the whole of a claim for an unspecified amount of money and offers a particular sum in satisfaction of this claim (r. 14.7).

The documents served on a defendant by the court are the claim form and particulars of claim issued by the claimant. To this, the court attaches a 'response pack' which is a set of documents on which a response to the claim can be made. These include a form for making an admission (PD 14, para. 2.1). It is now important to discuss these options.

26.5.1 Where the defendant admits the whole of a claim for a specified sum

There are three sub-categories of possibility here:

(a) If he can, he may simply pay the sum claimed in full together with the interest shown in the particulars of claim and the amount of fixed costs and court fee shown on the claim form within 14 days of service of the claim form. Payment must be made *direct to the claimant* and not to or via the court. This has the effect of bringing proceedings to a conclusion.

(b) Alternatively, he may in effect ask the claimant for time to pay, for example, request to be allowed to make payment by instalments, by sending form N9A (which is a part of the response pack) to the claimant, having completed not only details of the offer he is making, but also detailed information about his means. This enables the claimant to decide whether the offer is fair and realistic. How a claimant decides to approach such an offer will depend upon all the facts, the amount of payments and the time which it would take to repay the whole of the amount. A pragmatic claimant will have regard to all the circumstances of which he is aware and in particular to the limitations on the methods open to him for enforcing judgment anyway. In the cases of those who regularly have to pursue their customers or former customers for very substantial sums, there will usually be office policies and procedures dictating the extent to which they want to pursue further applications to the court, rather than accepting offers of modest instalments. In such cases, even offers of only a few pounds a month, so that it will take many years to repay the debt in full, are likely to be acceptable unless the claimant has reason to believe that the defendant is concealing some element of his means. If the claimant accepts the proposals he obtains judgment by filing a request in form N225 and judgment is then entered for payment of the amount specified at the rate offered by the defendant. If a claimant does not accept the proposal, he should still file request form N225, but give specific notice under r. 14.10 that he does not accept. The court itself will then go on to decide the time and rate at which payment should be made, which it will usually do from the information before it without the parties attending.

(c) If the defendant simply admits the claim, but does not seek time to pay or make any other proposals, the claimant can obtain judgment in form N225 and can specify the date by which the judgment should be paid or, if he himself is prepared to propose instalments, their amount and frequency.

26.5.2   Where the defendant admits only *part* of a claim for a specified sum

Here the defendant completes forms N9A and N9B (from the response pack) and they are to be returned to the court within 14 days of service. The claimant is then given the option of accepting the part admission in full and final settlement and entering judgment for it or refusing the admission in which case the claim goes on as a defended claim. The claimant has 14 days in which to consider the offer made.

A partial admission may in itself be of payment in full immediately or by instalments at some future time. There will be difficult choices for the claimant in such a case.

Unscrupulous defendants may attempt to obtain substantial discounts on sums that they properly owe by making tempting offers. Thus for example a defendant who really owes a debt of £5,000 may purport to admit only £4,000 on it, offer early payment and file a spurious defence as to the balance. It will then be for the claimant to decide whether a bird in the hand is worth two in the bush or whether to call the defendant's bluff, indicate refusal and press on. One thing that the claimant *cannot* do, generally speaking, is enter judgment for the amount that is admitted and press on for the rest. However, the practice and case law under the previous County Court Rules shows that it may be possible to persuade the court to give judgment on the part that is admitted if the amounts involved relate to *separate items or issues* (e.g., the defendant admits having received four items, but denies receiving a fifth). Here, the court may be persuaded to grant judgment for the four items, though the proper approach is to apply for *summary judgment* for that part of the claim. The procedure for this is described below.

26.5.3 The defendant admits liability on a claim for an unspecified sum

In this case he should complete form N9C (from the response pack) and return it to the court. The claimant may then request the court to enter judgment on liability with damages to be assessed. The court will enter judgment and give directions as to assessment of damages or disposal.

26.5.4 Where the defendant admits liability for an unspecified sum and offers an amount of money to satisfy the claim

Again, form N9C should be completed and sent to the court which will forward it to the claimant. He may then either accept the admission and enter judgment or may refuse it, in which case the claim continues as defended. It should be noted that this last procedure of offering a specified sum is one invited by the forms sent to the defendant, but is likely to happen rarely in practice. A defendant who is legally represented is more likely to pay the money into court under Part 36, which not only formalises his offer, but puts the claimant at risk as to costs if it is not accepted.

26.5.5 Enforcement of judgments where there is an instalment order

Where a time and rate of payment have been determined by the court, it will not be open to a claimant to seek to enforce the whole of the claim by other means, even if instalments are unpaid. Judgment can only be enforced in respect of unpaid instalments in such a case. If a claimant discovers that a defendant has misrepresented his means and assets, there is nothing to stop him from applying to the court to vary the timescale for payments so as to require payment of the whole amount forthwith or in much larger instalments. If the court accepts the application and varies the rate of payment the claimant can proceed to any appropriate method for enforcement of the outstanding parts.

26.6 Summary judgment (CPR, Part 24)

26.6.1 Introduction

We have considered above two different ways in which an action can end early to the satisfaction of the claimant. *Default judgment* occurs where the defendant either does not participate in the process at all or, having gone to the trouble of filing an acknowledgement of service, does not then follow it up with a proper defence in time. *Judgment on admission* comes about where a defendant accepts that he has no basis on which to defend the claim or some part of it. We are now going to consider a very important procedure which will also have the result of bringing a case to an early conclusion. This procedure, application for summary judgment, is likely to be used in a very significant proportion of cases, especially in relation to consumer debts.

Case management and fixed timetables will mean that the large majority of cases which proceed on the small claims track and the fast track ought to get to trial in well under a year from the date of commencement of the action. Multi-track cases will inevitably take longer, although much will depend upon the nature of the case. The court, for example, is likely to impose just as strict a timetable on a straightforward contract action involving £20,000 as it would have imposed on a fast track case.

In some kinds of action, especially in actions for debt, a defendant who is unscrupulous or impecunious could obtain credit for lengthy periods by delaying payment until proceedings are issued and by putting in an entirely spurious or speculative defence and spinning things out until trial. A defendant would have to think carefully about signing the statement of truth to verify his defence and risks prosecution for contempt if he deliberately states what is not true, but criminal prosecutions rarely result from civil trials. Even at trials where it is clearly demonstrated that one or other party has lied on oath in the witness box, it is most unlikely that criminal proceedings will ensue. The costs of spinning a case out until trial will inevitably be large and someone adopting this tactic will be ordered to pay those costs and interest, but even these may not be sufficient disincentive to an unscrupulous person to defer payment of debts. Indeed, it is not only the unscrupulous who might be driven to these tactics. The defendant may himself be in business and be in turn owed many bad debts and have serious cash-flow problems. Only by deferring payment of his own major debts, for example, to his trade suppliers, for as long as possible may he be able to hope to stay in business with the genuine objective of paying everybody eventually. He may be tempted to prevaricate and delay matters to the point where a claim is issued and even beyond, by advancing speculative defences in order to obtain many more months' grace.

The procedure which we are about to describe ought to prevent these tactics from succeeding. The purpose of summary judgment is to stop weak cases from dragging on and to eliminate issues as the case proceeds. The procedure will mainly be used by a claimant against a defendant, but it is vital to note that the procedure is also now available to a *defendant* to apply for an early summary judgment to dispose of a weak case against him. The procedure may also be invoked by the court of its own initiative.

26.6.2   The application under Part 24

Rule 24.2 provides that the court may give summary judgment against a claimant or defendant on the whole of a claim or on a particular issue if it considers that:

(a) the *claimant* has no real prospect of succeeding on the claim or issue; or

(b) the *defendant* has no real prospect of successfully defending the claim or issue; and

(c) there is no other compelling reason why the case or issue should be disposed of at trial.

It is also important to note that the court may give summary judgment against:

(a) a *claimant* in any type of proceedings; and

(b) a *defendant* in any type of proceedings except:
  (i)   proceedings for possession of residential premises against a tenant, a mortgagor or a person holding over after the end of his tenancy;
  (ii) certain kinds of Admiralty proceedings; and
  (iii) contentious probate proceedings.

26.6.3   Time for making the application

A *claimant* may only apply for summary judgment after the defendant has filed either an acknowledgement of service or a defence. If the defendant fails to do either, then the claimant will apply for a default judgment and the case will be brought to an end in that way. If a claimant is not aware of any conceivable defence open to the defendant, he may launch his summary judgment application immediately after he receives notice from the acknowledgement of service that the defendant does intend to defend; or he may wait to see what the defence is before doing so. It would usually be prudent to do the latter so that in the evidence he files he can deal with whatever is raised in the full defence. A *defendant* can only apply for summary judgment against the claimant once he has filed his acknowledgement of service.

As the objective of this procedure is to bring the case, or some issue in the case, to an early conclusion, application will normally be made at the start of the litigation process. The application should normally be made before filing the allocation questionnaire, or when doing so, in which case the court will not allocate to track. At the hearing for summary judgment, if the party seeking it succeeds so that it has the effect of bringing the proceedings to an end, no allocation is necessary. If the summary judgment application fails or only succeeds in part so that other issues remain, whether of liability or quantum, allocation will then be required.

There is in fact nothing to stop a party applying much later in the case for summary judgment and he might well do so if new information came to light which demonstrated conclusively that the basis of the defence was false. Generally speaking, however, an application will be launched early in the case.

If an application is made after filing an acknowledgement of service, but before the defence is filed, the defendant need not file a defence before the hearing (r. 24.4(2)) but he may do so if he wishes.

26.6.4 The procedure

The application is made by an application notice which must be supported by evidence (CPR, rr. 24.2 and 25.3(2)). The evidence will usually be either a witness statement perhaps with further documentary evidence, although if the application notice itself is verified by a statement of truth that may stand as the evidence.

The application must:

(a) identify concisely any point of law or provision in a document on which the applicant relies; and/or

(b) state that it is made because the applicant believes that the respondent has no real prospect of successfully defending the claim or issue to which the application relates,

and in either case state that the applicant knows of no other reason why the disposal of the claim or issue should await trial.

The application notice must also draw the attention of the respondent to r. 24.5(1), which is to the effect that if he wishes to rely on written evidence at the hearing (and oral evidence will not be permitted save in the most exceptional circumstances) he must file and serve the written evidence at least seven days before the summary judgment hearing.

If on receipt of the respondent's evidence the applicant wishes to put in further evidence in reply, he must file and serve it at least three days before the summary judgment hearing.

26.6.4.1 Applications by the defendant

We have mainly considered matters from the claimant's point of view, but it is likely that in many kinds of litigation defendants will apply for summary judgment in order to dispose of umeritorious claims against them at an early stage. Clearly this will be used against litigants in person who have launched cases for which there is no foundation in law, but it will also be used against legally represented parties where a defendant sees some prospect of having the case disposed of early because he has strong documentary evidence in his favour, e.g., there may be little factual dispute and the case turns entirely on a matter of law, and the defendant feels it can be disposed of by argument without a lengthy hearing. Similarly, if the defendant is relying on the Limitation Act 1980 as part of his defence, it may appeal to him to dispose of the Limitation Act issue early because if he is successful in his argument on it, the case will be brought to an end.

It should not be imagined that a summary judgment application always involves someone making an application which seems so straightforward that it can be disposed of in a 10-minute hearing. It is not unknown for summary judgment applications in commercial cases to be issued, the hearing time for which might be measured in days rather than minutes. Although the court will always be eager to see if the case can be disposed of early, it remains to be seen whether it will be prepared to allocate as long to a summary judgment hearing as it might have done to a full trial. One must always bear in mind the court's powers to manage a case so as to prevent excessive length and it may be that the court will often feel that it can give judgment on the basis of written materials without the hearing itself being unnecessarily lengthy.

26.6.5 The court's approach under Part 24

In the important case of *Swain* v *Hillman* [2001] 1 All ER 91, Lord Woolf MR stressed that a judge could summarily dispose of a claim or defence under Part 24 if it did not have a realistic, as opposed to a fanciful, prospect of success. In deciding whether to exercise such a power a judge should not conduct a mini-trial of issues which should be investigated at a full trial. The point of Part 24 was to enable the court to give effect to the overriding objective in Part 1 and to save expense and achieve expedition. If a claimant had a case that was bound to fail, it was in the claimant's interest to know that as soon as possible; likewise if a claim was bound to succeed, the claimant should be entitled to know that also.

The court may make the following orders:

(a) *Judgment on the claim*. This will be given if the applicant has satisfied the court of the merits of his position. If the summary judgment application related to the whole case and was brought by the claimant, the judgment given will be final as to liability and amount.

(b) *Assessment of damages*. If the summary judgment application was about liability only and assessment of damages is not possible, the court will give case management directions for dealing with the assessment of damages.

(c) *Case management directions*. If the summary judgment relates only to some aspect of a claim, the judgment appropriate to that will be given and case management directions will be given about the other parts of the case.

(d) *Dismissal of the claim*. If the summary judgment application was by a defendant and is successful, it will bring to an end that part of a claimant's claim to which it relates or if it was for the whole of the claimant's claim, the case will be brought to an end by the dismissal of the claim.

(e) The court may *dismiss the application*. This is not the same thing as dismissing either party's case. It simply indicates that the court was not satisfied that the applicant had proved his case or established the point of law he was arguing to the point where the opponent should be deprived of the chance of carrying on with the case to a full contested trial. It does not pre-empt the outcome of the case in any way and indeed, because the hearing will have been early, before all information may have been gathered and before other important procedural stages, such as disclosure of documents and witness statements, it in no way indicates the court's view that the person who applied for summary judgment will lose at trial. It simply recognises that it has not been established to a satisfactory standard at this early stage on the basis of documentary evidence alone that the applicant will succeed. Where the application is dismissed, the court will go on to allocate to track and give case management directions.

(f) The court may make a *conditional order*. It is now important to consider the difficult concept of 'conditional order'. Unfortunately, it is submitted with respect that the test set out in the basic rule has been considerably muddied and confused by the concept of 'conditional order' provided for in PD 24. A conditional order is an order which requires a party:

(i)   to pay a sum of money into court; or

(ii)   to take a specified step in relation to his claim or defence as the case may be and provides that that party's claim will be dismissed or his statement of case will be struck out if he does not comply.

The conditional order represents a midway stage between the court feeling that an application for summary judgment should succeed or fail. The unhelpful guidance given at para. 4 of the practice direction says:

Where it appears to the court possible that a claim or defence may succeed, but improbable that it will do so, the court may make a conditional order.

This is likely to cause considerable confusion. The test as set out in the basic rule required the respondent to a summary judgment application to discharge a burden of showing that the case should go on. With all respect to what is said in the Practice Direction, if the court concludes that 'it is improbable that a claim or defence may succeed' it should give summary judgment and not proceed to a conditional order.

The concept of conditional order appears to reflect a procedural possibility which existed under the previous rules where there was indeed a sort of halfway stage between the summary judgment application succeeding or failing, although the test for summary judgment was differently expressed. It often represented the situation where a claimant was, say, a supplier of goods and had not been paid by his trade customer and, when an action was launched, a somewhat thin or 'shadowy' defence would be submitted. If the court was unimpressed with the defence but could not entirely reject it, it would sometimes require a defendant to demonstrate his good faith by showing that his reason for defending was not simply that he could not afford to pay. The court would then require him to demonstrate that good faith by producing the sum of money and paying it into court funds to be kept there as a sort of security. In some kinds of litigation other conditions might be imposed as well as, or instead of, paying money into court, for example, requiring the defendant to give immediate disclosure of vital documents.

It will depend on the facts whether the court will find it appropriate to make a conditional order as a halfway house between success and failure. If a conditional order once made is not complied with, the terms of the order will usually stipulate that judgment may be entered at the expiry of whatever time was given for compliance with the condition.

26.6.6 Judgment on individual issues

It is open to the court to give summary judgment on 'a particular issue' as well as a whole claim. The court will expect, before someone applies for summary judgment on an individual issue, that that issue will determine an important part of the claim. Summary judgment applications will certainly not be appropriate about minor issues, for example, an attempt to obtain a favourable ruling on a point of evidence in advance of trial. The fact that a defendant may now take the initiative in applying for summary judgment is likely to lead to more imaginative defendants seeking to isolate and have determined preliminary points which may dispose of a claimant's case or a substantial part of it (e.g., striking out a particular aspect of a damages claim on the grounds that there is no basis for it in law). The example has also already been given of a defendant seeking to have a Limitation Act issue considered at a summary judgment application.

26.6.7 Claims for accounts, enquiries, specific performance and rescission

Although most summary judgment applications are made in money claims, there is a specific provision in PD 24 for applying for the remedy of summary judgment in claims where what is sought are accounts enquiries, specific performance or rescission. In the case of applications for specific performance and rescission, an application notice must have attached to it the text of the order sought by the claimant which clearly indicates the precise terms of what the claimant seeks. There are other minor differences including the fact that in applications for specific performance and rescission only four clear days' notice is needed rather than the usual seven.

26.6.8 Costs on summary judgment applications

Costs on a summary judgment application are specifically dealt with by Table 2 in Part 45 of the CPR. This provides for a fixed amount of costs where final judgment is given which for an amount of under £5,000 is £175.00 and over that figure is £210.00. This is in addition to the fixed costs on commencement.

The court does have a discretion to order otherwise and to give a party *assessed costs* rather than *fixed costs*. If it does decide to assess costs, it will inevitably proceed to a summary assessment of costs so as to bring the action comprehensively to an end. A party who hopes to persuade the court not to restrict him to fixed costs only, should prepare a costs schedule in the appropriate form and serve it at least 24 hours before the hearing. The court would be likely to give fixed costs if it were a very simple money claim, perhaps against a litigant in person where the purported defence could be disposed of at a short hearing. If something of greater substance is involved, necessitating a hearing of perhaps half a day, then the court would be unlikely to restrict the successful party to the very modest amounts of fixed costs and would summarily assess the costs. If the outcome of the summary judgment application does not dispose of the whole case, fixed costs will not apply.

26.6.9 Summary judgment at the court's own instigation

The court itself has the power to take initiatives to dispose of cases. The first time that a judge is likely to see a case file is at the allocation stage and if he concludes that one party's case or part of it is extremely weak, he may take the initiative and strike it out himself under r. 3.4. The party affected will have the right to apply to have the matter reconsidered as described in **26.3** under the terms of r. 3.3. If a district judge does not see the case as being so weak as to be capable of disposal under r. 3.4, but still unlikely to succeed, he may fix a summary judgment hearing and require both parties to file and serve their evidence at least seven days before the hearing. The court will then proceed of its own initiative requiring the respondent to satisfy the court as to its case on the same test previously described.

26.7 Summary proceedings for possession of land

There is a special procedure for obtaining summary possession of land against persons who are unlikely to have any defence, e.g., squatters, 'travellers' and licensees of land whose licences have been terminated. The procedure is a drastic one and can be used to obtain very early judgment against occupiers, even where the names of all the occupiers are not known to the claimant. The order once obtained can be executed very swiftly by the sheriff. The procedure is under CPR, rr. 55.5/55.8.

26.7.1 Commencement of proceedings

The proceedings are commenced by a special claim form to which an acknowledgement of service is not required, supported by a witness statement or affidavit stating:

(a) the claimant's interest in the land;

(b) the circumstances in which the land has been occupied without licence or consent and in which the claim for possession arises; and (where appropriate)

(c) that the claimant does not know the name of any person occupying the land who is not named on the summons.

The claimant does not need to go to any trouble to ascertain the names of all, or any, of the occupiers of the land in question. Even though the claimant may believe that he does know the names of all the occupants, it is usually prudent to add a claim against 'persons unknown' and to state in his written evidence that there may be such other persons whose names he does not know. Otherwise the effect of any order made may be limited to those defendants named, and this may be unwise for obvious practical reasons.

26.7.2 Method of service of the claim

The method of service depends on whether any defendant has been named on the summons. A sealed copy of the summons and a copy of the evidence must be served on named defendants, either personally or by leaving them at or sending them to the premises, or in such other manner as the court may direct. Where the defendants are also 'persons unknown', then (in addition to service on any named defendant where necessary) the copy claim form and affidavit are served by fixing them to the main door or other obvious part of the premises and, if practicable, inserting further copies through the door in a 'sealed transparent envelope' addressed to 'the occupiers'. If the premises are land not including a building, then service of the summons is by placing stakes in the ground in conspicuous parts of the occupied land, to each of which is affixed a sealed transparent envelope containing the necessary documents.

26.7.3   The hearing

On the issue of the claim form an appointment is given for a hearing before the district judge to take place at least five days after the expected date of service in the case of residential property, and two days in the case of other land. It is possible in an urgent case to obtain an expedited hearing even more swiftly than this, by applying to the court once the claim form has been issued.

The hearing of the application is a summary trial and the district judge *must* make an order for possession if the claimant proves his case. The defendant cannot prevent summary judgment merely by raising vague issues, but he may raise a substantial defence, possibly requiring oral evidence, which will make the case not suitable for summary trial. In such a case the court should give directions for a full and early trial.

If the claimant succeeds, the judgment is in a special form, providing that the claimant 'do recover possession'. The judgment is enforceable against all occupiers of the premises, even those who may have entered into possession after the claim commenced. As an exception to the general rule, a Part 55 judgment can be enforced without first notifying all the occupiers of the land and (if the claimant applies within three months of the making of the order) without first obtaining the permission of the court. Enforcement is by the sheriff. The claimant should be in a position to make the premises secure after the sheriff has evicted the occupiers, to avoid further unlawful occupation.

26.7.4   Another practical possibility

The claimant may, if the premises are residential, seek the assistance of the police under s. 7 of the Criminal Law Act 1977, since a trespasser is guilty of an offence if he fails to leave on being required to do so by the displaced occupier. There is a power of arrest by a police constable in uniform.

In addition, under s. 61 of the Criminal Justice and Public Order Act 1994, the police have powers to remove trespassers from land, in particular, where either damage has been caused to the land or to property on the land or threatening, abusive or insulting words or behaviour have been used by any of those people towards the occupier of the land, or the persons in question have between them six or more vehicles on the land. This latter provision will often allow the police to clear travellers, although some police forces are reluctant to get involved in what they insist is a civil matter, unless there is evidence of criminal conduct.

26.8   Discontinuance and abandonment

A claimant may find himself in the position of having started proceedings only to find that he has overstated his case, has sued the wrong defendant, or cannot now produce the evidence required to prove his case, or that further research on the law shows that his claim will fail. It may sometimes only be clear that his claim has little prospect of success after he sees the evidence in the defendant's witness statements.

The first approach for a claimant in this situation would naturally be to attempt to negotiate with the defendant. A defendant may be willing to pay some sum even though the odds appear to favour the defendant heavily, simply to get rid of the costs and risk of the claim or the possibility of publicity. If even that is not possible, it may be possible for a claimant to negotiate an agreement that a defendant will not pursue any claim for costs if the claimant ceases the claim.

The timetables imposed by the court under the CPR will mean that a claimant may have to decide rapidly whether or not he wishes to pursue a case through each intervening stage as costs mount. If he decides that he wishes to discontinue the claim and the defendant will not agree to any compromise, then a claimant may bring his own claim to an end by discontinuance or abandonment.

26.8.1 The difference between discontinuing and abandoning: The procedure

Discontinuing refers to withdrawing the whole case. *Abandonment* arises where more than one remedy is sought or perhaps more than one head of damages. A claimant can abandon some part of his claim in this way, perhaps indicating, for example, that he now only seeks damages and not an injunction; or that he accepts that one of the claimed heads of damages is unarguable and he wishes to abandon it. He should do so in accordance with the rules on amendment of statement of case. Any costs which flow from the part of the claim which has been abandoned, for instance, because the defendant has incurred substantial expense in investigating that part of the claim, will have to be paid by the claimant. We shall now go on to consider discontinuance of the whole action.

A claimant may discontinue either:

(a) the whole claim (CPR, r. 38.1); or

(b) part of the claim (i.e., some of the causes of action contained in his statement of case).

In either case, if there is more than one defendant, discontinuance may be against some or all of them.

A claimant does not generally need the permission of the court to discontinue unless either:

(a) an interim injunction has been granted in relation to the claim; or

(b) any party has given an undertaking to the court in any part of the claim now being discontinued.

In either of these cases the court's permission has to be sought. In two other cases *either* the court's permission *or* the consent of other parties must be obtained, namely:

(c) if the claimant has received an interim payment, the court's permission or the defendant's consent must be obtained;

(d) if there is more than one claimant, the claimant wishing to discontinue must either obtain permission from the court or consent in writing from all the other claimants.

In cases where the court's permission is required, an application by application notice must be made. The point about requiring the court's permission is that in cases where an interim injunction has been awarded, or an undertaking to the court given, the court will have to consider the terms on which the injunction or undertaking should continue or lapse and relevant costs orders. In cases where an interim payment has been obtained, the court will have to consider the costs consequences and whether or not the interim payment should be repaid. In the case of there being more than one claimant, the court will want to consider the position of the parties and the liability of the claimant who is discontinuing for such parts of the claim as the other claimants intend to proceed with.

If consent is not required, i.e., the case does not fall in one of the categories above, a claimant discontinues by filing a notice of discontinuance in form N279 with the court and serving a copy on all other parties.

The notice of discontinuance that is filed at court must state that copies have been served on all other parties (CPR, r. 38.3(2)) and in cases where the consent of another party is required (i.e., those in (c) and (d) above) all copies of the notice of discontinuance must have copies of that written consent attached (r. 38.3(3)).

26.8.2 Costs on discontinuance

The claimant will be liable for the defendant's costs up to the date of service of the notice of discontinuance. However, on the small claims track there are no costs consequences of discontinuance and this seems to be the case however late in the day the discontinuance occurs unless the defendant can then show unreasonableness as discussed at **17.8** (r. 38.6(3)).

If only part of the claim is discontinued, the claimant's liability is limited to the costs of that part of the claim. The claimant will not have to pay these until the conclusion of the action unless the court in its discretion orders that they be paid at some earlier time.

Following service of notice of discontinuance, therefore, the defendant will usually seek to have his costs assessed by the court either by summary assessment in cases which have not progressed very far or, if more substantial costs have been incurred, by the detailed assessment of costs procedure described in **Chapter 33**.

26.9 Costs where a claim is compromised before proceedings are issued

As noted earlier in the text, where negotiations lead to an acceptable settlement, even before a claim has been issued (which is after all the objective of the pre-action protocol and the spirit of those protocols is to be observed even in cases to which they do not strictly apply), the usual provision in the agreement will be that the person who would have been the defendant, had the claim been issued, and who agrees to compensate the other party will pay other party's costs. If the costs cannot be agreed, even though everything else has been agreed, a person who would have been the claimant can apply to the court for an order that the potential defendant pay the reasonable costs, and the court can make that order and go on to assess the costs.

Chapters 27 to 32: Procedural complications

We have discussed, in approximately chronological order, procedure in straight forward claims, usually between a single claimant and a single defendant. We have usually avoided describing the various sidetracks and alternative options that might exist at several stages of a claim in the interests of trying to preserve a coherent narrative. It is now appropriate to discuss a number of procedural complications which may arise and the next series of short chapters considers the following:

Chapter 27 *Part 20 claims*. This involves a procedure whereby the defendant can bring in other parties.

Chapter 28 *Group litigation*. This term describes cases where there is an attempt to combine in one single set of proceedings claims by very numerous claimants.

Chapter 29 *Security for costs*. This is a procedure whereby a defendant can make certain kinds of claimant pay money into court as security for the potential costs of an action.

Chapter 30 *Special kinds of litigants (1)*. This chapter involves a discussion of the particular rules applicable in litigation brought by or against limited companies, partnerships, sole traders, clubs and estates.

Chapter 31 *Special kinds of litigants (2)*. This chapter is a discussion of the particular rules applicable to litigation brought by or against children and mental patients.

Chapter 32 *Part 8 claims*. This chapter describes a procedure which is different in very important respects from the main civil litigation procedure which we have been describing in all other chapters. The Part 8 procedure is used in cases where there is no substantial dispute on the facts and what the court needs to determine is mainly a question of law or of construction of a document.

Additional claims under Part 20

27.1 Introduction

So far we have mainly been considering straightforward claims between an individual claimant and an individual defendant where the only matter under consideration is the claimant's cause of action against that defendant. It is now appropriate to consider two further situations which will complicate the picture procedurally. These are:

(a) where the defendant wishes to make a claim of his own against the claimant; and/or

(b) where the defendant wishes to bring some claim against some third person, whether because he contends that it is that third person who should pay the claimant's claim in full, or at least contribute to it, or where he has some cause of action against that third person which is in some way connected to the claimant's claim against him.

27.1.1 Where the defendant wishes to make some claim against the claimant

This type of claim is called a 'counterclaim'. It can arise either out of the same facts as the claimant's claim or have no factual connection with it.

EXAMPLE 1

There is a road traffic accident and the vehicles of the claimant and defendant are in collision. The claimant commences a claim against the defendant; the defendant does not merely defend that claim, but brings his own counterclaim against the claimant, contending that he was entirely to blame and that he has caused the defendant injury.

EXAMPLE 2

The claimant seeks payment of an alleged debt from the defendant. After a meeting at the claimant's offices to attempt to negotiate settlement of the dispute, on his way out the defendant falls down the stairs because of a loose carpet and suffers a broken leg. When the claimant issues proceedings seeking payment of the debt it is open to the defendant to counterclaim for damages for personal injuries.

A counterclaim may be greater or lesser than the amount of the claimant's claim; it can arise out of facts before or after those constituting the claimant's claim; and it can even be brought about matters arising after the issue of the claimant's proceedings.

27.2 The procedure

Where a defendant wishes to make a counterclaim against a claimant, he simply files at court particulars of it (CPR, r. 20.4(1)). Normally this will be in a single document with the defence and the counterclaim following on after it. In the 'response pack' sent out to defendants with the claim form, when issued, there is a blank form of defence and counterclaim. This form would usually only be used by litigants in person and solicitors will draft their own documents. As long as it is filed at the same time as the defence, the court's permission to bring a counterclaim in the same proceedings is not required.

The following procedural points should also be noted.

(a) If there is more than one claimant, but the defendant only wishes to counterclaim against one of them, he is able to do so without the court's permission (although a copy of his counterclaim must also be served on the other claimants, so that they can consider their positions).

(b) If the defendant has already filed his defence before he decides to bring a counterclaim, he may still do so, but will now need the court's permission. We shall consider below the procedure for obtaining the court's permission and the matters which the court might take into account.

(c) What if a defendant wishes to counterclaim against the present claimant, but also contends that his counterclaim involves someone else not a party to the action? Suppose for instance that in Example 2 above, the meeting took place not simply at the claimant's offices, but at the offices of a firm in which the claimant was a partner with another individual, so that the defendant's counterclaim ought really to be brought against both partners in that business? In that situation a defendant must apply to the court for permission to counterclaim and for an order adding the other person as a defendant to the counterclaim (r. 20.5(1)).

27.2.1 Contents of a counterclaim

The contents of a counterclaim should look very much like a form of particulars of claim, that is, they should set out all the allegations in the same detail with the same formality, and conclude with a statement of truth.

27.2.2 Set-off

It is important to mention the nature of set-off, both because it is a technical term which will cause confusion if it is not explained and because the court will probably deal with things rather differently in terms of case management. If a defendant wishes to rely wholly or in part on a defence of *set-off* he may, by CPR, r. 16.6, include this in his defence. Put simply, a set-off is a counterclaim for a sum of money which arises out of the very same facts as the claimant's cause of action and goes to the root of those facts. A set-off is therefore a form of defence to the claimant's action and extinguishes any amount owed to the claimant up to the figure of the set-off. If the set-off is for a greater amount than the claimant's claim then the whole of the claimant's claim is extinguished and the defendant seeks judgment for the balance between the two sums in his favour.

A good example of a set-off is the case of *British Anzani (Felixstowe) Ltd* v *International Marine Management (UK) Ltd* [1980] QB 637. The claimant landlord sued the tenant for arrears of rent. The defendant claimed by way of set-off damages for breach of the landlord's covenants to do essential repairs. The effect of the breaches by the landlord was to diminish the rental value of the land to the tenant and the court held that this was a proper case of set-off. Accordingly it only gave judgment for the difference between the value of the two figures. Another example is s. 53(1)(a) of the Sale of Goods Act 1979, which expressly provides that in an action for the price of goods, damages for breach of warranty of quality (for example the price of doing repairs to the goods) may be set off against the debt.

In the case of set-off the sum claimed, whether the case involves a specified amount or general damages, must already be due at the date of commencement of the claimant's action. It is not proposed to say anything more about the term 'set-off'.

27.3 Defence to counterclaim

Where a counterclaim is filed and served, it stands in all respects as if it were a claim made by the defendant against the claimant. Accordingly, one cannot simply let it pass unchallenged and the claimant is required in his turn to file and serve a defence to counterclaim setting out what his defence to it is, which must be verified by a statement of truth.

27.4 Cases where the defendant claims against some other person

The former term for a case where the defendant wished to bring some other person into the action was 'third-party proceedings'. This term has not survived into the CPR, but it is probably still convenient to describe the extra party as a 'third party' in this chapter simply for the purpose of clarity.

27.4.1 When will such proceedings be appropriate?

They will be appropriate where there is some real connection between the claimant's claim against the defendant and what the defendant is claiming against the third party. No exhaustive test for this is now set out in CPR, Part 20, but the following are illustrations.

EXAMPLE 1: Claim for a contribution

C has been knocked down by a vehicle driven by D. D contends that he was not the only one responsible for the accident because another car driven by T swerved into his path, causing him to mount the pavement and hit C. D may therefore want to join T by a Part 20 claim. The consequence will be that although D will, in the law of tort, remain liable for any damages awarded to the claimant, he may, having paid those damages, be able to obtain a contribution if the court concludes that T bore a share of responsibility for the accident. Of course if in a negligence claim by C, D claimed that T had *wholly* caused the accident this would provide a complete defence for D and, if the court found that this was the case, D would be exonerated entirely. The action that the claimant should take to cope with this possibility is discussed below.

EXAMPLE 2: Claim for indemnity

C has just bought a new television from a retailer D. When first switched on it explodes, causing a house fire, damaging C's property and causing some personal injury. C issues proceedings against D claiming breach of condition of satisfactory quality. D's contract with T, the manufacturer of the television, provides an indemnity for such cases. He would therefore seek to add the manufacturer by a Part 20 claim.

It should be noted, as a matter of practice, that in this instance it is still open to D to defend the claim on the merits, for example, by contending that the television had been misused or tampered with or that the whole incident had been fabricated. More probably what would happen would be that once the retailer notified the Part 20 claim, the manufacturer T would take over the conduct of the retailer's defence since the manufacturer would be ultimately responsible for any damages found due. The retailer would then in effect, although technically remaining a party to the proceedings, drop out from them and the claim would be carried out between consumer and manufacturer as the person ultimately liable.

EXAMPLE 3: Other claims connected with the claimant's claim

Suppose that C, the claimant, a pedestrian, is knocked down by a vehicle driven by D (as in Example 1). D's car goes on to strike a wall and D himself is injured. D contends that the accident was caused or contributed to by another vehicle driven by T which swerved into his path. He will issue Part 20 proceedings against T, seeking not only contribution towards any damages he might be found liable to pay C, but in addition damages for his own claim.

27.4.2   Is the court's permission required?

As we have seen in the example at **27.2(c)**, if a defendant wishes to counterclaim against the present claimant and also against some new person, the court's permission is *always* required. Generally speaking, however, the making of a Part 20 claim, now called an 'additional claim', against some other person *not already a party* (a third party) does not require the court's permission provided that the additional claim is issued at court at or before the date on which the defendant files his defence. It will then be served on the person against whom it is made in accordance with the directions given by the court which will usually be for service within 14 days.

So long as a defendant appreciates the need for an additional claim, formulates it and gets it launched at an early enough stage in the proceedings, no application for the court's permission is necessary. The court will, however, subsequently review matters in the use of its case management powers, as to which see below.

The issue of whether or not the court's permission is required therefore usually depends on the speed and efficiency of the defendant's solicitors in formulating the additional claim.

It is also necessary to ensure that if litigation is being funded by a legal expenses insurer, approval has been obtained from the insurer to add a new party, since the costs may be substantially increased. If the litigation is being conducted under a conditional fee agreement, the addition of the extra party must be reflected in the agreement.

27.4.3   Claims between co-defendants

By CPR, r. 20.6, there is a special rule relating to claims for a contribution or indemnity between co-defendants. This would come about where the claimant has sued two or more defendants and one wishes to make a claim for contribution (that is, a payment of a proportion of any damages found due) or an indemnity (that is, full compensation for any damages found due to the claimant) from the co-defendant. In order to ensure that all issues are before the court with proper documentation, a defendant in that situation must file a notice containing a statement of the nature and grounds of his claim and serve it on the other defendant.

This might well arise in situations such as where the consumer affected by the television in the example in 27.4.1.2 had chosen to sue at the outset both retailer and manufacturer as co-defendants. If there was a contract between them, providing for an indemnity, the retailer would in the same proceedings tell the manufacturer that he claimed to be indemnified by him against any damages that might be found due to the claimant. This would not, as indicated above, stop him from defending the claimant's claim on the facts.

Claims for a *contribution* between defendants are much rarer. The court already has powers to apportion liability between defendants when giving its judgment and, strictly speaking, contribution notices are rarely required. Where, for example, a workman is injured on a building site, say, in a fall from scaffolding and it is unclear whether his claim really lies against his own employer, who is probably a small subcontractor, or the main contractor, or the subcontractor who erected the scaffolding or even the occupier of the site under the Occupiers' Liability Act 1957, a prudent solicitor will usually join in all four defendants. There is no need for the defendants to serve contribution notices on each other because the issue of apportionment of liability will be before the court anyway.

There may be cases where the amounts of contributions to claims are fixed in advance by contracts between parties and in those situations a contribution notice may be appropriate.

27.4.4   Where the court's permission to bring a Part 20 claim is required

If the court's permission is required because the additional claim is to be launched later than the time limit mentioned in 27.4.2, by CPR, r. 20.7(5), application may be made without notice to the other parties. The application will be made by an application notice supported by written evidence by virtue of PD 20, para. 2.1. That written evidence should state:

(a) the stage which the claim has reached;

(b) the nature of the claim to have been made by the Part 20 claimant or details of the question or issue which needs to be decided;

(c) a summary of the facts on which the Part 20 claim is based; and

(d) the name and address of the proposed Part 20 defendant (the 'third party').

Where delay has been a factor contributing to the need to apply for permission, an explanation of the delay should be given and a timetable of the action to date should be provided.

When the district judge receives that application, he will consider the papers before him. If he concludes that it is necessary to hear the *claimant's* views before deciding, he will list the application for an appointment. It will not at this stage be material for him to know what the potential 'third party's' views are.

27.4.4.1 The matters to be taken into account

When deciding whether to grant permission to bring an additional claim, the court will take a number of matters into account. If it decides that an additional claim is not to be permitted, this does not extinguish the defendant's claim against the third party. It is simply a decision by the court that the defendant must bring his claim against the third party in totally separate proceedings by issuing a claim form in which he, the defendant, is now the claimant. Even if the district judge has initially given his permission for the defendant to bring his additional claim, it is open to him to review that decision later, at the case management stage. He may decide that, in the light of new evid-ence brought, perhaps in view of the contents of the third party's defence to the additional claim and even in the light of what the claimant says, dealing with all matters in the same proceeding is inappropriate, and give directions that the additional claim be brought by separate proceedings.

By CPR, r. 20.9(2), the matters to which the court must have regard in deciding on the suitability of the proceedings for an additional claim are:

(a) the connection between the additional claim and the original claim made by the claimant against the defendant;

(b) whether the additional claimant (i.e., the original defendant) is seeking substantially the same remedy which some other party is claiming from him; and

(c) whether the additional claimant wants the court to decide any question concerned with the subject matter of the proceedings:

    (i) not only between existing parties but also between existing parties and a person not already a party; or

    (ii) against an existing party, not only in a capacity in which he is already a party, but also in some further capacity.

What the district judge will want to see is some sensible factual connection between the issues, so that in the case management of the whole set of facts the court can deal conveniently with all the issues and that there is likely to be some saving in time and costs. If the events are closely connected, as in the road accident example described in **27.4.1.1**, it will probably be useful for the court to decide on all the issues at the same time. This may not always be the case, however, even in that simple factual set of circumstances. One thing that the court will need to consider is the timetable for the case and to what extent issues can be dealt with separately. Consider the scenario described at **27.4.1.1**. It might be that the claimant had suffered very slight injuries and wanted to bring his litigation on quickly, whereas the defendant might have suffered catastrophic injuries such that his own case would not be ready for final resolution for, say, three years. The court would have to decide whether the issue of liability between all the parties could easily be decided at an early stage and the claimant's claim disposed of swiftly, while leaving the defendant's assessment of damages, if he showed that T was at all to blame, to proceed at a slower pace.

In other situations the court may conclude that even a straightforward counterclaim should go ahead in separate proceedings, for example, where the claimant's claim is a disputed debt, but the defendant has a personal injury action against the claimant.

It may be that the issues about the debt are so simple, and factually unrelated to the circumstances of the defendant's accident, that they could be disposed of by summary judgment or some other swift procedure.

The court has the full range of case management powers contained in Part 3 available to decide how matters should proceed.

27.5 Procedural steps after service of a Part 20 claim form

Where the additional claim is brought by counterclaim against the *claimant*, as indicated in **27.3**, he will need to file a defence to the counterclaim. The court will then consider what case management directions are appropriate.

Where an additional claim form is served on a person who is not already a party (that form of proceedings where the extra person has been described as a 'third party', see **27.4**) then the form must be accompanied by the full 'response pack' of forms, including forms for defending or admitting the claim and acknowledging service, and a copy of every statement of case which has already been served in the proceedings and such other documents as the court may direct (for example, if the court's permission was needed to start the additional claim, the court will probably direct that the statement of the defendant's evidence used to obtain permission be served).

Thereafter, once a defence is filed to the additional claim, the court will consider the future conduct of the proceedings and give appropriate directions, which must, so far as practicable, involve ensuring that the additional claim and the main claim are managed together.

27.6 Probable directions

It may be the case that very little complication is caused by the bringing in of a 'third party' or alternatively there may be considerable complexity. If it is the latter, the court may well call a case management conference in the near future, while perhaps requiring the parties to comply with some preliminary basic directions, for example, the disclosure of documents or even service of witness statements. It is now necessary to mention some peripheral matters.

27.6.1 More than one 'third party'

Although in the examples given above the defendant is shown as adding only one extra party to the proceedings, it is of course open to him in his turn to join in anyone he thinks responsible. For example, to adapt the scenario where the defendant swerves on to the pavement and strikes the claimant, because he feared the manoeuvre being carried out by a third party, he might perhaps allege that he swerved on to the pavement to avoid two other vehicles which collided, in which case he might join them both by additional claims as alternative 'third parties'.

27.6.2 'Fourth parties'

It is also possible for the person joined by an additional claim as a 'third party' once involved in the proceedings to himself seek to join other parties (who might also do the same). To take the example in **27.4.3** of the workman's accident caused by a fall from scaffolding, he might initiate the claim by simply suing his employer for damages based on an unsafe system of work. The employer, who was perhaps a small subcontractor at the building site, might join the main contractor, who he will say, had guaranteed to provide safe equipment such as scaffolding. Once joined, that employer might choose in his turn to join the scaffolding subcontractor, claiming that he owed the main contractor a duty to ensure that all scaffolding was safely erected; in due course the scaffolding subcontractor might claim to join the builder or main occupier of the site, claiming that the scaffolding had been properly erected, but had been tampered with by vandals overnight and that the provision of security for the building site was the responsibility of the builder or occupier, etc.

Although the scenario does now sound complicated, in fact by the time all the parties' statements of case are served and the appropriate defences filed, all the parties will be before the court and it will be easier for it to dispose of matters at the one trial than by permitting a series of trials. Since all the parties (other than the claimant) are likely to be insured, it will also greatly facilitate a reasonable compromise of the action.

27.7   Some special considerations for a claimant

Suppose that the claimant has issued proceedings against the defendant believing him to be entirely to blame.

Let us take again the scenario from **27.4.1.1** where the claimant is a pedestrian who while walking along the pavement is knocked down by a car driven by the defendant which mounts the pavement. The defendant contends that the reason he mounted the pavement was to avoid a car which swerved into his path on the wrong side of the road and which was driven by T.

In this situation if the defendant can show that what he says is true, he has a complete defence. There is no strict liability of course for motor accidents and if in the agony of the moment he took a reasonable course of action in mounting the pavement, it may be that he has not been negligent at all, however traumatic the consequences for the claimant, and the claimant will therefore fail. Although it is open to a defendant to draft a defence in this way, and take no other action against T, the defendant would be very rash to do so. If the court found that he was even 1 per cent to blame for the injury to the claimant, then he would have to pay the whole of the claimant's damages. As well as blaming T in his defence, the defendant will normally go on to issue an additional claim against T. This will obviously be the case if D has himself suffered some damage in the accident, but should be the case anyway.

Accordingly, he will be hoping to persuade a court to conclude that T was entirely to blame so that he, D, should be absolved from any responsibility to the claimant. If he fails to persuade the court to the required level, he will at least be hoping that the court will find substantial liability against T, enabling him to get a contribution to the damages that he himself will have to pay the claimant.

27.7.1   In that situation what should the claimant do?

It would be prudent for the claimant to amend his claim form and particulars of claim by seeking to show that D and T were jointly and severally liable. The proportions in which they were liable would not matter to the claimant. The claimant would seek to amend his claim form to make T a second defendant. The claims could then proceed neatly in tandem and the court at trial would have the power to apportion liability between D and T. (For the practice on amendment see **12.6**.)

27.7.2 Practical points

Where a new party is joined in a road accident case, it will be important for the claimant to have written a letter protecting himself under s. 152 of the Road Traffic Act 1988 and to have ensured that whatever funding arrangements or conditional fee agreement he has entered into reflects the addition of the extra party.

27.7.3 Costs

There ought to be no difficulty for the claimant in respect of costs for having joined the new defendant. Even if at trial the court decides that the new defendant should be completely exonerated, the original defendant can hardly complain about having to bear increased costs of joining the new defendant since the suggestion that it was appropriate to do so came from him, the original defendant.

'Class' or 'group' litigation

28.1 Introduction

It has become increasingly common in recent years for claims to be commenced with numerous claimants involved. The terms 'class action' or 'group action' are often used in respect of such cases, but it is important to distinguish the two.

28.2 Class actions

Properly speaking, the term 'class action' should only be used in a case where all the claimants have exactly the same rights based on the same facts. In its strict use, therefore, it should only be used of claims brought, for example, by a group of beneficiaries against a trustee for breach of trust, or perhaps in some cases of shareholders' claims against a company. It is in fact a misnomer to use it in the much more common situation where there are multiple claimants in a personal injury claim, and in such cases the term 'group action' is better.

28.3 Group actions

Group actions commonly come about in situations such as the following:

(a) 'Instant' disaster claims arising out of a common cause of action such as an aircraft, shipping or train accident, or a major fire, or a failure in crowd control, e.g., the Zeebrugge shipping disaster, or the Hillsborough football disaster.

(b) Claims arising out of defects in pharmaceutical products such as the 'benzodiazepine' litigation, where some thousands of claimants alleged harmful side effects and addiction arising from their use of various tranquilliser drugs.

(c) Claims arising out of environmental pollution causing disease.

(d) Claims against local authorities by children in their care who have suffered abuse of one kind or another due to the misconduct of employees of the local authority.

28.4 Procedure

In this text a full discussion of the very great practical and procedural problems associated with class and group actions is inappropriate. The court will manage them closely, first under its general case management powers under CPR, Part 3, particularly those rules which permit the court to make decisions about whether to try two or more claims on the same occasion, and consolidate proceedings. For proper group litigation, the court has extensive specialist powers under CPR, rr. 19.10 to 19.15. These provide that a court may make a Group Litigation Order ('GLO') and give proper directions for management of Group Litigation and that orders made by the court are binding on all cases in the group.

28.5   Practical difficulties

The practical problems of this kind of litigation are enormous. Even in the 'instant' disaster case, although perhaps the issue of breach of duty and causation will be identical for each claimant, the differences in quantum of damage, and even possibly of contributory negligence, may be extreme. Thus, to take the case of the Hillsborough litigation, while at its worst there were numerous victims who suffered fatal accidents, equally there were others on the fringe of the disturbance who suffered quite minor injuries such as broken fingers; in addition, some spectators suffered no physical injuries but sustained nervous shock, whether by viewing directly within the ground, or on television. The extremely difficult questions of liability for nervous shock went to the House of Lords in the case of *Alcock* v *Chief Constable of South Yorkshire* [1992] 1 AC 310.

Litigation continued until very recently, difficult issues having arisen not merely in respect of nervous shock to bystanders but as to the extent to which those involved in the emergency services, in particular, the police and ambulance workers, may themselves have a claim.

In pharmaceutical product cases, such as the tranquilliser cases, the issues are even more complex. There will be patients of different susceptibilities who have taken different quantities of the drug (or possibly in combinations of different tranquilliser drugs, sometimes made by different manufacturers) over very different periods of time and who may well have desisted from taking tranquillisers for certain periods during that time. Moreover, the issues of liability in such cases are increased because the question of relevant scientific knowledge or degree of proper pre-testing may vary from drug to drug and manufacturer to manufacturer. Thus this apparently simple issue of negligence may be very different in respect of each claimant on different facts. In addition, there may be different side effects and different issues of limitation in respect of each claimant.

28.5.1   Commencing a group action

In most such disaster cases notice is given through the legal press and elsewhere that the court considers it desirable that a 'group' should be constituted. In such a case there is usually service of a 'master' particulars of claim, with each individual claimant serving separate schedules of special damage; disclosure by the defendants is carried out once only to the solicitors for the steering group of the lead cases. (Of course each individual claimant will have to carry out disclosure separately of the factors relevant to quantum.)

After the group is finalised certain lead cases are selected to come forward as test cases. The very need to set up such 'groups' in itself causes enormous complications.

Thus in *AB* v *John Wyeth & Brother Ltd* (1992) *The Times*, 20 October 1992, the court had to consider the 'benzodiazepine' litigation referred to at **28.3** above. For such litigation to be manageable as a group there will have to be cut-off dates after which other interested claimants will not be allowed to join the lead group. If it were not so, claimants who have come forward early would be severely prejudiced by having to proceed only at the pace of the slowest to come forward. In these cases the court issues practice directions, usually reserving all actions concerned with the same defendants to a given master or judge for the procedural stages. That is what happened in the 'benzodiazepine' litigation where the judge in control, Ian Kennedy J, imposed cut-off dates after which persons should not be eligible to join in the group litigation. Those cut-off dates were in fact extended on several occasions, eventually to 31 August 1992, but even so many hundreds more persons came forward attempting to join the group after that date. The Court of Appeal upheld the judge in his refusal to permit others to join in the claims, holding that a cut-off date was essential for the expeditious monitoring of large group claims. It must be borne in mind that that does not in itself destroy the claims of those who come forward later. It is simply that they will have to proceed alone, or form a later group, subject to the problem of limitation periods and, of course, of obtaining funding to join the group. (It may well be, for example, that a legal expenses insurer would consider that it was unreasonable conduct to fail to come forward in time to join the first group, and assistance may be harder to obtain for those who have not been sufficiently alert or cooperative to do so, provided that their symptoms became known in time.)

The lead claims chosen after the control of the interim stages will go forward to try the primary facts. The problem is that, strictly speaking, such lead claims do not bind the parties to the other claims, unless they have positively agreed in advance that the decision is to bind them. Although, however, that is the legal position it is certainly possible that, if the lead claim is properly constituted, represents a good example of the problem, and is thoroughly and competently litigated, but the lead claimant loses, any other litigants in the group reliant on legal expenses insurance will have their insurers' support withdrawn as being unable to show a reasonable chance of success. In that way some practical effect will be given to the lead claim.

Costs sharing orders which provide that the costs will be shared in certain proportions can be made in order to make the group action more effective. There are serious complications in this, of course, where some claimants have legal aid and some do not.

28.6 Conclusion

Even before the coming into force of the CPR the courts consistently stressed that 'modern case management techniques' should be used as far as possible in group actions and that the so-called 'sporting theory of litigation' (according to which it is up to each claimant to make the best he can of all the tactical advantages available to him whatever the position of other claimants) has no place in such a scenario. Certainly the general powers of the court under the CPR do now enable it to take a very firm grasp on group litigation, but very difficult decisions will still have to be made about such matters as how groups are to be constituted, cut-off dates, sanctions for individual claimants failing to comply with 'group' orders and the like. The collapse of the tobacco group litigation coming not long after the similar collapse of the benzodiazepine litigation in which the majority of claimants failed, was widely heralded as being the end of group litigation. That is much too simplistic a view. Product liability cases were always likely to be the most difficult, and 'instant disaster' cases provide very different opportunities for group litigation to demonstrate its effectiveness. In any event, it is understood at the time of writing that other claimants who do not suffer the particular difficulties experienced by the leading claimants in the last tobacco litigation, in particular, problems arising out of the Limitation Acts, are presently forming new groups to pursue their claims.

28.7 The Human Rights Act 1998 and group litigation

It may be contended that an over-robust use of the court's case management powers so as, in effect, to cut off potential claimants from any relief by exclusion from group litigation because of failure to meet cut-off dates is open to challenge as being in breach of Article 6 of the European Convention, which guarantees a right to a fair trial. This is discussed generally in **Chapter 37** which deals with the 1998 Act and its practical consequences for civil litigation.

Security for costs

29.1 The impecunious claimant

In ordinary litigation, there is no protection for a defendant who is being sued by a claimant, however unmeritorious the claim, unless it is so unmeritorious that he can have the whole claim struck out at some early stage, for example, by applying for summary judgment. It would be open to an impecunious claimant to harass a defendant with expensive and time-consuming proceedings knowing that even though he loses at trial, the defendant is unlikely to be able to recover the costs awarded to him because of the claimant's impecuniosity. Unfortunately in the majority of cases defendants who are harassed in this way will have no real remedy, although if the facts are extreme it may be possible to obtain a 'wasted costs' order against the impecunious claimant's solicitors on the basis that they have assisted him in pursuing utterly groundless litigation. One such case which ended in this way was *Tolstoy Miloslavsky* v *Aldington* (1995) *The Times*, 27 December 1995, where the court concluded that the impecunious claimant's solicitors had improperly assisted him to bring a quite hopeless action for the purpose of harassing the defendant and ordered that a substantial proportion of the costs be paid by the claimant's solicitors personally.

There is one major exception to this rule. In certain circumstances the court can order that a claimant, as the price of continuing with his action, gives 'security for costs', usually by paying a substantial sum into court funds. This guarantees that he will be able to meet any costs order eventually made against him.

Before going on to consider CPR, r. 25.12, it is important to remember that part of the court's case management powers under r. 3.1(3)(a) includes the power to make an order 'subject to conditions including a condition to pay a sum of money into court'.

While initially this might seem to duplicate and override the rules relating to security for costs, this is not the case. The general principle is that a specific rule takes precedence over a general rule. The power to direct that a sum of money be paid into court is of general application. Certainly the purpose of the order may sometimes be to give security for costs, but usually this particular part of the court's case management powers will involve it applying a sanction for misconduct or non-observance of previous orders. At the time of writing there is little case law as to how and when this provision ought to be invoked. On the wording of the rule it can be used against either claimant or defendant at any stage of a claim for any proper purpose. It is suggested that it is more likely to be used against defendants than claimants, as provisions for ordering security for costs otherwise never apply against defendants.

One should also not lose sight of the fact that in the exercise of its overriding case management powers the court may take steps to see that weak cases do not progress very far in the system, whether by use of the powers to strike out part of a case or where the court orders a summary judgment hearing even if the defendant has not applied himself.

We now go on to consider CPR, r. 25.12.

29.2   Security for costs

Rule 25.12 of the CPR deals with security for costs. It substantially repeats a provision of the Rules of the Supreme Court and the objectives of the new Part are similar to those of the old rule. However, Lightman J in *Leyvand* v *Barasch* (2000) *The Times*, 23 March 2000, stressed that because there is a vital change in the criterion for ordering security, as indicated below, previous case law on orders for security of costs might no longer be applicable. This is of course the position generally when considering previous authorities in the context of the CPR, with some few exceptions.

29.2.1   Conditions to be satisfied

The court may make an order for security for costs under r. 25.12 if, by r. 25.13:

(a)   it is satisfied, having regard to all the circumstances of the case, that it is just to make such an order; and

(b)   (i)   one or more of the conditions in paragraph (2) applies, or

(ii)   an enactment permits the court to require security for costs.

(2)   The conditions are—

(a)   the claimant is an individual—

(i)   who is ordinarily resident out of the jurisdiction; and

(ii)   is not a person against whom a claim can be enforced under the Brussels Conventions or the Lugano Convention, as defined by section 1(1) of the Civil Jurisdiction and Judgments Act 1982;

(b)   the claimant is a company or other incorporated body—

(i)   which is ordinarily resident out of the jurisdiction; and

(ii)   is not a body against whom a claim can be enforced under the Brussels Conventions or the Lugano Convention;

(c)   the claimant is a company or other body (whether incorporated inside or outside Great Britain) and there is reason to believe that it will be unable to pay the defendant's costs if ordered to do so;

(d)   the claimant has changed his address since the claim was commenced with a view to evading the consequences of the litigation;

(e)   the claimant failed to give his address in the claim form, or gave an incorrect address in that form;

(f)   the claimant is acting as a nominal claimant, other than as a representative claimant under Part 19, and there is reason to believe that he will be unable to pay the defendant's costs if ordered to do so;

(g)   the claimant has taken steps in relation to his assets that would make it difficult to enforce an order for costs against him.

There are thus two separate tests. One must first show that a claimant is within one of the 'suspect' categories and thereafter the court has a discretion to order security if it is satisfied that it is just to make such an order. It should be noted that the categories of 'suspect' claimants are exhaustive. It is no use showing merely that a claimant is impecunious unless he also fits one of these categories. One cannot, for example, obtain an order that a claimant should give security for costs merely because he is believed to be on the verge of bankruptcy, unless he also comes within one of the above criteria, for example, r. 25.13(2)(g). We now go on to consider the categories briefly.

29.2.2 'Ordinarily resident out of the jurisdiction'

The rationale of this part of the rule is obviously based on the difficulty of enforcing a costs order outside the jurisdiction if a person has no assets within it. The question of 'ordinarily resident' is to be determined on a common-sense basis and it may not correspond to the concept of domicile in other matters, for example, tax or family law. A claimant may well work all the year abroad, but if he has clear roots in this country he may not be 'ordinarily resident' out of the jurisdiction. In any event, if he retains assets within the jurisdiction which could be used to enforce a costs order, for example, a house or business interest, then even if he is ordinarily resident out of the jurisdiction, the court would not make a security for costs order.

It is beyond the scope of this book to discuss in detail the Brussels and Lugano Conventions. They provide a mechanism for the mutual recognition of judgments with a number of European countries, including some outside the European Union. In *Fitzgerald v Williams* [1996] QB 657 it was held that it was improperly discriminatory to require an EU-based claimant to give security for costs simply on the grounds of residence. However, the court in that case did reserve consideration of whether it would receive evidence that procedures for enforcing costs orders locally were ineffective, notwithstanding the fact that the country was within the Brussels or Lugano Conventions and it may still be the case that that kind of point can be argued in view of the wording of CPR, r. 25.13(2)(a)(ii).

29.2.3 The claimant's address

Categories (d) and (e) are self-explanatory. If a claimant does not give an honest address on the claim form or changes his address with the objective of avoiding the consequence of litigation, these would be powerful factors in favour of making an order so long as it was otherwise just to do so. If the failure to state an address or misstatement was innocent, the court would simply require it to be corrected.

29.2.4 'Nominal claimant'

A claimant who sues in a representative capacity, such as a litigation friend, or executor is *not* a nominal claimant. The test is whether the claimant retains a genuine interest in the outcome of the litigation. If he does then he is not 'nominal' and no order for security for costs can be made. The case demonstrating this is *Envis v Thakker* (1995) *The Times*, 2 May 1995, where the claimant was nearly insolvent, but intended to use the proceeds of the litigation to distribute amongst his creditors to avoid bankruptcy. The court held that as he had an interest in the outcome of the litigation, he did not become a 'nominal' claimant, even though he would probably not keep any of the fruits of the litigation for himself.

29.2.5 'Company or other body'

Security for costs may be ordered against a company or other body, whether incorporated or not (such as a trade union or members' club), where there is reason to believe it will be unable to pay the applicant's costs if ordered to do so. Until the CPR this was dealt with only by s. 726(1) of the Companies Act 1985, which remains in force in relation to limited companies and to that extent overlaps with the general rule. Section 726(1) provides:

> Where in England and Wales a limited company is plaintiff in an action or other legal proceeding, the court having jurisdiction in the matter may, if it appears by credible testimony that there is reason to believe that the company will be unable to pay the defendant's costs if successful in his defence, require sufficient security to be given for those costs, and may stay all proceedings until the security is given.

Although the wording appears to be slightly wider than that in the CPR, it is clear that r. 25.13(1)(a) provides an overriding consideration of whether it is just in all the circumstances to make the order and it is submitted that there is now little difference between the test in s. 726 of the Companies Act 1985 and the general test under the CPR.

Hitherto it was a common tactic by defendants to try to stifle claims by small limited companies which would be put in a difficult position by the statutory provision. The reason would be that, quite understandably, such a company would usually have caused its accounts to be drawn up with the major objective of avoiding tax. Thus if, for example, very large profits would have been shown just before its financial year end, the company might well have decided to use much of those profits to buy additional stock, upgrade company vehicles and the like so as, quite legitimately, to avoid tax. When the company came to sue someone those accounts would be obtained by the defendant and might be ruthlessly used against the company to show that the company was not very profitable and therefore unlikely to be able to bear a large costs order should it lose the litigation.

29.2.6 'The claimant has taken steps in relation to his assets that would make it difficult to enforce an order for costs'

This ground does not require a dishonest intention and therefore the claimant who in the course of the proceedings genuinely intended to move his home and business abroad might be caught by it. Everything will depend upon the facts of any individual case. The principles may be similar to those to be used in the case of freezing injunctions. It would probably be appropriate for a defendant seeking to rely on this ground to demonstrate some general dishonesty, lack of good faith or evasiveness on the part of the claimant. One factor might be how much the claimant delayed before bringing the claim, and whether the claimant appears to be dragging his heels in pursuing the action once started.

29.3 What tests will the court apply?

The tests which were applied to security for costs applications under the previous rules usually involved a consideration of the following matters:

(a) whether the claimant's claim was apparently *bona fide*;

(b) what were the claimant's prospects of success (although the court always stressed that on an application for security for costs it would be impossible to go into the full merits of the claim in any depth);

(c) whether the defendant has made any admissions in part or whole;

(d) whether there has been a substantial payment into court, or Part 36 offer or open offer;

(e) whether, even if a claimant was outside the jurisdiction, he retained substantial property within it against which an order for costs could be enforced;

(f) whether the application was being used oppressively, for example, to stifle a genuine claim;

(g) whether if the claimant was a limited company, its lack of means might have been brought about by any conduct of the defendant such as the delay in payment (e.g., between a main contractor and a subcontractor). This tended to be a very important ground in practice where, for example, a subcontractor might be working almost whole time for a main contractor so that if the subcontractor was not paid, his own business would be in severe difficulties. Withholding payment unscrupulously could therefore be a weapon to cause a subcontractor to renegotiate or to drop other claims. If the subcontractor then eventually had to go to litigation, it would clearly be unjust for the defendant to use the subcontractor's impecuniosity, which had been brought about by the defendant, as a reason to obtain security for costs;

(h) finally, the court would examine the stage of the proceedings at which the application was made. To make this application credibly the defendant usually should apply quite early in the proceedings and the later an application is made the less likely it is that the court will order security.

Some, or all, of these factors might be relevant in determining the single criterion now applicable, that is, whether it is 'just' to make the order.

It is strongly suggested that in view of the Human Rights Act 1998 the court will have to consider very carefully an application for security for costs if the effect of it might be to stifle a claim about which there is any shred of credibility. It is suggested it might be a serious infringement of the right of access to the courts contained in the right to a fair trial stated in Article 6 of the European Convention to bar a claimant by a security for costs order with which he could not comply. The court will certainly take this into account carefully in future. Provided that proper consideration is given to this, an order for security for costs does not infringe Article 6 of the European Convention (*Nasser* v *United Bank of Kuwait* [2002] 1 WLR 1868).

29.4 The application

An application is made pursuant to CPR, r. 25.12, by application notice supported by written evidence. Where the court makes an order for security for costs it will:

(a) determine the amount of security; and

(b) direct:

    (i)   the manner in which; and

    (ii) the time within which

    the security must be given.

The amount to be awarded is in the discretion of the court, which will fix whatever sum it thinks just, having regard to all the circumstances. It will be necessary for the claimant to supply an estimate of the likely costs either for the whole action or up to a particular stage in the proceedings at which further applications for security can be considered. Under the Human Rights Act 1998 it is suggested that an important consideration now will be the amount which the respondent is realistically likely to be able to raise. A claimant who wishes to resist being ordered to give security for an amount which he thinks excessive will have to make full disclosure of his means. The usual order for security for costs will require the claimant to pay the sum in question into the court office, or sometimes to lodge an insurance bond for that amount or to open a joint account with the defendant's solicitors in the required sum. The order may go on to provide that if security is not given either that the claim is stayed, or more usually now that the claim will be struck out with a further order that the claimant pay the costs of the claim.

29.4.1 Further applications

Further applications can be made for security to be given if, for example, the first application only required the claimant to lodge security for costs up to a certain stage of the claim and it then becomes clear that the claim will continue to trial and involve considerably more expense so that the amount presently lodged in court is inadequate as security.

29.5 Security for costs and additional claims

Whilst in ordinary litigation it is not possible for a *claimant* to seek security for costs against a *defendant*, it is possible for security for costs orders to be made against a counterclaiming defendant. Thus if the defendant is himself bringing a counterclaim in those circumstances it is possible for the original claimant to get an order for security for costs against the defendant in his capacity as a Part 20 claimant, though the order must only relate to the costs of the counterclaim and not the proceedings as a whole.

29.6 Miscellaneous

There are other provisions which it is unnecessary to discuss here in CPR, r. 25.14, permitting a defendant to obtain orders for security against someone other than the claimant where the claimant has assigned his right to litigation or is in some way supporting the claimant's litigation. Further, in r. 25.15 there are provisions which may enable the court to order security for the costs of any appeal to be given by an appellant, whether he was the claimant or defendant in the court below. A full discussion of these is outside the scope of this text.

Special kinds of litigants (1)

In this chapter we consider the rules and practical considerations relevant to special kinds of litigants.

30.1 Limited companies

30.1.1 Legal personality

A limited company is a legal person and may bring and defend proceedings in any court.

A limited company may appoint a solicitor or may be represented at trial by any employee who has been authorised by the company, provided the court gives its permission, though if the company insists on appearing by a representative it is difficult to see how the court could refuse.

30.1.2 Service of documents

A claim form may be served on a company under s. 725 of the Companies Act 1985 by sending it by post to the registered office of the company. Unless the contrary is shown, the date of service will be presumed to be, if posted by first-class mail, the second working day after posting, and if posted by second-class mail, the fourth working day after posting. If service is effected by leaving the document at the registered office or putting it through the letter box there, service is deemed to be immediate.

A limited company may also be served under the provisions of the table in CPR, r. 6.5(6), either at its principal office or any place within the jurisdiction which has a real connection with the claim (see **11.4.4**).

30.1.3 Enforcement of judgments

A limited company may enforce a judgment or have one enforced against it (see **Chapter 34**). Where judgments or orders are made which require some personal compliance, however, then clearly there is some difficulty. For example, if it is desired to ask a company to attend court to provide information under CPR Part 71, or even to punish a contempt of court by a company, what is to be done? The answer is that in such cases it is up to the opposite party to select the relevant officer of the company and direct the order to attend court to that person. The same applies in the case of an application to commit for contempt of court. It is clearly appropriate to select the officer of the company most involved with the litigation, or with the contempt complained of. Although a limited company cannot, of course, be committed to prison, it can in its own right be fined for contempt of court (see **34.3**). It can also have its assets seized as a punishment, which is called *sequestration*.

30.2 Overseas companies

Foreign corporations which establish a place of business in Great Britain must, pursuant to s. 691 of the Companies Act 1985, within a month of the date of establishment deliver to the registrar of companies for registration, *inter alia*, the names and addresses of one or more persons resident in Great Britain authorised to accept service of process and notices on behalf of the company.

30.3 Corporations other than limited companies

Corporations, like limited companies, may sue and be sued in their corporate name. Service may be effected on the mayor, president, chairman, town clerk, secretary, treasurer or other similar officer. Orders for oral examination and applications for committal may be made against any proper person, as in the case of limited companies.

30.4 Trade unions and unincorporated employers' associations

Pursuant to ss. 10 and 127 of the Trade Union and Labour Relations (Consolidation) Act 1992, these bodies can sue and be sued in their own names.

30.5 Clubs

It is important to distinguish between proprietary clubs and members' clubs. A *proprietary* club (for example, a nightclub, and even if there is a so-called 'membership fee') is simply a business. It may either be a limited company, sole trader or a partnership and be sued accordingly. A *members'* club (e.g., a sports or social club), however, has no legal personality and cannot generally sue or be sued in its own name. If all the members of a members' club are similarly interested in the dispute, one or more of the members may sue on behalf of all of them in representative proceedings. If it is desired to sue a club then it may be necessary to obtain a copy of the club constitution or rules to ascertain against whom actions should be brought. The proper defendants are usually the trustees or committee of the club.

30.6 Partnerships

30.6.1 Comparison with limited companies

Limited companies are of course legal entities. They may, broadly speaking, litigate much as a private individual may litigate, and there are very few special rules appertaining to them. In the case of partnerships, however, there is a considerable procedural problem caused by the difficult status of the entity. A partnership or firm is not, as such, a legal entity, and neither is the firm name anything more than a mere expression (although it may for convenience be adopted throughout the litigation).

The particular difficulties caused by partnerships in civil litigation arise in three areas, namely:

(a) how they may sue or be sued;

(b) how they may be served with proceedings; and

(c) how judgments may be enforced.

The provisions of RSC, Ord. 81 in CPR, sch. 1, provide a comprehensive code relating to these and other particular areas of difficulty. The approximate county court equivalents are in CCR, Ord. 5, r. 9 in CPR, sch. 2.

30.6.2 Claims by and against partnership firms within the jurisdiction

Provided that the firm concerned carries on business within the jurisdiction, then:

(a) Two or more persons carrying on such business may issue a claim form in the name of the firm without setting out the names of all the partners, and may give as the address the place of business of the firm instead of the partners' private addresses.

(b) As defendants, a firm may be sued in the firm name without the necessity for the claimant to discover the names of the individual partners, and the firm may be described as of the address at which the business is carried on. A person who sues such partners in their firm name sues them as individuals, just as much as if he had set out all their names and addresses.

(c) If, however, there has been a change in the personnel constituting the firm between the cause of action and the issue of the claim, then suing in the firm name may cause difficulty. In such a situation words should be used to indicate that the action is brought against those persons who were co-partners at the time of accrual of the cause of action. It may be better, if possible, to name such partners. If there has been a dissolution, or partial dissolution, it is important to serve the proceedings individually on the persons who are alleged to have been partners at the time of the accrual of the cause of action.

30.6.3 Practical points and special cases

30.6.3.1 A sole trader

A sole trader is someone who either carries on business in his own name or some other name (for example, 'The Middlemarch Pet Shop').

A sole trader must sue in his own name, but can be sued in his trade name (RSC, Ord. 81, r. 9 in CPR, sch. 1; CCR, Ord. 5, r. 10 in CPR, sch. 2). If the claimant suing a sole trader believes that the name of the firm is not the trader's own, he ought to add, after the defendant's name in the title to the claim form, the words 'a trading name'.

30.6.3.2   Limited partnerships

Since the rules are silent as to the procedure to be adopted in the case of limited partnerships, service would probably be preferable upon the general partners in such a firm, and not on limited partners. Execution may, however, be made against the limited partners to the extent of the limitation.

30.6.3.3   Disclosure of partners' names

It is sometimes, particularly for claimants wishing to sue a firm, an important matter to identify the partners. This may be crucially important in the question of enforcing judgment against the private assets of partners. It is a particularly difficult question when actions are to be brought, for example, against family businesses, where it is by no means clear to the outside world which members of the family have the status of partners and which are mere employees. The other provisions of the general law, such as the disclosure of partners' names on business notepaper or at their main place of business, are very often ignored in practice. In such situations the rules (RSC, Ord. 81, r. 2 in CPR, sch. 1; CCR, Ord. 5, r. 9 in CPR, sch. 2) usefully provide that where a person is either suing or being sued by a firm, he may serve on that firm or its solicitor a notice requiring it or him forthwith to furnish a written statement of the names and places of residence of all the persons who were partners in the firm at the time when the cause of action accrued. If this notice is not complied with, an application may be made to the court for an order that the details should be given.

The application is made to a master or district judge. Although it is discretionary, it is difficult to envisage any proper reason for which it could be refused, given the likely motives for non-disclosure. In the case of claimant firms, the court may order that proceedings be stayed until such details are given. In the case of defendant firms, an order may be made compelling such disclosure, in the last resort by striking out the defence or committal.

30.6.4   Service of a claim form on a partnership

30.6.4.1   Methods of service

A claim form may be served by the following methods:

(a) personally, on any one or more of the partners; or

(b) by personal service at the principal place of business of the partnership on any person having at the time of service the control or management of the partnership business there (whether or not such person is a partner); or

(c) by sending a copy of the claim form by ordinary first-class post to the firm at the principal place of business of the partnership within the jurisdiction.

In addition to the above methods the House of Lords held in *Kenneth Allison Ltd* v *A.E. Limehouse & Co.* [1992] 2 AC 105 that it is open to a partnership to stipulate any other method by which it will accept service of proceedings even outside the relevant rules of court.

30.6.4.2 Service of notice of capacity

Where personal service is effected either on a partner or on the apparent manager of the partnership business, a written notice stating whether that person is served as a partner, as a person having control or management of the partnership business, or as both, must be served on that person. If no such notice is served then the person concerned is deemed to be served as a partner.

In such a situation, service will be valid even though that person is not a partner, for that person may then acknowledge service and deny partnership. Service will, nonetheless, be effective as against the firm, provided the proper notice is served.

30.6.5 Acknowledgement of service

The rules relating to acknowledgement of service seem complex but are in reality quite straightforward. The problems are partly caused by the substantive provisions of partnership law. The position is as follows.

30.6.5.1 Acknowledgement by partners

If persons are sued as partners in the name of their firm, service may not be acknowledged in the name of the firm but must be by the partners individually, although the action will continue in the name of the firm. Thus, an individual partner should acknowledge service individually with the description 'partner in the firm of', or 'trading as', or 'practising as' as in the firm name. Any partner has the right to acknowledge service.

30.6.5.2 Acknowledgement by a non-partner

If a person denies that he was a partner, he may acknowledge service of the claim form, stating in his acknowledgement that he does so as a person served who makes such denial. The acknowledgement of service, however, stands until it is set aside, i.e., judgment in default cannot thereupon be given, but either:

(a) the claimant may apply to the court to set the acknowledgement aside on the ground that the defendant was a partner or liable as such, or may leave that question to be determined at a later stage (it may be appropriate to direct that the issue be tried separately, e.g., under CPR, r. 3.1); or

(b) the defendant may apply to the court to set aside the service of the claim on him on the ground that he was not a partner or liable as such at the material time, or may serve a defence denying either liability as a partner or liability of the defendant firm. Thereafter, the court may at any stage order that the question as to the liability of that defendant or of the firm be tried in such a manner, and at such time, as the court directs.

30.6.5.3 Acknowledgement by a person having control or management

Where the claim form is served on the person who has control or management of the partnership business at its principal place of business, that person may not acknowledge service unless he is a partner in the firm sued. In other words, although service on the firm is effective on such a person if he is the manager, it is on the basis that he will forthwith bring the claim form to the attention of one of the partners who may then acknowledge service. Judgment in default can be obtained in such a case if no acknowledgement of service or defence is filed.

30.6.6 Judgment

Where a firm is sued in the firm name, judgment must be entered against the firm and not against the individual partners. Judgment cannot be entered against one partner separately in default of defence, nor can any judgment be entered in a claim against a firm so long as any partner in the firm is defending the claim on behalf of the firm.

30.6.7 Enforcing a judgment or order

See RSC, Ord. 81, r. 5 in CPR, sch. 1; CCR, Ord. 25, r. 9 in CPR, sch. 2; Chapter 34.

Execution upon a judgment or order against a firm may be issued:

(a) against the property of the firm within the jurisdiction (this is so whether or not the partners all participated in the proceedings against the firm);

(b) without permission of the court against the private property of any partner who:

   (i) has acknowledged service of the claim form as a partner; or

   (ii) having been served as a partner with the claim form, failed to acknowledge service of it in the action; or

   (iii) admitted in his defence that he is a partner; or

   (iv) was adjudged to be a partner;

(c) where a member of the firm was out of the jurisdiction when the claim form was issued, execution to enforce the judgment against that person may not be issued unless that person acknowledges service of the claim form as a partner, or was served within the jurisdiction as a partner or was, with permission of the court, given under CPR, rr. 6.17–6.21, served out of the jurisdiction with the claim form as a partner.

The above are the situations where the court's permission is not required to enforce judgment against the private property of partners. There is no requirement first to proceed against the partnership property so that if, for example, it is known that one partner is particularly wealthy, it is perfectly proper for the successful claimant to attempt to enforce the judgment against that partner's private assets only.

The court's permission to enforce a judgment against the private property of an individual partner is only required where a judgment has been obtained against the firm and none of the above-mentioned situations apply. Application is made for the court's permission by application notice, which must be served personally on the partner against whom enforcement is sought. If he then disputes liability, for example, by contending that he was not a partner at all or at the relevant time, the court may order the issue of whether or not he was a partner to be tried in any appropriate manner.

30.7 Proceedings by and against estates

If a claimant or defendant dies after the commencement of a claim, an application may be made under CPR, r. 19.1(4) that the claim be carried on by or against his or her personal representatives. Application is made by application notice with evidence in support. If a defendant dies during the course of a claim, it may well be the case that his personal representatives do not apply to take over the claim, in which case the claimant may apply for an order requiring them to do so.

If a cause of action survives for the benefit of a deceased person, the claim must be brought by all his executors or administrators as parties to the claim.

If the deceased was to have been the defendant in a claim which has not yet been issued and the cause of action survives, proceedings may be commenced against his estate. If personal representatives have taken out a grant of representation, they should be named as defendants. If, as is often the case, no person has taken out a grant of representation then a claim form may still be issued against 'the personal representatives of AB deceased', without naming them or needing to give an address. Once the claim is issued application should be made to the master or district judge for an order to carry on the proceedings and for a person to be appointed to represent the estate for the purpose of the proceedings (CPR, r. 19.8). It is very important that this step be taken, as without it the whole claim will become a nullity. If no person comes forward to represent the estate the court will appoint someone. Should the deceased have been the cause of a motor accident this is likely to be a representative of his insurer, or of the MIB; in other cases the Official Solicitor will be appointed.

Special kinds of litigants (2)

31.1 Children and patients

31.1.1 Commencement of proceedings

There are special rules concerning actions brought by persons who are not of full capacity to sue. These appear in CPR, Part 21. 'Children' are persons under the age of 18 and 'patients' are persons who are incapable of managing and administering their own affairs by reason of mental disorder within the meaning of the Mental Health Act 1983.

Both patients and children must have a 'litigation friend' to conduct proceedings on their behalf. The title on the claim form would read:

John Smith (a child by Mary Smith his litigation friend).

In the case of a mental patient there should be no reference to the fact that he is a patient in the title to the action which would simply read:

Susan Brown (by Peter Green her litigation friend).

A claimant who intends to sue a child or patient should name the litigation friend on the claim form and serve it on that litigation friend. If there had been pre-action negotiations, as will almost always be the case, somebody ought to have come forward to fulfil this role. It may be, for example, that the child in question is a 16-year-old motorcyclist who has caused an accident, in which case the insurance company will have been involved in the negotiations and will appoint a litigation friend to conduct the case.

If no litigation friend has been identified, then a claimant may still issue proceedings against a child or patient, but may take no step in the claim other than issuing and serving a claim form. The claimant must immediately apply to the court for the appointment of a litigation friend before the claim can be pursued further (CPR, r. 21.3(2)).

If a claim has been commenced by or against a person who subsequently becomes a mental patient, no further step in the claim may be taken until a litigation friend has been appointed (CPR, r. 12.3(3)).

31.2 Powers and duties of a litigation friend

A litigation friend may be:

(a) a person appointed under Part VII of the Mental Health Act 1983 to conduct legal proceedings in the name of the patient; or

(b) a person who can fairly and competently conduct proceedings on behalf of the child or patient and who has no adverse interest in the claim.

Moreover, all steps and decisions he takes in the proceedings must be taken for the benefit of the child or patient (PD 21, para. 2.1).

In the discussion that follows we will deal with the position of a child, litigation by children being far more common than that by patients, but the propositions and discussions are also applicable to patients. Clearly, children are more likely to be claimants than defendants and are more likely to be involved in personal injury cases than contractual disputes. Because of this the overwhelming majority of litigation friends are likely to be parents.

Care should be taken in the choice of a litigation friend in road traffic accidents. If the child has been injured while a passenger in a vehicle driven by a parent involved in collision with another party, then, however clear-cut the facts seem, it is probably inappropriate to have the parent/driver as litigation friend. The other driver may make some allegation to the effect that the accident was actually caused by the negligence of the parent, and however far-fetched the allegation may seem, an apparent conflict of interest arises. It might be appropriate in the child's best interests eventually to amend the proceedings to name his own parent as alternative defendant. Such steps in litigation are by no means unusual and should not be understood to indicate any personal hostility, since the child's claim will in the end be compromised or any damages awarded be paid by one or both of the insurance companies of the drivers concerned. Where a child is a passenger or there is any other indication that the parent might, even marginally, be considered blameworthy, it is better to choose the other parent or some other relative as the litigation friend.

Once a litigation friend is appointed he has the power and right to deal positively with the litigation in the child's interest. Usually he will discharge that duty by appointing a competent solicitor to, in effect, run the litigation. He has the right to make decisions about tactical and practical aspects and procedural compromises. Where it is intended to reach a final compromise of a claim other matters must be considered. These are described below.

31.2.1 Appointment of litigation friend without a court order

A litigation friend may act either with or without a court order. If a litigation friend comes forward to act without a court order then:

(a) if he wishes to act on behalf of a patient, he must file an official copy of the order or other document which constitutes his authorisation to act under Part VII of the Mental Health Act 1983;

(b) if he wishes to act on behalf of a child (or on behalf of a patient without the authorisation referred to above), he must file a *certificate of suitability* under r. 21.5(3) which:

   (i)   states that he consents to act;

   (ii)   states that he knows or believes that the claimant/defendant is a child/patient;

   (iii) in the case of a patient states the grounds of his belief and, if his belief is based on medical opinion, has attached any relevant documents;

   (iv)   states that he can fairly and competently conduct proceedings on behalf of the child or patient and has no interest adverse to that child or patient;

(v)   if the child or patient is a claimant, undertakes that the litigation friend will pay any costs which the child or patient may be ordered to pay in relation to the proceedings subject to any right he may have to be repaid from the assets of the child or patient.

The certificate of suitability must be signed in verification of its contents.

31.2.2   Appointment of litigation friend by court order

An application for a court order appointing a litigation friend may be made by any person who wishes to be the litigation friend or any other party to the litigation. The application must be supported by evidence. The evidence must satisfy the court that the proposed litigation friend:

(a) consents to act;

(b) can fairly and competently conduct proceedings on behalf of the child or patient;

(c) has no interest adverse to that of the child or patient; and

(d) where the child or patient is a claimant, undertakes to pay any costs which the child or patient may be ordered to pay in relation to the proceedings.

This will be important where the defendant is a child and the parent or guardian does not come forward to act. The claimant's solicitor should have attempted to identify a potential litigation friend, but it is open to him simply to apply to the court with no one specific in mind. Usually a representative of some insurance company will be appointed but if nobody comes forward, as the litigation cannot proceed without service of documents, the Official Solicitor may be appointed. Provision must always be made then for payment of his charges.

31.2.3   Change of litigation friend

It is open to a child or patient to change his litigation friend without the court's approval. This might happen, for example, where the original litigation friend moves away from the area and cannot represent the child's interest, or where there is a conflict of interest and the solicitor conducting the case advises that such a change should take place. Notice of change is all that need be given.

By virtue of r. 21.7, the court has the power to change a litigation friend or to prevent a person acting as litigation friend and in either case to appoint a new litigation friend in substitution for an existing one. An application for an order may be made by anybody and must be supported by evidence. The court may not appoint a litigation friend unless satisfied that the person to be appointed complies with the conditions which we have previously discussed. Any application for an order must be served on the present litigation friend or the person purporting to act as the litigation friend and the new litigation friend, unless that is the person applying.

This rule therefore governs the 'hostile' situation where perhaps a relative believes that the present litigation friend is not acting in the child's best interests and wishes to bring the matter before the court so it can decide whether he should be appointed instead. This happens very rarely in practice, but sometimes arises out of marital problems where one parent wishes to replace the other and occasionally where a more distant relative, for example, an aunt or uncle, believes that the child's parent is not acting in the child's best interest.

It should be remembered that the solicitor is in fact the representative of the child and not the litigation friend and it may sometimes be appropriate for the solicitor to initiate action, for example, where the present litigation friend refuses to get in touch or give proper instructions.

31.2.4 Termination of appointment of litigation friend

If a child (who is not also a patient) reaches the age of 18 the litigation friend's appointment ceases automatically. Where a party ceases to be a patient the appointment continues until it is ended by a court order (r. 21.9). The court will need to be satisfied as to the change of status of a patient, whereas the change of status of a child is simply a matter of arithmetic.

In either case, where the need for a litigation friend has ceased, the child or patient must serve a notice on the other parties stating this, giving his own address for service (which may very well continue to be the address of the solicitor who represented before), and stating whether or not he intends to carry on the proceedings.

If he does not do this within 28 days after the day on which the appointment of the litigation friend ceases, the court may on application strike out any claim or defence brought by him.

Once a child becomes 18 he has 28 days to consider whether he proposes to continue the action and from then on will bear the liability for costs himself. If he does nothing about it, the opposing party may apply to strike out his statement of case. The procedure of a child in deciding to continue a claim used to be called 'adopting' the claim, and although that technical term is not used in the rules, it is still a convenient way of describing it. Obviously a child with competent legal representation will have been advised well in advance of the need for this step and will usually be able to take it in time.

If a child 'adopts' a claim as described in the preceding paragraph, the future heading of any documents in the claim should contain the words, e.g., 'James Southworth (formerly a child but now of full age)'.

There is no corresponding requirement for a former patient to so describe himself for obvious reasons.

31.3 Compromise of a claim by or on behalf of child or patient

An adult is able to compromise a claim, whether by agreeing terms, accepting money paid into court or discontinuing the claim by agreement, without the court's approval. Sometimes the court's approval will be needed if the terms are to be embodied into a formal consent order, but even then the court will merely be concerned to scrutinise the order to see that it is properly drafted and within the powers of the court to approve.

However, under CPR, r. 21.10, in claims made by or on behalf of a child or patient or against a child or patient no settlement, compromise, payment, or acceptance of money paid into court is valid without the approval of the court. This rule means that, to take the most common situation, where a personal injury claim is brought on behalf of a child and the parties want to compromise it before trial, unless the defendant ensures that an application to the court is made for the court's approval, the defendant will be unprotected so that the child is not bound by it and may reopen the compromise at any time while he is a child or within three years of attaining the age of 18.

There may be exceptions to this where the amount is very trivial and the defendant's insurers are prepared to trust the child's parents to invest the money wisely for the child and the costs and court fee of bringing a case to court, even for the purpose of getting the court's approval, are disproportionate. A claim for a very minor incident to be settled by a payment of £300 or £400, for example, might possibly be in this category. Even here, however, defendants doing this are taking a risk. Generally speaking, therefore, the parties will apply for the court's approval.

This needs to be done even if no claim has yet started. In that case the application is made by the Part 8 procedure described at **Chapter 32**. If the claim has already started, then application is made by application notice requesting the court to approve the settlement or compromise.

At the hearing of the application the court will need to consider whether it approves the figure at which settlement has been achieved and go on to give directions concerning investment and control of the money ordered to be paid to the child or patient.

31.3.1 The rationale

The rationale for this rule is said to be:

(a) to protect children and patients against any lack of skill or experience in their legal advisers which might lead to settlement for inadequate sums;

(b) to provide a means by which a defendant might obtain a valid discharge from the claim;

(c) to ensure that solicitors acting for children or patients were paid their proper costs and no more so as to prevent overcharging;

(d) to ensure that money recovered on behalf of the child or patient was properly invested.

31.3.2 The application to the court

The information that the court requires is set out in PD 21, para. 6.2. It includes:

(a) whether, and to what extent, the defendant admits liability;

(b) the age and occupation, if any, of the child or patient;

(c) the litigation friend's written approval;

(d) in a personal injury case arising from an accident:

   (i)   the circumstances of the accident;

   (ii) any medical reports;

   (iii) where appropriate, a schedule of any past and future expenses and losses claimed and other relevant information;

   (iv) if considerations of liability are raised, evidence or police reports in criminal proceedings and details of any prosecution brought.

It should be noted that there is no requirement for *evidence* as such in the form of a witness statement, although there is no prohibition on supplying this evidence.

31.3.3 Practical steps

Where the defendant puts forward a satisfactory offer, or when an adequate payment into court is made, the steps that must be taken are first to ensure that the claimant's legal adviser has the necessary evidence on which properly to advise the litigation friend as to the adequacy of the sum offered. Accordingly, medical evidence and evidence relating to loss of earnings or future loss of earnings ought to be brought up to date, and a further counsel's opinion should be obtained unless there is already a relatively recent one as to quantum. It must be borne in mind that the issue is not necessarily what amount of damages would the claimant have obtained at trial if he were wholly successful, but whether the settlement itself is reasonable and is for the benefit of the claimant, having regard to all the circumstances including the risk of litigation, the potential delay, the desire of the parties to settle, the disinclination of the claimant to go to trial, and the difficulties in establishing liability or in resisting a finding of contributory negligence. If, taking all these matters into account, the claimant's legal advisers are minded to recommend compromise and the litigation friend is agreeable, action should be taken to obtain the court's approval.

If a Part 36 payment into court has been made, then although in principle the 'consideration period' is only 21 days, there is little doubt that longer would be allowed for the proper consideration of such a payment into court by those advising a child or patient. In such a situation, therefore, the best method of approach would be for the claimant's solicitor to write in 'without prejudice' terms to the defendant indicating that the offer is being seriously considered, and requesting positive agreement by the defendant to pay necessary costs in the period of delay, e.g., for obtaining further medical reports or counsel's opinion, even though this takes the claimant outside the 21-day period. Thereafter, an application should be issued immediately seeking approval of the compromise.

It is useful to consider the course of a typical hearing, and to take as an example a personal injury case, although the same considerations *mutatis mutandis* would apply to any other kind of claim for a monetary remedy.

31.3.3.1 The hearing

(a) At the hearing no oral evidence as such is called. The master or district judge should first be told whether there is any dispute on liability. If there is none, he need be told no more about the actual facts of the incident causing the injury. If, however, there is some issue on liability, then the nature of the evidence should be indicated by the claimant's solicitor or by both sides. The court should be told what evidence can be adduced and what witnesses are available, and the police report and witness statements, if any, may be produced. If counsel has advised on liability, that opinion should be placed before the master or district judge, so as to enable him to assess the claimant's chances of success in the action and the possible discount which should be given for contributory negligence, or the risks of litigation. There is no doubt that the master or district judge, in the time usually available on such an application, is unlikely to be able to look further into liability than the claimant's solicitors and the circumstances would be unusual where the master or district judge took a strongly different view on liability from them, especially if counsel has also advised. It is usually best that the defendant's solicitors also attend the hearing so that they may know what is said if, e.g., approval is refused or some point as to the drafting of the order arises.

(b) The second matter is the quantum of damages. It is crucial that full evidence be provided about the nature and extent of the claimant's injuries and their likely effect on health, education, enjoyment of amenities, future earning power and risk on the labour market. Medical reports should be comprehensive and substantially up to date. Full computations and, if necessary, documentary evidence of the items forming special damage, should be produced. Usually, a written opinion from counsel explaining, with reasons, why the amount offered should be accepted is supplied.

(c) Usually, the claimant and the litigation friend are required to attend the hearing especially as the master or district judge might wish to see the claimant, for example, to see any facial or other cosmetic blemishes or physical disabilities or to ask questions about continuing symptoms. If the litigation friend does not attend, his written approval of the settlement should be produced. The claimant's solicitor should be able to produce the claimant's birth certificate to prove date of birth and full name. Evidence of any change of name must be to hand. If the master or district judge is then satisfied by the proposed compromise, he will make the order approving settlement. If he is not satisfied he may, if the difference is only a modest one, express his misgivings and ask the parties if a short adjournment would be of any use. If so, he may adjourn briefly, even for 10 or 15 minutes, to allow the parties to talk outside the court. Prospects of concluding the matter may then largely depend, in a personal injury case, upon whether the defendant's solicitors have authority to offer more, or can get in touch with their insurance clients with a view to obtaining further instructions. If nothing can be achieved in a short adjournment, or if the disagreement is serious, the master or district judge may offer a longer adjournment to some future date. If, however, the defence are adamant that the offer cannot be increased, the application to approve the compromise will be dismissed and further case management directions given to take the case to trial.

31.3.4   Further practical points

31.3.4.1   Patients, children and the Court of Protection

The Court of Protection is a part of the court which has a very specialised jurisdiction dealing with aspects of protecting the interests and managing the assets of persons unable to manage their own affairs, in particular, mental patients, persons in 'persistent vegetative state', children with very substantial claims and the like.

If a claim is brought by the litigation friend of a patient under the sanction or direction of the Court of Protection, its approval should be obtained, but this does not absolve the parties from applying to the court where the claim is continuing for approval. In such a case, money recovered should be transferred to the patient's account in the Court of Protection. The decision whether or not to approve the settlement is that of the court where the claim is proceeding, whatever view has been taken by the Court of Protection. If the Court of Protection has not previously been involved, the master or district judge, after approving the terms of the compromise, will order (unless the amount recovered is less than £30,000) that the litigation friend should apply within a stipulated time to the Court of Protection for the appointment of a receiver.

31.3.4.2   Appeal

If the settlement is not approved by the master or district judge, either party (and presumably both, if both are still eager to settle) may appeal to a circuit or High Court judge.

31.3.4.3   The order

If the settlement is approved, then the order directs by, to whom, and in what amounts the money is to be paid, and how the money is to be applied.

31.4   Control of money recovered by a child or patient

Directions must be given by the court, and will usually be for the sum to be paid into the Court Funds Office to be invested and dealt with there. There may be exceptions. It may be appropriate to release a modest sum of money immediately for something which the child wants, especially if this is of some educational value, e.g., a school trip abroad or home computer. If the sum is very modest, it may be appropriate to have the money invested informally out of court, e.g., in the form of a building society deposit account. It is worth indicating here some of the principles involved in the directions that the court will give as to the money:

(a) The basic principle is that the damages should be applied for the purpose for which they were awarded; thus, if damages have been awarded for pain and suffering, injury and future disability but there is as yet no economic loss, neither capital nor income should be used for ordinary maintenance for the child. The fact that a child has recovered damages, say, for a broken limb, does not relieve the parents of their duties to support him, nor any public authority which might have a duty to maintain the child.

(b) If the damages represent the child's loss of support from a deceased parent under the Fatal Accidents Act 1976, then income on capital could properly be applied to ordinary maintenance. However, much would depend upon the position and means of the surviving parent and the global settlement which had been achieved in the action.

(c) In between these possibilities is the middle ground where there may be some element of economic loss which is continuing, e.g., if the child needs special nursing or attendance. As far as possible here, payments may be made out of income.

(d) The same principles apply, *mutatis mutandis*, to a patient.

The fund, if it is not to be applied immediately, should be invested as appropriate by the court, and there is no need here to consider the nature of the court's discretion in relation to this.

It ought to be noted that if the parent or litigation friend wants money from time to time for the welfare, benefit or education of the child, then an application can be made in a relatively informal way. The procedure to some extent differs locally, but usually application by letter will suffice. The applicant will be called for an interview with the district judge to explain more precisely the nature of the requirement for the child (e.g., private medical treatment, school fees, etc.) and the court will give its decision there and then. The court will not of course release the child's money simply to repay the parent for money which any normal parent would have expended for his or her child, e.g., to pay the child's share of a foreign holiday which the family would have taken anyway. The court will always be alert to prevent attempts to 'raid the child's money box'.

31.5 Costs and a child or patient

One of the original supposed justifications for requiring the court to investigate and approve settlements effected on behalf of children and patients was the risk of the solicitors behaving improperly with regard to costs. There are two bases for costs, the standard basis and the indemnity basis (see **Chapter 33**). In negotiations on behalf of a child it is sometimes possible to arrange for the defendants to offer payment of costs on the more generous indemnity basis in addition to their offer for damages. Even if this is not achieved, children's solicitors will usually formally agree to waive any further demand for costs from the child over and above what will be recovered from the defendant on the standard basis.

Rule 48.5 is a particular rule governing the position of costs payable to or by a child or patient. This applies in principle whether those costs are ordered at the end of a trial, or in consequence of a compromise.

Rule 48.5 provides a general rule that:

(a) the court must order a detailed assessment of the costs payable by any party who is a child or patient to his solicitor; and

(b) on an assessment under paragraph (a) the court must also assess any costs payable to that party in the proceedings.

However, PD Costs provides that the court need not order the assessment of costs where:

(a) there is no need to do so to protect the interests of the child or patient;

(b) another party has agreed to pay a specified sum for the costs of the child or patient and the solicitor acting for the child or patient has waived the right to claim further costs;

(c) the court has decided the costs payable to the child or patient by way of summary assessment and the solicitor acting for the child or patient has waived the right to claim further costs;

(d) an insurer or other person is liable to discharge the costs which the child or patient would otherwise be liable to pay to his solicitor and the court is satisfied that the insurer or other person is financially able to discharge those costs.

In other words it will generally be open to a solicitor to agree costs with the defendant on behalf of the child provided he waives any further claim to costs.

In this chapter it has been widely assumed that the child or patient is the *claimant* and that will be the case in the overwhelming majority of instances. In cases where a child or patient is a *defendant* the most likely scenario is a road traffic accident (e.g., a 17 year old motorcyclist) where the status of the defendant is unlikely to be material given that the case will be run and paid for by insurers. In the few cases where a child or patient is a defendant outside this scenario, the rules relating to compromises affecting the child or patient apply so that the court's approval is also required of any settlement made on behalf of the defendant child or patient.

Part 8 procedure: Cases where there is little dispute as to facts

32.1 Introduction

When the new rules were first being drafted, it was hoped to provide a single means of starting every kind of claim. Under the previous rules there had been several different methods and forms of procedure, depending on the nature of the dispute, and it was thought that introducing a single form of proceedings would go a great deal of the way towards simplifying civil procedure. The form of proceedings for all cases was intended to be the claim form procedure which the bulk of this text has been describing. Quite late on, however, in the drafting of the rules the virtues of one particular type of the old proceedings were recognised. This old form of proceedings was called 'originating summons' procedure and it has been restated in a modified form in what is now known as 'Part 8 procedure'.

The Part 8 procedure is for use in claims where either the lack of any factual dispute between the parties, or the nature of the relief or remedy sought would make the standard procedure inappropriate because it could become too long drawn out for the issues involved. Essentially the Part 8 procedure will be used where there is one point which requires the court's determination and does not involve a substantial area of disputed facts. It is quite possible that many claims under the Part 8 procedure will go straight from issue of proceedings to a single hearing within a very short time without the need for any of the other stages of claim form procedure, such as disclosure of documents, choice of expert witnesses, exchange of witness statements and the like. That is not to say that the Part 8 procedure is entirely restricted to very simple matters nor indeed that every case can be progressed to a final hearing in such a short time, but in the majority of cases that will prove possible.

32.2 Types of claim

The procedure in Part 8 may be used instead of the normal procedure where:

(a) a claimant seeks the court's decision on a question which is unlikely to involve a substantial dispute of fact; or

(b) some rule or practice direction requires or permits the use of the Part 8 procedure.

The initial choice therefore is always that of the claimant. There will be cases which are finely balanced as to whether the ordinary claim form or the Part 8 procedure should be used. In essence it will not matter greatly because under CPR, r. 8.1(3), the court may at any stage order that where a claim has been commenced by the Part 8 procedure it should continue as if the Part 8 procedure had not been used. In that case the court may give any directions it considers appropriate, and in particular will allocate the claim to a track. If the court staff think that a Part 8 claim has been issued where it is inappropriate, they will refer the matter to a district judge, who may give directions about the matter immediately without attendance of the parties.

32.3 Contents of the claim form

Where the claimant uses the Part 8 procedure the claim form must state:

(a) that Part 8 applies;

(b) the question which the claimant wants the court to decide or the remedy which the claimant is seeking and the legal basis for the claim for that remedy;

(c) if the claim is being made under some enactment, what that enactment is;

(d) if the claimant is claiming in a representative capacity, what that capacity is; and

(e) if the defendant is sued in a representative capacity, what that capacity is.

The types of claim in particular referred to in PD 8, para. 1.4, which are suitable for this procedure include:

(a) a claim by or against a child or patient which has been settled before the commencement of proceedings and the sole purpose of the claim is to obtain the approval of the court to the settlement;

(b) a claim for provisional damages which has been settled before the commencement of the proceedings and the sole purpose of the claim is to obtain a consent judgment;

(c) certain applications for depositions to be taken from witnesses where there are no current English proceedings;

(d) provided there is unlikely to be a substantial dispute of fact, a claim for a summary order for possession against named or unnamed defendants occupying land or premises without the licence or consent of the person claiming possession (see **26.7**).

Apart from the above instances, another very common use of the Part 8 procedure will be by mortgagees claiming possession against mortgagors for default in payment. Other common instances will be where there is no factual dispute between the parties, but they need the court's determination on a point of law or the matter of construction of some document, for example, where a home-made will has created some ambiguity which it needs a court order to resolve so that the estate can be distributed appropriately.

32.4 The procedure

The claim form N208 is issued at court. Service is undertaken by the same methods as appropriate for the usual Part 7 claim. If the claimant wishes to rely on any evidence, it must be filed in written form when he files the claim form and must be served on the defendant. The defendant must acknowledge service within 14 days, but no defence as such is necessary. Indeed PD 8 provides that an acknowledgement of service could be filed informally such as in a letter. If the defendant believes the Part 8 procedure is inappropriate because there may be a substantial dispute of fact, or for some other reason, he should state his reasons when he files his acknowledgement of service. If he fails to file an acknowledgement of service it is *not* possible for the claimant to obtain a default judgment in this case. The consequences are that although the defendant may attend the hearing of the claim, he may not take part in the hearing unless the court gives permission. If the claimant has filed some evidence and the defendant wishes to rely on written evidence, he must file it in his turn when he files his acknowledgement of service and thereupon the claimant may within a further 14 days serve further written evidence in reply.

32.4.1   Extensions of time

As will be observed, the time limit for a defendant to respond to a claim form accompanied by perhaps substantial written evidence is not very long. In the spirit of the pre-action protocols, although none strictly apply to this case, the parties should have corresponded in advance about the matter so that the defendant had ample warning of what the case was about. If he still has not got time to respond then by PD 8, para. 5.6, the parties may agree in writing to an extension of time but the agreement must be filed by the defendant with the acknowledgement of service and must not extend time by more than 14 days; an agreement to extend time for a claimant to file further evidence in reply must not extend time to more than 28 days after service of the defendant's evidence.

By the end of this stage, the court will give directions either of its own initiative or on the application of either party. The court may convene a directions hearing in a more complicated claim. There is no allocation to track as such. Directions are unlikely to include directions for disclosure of documents or exchange of expert evidence, since that would presuppose a substantial dispute of fact which may make the case unsuitable for the Part 8 procedure. If the district judge concludes that the case is inappropriate for the Part 8 procedure he will allocate to track and give further directions as to its progress. It is unlikely that he would do this without convening a hearing. If the case is indeed one entirely of law or construction of documents, a likely direction will be for the parties to file written arguments, explaining their respective contentions.

32.5   The hearing

If the district judge thinks that matters can proceed satisfactorily to a hearing without any further directions, a hearing date may be fixed. Indeed a hearing date may be fixed at the time of issuing proceedings where there is no dispute such as applications to approve child or patient settlements, or where, even though there may be a dispute, an early hearing date can be fixed because of the simplicity of the claim, such as applications by mortgagees for possession where the mortgagor is in arrears of payment.

If a hearing date is fixed, it is important to note CPR, r. 8.6, which provides:

(a) no written evidence may be relied on at the hearing of the claim unless it has been served in accordance with the rules or the court gives permission; and

(b) the court may require or permit a party to give oral evidence at the hearing and may give directions requiring the attendance for cross-examination of a witness who was given written evidence.

The implication is that all hearings will proceed on the basis of written evidence only, since the court's permission is required for oral evidence. However, since oral evidence is only likely to be material in a case where there is a dispute of fact, when asked to give permission the court will instead find that the claim is not suited to the Part 8 procedure and direct that Part 8 is not to apply.

32.6 Allocation to track

As indicated above, if the Part 8 procedure is followed, there is no allocation to track as such. The claim is treated as allocated to the multi-track, and the court therefore has full case management powers without restriction to give whatever directions it thinks appropriate, including, in compliance with the overriding objective, orders that the case be tried in a way that is appropriate to its complexity or the amount involved.

33

Assessment of costs

We considered earlier one of the most important matters at the outset of any piece of litigation (see **7.1**). This is the need to establish firmly with one's own client the basis on which he will be required to pay for a solicitor's time and expertise. In non-litigation cases that is the end of the matter. The client will expect to pay proper charges and these will not be recoverable from anyone else. In litigation, however, there is the extra element that the loser is usually ordered to pay some part of the winner's costs, which may vary from the whole amount down to a relatively small proportion. It is now appropriate to discuss the nature of and procedure for assessment of costs by the court.

33.1 Solicitor and own client basis

Suppose that a client objects to his own solicitor's bill. This could occur where the party has lost the case and therefore is not to receive any other contribution towards his costs; or even where he has won the case and, after receiving the amount due from the opposing party, the client is dissatisfied with the shortfall between that amount and the amount he has had to pay his own solicitor. In that situation a client is entitled to have his own bill assessed—in other words, to call upon his solicitor to justify to the court every aspect of the charges made in it.

A client wishing to put in motion this procedure must use the alternative claim procedure under Part 8 and obtain an order for costs to be assessed. When that order is made a solicitor must serve a 'breakdown of costs' which is in a prescribed form (Precedent P in the Schedule of Costs Precedents). On receipt of this, the client must indicate what points he wishes to dispute in writing within 14 days. The solicitor must then reply to that within a further 14 days.

The client may be satisfied on receipt of these documents. If not, he may request a detailed assessment hearing by lodging an application in costs form 21 and a hearing will then take place. The assessment of a solicitor's bill to his own client proceeds on the *indemnity basis*.

This basis provides that where the costs judge is left in any doubt about the propriety of some item charged for, or the rate at which it is charged, the benefit of that doubt is to be given to the solicitor. In addition, the court has to bear the following points in mind:

(a) In so far as reasonableness is concerned, it is deemed reasonable to incur expenditure on items which the client has expressly or impliedly approved.

(b) Amounts incurred are reasonable if the client also approved them in advance.

(c) It is, however, unreasonable to incur expenditure on unusual items unless the client was specifically warned in advance that those items might not be recoverable on assessment from the losing party.

The costs judge will delete or reduce items which have been unreasonably claimed by the solicitor and an order will then be made that the client pay the balance to the solicitor.

33.2   Costs between the parties

Here we consider the more important situation of the procedure by which a winner recovers as much as possible of the legal costs from a loser.

33.2.1   The compensatory principle

The English theory of damages in tort and contract is compensatory. It aims to put the aggrieved party in exactly the same position as he would have been but for the tort or breach of contract. Where this is a purely financial matter, as in the collection of a debt, the law can do precisely that. Where something not directly expressible in money terms happens, such as the infliction of personal injuries, then the law ensures the payment of financial compensation. The difficult problem is, however, that of the legal costs incurred by the innocent party in enforcing his or her legal rights. In strict theory the loser should be required to pay the whole of the winning party's legal costs, because otherwise the winning party is not in fact put in precisely the same position in which he would have been but for the tort or breach of contract because he will have had to expend some money of his own to enforce his right. In some jurisdictions it is actually the case that the loser must pay the whole of the winner's legal costs. In other jurisdictions, for example, the United States, there is usually no order for costs between the parties and the lawyer for the winning party will recover his costs only from his client, often by a contingency fee arrangement.

In England and Wales the provision for the loser to pay the winner's costs is something of a compromise between these two extreme positions. However, it is fair to say that because of the way in which the winner's costs payable by the loser are now assessed, it will often be the case that the winner's costs will in fact be recovered in full if the litigation has been conducted in a reasonable and efficient manner.

33.2.2   Conventional and negotiated costs

In litigation there is no right to costs. Costs are always in the discretion of the court, but certain conventions have been established and will usually be followed. The principal convention is that costs 'follow the event', i.e., that the winner is usually entitled to an order that the loser should pay his costs. This will be the case where the matter has been litigated as far as trial. However, if the parties reach a negotiated settlement at an earlier stage it is usual for the party who is putting forward the compromise to agree to pay the other party's costs. Refusal to make this offer usually leads to a counter-refusal to accept the offer of compromise.

Litigation may, of course, be terminated with no requirement for either party to pay costs to his opponent, for example, where a claimant sues a defendant who raises a counterclaim of an approximately equivalent amount and after a certain stage both parties realise that the costs of litigating outweigh the possible advantages. Each might agree to withdraw both claim and counterclaim on the basis that each pays his own costs.

33.3 The court's discretion in ordering costs

By CPR, r. 44.3, the court has a discretion as to:

(a) whether costs are payable by one party to another;

(b) the amount of those costs; and

(c) when they are to be paid.

If the court decides to make an order about costs then the general rule is that the unsuccessful party will be ordered to pay the costs of the successful party, but the court may make a different order (r. 44.3(2)).

In deciding what order, if any, to make about costs the court must, by r. 44.3(4), consider:

(a) the conduct of all the parties;

(b) whether a party has succeeded in part of his case even if he has not been wholly successful; and

(c) any payment into court or admissible offer to settle made by a party which is drawn to the court's attention.

In this context 'the conduct of the parties' is given a very wide meaning by r. 44.3(5). It includes:

(a) conduct before, as well as during, the proceedings and in particular the extent to which the parties followed any relevant pre-action protocol;

(b) whether it was reasonable for a party to raise, pursue or contest a particular allegation or issue;

(c) the manner in which a party has pursued or defended his case or a particular allegation or issue; and

(d) whether a claimant who has succeeded in his claim in whole or in part exaggerated his claim.

When deciding what orders to make the court is given great flexibility by the specific terms of r. 44.3(6). Although in a simple claim the loser will simply be ordered to pay the winner's costs, in more complex cases the court will have to investigate issues in a more detailed way. As a result of this investigation, the court may make orders including that a party must pay:

(a) a proportion of another party's costs;

(b) a stated amount in respect of another party's costs;

(c) costs from or until a certain date only;

(d) costs incurred before proceedings have begun;

(e) costs relating to particular steps taken in the proceedings;

(f) costs relating only to a distinct part of the proceedings; and

(g) interest on costs from or until a certain date, including a date before judgment.

Morever, when it makes an order for costs it may order an amount to be paid on account before the costs are assessed. If it is clear that a substantial case has been concluded entirely in favour of one party, the advocate for that party may submit that the loser should be ordered to pay a substantial figure straightaway and not await the outcome of the lengthy detailed assessment of costs process.

When considering assessment of costs, it is vital to remember that the court will seek to apply the overriding objective to ensure that disputes about costs are resolved as swiftly and economically as possible so that they do not form a vast area of satellite litigation, which was a common occurrence before the CPR.

33.4 Assessment

33.4.1 Introduction

At the end of the case where the loser has been ordered to pay the winner's costs, it will often be the position that the parties will negotiate to try to agree what this figure should be. Very often this is possible (see **33.5**). If, however, the parties cannot agree and the loser thinks that the winner's claim for costs is excessive, there is a further hearing in court where an officer of the court (called a *costs judge*, who in London is a specialist judge who deals only with disputed costs, whereas outside London this is merely one of the functions of a district judge) assesses the bill of the winner and determines how much of it the loser should be required to pay.

33.4.2 Bases of assessment

There are two bases of assessment:

(a) the standard basis; and

(b) the indemnity basis.

33.4.2.1 The standard basis

When costs are to be assessed on the standard basis by r. 44.4(2) of the CPR the court will:

(a) only allow costs which are proportionate to the matters in issue; and

(b) resolve any doubts it may have about whether costs were reasonably incurred or reasonable and proportionate in amount in favour of the paying party.

The reference to 'proportionate to the matters in issue' should not be understood as such a crude test as to make the costs relate directly to a percentage of the amount in issue. The amount involved in the claim is only one of a number of features, and even in smaller cases solicitors are not required to work at uneconomic rates. It does not follow that in small cases legal costs may not equal or exceed the amount about which the case was brought. In particular, the court should be wary of using the length of the eventual trial as a guide to what was proper to prepare for it. Careful preparation often reduces the time taken at trial.

The court will thus have to determine whether the sums claimed are for reasonable items (i.e., whether it is proper to charge for those items at all) and whether the amounts claimed for each item are reasonable.

(a) *What kind of items are likely to be attacked?* It is open to the paying party (the loser) to challenge each and every item. One item to which there is commonly an objection is the amount of time spent interviewing and advising the claimant. It is a well-known fact that claimants vary greatly in their degree of patience. Suppose that a claimant in a case called into his solicitor's office for a half-hour chat about the case every week over some months or years, even though nothing had happened on the case in the meantime. The solicitor naturally has to charge that amount of time to someone, and he will charge it at first to his own client. However, is it reasonable to require the loser to pay this sum? If the district judge determines that the number of hours spent in attendance upon the claimant is excessive and serves no real purpose in the case, he is likely to disallow any such hours charged for. The outcome, of course, will be that any items disallowed as against the paying party (the loser) will have to be charged by the solicitor to his own client (the winner). Thus a solicitor must always remind a client that he may himself have to pay for any excessive time which has been spent to little purpose.

Another item often attacked is the amount of fees paid to counsel for advising throughout the case. Solicitors who are recently qualified (and perhaps do not have a great deal of assistance or supervision in the office) often seek counsel's advice as a case proceeds about matters on which a more experienced solicitor would not need to seek assistance. Thus at various stages counsel may be asked to advise about procedural options, tactics, quantum of damages, and so on. The loser may contend on assessment that a competent solicitor would not have needed to take counsel's advice so often, or at all. If the costs judge agrees, those items will be struck off the bill.

One further point to be considered is the *indemnity principle* (which should not be confused with the *indemnity basis of costs*). This is the rule that a winner in litigation can recover no more from an opponent than he would have been liable to pay his own solicitor. This difficult area has already been considered in **Chapter 7**. However, when attacking a bill for costs, one must be aware that a great deal of litigation nowadays is funded by insurance companies. This may either be by general legal expenses insurance or, in personal injury cases, by the defendant's insurance policy, whether road traffic or employer's liability. Most of the big insurance companies have struck particular arrangements with the solicitors on their panel by which the solicitors are only entitled to charge at quite modest hourly rates, (nothing like their usual commercial rates to a private client). Rates as low as £65 per hour are not unknown. Accordingly, one will often require the court to inspect the terms of any retainer arrangement between an insurance-funded party's solicitor and the insurer concerned.

(b) *The reasonableness of the amount—hourly charging rates.* Local factors are very important here. Costs judges are well aware what are proper hourly charging rates for certain kinds of work in the locality, and rates may vary as between, say, London and the north of the country. So, if in routine litigation in the area in question solicitors are being permitted to charge, say, £120 per hour and the present case is a routine one, if the solicitor is claiming £150 per hour his bill will be disallowed or 'assessed down' by a corresponding amount. Thus, if he had claimed that he had spent 20 hours on the client's case in respect of which he was claiming £150 per hour, i.e., £3,000, the costs judge would reduce this claim to the going rate of £120 per hour, i.e., £2,400.

(c) *Application of the standard basis.* The standard basis of assessment is applied in the routine situation where the loser is required to pay the winner in litigation, whether the overall costs at the end of the case or, for example, on assessment of costs for any interim stage where a costs order has been obtained. It is thus the basis applied to a summary assessment of costs as well as a detailed assessment.

If a routine case has been efficiently conducted then it may be that the standard basis will enable the successful party to recover almost all of his costs from the loser, so long as the hourly rate to be charged is one which the local costs judge is willing to allow on assessment, and the solicitor can establish that everything he did in the conduct of the case was reasonable and proportionate. In such a case a successful claimant will receive his whole damages untouched by any reduction by way of payment of his own solicitor's charges.

33.4.2.2 The indemnity basis

The indemnity basis, as mentioned above at **33.1**, is a more generous basis and provides that where any doubts about charging some item arise in the case, the benefit of the doubt is to be given not to the paying party as in assessment on the standard basis, but to the party who is to receive the amount. This basis is only likely to be awarded where the loser's conduct has in some way been disapproved of by the court. In negotiations between parties for settlement, however, it may be possible sometimes to insist on payment of costs on this basis. It is often thought particularly appropriate when settling a claim for defamation, and also when acting for a child claimant. On an assessment on the indemnity basis there is no test of proportionality.

33.4.2.3 Summary

Those are the two bases of assessment between the parties. In many cases they will amount to precisely the same. The difference between them only really bites where the costs judge has a doubt about an individual item. If he is left in doubt as to the propriety of some part of a bill then, in the case of the standard basis he exercises the benefit of that doubt in favour of the loser, i.e., he strikes the item off the bill; in assessment on the indemnity basis he exercises the benefit of the doubt in favour of the winner, i.e., he allows the item charged for.

33.5 Costs: Assessment and agreement

(1) At the end of an interim hearing the court will usually go on to assess the costs summarily (see **33.6**).

(2) At the end of a trial on the fast track the court will also go on to assess the costs summarily unless there is some good reason not to do so.

33.5.1 Assessment of costs

(1) The process of summary assessment is briefly described at the end of Chapter 21 and at **33.6**. Even though quite substantial amounts may be involved, it is something of a 'rough and ready' procedure where the court will apply its own ideas of what are reasonable amounts of time to be expended at certain stages of an action and what are fair charging rates before coming to a conclusion. Often the process of summary assessment takes half an hour or less even if the bill of costs being assessed is £10,000 or more. Many consider this somewhat of a paradox given that the court may very well have taken a whole court day over a trial itself, involving a much smaller sum.

(2) At the end of a *multi-track trial* (or of a fast track trial if the losing party is able to convince the court that summary assessment would not do justice) there will be an order for detailed assessment. The procedure for this is described at **33.7** below.

Usually where there is a detailed assessment there will be a delay of some months before the hearing at which an officer of the court (in London called a 'costs judge', who is a specialist judge who deals only disputed costs, but outside London an ordinary district judge) assesses the bill of the winner and determines how much of it the loser should be required to pay. Before this hearing is reached the parties will naturally try to negotiate an agreed figure to save the delay and expense of this further hearing.

33.5.2 Agreeing costs

At the end of the litigation it is common practice for the loser to offer to agree costs. In such a case the winner's solicitor will prepare a list of the items which he is claiming and the rates at which he wishes to charge, and give some overall indication of the hours spent on the case, in letter form. There will then inevitably be some negotiation, whether by post, telephone or face to face. In the majority of cases a satisfactory agreement is achieved.

The reasons for agreeing costs are as follows:

(a) The process of assessment is lengthy and time consuming and one may well wait some months for a hearing.

(b) There is a court fee on assessment of costs to be paid by the losing party, which can be avoided by agreeing costs.

(c) There is the psychological factor that after lengthy litigation, when the judge pronounces final judgment (subject to any decision to appeal), both sides' solicitors are usually glad to treat the matter as over and turn their minds to the rest of their case load. To prolong a matter by continuing to argue about costs and to wait for what might be a lengthy assessment (involving perhaps a whole day in the case of a substantial bill) is unwelcome. The solicitor will have to retain the file as current and remember in detail its contents so as to be able to justify the work done at the assessment, and this is unwelcome in cases which have been for all other purposes laid to rest.

(d) Finality is also in both clients' interests. A winning client will not know his own net liability for costs until the amount which can be recovered from his opponent is ascertained. A losing client will be anxious to know his total liability for damages and costs to his opponent and costs to his solicitor (including those for dealing with the assessment process which may themselves be substantial).

Nevertheless, if agreement is not possible there will have to be an assessment hearing.

33.6   Interim hearings and the effect of the CPR

In principle, even quite weighty litigation might involve no interim hearings and matters might proceed straight from the directions given on allocation to trial. Even if the allocation directions do not deal with absolutely everything that needs to be considered, in carrying out the duty of cooperation imposed on the parties, it may be that they can supplement any gaps in the directions by agreement between themselves.

If there are interim hearings of any kind, they are likely to be one of two types.

(a) Hearings which the court has directed of its own initiative. The court may do this on allocation because even though both parties may have completed the allocation questionnaires thoroughly, it is not clear what directions ought to be given, bearing in mind how early the allocation process takes place. If it calls both parties before it to discuss the issues and give further directions, then the court will usually order 'costs in the case' so that the eventual winner receives the costs of that hearing from the loser. The same applies at case management conferences.

(b) Alternatively, the need for a hearing may reflect the failure of one party to have complied with a procedural step. This may be fixed of the court's own initiative, for example, where one party does not return an allocation questionnaire, or returns one inadequately completed, so an allocation hearing is needed; or it may be that a party does not fulfil a direction already given so that the opposing party needs to bring matters before the court to ensure that the timetable for trial does not slip. This might happen where the disclosure of documents offered is manifestly inadequate, leading to the need for the innocent party to apply for specific disclosure of certain documents.

At the outcome of these kind of hearings there will usually be a summary assessment of costs.

We have briefly discussed summary assessment of costs at the end of **Chapter 21** and the costs summary form is illustrated there. The matter is governed by a practice direction which applies to all short interim hearings including summary judgment applications. The basic procedure is as follows:

(a) At the conclusion of the hearing of every interim application the court should consider whether or not to assess summarily the amount of the costs of the application to be recoverable by one party from another.

(b) The general rule is that whenever a 'costs in any event' order is made (i.e., one reflecting fault by the losing party) the court should make a summary assessment of costs unless there is good reason not to do so (e.g., that there are substantial grounds for disputing the amounts claimed as costs so that justice dictates that they cannot be dealt with summarily).

(c) Where costs are assessed summarily, the court may (though this is unusual) make an order for payment by some specified date or by instalments. If no such order is made, assessed costs are payable within 14 days of the date of the order.

(d) A summary assessment order cannot usually be made where the paying or receiving party is a child or patient, or where the receiving party has public funding, although it can make such an order where the *paying party* has public funding. (However, see **7.5.7.1**)

(e) In order to facilitate the above, no later than 24 hours prior to the commencement of the hearing, any party who intends to seek a 'costs in any event' order must supply every other party and file at court a brief summary statement of the amount of costs he will seek to recover. That must show the amount and nature of any disbursements, including counsel's fees and the amount of the solicitor's profit costs, together with a statement of the rate and grade of fee earner and hourly rate charged. It is illustrated at the end of **Chapter 21**.

(f) If a party fails without reasonable excuse to serve and file the costs summary form, in principle the court will presume that no application for costs was intended. If at the conclusion of such proceedings nothing is said in the order about costs, that will be deemed to amount to an order for no costs of the application. In other words neither party will recover their costs of attending on that hearing and preparing for it.

Summary assessment of costs will be the norm in 'hostile' applications where some party is at fault. Those costs will be ordered to be paid 14 days after the hearing and those items of work will now be taken out of account in any dispute about the parties as to the rest of the cost of running the case.

33.7 Detailed assessment of costs

33.7.1 The basic procedure

Detailed assessment proceedings must be commenced within three months of the judgment, order, award or other determination giving rise to the right to costs (CPR, r. 47.7). That period may be extended or shortened by agreement of the parties. The process is begun by serving on the paying party a notice of commencement (form N252) together with a copy of the bill of costs in the approved form. The drafting of bills of costs is very specialist work and is done by *costs draftsmen* who are a sub-profession of the legal profession. Larger firms have a costs draftsman in house who prepares all their bills. Smaller firms go to freelance draftsmen, who work alone or in partnership and provide this service on a fixed fee, hourly rate or sometimes a commission basis, that is, a percentage of the bill as prepared, or as eventually assessed.

In any event, the form of bill and notice of commencement should be served, together with copies of counsel's fee notes, expert's fee invoices and written evidence of any disbursement exceeding £250.

The bill sets out items of costs claimed under various headings, including:

(a) attendances at court and on counsel;

(b) attendances on and communications with the client;

(c) attendances on and communications with the witnesses and expert witnesses;

(d) attendances to inspect any property or place;

(e) searches and enquiries;

(f) attendances on and communications with other persons;

(g) communications with the court and with counsel;

(h) work done in connection with arithmetical calculations of compensation and interest;

(i) work done on documents including preparation and consideration of documents;

(j) other work done incidental to the proceedings not already covered above.

The bill must be drafted in a user-friendly, consecutively numbered format and organised into a number of columns.

Various conventions apply about rates of charging, discussion of which is beyond the scope of this text. The most important of these is that the working hour is split into ten units of six minutes each and for routine letters and telephone calls the standard allowance is six minutes.

33.7.2 Points of dispute

When the party who has to pay the bill is served with the bill and notice of commencement, he must within 21 days serve *points of dispute* on the other party. These should be short and concise and should:

(a) identify each item in the bill which is disputed;

(b) state concisely the nature and grounds of the dispute;

(c) where practicable suggest a figure to be allowed for each item for which a reduction is sought; and

(d) be signed by the solicitor for the party serving them.

33.7.3 Default costs certificate

If the party who has to pay the bill fails to serve points of dispute within the permitted time, the receiving party can, on filing a request (form N254), obtain a 'default costs certificate' (r. 47.9(4)) which means that all the costs in the bill are allowed. The certificate includes an order to pay the costs. A default costs certificate can be set aside by the court if there is good reason. Twenty one days allows limited time to respond to what may be a very lengthy and detailed bill which requires a solicitor to consider his own file and take detailed instructions from a client, so some latitude may be allowed. The other party can, in any event, consent to extend this time by consent.

33.7.4 Reply

The party who has delivered the bill has the right to serve a written *reply* to any points of dispute answering the contentions made in them. That should be done within 21 days of service of the points of dispute. There is no obligation to do so and failure to do so does not amount to acceptance of any of the points of dispute.

33.7.5 The assessment hearing

The party whose bill it is must file a request for an assessment hearing within three months of the expiry of the period for commencing the detailed assessment (i.e., six months from the order for costs itself). There will then be a hearing at which the costs judge will hear argument on the points of dispute. This will involve going through the bill item by item, listening to the arguments, with the costs judge making each decision in turn and allowing or disallowing the item, or reducing it to the figure he considers reasonable. At the end of the assessment hearing usually the receiving party will be entitled to his costs of the assessment proceedings which will be added to the bill and assessed there and then. However, the court can make some other order having regard to all the circumstances, including:

(a) the conduct of the parties;

(b) the amount if any by which the bill of costs is reduced; and

(c) whether it was reasonable for particular items to appear in the bill or for particular objections to have been taken.

If neither the receiving party nor the paying party is funded by the Community Legal Service, the paying party may make an offer expressed to be 'without prejudice save as to costs of the detailed assessment proceedings' (i.e., a kind of Part 36 offer) which is kept secret from the costs judge. If at the end of the assessment proceedings the costs judge has reduced the bill below the amount of the offer, then he will take the offer into account and may order the party whose bill it was to pay all the costs of the assessment proceedings.

33.7.6 Failure to abide by time limits

If the party whose bill is due to be assessed fails to commence assessment proceedings or to request an assessment hearing in time, the paying party may apply in writing (by virtue of r. 47.8) for an order requiring the other party to take the appropriate action within such time as the court may specify. The court may make any order it thinks fit, but will usually require the party who has obtained the order for costs to commence the proceedings within a certain brief time or run the risk of having the bill disallowed entirely.

33.7.7 Final costs certificate

Within 14 days of the detailed assessment hearing, the party whose bill it was completes the bill, showing all the amounts eventually allowed and correctly computing the total with court fees and VAT and returns it to the court. The court prepares a 'final costs certificate' which demonstrates the total amount payable by the losing party.

33.8 A special case—fixed recoverable costs in road traffic claims where the claims are settled before proceedings are issued

As noted elsewhere in this text, where pre-action negotiations lead to a potential claim being settled without the issue of proceedings, it is still usual for the person who would have been defendant to agree to meet the claimant's reasonable costs of the early work in investigating the claim, putting it forward, collecting evidence and the eventually successful negotiations. If the parties cannot agree what the amount of the costs will be, even though they have agreed every other element of the compromise, there is a particular procedure whereby the claimant can apply to the court under

CPR 44.12A for the court to make an order for costs and to go on to assess those costs. The assessment then proceeds as a detailed assessment in the ordinary way.

Following successful negotiations between bodies representing solicitors who commonly act for injured claimants, and solicitors who act for insurance companies, a particular rule has been drafted which provides for a form of fixed costs in road traffic accidents worth less than £10,000 which are settled before the issue of proceedings. This is by virtue of CPR 45.7–12.

It provides that to avoid any of the time spent in arguing about the amount of costs, a fixed amount is recoverable by the claimant's solicitors.

That amount is the total of:

(a) £800.00 plus

(b) a sum equivalent to 20 per cent of the damages actually agreed up to £5,000 and plus

(c) a further sum equivalent to 15 per cent of the damages agreed between £5,000 and £10,000.

In addition, VAT is payable as are the costs of reasonable disbursements such as medical reports, medical records, a police report, an engineer's report, and the cost of a search of the DVLA. There is also provision where appropriate for a success fee to be claimed and for an appropriate after-the-event insurance fee.

There are other more detailed provisions which provide in addition for fees for counsel's advice, and the court fee on issue for those cases which would have settled before issue, but for the fact that the claimant is a child or mental patient (it will be remembered that one cannot settle such claims without the court's approval and thus proceedings for that at least are necessary); in addition where the claimant lives or works in certain areas and instructs a firm of solicitors who practise in that area, the recoverable costs may be increased by up to 12.5 per cent (this is to reflect claimants who live in high cost legal areas, such as inner London and who reasonably instruct local solicitors).

Finally, there is a saving provision in CPR 45.12 that the court will still entertain a claim for an amount of costs greater than the fixed recoverable costs if it considers that there are exceptional circumstances, which make it appropriate to do so.

This is a useful scheme, albeit one of limited application. It applies only to claims in respect of road traffic accidents which occurred after 6 October 2003 and resulted in a total claim of less than £10,000. Cases that are larger than that have no restriction on the costs that the court will award where appropriate, on detailed assessment. At the time of writing there is a proposal to extend this to simple workplace accidents, and this may come about in late 2006.

It should perhaps finally be noted as mentioned elsewhere in the text that originally the Rules Committee who drafted the rules were keen to see whether fast track costs as a whole could be capped at a particular sum, and one proposal was that such a sum should be defined by some reference to the amount recovered. As noted elsewhere in this text, that was thought unfair and unworkable because it is certainly true that it can sometimes be the case that one can have more difficult issues in litigation over, say, £6,000 than one can have for a claim for ten times that sum and therefore, it may sometimes be unfair to restrict costs to a figure which in some way is fixed by reference to the amount actually in question. This remains a difficult issue on which discussion and consultation continues because it is also the case that many judges find it unpalatable that after a case which has, say, run for only a year and resulted in the claimant who has suffered a modest whiplash injury recovering, say, £2,500, that the costs put forward as associated with the claim may be twice or three times that figure on each side. For the time being, therefore, although there is no present proposal to cap recoverable costs in claims that either settle some time after issue or either go all the way to trial, consultation is continuing, partly based on the model of agreement achieved in respect of the limited class of costs referred to above, with a view to attempting to fix costs generally in fast track cases. Any agreement or proposal is certainly some years away.

33.9 Personal liability of legal representatives for costs

By virtue of the Supreme Court Act 1981, s. 51:

> (6) In any proceedings. . . the court may disallow, or (as the case may be) order the legal or other representative concerned to meet, the whole of any wasted costs or such part of them as may be determined. . . .
>
> (7) . . . 'wasted costs' means any costs incurred by a party—
>
> > (a) as a result of any improper, unreasonable or negligent act or omission on the part of any legal or other representative or any employee of such a representative; or
> >
> > (b) which, in the light of any such act or omission occurring after they were incurred, the court considers it is unreasonable to expect that party to pay.

The procedure to bring these provisions into effect is contained in CPR, r. 48.7. The provisions mean that the court may order that where any costs are 'wasted', they may either be disallowed on assessment, i.e., the solicitor will have to bear them himself or, if the legal costs of one party have been increased by the improper act or omission of his opponent's lawyer, the legal representative of that opponent may be ordered to pay the first party's costs.

Under the predecessor to the present rule it was usually considered that for this draconian power to be used against the lawyer personally, conduct of an oppressive or improper nature was required. It is clear that now all that is required is simple negligence, and thus a solicitor who is merely sloppy or slow in the conduct of the case, or who misses some point by oversight may be called upon to pay the opponent's costs. Case law shows that the courts have not been slow to make this order against solicitors, and even (in an appropriate case) against a barrister where that barrister has advised on or persisted with some course of conduct in a case which is clearly improper. See, in particular, *R* v *Secretary of State for the Home Department, ex parte Abbassi* (1992) *The Times*, 6 April 1992 and, more recently, *Medcalf* v *Mardell*, LTL, 24 November 2000, CA.

Where a party wishes to claim a 'wasted costs order' from his opponent's solicitor or barrister, an application for this can be made at the end of the trial. Alternatively, an application can be made in the course of the assessment of costs. The procedure requires the issue of a separate application, giving the opposing solicitor adequate notice of the case to be met and indicating what the acts or omissions are on which the party applying proposes to rely.

The increased powers available since 1991 for the court to order wasted costs against an opponent's solicitor or counsel personally were initially taken up with enthusiasm, one might also say with glee, by the legal profession. In many instances such orders were very well merited and a useful reminder to solicitors and counsel that slow or slipshod work could be directly penalised against them irrespective of the outcome of the litigation between the clients. However, in *Ridehalgh* v *Horsefield* [1994] Ch 205, the Court of Appeal held that matters were on the verge of going too far and that the whole field of wasted costs was about to become what it described as 'a satellite form of proceedings'. The Court of Appeal laid down guidelines for making wasted costs orders. The court said that it could not be assumed in every case which was litigated without much prospect of success, or even where an interim stage was prosecuted without much prospect of success, that this was the fault of the lawyers for the litigant, who in most cases would be acting properly on their client's instructions. The threat of wasted costs orders should not deprive the unpopular or unmeritorious litigant of being legally represented. Moreover the benevolent purpose of public funding might be subverted by an excessive risk of wasted costs orders. Lawyers for publicly funded parties felt themselves to be specially at risk from wasted costs orders given that costs orders against their clients directly are unlikely to be enforceable.

It is incumbent on a court which is minded to make a wasted costs order against a solicitor or counsel to give him or her the opportunity on notice to show cause why such an order should not be made and to exercise any doubt in favour of the solicitor or counsel concerned.

33.10　Fixed costs

It will be recalled that a claimant is usually allowed to claim only fixed costs if the case terminates in early judgment or payment (see **Chapter 26**). Thus:

(a) The fixed costs endorsement must be completed on the claim form which claims a specified amount. If the defendant then pays the amount claimed together with interest if claimed and the amount allowed for fixed costs directly to the claimant within 14 days of service, those are the only costs which the claimant may claim against the defendant. In such a case the claimant will inevitably have to bear a further element of solicitor and client costs.

(b) If the claimant obtains judgment in default of acknowledgement of service, or of defence, again there is a specified allowance for fixed costs and these are all that the claimant will normally be able to obtain.

(c) In summary judgment applications there is a provision for fixed costs to be allowed where the claim is for a specified amount such as a debt. Nonetheless even in that case the court does have a discretion to award assessed costs. Much will depend upon how the actual hearing went. If the defendant was a litigant in person who turned up merely to put some inadequate argument which was easily disposed of, then fixed costs would probably be all that was allowed. If, however, a defendant was legally represented and had served numerous pages of evidence attempting to justify why summary judgment should not be given, there is no doubt that assessed costs would be awarded. The court would inevitably go on to assess the costs summarily there and then.

(d) For some kinds of work done at various other stages of an action there is provision in the rules for an amount for fixed costs only. This does not apply to most interim applications in a normal action but does apply to much of what is done after judgment, e.g., as to the costs allowable where application is made to enforce a judgment by garnishee, a charging order and so on.

(e) Where there is no specific provision in the rules for fixed costs the assumption is that assessed costs may be ordered, and this is always the case in a claim for unspecified damages even where the case ends early, e.g., by judgment in default of defence. This is because in such a case there will inevitably need to be a hearing to assess damages, even though the case is brought to an early end on liability.

(f) In fast track trials there are specific amounts of fixed costs for the advocate's fee for conducting the trial (see **14.6**).

(g) Only fixed costs will be allowed in cases on the small claims track unless the court finds that there has been unreasonable conduct. See **17.8**.

The amount of fixed costs to be allowed appears in a table in CPR, Part 45.

33.11 Appeals

There are limited rights of appeal in respect of costs orders. A party wishing to appeal must apply for permission to do so. In deciding whether to give permission to appeal the court will take into account whether:

(a) the ground of appeal has a reasonable prospect of success; and

(b) the costs of the appeal are likely to be disproportionate.

If permission has been granted there will then be an appeal held before a judge of the appropriate level, i.e., a Circuit Judge or High Court Judge.

Enforcement of judgments

34.1 Introduction

The Civil Procedure Rules unified High Court and county court procedure and imposed an entirely new procedural code on civil proceedings in England and Wales. Because of time constraints, it was not possible for the new rules to deal with every single aspect of civil procedure. The most important area where some of the previous rules continue to apply is enforcement of judgments. Some of the previous rules as to enforcement of judgments in the High Court and county court are preserved in CPR, schs 1 and 2 respectively. Some minor changes of terminology and a little rewriting into 'plain English' have taken place, but otherwise the rules there relating to execution of judgments by seizure and sale of goods are substantially as they have been for some decades. This leads to the awkward situation that whereas some methods of enforcement of judgments have been rewritten and incorporated into the CPR, as we shall describe shortly, those to do with *execution* (that is, seizure and sale of goods) are still awaiting revision. The reason why comprehensive new rules dealing with every method of enforcement were not originally promulgated in the CPR was partly because of the vast amount of rewriting that would have been necessary, but also because the whole procedure for enforcement of judgments has been under review. A number of working parties have been formed and consultation documents published. This is because, essentially, enforcement of civil judgments is more than a matter of civil procedure because it poses a jurisprudential, and even a moral, problem which involves considering how competing interests may be resolved, including the following aspects:

(a) It may cause a system of civil justice to be brought into contempt if a successful party has obtained a judgment which proves impossible to enforce (for example, where the judgment debtor is known to have assets but is sufficiently adept in concealing them or voluntarily alienating them by putting them in trust or giving them temporarily to a relative).

(b) To what extent should someone who has incurred a civil judgment devote part of his earning resources and life to satisfying that judgment in priority to other needs, for example, the legitimate needs of his family to be adequately supported and for him to be adequately housed?

(c) What proportion of the court's time and resources should be given over to ensuring that its judgments are enforced or should some procedure be adopted which depends on the initiative of individual judgment creditors?

(d) Are persons who obtain judgments in different categories of priority? For example, should more sympathetic consideration be given to an individual who has loaned a sum to another person in time of need which that other person now cynically refuses to repay, rather than, say, to finance companies who have loaned money at punitive interest rates in the full knowledge that the rates reflect a degree of commercial risk?

The interrelation of these problems together with a somewhat ramshackle collection of separate and unrelated methods for enforcing judgments, which themselves stand aside from bankruptcy procedures (which form a quite separate code and set of procedures for pursuing insolvent persons), have all caused serious difficulties. It may still be some while before enforcement of judgments is properly and fully brought within the CPR.

As with other aspects of procedure, the court will have regard to the overriding objective and case management powers under the CPR. In the main, enforcement of judgment procedures go along certain clearly defined tracks and are unlikely to lead to a number of hearings or the need for collection and filing of evidence.

In the light of that we go on to consider enforcement of judgments.

34.2 Practical considerations

34.2.1 Introduction

Civil judgments are not enforced automatically by either High Court or county court. This is the case whether the judgment is for payment of a sum of money or for an injunction. Even though in the latter case breach of the injunction is a contempt of court, it is still up to the affected party to instigate proceedings for committal for contempt. In the case of money judgments, failure to pay, or even deliberate refusal to pay, is not usually a civil contempt. Until the successful party (the *judgment creditor*) instigates one or other of the relevant court procedures to enforce the judgment against the losing party (the *judgment debtor*) the court will take no action.

In the light of the above it is vital to discuss with a claimant suing for a sum of money the possible problems at the outset, and to ensure that he appreciates that even success in obtaining a judgment does not necessarily mean that the money will be paid in full and promptly. Early enquiries about the financial status of a potential defendant are often essential to ensure that good money is not thrown after bad in pursuing hopeless debts.

In personal injury cases, and some other cases, the defendant in the main has the advantage of being insured (or having his judgment paid by the MIB). Provided the proper measures have been taken at the outset of the litigation, by way of giving notice either under s. 152 of the Road Traffic Act 1988 or by writing the necessary letters to the MIB, there is therefore unlikely to be any problem in enforcing the judgment. It must be borne in mind, however, that there are some kinds of personal injury actions where there may be no insurance, such as where a pedestrian or a cyclist causes a road accident, or where a claimant is suing under the Occupiers' Liability Acts.

34.2.2 Interest on judgments

In the High Court judgments carry interest at 8 per cent per annum. Alternatively, if the claim was founded on contract and the contract itself provides for interest to run after judgment, interest will run at the contractual rate whether higher or lower than 8 per cent.

In the county court the matter is governed by the County Courts (Interest on Judgment Debts) Order 1991 (SI 1991/1184), which provides:

(a) Interest will not run on judgments of less than £5,000.

(b) Interest will run at 8 per cent per annum on judgments of more than £5,000, but it is important to note:

(i)   where interest is claimed two copies of a certificate must be lodged with any request or application for enforcement, giving details of the amount of interest claimed and the sum on which it is claimed, the dates from and to which interest has accrued, and the rate of interest which has been applied;

(ii) where interest is claimed it ceases to run once enforcement proceedings have been commenced, except where those proceedings fail to produce any payment from the debtor in which case interest continues to accrue as if the proceedings have never been taken. This applies to all methods of enforcement and oral examination with the exception of proceedings under the Charging Orders Act 1979.

The unavailability of interest on judgments in the county court for sums of under £5,000 can obviously cause injustice and great annoyance to clients. If a judgment for £4,000 had been obtained in the High Court, interest would run at about £320 per annum. In the county court the same debt depreciates year by year without any provision for interest to compensate. For this reason it is important to remember that county court debts can be registered in the High Court and enforced there as long as they are for a sum of more than £600. Once registered in the High Court interest runs as if they were High Court judgments, and therefore a prudent judgment creditor's solicitor will immediately take this step.

Where it is intended to enforce a judgment by execution against goods, one may apply to transfer the judgment to the High Court by a simple administrative procedure involving production of a certificate of judgment. There is now a combined form which provides an application for the certificate of transfer and request for writ of execution against goods (see **34.3.1**). Where, however, it is intended to enforce the judgment by some other method such as a third party debt order, one needs to apply to a district judge on a formal application on notice to the judgment debtor. It would seem, however, that, given the bona fide reason for transfer, namely, the availability of interest on the judgment, there is no reason why a district judge should not grant the application in the usual case.

Above £5,000, interest runs at 8 per cent but subject to the major disadvantage that interest does not run for any period during which enforcement proceedings are being undertaken so long as any money is produced. Consequently, if one takes proceedings for an order to attend court to provide information under CPR, Part 71, followed by attachment of earnings, interest will not run for the total period provided some money is obtained. This is an enormous drawback capable of creating considerable injustice. The only exception is the case of charging orders where interest will continue to run.

34.2.3   Obtaining information about the judgment debtor's means

As indicated in **34.2.1**, it is always preferable to spend some time and trouble at the outset of litigation to ensure that a client appreciates that judgments are not automatically enforced, that you cannot get blood out of a stone, and that there is no realistic possibility of imprisoning a person for a civil debt. If the client is in business, for example, a builders' merchant supplying small builders, this is an opportunity to give him general commercial advice about his business procedures, e.g., to ensure that when extending credit to his customers he obtains proper references, full details of the assets and location of the assets of his customers, procures personal guarantees from the directors in the case of customers which are limited companies, and so on. Here, however, we consider the situation where either the litigation has become so long and drawn out that the information originally obtained is no longer valid, or perhaps where the client for reasons of speed instructed you to press on with the litigation immediately without making initial enquiries in the belief that the judgment debtor was a person of some means. There are essentially two different routes by which to proceed:

(a) non-judicial enquiries; and

(b) an order to attend court to provide information (CPR, Part 71).

34.2.3.1   Non-judicial enquiries

It is always open to a person to employ an enquiry agent to obtain a status report on an opponent or a potential opponent in litigation. The court is not involved and this can as easily be done before litigation as after judgment. In such cases private detectives have various means of finding information. Often an enquiry agent will undertake a certain amount of surveillance on an individual, for example, by following him to his place of work and then making enquiries there; trying to trace the whereabouts of his bank account and seeking to make enquiries there; seeing whether he owns his own home and, if so, attempting to procure an approximate valuation of it, etc. In the case of run of the mill debts, enquiry agents are unlikely to have recourse to the more elaborate options often employed in commercial investigations (e.g., clearing out the contents of a person's dustbin in the hope of finding useful material such as bank statements).

As well as this, in the case of limited companies, company searches may be undertaken which sometimes give some indication of the value of a company and the whereabouts of its assets. On the other hand, the kind of limited company that gets into trouble with bad debts is often the kind which, despite increased penalties, fails to keep its documentation at the Companies Registry up to date, so this avenue may be of only limited use. In addition it will be prudent to check the Register of Judgments, Orders and Fines, which is open to public inspection, to see if the intended opponent already has other judgments against him or her.

34.2.3.2   Orders to attend court to provide information (CPR, Part 71)

This form of order provides for a judgment debtor to attend court to be questioned about his means and assets. It is a time-consuming and often frustrating procedure, which should most certainly not be embarked upon in a case where one already has some idea about likely assets so as already to commend one or other method of enforcement. It will take, at the very least, some hours of a solicitor's time; and for reasons which will be explained below, will often involve travel to some distant court, for which only modest amounts will be allowed for costs, leaving one's client with a substantial shortfall of the actual cost involved in implementing this procedure.

The procedure for obtaining such an order is as follows. A judgment creditor's solicitor prepares an application which states the name and address of the judgment debtor, identifies the judgment which it is sought to enforce, and states the amount presently owing under the judgment; if the judgment creditor wishes the questioning to be conducted before a judge, stating this and giving reasons; and if he wishes for specific documents to be produced (such as wage slips, bank statements), identifying those documents.

Upon receipt a court officer considers the application and will usually provide for the judgment debtor to attend the county court of the district in which he (the debtor) resides or carries on business, unless for some reason a judge decides otherwise.

The order will provide for questioning to take place before a judge (rather than a court officer) *only* if the judge considering the request decides that there are compelling reasons to make such an order.

An order will be drawn up by the court officer requiring the judgment debtor to attend court at a time and place specified in the order and to produce any documents which the judgment creditor has reasonably required, and telling him that he will have to answer on oath any questions the court may require. The form of order will also contain a notice telling the judgment debtor that he must attend and that it will be a contempt of court which may result in imprisonment if he does not do so.

The order is to be served by the judgment creditor unless he is a litigant in person, in which case the order will be served by the court bailiff on the judgment debtor.

A judgment debtor who is ordered to attend court may, within seven days of being served with the order, ask the judge or creditor for a sum reasonably sufficient to cover travelling expenses. As the order will almost invariably be made for him to attend at his own local court, however, this sum will be very modest. It is purely for travelling expenses and need not include any amount for loss of earnings.

At the hearing the judgment debtor will be questioned on oath by a court officer, unless the court has already ordered that the hearing should be before a judge. The questioning is by reference to a pro forma, so that the questions range thoroughly over the whole area of a person's income, capital, and outgoings. If the judgment debtor, having attended, is awkward and refuses to cooperate, quite commonly the matter is then referred to a judge (there and then if one is available). The judge will see the judgment debtor and make it clear that he risks imprisonment if he does not cooperate.

Questioning is therefore done by a court officer; and a judgment debtor who has no previous experience of the system may be relatively relieved because he may imagine that he will be questioned by a judge in full wig and gown in open court, and is often pleasantly surprised to find he is questioned by an employee of the court service in some anonymous office.

The judgment creditor or his solicitor may attend and has the right to cross-examine and to examine any documents produced by the debtor.

An order for costs of the procedure will usually be made, although probably only in a very modest amount. This will be most unsatisfactory if the judgment creditor's solicitor has had to attend.

By the end of this procedure, if it has gone properly, information should have been obtained to assist the judgment creditor to decide which method of enforcement to choose next. It is possible, of course, that mere attendance at court may produce a negotiated offer by the judgment debtor to pay in a reasonable timescale by instalments, or even all at once. Such an offer can be recorded on oath in the course of the proceedings.

34.3   Enforcement of money judgments

As indicated in the introduction to this chapter, the following methods of enforcement remain in the form in which they were before the CPR. They are referred to in the general rule concerning enforcement of judgments, namely CPR, r. 70. After discussing the following methods, which are usually those which one tries first, we shall discuss the other methods now appearing at CPR, Part 72 and Part 73.

34.3.1   Execution

34.3.1.1   High Court writ of execution

See RSC, Ord. 45 and Ord. 46 in CPR, sch. 1.

Execution is the term describing the process whereby movable property of a judgment debtor may be seized to be sold at auction to satisfy the judgment debt, legal costs and, indeed, the costs of enforcement. To obtain this the judgment creditor's solicitor takes to the district registry where the judgment was obtained:

(a) two copies of a writ of execution;

(b) a form of request for the issue of execution;

(c) the judgment obtained together with (if the costs have already been assessed by the court, which is unusual) a copy of the costs judge's certificate;

(d) the court fee.

Enforcement against goods is undertaken under the writ of execution by an enforcement officer of the High Court. Perhaps surprisingly, the enforcement officer is not an employee of the High Court, or of the court service, but a private individual who holds himself out as available for this kind of work. Because of the importance of the job and the fact that high standards and complete honesty are required, there is a complicated procedure for obtaining appointment as an enforcement officer by application under Regulations made in 2004. These Regulations set out provisions as to the districts to which enforcement officers are assigned, how applications are to be made, and what fees can be charged. Those who obtain appointment are in the main persons who have already acted as sheriff's officers under the previous procedure which existed until 2004, and will usually be members of auctioneers' firms in private practice. The latter expertise is particularly valuable since it is often important for enforcement officers to know what second-hand items will fetch at an auction.

The procedure is without notice to the debtor. The solicitor simply produces these documents to the clerk at the counter of the district registry. The fee is taken and one form of the writ of execution is sealed and returned.

The judgment creditor then posts the writ to an enforcement officer of the area concerned with an initial fee. This is the area where the judgment debtor resides, or alternatively where he has the assets which it is intended to seize. It is customary when sending the writ to the enforcement officer to give him any information that might be of use to him in knowing what or where to seize, e.g., it might be that a status report has disclosed that the judgment debtor owns a certain car which he usually parks some distance away from his house.

The enforcement officer can seize any of the debtor's goods in the district which are sufficient to realise the judgment debt, interest, costs and expenses. Anything movable may be seized, including cash found on the premises. The officers have no right to force entry to residential premises, although they do have that right in the case of commercial premises. They do, however, have their means for ensuring that they are invited in without too much fuss.

In practice, when an enforcement officer receives a writ of execution he endorses upon it the precise date and time of receipt. If he receives different writs from different creditors relating to the same debtor, he is obliged to execute them in the order of receipt, and therefore with this method of execution the first one in may get the whole of the cake. In principle the officers go immediately to the debtor's house and seize valuables which they estimate will bring in the necessary amount at public auction. As an alternative to immediate seizure, they may make an inventory of the contents of the house which they propose to seize. This is called 'taking walking possession' and the officers indicate that they will return shortly (four days is a common period) to seize the goods and remove them unless the sum is paid. This is to provide a last chance for the debtor to obtain the money to pay the debt; something that he would usually be well advised to do since the goods at auction will fetch only a fraction of their probable value to the debtor personally. If the sum is not paid the enforcement officers will return and seize the goods. They will then be auctioned some days later, the intervening period giving the debtor one last chance to pay the debt.

If a party has obtained judgment with costs to be assessed later, since this is likely to take some weeks, it is common to issue execution immediately in respect of the judgment debt, and then again separately for the costs once assessed.

The enforcement officers will sell the goods at public auction and retain their own fees out of the sum involved (i.e., the judgment debtor in effect pays their fees—a feature which makes this method of execution particularly appealing). They will then send to the judgment creditor's solicitors the full amount of the debt, interests and costs (if appropriate at this stage), and return to the judgment debtor any excess received after auctioning the goods. The enforcement officer must retain the money received for 14 days under ss. 184 and 346 of the Insolvency Act 1986, but thereafter, if no bankruptcy proceeding are begun by anyone else, will remit the money to the creditor.

34.3.1.2   Warrant of execution in the county court

In the county court the request for a warrant of execution is filed together with a fee. In the county court the warrant of execution is executed by the bailiff of the court, a full-time civil servant. The bailiff in principle does much the same as the enforcement officers in the High Court, and the procedures are in other respects virtually identical. (See CCR, Ord. 26 in CPR, sch. 2.)

34.3.1.3   Execution of county court judgments in the High Court

Where it is intended to enforce a judgment by execution there are now restrictions as follows:

(a) A judgment debt of more than £5,000 can only be enforced by the High Court enforcement officer. Accordingly, if a party has a county court judgment for this sum it is necessary to register the judgment in the High Court (see also *Practice Direction (County Court Order: Enforcement)* [1991] 1 WLR 695). Under this procedure two copies of a certificate of judgment of the county court must be produced, sealed by that court, and setting out details of the judgment. The High Court will thereupon allocate a reference number, letter and year, and endorse that on the certificate. The case will then be entered in a special register at the High Court. Thereafter the certificate may be treated for enforcement purposes as a High Court judgment and interest at the judgment debt rate runs from the date of the certificate. The title of all subsequent documentation must be such as to reflect the transfer to the High Court, with the addition of the words 'transferred from the county court by certificate dated . . .'.

(b) Judgments for £600 or less can only be enforced by the county court bailiffs. Accordingly, a High Court judgment must be registered in the county court for that purpose.

(c) Between the figures of £600 and £5,000, enforcement may be by *either* bailiff or enforcement officer.

34.3.1.4 Permission to issue execution

It has been assumed in the foregoing that there is no permission required of the court to issue execution and that this can be done at the counter without the formality of any judicial decision by the district judge to permit it. In fact in some circumstances, none of which is relevant in mainstream litigation, permission of the court is required before execution can be issued. The most important one is where there is an attachment of earnings order in force (see **34.3.5**). With this exception, however, there are usually no difficulties in attempting several methods of enforcement of judgments simultaneously. The interrelationship between the various methods is discussed at **34.3.7**.

34.3.2 Third party debt order

A third party debt order under CPR, Part 72 is the appropriate method where the judgment debtor is himself owed money by another person, for example, where the judgment debtor is in business and is owed trade debts by customers, or indeed where anyone has a credit balance in any kind of bank or building society account, since such sums are in principle a debt owed by the bank or building society to the person concerned. Third party debt orders are a method of freezing and seizing such sums in the hands of the person who has them, and thus of bypassing the judgment debtor until it is too late for him to do anything about it.

34.3.2.1 Procedure for obtaining a third party debt order

To obtain a third party debt order, the judgment creditor's solicitor makes an application which must contain the following information: the name and address of the judgment debtor; details of the judgment sought to be enforced; the amount of money remaining due; if the judgment debt is payable by instalments, the amount of any instalments which are unpaid; the name and address of the third party; if the third party is a bank or building society its name, branch address and account number, if known; confirmation that to the best of the judgment creditor's knowledge the third party is within the jurisdiction and owes money to or holds money to the credit of the judgment debtor.

This information is filed at court and put before a district judge, who, if the application appears to be in order, will initially make an *interim third party debt order*.

The nature of this order is to fix a hearing to consider whether to make a *final* third party debt order, and meanwhile to direct that until the hearing the third party must not make any payment which reduces the amount he owes the judgment debtor to less than the amount specified in the order. In other words, it freezes the amount due in the third party's hands.

An interim third party debt order becomes binding on the third party when it is served on him. If the third party is a bank, the order should be served at both head office and the bank local branch where the account is, and thereafter be served upon the judgment debtor himself.

There is then a final hearing before a district judge in chambers.

Third parties commonly do not bother to attend the hearing but simply write in confirming that they will abide by any order made by the court. This is particularly the case with banks, who after all have no particular interest in the outcome of such matters. If, however, the third party disputes his liability to pay anything to the judgment debtor (i.e., says that there was no such debt or credit balance) then he will need to attend, and at the first hearing the district judge will then give directions as to how the issue of whether or not the third party owes money to the judgment debtor will be determined.

The judgment creditor, and usually the judgment debtor, will attend the hearing. The judgment creditor will be seeking to persuade the district judge to make the interim order into a final order (i.e., one directing that the money which has hitherto been frozen should be paid out to him). The judgment debtor may try to persuade the district judge that for hardship or other reasons this order ought not to be made. Usually, however, the order will be made final if there are admitted debts from third party to judgment debtor. Nevertheless, the making of the order is discretionary, and a common situation where the district judge will not make the order final is where it comes out that there are other unsecured creditors of the judgment debtor so that making the order would represent an unjust preferment of one creditor over another. This method should therefore be contrasted with execution, where the first in gets the whole cake (see **34.3.1.1**).

If there is no reason to the contrary and the order is made, it will be addressed to the third party telling him to pay the money over direct to the judgment creditor within a certain short time. This obviously absolves the third party from debts up to the relevant amount owed by him to the judgment debtor. If the third party fails to pay, the judgment creditor may take enforcement proceedings against him direct.

34.3.2.2 Arrangement for debtors in hardship

There is a further provision which permits the court to consider the position of a judgment debtor who is an individual, who is prevented from withdrawing money from his account with a bank or building society as a result of an interim third party debt order, where he or his family is suffering hardship in meeting ordinary living expenses as a result.

In that circumstance, where a judgment debtor finds out for the first time, say, that his bank current account has been frozen immediately after receipt of his monthly salary, he may make an application for a 'hardship order' by giving detailed evidence explaining why he needs a payment of an amount which he requests and verifying that by a statement of truth. The court will then fix a hearing to consider the position and, if it is satisfied about the bona fides of the application, may permit the third party to make one or more payments out of the account for the benefit of the judgment debtor. A hearing must be fixed, at which the judgment creditor will be given the opportunity to attend and put his point, for example, saying that the application is based on untruth and that no hardship is being experienced, or that it is a deliberate attempt to defeat the purpose of the third party debt order.

The court will be alert to attempts to defeat the judgment creditor by untruthful information and will be likely to examine carefully any suggestions of hardship.

34.3.3 Charging orders

Charging orders (CPR, Part 73) are not strictly speaking a method of enforcing a judgment, but rather a means of obtaining security for it which can subsequently be turned into enforcement by an application for an *order for sale*. Where a judgment debtor owns land (even if he owns it jointly with some other person) a charging order can be obtained on his interest in the land. The same applies to various other kinds of assets, in particular stocks and shares, where an equivalent order (called a 'stop order') may be obtained.

Information as to ownership of land is often obtained via orders to obtain information or through an enquiry agent. While in the case of unregistered land there is no method of being positive as to the ownership of legal estates, in the case of registered land there is now open access to the Land Register. It is thus possible to do an index search with an application for office copies of the proprietorship register of any property which it is suspected the judgment debtor owns.

Under reforms recently announced, the Land Register will shortly provide even more useful information to the judgment creditor because in the near future it will show the last price paid for the property concerned.

34.3.3.1 Procedure

The method of application for a charging order is in two stages. An application must be prepared by the judgment creditor's solicitor which:

(a) identifies the judgment and states the amount unpaid at the date of application;

(b) states the name and address of the judgment debtor;

(c) gives full particulars of the subject matter of the intended charge (i.e., the address of the land concerned);

(d) verifies that the interest to be charged is owned beneficially and not as a trustee by the judgment debtor;

(e) states whether the judgment creditor knows of any other creditors of the judgment debtor.

It is common to attach to the statement in support of the application a copy of the proprietorship register of the land to demonstrate that it is indeed owned by the judgment debtor.

The documents are considered by the district judge without a hearing, and he will make an *interim charging order* imposing a charge on the judgment debtor's interest in the asset to which the application relates and fixing a hearing to consider whether to make a final charging order.

When made the interim charging order should be registered at the Land Charges Registry if the land is unregistered, or protected by notice or caution at the District Land Registry in the case of registered land. This will have the effect of preserving priority for the judgment creditor's charge.

The hearing date fixed by the charging order must now be served upon the judgment debtor. It invites him to attend the hearing to show cause why the order should not be made final.

At the hearing, as with third party debt orders, the district judge has a wide discretion as to whether or not to make the charging order final. The burden of showing cause why it should not be made final is on the judgment debtor. However, since with this form of application it is for the judgment creditor specifically to say whether he knows that there are other creditors, it is always a relevant consideration to ensure that the making of a final charging order should not give the judgment creditor presently applying for the charging order unjust preferment over other creditors in the pipeline. The fact that the land is jointly owned or is, for example, a family home is not really a relevant consideration at this stage, however. It will certainly become so should any application be made to enforce the charging order by order for sale (see **34.3.4**).

As indicated above, a charging order is not in itself a method of enforcement; it is a way of obtaining security for a debt and of preserving priority over other subsequent encumbrances. Usually charging orders can be described as a 'slow but sure' way of enforcing a debt. Interest will run at the judgment debt rate (or at any higher rate stipulated by the contract creating the debt).

34.3.4 Enforcement of charging order by order for sale

By virtue of CPR, r. 73.10, a charging order may be enforced by applying to the court for an order for sale. This is a separate application and the claimant must use the Part 8 procedure, but it should be made to the court which made the charging order, unless that court does not have jurisdiction to make an order for sale. (See below concerning the relative jurisdictions of the county court and High Court.)

The claimant must file written evidence in accordance with the Practice Direction which, put shortly, requires a statement identifying the charging order and the property sought to be sold; stating the amount in respect of which the charge was imposed and the amount due at the date of issue of the claim; verifying the debtor's title to the property charged stating the names and addresses of any other creditors and, if known, the amount owed to them; and giving an estimate of the price which will be obtained on sale of the property.

There is a sample form of order at Appendix A to PD 73.

It is important to note that if the amount involved is more than £30,000, application should be made *not* to the county court which made the charging order but to one of the High Court Chancery District Registries, which are situated only in Birmingham, Bristol, Cardiff, Leeds, Liverpool, Manchester, Newcastle-upon-Tyne and Preston, or to Chancery Chambers at the Royal Courts of Justice.

The matter will come before a district judge in chambers for consideration, and at that time he will have regard to s. 36(2) of the Administration of Justice Act 1970. This provision is relevant in the case of all applications to enforce legal charges by order for possession or sale, and thus is the one relevant also where building societies attempt to repossess dwelling houses. Under s. 36(2) the court may adjourn the proceedings, or, on giving judgment or making an order for delivery of possession, may stay or suspend execution of the judgment or postpone the date for delivery of possession for such periods as the court thinks reasonable.

This gives the district judge a very wide discretion indeed to take into account the interests of anyone presently in the house. Thus if, for example, there is a substantial equity still in the property, the debt is a private one incurred by the husband (especially if the husband has now left the home) and the property is a home for small children, the district judge is likely to adjourn the application for some months, and thereafter possibly to stay or suspend execution of the judgment or order. On the other hand, an order adjourning the proceedings or suspending execution should in principle be made only if 'the mortgagor is likely within a reasonable time to pay any sums due under the mortgage'. All the circumstances have to be taken into account and the legitimate interests of the judgment creditor must not be overlooked. Thus in *Austin-Fell* v *Austin-Fell* [1990] Fam 172 the court concluded that an abandoned wife's interest in the property should not totally override that of the Midland Bank plc which was legitimately seeking to enforce a civil debt owed by her husband. The effect was that the charge remained on the property but was not to be enforced until the youngest child left education. It must be pointed out, however, that in such a case, with interest running on the judgment debt for over a decade, unless property prices also improved over that decade, at the end of that time the wife would be likely to receive a much reduced amount in respect of her husband's share of the sale of the property. Such considerations may be important in an era of fluctuating property prices.

34.3.4.1   Costs

It will be observed that by the time one has obtained a charging order and thereafter embarked on quite separate proceedings seeking an order for sale, a good deal more money will have been spent on costs. It is possible that the bulk of these will be recoverable if the application for sale is successful and there is adequate equity. If this is not the case and there is diminishing equity in the house, other potential encumbrances and the use of the property as a family home, it may be that this method of enforcement seems less desirable. Of course, it is always possible to obtain the charging order with a view to ultimate security for the debt while not immediately embarking on the further stage of applying for an order for sale.

34.3.5   Attachment of earnings

Attachment of earnings is in some respects the least desirable of the methods considered so far. It is available only in the county court (CCR, Ord. 27 in CPR, sch. 2), although it is of course possible to transfer a High Court judgment to a county court for enforcement. It is a means of ensuring that regular sums are deducted from a judgment debtor's salary by his employer and remitted direct to the county court for onward transmission to the judgment creditor. The procedure is only desirable in the case of a person with no assets worth charging or seizing but who appears to be in regular, well-paid employment and does not have many dependants. If none of these conditions obtains, then attachment of earnings may be a frustrating and long drawn out procedure, notwithstanding that in principle once application for it is made the judgment creditor need take no other positive steps but can leave the court to run the procedure itself, and thus costs can at least be kept modest.

A further drawback of the attachment of earnings procedure is that, while it will often run on for many years, interest on the judgment debt ceases under the provisions for interest previously described (see **34.2.2**).

34.3.5.1 Application for attachment of earnings

Application is made to the county court for the district where the debtor resides. This has attached to it a form of reply which is a questionnaire to the debtor seeking details of his employment, income and financial liabilities. It also invites the debtor to pay the amount due direct to the judgment creditor as a way of avoiding an attachment of earnings order. Some persons in employment may choose to do this because one effect of an attachment of earnings application is to bring their debt to the notice of their employers and this may prove personally embarrassing.

If the debtor does not pay at once he must return the questionnaire to the court which, in the light of the information given, will make an attachment of earnings order. If the court officer who administers the procedure feels he has sufficient information, he may make a provisional attachment of earnings order and give notice of it to the creditor and debtor. If neither party objects the provisional order becomes final. However, if either objects in writing within five days of receiving the notice there will be a hearing at which the district judge considers the matter on hearing oral representations.

If a judgment debtor does not return his questionnaire, he may be committed to prison for up to 14 days; similarly, if he is ordered to attend the hearing for an attachment of earnings application, he may be committed to prison for up to 14 days for non-attendance. In principle the court itself puts these procedures into operation and the judgment creditor need not take any initiatives.

Although these penalties are provided by the Attachment of Earnings Act 1971, in reality the court is very slow to commit someone to prison. Whatever degree of non-compliance with, or outright defiance of, court orders there is, many courts give debtors several chances to comply before committal is imposed.

34.3.5.2 Contents of the order

When the court has sufficient information it will make an order specifying two matters. These are:

(a) the normal deduction rate (NDR); and

(b) the protected earnings rate (PER).

The latter is the minimum which the debtor needs to earn to achieve subsistence level for himself and his dependants, if any. Once he has earned that net figure in any given week, the excess over that figure up to the maximum of the normal deduction rate will be deducted by his employer for transmission to the county court. Thus, in the case of an employee who earns the same sum every week, the deduction at the normal rate will be made regularly by the employer who will then send the money direct to the county court. The employer may also make a modest charge for administrative expenses. If the employee's earnings are seasonal or vary with overtime or bonuses, however, then if in any given week his pay sinks below the protected earnings rate no deductions will be made for forwarding to the county court; if only a slight surplus over the protected earnings rate is earned, then only the surplus will be sent on. There is no provision for making up previous shortages in subsequent weeks, even if extra bonuses take the earnings substantially above the protected earnings rate in a following week.

If the order is made it is directed to the employer on whom it is served by the court, together with an explanatory leaflet giving details on how to operate the system.

34.3.6 Costs of previous abortive enforcement

It is possible to obtain the costs of previous abortive enforcement proceedings, for example, if, say, a third party debt order attempt fails because the debtor cleared his bank account the day before service of the order. An affidavit must be prepared explaining the circumstances and amounts involved, to be lodged at the appropriate time and the district judge will then, without a hearing, allow the amount he thinks appropriate. See *Practice Direction (Enforcement Costs: Recovery)* [1991] 1 WLR 1295.

34.3.7 Cumulative or alternative methods of enforcement

When one comes to weigh the different methods of enforcement against each other, much depends on the amount of accurate information to hand. There is in principle no objection to using the various methods simultaneously or cumulatively, except that a party needs the permission of the court to levy execution while an attachment of earnings is in force. Having said that, there would be nothing to stop a judgment creditor taking steps to obtain a third party debt order on a bank account, sending the enforcement officer in to execute judgment against movables such as furniture, a car or trade stock, and obtaining a charging order on premises, all at the same time. Care would have to be taken in the completion of the relevant documents but if, for example, each method in turn appeared likely to raise more than had been anticipated, then it would be a simple matter to desist from the third party debt proceedings once the enforcement officer informed the judgment creditor of the price obtained at auction; or, if the third party debt order were achieved first, the enforcement officer could be instructed to withdraw from possession. Care must be taken in the latter instance, however, to ensure that the judgment creditor is aware that in such circumstances the enforcement officer will be entitled to his full fees, which can be very substantial and in that instance may not, in principle, be reclaimed from the judgment debtor.

The advantages of each of the methods are as follows:

(a) The advantage of execution is that it is by far the swiftest method of enforcement. The enforcement officer is likely to execute the writ within a very short time and, if there are indeed goods worth seizing, a very satisfactory outcome may be obtained. The officer may in particular be given the money by the judgment debtor at a very early stage to avoid seizure.

(b) So long as one is certain that there is sufficient money, a third party debt order is perhaps the neatest method of all. It will take effect relatively quickly and it procures the debt in cash form.

(c) Charging orders, as indicated at **34.3.3.1**, are a slow method of obtaining security for a judgment debt. They are at their most effective when there is a large equity in the house or business premises and the judgment debtor is the only owner of the premises. In such a situation enforcement by order for sale will be effective, and since interest continues to run from date of judgment to final receipt of money this method can be very satisfactory. The method becomes markedly less satisfactory if there is no great equity in the house, the premises are jointly owned with another, or the premises are used as a family home.

(d) Attachment of earnings is the least satisfactory method of enforcement. Interest does not run even though it may take many years to recover the money; if the judgment debtor changes jobs then the procedure may need to be reinstituted each time; and there may well be substantial delays in getting the initial order in the event of non-cooperation, which is only rarely punished by imprisonment despite the terms of the Attachment of Earnings Act 1971. On the other hand, with certain kinds of employees this application may bring about payment in full because of their embarrassment at having their employers know about their civil debt; and the draining effect of having potentially substantial slices of one's earnings deducted at source over many years may make a debtor who is able to do so prefer to dispose of the matter by early larger payments, or even by obtaining finance to pay the whole debt.

34.3.8   Bankruptcy of individuals (and company liquidation)

Lastly, we should mention one method of enforcement which is the most successful of all in some cases but which is outside the scope of this text, i.e., bankruptcy. The threat of bankruptcy proceedings may be very successful against persons whose occupation makes it difficult for them if they have been adjudged bankrupt (e.g., professionals or company directors). As a method of enforcement it can be virtually instantaneous, the preliminary notice sometimes bringing payment in full. If the procedure itself has to be embarked on, though, it has serious defects.

Bankruptcy can only be used in the case of debts over £750; and whereas with other methods the initial outlay in terms of court fees is not great, in the case of bankruptcy the initial outlay is over £450 because a deposit must be left in respect of the official receiver's fees. Another defect is that whereas with other enforcement procedures, especially execution against goods, in principle the first in gets the whole of the cake (and even in the case of third party debt or charging orders, if the judgment creditor does not know of the existence of other creditors it may be that he gets in first and gets the whole), the nature of bankruptcy is to bring all creditors forward. Thus a particular creditor may in the end receive only a modest proportion of the debt owed, depending on the assets available.

Bankruptcy is said to be less of a stigma now and indeed in most cases a discharge from bankruptcy can be obtained in only a year provided reasonable cooperation is shown with the trustee in bankruptcy. This has the effect of 'writing off' the debts (NB. This does not apply to student loans!) However, notice of bankruptcy is kept on one's personal credit file for many years and it will make it very difficult to obtain credit in most forms. Increasingly intended employers search credit files also and a past bankruptcy may be a serious handicap in obtaining some kinds of jobs. The threat of bankruptcy in many cases is therefore more effective than the reality for many creditors.

34.4   Enforcement of judgments to do or abstain from doing any act

34.4.1   The order of committal

RSC, Ord. 45, r. 5 in CPR, sch. 1, states:

Where—

(a) a person required by a judgment or order to do an act within a time specified in the judgment or order refuses or neglects to do it within that time...or

(b) a person disobeys a judgment or order requiring him to abstain from doing an act, then . . . the judgment or order may be enforced by . . . an order of committal against that person or, where that person is a body corporate, against any [director or other officer of the body].

This then is the procedure for enforcing an injunction or undertaking. Where the injunction granted is *prohibitory*, any further act of the kind restrained will give the basis for an application for enforcement by committal; where the injunction is *mandatory* (e.g., to pull down a wall wrongly erected barring a right of way) then it is essential that the order fixes a specific time for doing the positive act. If the order does not fix such a time then a further application to the court must be made for a time to be fixed before application to enforce the injunction by committal can be made.

34.4.2   The penal notice

The order containing the injunction must be endorsed with a penal notice. The wording relevant in the High Court is as follows:

Disobedience to this order will be a contempt of court punishable by imprisonment.

In the county court the wording is:

Take notice that unless you obey the directions contained in this order you will be guilty of contempt of court and will be liable to be committed to prison.

34.4.3   Service of the order

It is usually essential as a prerequisite to enforcement by committal that the order should have been served. The order containing the penal notice must be served personally on the person required to do or abstain from doing the act in question, and service on the solicitor on the record will not usually do. However, an order requiring a person to abstain from doing an act may be enforced notwithstanding that service of the copy of the order had not been effected if the court is satisfied that pending such service the person against whom or against whose property it is sought to enforce the order had notice thereof, either by being present when the order was made or by being notified of the terms of the order, whether by telephone or otherwise. In addition, without prejudice to its general powers, the court may dispense with service of a copy of an order under the rules if it thinks it just to do so (RSC, Ord. 45, r. 7(7), in CPR, sch. 1).

Despite this last provision, the courts are usually very assiduous in seeing that there is strict observance of the rules about service because the liberty of the subject is at stake. In a clear case, however, and with a gross breach, e.g., one involving violence, it may be that the court can be prevailed upon to dispense with service.

34.4.4   Undertakings

An undertaking given by the defendant to the court is for all purposes as good as an injunction, and indeed is better in the sense that (strictly speaking) there is no need for the undertaking to be incorporated in any court order or served on the defendant. It is preferable, of course, that the undertaking is incorporated in such an order endorsed with a penal notice and served personally, but nonetheless the court has jurisdiction to proceed to enforce an undertaking by committal notwithstanding non-service if satisfied that the person who gave the undertaking is aware of its contents and the consequence of disobedience (*Hussain* v *Hussain* [1986] Fam 134).

34.4.5 Procedure on an application for committal

In the High Court application is made in the court where the case has been proceeding, on notice of application under RSC, Ord. 52, r. 4 in CPR, sch. 1.

The notice of application must state clearly the grounds of the application and describe the contempt in question. It must be accompanied by a copy of an affidavit in support sworn by someone who has personal knowledge of the matters constituting the alleged contempt. However, the notice itself must contain details of the contempt and it is not enough if the information is contained only in the affidavit.

The application notice and the copy affidavit must be personally served on the defendant. If it is sought to commit a director of a limited company, service must be on the company and on the director concerned.

34.4.6 The hearing of the application

Since an application for committal to prison is one involving the liberty of the subject it takes precedence over the rest of the day's business in the court. It is for the applicant seeking the committal to show on the criminal standard of proof that the contemnor is guilty. The court will then consider the whole matter.

It is often said that it is the paramount consideration of the court to ensure compliance with its orders, and if some other method than committal to prison can be undertaken then it may be that that will be the preferred outcome. For example, if the injunction requires a person to vacate a certain piece of land it may be that the judgment can be enforced by a procedure called a writ of possession rather than by committal. It may also be that a contemnor will be allowed to purge his contempt by an apology and an assurance that he has already obeyed, or will immediately obey, the injunction or comply with the undertaking concerned. In those instances the court may well suspend imprisonment or any other penalty it imposes. The court has the power to impose fines of unlimited amounts in addition to or instead of committal to prison.

Under the Contempt of Court Act 1981, committal may be for a fixed period of up to two years. The order must be scrupulously drawn up. There is a long series of Court of Appeal authorities where orders for committal to prison have been set aside because of sloppiness in drafting the order, in particular as to the facts found by the judge and the nature of the contempt. This should be carefully borne in mind.

As mentioned above, a person committed may in principle make an application to purge his contempt and be discharged. Now that committal is for a fixed term, however, this is unlikely to meet with great success.

34.4.7 Practice and procedure in the county court

The practice and procedure in the county court are substantially the same as in the High Court, but in the county court a district judge has powers to commit for contempt in certain circumstances, and to allow discharge from imprisonment (CCR, Ord. 29, r. 3 in CPR, sch. 2).

35

Alternative dispute resolution

In this chapter it is not intended to deal with all possible forms of ADR, but to indicate very briefly some of the current dispute resolution processes. Usually these processes fall into one of the following categories:

(a) negotiation;

(b) adjudication;

(c) mediation.

It is part of the function of the court and an important aspect of dealing with a case justly to seek to have disputes resolved as economically and swiftly as possible. Sometimes this will involve the court encouraging the parties to have recourse to alternative dispute resolution and it is intended briefly now to discuss this.

35.1 The emergence of ADR

Recent years have seen the growth of 'alternative dispute resolution' ('ADR') in, for example, family disputes and in commercial and other civil disputes. The term 'alternative' (as in comedy or medicine) may appear to suggest a non-conformist approach to dispute resolution, but this is not the case. ADR offers a range of additional resources to complement the present litigation system and is seen as widening the scope of available forms and processes rather than displacing litigation. Public expectation and professional attitudes tend to regard litigation as a first rather than a last resort, but the costs, delays and risks of litigation have made the possibilities of other means of resolving disputes attractive. A superficial attraction may be that parties hope even to dispense with lawyers in settling their difficulties, but regrettably, where there is any substance in the claim or any complexity in the law, it is rarely possible for lawyers to be dispensed with. Moreover, if one party thinks that he can act for himself but his opponent has competent legal representation, the party without a lawyer is likely to be at a substantial disadvantage, however informally the parties have agreed to resolve their dispute.

In reality most court proceedings are eventually settled or abandoned. Relatively few cases (perhaps as few as 3 per cent) actually reach trial where a claim has been issued. Given that, it is apparent that at some stages in the litigation process the parties are brought to compromise. Thus it is argued that sensible people ought to be able to find some way of getting to the stage of compromise without having first incurred the expense and delays of litigation. Attempts to find alternative methods of resolving disputes can lead to illusory benefits, however. Unless some method is found of ensuring that binding procedural orders can be made on the parties, and that the outcome is also binding, it may be that a great deal of time and expense is wasted in trying alternative methods only to find that the parties need to have recourse to litigation eventually anyway. In addition, if either of the parties is recalcitrant or unscrupulous, formal litigation may be the only proper option for his opponent. Sometimes one of the parties will be of sufficient size and wealth to find the costs of litigation a positive tactical advantage because of its deterrent effect on potential opponents. This seems particularly to be true of some large companies, especially privatised utilities, who tend to have a most uncompromising attitude to claims made against them from their disgruntled consumers.

From summer 2006 a new provision in the Practice Direction on pre-action protocols requires the parties in every case to consider the possibility of alternative dispute resolution before beginning litigation.

35.2 Negotiation

Negotiation is the process of discussing or dealing with a matter with a view to arriving at a mutual agreement, settlement or compromise. It is how we all arrange our affairs with one another in everyday life and in business, by establishing areas of agreement and reconciling areas of disagreement. There are various styles and approaches to negotiation used by solicitors which we have already considered at briefly at **9.6**.

35.3 Adjudication

Adjudication involves a third party making a decision which is binding on the parties, by litigation through the courts or by some other procedure, such as arbitration, or expert determination, which we shall now consider.

35.3.1 Litigation

Litigation is the action of carrying on legal proceedings within the court system. The traditional system provides established court procedures, rules of evidence and the application of substantive law and precedent. The neutral 'decision makers' are the judges at every level. The decisions made in this process, with which the rest of this book is largely concerned, are final, subject to appeal or review.

Outside the formal court system a variety of tribunals also provide finality in their decisions on the rights of parties, e.g., between individuals as in the case of employment tribunals; or between an individual and the State as in the case of immigration judges and the Asylum and Immigration Tribunal.

35.3.2 Arbitration within the court system

In the High Court it is possible to apply for a judge to deal with matters as an arbitrator (sometimes called an 'umpire') in commercial cases, giving the parties the benefit of commercial understanding, legal and judicial skills and the arbitration-type procedure with greater speed and informality. Unfortunately, the listing of cases in the commercial list of the Queen's Bench Division (usually known as the 'Commercial Court') is currently under a great deal of pressure due to lack of available judges, and it would not greatly expedite matters to attempt to use this procedure. Moreover, in such cases all the usual interim procedures are available, such as disclosure, orders for exchange of expert evidence, and even interim injunctions, and thus there may be just as much legal expense and complexity.

35.3.3 Arbitration outside the court system

Arbitration outside the court system usually comes about where in the contract between them the parties has already provided that disputes shall be subject to arbitration. In such a case arbitration is usually subject to the terms of the Arbitration Act 1996 and to the common law. However, it is possible for the parties to an arbitration agreement to exclude many of the rules under the Act and to substitute their own and to specify in particular what procedure is to be followed and what the powers of the arbitrator shall be.

Except in certain specialist trade or commodity disputes, arbitrations in the UK tend in fact to be conducted along similar lines to litigation procedures, applying the same interim processes, e.g., disclosure of documents, and even the formal rules of evidence. Thus such cases are likely to involve substantial delay (although perhaps not quite on the scale of formal litigation) and costs of a similar nature to those in conventional litigation. The powers of an arbitrator to award costs in such cases are usually the same as in court cases. The advantages are that in choosing the arbitrator the parties may select a specialist in the field of the dispute, who may not be a lawyer, and who will proceed at an agreed pace. His availability for dealing with interim matters is likely to be somewhat greater and more flexible than that of a judge. In addition, arbitration is usually conducted in private, which is often preferred by the parties in some kinds of commercial disputes.

If the arbitrator is not a lawyer it is possible for legal issues to be referred to the court during the course of the arbitration for separate decision. Although an arbitrator is usually granted some interim powers, e.g., to direct disclosure and exchange of witness statements, he will not have the power to make orders for interim injunctions. In such cases, however, it is possible to apply to the High Court for any order which is appropriate and which the arbitrator has no power to make. This intermingling of arbitration and High Court is in itself illustrative of the fact that there may be little cost saving. The usefulness of a specialist adjudicator and the greater speed of the proceedings may, however, be sufficient justification for arbitration. The decision made by the arbitrator is usually binding on all the parties. There is a limited right of appeal on questions of law and occasionally there may be the possibility of judicial review if some wholly inappropriate procedural error has been made.

If the parties have an arbitration clause in the relevant contract, then it will take effect and the court will, under s. 9 of the Arbitration Act 1996, stay the proceedings forcing the parties back to arbitration. Despite s. 9, however, the court does have a discretion to allow the court action to proceed, especially where there is a suggestion of fraud or fraudulent conspiracy between some of the parties, or where the case entirely turns on a matter of law. The fact that there is no real defence despite an arbitration clause and that the claimant wishes to proceed in court in order to obtain the advantage of summary judgment, may in particular be a reason for allowing an action to proceed despite an arbitration clause (see *Archital Luxfer* v *A.J. Dunning & Son (Weyhill)* [1987] 1 FTLR 372). If there is no arbitration agreement between the parties they may, of course, subsequently to the dispute arising, agree to refer the matter to arbitration. Various associations provide arbitration services, including, e.g., the International chamber of commerce, local chambers of commerce and the Chartered Institute of

Arbitrators. Trade associations also often offer arbitration, e.g., to the purchasers of package holidays which have gone wrong.

35.3.4 Expert determination

This is a final alternative to arbitration. It occurs where the parties have agreed in the contract that disputes (usually of a scientific or technical nature) arising under the contract may be resolved by a chosen expert nominated in the contract or to be chosen by a method described in the contract. The expert's decision will be final and binding on the parties. Such agreements usually provide that the expert will *not* act as an arbitrator, so that the Arbitration Act 1996 will not apply and the expert will not have to follow arbitration rules and procedures, nor will there be any appeal.

35.4 Mediation and conciliation

35.4.1 Mediation

Mediation is a non-adjudicatory process by which the parties engage the help of a neutral third party to resolve their dispute by negotiated agreement. Since the mediator has no power to deliver a binding decision or impose it on the parties, this may therefore be a helpful alternative in some kinds of case. The fact that if no agreement is eventually reached acceptable to both parties, either may resort to litigation, means, however, that there may be an unwelcome delay (and indeed extra expense, since both parties are likely to wish to consult their lawyers at certain stages of the process, or even have them directly involved with the mediator). The parties reserve their rights to resolve the matter by adjudication if they cannot do so by mediation.

Mediators' fees may also be substantial, at least £1,000 per day and possibly several times this figure.

35.4.2 Conciliation

Conciliation is a term often used interchangeably with mediation, but it has a slightly different meaning having been defined as a 'process of engendering common sense, reasonableness and agreement'. It is often viewed as a more general form of third-party intervention of a facilitative nature, whereas mediation is seen as a more specific form of this, involving (as in employer–employee disputes) the mediator playing a significant role in suggesting possible solutions. Conciliation is used in a number of fields, in particular, in the case of industrial disputes (by ACAS), and indeed at the start of ordinary employment tribunal proceedings. Likewise, there are possibilities of conciliation in separation and divorce and children's issues, and sometimes in community issues.

35.4.3 Other procedures

There are other possibilities as well as the methods described above which may assist in bringing disputes to an end without formal litigation. New procedures are being developed all the time in the case of commercial dispute resolution. Two other procedures which may assist are:

35.4.3.1 Early neutral evaluation

This is a process in which a neutral professional, usually a lawyer but possibly an expert from within a given industry, hears or reads a summary of each party's case and gives a non-binding assessment of his view and the probable outcome of the dispute. This can then be used as a basis for settlement or further negotiation. If it is not acceptable the parties can then take any further step that they wish, for example, full mediation or go straight to litigation.

35.4.3.2 Med-Arb

This is a combination of mediation and arbitration where the parties agree to mediate but if that fails to achieve a settlement the dispute is referred to arbitration. One variant of this hybrid form is where the same person acts as mediator and arbitrator.

35.5 When should ADR be considered?

If ADR is to be an effective complement to litigation, the circumstances in which it will be appropriate, and those when it will be inappropriate, must be considered. Mediation or other ADR procedures may be preferable to litigation in a wide range of business or personal relationships, particularly if the relationship is a continuing one. This is particularly the case in partnerships or as between company and shareholders. It may also be the case between persons who are frequently in a contractual relationship where they do not wish one dispute to sour what has otherwise been a satisfactory working situation, as between contractor and subcontractor, publisher and writer, and the like. ADR should particularly be considered where the issues between the parties arise from a breakdown in communications, misunderstandings about procedures to be adopted or differences on technical issues, especially in the construction industry. Confidentiality is often a very big advantage and since mediation will not involve lawyers at all there will be a considerable cost saving, which is always a consideration. Legal advice is often essential, however, at least at the outset of mediation or conciliation procedures, in order to ensure that the parties clearly understand the extent to which decisions made in the process are likely to be binding, and to what extent concessions made for the purpose of conciliation might be held against them should later formal proceedings need to instigated. Full legal advice may need to be given, for example, about the extent to which acknowledgement of errors in working practices might have further tort or insurance complications and even provide a basis for future liability in unrelated litigation. The difficulty of these subordinate issues is sometimes a powerful feature against alternative dispute resolution, at least between individuals; although in the case of disputes between companies, who will receive thorough and competent initial advice, there may be a great deal to be said for it.

Clearly there are circumstances where alternative dispute resolution is unlikely to be suitable once negotiations have broken down. This will be true of most personal injury litigation and in cases where immediate enforcement of a court order may be necessary, i.e., in almost every case where an injunction is likely to be sought.

35.6 ADR and the Civil Procedure Rules

The CPR make little specific provision for ADR except at r. 1.4(2)(e), which provides that the court's active case management duties include:

encouraging the parties to use an alternative dispute resolution procedure if the court considers that appropriate and facilitating the use of such procedure.

In some cases, the court may make limited enquiries of its own motion, but typically one or both of the parties are likely to propose an ADR before the court will consider it worthwhile to intervene. A stay for other forms of procedure to be considered is always a possible option, but the court will be anxious to ensure that this is not simply used to buy time for fruitless negotiations. The parties are likely to be required to report back to the court before indefinite stays will be considered. The court may attempt to give some kind of timetable for the carrying out of the ADR so that it will be necessary for the parties to agree precisely what form this is to take and what the timetable for it is.

Particular initiatives in attempting to sponsor formal ADR schemes have been taken by a number of county courts, in particular the Central London County Court. The position of this court is in some ways anomalous because it has always had a more extensive jurisdiction than other county courts, and by its very location the nature of its clientele involves a higher proportion of business related disputes. Its ADR scheme initially seemed unsuccessful, but latterly the response of parties has been encouraging and the numbers seeking to involve themselves in formal ADR has considerably increased. This is a trend which may develop further and in other locations, but progress will inevitably be slow unless the CPR are drastically revised to provide more positive incentives (for example, by a provision that costs will be disallowed unless the parties can prove that they have in some way attempted ADR in an appropriate case—a provision which it seems to the writer is most unlikely to come about). However, increasingly, in cases which may be appropriate for ADR, the courts expect parties at least to give it serious consideration. So, in *Dunnett* v *Railtrack* (2002) *The Times*, 3 April 2002 (CA), it was said that where the court suggested ADR and one party turned that down out of hand, there could be 'uncomfortable' consequences in costs.

Later cases, however, have confirmed that the court will consider whether there was ever a realistic possibility of ADR succeeding. If there was not, no costs penalty for rejecting it will be imposed.

35.7 ADR providers

A number of organisations provide ADR services. They are independent of the courts and most of them charge fees (sometimes substantial) for their involvement in disputes. These fees, plus the possibility of continuing to need to employ lawyers for the alternative dispute resolution procedure, must always be borne in mind when considering the advantages.

Appeals in civil proceedings

Any civilised court system must have a system of appeals. A new system of appeals in civil proceedings was introduced in Part 52 of the CPR and this has greatly simplified procedure.

36.1 Nature of appeals

It is important to consider two different concepts of the term 'appeal'. Before the CPR there were two forms of appeal:

(a) *Rehearing*, in which it was as if the previous decision had never been and the appeal court would proceed to hear all the evidence again, and indeed any new evidence which had come to light meanwhile. Moreover, a party was not restricted to raising the arguments he had raised in the court below, but could raise new ones.

(b) *Review*, which means that the court to which the appeal was being brought would not rehear all the evidence, but would limit itself to an examination of some specific feature or features of the decision of the court below, for example, whether the judge had wrongly assessed the evidence, misapplied the law, or misconducted the hearing procedurally.

Moreover, there were many stages of the appeal process where appeals could be brought *as of right*, that is to say there was no filtering mechanism or requirement to obtain permission to bring appeals.

36.2 CPR, Part 52

Under the CPR the position is radically different. In the following terminology we will use the terms from Part 52 of the CPR, namely:

(a) 'appeal court' means the court to which an appeal is made;

(b) 'lower court' means the court or judge from whose decision an appeal is brought.

The basic principle is that an applicant (subject to very minor exceptions) now *always* requires permission to appeal. An application for permission to appeal may be made either to the lower court at the hearing at which the decision in question was made, or to the appeal court.

If the lower court refuses to grant permission, a further application must be made to the appeal court within 21 days.

36.2.1 Principles for grant of permission to appeal

Rule 52.3(6) states that permission to appeal will only be given where:

(a) the court considers that the appeal would have a real prospect of success; or

(b) there is some other compelling reason why the appeal should be heard.

An order giving permission to appeal may give permission either generally or only on limited issues or subject to conditions (r. 52.3(7)).

36.3 Hearing the appeal

In principle every appeal will be limited to a review of the decision of the lower court and rehearings will not be permitted unless the court considers that in the circumstances of an individual appeal it will be in the interests of justice to hold a rehearing (CPR, r. 52.11). Even in that case unless it orders otherwise, the appeal court will not receive oral evidence or evidence which was not before the lower court (r. 52.11(2)).

36.3.1 Principles for granting an appeal

Rule 52.11(3) states that the appeal court will allow an appeal where the decision of the lower court was:

(a) wrong; or

(b) unjust because of a serious procedural or other irregularity in the proceedings in the lower court.

36.3.2 Powers of the court on appeal

By r. 52.10 an appeal court has power:

(a) to affirm, set aside or vary any order or judgment made or given by the lower court;

(b) to refer any claim or issue for determination by the lower court;

(c) to order a new trial or hearing;

(d) to make orders for the payment of interest;

(e) to make a costs order.

36.4 One appeal only

Once an appeal has been determined it is normally not possible to appeal again to a higher court. Thus, for example, if there is an appeal from a district judge to a circuit judge, in principle that will be the end of the route of appeal and a further appeal may not be brought to the Court of Appeal unless the Court of Appeal itself gives permission. By CPR, r. 52.13(2), it will not give permission for this further appeal unless it considers that:

(a) the appeal would raise an important point of principle or practice; or

(b) there is some other compelling reason for the Court of Appeal to hear it.

This is an important change which is intended to end the proliferation of appeals which had previously existed. Until May 2000 there was no restriction at all on appealing from the decision of a district judge to a circuit judge (which would usually be by way of a complete rehearing) and there might then be a further appeal to the Court of Appeal. The object of the new provisions is to require permission to appeal in every case so as to provide a filter on unmeritorious appeals, to bring about the virtual ending of appeals by way of rehearing, and to restrict appellants to one appeal only.

36.5 Summary

The following are the routes of appeal:

(a) from an interim decision of a district judge in the county court to a circuit judge;

(b) from an interim decision of a district judge in the High Court to a High Court judge;

(c) from a decision on a small claims or fast track trial by a district judge to a circuit judge;

(d) from a decision on a fast track trial by a circuit judge to a High Court judge;

(e) from a decision by a High Court judge to the Court of Appeal.

36.5.1 Exception

There is one exception. Where a circuit judge gives a *final decision* on a multi-track claim (or highly exceptionally a district judge or master gives such a decision in a case where the parties have agreed to him having jurisdiction), any appeal is to the Court of Appeal and not to a High Court or other judge. For these purposes 'a final decision' is one that would finally determine the entire proceedings and therefore includes the trial itself; any assessment of damages; or any other final decision, including, for example, decisions on aspects of the claim which may have been tried separately, such as whether there is a Limitation Act defence.

This does not apply to orders giving summary judgment or striking out proceedings or a statement of case, because, although they might at first sight appear to have some element of 'finality', they do not finally determine the entire proceedings in the same sense and therefore it is right that the first level of appeal in such cases should be the normal one as described in the summary above.

37

The Human Rights Act 1998 and civil litigation

The Human Rights Act 1998 came into force on 2 October 2000. The effect of the Act is to incorporate into the law of England Articles 2 to 12, 14 and 16 to 18 of the European Convention on Human Rights and Fundamental Freedoms, together with Articles 1 to 3 of the First Protocol.

The Convention was brought into force some time ago in Scotland and Wales, by the devolution provisions, and in relation to Scotland has provoked a considerable body of case law already.

The purpose of this chapter is to discuss briefly some aspects of the Act and the Convention in so far as they will be relevant to English civil litigation.

37.1 The European Convention on Human Rights and Fundamental Freedoms (1950)

The Convention is an international treaty promulgated by the Council of Europe, which is a body of 43 member states. It has no direct connection with the European Union, although much confusion is caused by the fact that the Council of Europe is based in Strasbourg from where the European Union also carries out some of its functions. The Convention is 'European law' in a general sense and has often been applied directly by the European Court of Justice based in Luxembourg, which is an organ of the European Union. However, what we are chiefly concerned with in this chapter is the European Convention as administered by the most well-known part of the Council of Europe, namely, the European Court of Human Rights based in Strasbourg. It is not proposed to say anything further about the law of the European Union.

The Convention concerns civil and political rights. Economic and social rights are protected by the *European Social Charter*, which, although declaring those rights, cannot be invoked in court proceedings by individuals.

The reasons for the distinctions between the two kinds of rights are not always obvious. For example, the Convention does guarantee a right to education but does not guarantee a right to health care, although that is guaranteed by the European Social Charter.

The Convention's purpose is really to establish Europe-wide minimum standards, but still allowing to member States a very wide 'margin of appreciation' to decide on the content of their own substantive and procedural law. This is particularly true of matters of civil and criminal procedure and evidence, where wide discretions are accorded to member states. Thus it has been held that the Convention does not guarantee anyone the right to a job, promotion, welfare benefits of any particular kind, a pension, a degree, education of any particular kind, etc. However, where there *is* provision for something under national laws, then the provisions of the Convention may apply in respect of the mechanisms by which an individual may have his rights determined. For example, although there is no right under the Convention to a pension, if domestic law provides such a right then in any proceedings to decide on a claim to payment of the pension (for example, by judicial review, ordinary court action, or through any relevant tribunal system) the provisions of the Convention may apply, for example, under Article 14 (right not to be discriminated against on the basis of gender, etc.) or Article 6 (right to a fair trial), although for further comment see below.

37.2   The Human Rights Act 1998

Although the Human Rights Act 1998 came into force on 2 October 2000, for some time previously the courts paid direct attention to the European Convention in reaching their decisions in many cases. This was particularly true of Article 6 (the right to a fair trial). The English courts in fact treated the 1998 Act as if it were fully in force, because any appeal arising out of decisions taken at that time would be likely to be heard after 2 October 2000 and then would be subject to the 1998 Act. Recent law reports therefore often contain references to the Convention, sometimes in bare acknowledgement of its terms, in others by detailed examination of Strasbourg jurisprudence.

37.2.1   The Act and civil litigation

The Act does not entitle UK courts to disregard primary legislation which is incompatible with the Convention. However, if a court is satisfied that a provision is incompatible with a Convention right, it may make a *declaration of incompatibility*, though that may be made only by a court at the level of the High Court or above. (It remains to be seen whether when a district judge is sitting on High Court business, he will be entitled to make such a declaration.) A declaration of incompatibility does not affect the continuing validity or operation of the relevant provision, neither is it binding on the parties to the proceedings in which it is made, but it is within the contemplation of the Act that the legislature will then bring in prompt amending legislation.

To date there has only been one clear civil case in which there has been a declaration of incompatibility, by the Court of Appeal, and that was reversed by the House of Lords. In *Wilson v First County Trust Ltd* [2001] 3 All ER 229 the Court of Appeal held that a section of the Consumer Credit Act 1994, which in effect barred an action on a debt for entirely technical reasons, was disproportionate to the object sought to be achieved, and made a declaration of incompatibility, since the claimant was deprived of the right of access to a court and was therefore subject to a breach of Article 6 and also of Article 1 of the First Protocol, as he was inappropriately deprived of property. The House of Lords, however, at [2003] UKHL 40 held first that the 1998 Act could not be used in respect of statutes which came into effect before it. Moreover, the House of Lords held that in any case, on the merits section 127(3) of the 1974 Act rendered it compatible with the European Convention, given the significant social problems caused by money lending transactions. It was perfectly appropriate for Parliament to make compliance with certain formalities required by the 1974 Act regarding prescribed terms, an essential condition before enforcement of a debt could take place. There have been declarations of incompatibility in public law cases, discussion of which is beyond the scope of this text.

Under the Act the important sections for civil litigation are likely to be:

2. **Interpretation of Convention rights**

    (1) A court or tribunal determining a question which has arisen in connection with a Convention right must take into account any—

        (a) judgment, decision, declaration or advisory opinion of the European Court of Human Rights,

        [(b) and (c) opinion or decision of the Commission],

        whenever made or given, so far as, in the opinion of the court of tribunal, it is relevant to the proceedings in which that question has arisen.

3. **Interpretation of legislation**

    (1) So far as it is possible to do so, primary legislation and subordinate legislation must be read and given effect in a way which is compatible with the Convention rights.

6. **Acts of public authorities**

    (1) It is unlawful for a public authority to act in a way which is incompatible with a Convention right. . . .

    (3) In this section 'public authority' includes—

        (a) a court or tribunal, and

        (b) any person certain of whose functions are functions of a public nature. . . .

    (6) 'An act' includes a failure to act but does not include a failure to [introduce legislation].

7. **Proceedings**

    (1) A person who claims that a public authority has acted (or proposes to act) in a way which is made unlawful by section 6(1) may—

        (a) bring proceedings against the authority under this Act in the appropriate court or tribunal, or

        (b) rely on the Convention right or rights concerned in any legal proceedings, but only if he is (or would be) a victim of the unlawful act.

37.2.2 What is a 'public authority'?

By s. 6(1), the Act makes it unlawful for public authorities to act in a way which is not compatible with the Convention. A great deal of ink has been spilt on the issue of who are 'public authorities'. It has been suggested that this gives rise to strange anomalies. For example, the BBC may be a public authority and therefore if it transmits a programme which might breach someone's right of privacy, there could be a breach of the Convention; but ITV companies are not public authorities and therefore that may not be the case in respect of them. Bodies like the railway companies may be public authorities for certain purposes, such as when having responsibility for rail safety, but not for others, such as when managing their property portfolios. These technical problems may well not matter very much because of what is discussed in the next section.

37.2.3 The application of the Convention

Section 2 of the Act requires a court determining a question which has arisen in connection with a Convention right to take Strasbourg case law into account. That is not the same as stating that Strasbourg jurisprudence must necessarily overrule established English case law, but it is clearly an important factor.

The member States of the Council of Europe have all acknowledged the right of individual petition under Article 34 of the Convention. It is this right of individual petition that gives the Convention its teeth. Put simply, the obligations of the State under the Convention are not merely, by itself or by its various emanations, not to interfere with Convention rights, but also to act *positively* to protect Convention rights 'even in the sphere of the relations of individuals between themselves' (*X* v *Netherlands* (1985) 8 EHRR 235, para. 23).

A key difficulty will be whether it can be argued that the Convention has *direct horizontal effect*. That is to say, must it be applied in relation to the rights of, and private litigation between, individuals, or is it only of importance where there is a *vertical effect*, that is, in litigation involving public authorities and individuals? It is clear from Strasbourg case law that a State may be liable for failing to put in place a system which protects rights or provides the machinery by which victims may challenge the infringement of their rights and obtain an effective remedy. The extension of this— and this is of course supported by the fact that 'public authorities' are defined in the Act to include the courts—would be that a State is obliged to protect the private rights of other citizens even where the infringement is not directly by a public authority.

The problem has come most frequently before the courts so for in applications under Article 8 of the Convention which, amongst other things, protects the rights to respect for private life. There have been numerous examples of this, in the main involving celebrities claiming intrusion into their personal lives by the media. Some of these cases have led to the suggestion that Article 8 creates a new tort of 'breach of privacy'. In analysing the situation the courts have generally appeared to conclude that even if the intrusion is by someone who is not a 'public authority', such as, for example, a daily newspaper, the court will give horizontal effect to the Convention.

In a preliminary decision in *Douglas and Others* v *Hello! Ltd* [2001] 2 WLR 992, the Court of Appeal, whilst discharging an interim injunction forbidding the publications of photographs of the wedding of Michael Douglas and Catherine Zeta Jones in *Hello!* magazine, permitted the claim to go forward for damages on the basis that the claimants might establish at trial a new tort of invasion of privacy under Article 8.

However, when the case came to trial in February 2003, the trial judge expressly declined to find that Article 8 created a new tort of breach of privacy and, whilst findings in favour of the claimants, preferred to base his judgment on existing sources of law, in particular interference with contractual relations.

A variety of other well-known celebrities—including premiership footballers in cases involving disclosure of casual sexual relationships; and television celebrities alleging infringement by photographing them on holiday—and others have attempted to invoke the Act. It is indeed rumoured that some cases have been settled out of court by substantial payments of damages simply because newspapers were reluctant to create precedents this early in the life of the statute. In the well-known case of *Campbell* v *MGM Ltd* (2002) *The Times*, 29 March 2002, the High Court found a breach of the right to confidentiality for Naomi Campbell, the model, in the publication of certain information about her past addiction to drugs and attendance at Narcotics Anonymous. This decision was however reversed by the Court of Appeal which considered that the claimant had herself sought to put her private life in the public arena on many occasions and that it was only right in the circumstances that the whole picture could be put before the public. The House of Lords in a decision published on 5 May 2004 by a majority of 3 to 2 reinstated the decision of the High Court and thus 'created' a right of privacy, albeit in a narrow and unclear form. The damages awarded were very small indeed (£ 3,500).

It is fair to say that in all these cases the previous English law is usually the dominant factor in the decision, and Article 8 is cited in such a way as to indicate that it probably adds little to the existing English law. It is noteworthy that in the Naomi Campbell case the court paid more attention to the requirements of the Data Protection Act 1998.

In the continuing debate about whether the Human Rights Act will have full hori-zontal effect, regard should be had to the answers given by the Lord Chancellor in the debate in the House of Lords, in particular where he appeared to accept Lord Wakeham's reading of the Bill so as to enable or compel the courts to enforce a right of privacy under Article 8. The Lord Chancellor said:

It is right as a matter of principle for the courts to have the duty of acting compatibly with the Convention, not only in cases involving other public authorities, but also in developing the common law in deciding cases between individuals . . .

37.3   Interpretation of the Convention

Writings on the Convention refer to its *'jurisprudence constante'*. The doctrine of prece-dent, however, has a qualified relevance in Strasbourg case law, in particular, because it is said that the Convention is a dynamic organ and thus cases which came before the court in the year 2004 might well be decided differently to those which were decided in 1975, or even 1995. This may be particularly true of cases in areas where public atti-tudes are thought to have changed, for example, in respect of national laws relevant to sexual orientation (see *Lustig-Prean* v *United Kingdom* (1999) 29 EHRR 548).

The idea of a doctrine of precedent is given some force, however, by the conditions for admissibility of an application in Article 35(2) of the Convention, which provides:

The court shall not deal with any application that . . . is substantially the same as a matter that has already been examined by the court.

Case law under the Convention does tend to show, with respect, that the court is not always consistent and one cannot sometimes see a logical distinction between some cases which have been decided differently on very similar facts. Such differences can-not always be explained by change in social circumstances. In many cases to do with evidence and procedure, the Strasbourg court often retreats behind the formula that 'the assessment of evidence is a matter for the national courts' or even behind the so-called doctrine of *margin of appreciation*, a doctrine which allows national courts a wide discretion in some areas as to what will or will not be part of their domestic law.

Until November 1998 there were two tiers of procedure in Strasbourg, the European Commission on Human Rights which acted as a filtering and fact-finding mechanism and the European Court of Human Rights, which dealt with cases referred on to it by member States or the Commission (but not private individuals who had no right to take their cases further than the Commission if they were found inadmissible there). Since November 1998 the Commission has been abolished and there is now one full-time court. The full court sits with 17 members, but decision-making powers are accorded to smaller sections or chambers of up to seven members and there are now many dozens of cases being decided each month as opposed to the very small number of cases decided annually under the previous system. The diversity of the membership of the court and the number of chambers are unlikely to be an aid to consistency of decision-making.

37.3.1   Principles of interpretation

In interpreting the Convention there are certain well-established principles. Many rights under the Convention are accompanied by qualifying paragraphs and the general principle is that the Convention is to be construed *purposively*, that a right is to be construed expansively, and any qualification to that right restrictively. Without examining the voluminous Strasbourg case law, however, it would be difficult for anyone coming to the Convention for the first time to know whether a certain case was within or outside the Convention.

This is particularly so in the case of Article 8, which has provoked a vast volume of applications in matters to do with, *inter alia*, telephone tapping, a claimed right to privacy, illegal search, abortion, the refusal of abortion, the right to a homosexual relationship, the right to homosexuality in the armed forces, the right to refuse a medical examination, the right to refuse blood testing, contraception, the refusal of contraception, divorce, residence and access disputes, child care, many matters of immigration, deportation, the right of travellers to camp where they wish, and a huge range of cases involving prisoners' rights. In addition there have been a significant number of cases to do with the right to quiet enjoyment of property, including issues of whether such matters as interference with television reception, or excessive noise caused by the flight path to Heathrow might be a breach of Article 8. It is fair to say that at the moment such cases have always ended in favour of a restrictive interpretation of Article 8, in so far as it applies with interference with property rights. Nonetheless it would be right to say that the Article is so widely framed, both in the statement of a right and in the acceptable derogation under Article 8(2) as to appear not much more than a pious exhortation and the outcome of any given litigation under it remains difficult to predict.

37.3.2 Proportionality

In determining the relationship between rights and permissible restrictions, and sometimes in determining the balance between apparently competing rights, the Strasbourg Court usually has regard to the principle of *proportionality*. The concept of proportionality is also inherent in the CPR, for example, in the overriding objective, in relation to standard basis costs, and in disclosure of documents. In this sense, however, 'proportionality' probably involves a rather simpler test than that developed under the Strasbourg jurisprudence. Under the CPR the important element of 'proportionality' is really something like a cost-benefit analysis.

In Strasbourg jurisprudence the test of proportionality usually involves the consideration of whether the measure is 'necessary in a democratic society'. In the context of restrictions on a Convention right, therefore, this is usually interpreted to mean that there must be a 'pressing social need' for the measure involved. Particularly therefore in the context of judicial review of administrative action this will provide a different standard for examining the decision impugned.

The test of proportionality usually involves a consideration of the following further elements:

(a) Does the action in question impair the right or freedom in question to the minimum degree possible?

(b) Is the action specifically designed to meet the objectives pursued?

(c) The action must not be arbitrary, unfair or based on irrational considerations.

This sophisticated test has in fact been refined even further in some cases, but the additional considerations are probably easily enough subsumed in the general concept of fairness.

37.4   The Convention and civil litigation

It is proposed to consider at a practical level the way in which there is a direct impact on ordinary civil litigation now that the Act is in force. We do not intend to consider issues of substantive law, such as whether, for example, Article 8 of the Convention creates a tort of privacy, which is briefly discussed above. Despite the outcome of the Naomi Campbell case referred to at **37.2.3** above, it is likely that in due course there will be another high profile case between a celebrity who complains about media intrusion and the newspaper or television company involved. If the case is, on its facts, of a kind that the courts might perceive as more meritorious than Ms Campbell's claim, for example by a celebrity who has always shunned publicity in the past so that very substantial damages are involved then the case may well eventually go to the House of Lords and their Lordships will then have to consider more fully Article 8 (the right to respect for private life) and Article 10 (the right to freedom of expression). Once the parties have been to the House of Lords, nothing will stop them going on to Strasbourg, since nothing in the Act precludes a party from taking his or her case to Strasbourg after he or she has exhausted the remedies in the English courts, as the defendants are already seeking to do in the Campbell case.

Apart from the breach of privacy line of cases, Article 8 of the Convention has also proved to be the most popular in a variety of other contexts, including a large number of applications to do with local authority housing and homelessness, the claimant contending that the right to respect for family life includes to some degree or other a right to receive adequate housing. It is fair to say that as an argument this has found little favour with the courts, the courts generally considering that Article 8 adds nothing to English law.

From now on we intend to consider procedural aspects only.

The Human Rights Act 1998 has been prayed in aid in a large number of cases to do with English civil procedure. There appears, however, to be no clear-cut case where the courts have concluded that anything in the CPR or in the practice of the civil courts was in itself incompatible with the Act. The following, however, is a brief discussion of some issues which might arise.

The most important article for civil litigation will undoubtedly be Article 6 of the Convention, which provides:

In the determination of his civil rights and obligations . . . everyone is entitled to a fair and public hearing within a reasonable time by an independent and impartial tribunal established by law. Judgment shall be pronounced publicly but the press and public may be excluded from all or part of the trial in the interest of morals, public order or national security in a democratic society, where the interests of juveniles or the protection of the private life of the parties so require, or to the extent strictly necessary in the opinion of the court in special circumstances where publicity would prejudice the interests of justice.

37.4.1   Are the proceedings civil or criminal in nature?

The question of what is a 'criminal charge' is said to be an 'autonomous concept' in Strasbourg case law, which means that under the Convention the Strasbourg court will itself examine the true nature of the proceedings and will not necessarily accept the national label attached to them. Despite the way in which they arise there seems little doubt that proceedings for contempt in a civil context would be viewed as criminal proceedings; so would, for example, the decision to commit for breach of the Attachment of Earnings Act 1971.

The effect of this is that someone who is claimed to be in contempt of court in a civil context is entitled to all the protections relevant to criminal proceedings under the Convention. These are considerably more extensive than the requirements of the Convention for civil proceedings, including a right to cross-examine witnesses, presumption of innocence, and a right to legal aid. If these are not accorded to someone said to be in contempt, there will certainly be a breach of the Convention, notwithstanding that the contempt proceedings take place in a civil context.

37.4.2 'Determination of civil rights and obligations'

The meaning of this phrase has been rightly characterised as 'perplexing' and the case law on it is very difficult. Until recently the court distinguished between public law rights and private law rights, holding that public law proceedings did not entitle individuals to the protection of Article 6. This appeared to take out of the scope of Article 6 cases concerning, for example, immigration and nationality, prison discipline and disputes about State education.

More recent case law under the Convention has generally shown a more dynamic approach and a widening of the scope of what can be considered 'civil rights and obligations'. Older authorities may need to be viewed with care, therefore. The classic test for distinguishing public from private proceedings has tended to be whether the State is exercising a discretion or whether it is merely fulfilling a statutory obligation, even if some element of computation is required. In the latter case the case law would tend to show that the Convention does apply to proceedings concerning the dispute, for example, see *Lombardo* v *Italy* (1992) 21 EHRR 188, which was a dispute concerning the amount and terms of a judge's right to his pension.

37.4.3 Right of access to the court

In principle this is not infringed by a lawful arbitration clause, waiver or compromise, provided these can be considered 'unequivocal and not counter to any important public interest'.

37.4.4 Possible infringements of the right to a fair hearing

37.4.4.1 Limitation periods

The Court has accorded a wide discretion to the contracting States, many of which have considerably shorter limitation periods than our own. The same is true under some international Conventions, for example, those which limit the damages recovery in respect of property lost by an airline or in respect of claims arising out of personal injury on a ship where limitation periods are considerably shorter than general limitation periods in the UK.

The Court considered limitation periods in *Stubbings* v *United Kingdom* (1996) 23 EHRR 213 and concluded that a period of six years applicable in that case was not in breach of the Convention as depriving the litigant of access to the court.

37.4.4.2 Failure to comply with other time limit or procedural default

This is likely to be the most worrying aspect of the Convention for the general conduct of civil procedure. As has been observed at many places through this book, the CPR provide a wide range of powers and sanctions for the court to manage cases robustly with the objective of getting them to trial speedily and efficiently. This will lead to striking out of the case of parties who do not comply with procedural orders, or sometimes debarring the party from calling evidence from a particular witness or of a particular kind. Do actions of those kinds go too far in promoting the interests of speed and efficiency above the interest of a fair trial? If, for example, a party's case has been struck out, or he has been debarred from calling the evidence from the witness who is most important to him to prove his case, how can he have a fair trial?

This will be a difficult problem in which the court will have to balance competing considerations. It must be remembered that under the Convention there is a right to a fair trial 'within a reasonable time' and it could be argued that this should involve protecting the innocent party, who has not breached any procedural orders, from losing the date of trial which has already been fixed so that adjournments caused by the necessity to let the guilty party get his case in order should not be allowed. On the other hand, it must be recognised that if a fast track case gets to trial within the usual time frame, that is very swift justice indeed, moving from commencement to the end in well under a year. That is much faster justice than could be expected in most of Europe. It would be open to the court to conclude that too harsh a procedural regime sacrifices justice for speed and efficiency to an unacceptable degree. Obviously everything will turn upon the facts of a given case, however. In *Daniels v Walker* [2000] 1 WLR 1382, Lord Woolf MR observed that on the facts of that case anyway it had been irresponsible to raise human rights points when objecting to case management in relation to expert witnesses. That was undoubtedly the right decision on the facts of that case, but it remains to be seen how the English courts will approach matters under the Convention where there has been a strike-out for procedural default and it is suggested that this might well lead to the tempering of the fairly draconian regime which is often applied under the CPR.

The potential difficulty of this was suggested as long ago as *Re Swaptronics Ltd* (1998) *The Times*, 17 August 1998, where Laddie J queried whether a strike-out for procedural default might infringe the right to a fair trial under Article 6. In that case there was procedural default and the court held that a refusal to allow a party in contempt access to the courts simply by reason of the contempt, might well involve a breach.

It should be noted that some of the terminology in the CPR directly reflects Strasbourg concepts (e.g., equality of arms and proportionality). The English courts' current approach shown by the Court of Appeal in *Biguzzi v Rank Leisure plc* [1999] 1 WLR 1926 and further examined in *Axa Insurance Co. Ltd v Swire Frazer Ltd* (2000) *The Times*, 19 January 2000 and *Arrow Nominees Inc. v Blackledge* (1999) *The Times*, 8 December 1999 expressly adverts to Article 6, particularly in the latter case where the court held that if a fair trial could still take place notwithstanding a contempt, strike-out would be in breach of the Convention.

37.4.4.3   Security for costs

In itself this is not contrary to the Convention (See *Nasser v United Bank of Kuwait* [2002] 1 WLR 1868), though again it may be open to scrutiny. The tests for security for costs are vague, but require consideration to be given to whether it is 'just' to make such an order under CPR, r. 25.12. The tests used in deciding whether it is 'just' must always include a consideration of whether such an order would stifle a potentially genuine claim and thus deprive someone of access to the court. In *Tolstoy Miloslavsky v United Kingdom* (1995) 20 EHRR 442 the Court of Human Rights did not consider that an order to pay security for costs in the Court of Appeal totalling approximately £125,000 was in breach of the Convention, given that the Court of Appeal had carefully considered the applicant's prospects of success and concluded that they were remote.

37.4.4.4   Blanket immunity from suit

In *Osman* v *United Kingdom* (1998) 29 EHRR 245 the Court of Human Rights held that the immunity from suit of police forces for operational decisions, as applied in that case, infringed the right of access to the court and thus a fair trial. It is important to note that it was the striking out of the claim at an early stage as disclosing no cause of action that was material. If the case had gone on to a trial and the court had considered the competing public interest considerations and the individual facts of the case and had come to the same conclusion, e.g., confirming the rule in *Hill* v *Chief Constable of West Yorkshire* [1989] AC 53, it is unlikely that this would have infringed the Convention.

This decision clearly causes difficulty in a number of fields where there are well-established rules of law and is at present a powerful factor against the exercise of the court's powers in CPR, r. 3.4. It remains to be seen also whether, by extension, the Court of Human Rights would consider that a summary judgment application under CPR, Part 24, would amount to a 'hearing'. On the face of it it might well not do so, given that it is unlikely to be permissible to call oral evidence on a summary judgment application and that other directions which might assist the respondent to an application, e.g., for exchange of witness evidence and disclosure, will not have been undertaken.

The decision in *Osman* v *United Kingdom* (which has received a remarkable barrage of criticism) has been approved in *TP* v *United Kingdom* (2001) *The Times*, 31 May 2000, which found breaches of the Convention where UK law provided immunity from suit to local authorities from claims by children for whose care they were responsible.

The issue of blanket immunity from suit has been considered in a number of other cases, including, *Carnduff* v *Rock* [2001] All ER(B) 151, concerning whether a registered police informant had the right to sue and seek disclosure of documents in relation to informant's fees which were allegedly unpaid.

In a further imaginative attempt to invoke the Convention on matters of substantive law, in *Walters* v *North Glamorgan NHS Trust* [2002] All ER(D) 65 the High Court rejected an attempt to stretch the boundaries of the law of tort by applying Convention principles to substantive law issues and held that the law relating to nervous shock was perfectly consistent with the Convention and the fact that no damages would lie in the present case for a pathological grief reaction caused by the death of the claimant's son, as a result of clinical negligence, did not mean that the UK was in breach of Article 6.

37.4.4.5   'Equality of arms'

Although this term is nowhere mentioned in the Convention, it is an important concept in Continental legal systems and is certainly said to form an essential element of the requirements of Article 6. It involves the requirement that both parties be allowed to present their cases on equal terms. In what was widely believed to be a landmark case, *Airey* v *Ireland* (1979) 2 EHRR 305, the court held that the non-existence of legal aid in Ireland for judicial separation proceedings was in breach of the Convention, it being beyond the competence of the individual to pursue such proceedings. This is to be contrasted with Article 6(3), which positively requires legal aid to be available in criminal cases.

Despite *Airey* v *Ireland* the Court of Human Rights has in fact always shrunk from declaring that failure to provide civil legal aid for any particular class of case, or indeed at all, is a breach of the Convention. This is all the stranger in that some legal systems require the use of a lawyer before an action can be commenced and do not permit litigants in person.

There are a number of recent interesting decisions concerning the United Kingdom. In *Woodley* v *United Kingdom*, Application No. 28639/95, 9 April 1997 the European Commission of Human Rights concluded that there was no breach of Article 6 where the applicant had come forward too late to join the Myodil group litigation (which was litigation concerning the side effects of surgical investigative procedures involving thousands of claimants) and whose legal aid had consequently been discharged. Similarly in *McTear* v *United Kingdom*, Application No. 40291/98, 7 September 1999 (admissibility decision) the Court concluded that the fact that the applicant had been refused legal aid to pursue litigation in Scotland against Imperial Tobacco Ltd for damages arising from the death of her husband, was not in breach of the Convention, notwithstanding that the Court accepted that the litigation was complex, might be a test case, and on preliminary evidence was likely to be successful. (It was conceded that the applicant's legal representatives would continue to represent her on a pro bono basis and expert evidence was being provided free through an anti-smoking pressure group and these factors appear to have influenced the Court.) Finally, in *Smith* v *United Kingdom*, Application No. 49167/99, 28 September 1999 (*admissibility decision*) complicated litigation arose out of housing disrepair and involved claims for damages for personal injury and nuisance and eventually led to alleged contempt of court by a local authority which failed to comply with an injunction. The case went to the Court of Appeal on two occasions and the claimants acted in person because they were refused legal aid. The European Court still concluded that the applicants suffered no breach of their Article 6 rights because of the refusal of legal aid despite the fact that they were opposed by experienced counsel. The Court did, however, permit the application to proceed for further consideration, in respect of a separate allegation that the defendant local authority had been allowed to spin out the proceedings unfairly (the main proceedings lasted between 1988 and 1998) and that this was in breach of their Article 6 right to have the claim determined within a reasonable time.

However, in *McVicar* v *UK* (Application No. 46311/99) now reported at [2002] All ER(D) 79, the European Court of Human Rights held that the failure to provide legal aid for defamation proceedings was not a breach of Article 6, despite the complexity of libel law and procedure, the exclusion of witness evidence under procedural rules and the reversed burden of proof on the defendant. In that case the complainant referred to the fact that he had been subject to prejudice because, due to his own error and ignorance of the rules, he had not served proper witness statements in time. The court held that on the facts of the present case the complainant who was a well-educated and experienced journalist, was quite capable of formulating his own cogent arguments, and should really have understood the clear and unambiguous procedure for serving witness statements. English law of defamation, even with its reversed burden of proof in some cases, was held not to be inconsistent with Article 10, neither did the absence of legal aid affect the UK's liability.

In *Faulkner* v *United Kingdom* (1999) *The Times*, 11 January 2000 the applicant complained that the absence of legal aid for civil proceedings in Guernsey infringed the Convention and as part of a 'friendly settlement' the UK undertook to establish a legal aid system in Guernsey.

Finally, in *Steel and Morris* v *UK* (Application No. 6841/01), *The Times* 16 February 2005, the European Court of Human Rights held unanimously that the denial of legal aid to the defendants, the present applicants, in libel proceedings, which ran for 313 court days and was the longest trial in English legal history, was unfair. The denial of legal aid deprived them of the opportunity to present their case effectively before the court and contributed to an unacceptable inequality of arms, given the length of proceedings and the issues. The claimants had submitted that they were severely hampered by lack of resources, not just in the way of legal advice, but also when it came to administration, photocopying, note-taking and acquiring *expert* evidence. Throughout the proceedings the claimants, McDonalds, were represented by experienced leading and junior counsel and a number of solicitors. The applicant's rights under Article 6.1 had been breached.

It would be wrong to suggest from this case that denial of legal aid in all 'heavy-weight' proceedings must of necessity be a breach of Article 6.1. A great deal of the decision in this case is clearly specific to the facts, including the extraordinary length of trial, amount of documentation and level of representation by the opposing party. It would not necessarily follow that the court would now decide differently in the case of *McVicar* v *UK* above. Having said that, it would seem that cases such as the tobacco litigation might fall into the same category as the *Steel and Morris* case, given the resources of the defendant and the likely length and complexity of the trial.

The issue of equality of arms is a difficult one in both UK and Strasbourg jurisprudence. Rule 1.1(2)(a) of the CPR requires the court to ensure 'that the parties are on an equal footing': that this is not literally possible is underlined by *Maltez* v *Lewis* (1999) *The Times*, 4 May 1999, where the court declined to rule in advance that, because the claimant's barrister was only of seven years' call and the defendants would be represented by leading counsel, there was a breach of the principle of a 'level playing field' and proportionality.

The problem that will be most frequently encountered in small claims hearings is where one party has legal representation, or is perhaps represented by an experienced member of an insurance claims department and the other is acting in person. It is a problem familiar to district judges from well before the time of the CPR and may sometimes involve the judge attempting to supplement the deficiencies in one party's presentation of his case by taking a thoroughly interventionist approach. Although such cases are unlikely, in the nature of things, to lead to challenges under the 1998 Act the court must nonetheless be astute so far as possible to ensure a level playing field.

37.4.4.6 Right to a public hearing

The CPR anticipated and attempted to meet this requirement by the form of Part 39, and it is suggested that this is unlikely to prove controversial, although there will undoubtedly be complaints in individual cases, e.g., about small claims hearings which, albeit public in nature, have to be conducted in district judges' rooms, which contain inadequate facilities for many if any spectators.

It is clear, however, that if the court purports to offer a 'public hearing', this must be a reality. It is suggested that courts may need to review their security arrangements, because it is unlikely that a hearing in a private room reached through a security door to which there is no effective public access would be deemed to be sufficient compliance with the right to a public hearing. In *Storer* v *British Gas plc* [2000] 1 WLR 1237 it was held that it was not sufficient in employment tribunal proceedings merely to fix a notice on the door saying that proceedings were public when all the arrangements at the tribunal clearly indicated that this was not in reality the case.

However, the Court of Appeal concluded in *R (on the application of Pelling)* v *Bow County Court* [1999] 1 WLR 1807 that carrying on proceedings in a court which was in effect behind a locked security door because of local arrangements, was not in itself in breach of the Convention. It must be remembered that CPR, r. 39.2 gives a court the right to sit in private where it involves confidential information, including information relating to personal financial matters. This would justify all manner of hearings remaining in private, including most hearings relating to enforcement of judgments and perhaps 'debt collecting' litigation of many kinds.

37.4.4.7 Reasoned decision

Though nowhere referred to in the Convention it is well established that there must be a reasoned decision in civil cases. It is suggested it is unlikely that English practice will breach this principle.

37.5 Remedies under the 1998 Act

Section 7 of the Human Rights Act 1998 creates a new 'statutory tort' allowing an individual who claims that a public authority has acted or will act contrary to the Convention to bring proceedings against it. Such proceedings must be brought within one year unless the court decides to extend the period in its general discretion. Applications can only be made by people who are or would be 'victims' of the action in question and therefore litigation by pressure groups is not permitted.

By s. 8(1) of the Act where a court or tribunal finds that any act or proposed act of a public authority is or would be unlawful, it may grant such relief or remedy or make such order as is just and appropriate. Damages may be awarded only by a court which has power to award damages in civil proceedings and thus the criminal courts and tribunals which have no power to award damages cannot award compensation for breach of Convention rights.

Further by s. 8(3) no award of damages is to be made unless, taking all the circumstances into account, including any other relief or remedy granted, the court is satisfied that the award is necessary to afford just satisfaction to the victim of the breach of Convention rights.

37.5.1 The measure of damages

If deciding to award damages a court must, by s. 8(4), take into account the principles applied by the European Court. In fact the European Court's approach to damages is decidedly ungenerous. It appears to take little interest in arguments or procedures to establish damages and it is impossible to detect clear principles from past awards. There is no specific procedure requiring schedules of claimed damages with documentary evidence to support them and the court appears to pick figures out of the air usually in round sums.

It frequently concludes that damages, a right to which would be clearly established in English law, are 'merely speculative' and declines to find any causal link between the violation and financial loss. If there has been a breach of a person's right in a civil case it will usually refuse to speculate about what the outcome of the case might have been without that breach. For example, in *Osman* v *United Kingdom* (1998) 29 EHRR 245, where the applicants were claiming about the police's failure to protect their husband and father, who had been killed by a mentally disturbed offender, the Court decided on 'an equitable basis' to award each of the applicants the round sum of £10,000 without any analysis of whether this was meant to constitute damages for bereavement or loss of dependency.

It must be clearly understood that these principles on assessment of damages relate only to a 'pure' breach of a Convention right. If the Convention is prayed in aid as part of an existing cause of action, there is of course no reason to depart from the ordinary English principles for assessment of damages.

37.6 Summary

The Human Rights Act 1998 provides a vitally important new dimension in all aspects of litigation. It will be of huge importance for criminal litigation, and indeed historically more than half of all applications to the European Court in Strasbourg have arisen out of criminal proceedings. The fields of family law and immigration will likewise be potentially more high profile than civil litigation. However, the importance of understanding the framework of the Act and the Convention cannot be overstated. Procedural rules are likely in due course to be promulgated under the Act and these may include rules about citation of authorities. It will certainly not be enough, if one wishes to take a Convention point, to turn up with a vague argument referring to a single Strasbourg case. The Court of Appeal made its position clear on this in *Barclays Bank* v *Ellis* (2000) *The Times*, 24 October 2000, CA, in which the Court said that counsel wishing to rely on the Convention must provide the court with any decision of the ECHR on which reliance is placed and which would be helpful. Mere brief references to the Convention would not help the court, and arguments must be formulated and advanced in a thorough and plausible way. The profession will in effect have to master much of the Strasbourg jurisprudence in order properly to put Convention points. The courts will of course be alert to deter time-wasting by spurious points as a number of suggestions from the higher judiciary have already stressed. Access to the Strasbourg case law is therefore likely to be vital, and this can now be obtained relatively easily from various series of reports or indeed by accessing the European Court of Human Rights web site which is at **http://www.echr.coe.int**.

INDEX